Elements
of Economics

WALLACE C. PETERSON

UNIVERSITY OF NEBRASKA

Elements of Economics

W · W · NORTON & COMPANY · INC · NEW YORK

To Eunice

*without whom so many good
things would not have happened*

Contents

Contents

Preface

This text is designed as a concise introduction to the elements of economic analysis. The coverage and depth of analysis will serve the needs of the student who takes but one course in economics. For the student who finds the subject sufficiently interesting to go on to more advanced studies, the text should provide a solid footing. It is based on a one-semester course that has been offered with success for a number of years at the University of Nebraska-Lincoln. While planned for use in such shorter courses, it can readily be adapted to the longer course that involves additional reading.

There is probably no more certain way to interest the student in the basic propositions of economics than to relate them as accurately and as honestly as possible to the issues of our time. To achieve this objective, each major topic is introduced with a thorough probing of the key concepts and principles that belong to that particular body of economic knowledge. Immediately following are sections or chapters that relate the analysis to the great public issues of our day. Except for the limitations imposed by printing and production schedules, the policy matters treated in the text are almost as current as today's headlines.

As an illustration of this approach, two chapters (11 and 12) not only explain how prices are determined, but give the student an appreciation of the way in which the interaction of prices and competitive forces allocate resources in a market economy. The following policy chapter (13) explains government action designed either to modify or to correct the untrammeled workings of the market system. The constant interplay between theory and policy in relation to all the vital areas of macro- and microeconomics helps the student understand many of the powerful ideas and techniques that can be brought to bear on the vexing problems that beset society. For the ultimate value of economics is not just knowledge or understanding, but its use to better the human condition.

Because this text is designed either for the shorter course or for use with supplementary readings, it is necessarily selective rather than exhaustive in the range of topics covered. In choosing from the broad and complex array of material that modern economics encompasses, the utmost care has been taken to concentrate on the principles that are most enduring and, at the same time, most relevant to the many difficult issues our society confronts. Since, too, economics is often a difficult subject for the beginning student, clarity in the exposition of fundamental concepts, principles, and policies has had the highest priority. In the analytical material especially, statistical data are freely used whenever they can contribute to understanding. In both the analytical and policy chapters, historical material is frequently drawn upon, the object being not only to help the student appreciate economics as a growing field of study, but also to show how deeply its roots are embedded in our cultural heritage.

Among the important features of this text are simple and, I believe, unusually clear diagrams with accompanying commentaries; an extensive glossary of key terms, concepts, and principles; and suggested further readings at the end of the text. As aids to review, side headings have been liberally provided in the margins and sets of questions underscore the most important points developed in each chapter. The text deliberately seeks to be self-contained, an approach that gives the individual instructor maximum choice in the selection of supplemental readings, if any.

As is always true, a writer is indebted to many more persons than can be acknowledged adequately in a brief preface. But there are some whose special contribution cannot be overlooked. Among these are a number of my colleagues at the University of Nebraska-Lincoln, including Richard Felton, Harish Gupta, Ernst Kuhn, Campbell McConnell, Charles Lamphear, and George Rejda. Many times they gave willingly of ideas and suggestions. Harold Williams of Kent State University reviewed the manuscript in a detailed and constructive manner; his help was deeply appreciated. Valuable aid was provided from the outline stage to final manuscript by James S. Duesenberry of Harvard University, in his role as advisory editor to W.W. Norton & Company, Inc. Mrs. Dorothy Switzer, of the Bureau of Business Research at the University of Nebraska-Lincoln, was most efficient in locating needed statistical material. Mrs. Mary Berglund, Assistant in the Department of Economics, was helpful in a number of ways, including preparation of the glossary. I want also to thank the staff of W.W. Norton & Company; their skill and perception in editing is outstanding. Finally, I owe a special debt of gratitude to my wife Eunice, whose patient good humor helped in so many ways during the long period of gestation of this book. As is traditional, the sole responsibility for any errors in the text is mine.

Wallace C. Peterson

November, 1972

Elements
of Economics

1

The Nature
of Economics

WHEN PRESIDENT NIXON began his fourth year in office, more than five million Americans were out of work, including thousands of high-priced executives, new Ph.D.'s, skilled space scientists and engineers, as well as millions of ordinary skilled and unskilled workers. In two years the number of unemployed increased by 79 percent. For several years wages and prices had chased each other dizzily upward, leaving most citizens confused, worried, and little better off economically. For example, at the start of 1972 the average American worker's weekly pay envelope contained 27.6 percent more dollars than it had five years earlier, but a 23.2 percent increase in prices in the same period meant that he had experienced little real gain.

The drama of rising unemployment and rising prices was being played in the early 1970s against a background of ever more strident demands from many different sectors of society for more money and resources to meet a growing array of intractable economic problems. An unpopular Asian war was slowly being wound down, but the Pentagon stood ready to absorb any savings with a long shopping list of costly new items of military hardware. Welfare rolls across the land grew at a staggering pace, amid a growing clamor for fundamental reforms and demands that the country institute a system of guaranteed incomes. In nearly every

Stubborn economic problems

1

major city the situation was the same: the costs of government were accelerating because of the need for more and better schools, law enforcement, transportation facilities, pollution control, and housing, but traditional revenue sources were exhausted or even shrinking. Mayors joined with governors to demand that the federal government share some of its revenues with the states and cities. Ordinary citizens, buffeted by medical costs that never seemed to stop rising, heavy taxes, and burdensome interest charges, demanded government action for improved medical services, tax reforms, and better housing. "Nader's raiders" and other consumer groups roamed the land, harassing unscrupulous manufacturers and prodding the government to enact legislation to protect the consumer. Farmers, small businessmen, and teachers were insistent that attention and resources be directed to their problems.

Such was the economic scene in America in the early 1970s. Out of the clash of ideas and events comes the raw material for the science of economics. Since economic events pervade our lives, most of us have preconceived ideas about how the economic system works and what should be done about its many problems. But this does not necessarily mean that we have a good grasp of the nature of economics as a subject of study. We must begin with a clear understanding of what economics is all about.

What Is Economics?

There is no simple, universally accepted definition of economics. This is not surprising, for economics is a vast and complex body of knowledge that covers many facets of human behavior. But though economists differ on many details, there is agreement on the basic nature of the discipline. Let us briefly examine what three great economists of the past have had to say about this subject.

Alfred Marshall, a towering figure whose life and thought strongly influenced the development of economic thought in the nineteenth and twentieth centuries, offered the following definition:

> Political Economy or Economics is the study of mankind in the ordinary business of life; it examines that part of individual and social action which is most closely connected with the attainment and the use of the material requisites of well being. Thus, it is on the one side a study of wealth; and on the other, a more important side, a part of the study of man.[1]

Basic definitions

[1] Alfred Marshall, *Principles of Economics,* 8th ed. (London: Macmillan, 1925), p. 1.

Marshall's definition contains nearly all the elements that enter one way or another into the scope of modern economic analysis. Examine it closely.

A great American economist of this century, Wesley Mitchell, said:

> Economics is . . . social science; that is, it deals with the behavior of men in organized communities. Its special province is the behavior of social groups in providing the means for attaining their various ends.[2]

Perhaps the best definition of all is the title of the first basic treatise on economics, written by Adam Smith, generally regarded as the father of systematic economic analysis, and published in 1776, the year of the American Declaration of Independence. Smith's classic work is called *An Inquiry into the Nature and Causes of the Wealth of Nations*.

These definitions differ, but each deals with one or more of three key ideas that define the essential nature and boundaries of the subject.

First, economics concerns itself with the production, distribution, and use of valuable goods and services. Material goods and services are valuable in an economic sense because human beings want and need them. Some needs are so basic that men cannot exist without them; for example, food and water. Most of our wants, ranging from rock music to space travel, are products of a given time and society. But they are no less real than basic biological needs.

Satisfaction of wants and needs

Second, economics is the study of *scarcity*. From its beginnings, economics has stressed that all societies known to history have lacked sufficient resources (or means) to satisfy all the wants (or needs) of their members. The economist, therefore, is interested in finding methods that will allocate the scarce resources of a society so as to satisfy the maximum number of wants. More than the study of scarcity, economics is the study of *choice*. It is the rare individual who has enough money to satisfy all his conceivable wants. Most of us constantly face decisions that involve choosing between one good and another. It is essentially no different for a nation. As rich and powerful as the United States may be, it still has insufficient resources to solve the vast array of problems listed at the start of this chapter. No matter how much we might wish to, we cannot escape the painful need to make choices.

Scarcity and choice

Third, economics embraces a body of techniques and intellectual tools with which we can understand, analyze, and to a degree foresee future developments in the complex and ever-changing panorama of our dynamic economy. For example, members of

Tools for analysis

[2] Wesley Mitchell, *The Backward Art of Spending Money and Other Essays* (New York: McGraw-Hill, 1937), p. 254.

the President's Council of Economic Advisers must be able to forecast changes in the nation's gross national product (its total output of goods and services), suggest workable policies for coping with unemployment or inflation, and grapple with such diverse problems as tax reform, the elimination of poverty, America's balance of payments troubles, and adequate medical care for all citizens. Economics provides the skills to do these things.

A social science

Economics is one of the social sciences; like political science, sociology, anthropology, and social psychology, it is ultimately concerned with how human beings behave in organized societies. Although the economist usually talks in quantitative terms about the phenomena in which he is interested—prices, production, interest rates, wage levels, income, wealth, and so on—behind all the numbers lie complex patterns of human action and behavior. These are the patterns the economist must try to understand.

Why Study Economics?

Personal benefits

The study of economics, if honestly and vigorously pursued, yields great personal satisfaction. At almost every turn in our intricate contemporary society, the play of economic forces affects our lives and fortunes. As individuals and as members of a family we must work to earn a living, purchase goods, pay taxes, save money, buy insurance, educate our children, manage property or perhaps a business, provide for the economic hazards of illness and old age. All these personal matters are affected by powerful and often exceedingly complex forces in our economic system. The person who can assess the consequences of economic forces is obviously in a far better position with respect to his own affairs than the person who does not understand the basic nature of economic phenomena.

Social benefits

But we do not live alone, either as individuals or as members of a family. "No man is an island," the British poet John Donne wrote three centuries ago; we are part of a community, a state, and a nation. The affairs of these large social and political entities are, like our personal lives, always influenced by economic forces. If we are committed to the democratic ideal of self-government, then we must not only be interested in what is happening in our political, social, and economic environment, we must be able to judge what action should be taken to advance the well-being of society. Action rooted in ignorance usually leads to catastrophe. When most of the nations of Western civilization plunged into the Great Depression of the 1930s, an economic calamity of unprecedented scope heralded by the shattering crash of the American stock market in 1929, many governments tried to stem the worldwide collapse of prices, incomes, and employment. More often than not, though, the action they took in the early years of the depression worsened the situation, simply because the leaders did not understand the nature of the economic forces that had surged out of control. The democratic ideal is based upon faith that citizens collectively possess sufficient wisdom to cope with problems of ever-growing complexity and scope. Simply put, good citizenship today demands economic understanding and enlightenment.

Finally, the study of economics is a great and exciting intellectual adventure in its own right. Our economy is not a simple thing; to understand it requires skill, perseverance, and imagination, but enormous satisfaction awaits those who ultimately master the many facets of a vigorous and intricate economic system. This is as it should be. Philosophers have known for ages that intellectual and artistic achievements are the most noble and satisfying of all man's activities. Economics offers a pleasing blend of the purely intellectual and the artistic, for pure economic analysis has the rigor and symmetry of science and mathematics, whereas economic policy partakes more of the uncertain character of an art than a science. The policy maker must develop the skill to relate pure economic analysis to such real world problems as inflation, unemployment, and poverty.

*An intellectual
adventure*

What Do Economists Do?

If we agree that there are good reasons to devote time and energy to studying economics, the next question is how to go about the task. We might say that this is a question of finding out what economists do. Stated more formally, we are concerned here with the methods of economic analysis.

Getting the Facts: Description and Measurement

Before the economist can suggest a policy or course of action, he must describe and measure. Description in this context refers to the process of gathering information about economic activities and institutions. Description involves not only gathering the facts, but sorting them out and selecting the most representative. Even what might seem to be a relatively simple matter of describing what is seen requires judgment and discretion. Reality, economic or otherwise, is a complex mass of interconnected facts, some important and some not so important. To describe its essential features accurately, one must select those facts and relationships

Description

5

which, in his judgment, are representative. Economics has its roots in observation of the world. But do not forget that the ultimate concern in observation is with relevant facts, and relevance always remains a matter of judgment.

Measurement

To describe the economy by the selection of relevant facts is important, but not enough. Facts must be related to one another, and to do this they must first be measured. Economic behavior frequently manifests itself in ways that are subject to precise measurement. Thus, the economist can describe many activities of the economic system in numerical rather than verbal terms. One of the advantages that economists possess over other social scientists is that the data with which they work are often subject to quantitative measurement.

From Facts to Principles

To describe the economy and measure it quantitatively is only the beginning of the economist's work. His most important task is to determine what the facts add up to; that is, he must develop economic principles. Often called "theories" or "laws," economic principles are the instruments through which the economist achieves understanding of the way the economic system functions; they are the tools the economist relies on first and foremost when he analyzes data.

Definition of an economic principle

An economic principle is a broad statement that embodies a meaningful relationship between observed economic events; in short, it is a generalization. Economic principles pertain to the general behavior of groups and institutions because they reflect elements common to many specific situations. But an economic principle does not purport to describe the behavior of specific persons or institutions. Thus the economist asserts that, in general, consumers will buy more bread if its price is lowered, without attributing such behavior to any particular person. A "meaningful relationship" between observed events explains how and why economic events come about.

Economic principles are usually cast in the form of "if . . . then . . ." statements: if an economic event *A* takes place, then the economic event *B* will follow. Consider the principle illustrated by the consumer's reaction to the lowered price of bread. Other things being equal, a reduction in the price of a commodity will increase its sales. We are saying, in effect, that the reduction in price causes the increase in sales.

Causal relationships

Explanation must involve the discovery of causal relationships among the phenomena observed. One must proceed cautiously here, however, for the causes of economic phenomena are frequently difficult to identify clearly. The mere existence of an observable relationship between events does not mean that are causally related. In most rural areas the crowing of a rooster heralds the dawn, but few in this day and age would claim that the rooster's crowing causes the sunrise each day!

Economic principles, though sometimes quite simple, are more often complex and abstruse. But simple or complex, when a number of basic economic principles are brought together in a single, unified structure, the result is a *theory* of the economic system or a part of that system. Contemporary economists speak about the construction of economic models, by which they mean, essentially, building a framework of relationships that represents the economic system or some of its parts. For the purposes of this text the terms *principles, theories,* and *models* mean essentially the same thing—a structure of generalizations that explains the behavior of persons and institutions in the economy. For example, in Chapter 6 we will construct a basic model that shows how the nation's production and levels of employment and prices are determined. The model consists of a series of theoretical relationships which explain total expenditures by households, business firms, and governments in the economy, the sum of which is a key determinant of the total performance of the system.

Is Economics a Science?

Before we proceed, we should face a question often raised by the beginning student and by the public at large: Is economics a science? Are economists "true" scientists? These are important questions because both in the private and public aspects of our national life the economist's role is growing. There is hardly a government anywhere that does not have on tap a corps of economists upon whose advice it relies when grappling with complex economic issues.

The Meaning of Science

Many people find it difficult to define science with any precision, although they are very much aware that in today's society we are surrounded—and, perhaps, even overwhelmed at times—by the material fruits of scientific inquiry and progress. But what, precisely, is science? We may define it briefly as any area of human knowledge in which the results of investigation and observation are both logically arranged and systematically organized in the form of hypotheses or general laws which can be verified.

Definition

To understand the nature of science it helps if we realize that the Latin root of our modern English word "science" is *scire,* which means "to know." Science is fundamentally concerned with knowledge, but to know means to understand; to understand means *to be able to explain.* As the above definition suggests, scientific explanation requires the establishment of hypotheses and laws, which are general statements that formally point up the existence of cause and effect relationships between observable events. Professor Jacob Bronowski, a renowned mathematician, has said that the essence of all scientific activity lies in the discovery of relationships between phenomena.[3] This discovery is a creative experience, he says, and in essence it consists of finding uniformities or hidden likenesses in separate facts or experiences.

When the economist seeks to know, to understand, and to explain the economic system by constructing generalizations which embody causal relationships between observed economic events, he is as much a scientist as the physicist or chemist, who does precisely the same thing for matter and energy. The construction of generalizations that explain is the purpose of all scientific activity.

The Social Sciences

Economics is a *social* science, distinguished from the physical and biological sciences, because it is concerned with the behavior of human beings as members of organized societies. This is both important and troublesome. If we accept the notion that man is a free agent and thus able to control and modify his behavior at will, then economics must allow for a large element of unpredictability and even capriciousness in human behavior. How can the economist generalize and make useful predictions?

Patterns of Behavior

The answer is, in part, that in economics we are concerned with the behavior of the group, not the individual. Economic principles do not—and cannot—tell us how any individual will react in a particular situation, but they can frequently predict very accurately the way a group will react under a given set of circumstances. One reason for this is not hard to discover. When human beings live together in organized societies they must behave most of the time in orderly, hence predictable ways. Without order, civilization would be impossible. Thus, we find in civilized societies many thousands of recognizable and persistent patterns of behavior that serve as a basis for generalization and prediction. A simple example is the way our work habits are organized. Most people go to work in the morning and return home in the evening, which makes it possible to forecast quite accurately traffic patterns in a city at crucial times during the day. Such forecasts provide the necessary basis for traffic regulation and control.

Group behavior

[3] Jacob Bronowski, *Science and Human Values* (New York: Julian Messner, 1956), p. 23.

Another reason why it is possible to make predictions concerning the behavior of large groups is the phenomenon known as the statistical law of large numbers. Essentially, this law states that if the action or movements of a very large number of individual items is analyzed the random movements of the individual items will be found to cancel one another out, resulting in a pattern of behavior which in statistics is described as a *normal distribution* or a *normal curve*. Such a curve is illustrated in Figure 1-1. This

Is Economics a Science?

Law of large numbers

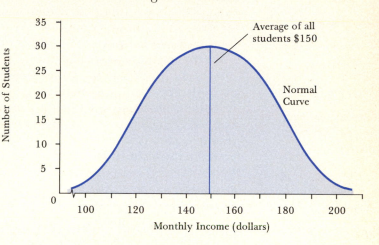

FIGURE 1-1

The Normal Curve: Distribution of the Monthly Income of College Students.

This bell-shaped curve shows that the income for most students in the sample is between \$120 and \$180 per month. Only a few out of the sample have incomes either above or below this range.

type of analysis is useful for predicting the behavior of a group when the behavior of the individual entities that make up the group is governed by many small factors. Such behavior patterns, for example, are the basis for all types of insurance. Of course it is not possible to predict when any particular individual will die or whether any specific house will burn to the ground, but if a large number of observations are made and the law of large numbers applied to the observations, surprisingly accurate predictions can be made about how many persons in a particular age group can be expected to die, or how many houses in an area can be expected to burn, within a stipulated time period.

One final point must be stressed. Most of us would agree that man is a free agent, with not only the power of thought, but the ability to learn from experience. Because of this he can consciously and purposefully bring about change in society—that is, he can establish new and different behavior patterns. As a practical consequence, scientific prediction based upon generalization is inherently more risky in economics and the other social sciences than in the natural sciences. This does not mean, however, that there are not important uniformities in human behavior which the economist can discover. A science of economics is quite possible, even though at times it may appear far less exact than such sister disciplines as physics and chemistry.

Risks in prediction

Some Characteristics of Economic Principles

Now that we have discussed the scientific character of economics, let us consider further some properties of economic generalizations. Principles in economics always rest upon assumptions or postulates, which are generally of two kinds. First, there is an assumption about what determines economic behavior in a particular situation. In our example of an increase in sales of bread following a reduction in its price, the underlying assumption concerns the motivation of consumers. Here it is assumed that consumers desire to maximize the satisfactions they derive from the expenditure of their incomes; "getting the most for your money" is a cliché that tells us much about consumer behavior. It is important to realize that underlying assumptions may be explicit or implicit, clearly stated as a part of an economic principle, or contained within the principle but not clearly stated. It is essential to be aware of the assumptions on which an economic principle is grounded.

Ceteris Paribus: Other Things Being Equal

A second type of assumption normally associated with economic principles is the idea of *other things being equal,* often expressed in the Latin phrase *ceteris paribus*. With this assumption the economist mentally holds all other relationships in abeyance while he investigates one particular relationship. Again, recall our bread example. *Other things being equal,* a reduction in the price of bread will increase its sales. This means that as long as any other possible factor (such as the supply of butter) that might influence consumer purchases of bread remains unchanged, price becomes the sole variable which determines the amount sold. The *ceteris paribus* assumption is the economist's intellectual equivalent of the controlled laboratory experiment frequently available to physical and biological scientists. In the laboratory the investigator may hold physical conditions such as temperature, humidity, and atmospheric pressure constant while he investigates certain specific relationships.

Unfortunately for economics and the other social sciences, the controlled laboratory experiment is rarely available to the investigator. The domain of the economist is the complex, real economic system, and he cannot hold parts of it in abeyance while he examines certain specific relationships. Partly for this reason, principles in economics and the other social sciences may be much less precise and exact than those in the biological and physical sciences. We shall return to this theme shortly.

The Question of Realism

The role of the underlying assumptions in economics is to set forth the limiting conditions under which the theoretical principle will apply. An important related issue concerns the realism of the underlying assumptions. Contrary to what one might think initially, the underlying postulates of economics do not have to be perfectly realistic to be useful in constructing meaningful generalizations. For example, economists have built an extremely valuable body of theory upon the simplifying assumption that business firms in the economy are seeking to maximize an entity defined as "profit." This is, at best, only a partial truth, for the forces that motivate the business firm in the actual economy are more complex; nevertheless, an assumption of this kind, even when only partially true, can open the door to powerful insights into the behavior of the economy.

Abstraction

Economic principles are abstract. This can be a difficulty. People unfamiliar with the methods of science tend to assume that because theoretical analysis is abstract it is necessarily unreal, and thus not useful. Nothing could be further from the truth. Abstraction is vital to the entire process of theory construction. When we abstract we draw out of the complex forces that constitute reality only those elements thought to be of strategic importance for understanding how things actually work in whatever part of the world we are studying. An ordinary road map provides a practical example of abstraction. It does not reproduce the landscape like a photograph, but represents the key features of the terrain necessary to guide the driver to his destination as efficiently as possible.

Simplifying reality

Abstraction has been defined as the process of forgetting unimportant details. The objective of theory construction in economics and other sciences is not to achieve a photographic reproduction of a portion of reality, but to create an oversimplified—or abstract—picture that will make the complexities of the real world intelligible to us. The student who truly understands the nature and purpose of abstraction in economic analysis will have taken a giant step toward mastery of the subject.

Prediction

Economic principles serve as predictive devices. This is inherent in their nature because, as we have seen, theoretical statements in economics usually take the form "*if* you do this, *then* such and such will follow." In other words, a theoretical principle enables

A means of control

11

us to state what will happen under certain circumstances—to predict. Obviously if we can predict the form an event will take under a particular set of circumstances, we are in the fortunate position of being able to exercise some degree of control over the event. The predictive element in economic generalizations is especially relevant to economic policy, for without a knowledge of what will happen under a particular set of circumstances there is no way to bring about, influence, or prevent a specific event. For example, if we understand how consumers may change their spending because of changes in their income, some control over spending in the economy can be exercised through government tax policy since increases (or decreases) in taxes leave consumers with less (or more) money to spend.

Forecasting

A word of caution is in order here. Be careful to distinguish between economic prediction and economic forecasting. When an economist prepares a forecast, he attempts to determine precise future values for economic variables on the basis of known values for other variables. Economic forecasting implies that the precise form of a relationship between observed economic variables is known to the forecaster. For example, he might attempt to report exactly how much the sales of a particular make of automobile would increase if the manufacturer reduced its retail price by $100. The forecaster presumably knows the exact relationship between price and quantity sold for a particular commodity or service. Economic prediction, on the other hand, is much broader and less precise; it merely tells us that certain events will follow if certain circumstances are present. Thus, an economic prediction need tell us only that the sale of automobiles will increase if their price is reduced. In general, economic principles predict more about the direction in which events will move as a result of particular circumstances than they do about the magnitude of changes that may ensue.

Prophecy

The act of prophesying should not be confused with either prediction or forecasting. A prophecy is a speculative judgment about the future. For example, an observer of the economic scene might reasonably say, "I expect that next year most prices will be higher because consumers will spend a larger proportion of their current incomes." This is a reasonable statement, but it is a prophecy about future consumer behavior rather than a prediction or forecast of what will happen to prices if consumers behave in a certain way. Prophecies, as in the example just cited, may often embody an element of prediction based upon some general economic principle. But it is nevertheless essential to clear thinking in economic analysis always to be able to distinguish one from the other.

Presenting Economic Principles

There are three basic ways to express economic principles: verbally, as equations, and graphically.

Verbal Description

Very little need be said about the verbal expression of an economic principle. It involves a descriptive statement of the essential relationship embodied in a particular economic principle. To illustrate, a fundamental principle in economics is the law of demand, which states that *other things being equal,* the quantity sold of any commodity or service will vary inversely with its price, increasing when the price falls and decreasing when the price rises. This is a straightforward statement of an economic principle, describing the reaction of consumers—or buyers—to a change in the price of a good or service. We have already described this principle in action: recall what happens to the sales of bread when its price is lowered. We will rely most heavily on the descriptive form of presentation in this text.

Equations

Principles can just as well be expressed in mathematical form as an equation. Take the law of demand; it embodies the thought that one thing (quantity sold) depends upon another (price). To express this idea in mathematical form we employ the concept of a *functional relationship*. If two variables are related so that the value of one depends upon the value of the other, then we say that a functional relationship exists between the two.

Functional relationship

To illustrate this, we can express the law of demand in the form of this equation:

(1) $$Q_d = f(P)$$

Here Q_d represents the quantity demanded of a particular commodity or service and P represents its price. The equation should be read: "The quantity demanded of such and such a commodity is a function of its price." Note, first, that this tells us that quantity demanded depends upon price, which means that the value of

13

Q_d is determined by the value of P. In addition, note that the mathematical statement of the principle of demand cannot *by it-self* tell us anything about the form that the relationship between Q_d and P takes. The equation does not, in other words, reveal whether Q_d increases or decreases as P changes in value. For this we need to know more about the relationship under analysis than is given to us by the bare mathematical statement that a functional relationship exists between Q_d and P. As matter of fact, the economic law of demand we have been discussing says that the quantity demanded (or sold) of any commodity or service will vary inversely with its price. Translated into the language of mathematics, this means that Q_d is a decreasing function of price: as P increases Q_d will decrease.

Equations that show a functional relationship between economic variables are sometimes described as behavior equations, because they describe how one economic variable or magnitude can be expected to behave in response to changes in another variable or magnitude. Since they are the mathematical expression of an economic principle, it should be evident that they do much more than merely define; they *explain*.

Behavior equations

Another form of equation often encountered in economics is the identity equation. An identity equation defines one variable in terms of other variables; it states an equality that is true by definition. For example, we shall subsequently discuss the total output of the economy, usually called the *gross national product,* which by definition consists of the sum total of investment, consumption, and government expenditures in a closed economic system. An equation stating this fact is called an identity. For example:

Identity equations

$$GNP = C + I + G$$

Both identity and behavior equations play important roles in economic analysis, but it is vitally important not to confuse the two. Definitions in economics are frequently presented in the form of identities, but economic principles—or theories—can only be presented in the form of behavior equations, that is, functional relationships.

Graphs

Economic principles may also be presented in graphic form. Logicians might argue that graphical presentation is simply another form of mathematical presentation. This may be correct, but in economic analysis at least, graphical media are used to such an extent and in such a variety of ways as to justify regarding them as a separate and distinct method of presenting economic principles. A graphical presentation of economic data and principles usually begins by drawing two axes at right angles to each other (Figure 1-2). The point of intersection of the two axes is called the *origin* and the horizontal axis—known mathematically as the *x* axis—is called the *abscissa,* while the vertical axis—known mathematically as the *y* axis—is called the *ordinate.* Distances measured to the right and upward from the point of origin on either the abscissa or the ordinate will have positive values, while distances measured to the left or downward on the two axes will have negative value. In economic analysis it is conventional to measure price, income, and other magnitudes representing monetary values on the ordinate, and physical quantities such as output and sales on the abscissa.

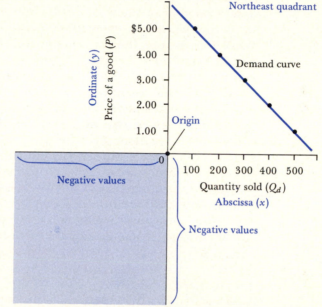

FIGURE 1-2

Graphic Analysis: The Law of Demand.

The graph of the demand curve shows that more of a good will be sold as its price falls. Since most economic values are positive, the graphic presentation of economic principles almost always uses only the upper right-hand quadrant of this type of diagram.

In Figure 1-2 the economic principle embodied in the law of demand is depicted by a line which slopes downward to the right. This line shows that the quantity sold Q_d increases as the price P declines. Since this particular economic principle is generally relevant only to positive values for both the variables involved, the graphic presentation of the principle is confined to the upper right-hand—or "northeast"—quadrant of the diagram. Negative values for a price are unrealistic, as this would mean paying people to consume the good, but the price can go so high that no sales will be made.

As we shall see, the overwhelming majority of the relationships in beginning economic analysis involve only two variables (and hence can be represented in a two-dimensional chart). These variables generally have positive values, so that our graphic presenta-

15

tion will be limited mainly to the upper right-hand quadrant of the chart. In fact, most of our diagrams will show only that quadrant.

Limitations of Economic Principles

When properly employed, economic principles and their varied forms of expression are extremely powerful tools for understanding the functioning of the economic system. But like any tools they have certain limitations.

Approximation of
real world

First, and perhaps most important, economic principles are an approximation of the real world, and should not be misconstrued to *be* the real world. They are a means by which we try to understand the complexities of the real world economic system. Their validity rests upon the good judgment of the observer in selecting the strategic relationships he believes best illuminate the behavior of the economic system.

Positive vs.
normative science

Second, economic principles, particularly when incorporated into somewhat complex models, should not be misinterpreted to represent ideals or norms of behavior. We should not, in short, confuse the theoretical propositions of economics with propositions concerning what ought to be. Nearly a century ago, J. N. Keynes,* a distinguished British economist, pointed out that much confusion would be avoided if we remembered the distinctions between positive economics, normative economics, and the art of political economy. His distinctions remain useful and valid today. Keynes defined a positive science as "a body of systematized knowledge concerning *what is*"; a normative science as "a body of systematized knowledge discussing criteria of what *ought to be*"; and an art as "a system of rules for attainment of given ends." [4] The student who remembers these differences will not be troubled by confusion between economic analysis, the economic goals of a society, and the use of economic policy to attain these goals.

An evolving body
of theory

Finally, it should be understood that economic principles are always in the nature of unfinished business. One should not view the existing body of economic doctrine and relationships as a completed structure capable of yielding correct answers to all the economic problems of our society. On the contrary, our knowledge and understanding of economic behavior evolve and change, often in response to pressures generated by human progress; new and taxing economic problems are constantly thrust before us. To a very large degree the fascinating story of the development of a

* The father of John Maynard Keynes.

[4] John Neville Keynes, *The Scope and Method of Political Economy* (London: Macmillan, 1891), p. 34.

systematized body of economic theory over the past two hundred years reflects the vast array of bewildering problems with which Western societies have had to grapple since the beginning of the Industrial Revolution.

The Issue of Validity

Our discussion of the nature and character of economic principles would be incomplete without touching upon the crucial question of validity. How can we determine the validity of a particular economic principle? How do we recognize truth or falsity in an economic theory? No questions about economic analysis are more important than these, for unless we have confidence in the validity of economic principles, their usefulness as instruments for penetrating the often murky complexities of the real world economy is destroyed.

Logic

The validity of any theoretical proposition rests first on logic. The observer must employ logic correctly in drawing conclusions and seeing the implications of a given set of assumptions concerning the determinants of economic behavior. If the rules of logic are not applied correctly, then an economic theory cannot be valid, however accurate its underlying assumptions.

Observation

Even more important, the ultimate test of any principle, theory, or generalization is reality or empirical observation. Does the theory truly explain what it sets out to explain? A valid economic principle must be consistent with the facts as we can observe them. Reality is the ultimate test of all scientific propositions, not just those of theoretical economics.

To illustrate, let us return once more to the law of demand. Essentially, this principle is a proposition about the way people will behave in their buying activities when confronted with a change in the price of the commodity or service they contemplate purchasing. The issue of validity is a simple one: do people actually behave in this fashion? Do they actually buy more bread when the price is lowered? The only way to answer this question is to look at actual behavior as objectively as possible and see if the principle agrees with the facts we observe.

A word of caution is necessary here, for though "the observation of reality" as a way to determine the validity of an economic

17

principle sounds easy, it is extremely difficult. First, all principles in economics—as well as other disciplines—rest upon the assumption of "other things being equal." In the real world other things are seldom equal, and it takes a high degree of skill and astuteness in an observer to trace the line of causation for a particular economic happening.

Second, and as pointed out earlier, the economist cannot make a laboratory experiment to assess the validity of his theoretical propositions. The great nineteenth-century philosopher John Stuart Mill said that in economics, as in the other social sciences, evidence for the validity of a principle or theory must depend upon "the limited number of experiments which take place (if we may so speak) of their own accord, without any preparation or management of ours; in circumstances of great complexity and never perfectly known to us." [5] It would be difficult to find a better statement of the obstacles to verification in economics. But, no matter what obstacles are encountered in our search for evidence, we must stick to the rule that experience is the ultimate test of any economic theory.

One final point needs stressing. Even though observed reality provides the ultimate test, it does not follow that observation can conclusively prove that a theory is true. There is a limit to the number of observations one human being can make; hence the possibility always exists that future observations by another person will refute a particular theory. It is thus best to regard all theoretical propositions in economics as tentative hypotheses, ever subject to change by the facts of experience, but never subject to final, authoritative proof.

Economic Policy and Its Formulation

We have cited the distinction between economics as a positive and a normative science. While economic analysis in a positive sense is concerned primarily with understanding the functioning of the economy, in a social sense, economic analysis must ultimately contribute to the solution of real economic problems. This is why society will devote time, money, and human resources to the development of a body of abstract economic principles. Arthur M. Okun, a former chairman of the Council of Economic Advisers, wrote,

> The economist's influence is best known in the area of policy to influence overall business conditions. The tasks of promoting pros-

[5] John Stuart Mill, *Essays on Some Unsettled Questions of Political Economy* (London: Longmans Green, 1877), p. 147.

perity and avoiding recession, curbing inflation and achieving price stability . . . have long been recognized generally as the territory of the economist. However skeptical the public may be about the ability of economists to solve these problems, it does not know any group that is more reliable.[6]

As usually understood, the term *policy* refers to a course of action designed to bring about some specific objective. Edwin G. Nourse, first Chairman of the President's Council of Economic Advisers, has defined economic policy as:

> . . . . a sophisticated—that is, an intellectual rather than emotional —way of defining ends to be sought and adopting promising means of pursuing those ends. Perceiving business life as a complex social process about which, in spite of its vagaries, we have some hard-won understanding, policy-making expresses a faith that we have some measure of control over the outcome.[7]

National Goals

Policy in economics has two major aspects. One concerns the ends that we seek as a nation. This is ultimately a matter of values and has to do not only with what we expect from the operation of our economic system but also with the broad and difficult question of how we as a people reach some measure of agreement on our goals and their priorities. Any listing of national goals which Americans would agree are legitimate objectives of economic policy probably includes at minimum the following:

Major objectives of economic policy

1. Maintenance of full employment
2. An adequate rate of economic growth
3. Stability in the general level of prices
4. Freedom for businessmen, employees, and consumers to pursue their own economic interests and activities
5. Equity in the distribution of income
6. Economic security for the aged, the orphaned, the ill and disabled, and the victims of unemployment
7. Efficiency in the overall functioning of the economy
8. Stability in our trade and payments relations with other countries

This list is by no means exhaustive. But it is comprehensive enough to indicate something of the nature of the goals of our society. Several aspects of these goals should be noted. First, few, if any, of them can be stated with quantitative precision. What, for example, is the exact meaning of full employment? What is an

[6] Arthur M. Okun, *The Political Economy of Prosperity* (New York: Norton, 1970), p. 2.
[7] Edwin G. Nourse, *Economics in the Public Service* (New York: Harcourt Brace, 1953), p. 6.

"adequate" rate of economic growth? How stable must prices be before we can say we have stability in the price level? What constitutes fairness, or equity, in the distribution of income? These are tough questions about which there is much debate.

Second, the goals themselves may be in conflict; to a degree, at least, we may be able to attain certain of them only at the expense of others. For example, the desire for price stability or greater fairness through a more equal distribution of income may conflict with what is needed to attain a higher rate of economic growth. Economic analysis cannot always supply precise and correct answers on these matters, yet society and its policy makers cannot escape the need to make choices whenever there is a conflict between goals.

Establishing priorities

Finally, it is important to realize that the relative priorities of specific goals will necessarily vary from society to society and over time in the same society. In an underdeveloped nation such as India, achieving a high rate of economic growth may be so critically important that all else is secondary to it, but in a more developed nation like the United States other goals may rate a higher priority. Further, within the United States during the last four decades there has been a decided shift in the priority ordering of our economic objectives. During the Great Depression of the 1930s, for example, the overriding objective of public policy was the restoration of full production and full employment, but during the 1940s our interest shifted to the problems of wartime production during World War II and postwar reconstruction after it. Throughout the 1950s policy makers in the federal government were concerned primarily with inflation and price level stability, but in the early 1960s attention shifted to the rate of economic growth and to maintaining a high level of employment in a growing, dynamic economy. In the 1970s our priorities are increasingly directed toward finding the resources to revitalize our urban areas and improve the quality of life for all citizens. At the top of the list are programs to save the physical environment and to make adequate income, housing, medical care, and education available to all.

Means to Attain Goals

Choosing among alternative means

Another major aspect of policy in economics concerns the means used to attain goals upon which the society has reached consensus. Means must be compatible with the fundamental democratic values of our society, but there frequently exist alternative means for the attainment of a particular objective. For example, to attain full employment a modern, developed society may employ *fiscal policy,* using government expenditures and taxes to influence the level of economic activity, or *monetary policy,* using changes in the money supply and the rate of interest to achieve the same ends. It is the policy maker's job to select policy instruments that will best achieve the desired objective.

This brings us face to face once again with the crucial importance of economic principles—or theory—to the policy maker. He cannot select the appropriate means to achieve stated goals without a thorough understanding of the way the functioning of the economic system is affected by specific actions. But this, in the final analysis, is the purpose of all theory. To illustrate, the intelligent use of fiscal policy demands knowledge of the way changes in taxation, public expenditures, or both affect the performance of the economy. The same may be said for changes in the money supply or the rate of interest. In short, the role of theory in policy formulation and application is crucial; it defines the means we can employ and the results we can expect to achieve.

Some Suggestions on Studying Economics

Before plunging into the formal analysis of the economy, a few suggestions about how to proceed and what to look for may be valuable. It is important, first of all, not to underestimate the difficulty of the subject; economics is demanding. Yet there is no reason to be frightened by it. Economics, like mathematics, develops in a logical, building-block fashion. You must master each step in the analysis before moving on to the next. The system of economic analysis to be developed in this text is a logical and imaginative construct of the human mind. Mastery of the system will be a source of pride and satisfaction.

Vocabulary

Like all intellectual disciplines, economics has its own specialized vocabulary—or jargon—which must be mastered for comprehension of the subject. In fact, the pathway to understanding in economics will become much easier if you try to understand the precise meaning given to the terms used in economic analysis. Many will seem familiar, for they are also a part of the vocabulary of our daily speech. But often their meanings differ in the two realms. This should not concern a college student, for only the uneducated believe a word can have a single hard-and-fast meaning. A vital part of education lies in learning to use language skillfully, with appreciation of the nuances that make the English language such a marvelously expressive vehicle for thought.

Traps in Logic

There are also some rather well-known pitfalls in logic that the beginning student should know about. One of the most common is an assumption that what is true for a part of a thing must also be true for the whole to which the part belongs. This is known as the *fallacy of composition*. Often in economic analysis, things that may be true for the individual entities of the economic system, namely business firms or households, will not necessarily be true for the system as a whole. One of the best known examples of this is the "paradox of saving," which asserts essentially that though it may be a good thing for the individual to save some of his income, it does not necessarily follow that it is always a good thing for the whole society to save. We shall hear more of this later.

Another common fallacy in logic is often stated in its Latin form, *post hoc ergo propter hoc,* which means "after this, therefore, because of this." "Post hoc" reasoning mistakes a sequence of events for a cause and effect relationship. This fallacy is most likely to appear in areas that concern government action and the overall level of economic activity. For example, the national government might cut taxes to increase employment and stimulate a depressed economy. This would be an appropriate measure, and it might be followed by a drop in unemployment and a rise in the national income. The economically unsophisticated might immediately conclude that, because it came first, the tax cut was the cause of the recovery. But this is not necessarily true. The forces making for an economic recovery might have gathered momentum prior to the decision to make the tax cut; the timing of the tax cut in relation to economic recovery may have been purely coincidental. Very careful analysis of events that succeed one another is necessary before one can be sure that a particular event is necessarily the cause of a subsequent event.

A logical error which is, perhaps, a universal human failing is the tendency to generalize on the basis of a limited number of observations. This tendency is especially strong in economics, primarily because in our daily lives we accumulate a steady stream of economic experiences; being human, we tend to apply this personal experience to the economy as a whole. The result may be a false analogy between individual experience and experience applicable to the economy as a whole, which leads us back to the fallacy of composition. A common example is the widespread belief that because an individual who consistently spends more than he earns may go bankrupt, similar behavior on the part of a national government will inevitably "bankrupt" the latter.

Finally, you must make a conscious effort to approach economics objectively. Because economic phenomena touch our personal lives in so many important ways, the subject is charged with emotion. As a consequence we frequently bring to it our built-in conceptions about economic activity and economic issues, many of which are wrong and must be unlearned. An open, inquiring mind is the most important single asset for the profitable study of economics!

Questions for Review and Discussion

1. Discuss reasons why the study of economics is relevant to an understanding of the modern world.
2. What are the three key ideas that define the essential nature and boundaries of economics as a discipline?
3. What makes a good or service valuable in an economic sense?
4. Is economics a science? Why or why not?
5. What are the important characteristics of a social science? Is economics an example?
6. How do we express economic principles in a mathematical way?
7. Discuss the difference between identity and behavior equations. Give an example of each.
8. What is the important distinction between positive economics and normative economics?
9. What do you consider to be some of the important economic problems in the United States today? What makes them economic in nature?
10. Give an example of an economic policy in effect in our nation today. Why is policy an important aspect of economics?
11. Discuss the shift in priorities of economic objectives from the 1930s to the present day (in the United States).
12. What kinds of logical fallacies are common in economics? Give an economic example of these errors in reasoning.

2

An Overview of the Economy

As THE TITLE SUGGESTS, this chapter will take a comprehensive look at the contemporary economic system. This will give us a better idea of the forces at work in our economy; it will also enable us to pursue in greater detail the theme of Chapter 1—the nature and boundaries of economics.

At this point in your study of economics you may be apprehensive about the complexity of the terrain before you. The modern economy *is* astonishingly complicated. But, with the help of economic theory, we can sort out the main features of the economy and reduce the complexity of the real world to relative simplicity and order.

Logically, an overall analysis of contemporary economic society begins with a condition central to all economic systems ever known to man—the fact of scarcity. If scarcity were not all-pervasive in human life there would, of course, be no need for a science of economics. But it will probably be a long while—if ever—before scarcity is no longer the lot of human beings. We introduced the notion of scarcity in Chapter 1; let us pick up where we left off.

Goods and Services

The United States learned bitterly and painfully in the late 1960s and early 1970s that it could not divert men and materials into war in Southeast Asia and at the same time meet pressing demands at home for better cities, transportation, education, welfare reform, pollution control, and many other domestic needs. Here was the richest nation in the world, hamstrung in its efforts to achieve a better standard of living for all its citizens. Why? At the root was what has been called the "fundamental economic problem," the inability of any economic system yet devised by the wit of man to satisfy all the demands that human beings place upon it. And this can be attributed, in a word, to scarcity.

The fundamental economic problem

When we say that scarcity is a dominant fact of human existence we are, in effect, saying that the material (or economic) wants of human beings are virtually unlimited, but that the means through which wants are satisfied are not unlimited. But we must determine what the economist has in mind when he talks of "wants and means" if we are to understand the basis of the science of economics.

To begin, note the emphasis we have given to material (or economic) wants. Essentially, the economist is interested only in wants that require for their satisfaction the consumption of goods and services. Economics is not concerned directly with philosophical, spiritual, or esthetic wants except to the extent that their satisfaction involves using up goods and services. What do we mean by "goods and services"? The basic distinction between a *good* and a *service* is that a good is tangible and a service intangible. Food and clothing are goods which we consume to satisfy such basic wants as physical survival and shelter from the elements. In contrast, medical and dental care are called services, but they satisfy wants no less real than hunger and protection. Both goods and services must normally be produced (or created) through the use of human labor and material resources such as land, buildings, and machinery. To possess economic value, goods and services must be scarce relative to the demand for them. Thus, an economist thinks of goods and services as things that are scarce, that normally are produced, and that satisfy human wants.

Goods contrasted with services

We come now to a paradox that puzzled even Adam Smith, the founder of the science of economics. Any good or service that can satisfy some human want is useful; in the economist's term, it has utility. But it does not follow that because something is useful it necessarily has economic value. Air is a highly useful commodity, but under normal circumstances it is so abundant that it has no

The paradox of value

25

economic value. This statement is less true today than it has been in the past, for in many modern cities clean and unpolluted air is becoming increasingly scarce. Still, we consider air to be virtually limitless and freely obtainable. Emeralds, on the other hand, are not particularly useful in any practical sense, but they are highly valuable. The factor that makes a difference is their scarcity relative to the desire for them. This is called the *paradox of value;* it helps us understand why utility and economic value are not necessarily the same thing, as well as why scarcity is the key to understanding economic value.

The Source of Wants

Basically, all wants originate at one of two levels, either *biological* or *social.* Biological wants come from our most basic needs as human beings. At the most primitive level imaginable men need food and shelter. Economics would be a relatively simple science if it only had to concern itself with the satisfaction of our basic biological requirements. Such is not the case. The overwhelming proportion of our wants are social; they arise out of the standards and behavior patterns that civilized society imposes upon us.

Individual Wants

Economists frequently say that our wants are insatiable. Obviously this does not mean that any one person's desire for a particular thing at any one time cannot be satisfied. It does mean that the totality of human wants appears to be open-ended, capable of indefinite expansion. In the contemporary world wants are not only complex, but also appear to be subject to a process of "continuous creation" whose roots and workings are not fully understood. Advertising is a prime mover in this process. Through commercials on television and radio, words and pictures in magazines, newspapers, and on billboards, the nation's manufacturers try hard to interest the consumer in their products. But many other human activities also play a significant role in the creation and expansion of wants. Education clearly figures in this process, for it both transforms and expands the individual's storehouse of wants. For example, as a student learns about music, gaining greater depth, range, and appreciation of musical forms, his demand for the means to satisfy growing musical wants will expand from, perhaps, a simple phonograph or radio to elaborate and expensive equipment that will reproduce all conceivable musical forms with concert hall fidelity.

Collective Wants

Wants can be collective as well as individual. We usually consider
wants as phenomena related to our needs and desires as individual human beings. But many of our wants derive from the fact
that we live in organized societies. Such wants are collective not *The needs of
organized society*
because individuals fail to get enjoyment through their satisfaction, but because in organized societies many needs cannot be satisfied for one individual unless they are simultaneously satisfied
for all individuals. Take streets and roads, for example. Any individual who uses a roadway obviously derives a benefit from it, but
the only practical means to provide such a benefit to the individual is to make the roadway available to all individuals. Highways are clearly a response to a collective want as much as they
are to an individual want. Individuals may be inconvenienced by
provision for collective wants, as, for example, when a street or
highway cuts through a portion of a person's private yard. The social gain must be balanced against the private loss.

Is it a good thing for human wants to continue to expand in
apparently inexhaustible fashion? It is clear immediately that this
is not really an economic question at all; rather, it involves value
judgments having to do with the question of what ought to be. In
one sense the issue may be purely academic, for whether we like
it or not there seems little doubt that human wants will grow un-
abated. The continued expansion in wants, particularly in the
last century, is to a large degree a consequence of spectacular
growth in our ability to satisfy them. We continue to create new
wants in the process of striving for ever higher living standards.
In the final analysis, this is the meaning of economic progress.

We think of material progress, which most people still regard
as a good thing, as a continued increase in our ability to provide
goods and services to a growing population. Nevertheless, there *Material progress*
are serious scholars who are concerned with a different facet of
this issue: the possible danger that a highly developed economy
like that of the United States devotes too many resources to satisfying a growing quantity of essentially frivolous private wants,
neglecting more serious collective wants. A Harvard University
professor, John Kenneth Galbraith, is the best-known American
exponent of this thesis. We shall return for a closer look at his
views in Chapter 4.

Resources: Labor, Land, and Capital

We have seen that the nub of the economic problem is the necessity to choose among various goods and services. But where do the

27

goods and services consumed in an advanced economy come from? They rarely exist in abundance in nature. So most goods and services must be created (or produced), a process which requires *resources*. And resources are scarce.

To the economist, resources are all things used and necessary in the production of economically valuable goods and services. This extremely broad definition, to be useful for analysis, must be made more specific. In a fundamental sense, resources consist of human energy expended in production and material things employed in conjunction with such human energy. Thus, a man building a house expends energy—work—and uses tools—material things—to aid him in his task. This is, perhaps, the most basic classification of resources imaginable. The economist defines human energy used in production as *labor;* it may be either mental or physical, just so long as it is directed toward the production of a good or service. Material things used in production are either *man-made* or *natural*. All natural things, including land, minerals, and water, are lumped together under the term *land,* whereas man-made things required for production are called *capital*. It is most important to understand that in economics the word capital normally refers to tools and structures used in conjunction with human labor to produce goods and services. Capital in this sense should not be confused with its use in the more popular sense of money. The three types of resources used in production—labor, land, and capital—have traditionally been called *factors of production,* for they represent the basic elements that must be combined to produce goods and services.

*Factors of
production*

But resources have other important characteristics beyond their scarcity. In general, resources are versatile; most resources can be employed for different uses. Agricultural land, for example, may be used to produce wheat or corn, while human labor, as most of us know, is adaptable to a wide variety of tasks. Further, as previously suggested, resources may be combined in the process of production.

*Versatility of
resources*

There is a final point about resources that no modern society can afford to overlook. Resources can be depleted—or used up—in production and thus must be replaced. Land, minerals, and water resources are subject to exhaustion and depletion from use, while human beings age, become sick or suffer injury, and ultimately retire or die, thus leaving the work force. Man-made instruments of production—buildings and tools—will eventually wear out through use, as well as on occasion be destroyed by chance events, such as accidents, fire, natural catastrophes, or war. Often the productive process itself may destroy resources, as happens when waste products are carelessly discharged into lakes and rivers, causing polluted conditions that contaminate the waters and destroy marine life. The growing threat to our environment

*Depletion of
resources*

is making us more aware of the need to conserve as well as replace our natural and man-made resources. In any event, all human societies must not only recognize the essentially perishable nature of all economic resources, but devise means to replace resources as they are lost in the course of production.

Technology and Time

Resources in the form of human labor, man-made capital instruments, and land are the basic factors in the productive process, but they are not the whole story. Two other non-material elements are also vital to our understanding of economic production. These are *technology* and *time*.

In a broad sense technology is the entire stock of man's knowledge. A more usable definition for economic analysis is the human knowledge and skill a society can bring to bear when combining economic resources in production. Thus, we can think of any society as possessing at a particular time a given stock of knowledge and skill to draw upon when resources are combined to produce goods and services. The greater the size of this stock, the more effective will be the productive process.

Technology

In a practical sense the stock of human knowledge is not just embodied in man himself. It exists in accumulated form in books and other written material we find in libraries. It is also reflected in the kind of capital goods—tools, machines and buildings—a society uses. As a matter of fact technological advance in a society is more likely to be revealed in a sharp and dramatic fashion through the kind and variety of capital goods at its disposal than through any outward characteristic of its people. In sum, technology is a complex phenomenon involving man's knowledge, his effectiveness in embodying this knowledge in machines, and, finally, his skill in combining his own labor with machines and available natural resources to produce economically valuable goods and services.

To make technological progress, a society must improve the effectiveness with which resources are combined in production. The existing stock of knowledge and skill may be spread more widely throughout the society by investment of resources in education. This may be formal or informal, as through on-the-job training. An interesting aspect of the phenomenon of knowledge is that the process of sharing in no way diminishes the amount originally in the possession of the person or persons who share their stock with others. This is not the case with material resources or money. One quite practical consequence is that economically advanced societies can assist less advanced nations at little real cost to themselves.

Technological progress

29

Another path to technological progress is to allocate resources to expand man's command of the process of production. This is commonly known as *research,* and typically classified as *basic* or *applied.* Basic research enlarges the stock of knowledge in a general sense, while applied research is directed toward specific practical objectives. Discovery of the laws of motion as applied to physical bodies was the product of basic research, whereas the use of such laws to place men on the moon involved applied research. The distinction between the two is often difficult to draw in practice. For the economy, research of either type may result in technological progress. Since research is the production of new knowledge, it requires resources like any other type of production. Thus the amount of new knowledge that any society can produce is limited by the scarcity of available resources.

Time

To think of time as an economic resource may, at first, seem strange. But time is the most precious and scarce of all resources, if only because all human activities seem to be related to the passage of time. Time enters economic analysis simply because production must always take place within certain time limits. Organizing resources to produce a continuous flow of economically valuable goods and services is a time-consuming process.

Efficiency

The element of time lies behind a concept that is highly significant for economic analysis, the idea of *efficiency.* To the economist, efficiency means getting the maximum output of economically valuable goods and services from a given combination of economic resources in a minimum of time. If time is in short supply, like all other resources, efficiency in production increases with every saving of time expended per unit produced. Time expended per unit of production is not the only criterion of economic efficiency, but it is an ever-present consideration.

*Capital goods and
consumer goods*

Time also enters the economic process in another important manner, which has to do with the creation of capital goods. Since capital goods are man-made instruments (tools, machines, and buildings) whose primary use is to produce goods and services used directly to satisfy wants (i.e., consumer goods and services), their creation—or production—also uses scarce resources, including time. If a factory is to be built to produce a new type of automobile and if resources are fully in use, then the factory can be built only by temporarily diverting some resources from the production of consumer goods and services. Building the new factory lengthens the production process, because additional time has to elapse before the factory is completed and can be used to produce the new model car. The problems involved in this type of decision are complex and we shall defer a fuller treatment of them until Chapter 6. At this point, it is important to understand that the decision to produce more capital goods here and now involves balancing the costs in resources and time diverted from the current production of consumer goods and services against the gain expected in the form of an enlarged future supply of consumer goods and services. From this standpoint, time is a comparison of present costs against future benefits.

The Economic System

An economic system is, in the last analysis, an arrangement whereby choices are made and wants are satisfied. This is true whether we are speaking of the mixed "free enterprise" system usually said to characterize the American economy, or the more centrally directed type of economic system found in the Soviet Union, the countries of Eastern Europe, and the People's Republic of China.

Essentially, *an economic system is a set of arrangements through which a society mobilizes its resources and technology to produce the goods and services necessary to satisfy its wants.* All economic systems involve the organization of activity to produce goods and services and satisfy a maximum of wants, individual and collective. This definition encompasses all the essential elements of an economic system. But to go beyond simple definition, we need to examine several aspects of the structure of the economic system. *Definition*

All economic systems rest upon a basic physical structure which involves a flow of the services of economic resources to productive units (firms and government) and a reverse flow of goods and services to those who own the resources. The flow of services of economic resources and the counterpart of output flow is the "real" side of economic activity. The real flow, though, has a monetary equivalent in the form of payments made to the owners of economic resources to secure their services, and expenditures made by these owners for the purchase of goods and services from the producing unit. This physical structure is common to every society, including the most primitive, because all societies must mobilize resources to undertake the production necessary to make goods and services available to satisfy wants. Figure 2-1 shows in simplified fashion the underlying physical structure of an economic system in terms of the flow of services of economic resources, the flow of goods and services, the flow of payments to resource owners, and the counterpart flow in terms of expenditures for the economy's output. *Flows*

Sectors of the Economy

It is convenient to divide an economic system into a number of sectors, the nature of which is determined both by their characteristic outputs and decision-making processes. A mixed "free-enter-

The market sector

prise" economy, such as the United States, consists of three major sectors.

First, there is a market sector in which individual demands are normally satisfied by privately owned business enterprises operating in response to the profit motive. A rough estimate is that about 80 percent of employment and output in the economy originates in the market sector, which, it should be noted, includes the activities of giant corporations like General Motors as well as those of the small corner grocery store.

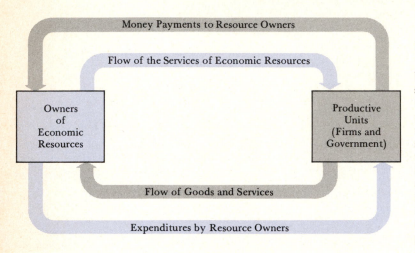

**FIGURE 2-1
The Structure of an
Economic System.**

The economic system has been compared to a gigantic sausage machine into which we pour the services of economic resources and out of which come the goods and services that satisfy our wants. This is the inner ring in the figure. The outer ring shows this two-way flow in money terms, for only through money can we measure the magnitude of what goes in and what comes out.

The public sector

Second, there is a public sector, in which decisions of a collective (or public) nature predominate. This, of course, is the realm of government. Its primary concern is getting resources to create goods and services that are essentially social in character, although a major task of modern governments is to transfer income among the different groups within the private sector of the economy, as, for example, when pensions are paid to retired persons through the Social Security system, or an unemployed worker collects unemployment compensation. For other expenditures, governments normally receive an equivalent value in exchange, as when they hire workers or buy goods needed to carry out public functions. These are discussed in depth in Chapter 4.

The not-for-profit sector

Finally, and of increasing importance, there is a not-for-profit sector, embracing a large and growing variety of economic activities, many of which are services. This sector includes enterprises such as private hospitals, consumer cooperatives, foundations, research organizations, privately funded museums and libraries, as well as a host of other types of activity, all engaged one way or another in producing goods and services for the public, but normally on a nonprofit basis. In the United States the not-for-profit sector has grown significantly in recent years, even though the overwhelming proportion of goods and services utilized in the economy is still produced in the private sector. In recent years about 5 percent of the nation's total employment is to be found in the not-for-profit sector. The public sector and the not-for-profit sector are major end-users of the goods and services the private sector produces. All three sectors need labor and other resources to produce the kind of goods and services we normally associate with their activities. In the private sector prices provide the revenue business firms need to acquire resources, while taxes and borrowing serve this function in the public part of the economy. In the not-for-profit sector, revenues are usually obtained by a combination of private contributions and prices, often with the aid, through grants, and tax relief, of government. Figure 2-2 depicts relationships between the three sectors.

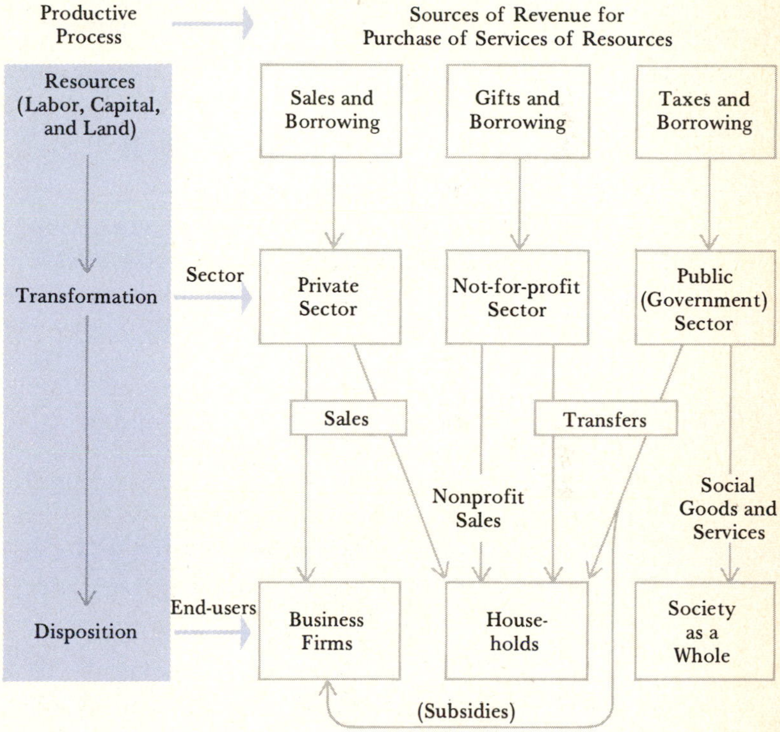

FIGURE 2-2
The Private, Public, and Not-for-Profit Sectors of the Economy.
All three sectors utilize land, labor, and capital resources to produce their outputs, but they have different sources of revenue to finance the purchase of their resources and different methods of distributing their output to the final users.

Productive Process → Sources of Revenue for Purchase of Services of Resources

Resources (Labor, Capital, and Land)

Sales and Borrowing | Gifts and Borrowing | Taxes and Borrowing

Transformation — Sector → Private Sector | Not-for-profit Sector | Public (Government) Sector

Sales | Transfers

Nonprofit Sales | Social Goods and Services

Disposition — End-users → Business Firms | Households | Society as a Whole

(Subsidies)

The Ownership of Resources

Economic systems also possess an underlying value structure, a way in which people would like their economic system to be organized. The system of ownership in any economic system is the key to understanding this value structure. For example, one basic difference between a private enterprise system, such as we have in the United States, and a socialistic system of the Marxian variety,

Private vs. collective ownership

33

such as exists in the Soviet Union, is in the realm of ownership.
Our laws and customs permit individuals to own economic resources in the form of land and capital. Human beings are not
owned by other humans except in a slave society. In the Soviet
Union, on the other hand, basic productive resources cannot be
owned privately; they are owned collectively through the state.
Collective ownership in the Soviet Union does not extend to personal or family goods, such as houses, small plots of land, and a
variety of others, including durable goods such as refrigerators
and automobiles. But it does embrace all major instruments of
production in the form of land and capital. The prevailing system
of ownership is rarely a simple black and white matter; collective
and private ownership arrangements exist side by side to some extent in nearly all societies.

Coordinating Mechanisms

A second attribute of an economic system pertains to the kind of
coordinating mechanism through which economic activity is organized. The system that predominates in the United States is
built upon the foundation of impersonal market forces, dominated by individual decisions on consumption, the disposition of
income, and the level of production. The private market serves as
a vast coordinating mechanism that translates individual decisions
into a variety of outputs. In contrast, the Soviet system is organized on the basis of central direction and control of economic activity.

There has been some tendency for these two systems to grow
more alike. Increasingly in recent years, for example, the Soviet
Union has experimented with various types of market arrangements as an organizing device for economic activity, although it
has in no way abandoned its fundamental Marxist tenet that the
ownership of economic resources should be vested in society as a
whole, namely the state.

Incentives

A third important attribute centers on the drives or incentives
that make the system operate. In the United States and other
Western nations, the basic motivating forces stem from a desire to
maximize some type of private interest, such as profit or personal
income. For example, in a market economy the manager of a private business firm will try to make as much money as possible by
producing and selling goods or services he thinks consumers want.
His counterpart in a centrally planned economy like that of the
Soviet Union may be motivated primarily by a desire to fulfill tar-
gets set down in a general plan, rather than the needs originating

with specific customers. In some underdeveloped countries, maximization of social objectives appears to be the dominant force in making the economic system work. In such systems, a key problem is determining what is a proper collective or social objective, particularly if the society's political organization is not democratic. All these attributes together provide the ideological basis of the economic system. But one must be careful here. The ideology professed within an economic system and the practices in the system may not always agree. Nevertheless, ideology reflects how people think economic activity ought to be organized, and that is frequently as important as how the system is actually organized.

Technical Features

Another way to examine the basic structure of an economic system is by reference to various technical features of the economy. These are, in general, common to all economic systems, but the degree of their development is frequently the major difference between more and less advanced economies in the world. Four of these technical features are especially important.

First, there is the use of capital (or capital goods) in the process of production. The word "capitalism" has come to mean in the popular mind a free enterprise, or market, system; in economics, the term often refers to a system that makes extensive use of capital goods in the process of production. In this special sense all modern economies, no matter what their ideological structure, are capitalistic.

The use of capital

Second, all contemporary economic systems accord an extensive role to technology and science in the production of goods and services. As a matter of fact, probably the most important single difference between an economically advanced nation like the United States and an underdeveloped economy such as India is the extent to which Americans apply modern science and technology to the production of useful goods and services.

Applications of science

Third, all economic systems are characterized by specialization in production. Adam Smith was among the first to observe this characteristic, stressing it as a major source for improvement in the productivity for labor, and hence, the welfare of society. Specialization usually increases the effectiveness of any kind of labor applied to production, thus making possible a greater output for any given input of labor.

Specialization

Finally, all modern economic systems make extensive use of money, one of the most important social inventions of mankind. Money does several things, but one of its most important functions is to serve as a medium of exchange, obviating the need to resort to the clumsy and inefficient barter system, in which goods are exchanged directly for other goods.

Money

The Central Problems of the Economic System

Allocation of Scarce Resources

Certain central problems, rooted in the fact of economic scarcity, confront all economic systems. First, every economic system must find some way to allocate its scarce resources among alternative uses. It must determine what goods and services are going to be produced, how much is to be produced, and how it is to be produced. Should we produce more automobiles and fewer houses? Should we build up our armaments at the expense of improvements in our cities? If we increase our production of motor boats, can we also expand our production of food? Should we produce electricity through steam or atomic power? Such questions point to some of the complex issues involved in these decisions.

Deciding what is to be produced also means deciding what is not to be produced, given limited resources. A rational economic system has to have a method for allocating its scarce resources to satisfy as large a number of alternative wants as possible. Answering the questions of what is to be produced, how much is to be produced, and how it is to be produced, is the essence of the resource allocation problem which confronts all economic systems.

Distribution of Income

The second major task an economic system is to provide for the distribution of the income created by the process of production. As Figure 2-1 showed, when production takes place money income equal to the value of production is created, since resource owners are paid for the services of the resources they own. The economic system also provides for the distribution of output, which, in the final analysis, is the *real* income of the society. This is what economists call income distribution.

One way in which individuals exercise a claim on the output of society is by exchanging the *services* of the resources they own for *income payments* from business firms and other entities which organize the process of production. So the structure of resource ownership is very significant in determining how the output is distributed to the members of any society. Most people "own" only their own labor power, but for a minority, ownership of capital and land is a major source of income. People without labor power currently in demand or property must depend upon transfer payments for income.

Efficiency

The third major task of an economic system is to attain efficiency. Economic efficiency has two dimensions. We have already mentioned that efficiency in the allocation of resources means that the society ought to achieve with its resources the maximum output of the things its citizens want. From this idea economists developed the concept of optimum allocation of resources, a situation in which no greater output can be obtained by any rearrangement in the pattern of resource use. Efficiency in resource use also means that the resources ought to be fully utilized, for whenever unmet wants exist, a failure to use some resources implies waste. This is the basis for the view that the nation's labor force ought to be fully employed, an idea that has dominated much economic thinking since World War II. Finally, efficiency implies that the system ought to provide for a satisfactory rate of economic growth, because the continued expansion of wants means that new wants will be satisfied only if the economy's real output grows.

Stability, Security, and Other Goals

There are still other important objectives for an economic system, some of which may be briefly mentioned. One is stability in output and employment, as well as in the general level of prices. The intensive debate over how best to get full employment without inflation, which dominated much public discussion of economic issues in the early 1970s, reflected this concern. An upshot of this debate was President Nixon's New Economic Policy, announced on August 15, 1971. In Phase I of this policy the government clamped down on wages and prices by freezing them at their levels on the date of the President's announcement. The freeze was subsequently relaxed. Under Phase II of the New Economic Policy business firms could raise prices and wages, but only within clearly defined limits. Whether the policy succeeded in halting inflation and increasing employment still remains unclear. The economic system in most modern nations is expected to offer a minimum level of economic security and well-being to all citizens. This means that society and this system must protect the family and individual from adverse social and economic forces. The drive for economic security has led to the emergence of the modern welfare state, a term which has come to symbolize the government's assumption of responsibility for old age pensions, employment compensation, medical care, and provision of income for persons and families unable to participate effectively in the productive process.

We also want the economic system to maximize freedom, particularly the freedom of the consumer to choose what he wishes to consume and to spend his income as he desires. In a market system, freedom of the individual enterprise to pursue its own goals of profit and production should be maximized. Further, we expect the economic system to be equitable, in that the distribution of income ought to be reasonably fair, although this is a difficult matter to determine. The same applies to the tax structure, as both its benefits and burdens ought to be fairly apportioned among all taxpayers.

Finally, many economic systems support the idea of *consumer sovereignty:* the ultimate decisions as to what will be produced rest with the consumer. Even centrally directed economic systems frequently adhere in principle, though not so much in practice, to this notion.

It is somewhat traditional in economic analysis to think of economic systems as being loosely arrayed along a spectrum, ranging from highly decentralized systems at one extreme to highly centralized systems at the other. A highly decentralized system is described as a market economy, because in this type of economy the basic decisions which lead to a solution of the fundamental problems discussed earlier arise out of the operation of impersonal market forces. In Chapter 3 we shall examine in detail the impersonal market as an instrument through which economic activity is organized. In many respects, the United States approximates the ideal of a pure market economy, just as the Soviet Union approximates the ideal of a centrally directed economy. In reality, of course, neither the American nor the Russian economic system is a pure system; both contain many elements characteristic of economies at the other end of the spectrum. Thus, many economists feel that it is most realistic to describe the American economy as a mixed system, although private ownership and market principles dominate.

Questions for Review and Discussion

1. Explain the paradox of value. Why is it important in the study of economics?
2. Discuss whether there is still a problem of scarcity in our economy.
3. What is the nature of an economic resource? Name some economic resources.
4. Why are technology and time considered important to the productive process?
5. What economic choices must a society make?
6. What do we mean by efficiency in the use of economic resources?
7. What are some basic characteristics of an economic system?

8. Give an example of an activity included in the not-for-profit sector. Give reasons for your choice.

9. What are the basic motivating forces that make the market system operate?

10. In what sense are all modern economic systems capitalistic?

11. What are the three major problems any economic system must solve? Do you think our economic system has solved them?

12. What do we mean by a highly centralized economic system? A highly decentralized economic system? Give an example of each.

3

Principles of
the Market
Economy

IN CHAPTER 2 we took an overview of the economic system. In this chapter we shall sharpen our focus on the essential features of a market economy. Again we stress that even though the principles of the free market dominate the organization of economic activity in the contemporary United States, no economy is organized wholly on a market basis.

The Market Economy in Action

Network of prices

In a market economy the actions and reactions of individual economic units (business firms and households) are related to one another through a network of relative prices. Assume that consumers this year decide to spend more than previously for new automobiles. What happens in the economy? An expanded demand for cars will lead to increased use of steel, rubber, fabrics, plastics, and other raw materials, not to mention a need for more workers.

Changes take place in the prices for all these materials, as well as the wages paid labor. Ultimately, the price changes affect not only the price of automobiles, but also the price of other commodities such as household appliances, that can be produced with the same industrial raw materials used in automobile production. When the full effects of an increase in demand have worked their way through the economic system, the price of cars may have risen somewhat relative to other commodities, leaving an impact on subsequent consumer spending plans. Changes in the price of one commodity in relation to another are signals to the business community, suggesting that production of some goods or services should be expanded and others curtailed. In this manner individual spending decisions and prices interact to guide production decisions in a market system.

Market and Price

A market economy works through the price system. Because markets exist for a nearly infinite variety of goods, services, and economic resources, there also exists a gigantic interlocking network of markets and prices, which serves as the mechanism for organizing economic resources and producing goods and services to satisfy human wants. The price system, in other words, coordinates the desires of buyers and the response of sellers. A market economy works through decentralized decision-making, responding to thousands of decisions which, though independent, are nevertheless coordinated through the price system and ultimately determine what is going to be produced, by what means, and in what quantity.

The meaning of market

Let us examine more carefully the meaning of both "market" and "price." A market may be defined as any area or place where there is interaction between buyers and sellers. Thus its geographic limits may be extremely narrow or extremely broad. Some markets are strictly local, while others are worldwide. The essential feature of any market is that buyers and sellers are free to interact so that a price is established for the commodity or service being exchanged. The local drug or grocery store is a market whose boundaries are the neighborhood. The stock market, which exists for the buying and selling of securities, is nationwide. Markets for wheat and corn are frequently worldwide in scope, even though much of the actual buying and selling takes place in organized exchanges such as the Board of Trade in Chicago.

Economists distinguish between two broad categories of markets: markets for the exchange of goods and services whose purpose is to satisfy consumer wants, and markets for the exchange of services or economic resources. Economists describe the first as

Product vs. resource market

41

the *product* or *commodity market* and the second as the *resource market*. Note that the term "product market" encompasses the market for services as well as for commodities.

Everyone is familiar with the notion of price as the money sum paid for a specific quantity of a particular good or service. Most of the time economists use the word "price" in this commonsense way. But it also has a technical meaning. In formal economic language, price is a ratio reflecting the exchange value of goods and services; it measures the ratio at which goods and services will exchange for one another. If, for example, the price of a loaf of bread is 30 cents and the price of a pound of coffee is $1.20, it means that the ratio of exchange of bread for coffee is four to one. Four loaves of bread have a value equivalent to one pound of coffee. In a barter system, four loaves of bread would be brought to the marketplace and exchanged for one pound of coffee. But in a price system we can avoid this clumsy process of direct exchange. Price measures exchange value in monetary terms, since money is the only common denominator we have to measure the value of all goods and services exchanged through market processes.

Markets exist in all countries, whatever the nature of their economic system. They exist in the Soviet Union just as much as in the United States. When and wherever goods and services must be exchanged, a market is a simple, effective, and efficient device for bringing together those who produce and those who want to acquire goods and services. Organization of most economic activity on the principles of the market system is quite a different matter.

Key Institutions in a Market System

What is essential for the existence of a market economy? And how far can we push market principles as a technique for the organization of economic activity? We have seen that no economy is organized wholly on the basis of market principles; thus, we must examine whatever limits may exist for using market techniques for the economic organization of society.

A market system rests on a set of social institutions. These are private property in the ownership of economic resources, freedom of enterprise and occupation, and freedom of choice in consumption. Private property in the ownership of economic resources means that private citizens are permitted both to own and to use material resources according to their own desires and wishes. Economic resources in the form of land or capital may be owned by individuals, or by legally recognized private entities such as corporations, cooperatives, trade associations, and labor organiza-

Price as a ratio

Private property

42

tions. Private ownership is distinguished from public (or collective) ownership, wherein ownership rights and control are vested in government—at the local, state, or federal level. In the United States public ownership is not uncommon, particularly at the municipal level, for electric power production and distribution and some transportation systems. Ownership at the national level is not so common; the Tennessee Valley Authority, a major enterprise for the production and distribution of electrical power in the southeastern United States, is a public rather than a private corporation. The communication satellite system, "Comsat," and the recently reorganized U.S. postal system are examples of semipublic corporations in which ownership may be divided between the public and private sectors. State ownership of material resources (exclusive of personal effects such as houses, automobiles, and other forms of personal property) is a distinction between a socialist (or communist) economy and a market economy. Often there is confusion on this point, because socialist and communist economies use markets as mechanisms for the exchange of goods. But, as we noted in Chapter 2, they should not be described as market economies because the state or state-controlled bodies such as collectives own most nonhuman economic resources.

Freedom of enterprise and occupation means that the individual may choose to employ all the resources and talents at his disposal in response to the demands of the market as he interprets them. Obviously the individual must operate within the legal framework of the society. Mine owners are required to operate their mines in accordance with safety standards set down in state and federal laws, although as newspaper reports of mine explosions and tragedies testify, frequently they do not. Textile manufacturers today must provide comfortable and safe working conditions for their employees, a condition that contrasts sharply with the sweatshop conditions of the nineteenth and early twentieth centuries. Air transportation is very carefully controlled and regulated for the sake of safety. These few examples illustrate not only that resources should be utilized within a legal framework, but that imperfections remain in the system. Freedom of enterprise permits the private businessman to acquire resources and organize them according to his judgment and produce goods and services in response to market forces. He does this with the expectation that he will make a profit or earn an income for himself. Freedom of enterprise also means, of course, that individuals may enter any occupations that they desire, assuming they have the necessary ability. In theory, persons are free to use their own talents in any way they choose to meet needs expressed through the market, although the reality is often different, especially for minorities.

The third essential institution of a market system is freedom of

Key Institutions in a Market System

Freedom of enterprise and occupation

43

choice in consumption. Essentially this means that every household or consumer is free to spend its income according to its own tastes and desires. It is through the exercise of free choice by the consumer, within the constraint of available income, that individual wants are given expression in the market. In this manner they play a strategic role in guiding resources into alternative uses. The principle of freedom of choice in consumption is called *consumer sovereignty*. Ultimately the consumer determines how the economy uses its resources and which wants are going to be satisfied.

The actual operation of these key institutions of the market system is not without serious limitations and deficiencies, in the United States and all market economies. Ownership of nonhuman resources in the form of land or capital is severely limited by the individual's income; the "right" to own property means nothing to the person who cannot afford to buy it. Freedom of enterprise, too, is limited in practice by the fact that in many industries—automobiles, steel, rubber, chemicals, etc.—production is dominated by giant corporations, and it is frequently difficult, if not impossible, for small new firms to enter these industries. Finally, it should be obvious that the ideal of freedom of choice in consumption depends upon an adequate income. For the poor and near-poor it means very little.

The Nonmarket Economy

Before we pursue further the analysis of the workings of a market system, we will consider for the sake of comparison the role of the institutions just discussed in nonmarket economic systems. What of the ownership of economic resources? In the Soviet Union, for example, there is generally no private ownership of economic resources; the major portion of productive resources is controlled by society at large. Such ownership is not necessarily limited to the state. The collective farm is a characteristic form for the organization of agricultural production in Russia; in this arrangement the collective is the unit in which ownership resides.

With respect to freedom of occupation, government in a nonmarket system may exercise somewhat more control of entry into particular occupations than is customary in market economies. Nevertheless, in nonmarket societies like the Soviet Union there exists a large measure of freedom with respect to the occupations people may enter.

On the matter of consumer sovereignty, the consumer in nonmarket systems acquires income through work and transfers, as does his counterpart in market economies, but not through ownership of nonhuman economic resources. He is generally free to spend his income for whatever goods and services may be available. In the nonmarket economy, though, the government will control consumer spending more through controlling what is produced—that is, through central planning—than by direct controls on household spending behavior. In recent years, the Soviet Union and other countries in Eastern Europe have moved toward allowing markets to reflect the desires of the consumer, a development which has been possible because these nations have become more affluent and thus better able to supply consumer wants. Even though top priority is still given to production of heavy industrial goods, a limited consumer sovereignty has emerged.

Government in a Market System

What role does government play in a so-called pure market system? In principle its role is strictly limited to establishing the legal framework within which economic activity can be organized and take place. Specifically, government's key function would be to establish the right to private individual ownership of material resources, including the right to use them for economic purposes. Furthermore, it should make certain that this right is enforced and that resources are used in accordance with the society's basic laws. Government's role in an economic sense is highly limited, simply because a "pure" market system presupposes that ultimately all decisions will be made on the basis of private responses to private actions. This, of course, is a hypothetical extreme, not the reality. Actually no economy that is purely a market economy with respect to every activity has ever existed in all history. Nevertheless, the notion of a limited role for government in a hypothetical "pure" market system is the basis for the policy concept of *laissez-faire,* which means that the government should let things alone and allow economic activity to go forward in response to individual and private motives.

Laissez-faire

Motivating Forces in a Market System

The Pursuit of Self-Interest

To answer the question of what makes a market system work, it is instructive to take another look at the theories of Adam Smith. His monumental work, *The Wealth of Nations,* was not only the first systematic treatise in economics—the first textbook, if you will—but also provided a fundamental explanation of how a mar-

The "invisible hand"

ket system operates. Smith outlines the basic institutions of private property, freedom of choice in consumption, and occupational and enterprise freedom, He also sets forth two essential principles for the operation and control of a market economy. In his view the basic motivating force of a market system—what he calls "the invisible hand"—is the pursuit of self-interest. This is what makes the system function; it is what makes the system:

> . . . by directing industry in such a matter as its produce may be of the greatest value, *he* [the businessman] *intends only his own gain,* and he is in this, as in many other cases, led by an *invisible hand* to promote an end that was no part of his intentions . . . By pursuing his own interest he frequently promotes that of the society more effectually than when he really intends to promote it.[1]

Smith's concept of an "invisible hand" does not imply a supernatural force. It merely means that the desire of the individual, whether a consumer or a businessman, following his own interest and seeking to maximize his economic gain, imparts the basic motivation to the market system. Consumers try to maximize their satisfaction from the consumption of goods and services, business firms and their owners try to maximize their profits, and those who own resources and supply their services to the market try to maximize their incomes.

Competition

The absence of economic power

But what is there to make the system operate in the interest of the society as well as the interest of the individual? Consider the second important principle in the *The Wealth of Nations*. Adam Smith argues that self-interest works not only in the individual interest but also in the social interest—that is, it promotes the ends of society as well as those of the individual—as long as *competition* exists in the economic system. What do we mean by competition? In normal usage it connotes rivalry, as, for example, when two athletic teams compete to win. Its meaning in economics is different: it is a situation in which no single buyer or seller in a market can by his own effort control the price of what he buys or sells. When competition exists, the participants in the market are without economic power, for economic power stems basically from the ability to influence or control price.

If participants in the market cannot control price, they also lack the power to pervert the workings of the market in a way that promotes their self-interest to the detriment of the public interest. This is the social significance of the economic concept of competition. Competition must be present if a market system built upon the pursuit of self-interest is to maximize simulta-

[1] Adam Smith, *An Inquiry into the Nature and Causes of the Wealth of Nations* (New York: Modern Library, 1937), p. 423.

neously both individual and social interest. This point is of fundamental significance. We conclude, then, that the pursuit of self-interest and the presence of competition are the twin pillars of the market system. Only if both conditions are present is there any assurance that a market system will operate in the social interest.

A Model of the Market Economy

We have seen that the market economy is a network of markets and prices reflecting, on the one hand, the preferences of consumers, and, on the other, producers' response to those preferences. To clarify the operations of this network we need to construct a model that links the markets which measure the demand for and supply of goods and services that directly satisfy wants (commodity markets) to the markets which measure the demand for and supply of the economic resources necessary to produce the goods and services that satisfy wants (resource markets). In the commodity markets, prices reflect the relative importance to consumers of the vast array of goods and services offered for sale, whereas in the resource market, prices mirror both the money cost of these resources to the producers, as well as their relative importance in the productive process. Figure 3-1 is our model of this network.

Demand and supply of resources

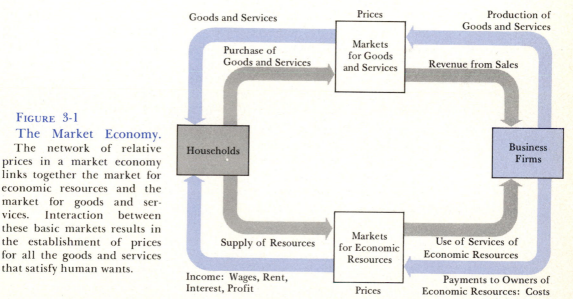

FIGURE 3-1
The Market Economy.
The network of relative prices in a market economy links together the market for economic resources and the market for goods and services. Interaction between these basic markets results in the establishment of prices for all the goods and services that satisfy human wants.

If you look at the left side of the figure, you will see that the demand for the goods and services which directly satisfy wants orig-

47

inates with households (or consumers) and that the goods and services supplied to meet these wants come from the producing units (or business firms) of the economy. The interaction of these forces results in prices for all final goods and services that directly satisfy human wants. Shift now to the right side of the diagram. There you see that the demand for economic resources originates with the producing units (the business firms), but these resources are supplied by those who own them. In the diagram, ownership of resources resides in the households.

Our model assumes a "pure" market system in which resource ownership is in private hands, and for the sake of simplicity it is assumed that only households own resources. Reality is far more complex, of course, because of the existence of corporations and other large entities, both public and private, which do in fact own economic resources. Nevertheless the interaction in this segment of the economy between the demand for resources and their supply establishes prices for the services which the resources provide. These prices reflect not only their absolute value and hence their cost to a user, but also the relative importance of different types of resources for the productive process.

The Market System and the
Central Economic Problems

In Chapter 2, we discussed the central problems confronting any economic system. Let us review them here and then look at the way the market system copes with them.

1. To allocate scarce resources among alternative uses means that decisions must be made about what is to be produced, how it is to be produced, and in what quantity.
2. To achieve a fair distribution of income requires decisions as to how output is ultimately allocated among the society's citizens.
3. To provide for economic growth means that choices must be made between work and leisure and between the production of capital goods and the production of consumer goods and services.

The features common to all of these problems are, of course, scarcity and choice.

Resource Allocation

We turn first to the question of how the market system allocates resources among alternative uses. What is important is not the absolute price of a particular good or service, but the structure of relative prices for all goods and services. At a given time, relative prices reflect consumer preferences among the goods and services the economy produces. Relative prices govern the response of producers to these preferences, which ultimately determines how society's resources are being allocated. A change in consumer preferences, whatever the reason for the change, results in a different pattern of relative prices. Such a change is a signal for producers to alter the pattern of resource use. For example, if automobile prices rise relative to the prices for electric refrigerators because of a change in consumer preferences, ultimately more resources have to be allocated to automobile production and fewer to the production of refrigerators. Obviously minor and short-term fluctuations in relative prices will not have a significant impact on resource use, but marked and persistent changes in the price structure will have such an impact. A persistent increase in the relative price of automobiles will bring more steel, rubber, other materials, and labor into automobile production relative to refrigerator production. In this way the price mechanism changes the pattern of resource use in the society. But as the pattern of resource use changes, the composition of final output also changes, which means that the price system determines what is being produced and in what quantity.

Efficiency

How does the price system insure efficiency in production? As already pointed out, the market system establishes prices for resources used in production; these are costs for the producer. If we assume that competition exists and that producers act to maximize their incomes (i.e., profits), it follows that each individual producer will not only be forced to use the most effective production techniques, but will have to find the most efficient combination for the resources used in production, given the prices he must pay to get the resources. The market system, when competition exists, forces the producer to achieve the maximum output of goods and services wanted by consumers with the least input of resources.

Income Distribution

The market mechanism, working through the interaction of the demand for resources and their supply, establishes absolute and relative prices for their services. How does this bear on the distribution of income to those who participate in the productive process? The income a person gets depends upon both the price paid for the services of resources he owns and the extent to which his resources are employed. Both are determined by the market system. Income distribution in a society at large therefore depends

Maximum output with least input

upon the pattern of resource ownership existing in that society, the prices established for the services of the resources, and the level of resource use.

The amount of money income obtained by the resource owner determines the size of his claim upon society's real output. A market-determined distribution of income means that a person who does not have resources at his disposal which can command a price in the market is, in effect, excluded from obtaining a money income. But no modern society ignores the plight of those who do not own resources that will command a price. Nonmarket arrangements have to be made to provide money income for these persons. These arrangements may be both public and private. A simple example is the situation of a worker reaching a mandatory retirement age. If he is without other resources that will yield an income, he may be entirely dependent upon a retirement income provided through a system of social security. Income received in this way is normally described as *transfer income;* through taxation society transfers income from those who participate directly in the productive process by virtue of resource ownership to those who cannot participate because they no longer possess resources with economic value.

Economic Growth

Economic growth means the systematic expansion over time of the volume of goods and services produced, both in total and on a per person basis. To have economic growth there must be a continuous increase in the input of resources. How does the market system promote growth? In the simplest sense the market must resolve the question of how the work force allocates time between work and leisure and how resources are allocated between the production of consumer goods and services and the production of capital goods (instruments of production). This is so because growth demands both more work and more capital.

Let us turn first to the issue of work versus leisure. As we have seen, the resource market establishes a price for the services of all resources, including labor. Workers, both manual and intellectual, confront the choice of how much to work at a particular price (or income) as an alternative to leisure. (This assumes, of course, that employment is available if desired.) Leisure is like a commodity in that it provides satisfaction and enjoyment to the individual, and thus has a positive value. The choice between work and leisure must be made by comparing the monetary gain from work—the wage or salary obtainable—with the satisfaction lost by surrendering some leisure. The need to maintain a basic living standard dictates that everyone must devote a minimum amount of time to work, but as a society becomes increasingly wealthy, the choice between work and leisure grows more significant.

The resource market also establishes prices paid for the services of capital goods. Interest rates are a good proxy for the prices for the services of capital, chiefly because the acquisition of capital by business firms often involves borrowed money. Firms which purchase capital goods with borrowed money must compare the expected profit on the capital with what it costs them to borrow the money. The latter is measured by interest rates. For example, the expected profitability for a particular machine may rise because of an increase in demand for the commodities produced by using the machine. If this happens, business firms will increase their demand for these machines, assuming they can borrow money at a known interest rate at that time. On the other hand, a fall in interest rates, which reduces the cost of borrowed money, may stimulate demand for more capital goods simply because the decrease in the cost of borrowed funds makes some capital potentially more profitable to use. Thus, when the expected profitability of capital goods increases or when interest rates fall, the economy may increase production of capital goods relative to consumer goods and services. The reverse may happen when profitability expectations collapse or interest rates increase. Then the production of capital goods relative to consumer goods may decline. These interactions between profit expectations and interest rates reflect a society's changing preferences for current as compared to future consumption. If production of capital goods is increased relative to the output of consumer goods and services, this means that society has chosen to consume less now in exchange for more consumption in the future. The opposite decision is made when there is a relative decline in capital goods output. This is not decided by a referendum or through a master plan; it emerges from the interaction of prices in a market system.

Limitations of the Market System

Unmet Social Wants

The market system mechanism is admirably suited to the production of goods and services that satisfy the *individual's* wants. But how far can market principles be pushed to satisfy social wants? As it turns out, the market is neither efficient nor usable for the satisfaction of social wants. Government is the chief instrument for this purpose, and the process by which governments achieve their economic goals will be the main theme of Chapter 4.

Unequal Income Distribution

A second limitation of the market system centers on the distribution of income. Our earlier discussion stressed that the market mechanism distributes income—money and real—on the basis of an existing distribution in the ownership of economic resources. Further, a market system only responds to wants that are expressed through money expenditures. Obviously one must have a money income or access to money to satisfy his wants; any person without an effective command over some resource needed in production is excluded by the market system from receiving any income. This is not tolerable. Its correction requires extramarket arrangements, such as construction of a system of transfer payments to provide income to those without resources. But the matter does not end here, simply because a market system does not assure that the existing distribution for the ownership of economic resources is either equitable or desirable. All a market system can do is distribute income on the basis of the existing ownership of economic resources. The composition of output and the allocation of resources reflects this distribution. Whether a given distribution of resource ownership is satisfactory and just is a broad and extremely important social issue. Its resolution involves values and extramarket means. It is very important to understand the limitation involved here, and the extent to which we can push the market principle in relation to income distribution.

Social Costs and Social Benefits

A third limitation to the market system is its frequent failure to reflect adequately social benefits and social costs in contrast to private benefits and private costs. As we have seen, the market system establishes a network of prices for goods and services and the resources entering into their production. The structure of relative prices reflects the benefits individuals expect from consumption as well as the costs business firms incur in producing goods and services. These costs, though, are the private costs of the producer. A social cost is a disadvantage to society which results from private production but is not necessarily reflected in the money costs to the individual producer of acquiring resources needed for production. For example, a manufacturing plant may dump its industrial wastes into a stream to the disadvantage of all because of the resulting pollution of the stream. For the individual manufacturer the only costs are the money he pays for labor and other resources needed for production. But to the extent that the stream is polluted there are social costs involved in production which the market system will not measure. In this situation the environment absorbs social costs to the detriment of everyone; the polluter escapes without paying for the damage he has done. Thus, there is a real gap between private money costs of production and social costs of production.

The growing awareness of serious pollution problems makes it more and more important to confront the issue of the gap between social and private costs. Because nothing within the market system forces a producer to incorporate real, social costs into his money costs of production, society must resort to some kind of extramarket arrangement, such as a law or regulation to forbid a manufacturing firm from dumping its industrial wastes into a stream, or a fee charged the manufacturer to cover the expense of cleaning the water.

A social benefit, in contrast to a private benefit, is a gain that accrues both to society as a whole and to individuals, but for which an individual does not have to pay directly. A well-known example of a social benefit is education. Education clearly benefits the recipient; most people are willing to pay a price for this service because of its likely payoff. However, it is equally clear that an educated population confers benefits on the whole society which extend beyond the benefits to its individual members. There is, in other words, a spillover effect from the individual's consumption of this particular service that makes it desirable to produce education at some level on a social basis; hence the American system of public schools, colleges, and universities. In principle, we could rely on the market as the mechanism for the production of education in our society, creating a situation in which only those who could pay would be able to consume education. But because we perceive that spillover benefits us, it becomes justifiable and essential to produce education by a public rather than a market technique.

As a general proposition we can state that social benefits may result whenever any transaction involving consumption by an individual has third party effects. Laws that require compulsory vaccination offer an example of third party effects. An individual is vaccinated and because he benefits is willing to pay for the vaccination. But because vaccinations protect everyone by reducing the incidence of disease, there are third party benefits and, thus, a social gain separate and distinct from the individual gain. Whenever such a situation exists, the possibility arises that a gap may emerge between social and private benefits. There is no easy formula to measure this gap, or to lessen it through appropriate public policy means. Because it exists, however, the market system cannot be the only instrument for the production of goods and services.

Limitations of the Market System

Social benefits and private benefits

Spillover effects

Third party effects

53

Breakdown of Competition

Some critics of the market system argue that there is a tendency for competition to break down, severely hampering the social effectiveness of the market system. When economic competition exists, business firms have no direct control over the prices they pay for the services of the resources they use or the prices they get for the commodities and services they produce. For the producer this is not a comfortable position. Historically most producers, perhaps by instinct, try to change these conditions and gain some measure of economic power for themselves. This is achieved when they acquire some control of the prices paid for resources used or goods and services sold. The methods have been many and varied, ranging from informal agreements among producers to grabbing complete control over the supply of a valuable resource. It is reported, for example, that the International Nickel Company, a Canadian firm, owns about 90 percent of the world's known reserves of nickel. In the United States, monopoly in the strict sense of a single business firm controlling all output is rare, but there are many industries in which one firm dominates the industry. For example, General Motors accounts for about 85 percent of the locomotive and intercity bus market, while Western Electric has a comparable hold on the market for telephone equipment.

Another factor that tends to bring about the breakdown of competition stems from the use of modern technology in production. Many products must be manufactured in units that are large in size relative to the total market for the product. Technology often results in what economists describe as *economies of scale,* meaning that real savings in production costs result as the scale (or size) of the production unit is increased. From a social standpoint, the loss may be the breakdown of competition, because as production units increase in size, their managers (or owners) acquire increasing amounts of economic power in the form of control over the prices of the goods and services they produce or the prices they pay for the resources they use. Society must choose between gains in efficiency resulting from economies of scale and losses that result when competition breaks down and private economic power emerges. This kind of social choice cannot be resolved on the basis of a simple formula.

Basic Analytical Tools:
Supply and Demand Schedules

It is one thing to *describe* how the market system operates; it is another to *analyze* the process of price determination. To get to the root of the process the economist, like any scientist, relies on a set of special techniques and tools. One of the most important of these is the concept of a *schedule,* a device to depict a relationship between two economic variables. In Chapter 1 we defined a functional relationship as one in which the value of one variable depends upon the value of the other variable. A functional relationship is most frequently expressed as a schedule in the form of a table or graph. Demand schedules and supply schedules depict key functional relationships for analysis of the process of price determination.

The Demand Schedule

To the economist, demand for a commodity or a service does not mean simply desire. Demand means desire plus the ability to buy. In an economic sense demand is a relationship between the price of a commodity (or service) and the amount of commodity (or service) that will be purchased at a given price. But demand is something more than the quantity of a commodity that people will buy at a specific price; it is a schedule showing the amounts of the commodity (or service) that users will purchase at different prices during a known period of time. Hence the term *demand schedule.* Table 3-1 shows a hypothetical demand schedule for wheat. Study this table carefully. It shows the quantity of wheat that buyers are ready to acquire, given different possible prices per bushel. The data from Table 3-1 are plotted in Figure 3-2,

TABLE 3-1
Demand Schedule for Wheat in Kansas
(Million Bushels)

PRICE OF WHEAT (PER BUSHEL)	DEMAND FOR WHEAT (MILLION BUSHELS)
$1.38	215
1.37	217
1.36	219
1.35	221
1.34	223
1.33	225
1.32	227
1.31	229
1.30	231

where the demand schedule depicts a relationship between two variables, the price of wheat and the quantity of wheat demanded. In this relationship the quantity of wheat demanded is a function of the price of wheat, which means as a practical matter that the number of bushels of wheat sold depends upon the price of wheat—not the other way around. This is an important point.

Also note that the schedule shown in both the table and the

diagram is constructed so that more wheat will be sold as its price declines. Presumably this is the way most buyers behave, buying more when the price falls and less when the price rises. We shall analyze the reasons for this behavior later. Right now, though, we must mention that other things besides price affect the willingness of people to buy a specific quantity of a particular commodity: for example, the availability of an acceptable, or even better, substitute. No one would deny this. Nevertheless, for the purpose of shaping an analytical tool that is essentially abstract in character and can be used to explain price determination, we eliminate from our analysis all considerations other than price which influence the quantity of a commodity (or service) purchased. This permits us to concentrate on the basic relationship between quantity demanded and price, a procedure which assumes that price is the most important of all possible variables that might affect the willingness of a buyer to acquire a fixed quantity of a particular commodity or service.

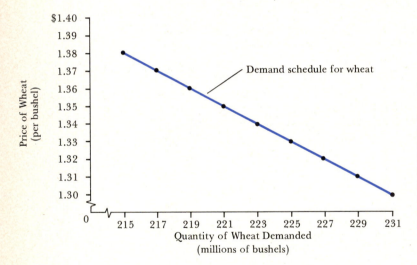

FIGURE 3-2

Demand Schedule for Wheat in Kansas.

This schedule shows the inverse relationship between the quantity of wheat demanded and its price. A drop in the price from a high of $1.38 per bushel to a low of $1.30 will increase sales by 16 million bushels. An increase in price will have the opposite effect.

In any discussion of demand it is important to understand clearly the distinction between a change in the quantity of the commodity purchased as a result of a change in price, which is shown graphically as a movement downward or upward along the schedule given in Figure 3-2, and a change in demand. In ecomomic analysis the latter means that at all possible prices buyers will purchase more or less of the commodity (or service) than previously. A change in demand is illustrated graphically by a shift in the entire schedule showing what buyers intend to do at various prices. In Figure 3-3 the schedule is shown being shifted to the right, which is an increase in demand. The second schedule indicates that at all of the possible prices shown on the vertical axis buyers will purchase more bushels of wheat than previously. There has been an increase in demand.

FIGURE 3-3

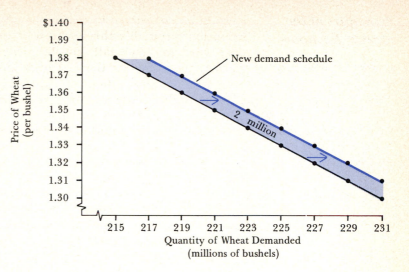

Increase in the Demand for Wheat.

At every price, 2 million more bushels of wheat will be sold than previously, a consequence of the increase in demand depicted by the shift to the right in the demand schedule. For example, at a price of $1.38 sales of wheat will be 217 million bushels instead of the 215 million bushels sold at $1.37.

The Supply Schedule

The demand schedule depicts how buyers are expected to behave in a market situation; a *supply schedule* does the same thing for those who supply goods (or services) to a market. Like its demand counterpart, it shows in relation to price the quantity of a commodity (or service) that will be offered to prospective buyers at different prices during a period of time. Such a schedule for wheat is shown in Table 3-2 and depicted graphically in Figure 3-4. The basic difference between the supply schedule and the de-

Price and quantity supplied

TABLE 3-2
Supply Schedule for Wheat in Kansas
(Million Bushels)

PRICE OF WHEAT (PER BUSHEL)	SUPPLY OF WHEAT (MILLION BUSHELS)
$1.38	227
1.37	226
1.36	225
1.35	224
1.34	223
1.33	222
1.32	221
1.31	220
1.30	219

mand schedule is that the former is constructed to show that normally suppliers offer more units to sell as the price of the commodity (or service) increases. Typically the cost of producing a commodity (or service) increases as more units of it are produced; consequently the supplier has to have a higher price to induce him to supply more units to the market. This is what the supply schedule shows.

57

Obviously supply, like demand, will be influenced by factors other than price. Nevertheless, we follow the same procedure employed with demand to show that price is the most important single factor influencing the quantity of a commodity (or service) offered in a market at a particular time. Typically a supply schedule for a commodity (or service) tends to have a positive slope, while the demand schedule has a negative slope.

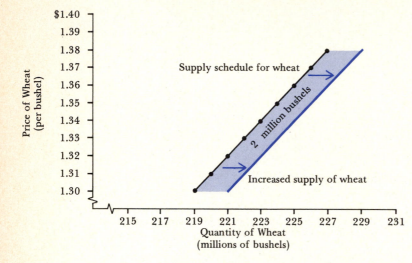

**FIGURE 3-4
Supply Schedule for Wheat in Kansas.**

The supply schedule shows that as the price of wheat increases, farmers will produce more. Thus, a price increase from $1.30 to $1.38 per bushel would result in Kansas wheat farmers putting an additional 8 million bushels on the market. The colored line in the diagram shows an increase in the supply of wheat, which means that more wheat will be produced at each possible price.

The schedules just discussed are often described as the "law of demand" and the "law of supply." The word "law," used in this way, is a misnomer because it implies a fixed and immutable relationship. This is not true. All economic relationships, as Alfred Marshall said, are expressions of a tendency:

> the term law then means nothing more than a general proposition or statement of tendencies, more or less certain, more or less definite. Many such statements are made in every science: but we do not, indeed we cannot, give to all of them a formal character and name them as laws.[2]

It is well to keep this point in mind as we discuss not only the "laws" of demand and supply, but all other laws or principles that are important in economic analysis.

Determination of Price

Equilibrium price

If we bring together the demand schedule shown in Figure 3-2 and the supply schedule shown in Figure 3-4, we will be using these analytical tools to explain how price is determined in a typical market. This is done in Figure 3-5. Note in the diagram that

[2] Alfred Marshall, *Principles of Economics*, 8th ed. (London: Macmillan, 1925), p. 33.

the point of intersection of the two schedules is shown on the vertical axis as P_e. This indicates an *equilibrium* price which, if nothing disturbs the position of the schedules, will ultimately prevail in this particular market. At this price, note also that on the horizontal axis the quantity is marked as Q_e. This is the amount of wheat being demanded by buyers at the price P_e and also the amount being supplied at this price. Since the two are

FIGURE 3-5

Determination of the Equilibrium Price of Wheat in Kansas.

The interaction of demand (*dd*) and supply (*ss*) works to establish an equilibrium price in the wheat market of $1.34 per bushel, at which price sales will total 223 million bushels. At any higher price, supply offered will exceed quantity demanded and the market price will fall. At a lower price the reverse will happen.

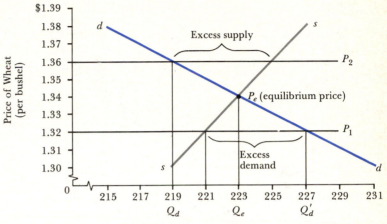

Quantity of Wheat Supplied (millions of bushels)

equal there has to be an equilibrium (or balance) between the wishes of buyers and the response of suppliers. This price is an equilibrium price because it clears the market by balancing the behavior of buyers and sellers.

What will happen if a different price for wheat momentarily exists in this market? Note what takes place in the diagram if the market price is momentarily above the equilibrium price, say at the level P_2. First, at P_2 the quantity of wheat demanded equals the distance OQ_d, shown on the horizontal axis. At this price the quantity suppliers offer on the market exceeds what buyers are willing to purchase. The inevitable result is an excess of supply, which drives the price down, because some buyers will accept a lower price for their wheat in order to dispose of it. As the price goes down, more buyers enter the market. This process continues until an equilibrium price is established and the market is cleared. At this point, price will be P_e with the quantity demanded and quantity supplied equal to OQ_e.

Let us examine the opposite type of situation, one in which the market price for wheat is below the equilibrium price. Price is now at P_1. If this is the way things stand, the quantity demanded at P_1 equals the distance OQ'_d as shown on the horizontal axis, and quantity supplied equals the distance OQ'_s, also shown on the horizontal axis. This situation is the exact reverse of the one

59

described earlier, in that the quantity demanded exceeds the quantity supplied. Some buyers will have to go without because there is not enough supply entering the market at this price to satisfy all buyers. In consequence, the price of wheat will be bid up as buyers compete with each other for the limited supply. But as the price rises, some buyers will leave the market, and additional supply will enter the market, a process that continues until the market again attains an equilibrium P_e. The interaction of buyers and sellers drives the market toward equilibrium, a situation in which there is a price that will clear the market.

Reflect a moment upon the concept of an equilibrium price. As the discussion and diagrams indicate, an equilibrium price equates quantity demanded and quantity supplied. Once equilibrium is attained, and as long as the demand and supply schedules are unchanged, the equilibrium price will not change. The market will be in a state of balance, which, theoretically, would continue indefinitely so long as no external disturbance shifts the position of the demand and supply schedules.

The equilibrium concept must be employed with caution: it is extremely difficult in reality to determine if a given actual price is an equilibrium price. Economists observe prices in a variety of market situations, but there is no easy way to discover the equilibrium price in a particular situaton. Nevertheless, the concept is highly useful for understanding price and its determination.

Our discussion of price determination enables us to formulate several general principles pertaining to price behavior in various market situations. These "laws" of price behavior may be stated as follows:

    1. In a competitive market there is a tendency for price to move toward a level which equates quantity demanded and quantity supplied. (This is simply a formal restatement of the point made about the nature of an equilibrium price.)

    2. An increase in demand (a shift in the position of the entire demand schedule) will, with supply unchanged, cause price to rise. A decrease in demand, with supply unchanged, has the opposite effect, namely to reduce price. In short, an increase in demand, other things being equal, will increase price, and a decrease in demand, other things being equal, will reduce price.

    3. An increase in supply (a shift in the position of the entire supply schedule) will, with demand unchanged, cause price to fall. On the contrary, a reduction in supply, with demand unchanged, will cause an increase in price. As above, an increase in supply, other things being equal, leads to a reduction in price, and a decrease in supply, other things being equal, leads to an increase in price.

Questions for Review and Discussion

1. Explain the importance of the price system to our market economy.
2. Name several social institutions that are important in a market economy. Justify your choices.
3. What function does the government perform in our market economy? Does the *principle* of the government's role differ from reality?
4. Define "competition" as it is used in economics. What role does it play in our economy?
5. Why are we concerned with the consumer's preference in our study of economics? How important do you think it is?
6. How does a market system allocate scarce resources?
7. Discuss some limitations of the market system. How important are these limitations?
8. Give an example of a social cost. A social benefit.
9. Discuss factors that tend to bring about the breakdown of competition in our economy.
10. What information do demand and supply schedules convey?
11. Explain how Alfred Marshall used the term "law" in conjunction with economic principles.
12. Why is an equilibrium price said to be one that clears the market? Don't all prices do this?

4

Principles of the Public Economy

WE HAVE SEEN that a market system rests upon private motives, the most important of which is the pursuit of self-interest. When economic activity is organized in this fashion, the system responds to private and individual needs. But since there are limits to the extent to which economic activity can be organized around the principles of a market system, some portion of economic activity must be organized on a different basis. This brings us to the role of the public sector or government. Governments, which exist in all modern societies, undertake important economic functions that cannot be performed adequately by the market system. In this chapter we shall consider the role and principles of the public economy—that is, economic activity organized through governmental action.

Specifically, we are interested in the following questions: What is the nature of the public economy? What is the rationale for the public economy? What are the basic functions of the public sector? How is the public sector supported?

The Public Economy and Its Rationale

Why are highways generally constructed by governmental action, whereas automobiles are built by private firms? This is a simple question and the answer may seem obvious; nevertheless, it helps us sort out the basic differences between the public and the private sector. First, the public sector is concerned with social rather than private wants. (Highways are open to all drivers, though certain vehicles, such as trucks, may be banned on some roads.) Second, since the output of the public sector is not allocated to the users through the market process, prices do not play the same role in the public sector as they do in the private sector. (Normally, highways are made available without direct charge to drivers). Note, however, that this does not mean there are no costs for public services. Third, resources are allocated for public purposes by a different process from the one used in the private sector. (Highway construction and maintenance funds come from federal, state, and local governments.) In the public sector taxes are the chief instruments of resource allocation, whereas in the private sector the price mechanism determines whether resources are to be directed to a particular purpose.

*The public sector
vs. the private
sector*

Some form of government has existed as long as human beings have lived together in any organized way. A minimal level of government is necessary to establish and enforce the basic rules of group behavior. These rules are the standards the group imposes upon the individual; they are the bedrock of government. Adam Smith understood not only that government was necessary, but that it has a complex and important role in the economic system. He did not think that the functions of government ought to be held to an absolute minimum. In *The Wealth of Nations* he listed the following major tasks for government:

*Adam Smith on
government*

1. ". . . protecting the society from violence and invasion by other independent societies . . ." This means providing for national defense.

2. ". . . protecting . . . every member of society from the injustice or oppression of every other member of it . . ." This means establishing a framework of law and order.

3. ". . . erecting and maintaining those public institutions and public works, which . . . are, however, of such a nature that the profit could never repay the expense to any individual or a small number of individuals and which it therefore cannot be expected that any individual or small number of individuals should erect or maintain." This refers to activities in any society which the market system will not or cannot perform adequately, but which are nev-

ertheless necessary and thus must be done by government. Highways fall into this category.

4. The duty of meeting the ". . . expense necessary for enabling the sovereign to perform his several duties . . ." These expenses vary depending upon the form of political structure. Although Smith refers to a sovereign (his country, of course, was ruled by a king), his statement means in modern terms that government must receive and disburse the funds that are essential to its operation.[1]

John Stuart Mill accorded government an even more sweeping role in his *Principles of Political Economy*. He said that in a given age or nation there is ". . . scarcely anything really important to the general interest, which it may not be desirable, or even necessary, that the government should take upon itself, not because private individuals cannot effectually perform it, because they will not." [2] Economists since Smith and Mill have elaborated and refined their thinking on the role of the state in a market economy. Among contemporary economists the greatest contrast on this point is between the views of Professor Milton Friedman of the University of Chicago and Professor John Kenneth Galbraith of Harvard University. Professor Friedman, onetime economic adviser to the conservative Presidential candidate Barry Goldwater and to President Nixon, believes strongly that the market can perform most functions now carried out by government, including education, provided all individuals in society have at least a minimum money income. In contrast, Professor Galbraith, a former chairman of the liberal Americans for Democratic Action and adviser to President Kennedy, is best known for his "theory of social imbalance" in which he argues that the public sector has been starved in comparison to the private sector in the post-World War II era.

The Basic Framework

In normal usage the word "government" refers to the political organization of society, and its role is to establish the rules by which the society lives. The structure of government may be determined by a basic document such as the Constitution of the United States, or it may, as in England, develop from a body of law and custom without a specific written constitution. In the United States the boundaries of governmental action have shifted through time partly as a result of judicial interpretation of the

---

[1] Smith, *Wealth of Nations,* pp. 653, 669, 681, 766.

[2] John Stuart Mill, *Principles of Political Economy,* vol. 2 (London: Longmans Green, 1886), p. 606.

Constitution and partly as a result of legislative and executive actions which have gone unchallenged in the courts. This is especially true in the economic realm; the scope of governmental intervention in the operation of the economic system has been consistently broadened by decisions of the United States Supreme Court and the lower federal courts. While nothing in the Constitution gives the federal courts the authority to rule on the constitutionality of legislative acts, this practice has developed over time.

As far as the economic system is concerned a government sets forth the basic framework of rules, laws, and regulations within which all economic activity must take place. In a sense, the government establishes the rules of the game which determine both the conditions under which the economic system will function and what kind of economic system a society will have. Specifically, in the American experience, government through the constitutional process determines the nature of property rights, without which the market system would not be able to function; it upholds these rights through the practice of enforcing contracts; it maintains the competitive conditions in the economic system by various legislative acts; and it uses its broad police powers to maintain a framework of law and order, without which it would be impossible for private decision-making in the market system to operate constructively.

The Satisfaction of Social Wants

Next to establishing the basic framework for the political and economic organization of society, the most important function of government, currently and historically, is to provide the goods and services necessary to satisfy social—or collective—wants. In this connection, keep in mind the distinction between the wants themselves and the goods and services which are the means to satisfy them. In a democratic society, the identification of social wants is believed to take place through the political process. The people elected to office largely determine what governments (at all levels) do; they, in effect, determine what social wants are to be satisfied. This is true whether we speak of sending men to the moon, building a supersonic transport airplane, or more prosaic tasks such as keeping streets and highways safe and clean. Since social wants represent the desires of all citizens in a society, government is the instrument through which these wants can be satisfied.

A democratic society does not think of government as having wants independent of those of the society at large. This is the

The political process and social wants

ideal rather than the reality, for the modern state is a complex bureaucratic entity. The reality, as every student of modern government knows, is that particular parts of a government may promote actions that serve their own bureaucratic interest more than the general interest.

Indivisibility of Social Wants

Before analyzing the process by which social wants are satisfied, we will review and extend the remarks we made about social goods and services in previous chapters. We have stressed that a key characteristic of a social good is its indivisibility. The benefits it offers are indivisible in the sense that if one person receives them all persons will receive them. National defense is a good example. On the local level, so are fire and police systems. One can readily imagine the chaos and tragedy that would result if these services were available only on a private "fee for service" basis in which no aid would be rendered unless a family or individual could make payment then and there. To put it differently, a good is indivisible whenever its benefits cannot be priced and consumed individually. A social good also involves a situation in which one individual's consumption of the good does not normally interfere with or reduce the possibility of consumption by another person. If Mr. Smith uses the public parks normally, this does not exclude Mr. Brown's use of the public parks. The word "normally" is stressed because under some circumstances the crowding of public facilities may change this situation. But usually this is not the case, although major freeways in large cities often become so jammed by peak hours that some people may be excluded—or frightened—from using them!

Because of indivisibility, it is impossible to reduce the benefits from a social good to an individual basis and thus charge a price for the consumption of the good. This is possible in the market sector, where goods and services are priced and consumed on the basis of the benefits the individual believes he receives from consumption of a particular good or service. When we cannot measure benefit on an individual basis and link it to price, it becomes impossible to apply the *exclusion principle* to the good or service in question. This principle, which does apply in the private market, asserts that a person who is unwilling or unable to pay the current price for a commodity or service is excluded from its consumption. But for social goods and services with indivisible benefits, there is no way to exclude anyone from their consumption by using prices. It follows that there is no reason why the individual will pay voluntarily for the benefits received from social goods and services. Consequently, social goods and services will not be produced except by government, which has the power to finance

*The exclusion
principle*

them through taxation, provided of course that the legislative branch is willing to vote the necessary taxes.

Social Goods versus Semi-Social Goods

The foregoing comments apply to pure social goods and services, which are wholly indivisible. We must distinguish between pure social goods and semi-social goods. The latter possess some of the attributes of both social and private goods, and therefore are only partially indivisible, which means they can be priced to a degree on an individual basis. Education, low-cost housing, medical care, are semi-social goods. Even though some of these goods and services are divisible and consequently suitable for individual pricing and production through the market, the market process alone does not produce enough of them to meet the needs of society. Thus they are partly produced in the public sector and partly in the private sector. This division is made by the political process. Decisions concerning, for example, the amount of public schooling we shall have, how much subsidized rental housing there shall be, and who shall receive subsidized medical care are political rather than market decisions. This does not imply that either type of decision is superior.

Examples of semi-social goods

In contrast to both pure social and semi-social goods, purely private goods are wholly divisible and derive completely from private wants. Purely private goods are normally produced in the market sector, although the supplier may be a public body. For example, generation and sale of electrical power by a municipality is a matter of private versus public ownership, rather than a private versus a social good, for clearly electricity is consumed individually. It is not indivisible, in other words.

External Effects

Both the production and consumption of goods and services often involve external effects, or externalities. These are economic gains or losses experienced by an economic unit—a person, a household, a business firm, or the community—not immediately and directly involved in either the production or the consumption of a particular good or service. We saw in Chapter 3 that when a factory pollutes the water in the process of producing goods and services the community bears a social cost. Water pollution is a loss for the community, the cost of which is not absorbed by either the producer or consumer. As we also noted in Chapter 3, an external *gain* takes place when a third party benefits from a transaction in which it has not participated directly; we pointed out that vaccination yields social benefits in addition to the protection afforded the individual who is immunized. So-

67

ciety obviously benefits when a contagious disease is kept under control.

Thus, some goods and services are social because their production or consumption may entail substantial external economies. These economies may be sufficiently important to justify their production through the public sector rather than by the market. For example, the main reason why most education is provided through the public sector is not because education is totally indivisible, but because the production of educational services by the private market would almost certainly result in an insufficient educational output.

A third major feature of social goods and services is that they are exhaustive. This means that they use resources. In this respect they are no different from private goods and services; production of any kind of a good or service uses up resources in the form of land, labor, and capital. The difference is in the way resources are allocated to the public sector as compared to the resource allocation process in the private sector. For public purposes, taxation is the basic means of obtaining the resources needed for production of social goods and services. Note, too, that taxes are not limited to financing production of social goods and services by governmental units, because some government expenditures take the form of transfers such as old-age pensions for retired people, income provided through Medicare, and unemployment compensation. Other transfers from government take the form of subsidies to industries, as in the defense field where not enough output will be produced if decisions are left entirely to market forces. Many farmers also receive subsidies in the soil bank program, where farmers are paid by the government to leave some of their land unplanted to conserve its productive potential (and to reduce the surplus that often develops in such crops as wheat and corn).

Obtaining social goods (margin note)

Benefits and Costs

For most privately produced goods and services, separation between benefits and costs does not exist. The cost to the user of a good or service is its price, which means that the individual user can judge at the time of purchase whether the benefits are worth the price he must pay. But social goods and services are usually distributed to society without any charges based upon benefits received. Consequently there is no simple, direct way for consumers of social goods and services to compare benefit to cost. Costs are met by taxes, which normally, too, are separated in time from the benefit obtained. This lessens the likelihood that the user can make an effective comparison of costs and benefits.

The Size of the Public Sector

What proportion of the nation's total output of goods and services is directed toward satisfaction of social wants? In 1971 the gross national product of the United States totaled $1,046.8 billion, of which 22.3 percent or $233.1 billion was used by federal, state, and local governments to purchase goods and services. These governmental purchases constitute the resources acquired for the production and distribution of social goods and services. The breakdown between federal expenditures and state and local expenditures shows that the federal government accounted for 9.3 percent of the nation's output of social goods, as compared to 13.0 percent for state and local governments. Expenditures for military and defense purposes absorbed 73.2 percent of the expenditures by the federal government for goods and services.

Federal, state, and local expenditures

Growth of the Public Sector

Table 4-1 shows the trend of government purchases of goods and services over the period 1929–1971. These data show significant growth over this period in the relative importance of the public sector and the share of social goods and services in the economy's total output. In 1929 purchases of goods and services by the public sector for all purposes absorbed 8.2 percent of the national output, whereas by 1971 this proportion has risen to 22.3 percent.

TABLE 4-1
Government Purchase of Goods and Services
Selected Years: 1929–1971
(Billions of Current Dollars)

YEAR	FEDERAL GOVERNMENT	STATE AND LOCAL GOVERNMENTS	TOTAL PURCHASES	TOTAL PURCHASES AS A PERCENT OF OUTPUT
1929	$1.3	$7.2	$8.5	8.2%
1935	2.9	7.1	10.0	13.8
1940	6.0	8.0	14.0	14.0
1945	74.2	8.1	82.3	38.8
1950	18.4	19.5	37.9	13.3
1955	44.1	30.1	74.2	18.6
1960	53.5	46.1	99.6	19.8
1965	66.9	70.1	137.0	20.0
1970	97.2	122.2	219.4	22.5
1971 [1]	97.6	135.4	233.1	22.3

[1] Preliminary.
Source: *Economic Report of the President,* 1972.

Before discussing some reasons for the growth of the public sector, let us examine a breakdown of total private consumption and social consumption (public expenditures for goods and services) that reflects our earlier comments on the division of social goods into pure social goods and semi-social goods. This is done in Table 4-2, where these expenditure totals are divided into the consumption of purely private output, purely public output, and semi-public output. The data in Table 4-2 show little recent change in the composition of consumption expenditures when measured this way.

TABLE 4-2

National Consumption by Type of Good and Service
in 1952, 1963, 1970
(Current Dollars and Percent)

TYPE OF CONSUMPTION	DOLLAR VALUE (BILLIONS)			PERCENTAGES		
	1952	1963	1970	1952	1963	1970
Private	$219.7	$375.8	$615.8	73.0%	75.3%	73.7%
Purely Public	53.1	69.6	137.3	17.7	13.9	16.4
Semi-Public	28.0	53.8	82.1	9.3	10.8	9.9
Total	300.8	499.2	835.2	100.0	100.0	100.0

Source: Bernard P. Herber, *Modern Public Finance* (Richard D. Irwin, 1967), p. 47, and *Survey of Current Business,* July, 1971.

In 1970, 73.7 percent of total consumption consisted of purely private goods and services, 16.4 percent was purely public, but 9.9 percent represented semi-public goods and services. There was little change in this distribution between 1952 and 1970. The higher proportion of consumption of a purely public nature in both 1970 and 1952 as compared with 1963 is accounted for by the Korean and Vietnam wars. The term "consumption" in this context designates all private and public expenditures that use up resources, but do not add to the nation's stock of real wealth. No judgment is implied as to whether the type of consumption involved—i.e., military expenditures—is good or bad.

The breakdown in Table 4-2 does not measure the ultimate origin of the goods and services which are the resource inputs for social output. In the American economy the overwhelming proportion of all goods and services produced and sold originates in the private sector, even though ultimately some goods enter the public sector as a part of the social output. For example, the materials entering into highway construction are produced in the private sector, although the total outlay in any period for road building is a part of purely public output.

One of the most important reasons for the growth of expenditures for social goods and services in this century has been war. As the data in Table 4-1 clearly indicate, most of the growth in the purchase of goods and services by the federal sector has resulted from war and defense activities. In the post-World War II period, federal purchases of goods and services for war or defense purposes climbed to and remained at about 75 to 80 percent of the national government's total outlay for goods and services. Figure 4-1 shows the impact of war and defense spending since 1929 by computing these and other types of outlays as a percent of the nation's potential output, the latter being equal to the gross national product adjusted upward by the proportion of the labor force unemployed. The figure also shows in dramatic fashion the output lost because of the Great Depression of the 1930s.

The Size of the Public Sector

Impact of military spending

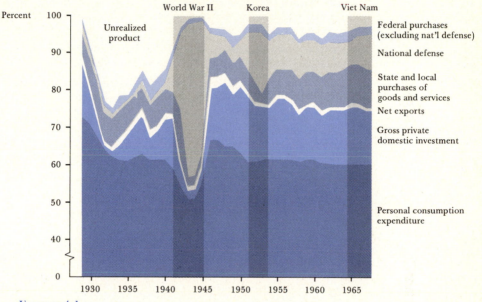

FIGURE 4-1

War, Defense, and Other Expenditures as a Percent of Potential Output.

The impact of World War II and enlarged military expenditures in the postwar period has been a smaller share of the nation's total output potential for personal consumption outlays. This has clearly been a case of trading guns for butter, as compared to the pre-1930 allocation of the nation's output. (Source: Kenneth E. Boulding, *War Industry and the American Economy*, 1970.)

A second important factor in explaining the enlarging demand for social output is the growth and complexity of society. As society becomes more industrialized and urbanized, there is a corresponding growth in social needs which must be met through an enlarged public sector. Urban living is simply more complicated than rural living. As large numbers of people come to live together in a small area, there must be extensive public investment in a variety of facilities, including sewer and waste treatment systems, mass transit, education, health care, public safety, libraries,

Industrialization and urbanization

71

parks, roads, and airports. Some economists have suggested that there is a basic economic principle applicable here. Adolf Wagner, a German fiscal theorist of the nineteenth century, said there is an inherent tendency for the public sector of the economy to grow larger as the economy itself develops. Although there is substantial empirical evidence to support this idea, Wagner did not say whether there is any limit to this process.

Social Balance

The question of the relative size of the public sector has become a source of sometimes heated controversy in recent decades.

The Affluent Society

The debate centers on the issue of social balance, an issue we encountered in Chapter 3. Let us take a closer look at the debate here. Social balance refers to the relative distribution of resources and the nation's output between production of private goods and services and public goods and services. The concept was brought into lively discussion by John Kenneth Galbraith's influential and stimulating work, *The Affluent Society*, which argued that too few resources were being directed to the production of essential social goods, whereas too large a share of output was directed to private goods often of a frivolous and unimportant nature. Galbraith explained this tendency partly by the fact that benefits and costs are separate for social goods, which is not necessarily the case for private goods and services. Critics of the Galbraith thesis argue that credible evidence of this kind of misallocation of resources does not exist. Actually the question of how large a share of the national output ought to be allocated to the public sector for production of social goods cannot be resolved in a definitive way. No magic percentage figure exists to set an upper limit for the production of social goods and services relative to those being turned out in the private sector. If there are limits, they must depend upon circumstances peculiar to a particular time and situation. During World War II, for example, nearly half the output of the American economy was channeled into the public sector for war purposes, a condition which probably could not be sustained for long in peacetime.

The Public Sector and the Distribution of Income

Another key function of the public sector in the modern economy is to influence the distribution of income in society. This distribution relates primarily to money incomes received by individuals and family units: who gets what and why. Our concern is with the ways in which the public sector may change the distribution of money income.

Methods of Income Distribution

Recall the two basic distribution processes for money income One involves participation in the productive process through ownership of economic resources; market forces are the instruments of income distribution. The other involves transfer payments; government provides income to persons who do not participate in production.

Distribution of income through market forces depends upon two things. The first is ownership of economic resources, for without ownership no income can be generated through the market process. It is the demand for the services of economic resources that gives rise to payments, which are income for the owners of the resources. The second is the extent to which resources are actually employed. Idle resources have little value. They always represent a potential for output, but unless they are used they will not yield any income for their owners. Without the use of resources, resource ownership means nothing. These major determinants of income distribution in the market process are influenced by other variables, including innate human abilities, educational opportunities, the degree of mobility possessed by resource owners, and finally, whether resources are controlled by many or few owners (that is, the extent of monopoly).

The extent to which income accrues to individuals through transfer payments is determined primarily by public policy. The fundamental issue concerns the proportion of the income derived from production that ought to be transferred to individuals and families. The best measure of the amount of income which originates through production is the *national income*. Transfers expressed as a percentage of the national income offer an estimate of the amount of income from production being transferred through government activity. Table 4-3 shows transfers in both absolute amount and as a percent of the national income for selected years, 1929–1971.

Note that we are not concerned with transfers within the family, a normal part of the economic process. Usually only one or two members of a family work; others in the family receive income because the wage earners in the family transfer income to them. Intra-family income transfers are not directly affected by public policy to an appreciable extent.

The Lorenz Curve

To understand the impact of public policy on the distribution of income, we need some measure of income distribution. The best

TABLE 4-3

Transfer Expenditures to Persons
Selected Years: 1929–1971
(Billions of Current Dollars)

YEAR	FEDERAL TRANSFERS	STATE AND LOCAL TRANSFERS	TOTAL TRANSFERS	TOTAL TRANSFERS AS A PERCENT OF NATIONAL INCOME
1929	$0.7	$0.2	$0.9	1.6%
1935	0.6	1.2	1.8	3.2
1940	1.4	1.3	2.7	3.3
1945	4.3	1.3	5.6	3.1
1950	10.8	3.5	14.3	5.9
1955	12.4	3.7	16.1	4.9
1960	21.5	5.1	26.6	6.4
1965	30.3	6.9	37.2	6.6
1970	61.2	14.4	75.6	9.5
1971 [1]	73.4	17.0	90.4	10.6

[1] Preliminary.

Source: *Economic Report of the President,* 1972.

*Lorenz curve as
measure of income
distribution*

known device is the *Lorenz curve,* (Figure 4-2), which arrays on one axis the percentage of spending units in the economy (normally the family unit) and on the other axis the percentage of income received by these spending units. The Lorenz curve in Figure 4-2 shows the distribution of money income in the United States in 1968. The 45-degree line in the diagram is called the line of equal distribution, because it shows the distribution of income if income were divided equally among all spending units.

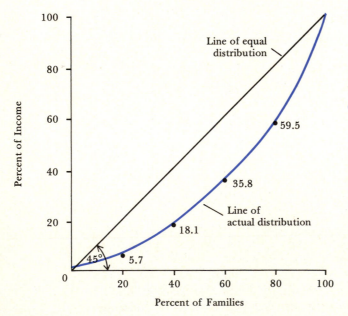

FIGURE 4-2

The Distribution of Money Income in the United States (Families Only): 1968.

The Lorenz curve arrays income on the vertical axis and family units on the horizontal axis to show the proportion of total income received by a given proportion of family units. The closer the line of actual distribution is to the 45-degree line, the more equal the distribution of money income. (Source: *Statistical Abstract,* 1970.)

This is not the situation, though. The second line in the diagram represents the actual distribution, showing less than complete equality in the distribution of income. For 1968, the Lorenz curve reveals that the lower 20 percent of the spending units received 5.7 percent of the total income; 40 percent of the spending units received 18.1 percent of the total income; 60 percent received 35.8 percent; and 80 percent received 59.5 percent. The 20 percent at the top received the remaining 40.5 percent of the income total. Economists and statisticians concerned with measurement of income distribution in our society point out that there has been no significant change in the distributional pattern ever since World War II, although all spending units have experienced absolute increases in their income in this period.

The Lorenz curve is also used to show the distribution of wealth in the economy. Wealth in this context refers to property and other privately held claims upon the assets of the society, including bonds, stocks, and money. A Lorenz curve of this type is shown in Figure 4-3, using net worth as a measure of personal

Lorenz curve as measure of wealth distribution

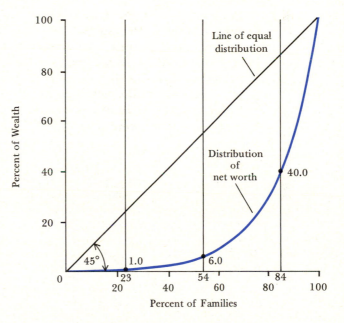

FIGURE 4-3

The Distribution of Wealth in the United States: 1953.

Contrast this Lorenz curve with that shown in Figure 4-2. The important point is that there is much greater inequality in the distribution of wealth (net worth) than there is in the distribution of money income. [Source: Robert J. Lampman, *The Share of Top Wealth-Holders in National Wealth, 1922–56* (Princeton, N.J.: Princeton University Press, 1962).]

wealth. It is apparent that the distribution of wealth in the society is significantly more unequal than the distribution of income. A larger proportion of total claims upon the assets of the society is held by a smaller proportion of the total population than is true for the receipt of income.

Little is actually known about what has happened to the distribution of wealth in the United States since the early 1950s. Pioneering work by Professor Robert Lampman of the University of Wisconsin indicated that there had been some slight decline in the extreme inequality in the ownership of wealth between 1922 and 1956, a period in which the share of personal wealth owned by the very wealthy—the top 1 percent of all wealth holders— dropped from 32 percent to 25 percent. But Lampman's research also found that in every peacetime period in which there was growth in the national output the share of the very wealthy in the ownership of personal wealth also increased. Thus it seems likely that since the early 1950s the share of the top wealth holders in ownership of the nation's assets has moved back toward the level that prevailed in the early 1920s.

Changing Income Distribution

Basically a government changes the distribution of income by the taxes it levies and the transfer payments it makes. Taxes reduce the disposable income available to individuals and families. Transfers have the opposite effect, increasing the amount of disposable income available to the society. Transfers to persons do this directly, whereas subsidies to industries do it indirectly. In principle, then, the public sector alters a market-determined distribution of income by the kinds of taxes levied and the transfer expenditures undertaken. For example, the distribution of income could be made less unequal by a combination of taxes that fall primarily upon upper income groups and transfer payments directed mainly at the lower income groups. On the other hand, if the government taxed some persons in order to subsidize particular industries, the effect might be a less equal distribution of income. Table 4-4 shows the distribution of both benefits (estimated) and taxes by income class, a comparison which must be made to gain any overall grasp of the impact of total government activity on the distribution of real income in the nation.

Although taxes and transfer payments are direct ways to change income distribution, they may also work indirectly. For example, a change in the tax law affecting inheritance may alter the ownership of nonhuman resources, which in turn will ultimately affect income distribution. The government also affects income distribution by making educational opportunities available to the population at large. Undoubtedly, the introduction of free public education reduced income inequality because it opened the way for an increasing number of people to participate effectively in the economic process. Government actions which affect the extent of monopoly in the economy or the mobility of economic resources may also have an impact upon the distribution of income. Monopolies, for example, can generally command higher incomes than businesses which have to face competition; thus if the government breaks up monopolies, income distribution may become

TABLE 4-4

Taxes Paid and Transfer Payments
Received by Income Class: 1968
(Billions of Dollars)

INCOME CLASS	TAXES PAID	TRANSFER PAYMENTS RECEIVED	TAXES MINUS TRANSFERS
Under $2,000	$3.1	$6.6	$—3.5
$2,000–3,999	8.2	11.5	—3.3
4,000–5,999	14.7	9.3	5.4
6,000–7,999	23.4	6.7	16.7
8,000–9,999	27.4	5.2	22.2
10,000–14,999	65.5	8.6	56.9
15,000–24,999	57.1	5.7	51.4
25,000–49,999	29.7	1.9	27.8
Over $50,000	24.9	0.2	24.7
Total	$254.0	$55.7	$198.3

Source: Bureau of the Census.

somewhat less unequal. If some workers lack the means to move from areas where jobs are scarce to areas where jobs are more plentiful, their share of the national income will be adversely affected. Consequently, any action, such as a program of relocation loans, which increased the ability of workers to take advantage of job opportunities might lessen income inequality.

The Question of Equality

The underlying question is the extent of equality in income distribution deemed to be just by a society. This question does not permit an objective answer; the whole issue is loaded with subjective values. History suggests, however, that most people agree in principle that movement toward more equal income distribution is better than movement in the opposite direction. To achieve greater income equity means that the structure of both taxes and transfer payments must be progressive. Such a structure is illustrated in Figure 4-4, which shows that the proportion of income paid in taxes increases as income increases, whereas the proportion of income received as transfer payments declines when income rises.

*Progressive taxes
and transfers*

A progressive tax and transfer structure clearly would reduce inequality in the distribution of income, but the extent of the change would depend on the income level at which a break-even point between taxes and transfers occurs. The proportion of the income acquired through the process of production that ought to be transferred to nonparticipants in the economic process is ultimately a matter of social policy, which a democratic society must

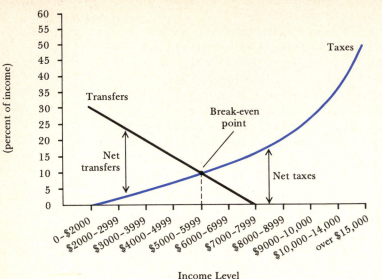

FIGURE 4-4

Progressive Structure of Taxes and Transfer Payments.

The figures in the diagram are illustrative, not actual. They show that up to an income range of $5,000–$5,999 families receive more income from transfer payments than they pay in taxes, thus making a net gain from the combined effect of transfers and taxes. Beyond this income bracket families pay out more in taxes than they receive in transfers.

decide through the political process. What the economist can—and should—point out is that in a society which experiences meaningful economic growth it becomes increasingly possible to transfer a larger proportion of the national income without impairing either the standard of living or the economic effectiveness of participants in the market process. This is a point frequently overlooked by over-zealous advocates of a "no growth" society. Unless they are willing to freeze the existing distribution of income and wealth—which is probably not the case—a slowdown or cessation of economic growth cannot help but intensify the conflict over the distribution of the national income.

Charity

The economist must also stress that throughout history no society has depended wholly on the market process to distribute income. In all societies there are persons who cannot participate in the productive process; consequently, if income distribution depended only on the private market, some people would be without income and left to starve. Most societies do not tolerate this condition, working out a variety of extramarket arrangements to distribute income to those who cannot take part in production. The oldest of these arrangements is private charity, which in poor countries may mean little more than begging.

The Public Sector and Economic Stabilization

Another major function of government is to maintain conditions favorable to full employment, price stability, and a satisfactory rate of economic growth. This function is the most recent addition to the agenda of the modern state.

Direct concern by the public sector with production and the employment level results primarily from the experience of the Great Depression when unemployment at its worst reached approximately 25 percent of the labor force. The catastrophe of the 1930s was directly responsible for enactment by Congress of the Employment Act of 1946. By making the federal government responsible for maintaining high levels of employment and maximum purchasing power, the Employment Act committed the federal government to policies that result in full employment in the economic system. It also established the President's Council of Economic Advisers, which brought economists into a key role in government planning and policy making.

During the 1950s the American economy grew sluggishly, particularly compared to the fast pace of the leading economies in Western Europe and the Soviet Union during that decade. This experience forced the federal government to concern itself with the rate of economic growth, including development of policies to improve and even stimulate the economy's rate of growth. In the late 1960s and early 1970s inflation emerged as the nation's most urgent economic problem, primarily as the result of the military buildup and the diversion of resources to the war in Vietnam after 1965. Consequently, public policy measures shifted away from growth and toward inflation control as a major objective.

The post-World War II era has thus seen increasing concern at different times with one or more of the facets of the economy's aggregate performance, namely the employment level, the rate of economic growth, and the price level. These problems have not been resolved because economic management has not yet achieved both full employment and an adequate rate of growth without inflation. We will have more to say about them later. But, as we have seen, the notion that all economic growth is necessarily good, easily accepted in the 1950s, is being widely challenged now, particularly since much growth brings with it undesirable social costs in the form of pollution, urban overcrowding, and ecological damage. These are some of the yet unresolved issues of public policy in this nation.

Taxation and the Public Sector

The Employment Act of 1946

Growth and inflation after World War II

Taxation and the Public Sector

To carry out its functions, the public sector must have access to real and money resources. Taxation supplies most of the revenues for governmental activities. For normal operations and for the long run, taxation is the primary revenue source for any governmental unit, although, like business firms and individuals, governments borrow money. Borrowing should not, however, be viewed as a permanent revenue source for the government, just as it cannot be a permanent source of revenue for the household or business firm.

Taxes are compulsory payments by citizens to their government. Taxation is an attribute of sovereignty because the power to tax is inherent in the concept of a sovereign state; it is one of the fundamental attributes of the political state in contrast to the household, the private business firm, or any other organization in modern society. Only the state possesses the power to tax. In an economic sense and from the viewpoint of society as a whole, taxes are a claim upon the currently produced income and output of the society. There is no other continuing source for taxes than what society currently creates as income. Taxes on wealth, such as inheritance taxes and capital gains, present a special case, but not a departure from the fundamental idea that ultimately taxes come from income. The worth of any asset depends upon its expected income; hence taxes on wealth are an indirect way of getting at income because they will reduce the future income-producing ability of the asset subject to the tax.

The Basic Forms of Taxation

There are a variety of ways in which governments can levy taxes, but they can be lumped under three categories. The state may tax income directly, either personal or corporate income. The state may also tax transactions, as through various sales and excise taxes. These taxes may be either general or selective; they may apply to all transactions or sales, or only to selected ones. Finally, the state may tax property, including claims to property. Claims to property—as distinct from property itself—include debts, equities, deeds, and money held by individuals and business firms. Income, sales, and property taxes are simply different ways to reach the same objective, namely to enable the public sector to claim a part of society's real output and money income.

One new type of tax that Americans will be hearing about in the next few years is the *value-added* tax, or VAT as it is known for short. This tax is widely used in Western Europe. Essentially it is a tax on the difference between gross sales and material costs —value added—as measured at each stage in the production process. It is a tax on transactions, and if enacted by the federal government would amount to a national sales tax. The main difference between this type of sales tax and that commonly in use in the states is that in the value-added tax the amount of the tax is built into the price of the final product and not added on at the time of a sale, as is the practice with most state sales taxes.

Sources of Taxes

Table 4-5 shows recent data on the major sources of tax revenue for federal, state, and local governments in the United States. These taxes are grouped according to the basic classification for taxing income, transactions, or property and claims to property. The data in this table show dramatically that the federal government depends overwhelmingly upon taxes on income, whereas the states look primarily to taxes on transactions for revenue, and property taxes are most important for local government.

TABLE 4-5
Sources of Tax Revenue for Federal,
State, and Local Governments, 1969–70
(In Percent)

TYPE OF TAXATION	FEDERAL GOVERNMENT	STATE GOVERNMENTS	LOCAL GOVERNMENTS
Income	84.4%	26.9%	4.2%
Transactions	12.5	56.8	7.9
Property	—	2.3	84.9
Other	3.1	14.0	3.0
	100.0	100.0	100.0

Source: U.S. Department of Commerce, *Government Finances in 1969–70.*

A recent political debate centered on the idea of revenue sharing, which means having the federal government turn back some of its revenues on an unrestricted basis to state governments. This is not entirely new, because the federal government has been granting aid to the states for a long time; but grants-in-aid are earmarked for specific purposes. The new feature of the recent debate involved *unrestricted* grants to the states from the federal government, based upon some fixed proportion of federal revenues. Proponents of revenue sharing also required that the states funnel some of the money they will receive to local (city and county) governments, now heavily dependent upon property taxes, which do not expand adequately with local needs.

Revenue sharing

The Tax Base and the Tax Rate

Certain technical features of tax systems must be understood. One of these is the *tax base,* the object of taxation; it may be income for an income tax, transactions for a sales tax, or a property or claim to property for a property tax. The problem of defining a tax base is both economic and legal, particularly with respect to taxation of income in any form. Another concern is the *tax rate*

Proportional, progressive, and regressive rates

and the *rate structure*. Rate is the proportion of the value of the tax base claimed by the state as a tax. For example, an income tax rate of 10 percent means that 10 percent of income (however defined) is taxed. A 3 percent sales tax means 3 percent of the value of sales is taxed. The rate structure determines what happens to the tax rate as the base changes. A rate structure may be *proportional, progressive,* or *regressive.* In a proportional rate structure the rate does not change as the base changes. For example, an income tax constructed so that the rate is 10 percent without concern for the size of the base is a proportional tax. On the other hand, a structure in which the rate increases as the base increases is a progressive tax. This idea is most familiar to many people in connection with the income tax. The federal income tax has a progressive rate structure: as the base (income) increases, the rate at which the base is taxed also increases. In a regressive tax structure, the rate declines as the base increases. Very few taxes are designed to be regressive in principle, although taxes on transactions, such as a sales tax, are regressive in practice. This is because savings are not subject to sales tax. It is well recognized that as incomes get bigger, a growing proportion of income is saved. Since a sales tax applies only to the part of an income that is spent, the actual proportion of income taxed under a sales tax will decline as the income gets larger.

The Impact of Taxes

Finally, there are questions relating to the *impact* and the *incidence* of a tax. Impact is the point in the economic system where the tax is initially levied. For example, the impact of a sales tax may be on a retail merchant, as he or she is the person charged legally with making the payment of the tax to the government. The incidence refers to the ultimate burden of the tax; it is a matter of who finally pays. The ultimate burden of most sales taxes is believed to be upon the consumer, primarily because the retailer (or the wholesaler or manufacturer) can often shift the tax forward through higher prices. This is what would happen with the value-added tax. Sometimes, though, transaction taxes are shifted backwards from a retailer to a supplier or even to resource owners.

Some Basic Issues in Taxation

The question of standards to be applied in the tax system is probably as old as government itself. Adam Smith in *The Wealth of*

Nations laid down four maxims with respect to taxation which largely remain valid today.[3]

1. The subjects of every state ought to contribute toward the support of government, as nearly as possible, in proportion to their respective abilities.

2. The tax which each individual is bound to pay ought to be certain and not arbitrary.

3. Every tax ought to be levied at a time, or in a manner, in which it is most likely to be convenient for the contributor to pay it.

4. Every tax ought to be so contrived as to take and keep out of the pockets of the people as little as possible, over and above what it brings into the public treasury of the state.

There is little disagreement with these maxims, particularly the latter three, although the issue of equitable taxation (the first maxim) is not readily resolved. To speak of equity in taxation is to speak to the problem of distributing the ultimate burden of the tax system. The issues are who shall pay taxes and in what amount, and there is no universal agreement on how this is done. In the years since publication of Smith's famous treatise, however, several principles have emerged and been applied toward the goal of achieving equity in taxation.

The three major principles concerned with equity in the distribution of the tax burden are the principle of equal treatment for taxpayers equally situated; the benefit principle; and the principle of ability to pay. It must be underscored that these principles do not offer a final answer, but they do provide some rough-and-ready guideposts.

Equal Treatment for Equal Situations

The first principle is that taxpayers equally situated should be equally treated. It is difficult to apply this principle literally because as a matter of fact and of necessity all societies discriminate in a variety of ways with respect to the tax base. For example, at the federal level, income from oil or gas production is taxed differently from other income; individuals who may have the same income but whose circumstances differ in other respects—for example, family size—are taxed differently.

The principle means essentially that any discrimination or classification applied to either the tax base or the economic status of some taxpayers ought to be reasonable and in itself equitable. What constitutes reasonableness and equity in this connection is a matter for interpretation by both administrative authority and the court system. As this principle is applied to taxation it means that individuals or groups should not be subject to arbitrary or

Reasonable taxation

[3] Smith, *Wealth of Nations*, pp. 777–778.

capricious differential tax treatment. It does not completely rule out discrimination with respect to the tax base or the treatment of people in a particular classification.

The Benefit Principle

The benefit principle states that people ought to pay taxes in proportion to the benefits they receive from public activity. This principle comes closest to the application of market principles to the financing of government activities. One of the advantages of this principle is that it ties tax decisions closely to expenditure decisions, avoiding the difficulties that stem from a separation of the costs and benefits for governmental activities. One of the best known applications of the benefit principle is the use of motor vehicle and gasoline taxes to finance street and highway construction. Another use of the principle is in making assessments against property whose value is improved as a result of public expenditures, as in paving of a street or sidewalk adjoining the property.

Note, however, that the use of the benefit principle does not necessarily reduce costs and benefits to an individual basis. Street financing is a case in point. Streets and highways remain collective goods, for which there is no charge for use on an individual basis. The exception is a toll road, on which payment is made directly for use. As a practical matter, the benefit principle can only be applied to a group—automobile owners, for example—that can readily be identified with the benefits they get from a public activity, such as streets and highways. Actually, the benefit principle has a limited applicability because of the extreme difficulty of measuring benefits in relation to users for most govermental purposes. This is another instance of the indivisibility of public goods.

Ability to Pay

The third and perhaps most important principle of taxation is ability to pay. This principle is widely accepted as the proper way to attain equity in taxation. Simply put, the principle says that people ought to be taxed in accordance with their ability to pay. This is essentially Adam Smith's first maxim. Even though the principle is widely recognized, its application involves a number of complex problems. The first is definition.

Historically, both wealth and income have been the most important measures of ability to pay. Income is the ultimate source of ability to pay, although wealth may be a source of income and thus a kind of proxy for ability to pay. For the individual, as distinct from society as a whole, claims to wealth as well as wealth itself are a source of income. This helps explain why property taxes emerged in the nineteenth century as a major source of revenue, especially for local governments. Then the United States was largely agricultural, and land, the most important single form of wealth, was also the major resource used in production and the creation of income. Taxation of land in the nineteenth century was an effective way to tax income. Today this is no longer true, and consequently the continued reliance of local governments on the property tax is an anachronism. Property taxes too often do not get to the real source of tax-paying ability, namely income, a point that President Nixon recognized in his 1972 State of the Union address.

Most tax authorities now recognize income as the most suitable measure of ability to pay, even though our tax system does not fully reflect this. Too often the tax system, at federal, state, and local levels, does not apply any principle designed to attain justice in the distribution of the tax burden; rather it reflects simple expediency, as governments try to obtain the greatest revenue with least protest from the taxpayer. Nevertheless, income remains the most suitable measure of ability to pay. The real problem is how to define and measure income for tax purposes, a matter which is both complex and controversial

Expediency

Once income is accepted as the best measure of ability to pay, assuming a satisfactory definition of income is reached, the appropriate rate structure for the tax system must be determined. Generally, the United States and other Western nations accept the principle of progressive income taxation. Some economists argue that the philosophical justification for a progressive income tax is fairly shaky, but as a matter of fact, progression in the rate structure is probably accepted more for pragmatic than philosophic reasons. It is believed, in general, that it is better to have a tax system that tends to reduce rather than increase inequality in income distribution. A non-progressive rate structure for taxing income would not have this result.

Questions for Review and Discussion

1. Discuss the reason why automobiles are usually built by private firms and highways are usually built by governments.
2. What do we mean when we say certain social goods are indivisible? Give an example of such a good or service.
3. What is the distinction between a pure social good and a semi-social good? Give an example of each.
4. Give reasons why most education is provided through the public sector rather than the private sector. What characteristic of social goods is responsible for this?

5. Give reasons for the growth of expenditures for social goods and services in the U.S. economy in the past fifty years.

6. How is income distributed by market forces? What does the Lorenz curve tell us about income distribution?

7. What methods does the U.S. government use to change the distribution of income?

8. What does it mean to say that one function of the U.S. government is stabilization?

9. What is the greatest source of federal tax revenues? Of local government tax revenues?

10. Explain the benefit and ability-to-pay principles of taxation.

11. How well do our present taxes—federal, state, and local—conform to the maxims laid down by Adam Smith nearly two hundred years ago?

12. Explain the difference between the tax rate and the rate structure.

5

National Product and Its Measurement

IN THIS and the next three chapters we begin to analyze the forces which determine the performance of the economy as a whole. We have two major objectives: first, to understand the meaning of the widely used statistical magnitudes of output, employment, the price level, and the rate of economic growth; and second, to understand how the economy's performance can be influenced by public policy. We start with measurement.

Economists use the term *national income and social accounting* to describe the series of statistical techniques developed in the United States and most other modern nations for measuring economic performance. In the United States serious study of national income measurement developed during the 1920s and earlier, but progress in this branch of economics was strongly accelerated during the Great Depression. During World War II measures of the national product and the national income proved extremely useful in determining how to allocate resources in an economy marked by widespread shortages.

National income and social accounting

87

An accounting system for the national economy is similar to an accounting system for an individual business firm. It provides a numerical record of what transpired during a particular period. For the national economy the normal accounting period is the calendar year, although data are compiled more frequently for special purposes. As with the business firm, total expenditures and their allocations are in balance. In the United States the National Income Division of the Department of Commerce has primary responsibility for compiling and publishing data on the performance of the economy as a whole.

Income and Wealth

Income and wealth are two concepts crucial both to an understanding of the economic process and to economic analysis. When the economist refers to the income of the economy as a whole he refers to a flow of output. Income is a flow phenomenon because it is measured over a period of time, another illustration of how time enters into economic analysis. When we say that the national income is a flow of output we mean that it is made up of the volume of economically valuable goods and services produced during a particular time period.

Income: A Flow

*Total production
in a period*

Income, or the output flow, is the most important single measure of economic performance at our disposal, because the total production of economically valuable goods and services in an economy during a period determines what living standards can be attained during that period. This output flow represents the total of goods and services available to satisfy all the demands that may be made upon the resources of the economic system.

Typically, the flow of production is measured by the money value of the goods and services that make up the flow. This can be a problem, in part because money is not a stable measuring rod: its value fluctuates in response to changes in the general level of prices. We must therefore devise a technique that takes such changes into account to compare the flow of income for an economy in two different time periods.

Wealth: A Stock

The concept of *wealth,* a term less widely used than income, is nonetheless highly significant in economics. In contrast to income, which is a flow phenomenon, wealth is the stock of material things possessing economic value that exist at an instant in time.

We measure the wealth of a society with reference to a particular point of time. Table 5-1 contains estimates of the national wealth of the United States for selected years. Note that the concept of wealth does not include services, which, being intangibles, cannot exist over time; services must be utilized at the moment at which they are produced.

TABLE 5-1
National Wealth in the United States
(Selected Years)

	YEARS				
	1900	1929	1948	1958	1967
Total National Wealth (billions of current dollars)	$88	$439	$928	$1,703	$2,828
Per Capita Wealth	$1,145	$3,586	$6,274	$9,698	$13,854
Ratio of total wealth to Gross National Product	5.2	4.3	3.6	3.8	3.6
Population (millions)	76.8	122.4	147.9	175.6	200.3

Source: *Statistical Abstract of the United States, 1970.*

For the economy as a whole, a distinction must be made between wealth and various claims to wealth, such as shares of stock, debts, or other ownership instruments. This distinction is important because we frequently form an overall picture of an individual's assets by lumping together items of physical wealth with various claims that may be in his possession. This will not do for the economy as a whole; if we followed this procedure many things would be counted twice. For example, if the market value of all the outstanding shares of General Motors stock were added together with an estimate of the value of the physical plant of the corporation, the result would be double-counting, for the value of the stock itself includes the value of the General Motors physical plant.

Finally, a word should be said about the peculiar role money plays in this connection. The individual considers the money he has on hand part of his total wealth. But from the standpoint of the national economy, money is not wealth but a generalized claim to other assets. We shall discuss the various aspects of money and its use in the modern economy later in much greater detail.

The Relationship Between Income and Wealth

The key relationship between income and wealth provides the conceptual basis for important aspects of our national income and social accounting system. Since income is a flow phenomenon, the

89

natural question is how society disposes of this flow. Aside from services, for which production cannot be separated from consumption, the answer is quite simple. Output produced during a period of time must either be used up, that is, consumed, or not used up. In the latter case, saving has taken place.

But if some part of the economy's output in a period is not consumed, what happens to it? Any part of current output which is not consumed in a given period is necessarily added to the economy's stock of wealth. The stock of goods on hand at the beginning of the production period will be increased at the end of the production period by the exact amount of output not consumed during that period. Figure 5-1 shows this process by means of a

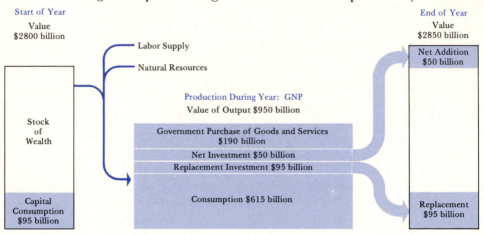

FIGURE 5-1

The Relationship Between Income and Wealth.

The diagram shows that at the start of a hypothetical year the economy's stock of wealth totaled $2,800 billion and that during the year $950 billion in goods and services were produced. The economy used up $900 billion, leaving $50 billion as a net addition to the stock of wealth, which at the end of the year totaled $2,850 billion.

diagram. The economist describes an increase in the economy's stock of wealth as the act of investment. Investment basically means the process of adding to the economy's stock of economically valuable goods. These goods, it should be understood, may take a variety of forms; they may be goods in process, raw materials, or finished goods, on the shelves and in the storerooms of business firms, which have not yet passed into the hands of the ultimate users.

It is important to understand that we are looking at this process in an *ex-post* sense. *Ex-post* means looking at an event after it has happened. After the fact, it is clear that *the act of saving is identical with the act of investment.* Saving and investment are the two sides of the same coin. To put it differently, saving takes place in the economic system whenever all of the current output is not consumed, and, in similar fashion, investment takes place when there has been a net addition to the economy's stock of wealth. Thus, in an *ex-post* sense saving and investment are always identical.

We have defined saving as non-consumption and investment as adding to the economy's stock of goods. These are fundamental definitions. It should be mentioned, however, that complications arise from the introduction of money into the process, as well as from taking into account the intentions of those who do the saving in the economy as well as those who do the investing. The economic concepts of saving and investing differ significantly from popular notions. We will deal with these various complications later; they need not at this point obscure our understanding of the basic relationship between saving and investment.

The Key Components of National Output

We have seen that the output flow can be divided into a part which is consumed and a part which is not consumed. It can also be divided among four major output categories, which provide the basis for the most effective measures of output that economists have yet devised. We shall discuss each of these output categories individually and then discuss the actual measures of the economy's performance.

Consumer Goods and Services

The first major category is consumer or consumption goods and services, which are defined as that part of current output designed directly to satisfy human wants. They include such diverse goods and services as automobiles, food and beverages, clothing, household equipment, rents, transportation services, and the services of physicians and lawyers. In contrast, machines and equipment purchased by business firms are not consumption goods. It is the general practice in the American economy to measure the output of consumer goods and services by the amount spent on them by households and private nonprofit institutions. The United States Department of Commerce classifies consumer goods and services in three sub-categories:

*Durables,
non-durables,
services*

    1. consumer durables, such as automobiles, household appliances, household furniture, and other goods which can be expected to last more than a year;
    2. consumer non-durables, mostly food and clothing, which are commodities consumed within a year;
    3. services, which are "consumed" at the time of purchase.

91

We will use the letter C to designate the output of consumer goods and services in a period.

Investment Goods

A second major category in the output flow is investment goods. In a broad sense, this category includes all additions to the economy's stock of wealth during a period. This was the basic meaning that we gave to investment earlier in our discussion of the relationship between income and wealth. But current practices in national income and social accounting have led to some modification of this concept, primarily because of the statistical difficulty of gathering the information on all additions to wealth. Therefore, the investment goods category of the output total is limited in actual practice to the following:

1. All purchases by business firms of new structures and equipment.
2. All purchases of new houses for residential purposes.
3. All changes in inventories held by business firms.

The first category of investment expenditure obviously consists of additions to the stock of productive instruments. For example, a printer acquires a new high-speed press or an auto manufacturer gets a new stamping machine. The purchase of a new house is an addition to the stock of wealth, even though in the minds of many people it is probably a consumer good rather than an investment good. Changes in inventories represent changes in the stock of goods in process or on hand and fit readily into our basic definition of investment as involving a change in the economy's stock of wealth.

One qualification of the investment category is in order. Included in investment necessarily are replacements for capital instruments which have worn out. Production requires the use of capital and these instruments, like any physical good, will wear out or become exhausted through use. Consequently, the total investment expenditure in any given period of time cannot be added to the economy's stock of wealth. Some part of it must be designated as replacement investment. The excess of the investment total above the amount needed for replacement purposes is net investment; it represents the amount of investment goods at the economy's disposal for adding to its stock of wealth in the form of equipment, buildings, and inventories. We shall designate investment by I.

Government Purchases of Goods and Services

The third major category in the output stream consists of goods and services purchased by government units in the economic system. Government units, state and local as well as federal, purchase goods produced by the private sector of the economy and an array of labor services. These represent the share of the output total being utilized by the public sector. As we pointed out in Chapter 4, the output of the public sector is basically collective. Government purchases of goods and services are therefore the inputs necessary for the production of collective goods and services.

The output of the public sector is distributed on a different basis from that of the market sector. Valuation of social goods and services is difficult because in most instances these goods and services are not sold in individual units to the ultimate users at a price, as is true for most privately produced goods and services. We must measure the cost of the input of goods and services required for this output in order to get a measure of its value to society as a whole. What governments pay for the goods they buy from private firms and what they pay their employees are the costs of the input of the public sector. Consequently, in modern systems of national income and social accounting, government purchase of goods and services has become the best measure of output originating in the public sector. The letter *G* will be used in referring to this category of the output total.

Transfer Expenditures

Transfer expenditures occur at all levels of government, and differ from the purchases of goods and services in that they do not absorb a part of the national output. As we have indicated, these expenditures are called transfers because, in effect, they bring about the transfer—or shift—of income from one individual or one social group to another. The government is the instrument through which such a redistribution of income is effected.

Transfer expenditures on the federal level are financed by taxes paid by individuals and business firms. The basic difference between a transfer payment and government purchase of goods and services is that in the latter instance the government receives an equivalent value in goods or services for its money outlays. In a sense transfers may be viewed as negative taxes because they represent a one-way flow of income from the government to the individual, whereas taxes represent a one-way flow of income from the individual to the government. It is important to understand that we are not saying that transfers have no influence on the level of economic activity; both transfers and taxes are important in this respect. But transfers do not enter directly into output totals as do government purchases of goods and services. Their influence on output is exercised indirectly by affecting the disposable income available to the public. We shall expand on this point shortly.

Negative taxes

Net Exports of Goods and Services

The final major category into which we can divide the output total is usually described as net exports. Net exports equal the difference between a nation's exports of goods and services and its imports of goods and services. Exports of goods and services measure purchase of the national output made outside a nation's borders, while imports are expenditures made by its residents for the output of other countries. As long as there are no transfers of income to or from foreign residents, net exports are the same as net foreign investment. If a nation's exports exceed its imports, then net foreign investment will be positive, but if its imports are in excess of exports then net foreign investment will be negative. We shall designate net exports by X_n.

Expenditures and End-Users

The magnitudes of the categories of the output stream are measured by the expenditures made for them by *end-users*. The end-users of consumer goods and services are households and non-profit institutions; for investment goods, business firms are the end-users. For government purchases of goods and services, the end-users are obviously the governmental units of the economic system, while for net exports we may say that the rest of the world constitutes the end-users. If net foreign investment is positive it means a part of the output stream has gone abroad; if it is negative, it means that there has been a diversion of output from the rest of the world to the national economy.

The Gross National Product

We now have the necessary background to discuss actual measures of income and product currently in use in the modern economy. We have already introduced the most important of these: the gross national product or GNP. The gross national product is the value in current prices of all final goods and services produced by the economic system during a designated time period, normally the calendar year. It is the best known and most widely used single measure of the economy's performance.

The gross national product measures the total output of economically useful goods and services during the relevant time period. The output total is called "gross" because the capital goods consumed or worn out during the process of production have not been deducted from the total, and "national" because it refers to productive activities that originate with the residents of a nation.

TABLE 5-2
Gross National Product for the United States: 1971[1]
(Billions of Current Dollars)

ITEM	AMOUNT [2]
Personal Consumption Expenditures	$662.2
Durable Goods	(100.4)
Nondurable goods	(278.8)
Services	(283.0)
Gross Private Domestic Investment	150.8
Plant and Equipment	(108.2)
Residential Structures	(40.6)
Inventory Change	(2.1)
Government Purchase of Goods and Services	233.1
Federal	(97.6)
State and Local	(135.4)
Net Exports of Goods and Services	0.7
Exports	(65.5)
Imports	(64.8)
Gross National Product	*1,046.8*

[1] Preliminary data.
[2] Details may not add to total because of rounding.
Source: *Economic Report of the President*, 1972.

The standard procedure for measuring the gross national product is to sum up the flow of expenditures made during the time period by the end-users for the four output categories discussed in the previous section. Table 5-2 shows the GNP data in detail for the United States in 1971. There are several aspects of GNP that warrant emphasis.

Goods and Services

First, gross national product is a measure of currently produced goods and services; that is, it relates to all production taking place within the current production period. For national income and social accounting this is normally the calendar year.

Second, it measures final goods and services. In national income and social accounting the practice is to distinguish between *final* and *intermediate* goods and services. The latter are goods purchased for resale. This distinction is made to avoid double-accounting. Since the GNP is obtained by summing up expenditure totals, all intermediate goods and services must be excluded

Final vs. intermediate goals

95

from this process; otherwise we would be counting many things twice. For example, the price of bread includes the price of the flour needed to make the bread and the price of the wheat needed to make the flour. Wheat and flour are intermediate goods if they are incorporated into the bread; we do not want to add their prices into our product totals along with the price of bread to get a measure of output. If we counted the price of flour and wheat as well as the price of bread, the total would overstate the amount of production taking place. Flour, of course, may be a final product if it is sold directly to the housewife. Even wheat may be a final product if, for example, it is exported.

Prices

Third, the gross national product is normally measured in current prices, which we define as the prices prevailing in the current production period. This may pose a problem if we wish to compare the gross national product of two different periods, because the purchasing power of the dollar fluctuates, a consequence of changes in the general level of all prices. We shall discuss in a subsequent section the technical details involved in adjusting for price level changes.

Imputed Values

Fourth, the gross national product measure is largely, though not wholly, limited to production reflected in market transactions. Certain types of productive activity, for example, the labor of the housewife, will be excluded from our gross national product total. In other words, the figures tend to understate the actual amount of productive activity taking place in the economic system. To a degree the United States Department of Commerce compensates for this by including some "imputed" values in its calculation of gross national product. The most important of these are the value of food produced and consumed on farms, the rental income of owner-occupied houses, and certain other non-monetary transactions. For example, in 1970, the value of food produced and consumed on farms was $748 million, while the estimated rental income of owner-occupied homes was $59.6 billion.

Finally, let us stress again that the gross national product is a measure of output as reflected in the spending flows of the major spending entities in the economy. Hence it is not only a measure of gross spending and output in the economy in the period, but also a measure of gross income, for the basic fact is that production and output are the source of money income in any society. One should be cautious here, though, because not all of the gross money income created by the productive process is necessarily received as income by individuals. As we discuss several alternative

Measurement of the Alternative Approach to Gross National Product

Another way to derive the gross national product is to sum up the charges against the output flow, the allocations made against the gross national product in terms of what it costs the society to obtain that amount of output. Three types of charges are worth examining in detail, and several relatively minor charges on the allocation side of the GNP will receive brief mention. The data of Table 5-3 summarize both the expenditure and the allocations side for the gross national product for 1971.

TABLE 5-3

Gross National Product: Expenditure
Flows and Charges: 1971[1]
(Billions of Current Dollars)[2]

EXPENDITURE FLOWS		CHARGES AGAINST GNP	
1. Personal Consumption Expenditures	$662.2	1. Compensation of Employees	$641.8
2. Gross Private Domestic Investment	150.8	2. Proprietor's Income	68.4
3. Government Purchase of Goods and Services	233.1	3. Dividends	25.5
4. Net Exports of Goods and Services	0.7	4. Corporate Profits Tax Liabilities	33.5
		5. Undistributed Profits	21.7
		6. Rental Income	24.2
		7. Net Interest	35.6
		National Income	**$850.8**
		8. Minor Adjustments	1.3
		9. Indirect Business Taxes	102.1
		Net National Product	**$951.6**
		10. Capital Consumption Allowances	95.2
Gross National Product	$1,046.8	**Gross National Product**	**$1,046.8**

[1] Preliminary data.
[2] Details may not add to total because of rounding.
Source: *Economic Report of the President*, 1972.

Factor Costs

The largest single charge against GNP comes under the heading of *factor costs,* the necessary payments that must be made either in money or in kind (for example, food or lodging supplied by an employer) to secure the services of the factors of production. Factor costs are the major source of income for individuals in the economic system. Obviously, payments must be made to the owners of the resources whose services are utilized in the production of all goods and services. It is the current practice in the United States system of national income and social accounting to distinguish seven types of factor costs which enter into the allocations side of the gross national product.

1. *Compensation of Employees.* Under this heading are lumped all wages, salaries, and income in kind paid for labor and, in addition, certain supplements to wages and salaries. The latter include contributions made by employers under the Social Security system, employer contributions to private pension plans, and various minor forms of labor income or fringe benefits, such as compensation for injuries and the pay for individuals in the military reserves.

2. *Proprietors' Income.* This category covers the monetary earnings and income in kind which accrue to all unincorporated business enterprises in the economy. Thus, proprietors' income is a measure of the profits of individual proprietorships, partnerships, and producer cooperatives.

3. *Dividends.* The portion of corporation profits paid out to shareholders during the current income period is included in this figure.

4. *Corporate Profits Tax Liability.* This item consists of the total of federal and state taxes levied against the earnings of all corporations in the economy.

5. *Undistributed Profits.* This factor element constitutes the share of corporate profits which is neither paid out to the shareholders as dividends nor collected as taxes by federal and state governments. The sum of this item, dividends, and corporate profits tax gives the total corporate profit in the income period.

6. *Rental Income of Persons.* This is equal to the money income received by persons from the rent of real property, such as buildings and land.

7. *Net Interest.* This measures income in the form of interest payments received by individuals and business firms in the economy, with the exception of interest payments by government and by consumers. The latter includes interest paid on home mortgages and installment plan purchases. The Department of Commerce maintains that interest on the public debt and interest paid by consumers are not a part of current production; hence these items are not treated as a factor cost. The interest included as part of the national income should represent interest on money borrowed and used to secure the services of economic resources.

The sum of the seven factor costs is the *national income,* which is defined as the factor cost of producing the goods and services that enter into the total of GNP in any particular period. Factor costs constitute approximately 80 percent of the total on the allocation side of the gross national product.

The other two major charges against the gross national product are classified as non-income charges because they do not constitute a source of income payments to individuals in the economy. These are *indirect business taxes* and *capital consumption allowances.*

Indirect Business Taxes

Indirect business taxes are all taxes levied on business firms with the exception of corporate income taxes. Taxes which fall in this category are general sales taxes, other excise or selective sales taxes, such as on cigarettes or liquor, and real property taxes paid by business firms. These taxes are called indirect because it is assumed that business firms treat them as a part of the cost of doing business; hence they will be included in the sale price of the final goods and services produced. The assumption is, in other words, that all taxes other than income taxes are shifted forward and reflected in expenditures for the various component parts of gross national product. Thus they must appear on the allocations side of the GNP, but they cannot be considered factor costs because such taxes accrue to the government and it is not the present practice in national income and social accounting to treat government as a factor of production.

General sales tax, other excise taxes, and real property taxes

Capital Consumption Allowances

Capital consumption allowances, as the term implies, are a monetary measure of the quantity of physical capital used up during the production period. We have noted that in the course of the productive process capital goods inevitably wear out. The amount by which the economy's stock of real capital is depleted during the current income period is measured by capital consumption allowances.

The figure shown in the gross national product account is derived from business records for depreciation, which may not accurately represent real depreciation in an income period. Depreciation is a sticky concept in some ways. For the business firm it is a way to write off the cost of an asset used by the firm, such as the cost of an automobile supplied for use by a salesman. Federal tax laws permit business firms to deduct a percentage of the purchase price of an asset as allowable depreciation over a designated period. This permits the firm to recover tax-free the cost

Depreciation

of capital. But in an economic or real sense, the concept refers to the actual physical wearing out of the asset. However, this is the best approximation that present statistical techniques permit for estimating the consumption of capital in the income period. To view it in another way, capital consumption equals the amount of current output that must go to replace capital, or replacement investment. If this figure is deducted from the outlay for gross private domestic investment found on the expenditure side of the GNP, the result will be an amount equal to net investment in the income period.

Minor Adjustments

The minor charges mentioned earlier consist of certain relatively small adjustments that must be made to take into account the role of subsidies in the economy, the surplus or profits that some public enterprises may obtain, and business transfer payments. Subsidies may be necessary on occasion to secure certain outputs or services, as has been the case with airlines and ocean shipping. In Table 5-3, these other charges are lumped together under the single heading "minor adjustments," which also includes the statistical discrepancy resulting from the fact that the totals obtained from the allocation side will not necessarily always equal the totals obtained from the expenditure side.

In summary, there are two alternative approaches to measurement of the gross national product (review Table 5-3). On the product side we have the expenditure flows reflected in totals for consumption, gross private domestic investment, government purchases of goods and services, and net exports. On the allocation side of the table we show the three major categories of charges in the form of factor payments, indirect business taxes, and capital consumption allowances, plus the entry for minor adjustments. Expenditures totals and charges totals are the two ways of looking at the same phenomenon, the flow of output in the economy.

Major Uses and Limitations of the
Gross National Product Measure

Before discussing some other important aggregates pertaining to national income and product, let us comment on the most important uses as well as some of the limitations inherent in GNP as a measure of total output for the economic system. The gross national product figure is particularly useful because it shows the composition, in terms of consumption, investment, government purchases of goods and services, and net exports, of the overall expenditure flow in the economic system. A knowledge of the magnitude of these flows and of changes in them is indispensable for economic analysis and policy formulation. GNP provides vital information on the outcome of economic activity in terms of the size, the composition, and the ends of our productive activity. In addition, it has been increasingly apparent in recent years that statistics on output are absolutely necessary for our understanding of the forces which determine the overall level of economic activity. Nonetheless the GNP measure is subject to a number of limitations that must be considered when using national income statistics.

Economic versus Social Values

Since the gross national product is measured in terms of the market valuation placed on current productive activity, it does not measure the social value of any activity. This means that the price put upon an activity by the market process may not necessarily reflect the value of that activity to society in a more fundamental philosophical sense. For example, a society may spend equal amounts for education and entertainment. Gross national product data include both expenditures in the total and show no distinction concerning their relative value. Yet it might be argued that education has a distinctly greater social advantage than entertainment. Expenditures for the Vietnam war illustrate this point most strikingly, as they were counted as a part of the national output. Not many would argue strongly that such outlays contributed significantly to our real welfare. Obviously, we are dealing here with subjective phenomena which carry us into the realm of value judgments. Issues of what ought to be involve relative social values and there is no simple way to quantify the social value of the national output. Divergence between market value and social value is a prime topic of controversy and debate in modern society.

Social value

Economic versus Social Cost

Most of this applies also to the distinction between economic and social costs. The economic costs of producing the national output are reflected in factor costs, indirect business taxes, and capital consumption allowances, which together make up the allocation side of the GNP. Social costs, as we have seen, are intangibles which, in fact, do constitute a part of the real cost of obtaining a given national output. Economic and social accounting simply has not advanced to the stage at which a numerical figure can be placed upon the social costs of the output. But we are increasingly

Social costs

101

aware of the phenomenon of social costs as we struggle to find ways to counteract the smog that pollutes most of our great cities, to halt the destruction of the natural beauty of the countryside, and to stop the contamination of our rivers and lakes. These unwanted by-products of the rapid economic progress of American society in recent decades remind us that social costs, intangible and elusive as they are, nevertheless are real costs that must ultimately be reckoned with in any form of economic analysis. But there is no universal agreement on their statistical measurement; hence they cannot be included in the gross national product. If they could be included, we would have a very different idea of what it costs to produce the vast array of goods and services the economy pours forth each year to maintain our high standard of living.

One type of social cost, though, will probably soon find its way into our national accounting system. This is *recycling*. Among the real social costs of our ever-rising GNP is the enormous amount of waste thrown out each year by our industrial system—from old newspapers, tin cans, and bottles to the noxious and dangerous fumes given off by some industrial and manufacturing enterprises. We are increasingly aware that these wastes must be recycled, returned as raw materials or inputs into the manufacturing process. How to do it remains unclear in many instances, but the costs of doing it can and will be reflected in the value of final goods and services produced.

Recycling

The Value of Leisure

Any analysis of the economic welfare of a nation or an individual must give some attention to leisure. Over the last century the length of the work week has fallen drastically in every modern nation, and virtually everyone would agree that this represents a genuine improvement in welfare. One difficulty with the gross national product aggregate, though, is that it does not provide for measuring the value to society of the leisure time available to its members. Morever, aggregate statistics cannot tell us the valuation society might place on an exchange of more leisure for fewer goods and services, or less leisure for more goods and services. Yet this is obviously an important economic question which we confront in various forms at the national as well as the individual level.

Qualitative Changes in the National Output

Another limitation of the GNP data is that they do not measure qualitative changes that may have taken place in output over a period of time. The valuation of output depends on the prices that prevail for the goods and services produced, as well as the physical quantity actually turned out. However, if the quality of a commodity or service has improved during an interval of time there may have been a significant real improvement in welfare which is not reflected in the GNP. The statistical data can only reflect a physical change in output or a change in the price at which a particular part of the output is valued. To illustrate, there have been important qualitative changes in the automobile over the last dozen years which may more than offset, in some instances, any change in the price of the automobile. Among these we might include dual braking systems, the use of disc brakes, automatic transmissions, and the radial tire, to mention but a few. Not all such changes come willingly from manufacturers; some resulted from pressures by consumers and consumer groups, such as "Nader's Raiders." To the extent that this is actually the case, improved welfare as a result of qualitative changes is not accurately reflected in the statistics. Unfortunately, at its present stage of development national income and social accounting does not yet have any satisfactory technique for measuring qualitative changes in the product totals.

The Composition of Output

The GNP figure is also limited by the fact that aside from the broad breakdown between consumption, investment, government purchases of goods and services, and net exports it tells us nothing about the composition of the output total. Yet most economists would agree that the state of material welfare is obviously affected by the composition as well as the total size of a given output. For example, in the Vietnam War, as in other wars in which this country has engaged, there was a significant increase in the absolute size of the nation's product as a consequence of stepped-up production of material for war purposes. The gross national product total faithfully reflected this increase in output, but told us little or nothing about its composition. From a welfare standpoint, war frequently means a reduction in the levels of consumption; people are required to tighten their belts and give up butter for guns. Although the war in Vietnam did not lead to shortages of consumer goods, skimping on badly needed public expenditures was a major cost of the war. Money that might have been spent on reconstructing cities or cleaning up streams was channeled instead into the manufacture of armaments and the maintenance of a large fighting force. Thus, one can hardly say that material welfare has been enhanced under such circumstances even though there has been absolute increase in the size of the GNP. To judge the welfare implications of any given output total we need to know more than its mere size; we must know something about its internal composition.

103

The Distribution of the National Output

Gross national product statistics tell us the size of the total output and show how much is being devoted to consumption and other purposes, but they do not tell us how output is being distributed among the members of the society. Welfare is related to the distribution of the national output, to who gets what share and why. We cannot ignore distribution when we are attempting to analyze the welfare implications of the gross national product. It is true that the allocation side of gross national product data reveals how the national income is distributed in the form of wages, rents, interest payments, profits, etc., but this does not tell us how that output is distributed among persons. For example, the salary of a bank president and the salary of a teller are lumped together under the same heading of wages and salaries, although the president may receive an income many times larger than the teller. It is important to understand that there are no wholly scientific criteria for determining the proper distribution of output and income in society. Nevertheless, knowledge of the actual distribution in relation to a concept of how it ought to be distributed is necessary to evaluate fully the economy's performance with respect to the economic well-being of its citizens.

Output Per Capita

*Per capita output
vs. GNP*

Finally, gross national product data are limited because they represent the total output of the society and do not tell us what has happened to output per person. Yet, for the analysis of economic well-being, output per capita is often more meaningful than total output, because an improvement in material well-being over time requires that, on the average, more goods and services be available for each person. If a society's rate of population growth exceeds the rate at which its output is increasing, then the society will not experience an improvement in material well-being with a growth in total output. On the contrary, economic well-being will be reduced. So it is necessary to take into account per capita changes in the gross national product as well as total changes if we are going to make comparisons over a number of years. This is by no means an academic question; many societies in the poorer parts of the world are trapped in poverty by their inability to increase the production of goods and services at a rate in excess of their annual increase in population.

Other Measures of Product and Income

Our discussion so far has primarily dealt with the gross national product, the most widely used of the major national income measures. But there are a number of other important measures of both output and income which are utilized by the government. We shall consider them briefly.

The Net National Product

The Department of Commerce defines net national product as the market value of the net output of final goods and services produced by the economy in the income period. It is a measure of the nation's output after allowance has been made for the consumption of capital during the current process of production. Net national product is obtained by deducting capital consumption allowances from the gross national product, although the usefulness of the net national product figure is limited by the fact that such allowances, as we have seen, do not necessarily reflect the real depreciation of the economy's capital stock.

The National Income

Earlier, national income was defined as the sum of the factor costs incurred during production of the economy's current output. Specifically, the Department of Commerce calls national income the aggregate return to labor and property which arises from the production of goods and services by the nation's economy. The national income is also described as the net national product at factor cost because it measures the factor costs involved in the production of the net output total. As pointed out on page 99, national income accounts for about 80 percent of the value of the GNP.

Net national product at factor cost

National income is an important concept because it represents for the economy as a whole the amount of income earned by owners of economic resources (land, labor and capital) in return for supplying the services of these resources to the productive units of the economic system. As such, it is the major source of money income or spending power for the purchase of most of the national output. The simplest way to derive the national income figure is to deduct indirect business taxes and the other minor adjustments from our net national product total.

Personal Income

Although national income is the income earned by the owners of economic resources through participation in the productive process, it does not measure money income actually received by persons and households during the income period. The reason is that a portion of factor income is not actually received as money income by persons or households; some is withheld for taxes or contributions to pensions and insurance programs, among other things. On the other hand, some households and persons receive money income that has not been earned by supplying the services of economic resources to the productive process. This consists of transfer payments and interest income received from consumers and government. The Department of Commerce defines personal income as the current income received by persons from all sources, including transfer income from government and business. This measure is normally computed before taxes except for individual contributions to social insurance.

The usual way to obtain the personal income measure is to deduct from the national income the major categories of earned factor income that are not actually received as money income by persons or households; to this figure are added transfer incomes received from business and government. The major deductions include contributions to social insurance (such as Social Security payments), corporate profits tax liability, and undistributed corporate profits. The major forms of transfer payments which must be added in are: interest on government debt, pensions paid to retired persons, unemployment compensation, various forms of relief benefits, and benefits extended to war veterans. Interest paid by consumers must also be added in because it is not treated as a part of current production, and thus, is not a factor cost.

Disposable Income

The final widely used measure of income is disposable income, which is the income remaining to individuals after deduction of all taxes levied against their income and their property by all government entities in the economy. It is obtained by deducting such taxes from the personal income total; it represents a measure of the after-tax purchasing power in the hands of persons and households. The last two measures of income discussed, personal income and disposable income, measure the flow of money income to persons and households, while the first three are measures of product flows, although of course they also record money incomes earned in the process of production.

The interrelationships between the income and product flows are shown in the diagram in Figure 5-2. The student should study

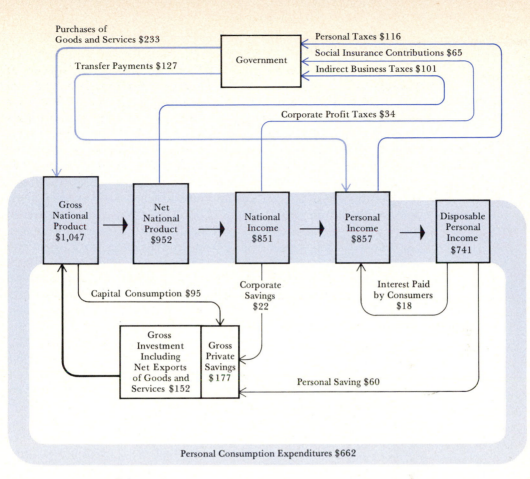

FIGURE 5-2

The Relationship Between Product and Income Flows: 1971. (Billions of Dollars)

This flow chart pictures the relative size in 1971 of the various components of the gross national product and how they are related to one another. The flow depicts the various deductions and additions necessary to derive the other income measures, net national product, national income, personal income, and disposable income, from the gross national product figure. (Source: The Twentieth Century Fund, 1971.)

this carefully; it shows not only the nature of these five measures of economic performance but how they are related. The data in Figure 5-2 are rounded to the nearest whole number. We begin with the GNP for 1971, from which the flow chart shows $95 billion in capital consumption allowances is deducted to arrive at the NNP figure of $952 billion. Note that the capital consumption allowance figure becomes a part of the gross saving flow. From the NNP $101 billion in the form of indirect business taxes is next deducted, yielding a figure of $851 billion for the national income. The indirect business tax total becomes a part of tax receipts which flow into the government sector and are the major source of finance for government expenditures for goods and ser-

Relationships of income and product flows

107

vices and transfer payments. The transition from national income to personal income is accomplished by deducting from the national income total undistributed corporate profits, which become a part of the savings flow, and corporate profits taxes and social security taxes, which are a part of the government receipts flow, and adding in transfer payments, which originate with government. The result is a figure for personal income: $857 billion. Finally, from personal income there are deducted personal tax payments in the amount of $116 billion to arrive at disposable personal income. This income figure is divided into $662 billion for consumption outlays, $18 billion for interest paid by consumers, and $60 billion for personal saving. The return flow of expenditures by government (goods and services), business firms (investments), and consumers (consumption goods and services) adds up to the value of the 1971 GNP of $1,047 billion.

Gross National Product and the Price Level

Converting current prices to constant prices

We have pointed out that the normal procedure of the Department of Commerce is to measure output in prices prevailing during the current income period. But from one income period to another, the prices for individual goods and services will vary, as does the average of all prices. This creates a difficult problem because we must take such changes into account to compare GNP in different years. Economists have devised ways to do this. The basic technique is known as "deflating" for price level changes, which means converting gross national product as measured in current prices to gross national product measured in constant prices. It is difficult to compare the GNP in 1960 with the 1972 figure because the price level may have changed during this time. Our problem is solved if we find a way to convert the gross national product data for both years either to prices of 1972 or of 1960. Deflating for price level changes does this. If we make such a change, then a comparison of gross national product data for different dates will reflect real changes rather than monetary changes in the value of output, which are due to inflation or its opposite, deflation.

The Price Index and Deflation

The method is to divide gross national product data in current prices by an index of the price level. In this context the index should measure overall changes in the general price level; this is what we are interested in when concerned with the performance of the economy as a whole, although any index must necessarily be a composite of many thousands of individual prices.

$$GNP_{1972} = [O_{1972} \times P_{1972}]$$

$$O = \text{Output}$$
$$P = \text{Price level}$$

$$Index_{1972} = \frac{P_{1972}}{P_{1958}}$$

$$P_{1958} = \text{the base year}$$

3.

Divide GNP_{1972} by $Index_{1972}$:

$$(a) \quad \frac{GNP_{1972}}{P_{1972}/P_{1958}} = \frac{[O_{1972} \times P_{1972}]}{P_{1972}/P_{1958}}$$

Which equals:

$$(b) \quad [O_{1972} \times P_{1972}] \times \frac{P_{1958}}{P_{1972}} = [O_{1972} \times P_{1958}]$$

which is 1972 output in 1958 prices

FIGURE 5-3
Deflation Procedure.
    The algebraic steps shown explain why the process of dividing GNP measured in current prices by the appropriate price index will convert the figure to prices for the base year of the price index.

A price index is a statistical device for comparing the amount by which one or more prices have changed during a given period of time. Some specific year is chosen as the base year or specific point of reference. Prices in all other years are measured as a percentage of the price in this base year. Suppose, for example, that the price of a loaf of bread was $.25 in the selected base year of 1960, and that in 1972 the price of bread was $.30. Since the price had increased by 20 percent, it would be correct to say that the price of bread in 1972 was 120 percent of the base year price of $.25. Thus, the price index for bread in 1972 is 120, since the price index in the base year of 1960 must be 100 or 100 percent.

The problem grows more complex when we try to construct an index to represent not just the change in the price of a single commodity but change in the price of all commodities and services over a period of time. There is a formidable statistical problem involved in the construction of such a general index. The technique involves weighting prices of various typical commodities (what the economist calls a market basket) in accordance with the relative importance of the goods and services they represent. If this is done carefully and accurately, the index will reflect change in all prices and can then be used to deflate the gross na-

The market basket

109

tional data. Obviously the economist or statistician who constructs a general price level index must have an extensive knowledge of the composition of output so he can assign a proper weight to the different categories of goods and services entering into the index being constructed.

The most widely known price index is the index of consumer prices, often described in the press as the "cost of living" index. Among the major items included in this index and weighted according to their relative importance in consumer budgets are food, housing (including rent), clothing, transportation, medical care, personal care, reading and recreation, as well as other goods and services. The base year for the consumer price index is 1967. Another important price index is the "GNP deflator," which actually consists of a general price index for the entire GNP and a series of individual indices for each of the component parts of the gross national product. It uses 1958 as a base year.

The underlying reason for dividing gross national product data in current prices by an appropriate price index to convert these data to the prices of the base year of the index is revealed by the example presented in Figure 5-3. This figure shows the algebraic steps involved in this procedure. Study this simple arithmetical example until it is clear exactly what has been done and why. Table 5-4 shows gross national product data for the United States in both current and constant prices for selected years since 1929. This table also contains the price index used to deflate the gross national product in current dollars.

TABLE 5-4
GNP in Current and Constant Prices:
Selected Years
(Billions of Dollars)

YEAR	CURRENT PRICES	CONSTANT PRICES *	PRICE INDEX **
1929	$103.1	$203.6	50.6
1935	72.7	154.3	42.6
1940	99.7	227.2	43.9
1945	211.9	355.2	59.7
1950	284.8	355.3	80.2
1955	398.0	438.0	90.9
1960	503.7	487.7	103.3
1965	684.9	617.8	110.9
1970	974.1	720.0	135.3
1971 [1]	1,046.8	739.5	141.6

* 1958 dollars.
** 1958=100.
[1] Preliminary.
Source: *Economic Report of the President,* 1972.

Questions for Review and Discussion

1. Distinguish between the concepts of income and wealth.
2. How does an economist define investment? What is net investment?
3. Why can transfer payments be viewed as negative taxes?
4. Why is the GNP a measure of the value of *final* goods and services?
5. Why is the measure of a nation's gross output the same as the measure of that nation's gross income?
6. What kinds of labor are not included in the GNP measure?
7. What are some of the major social costs excluded from present practices of national income and social accounting?
8. What method might be devised to include in the GNP a figure representing the value of leisure?
9. How does net national product differ from GNP? From national income?
10. What useful information is obtained from computing national output per capita?
11. What corrections are needed when comparing the GNP of the present period with GNP in an earlier period?
12. Explain how a price index is constructed.

6

Principles
of Output
Determination

In Chapter 5 we were concerned with measuring the economy's performance. We now go beyond description of the output level to examine the basic forces that determine both income and employment in the modern economic system. This branch of economic analysis is often defined as *income and employment theory,* a designation which reflects the high correlation between output and employment for the economic system as a whole. The relationship between output and employment from 1950 through 1970 is illustrated in Figure 6-1, which shows for each of these years employment in millions of workers on the vertical axis and output in billions of constant dollars on the horizontal axis.

What is involved in analyzing the determinants of income and employment? First, we must identify the key factors which explain why output at any time is at a particular level. Second, we must show how variables are related to one another. When we do this we are, in effect, constructing a theory to explain the process of output determination in the modern economic system.

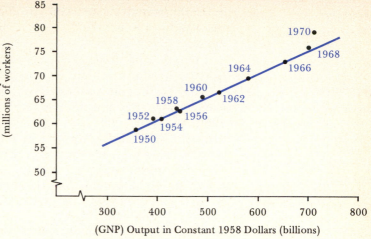

FIGURE 6-1
Output and Employment: 1950–1970.

The line fitted to the actual data on both real output (GNP in 1958 dollars) and civilian employment shows that there is a close correlation between changes in output and changes in employment. When output rises, employment rises, and when output falls, employment falls. (Source: *Economic Report of the President,* 1971.)

Types of Changes

The overall performance of the economic system can be assessed either on the basis of short-term or long-term changes in output and employment. Short-term changes take place within the existing productive capacity of the economic system. While there is no precise measure of the short term, in general four to five years may elapse before a nation's productive capacity is significantly altered. Long-term changes involve alterations in the capacity of the economic system that belong under the heading of economic growth. This chapter will primarily treat changes taking place within the limits of the economy's existing productive capacity, reserving long-term changes for Chapter 8.

Short-term and long-term changes

Productive Capacity and the Supply of Output

The concept of productive capacity is the logical point at which to begin. Essentially, productive capacity is the potential of the economic system for production of economically valuable goods and services. Note carefully that capacity is not output; it is a potential for output which is only realized when put to use. It must be stressed, too, that even in the short term the capacity of an economy is not an exact or fixed magnitude. In most economic systems there is some flexibility in the maximum ouput obtainable over short periods of time. Nevertheless, every economy has

113

some absolute upper limit on the output obtainable which represents the system's maximum productive potential. If this upper limit did not exist, the "economic problem" of scarcity would obviously disappear.

Potential GNP

The concept of productive capacity has been resorted to frequently by the President's Council of Economic Advisers (CEA). The Council defines productive capacity as the potential gross national product at a minimum level of unemployment. In the early 1960s potential GNP was equal to the volume of goods and services the economy would produce if unemployment in the economy were no higher than 4 percent. Potential GNP was first used as an important tool of economic analysis in the 1962 *Report* of the Council, because at that time research undertaken principally by Arthur Okun, then on the staff of the Council, revealed a significant gap between actual output and potential output. From 1962 to 1965, a major objective of economic policy was to eliminate this gap and thus raise actual output up to potential output. After 1965, the problem was reversed, as actual output ran ahead of potential, creating strong inflationary pressures in the economy. Beginning in early 1970, as restrictive measures applied during 1969 by the Nixon administration began to take hold, actual output fell below the potential once again. Figure 6-2, taken from

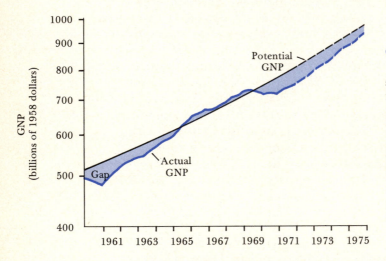

FIGURE 6-2

Potential and Actual GNP: 1960–1975.

This updated diagram shows the effect of the 1970 recession on the nation's output, as it dropped sharply below the potential during that year. Even with a projected 6 percent rate of growth, actual output will lag behind the potential for some time to come. (Source: *Economic Report of the President,* 1970, updated.)

the 1970 *Report* of the Council and updated through 1971, traces potential and actual output over the period 1960–1971, with projections through 1975. For the latter, a 6 percent rate of growth was used.

In any analysis of the productive capacity of the economic system, two questions arise. First, what determines the size of the economy's productive capacity? Our answer will be relatively brief here as we shall return to this question in Chapter 8. It should be pointed out, though, that this is one of the most crucial contemporary economic questions. Nations the world over are desperately seeking to expand their productive capacity. Second, what explains the use of productive capacity? The main concern of this chapter is to develop a theoretical system which will explain the conditions under which productive capacity comes to be used.

Productive Capacity and Its Measurement

Explaining the determinants of an economic system's productive capacity is one of the most complex of all economic problems, although the basic factors involved can be readily identified. As a matter of fact, it is much easier to identify the determinants of productive capacity than to explain their impact. In the simplest sense the productive capacity of any economic system depends upon the quantity and quality of the resources available to the economy, and also upon what was defined as technology in Chapter 2: the skill and efficiency with which these resources are brought together for the purpose of production. Technology is a stock which can be increased through investment, and as it is increased the productive capacity of the society expands.

Labor and Capital Productivity

To the economist, the productivity of a particular resource is the output produced on the average per unit of the resource employed. Thus, productivity of labor refers to the output of goods and services per unit of labor utilized in the production process. The concept is not only used in economic analysis but widely discussed in the public press; no discussion between union and management is complete without some reference to labor productivity. As might be expected, the productivity of capital means the amount of output associated on the average with each unit of physical capital employed in the production process.

Output per unit of resource used

Capital productivity and labor productivity are highly useful concepts for certain types of economic analysis. But a word of caution is in order here. One must not jump to the conclusion that the whole of the output associated with the employment of a particular type of resource such as labor or capital is to be attributed to qualities inherent in the unit of the factor employed. Production is created through the cooperation of all the factors of production; when we measure the productivity of capital or labor or any other resource, in the manner just described, it is merely a way to derive an average which measures output in terms of the inputs of one particular resource. A measure of labor productivity

115

can be obtained, for example, by dividing output by the number of hours worked over a period of time. This yields an output per man-hour figure, a magnitude widely used today. But such a measure also reflects the amount of capital, land, and technology which enables an hour's worth of labor to produce on the average a given quantity of product. The value of the labor productivity concept lies in the fact that it gives a reasonably good estimate of the productive capacity of the economy.

Measuring Productive Capacity

*Multiplying labor
productivity by
labor supply*

One of the most direct ways to measure the productive capacity of the economic system is to multiply the productivity of the labor force, measured as output per man-hour, by the number of man-hours of productive effort expected to be available from the labor force. The product of these two variables gives us a measure of the productive potential of the economic system. In symbolic terms productive capacity, which we shall designate by the capital letter Q, is equal to Pr, which is our symbol of the productivity of labor, times N', which is the labor supply, or man-hours of productive effort forthcoming. Thus, $Q = (Pr \times N')$.

*Projecting GNP
at annual rate*

A different method for determining productive capacity was employed by the Council of Economic Advisers (Figure 6-2). The early CEA measure of potential GNP was obtained by the relatively simple technique of projecting forward a figure for real GNP at a specified annual rate. To illustrate: in 1955 the CEA found that the unemployment rate was at 4 percent, which in its judgment represented full utilization of the economy's productive capacity. The 1955 GNP was projected forward at an annual average rate of growth of $3\frac{1}{2}$ percent, which was assumed to be the rate of growth necessary to maintain full employment. This $3\frac{1}{2}$ percent trend rate for the growth of potential output was used until 1962; in 1963 the Council raised the trend rate to $3\frac{3}{4}$ percent. In the late 1960s the trend rate for potential GNP was raised to 4 percent. For the projected GNP for 1970–1975, the Council moved to a 3.8 percent unemployment rate and a 4.3 percent rate of growth for potential GNP. In arriving at the appropriate growth rate to establish the trend of potential output, the CEA takes into account the growth rate of the labor force, the annual growth rate of labor productivity for the entire labor force, and the downward trend in hours worked per year. Either method described should result in a reasonable estimate of the economy's productive capacity, providing the analysis begins with accurate figures on both the productivity of labor and the size of the labor force.

The Use of Capacity

Through the use of productive capacity enough goods and services are brought into existence to satisfy the wants of the members of the economic system. As already pointed out, productive capacity is merely potential for production. If it goes unused no one will benefit. What determines the extent to which productive capacity will be used?

Aggregate Supply and Demand

Private firms in the economy produce goods and services in the expectation that demand for the output they produce will be sufficient to sell the goods and services at prices that will cover their cost of production, including a return or profit to the firms. The key word is expectation. It is the expectation of sufficient proceeds from the sale of the output to cover the costs of producing (including profit) which leads firms to act. The amount produced by all firms in the economy in a period in response to demand expectations we define as *aggregate supply*.

Expectation

When we say that the expectation of demand is the essential condition to bring productive capacity into use, we are saying, in effect, that the key to output determination within the limits of existing productive capacity is the volume of *aggregate demand* that producers anticipate during the income period.

Let us examine closely what aggregate demand means. As a first approximation we state that, for the economy as a whole, aggregate demand consists of the total flow of expenditures for goods and services in the income system during a given time period. This flow of money expenditures originates with the major spending entities which make decisions on the ultimate uses of the national output. These are households and nonprofit institutions, business firms, governmental units, and what we have called "the rest of the world." The decision to spend is a decision to use part of the national output. The household sector purchases the consumer goods and services produced; the business sector purchases the capital or investment goods produced; the government sector purchases the goods and services necessary to provide governmental units with the inputs to create collective (or social) goods and services; and finally, the rest of the world purchases the net exports of the economic system. Note that the spending streams which constitute the demand for the economy's output correspond to the major components of the gross national product discussed in Chapter 5. The ultimate users, in other words, are those

*Aggregate demand
as measure of
expenditure*

117

who purchase the final goods and services which constitute the nation's gross national product. In symbolic terms aggregate demand, which we designate by DD, consists of the sum of consumer goods C, investment goods I, government purchases of goods and services G, and net exports (X_n). As an equation:

$$(1) \qquad\qquad DD = C + I + G + X_n.$$

A Restatement of the Analysis

Let us pause briefly here and compress the essential points on the use of capacity. We start with the proposition that at any given time the economy possesses a capacity for the production of goods and services. This capacity is brought into use, which is to say potential is transformed into actual output, whenever aggregate expectations among enterprise managers are such that output produced can be sold at prices that will cover production costs, including a return to the enterprise in the form of a profit. Aggregate demand depends upon the spending decisions made by the major spending entities of the economic system, namely households, firms, government units, and the rest of the world.

*The decision to
produce and the
decision to spend*

One highly important consideration emerges from this discussion: the output level in a market economy depends upon two distinctly different types of decisions. There is a decision which originates with the firm—or on the supply side—and involves whether to undertake production. There is another decision which originates with those who use or are the final users of the economy's output—households, firms, government, and the rest of the world—and involves whether to spend in order to acquire a portion of the output. Production decisions and spending decisions and the interactions between the two are the heart of the matter insofar as levels of output and employment are concerned.

What we have stated thus far does not yet constitute a clear and full explanation, or theory, of how the output level is determined, but it does enable us to construct the basic framework for such a theory. To do this we must both identify the key determinants of output—productive capacity, aggregate supply, and aggregate demand—and show how these aggregates interact.

The Aggregate Supply Schedule

We shall begin our discussion with the concept of the *aggregate supply schedule*. In our discussion of capacity, the amount of output that all firms produced in an income period in response to their demand expectations was defined as aggregate supply. This is correct, but this factual statement of what may actually take place in an income period does not provide us with the kind of analytical tools we need to solve the problem of output determination. For this we must introduce the idea of aggregate supply as a schedule. An aggregate supply schedule shows the amount of output that all firms will produce, given varying sets of expectations concerning the level of aggregate demand. For the sake of simplicity in this phase of our analysis, let us assume that both output and expected total demand are computed in constant prices. This procedure should be recognized for what it is: an analytical oversimplification. In reality, output for the economy as a whole and the price level generally move together and in the same direction, especially as the economy approaches full employment.

We start with a diagram in which the value in constant prices of alternative levels of the gross national product is plotted on the horizontal axis and expected demand (the amount of proceeds expected from the sale at output) on the vertical axis. The aggregate supply schedule is depicted graphically by a 45-degree line *OZ* which is shown in Figure 6-3. Since at any and all possible levels of the gross national product (within reasonable limits set by existing productive capacity) firms in the aggregate must get back all costs incurred in the production of output, the level of expected aggregate demand required to justify the production decision necessarily equals the value of the output. Under our as-

Aggregate supply: a 45° line

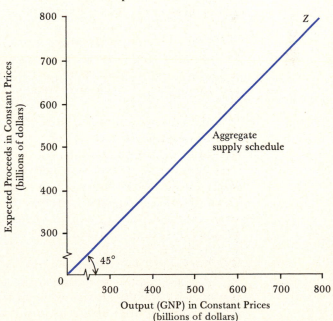

FIGURE 6-3
The Aggregate Supply Schedule.

The data plotted on the vertical axis tell us the amount of revenue or proceeds that business firms in the aggregate must get back to justify continued production in the amount depicted on the horizontal axis. The data on both axes are in constant prices. Output should be interpreted as responding to expected proceeds. (Data given in constant dollars.)

sumption that output is valued in constant prices, the locus of all points representing an identity between output and proceeds equal to charges against GNP must be on the 45-degree line. This line represents an aggregate supply schedule.

It must be stressed that a schedule of aggregate supply as depicted in Figure 6-3 represents intended rather than realized value. In other words, whether or not any particular value for the gross national product becomes realized in any given income period depends on expected demand as viewed by suppliers. Economists define the output values embodied in the schedule described above as *ex-ante* values: they are reckoned before the fact in contrast to *ex-post* (or after the fact) values.

The Aggregate Demand Schedule

In the theoretical model of income determination that we are constructing, our second strategic concept is the schedule of aggregate demand. In both reality and theory such a schedule is separate and distinct from the aggregate supply schedule, for obviously decisions to use output—decisions to spend—are made separately from and by different entities than those who make the decisions to produce output. We said earlier that aggregate demand consists of the total flow of money expenditures in the economic system during a given time period. But as was true of aggregate supply, the volume of total expenditure we may measure during a specific period of time is not sufficient for analytical purposes. What is required for analysis is to view aggregate demand as a schedule showing the total expenditures that will be forthcoming from the spending entities of the economic system at every possible level of the gross national product. Such an aggregate demand schedule is depicted by the line *DD* in Figure 6-4.

*Response of
spending units*

The aggregate demand schedule *DD* shown in the figure should be interpreted somewhat differently from the aggregate supply schedule (*OZ*). Recall not only that a schedule is a graphic representation of the relationship between two variables, but that normally one of these is thought of as the independent variable and the other as a dependent variable. With respect to the aggregate supply schedule, total output, shown on the horizontal axis, should be seen as responding to variations in total expected expenditure as measured on the vertical axis. The aggregate demand schedule, on the other hand, should be viewed as representing the response of spending units to the various levels of real output which may prevail in the economy. This response is found on the vertical axis.

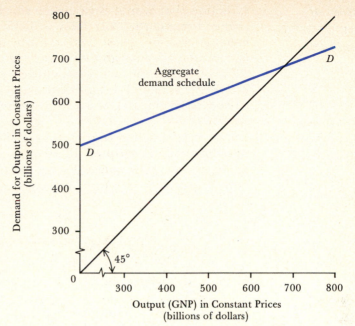

FIGURE 6-4

The Aggregate Demand Schedule.

In this figure the data plotted on the vertical axis represent the sum of spending by households, firms, governments, and the rest of the world—their demand for the output being produced. The diagram should be interpreted to show demand responding to the actual output produced, which is measured on the horizontal axis.

The rationale for viewing aggregate demand in this fashion lies in the fact that total output (the GNP shown on the horizontal axis) is the most important single source of purchasing power for the major spending entities of the economic system. It is not the only source because firms, households, and governments may draw upon financial assets accumulated from prior income periods or new purchasing power may be created by the banking system, but it is by far the most important and consistent source for spending. Like the aggregate supply schedule, the aggregate demand schedule slopes upward to the right although its slope is less steep than that of the aggregate supply schedule. The general upward slope of the *DD* schedule is explained partly by the fact that as GNP increases more expenditure will result because a larger output puts more spending power into the hands of the owners of economic resources. But a fuller understanding of the nature of the aggregate demand schedule awaits our analysis of the concept of the equilibrium level of output.

Slope of the aggregate demand schedule

The Equilibrium Level of Output and Employment

We define an equilibrium level of output as an output at which the aggregate demand and aggregate supply schedules are equal.

121

It is, in other words, a situation which shows no disposition to change because the underlying economic forces are balanced. Remember that the idea of an equilibrium level of income is primarily an analytical concept; rarely, if ever, does actual output in the economy reach such a state of rest that we know for certain it is in equilibrium. The equilibrium level of output as a concept is analogous to the idea of an equilibrium price discussed in Chapter 3.

*Nature of
equilibrium*

The nature of the equilibrium is illustrated in Figure 6-5. In this diagram, equilibrium in output exists at the intersection of the aggregate demand and the aggregate supply schedules. At this point aggregate demand and aggregate supply are in balance.

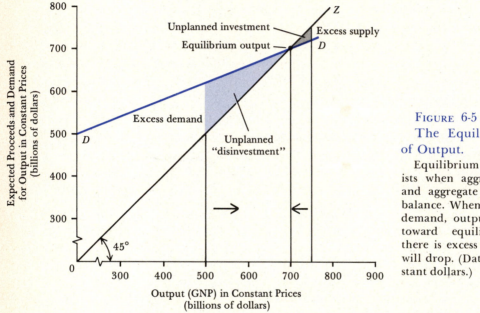

FIGURE 6-5
The Equilibrium Level of Output.

Equilibrium in output exists when aggregate demand and aggregate supply are in balance. When there is excess demand, output will expand toward equilibrium; when there is excess supply, output will drop. (Data given in constant dollars.)

What does this mean? At this particular level of output the expectations of the producers are being realized; the flow of money expenditures originating with the spending units is just sufficient to match the proceeds expected and required by the producers in the aggregate. This being the case, there is no reason for income to change, as long as it is assumed that these conditions will continue into the future. To put it slightly differently, at the point of intersection of these two schedules spending rates and output rates are in balance; hence there is no need for either to change.

Supply Exceeds Demand

To understand fully the nature of equilibrium, let us examine what takes place in our model of the economy assuming aggregate demand and aggregate supply are not in balance. Suppose, for example, that the aggregate expectations of firms in the economy are such that during the income period they produce an output equal to Y_2 in Figure 6-6. Note first that at the output Y_2 the aggregate supply schedule lies above the aggregate demand schedule; in other words, the OZ line is above the DD line. This means that the value of the goods and services actually supplied in this period is in excess of the amounts that households, firms, governments, and the rest of the world intend to spend to acquire output in the same period.

The Equilibrium Level of Output and Employment

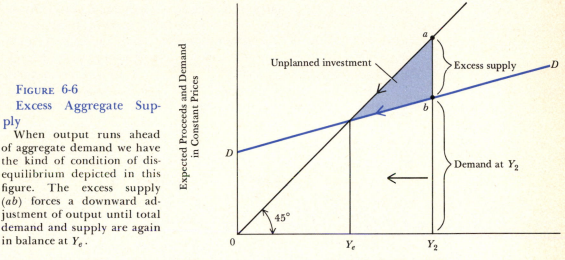

FIGURE 6-6

Excess Aggregate Supply

When output runs ahead of aggregate demand we have the kind of condition of disequilibrium depicted in this figure. The excess supply (ab) forces a downward adjustment of output until total demand and supply are again in balance at Y_e.

At this point, a word of caution. Keep firmly in mind that this diagram endeavors to show what happens during a particular income period. Thus, the diagram has a time dimension attached to it but it requires imagination to understand and be aware of this dimension. Both the horizontal and vertical axes in the diagram measure rates, the rate of output per income period and the rate of expenditure per income period. The diagram is so abstract that we do not normally need to define precisely the amount of time involved, although if we are thinking in terms of the gross national product as our measure of output, obviously the time of period will be the calendar year. Thus Y_2 in Figure 6-6 may represent the gross national product in a particular calendar year.

The time dimension

The excess of the schedule OZ above the schedule DD at the output level Y_2 means, in effect, that current production in this income period exceeds the demand for the output. Consequently, we have disequilibrium because spending intentions fall short of output produced. The most obvious result is that a part of the current output will be unsold. In other words, we will have ad-

123

**Principles of
Output
Determination**

*Unintended
accumulation of
goods*

ditions to the economy's stock of goods at some point in the production process. The important thing to note is that these accumulations of goods (or inventory changes) are not desired by producers in the economic system. An "unforeseen" or "unintended" increase in investment will take place because aggregate demand falls short of aggregate supply. Since the output has been produced, it exists somewhere in the economic system, but since it is not being taken off the market by the end-users in the economy's output, it must take the form of unplanned inventory accumulation. The volume of the unplanned inventory buildup is measured in the diagram by the distance by which aggregate supply exceeds aggregate demand, which is *ab* in the figure. This accumulation bears out what was said in Chapter 5 about investment in relation to the economic system as a whole. Investment takes place in the economic system whenever there is a buildup in the economy's stock of wealth, which is exactly what happens whenever some part of current output is not disposed of through the market process.

Regaining Balance

What happens next? Since firms cannot change what has already been done (output in the current production period), they will change their plans for the next production period. Production plans will be revised downward in the hope that output will come closer to sales and, thus, more nearly be in equilibrium in the next period. In the diagram this means that for the next period output will fall somewhere to the left of Y_2. This output may or may not yet equal aggregate demand because as the output falls, aggregate demand also declines; this is shown by a movement downward along the aggregate demand schedule. However, as we move down the aggregate demand schedule *DD* it can be seen that the rate at which aggregate demand declines is less than the rate at which output falls as we move down the *OZ* schedule. Therefore, even though output may be falling there is some point, shown by the intersection of the two schedules, at which an equilibrium becomes possible. In reality we can expect firms to continue to adjust their production downward until they reach the point at which aggregate demand equals or exceeds aggregate supply.

Demand Exceeds Supply

The opposite situation will prevail for the economic system if, in an income period, output produced falls short of aggregate demand. In Figure 6-7 this is the situation at the output level of Y_1, an amount less than the equilibrium. In the aggregate, firms

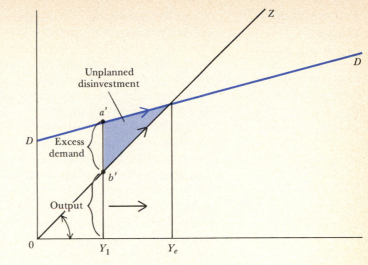

FIGURE 6-7

Excess Aggregate Demand.

When aggregate demand runs ahead of aggregate supply we have the kind of disequilibrium condition depicted in this figure. The excess demand ($a'b'$) forces an upward adjustment of output until total demand and supply are again in balance at Y_e.

Output in Constant Prices

produced fewer goods and services than the quantity desired by all spending entities in the economic system. Diagrammatically, aggregate demand lies above aggregate supply. Additional spending is being injected into the income system beyond the quantity generated by and equal to the output produced. This added purchasing power may come either from new money created by the banking systems or through drawing down financial assets carried over by spending units from previous income periods. Borrowing or assets may, for a time, provide additional spending power in excess of the spending power generated by the production process.

The difference between aggregate demand and aggregate supply is met by a reduction in the economy's stock of goods on hand. This is the distance $a'b'$ in the figure. This is called disinvestment. To put it another way, current demand in the aggregate exceeds current output, and since price changes are ruled out by the manner in which the diagram is constructed, the goods needed to satisfy the excess of demand over supply must come from goods in existence at the start of the production period rather than from current production. This is why we speak of disinvestment taking place in the income period. Disinvestment is the opposite of investment; it represents a drawing down of the economy's stock of wealth.

Disinvestment

Regaining Balance

As may be surmised from our earlier discussion, firms discover that in the current period their production plans fall short of the spending plans of consumers, business units, government, and the

125

rest of the world. So they revise their production plans upward at the earliest possible opportunity. In the framework of our model, this will be the next production period. The process of adjustment will continue until an equilibrium is reached, when aggregate demand no longer exceeds aggregate supply, which again is represented by the intersection of the aggregate demand and the aggregate supply schedule.

The foregoing discussion of the process of adjusting output to equilibrium is illustrated in Table 6-1 by a simple mathematical example. The first column shows the amount of employment associated with each possible level of income or output; thus we can see how employment and output vary together. The second column is the aggregate supply schedule, which shows the varying amounts of output which the economy can produce, up to a maximum representing the economy's short-term capacity. This is an aggregate supply schedule because for each of the output levels shown, producers' costs (including profit) are exactly equal to the value of the output produced. Column three is the aggregate demand schedule, which indicates the totals that all spending units are prepared to spend at each possible output tabulated in the second column. Finally, the data indicate the direction in which output and employment will change in response to the difference which may exist between aggregate demand and aggregate supply at various levels of the latter.

The Principle of Aggregate Equilibrium

The data of Table 6-1 reveal that there is only a single income level at which total spending in the economy is just equal to the value of total output. This condition occurs when output reaches $700 billion and employment 78 million. At all other potential production levels within the limits set down in the table, disequilibrium exists. Either aggregate demand exceeds aggregate supply, or the reverse. According to these data an excess of aggregate demand over aggregate supply causes an expansion in production and employment, but if aggregate demand falls short of aggregate supply, output and employment will fall. This is the first and most basic principle of income determination of modern economic analysis. In its importance and simplicity it is analogous to the principle of demand and supply in the determination of market price.

Note that the economy at any and all possible levels of output never fails to generate sufficient spending power to clear the market of the goods and services actually produced in an income period; there is no assurance, however, that the decisions to spend

TABLE 6-1
Adjustment to Equilibrium
(Billions of Constant Dollars)

EMPLOYMENT	AGGREGATE SUPPLY	AGGREGATE DEMAND	
58	$300	$500	
60	350	525	
62	400	550	
64	450	575	*Excess Demand*
66	500	600	Output Will
68	550	625	Expand
70	600	650	
72	650	675	
78 ⟶	700 ⟵	⟶ 700 ⟵	*Equilibrium*
80	750	725	*Excess Supply*
82	800	750	Output Will Contract

the income generated by the process of production will, in the aggregate, necessarily equal the value of output. In our simplified example there is only one output at which this happens and that, of course, is what we call an equilibrium output. The idea of overproduction is not economically meaningful if we mean only a failure of the economic system to generate sufficient purchasing power to buy back the goods and services produced. The economy always does this, but decisions to spend may exceed or fall short of decisions to produce, primarily because spending decisions are not made by the same people who make the production decisions. This is the fundamental reason why aggregate demand and aggregate supply may not be in balance. Finally, let us stress that nothing in the mechanism just explored guarantees that output will necessarily rise to a level that yields full employment. This is a key lesson of modern economic analysis.

The equilibrium output

Change in Output and Employment

Further examination of our simple geometrical and mathematical model of income determination shows some meaningful aspects of change in the economic system. In general, change in output, employment, or both, results whenever the aggregate demand and aggregate supply schedules are *not* in equilibrium. Output (and employment) rises whenever aggregate demand exceeds aggregate supply and falls whenever the reverse is the case. We can go beyond this principle, though, and explain that there are two basic types of change encompassed in our relatively simple model of in-

Movement toward equilibrium

127

come determination. As just discussed, there is change in the
form of a movement of output and employment toward an equilibrium level. This results when the position of the aggregate demand schedule relative to the aggregate supply schedule is known
and aggregate demand and aggregate supply are not initially in
balance.

The second type of change is the adjustment of output and employment to a new equilibrium. Change of this nature takes place
following the shift of the aggregate supply schedule to a new position. Subsequently, we shall discuss reasons for a shift in the
position of the schedule, but here it suffices to point out that
when a shift takes place—either upward or downward—the result
disturbs a pre-existing equilibrium and, thus, the system must adjust to a new equilibrium position.

Even though we can measure change in the economic system
very accurately with the techniques of national income and accounting we cannot readily distinguish statistically the kind of
change that may be taking place. We cannot tell from statistical
evidence alone whether a given change is, in effect, a movement
of the system toward an equilibrium, given the position of the aggregate demand schedule, or a movement of the system to a new
equilibrium, following displacement of the aggregate demand
schedule.

*Movement toward a
new equilibrium*

The Principle of Aggregate Demand

The discussion pursued to this point concerning the determination of the economy's output has enabled us to derive a second
basic principle of modern economic analysis. This principle is
that, in the short run, output and employment depend primarily
upon the level of aggregate demand. The implication of this statement is that to understand how the aggregate economy really
works, we must, so to speak, go behind the aggregate demand
schedule and explain what determines its level in a particular situation or at a particular time. But in order to do this we must
understand and analyze the magnitude of the component parts of
the aggregate demand schedule and how they relate to one another. If we can do this with some success and put our findings together, we will have constructed a theory of aggregate demand,
which can be used to explain how changes in output and employment come about. We shall begin our analysis with the consumption component of the aggregate demand schedule.

*Output and
employment
dependent upon
aggregate demand*

Determinants of Consumption Expenditure

The most important economic hypothesis concerning the determination of aggregate consumption expenditures is that the

volume of these expenditures is determined primarily by income itself. More accurately, aggregate consumption depends upon disposable income available to the consumers and households in the economic system which, in turn, depends upon the size of output (GNP). This is the major finding of several decades of research by economists and statisticians into the behavior of both individual households and consumers in the aggregate in the economic system.

This hypothesis was originally formulated in the 1930s by the British economist John Maynard Keynes. In *The General Theory of Employment, Interest, and Money,* Keynes postulated a "fundamental psychological law" of consumer behavior. Keynes' "law" stated not only that consumption depended primarily on income but also that when income increased or decreased consumption would also increase or decrease but not to such a great extent.

Keynes' fundamental psychological law

Note carefully that the economist does not say that income is the only determinant of consumption, but simply that it is strategically more significant than any other possible determinant. A little thought brings to mind other variables that may influence consumption, such as prices, expectations of future income, expectations of price changes, tastes, and the like, but economists are less sure of the exact manner and degree in which these variables exercise an influence on consumption spending. They are reasonably certain, however, that income is the prime determinant of such expenditure. We should stress, too, that when, following Keynes, economists set forth a relationship between income and consumption they do so on the assumption of "normal" conditions, by which is meant the absence of war, revolution, or other serious social upheaval.

The Consumption Function Concept

The idea that consumption is determined primarily by disposable income takes on a formal theoretical expression in economic analysis in the concept of the *consumption function*. This is a schedule showing total consumer expenditures forthcoming at various levels of disposable income. Figure 6-8 illustrates it graphically. Disposable income on the horizontal axis is plotted against consumption outlays on the vertical axis. The slope of the schedule is shown as less than 45 degrees, which adheres to Keynes' fundamental psychological law that consumption outlays always change by a smaller absolute amount than does income, even though the consumption outlays are clearly dependent upon income.

Since disposable income bears a reasonably fixed relationship to the gross national product, we can also postulate that for every possible level of GNP there will be a corresponding level of disposable income, and hence, consumption. The relationship of disposable income to GNP depends upon the structure of taxes,

Disposable income, consumption, and GNP

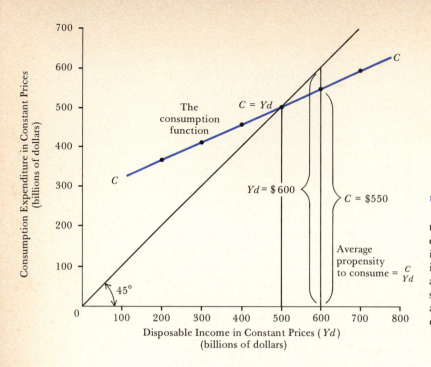

FIGURE 6-8
The Consumption Func-
tion.

The schedule CC illus-
trates the hypothesis that
consumption depends upon
income and that it changes as
income changes, but not by
as much. In this figure consumption is related to disposable income. (Data given in
constant dollars.)

transfers, and other forms of income withholding in the economic
system in a particular period. Once we know the relationship between gross national product and disposable income, we can construct a schedule showing how consumption varies with changes
in the gross national product. A schedule of this kind, shown in
Figure 6-9, is a vital element in the construction of an aggregate
demand schedule.

Before we turn to the determinants of the other major components of the aggregate demand schedule, two important technical
attributes of the consumption-income relationship must be examined. The first is the *propensity to consume,* which is the proportion of any given income level spent for consumption purposes. If
we are talking about the relationship between consumption and
disposable income, then the propensity to consume refers to the
proportion of disposable income spent on consumer goods and
services; whereas if we are thinking of the relationship between
consumption and the gross national product, we have in mind the
proportion consumed out of the gross national product. In either
case, the propensity to consume is a ratio which indicates the proportion of income, however measured, absorbed by consumption
outlays. Table 6-2 shows GNP, disposable income, and consumption as well as the propensity to consume out of both GNP and
disposable income for the period 1929–1970.

The second technical attribute of this relationship is the *marginal propensity to consume* (MPC), which is a technical name
for Keynes' fundamental psychological law. It is the proportion of

*Propensity to
consume*

130

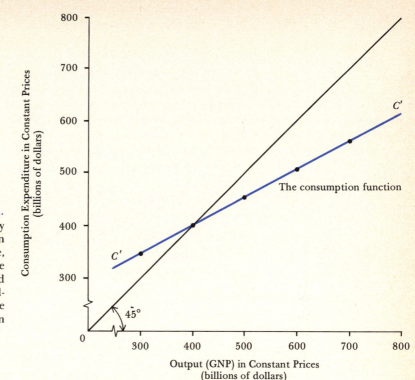

FIGURE 6-9
GNP and Consumption.

If there is a reasonably fixed relationship between GNP and disposable income, then there will also be one between consumption and GNP. This relationship is illustrated in the figure by the schedule *C'C'*. (Data given in constant dollars.)

TABLE 6-2
GNP, Disposable Income, and Consumption:
Selected Years, 1929–1970
(Billions of Current Dollars)

YEAR	GNP	CONSUMPTION	C/GNP	DI	C/DI
1929	$103.1	$77.2	74.9%	83.3	92.7%
1935	72.2	55.7	77.1	58.5	95.2
1940	99.7	70.8	71.0	75.7	93.5
1945	211.9	119.7	56.5	150.2	79.7
1950	284.8	191.0	67.1	206.9	92.3
1955	398.0	254.4	63.9	275.3	92.4
1960	503.7	325.2	64.6	350.0	92.9
1965	684.9	432.8	63.2	473.2	91.5
1970	974.1	615.8	63.2	687.8	89.5

Source: *Economic Report of the President,* 1972.

any given increment of income spent for consumption purposes. The concept of the marginal propensity to consume is illustrated in Figure 6-10. This shows that with an increase in income of $100 billion—from $300 to $400 billion—consumer expenditure will increase by $50 billion. Thus, 50 percent of any increase in disposable income will be spent for consumer goods and services. The concept is equally applicable to a decline in income. If we

Marginal propensity to consume

131

refer to the relationship between consumption and disposable income, then the appropriate concept is that of the marginal propensity to consume out of disposable income; whereas if we are concerned about changes in consumption and changes in the gross national product the appropriate concept is the marginal propensity to consume out of the GNP. Figure 6-10 shows the marginal propensity to consume out of disposable income. The marginal propensity to consume provides a means of analyzing the magnitude of changes in output which result from shifts in the aggregate demand functions. Its value is normally less than unity. That is, less than 100 percent—or the whole—of any increase in income will be spent for consumption purposes. This of course is the essence of Keynes' law. The marginal propensity to consume also forms the basis for the principle of the multiplier, an interesting economic phenomenon which we shall encounter shortly.

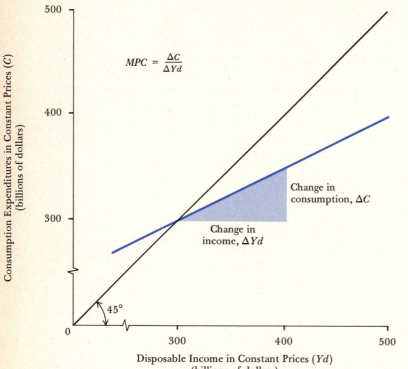

FIGURE 6-10

The Marginal Propensity to Consume.

The slope of the line is the ratio of a change in consumption (ΔC) to a change in income (ΔYd). This is the marginal propensity to consume, illustrated by the shaded triangle in the figure.

Investment Outlays

A second major component of the aggregate demand schedule consists of the investment expenditures that originate with the firms in the economy. Investment expenditures are outlays for new equipment, new structures, along with changes in inventory. Inventory changes may, of course, be negative in any income period; that is, inventory may be reduced rather than built up. Essentially, investment expenditures are undertaken in the expectation that increased capital, in the form of equipment, buildings, or additions to the stock of goods on hand, will be profitable.

Investment expenditures or capital outlays differ from consumer expenditures in one highly important respect: they normally have a life span extending beyond the current income period. This is certainly true for buildings and most machinery or equipment items, although it is not necessarily always the case with inventory expenditures. However, the fact of durability significantly influences the nature of investment spending; it means the firm must take into account expected profitability over the entire life of the added asset. And since the future in the economic world is uncertain under any conditions, a high degree of uncertainty attaches to investment decisions. The profitability of an additional item of capital of any kind inevitably will be affected through its physical and economic life by many factors, including technological change, increases or decreases in the costs associated with the use of the capital good, tax policies of government units in the economy, changes in the general level of prices for consumer goods and services, and changes in consumer tastes. For example, in the spring of 1971 the Nixon administration approved allowing business firms to depreciate their investments in machinery at

The Principle of Aggregate Demand

Life span of investment expenditures

Uncertainty of investment decisions

FIGURE 6-11

Gross Investment Expenditure: 1947–1971.

Investment expenditure has exhibited a marked degree of instability in the post-World War II era, save for a strong and smooth expansionary upsurge in the first half of the 1960s. (Source: *Economic Report of the President*, 1972.)

an accelerated pace, the objective being to make certain types of investment more profitable and, thereby, increase investment spending. The uncertainty inherent in investment decisions has led economists to conclude that the investment component of the aggregate demand function is subject to widespread fluctuation and statistical evidence supports this view. Figure 6-11 shows fluctuations in total of gross private domestic investment since 1947. Investment can be seen as a factor which imparts instability to the economic system as a whole.

To summarize, the investment component of aggregate demand is based upon *expected* profitability (or yield) of the investment in question. And expected profitability is founded on highly uncertain knowledge of the future. Speaking about the investment decision, Keynes said:

> The outstanding fact is the extreme precariousness of the basis of knowledge on which our estimates of prospective yield have to be made. Our knowledge of the factors which will govern the yield of an investment some years hence is usually very slight and often negligible. . . .[1]

Rate of interest

One particular factor which economists heed in relation to investment spending is the rate of interest. When a firm acquires a new structure or machine, or adds to its inventory, it must spend money for this purpose; it either spends money of its own or it borrows in the market. When it spends its own money it forgoes the opportunity to lend these funds to someone else at the prevailing rate of interest, but if it borrows in the market it must pay the going rate of interest. Thus, the rate of interest is a measure of the financial cost to the firm of acquiring new assets. The business firm will compare the rate of interest to the expected profitability of the asset expressed as an expected rate of return on the cost of the asset in order to determine whether it is worthwhile to go ahead and acquire the capital good. For example, the interest rate on high-grade corporate bonds in early 1972 was a little above 7 percent. This meant that a corporation contemplating a new plant would have to get back more than 7 percent as a return on its investment before it would consider borrowing the money to finance the construction of a plant. The return on investment is calculated after deduction of additional costs—labor and raw materials, for example—that the firm will incur in connection with the operation of the new plant. Economists use the term "marginal efficiency of capital" to describe expected profitability as a rate of return.

[1] John Maynard Keynes, *The General theory of Employment, Interest and Money* (New York: Harcourt Brace, 1936), p. 149.

Government Expenditures

Government purchases of goods and services make up the third major component of the aggregate demand schedule. The level of total government expenditures depends upon an enormous array of factors, many of which are non-economic. In the United States government units operating at three levels (national, state, and local) all engage in collective activities and acquire goods and services to carry out these activities. Unlike the relationship between consumption and income or investment and the rate of interest, there is no simple and direct relationship between government purchase of goods and services and other economic variables such as income, expectations, the price level, or employment.

The federal government often varies its taxes or expenditures in direct response to current economic conditions—as the Nixon administration proposed following the President's announcement of a New Economic Policy in August of 1971. Nevertheless many of its expenditures are determined by other considerations, a fact even more pronounced for state and local governments. At the national level, for example, spending for defense, for space exploration, for economic security, including welfare outlays, are major claims upon the resources of the federal government. The magnitude of these claims is determined only in a marginal way by current economic conditions. For purposes of economic analysis most government expenditures are said to be autonomous, which means they are independent of other economic variables that are a part of the model of the economic system developed in this chapter. In Chapter 9, which focuses on government and the national output, we shall examine in greater detail some of the major factors which influence both the level and change in government expenditures.

Net Exports

A brief word about the fourth component of aggregate demand, the size of net exports, is in order. Since net exports are the difference between the exports and imports of a country, they depend as a spending component of the aggregate demand schedule in part on what happens in the rest of the world and in part on what happens in the domestic economy. Generally speaking, our exports expand when income in the rest of the world is increasing and our imports rise when domestic income is rising. However, other variables may influence the export-import balance; in 1970, a recession year, our imports rose, a development due in part to continued inflation in the American economy which made imports more competitive. The inflation of recent years has also slowed down the growth in American exports.

A Complete Model of Output Determination

Now that we have examined each of the individual components of the aggregate demand schedule we can construct a complete model for determination of the gross national product. This is done graphically in Figure 6-12 and numerically in Table 6-3. Essentially the process is as follows: First, we draw a consumption-output schedule, which relates consumption to the gross national product, as was done earlier in Figure 6-9. For simplicity's sake we assume that the other three components of GNP, namely investment expenditure, government outlays for goods and services, and net exports, are autonomous with respect to the level of the GNP. This is an oversimplification but it permits us to see the essentials of our model of income determination in the clearest fashion possible.

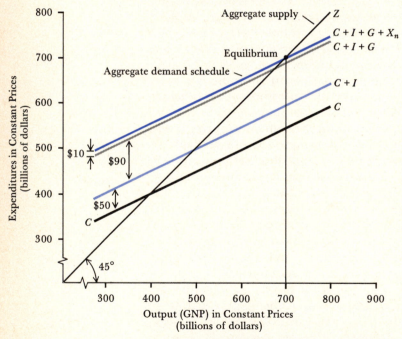

FIGURE 6-12

A Complete Model of Output Determination
Using the data from Table 6-3, this figure shows how the complete aggregate demand schedule is constructed by adding autonomous amounts for investment, government expenditures, and net exports to the consumption function. Equilibrium is at the point of intersection of aggregate demand and aggregate supply, namely $700 billion. (Data given in constant dollars.)

Since our other variables are assumed independent of any particular magnitude for the gross national product, we can depict them in graphic form by adding to the consumption output relationship a series of parallel schedules, each one of which represents a value for each of these components. Thus, we add to the consumption schedule C an amount representing fixed investment, which gives us the line $C+I$ in the figure; to this we add

Building the
aggregate demand
schedule

136

TABLE 6-3
A Complete Model of Output Determination
(Billions of Constant Dollars)

AGGREGATE SUPPLY (Z)		CONSUMPTION (C)	INVESTMENT (I)	GOVERNMENT PURCHASE OF GOODS AND SERVICES (G)	NET EXPORTS (X_n)	AGGREGATE DEMAND $(C+I+G+X_n)$
$300		$350	$50	$90	$10	$500
350		375	50	90	10	525
400		400	50	90	10	550
450		425	50	90	10	575
500		450	50	90	10	600
550		475	50	90	10	625
600		500	50	90	10	650
650		525	50	90	10	675
→700	Equilibrium	550	50	90	10	700←
750		575	50	90	10	725
800		600	50	90	10	750

another line representing the amount of government purchases for goods and services, which gives us the schedule $C+I+G;$ and, finally, we add a third line representing net exports, which gives us the final schedule, $C+I+G+X_n$. This becomes the aggregate demand schedule in our graphic model. As in an earlier example (Figure 6-5), equilibrium is the point of intersection between the schedule of aggregate demand and aggregate supply. At *any* other level of gross national product, aggregate demand and aggregate supply will not be in balance and a disequilibrium will prevail.

Table 6-3 shows the same results in simplified numerical form. Column one in the table represents possible levels of the gross national product, or the aggregate supply function. Column two shows how consumption expenditure changes with change in the size of the gross national product. Column three represents autonomous investment; column four shows a fixed amount of government expenditures for goods and services; and column five represents a fixed level for *net* exports. Column six is the sum of columns two through five and, as such, constitutes an aggregate demand schedule. A quick examination of the data in the table shows that there is only one equilibrium point given by these data, which is that point at which aggregate demand and aggregate supply are equal. This is $700 billion.

The model we have just developed helps answer one of the questions posed earlier. Why is the slope of the aggregate demand schedule less than that of aggregate supply? We start with the fact that the consumption component of aggregate demand does not increase (or decrease) at the same rate as the gross national product itself. By adding to consumption fixed amounts representing

Disparity between slopes of aggregate demand and aggregate supply

137

investment, government purchases, and net exports we end up with a schedule whose slope is necessarily less than that of the aggregate demand function.

Further examination of this model reveals another reason for the disparity between the slopes of aggregate demand and aggregate supply. This arises out of the requirements for stability in the economic system. If the slope of the aggregate demand schedule were steeper than the aggregate supply schedule the economic system would be inherently unstable. Figure 6-13 depicts this possibility. True, an equilibrium would be possible at the output represented by intersection of the two schedules, but at any other output the economy would be in a state of continuous disequilibrium with no possibility of aggregate supply and aggregate demand ever becoming equal again. Examine the model carefully to convince yourself of the logic of this position and the reasons for it.

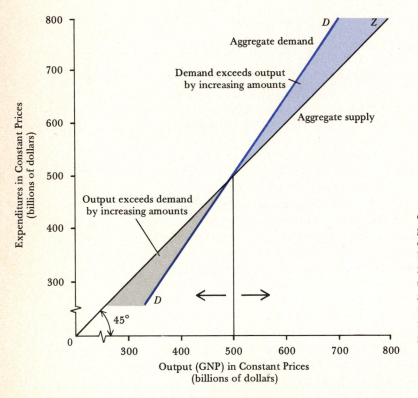

FIGURE 6-13
Unstable Equilibrium.

If aggregate demand increases more rapidly than aggregate supply, a stable equilibrium becomes impossible. At any income above $500 billion, demand continually runs ahead of supply; at any income below that figure, demand will always fall short of supply. (Data given in constant dollars.)

Saving and Investment

There is an alternative way to show how equilibrium is established. Up to now we have utilized the concepts of aggregate demand and aggregate supply, showing that equilibrium exists at the point of intersection of these schedules. But the idea of an income equilibrium can also be demonstrated by use of an aggregate investment schedule and an aggregate saving schedule, assuming for the sake of simplicity a system with neither government purchases of goods and services nor net exports.

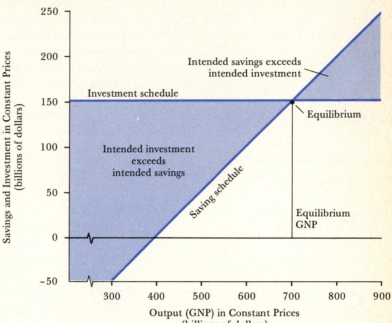

FIGURE 6-14

Equilibrium of Savings and Investment.

At every level of income *less* than $700 billion, intended saving is less than intended investment, which means there will be inventory disinvestment and thus an expansion of output. At any income level *greater* than $700 billion the reverse will hold; intended saving will exceed intended investment, leading ultimately to a fall in income. Model assumes no government expenditures and no taxes. (Data given in constant dollars.)

This alternative approach to determination of the income level at equilibrium is illustrated in Figure 6-14, in which GNP is measured on the horizontal axis and saving and investment are measured on the vertical axis. The saving schedule is the counterpart of the consumption schedule shown in Figure 6-9, because without government expenditures for goods and services or net exports, the difference between consumption and the gross national product must necessarily be saving. Thus it is possible to draw a schedule showing the amount of saving that will be forthcoming at every income level. The horizontal line in the diagram represents investment outlays, on the assumption that these outlays are autonomous with respect to gross national product. These two schedules intersect at a point which represents the equilibrium income level; this point corresponds to the equilibrium shown in Figures 6-5 and 6-12.

Saving equals the difference between consumption and GNP

Planned Saving and Investment

What is the significance of this point of intersection when equilibrium is depicted in terms of schedules of aggregate saving and aggregate investment? Essentially, this diagram shows that an equilibrium value for GNP requires that planned (or *ex ante*) savings be equal to planned (or *ex ante*) investment, since it is intended values which are embodied in the two schedules shown. At any other level of GNP the schedule (or planned) values for saving and investment will not be equal. For example, to the left of the equilibrium GNP is a situation in which intended investment exceeds intended savings; this is the same as saying that aggregate demand is in excess of aggregate supply. The consequence will be an expansion in the income level. To the right of the intersection of the schedules shown in Figure 6-14, the situation is reversed: intended saving is in excess of intended investment. In this case aggregate supply exceeds aggregate demand. The consequence will be a decline in the gross national product and with it the amount of employment.

Actual Saving and Investment

Equilibrium defined in terms of saving and investment schedules is useful in helping us understand a point raised earlier, namely

that actual (*ex post*) saving and investment in the aggregate are always equal. This is true even though it is also true that planned saving and investment are not necessarily equal except when the GNP is in equilibrium. The fact that actual saving and investment must be equal, where planned saving and investment are not necessarily equal appears, at first glance, highly puzzling. But there is really no mystery here. Examine, for instance, the situation in which GNP is momentarily in excess of its equilibrium value. Such a situation exists at any output above the output represented at the point of intersection shown in Figure 6-14. At any such output there will be unintended investment in the economic system in the form of unforeseen inventory accumulation. In Figure 6-14, planned saving is in excess of planned investment at any output greater than the equilibrium output, but actual saving and actual investment values are brought into equality by the phenomenon of unintended inventory changes.

On the other hand, if we find during the output period that aggregate demand exceeds aggregate supply, there will be unforeseen disinvestment, or a drawing down of stocks of goods accumulated from an earlier production period. In Figure 6-14, this means that intended investment is in excess of intended savings, but the equality between actual saving and investment is brought about by the inventory disinvestment which reduces actual investment in the period below the intended level. The mechanics of this analysis require careful thought, but once these are understood no difficulty should be experienced henceforth in understanding the sense in which saving and investment for the economy are always equal and the sense in which they may not be equal. Table 6-4 illustrates the establishment of equilibrium with a simple numerical example showing the interaction between intended saving and investment. When planned investment exceeds planned saving, aggregate demand will exceed aggregate supply and the income level will rise. But when planned saving is in excess of planned investment, the opposite will be true and the income level will fall. Consequently, equilibrium is possible only where planned investment and saving are equal.

TABLE 6-4
Equilibrium of Savings and Investment
(Billions of Constant Dollars)

GNP	PLANNED SAVING		PLANNED INVESTMENT	UNPLANNED * INVESTMENT	ACTUAL ** INVESTMENT
$300	$−50		$150	$−200	$−50
350	−25		150	−175	−25
400	0		150	−150	0
450	25		150	−125	25
500	50		150	−100	50
550	75		150	−75	75
600	100		150	−50	100
650	125		150	−25	125
700	150	Equilibrium	150	⟶ 0 ⟵	150
750	175		150	25	175
800	200		150	50	200

* Negative value indicates *disinvestment*, i.e. a drawing down of stocks.
** Equals Planned Saving.

Leakages

In our discussion up to now, the difference between consumption and the gross national product was absorbed on the expenditure side by investment and on the non-expenditure side by saving. Further, we saw that equilibrium in the system as a whole requires equality between the intended values of these two variables. In reality, this is a vast oversimplification, because the difference between consumption and GNP also encompasses on the expenditure side both government purchases of goods and services and net exports, and on the allocation side some of the economy's gross income which is neither consumed nor saved, and hence absorbed by taxes. What is being said, in effect, is that once consumption expenditure is subtracted from the gross national product, equilibrium for the economic system as a whole requires that other expenditures (investment, government purchases of goods and services, and net exports) must offset any leakages out of the income stream in the form of either savings or taxes. The latter are leakages because they represent non-expenditure of current income for output currently produced. Equilibrium cannot be maintained unless these leakages are offset by a form of expenditure other than the purchase of consumer goods and services. It is well to keep these points in mind as we pursue our analysis further, even though they do not alter the basic principles involved.

The Multiplier Principle

The movement of the economic system from one equilibrium position to another, as we have seen, results from a change in the position of the aggregate demand function. It has been found that whenever the aggregate demand schedule shifts because of any autonomous change in expenditure there will be a *multiplier* effect because the total and ultimate change in output will be greater than the amount by which the aggregate demand schedule has shifted. In this section we shall examine the nature and source of this multiplier effect. At first glance it seems somewhat complex, but as we explore it we shall see that it is rooted in logic and common sense.

*The multiplier
at work*

To illustrate the multiplier at work, let us postulate in diagrammatic form a simple economy which has only two forms of expenditures, consumption and investment. The essentials of this economic system are illustrated in Figure 6-15, which plots a con-

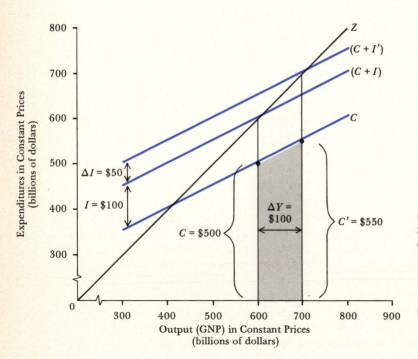

FIGURE 6-15
The Multiplier Effect.

The autonomous shift in the investment schedule by $50 billion leads to an increase in output of $100 billion; thus there is a multiplier effect of 2 associated with this change in investment. (Data given in constant dollars.)

sumption schedule to which is added a fixed quantity for autonomous investment. The consumption schedule plus the fixed amount of autonomous investment gives us the aggregate demand function $C + I$. In our hypothetical model the equilibrium income level is at the intersection of the $C + I$ schedule and OZ, the supply schedule. What will happen in the event of an autonomous upward shift in the aggregate demand function? In this example, aggregate demand shifts because of an autonomous increase in investment outlays. Diagrammatically, the outcome is a shift for the economy from one equilibrium position to another, the latter being at a higher level of output and employment than the former. Close scrutiny of the diagram in Figure 6-15 shows that the change in output (depicted on the horizontal axis) is greater than the amount by which aggregate demand shifted upward as a consequence of the autonomous increase in investment. This is the essence of the multiplier effect, which, technically, we may define as the ratio of a *change* in output to a change in aggregate demand.

A Chain Reaction: Spending and Responding

Why is there such an effect? The answer is deceptively simple. When there is an autonomous increase in spending—or shift in aggregate demand—in the economic system there will be important secondary effects flowing from the initial increase in expenditure. In our example, the autonomous increase in spending is in the form of more investment outlays, which come about because business firms anticipate that it will be profitable to acquire more capital goods, structures, or inventories. But the additional expenditure which flows from those who want to acquire more capital accrues as money income to those who supply the capital. It does not really matter whether the capital is in the form of equipment, structures, or inventories. The suppliers of capital goods, finding their own incomes increased, will spend a part of this increase in income on consumption goods and services. This, of course, is Keynes' fundamental psychological law at work. But as the suppliers of capital goods increase their own consumption expenditures, their income is added to the suppliers of these goods and services, who in turn increase their consumption outlays because of higher income. In effect, the initial increase in expenditure which originated with the increased demand for capital sets off a chain reaction of spending and responding in the form of increased demand for consumer goods and services. To put it in another way, there will be induced consumption expenditures resulting from the initial first round increase in investment expenditures, and it is the sum of the induced expenditures and the initial increase in investment expenditures which gives us the overall multiplier effect for the whole economy. If there were no induced consumption outlays as a result of higher spending for investment goods there could not be a multiplier effect, for the total increase in the gross national product would necessarily be limited to the increase in investment expenditures. But this is not the case.

The Size of the Multiplier Effect

Interaction of the
marginal propensity
to consume and the
multiplier

What determines the overall size of the multiplier effect? To answer this we need to return to an idea introduced earlier, the marginal propensity to consume out of the gross national product. This is the proportion of any increment in the GNP that is absorbed by consumption expenditure. If the value for the MPC is, for example, fifty percent, then for every additional dollar of GNP generated by new expenditures for investment goods, the suppliers of these goods will increase their expenditures for consumer goods and services by fifty cents. As they do this, additional income will be received by those who supply the consumer goods and services, and they, in turn, will increase their purchases of consumer goods and services in like proportion. Thus, we can see not only how the chain of spending and respending begins, but also how as it spreads throughout the economy it gets smaller and smaller until ultimately it becomes negligible in size. At this point the multiplier effect is, for all practical purposes, at an end. It should be noted, too, that if the marginal propensity to consume is not less than 100 percent, the increase in spending in the economic system would be infinite, which would have disastrous consequences. The fact that the marginal propensity to consume is typically less than 100 percent saves the economic system from serious problems whenever there is a shift in the level of the aggregate demand schedule.

The Multiplier Process in Action

Table 6-5 gives a simple example of the multiplier process at work, using the assumptions embodied in Figure 6-15. The data of Table 6-5 show the economy initially in an equilibrium position in which planned saving and planned investment are equal. We then assume there is an autonomous increase in investment outlays of $50 billion. The table traces the sequence of events following this increase in investment expenditures. The assumed value for the marginal propensity to consume in our example is 50 percent. After an infinite number of periods the total increase in GNP in this hypothetical situation is twice as large as the initial increase in investment expenditure. The latter measures the increase in aggregate demand. The multiplier in this instance has value of two. The reason is that an autonomous change in aggregate demand which issued from a change in investment expenditure caused twice as large an increase in the gross national product.

TABLE 6-5

The Multiplier Process *

(Billions of Current Dollars)

PERIOD	GNP	CONSUMPTION (*C*)	CHANGE IN CONSUMPTION (Δ C)	INVESTMENT (*I*)	CHANGE IN INVESTMENT (Δ I)	CHANGE IN OUTPUT ΔGNP
0	$600	$500	—	$100	—	—
1	650	500	—	150	$50	$50
2	675	525	$25	150	—	25
3	688	538	13	150	—	13
4	695	545	7	150	—	7
5	699	549	4	150	—	4
∞	700	550	1	150	—	1
Total	—	—	$50		$50	$100

* Lag of 1 period assumed for change in consumption as a result of a change in income. The value of the MPC=.5. The value of the multiplier is 2. Figures are rounded to the nearest whole number.

The realism of the example chosen can be underscored by examining the 1963 *Annual Report* of the President's Council of Economic Advisers. In this report the CEA was concerned with showing what would be the effects on the economic system of a cut in personal and corporate income taxes. A tax cut was urged at that time to stimulate the economy's growth. A tax reduction would have roughly the same effect as an increase in investment, as shown in our example, because a tax cut puts more disposable income into the hands of the consumer or creates a more favorable climate for investment expenditure. The result is to raise the level of aggregate demand. It is interesting to note that the Council of Economic Advisers found that for each additional dollar of the gross national product generated by a tax cut there would be fifty cents more in added consumption expenditure. This is equivalent to a marginal propensity to consume out of the gross national product of two, the same figure used in our hypothetical example. In its 1963 *Report* the Council pointed out that "the additional expenditure on consumption that is brought by the rise in GNP generates in further production which generates additional income and consumption and so on in a continuous sequence of expansion which economists call 'the multiplier process.' The multiplier applicable to the initial increase in spending with account taken of the various leakages works out to roughly two." This is a good example of a recent and important practical appli-

Effects of a tax cut

145

cation of the principle of the multiplier in the realm of economic policy.

It should now be apparent that the actual value of the multiplier depends upon the size of the marginal propensity to consume. If people had been willing to spend a higher proportion of any additional income on consumer goods and services, the value of the multiplier would have been increased correspondingly because the total of induced consumption expenditures resulting from the initial instrument of expenditure would be larger. If we designate the multiplier as k and the marginal propensity to consume by MPC we can express its value in a simple mathematical formula as follows:

(2)
$$k = \frac{1}{1 - MPC}$$

Marginal propensity to save

This formula states that the multiplier is equal to the reciprocal of one minus the marginal propensity to consume. Since we assumed in the example that the only form of non-expenditure present in the system is saving, it follows that one minus the marginal propensity to consume equals the *marginal propensity to save*. The latter is the percent of any increment of income saved. Note that since saving is leakage from the income stream, in effect the multiplier has a value equal to the *reciprocal* of leakages from the income stream expressed as marginal propensities. In a more complex system in which some leakages take the form of taxes in addition to saving, we must take this into account. Those interested in the algebraic derivation of the multiplier will find an explanation in the appendix to this chapter. For the present, though, it will suffice to point out that in a simplified system the multiplier equals the reciprocal of the marginal propensity to save. The practical significance of this is the *larger* the marginal propensity to save (or the smaller the marginal propensity to consume) the *less* will be the multiplier associated with any increment of aggregate demand. The reverse, of course, is also true.

Appendix: The Algebraic Derivation of the Multiplier in a Simple System

1. $Y = C + I$. The basic identity, assuming no government expenditures for goods and services, no taxes or transfer payments, and no exports or imports.

2. $\Delta Y = \Delta I + \Delta C$. This follows from the basic identity.

3. $\Delta C = MPC \cdot \Delta Y$. The change in consumption depends upon the change in income and the value of the marginal propensity to consume.

4. $\Delta Y = MPC \cdot \Delta Y + \Delta I$. Substitute $MPC \cdot \Delta Y$ for ΔC in equation 2.

5. Algebraic manipulation of equation 4.
   (1) $\Delta Y - MPC \, \Delta Y = \Delta I$
   (2) $\Delta Y \, (1 - MPC) = \Delta I$
   (3) $(1 - MPC) = \Delta I / \Delta Y$
   (4) $\Delta Y / \Delta I = \dfrac{1}{1 - MPC}$. Rearrange equation (3).
   (5) $\Delta Y / \Delta I = k =$ the multiplier.

Questions for Review and Discussion

1. What is the basic difference between the short term and the long term with respect to the general level of economic activity?

2. Explain why productive capacity is defined as potential for output. How can productive capacity be measured?

3. In what way is aggregate supply related to the expectation of demand? Where do decisions concerning aggregate demand originate?

4. Explain how economists analyze aggregate supply and aggregate demand as schedules. What is the value of the schedule notion as applied to these concepts?

5. What is the meaning of an equilibrium level of output and employment? Use schedules to demonstrate how equilibrium is brought about.

6. If the actual GNP in any year is less than the potential equilibrium for that year, why will forces be set in motion that tend to increase the GNP?

7. John Maynard Keynes developed a "fundamental psychological law" of consumer behavior. What is the nature of this law and what significance does it have for explaining the income and employment level?

8. Why is it that income is more important than most other variables in determining the level of consumption, but the rate of interest seems to be the variable of most significance with respect to determining the volume of investment expenditure?

9. Why do economists generally say that government purchases of goods and services are "autonomous"? Is this a valid assertion?

10. What is the difference between an *ex post* and an *ex ante* identity of saving and investment? Can these differing concepts of equality between saving and investment be reconciled?

11. Whenever there is an autonomous shift in the aggregate demand schedule, income increases by some multiple of the change in ag-

147

gregate demand. Explain the origins and principles of this multiplier effect.

12. Explain fully the difference between an output and employment change that means movement of the economic system toward an existing equilibrium position and one that means movement toward a new equilibrium position.

7

Money, Banking, and the Economic System

THERE IS PROBABLY no subject in economic analysis both more intriguing and mystifying to the layman than money. No modern economy can function effectively without money and an efficient system to control its circulation. But the nature and workings of a monetary system remain, unfortunately, too much of a mystery for too many people. Our task in this chapter is to dispel some of this mystery by a close analysis of money and how it fits into the economic system.

The Nature and Functions of Money

Money is probably as old as civilization itself, but there is no exact or simple definition for it. The best way to explain money is through reference to its major functions. It is a social invention whose primary purpose is to facilitate the economic processes of production, exchange, and consumption. It is a man-made ar-

149

rangement continuously subject to evolution and change. Although all of us know people who seem to "worship" money, there is nothing sacred or immutable about any type of monetary system. Throughout human history money has taken a variety of forms and been put to many uses.

We can trace two important evolutions money has undergone. The first is an evolution in form. What we regard as money has changed from a metal with an intrinsic value (for example, gold or silver), to various abstract claims without intrinsic value. One such claim is the modern checking account (technically called a demand deposit); in a literal sense, the money one deposits is a mere entry on the books of a bank. The second is an evolution in supply; whereas at one time the amount of money in circulation was determined by market forces largely beyond governmental control, now the money supply is primarily under the direct control of government. In effect, the evolution of money in practically all countries has been toward a fully managed system. Society exerts control over the amount of money in circulation; it also determines the value of the monetary unit in the economy.

The Primary Functions of Money

The oldest and no doubt most useful definition of money is in terms of its major function. Basically money is anything which serves as a medium of exchange, a means to carry on the purchase and sale of things having economic value. This definition can be traced back at least as far as ancient Greece. In his *Ethics* Aristotle stated, ". . . [money] is therefore indispensable that all things which can be exchanged should be capable of comparison and for this purpose money has come in, and comes to be a kind of medium, for it measures all things . . ." The medieval philosopher Thomas Aquinas said essentially the same thing: "To the end that the products of various workers may be equated and exchange thus made possible, all those goods which can be exchanged must be made comparable to each other in some way so that the greater or lesser value of each can be known. To this end money—that is, coin—was invented by which the price of such things are measured." Both Aristotle and Aquinas expressly state the most fundamental of all the characteristics of money: it is a medium of exchange. Odd as it may seem, these comments from the ancient and medieval world come as near as any to a specific definition. Most modern economists believe that money ought to be defined precisely, but also agree that it is nearly impossible to do so.

A second important function of money is implied in our first definition. Money serves as a standard of value. When comparisons need to be made between the value of different things, money is often the best measure available. Thus, when we say a loaf of bread costs $.35, we know almost instinctively what the loaf is worth in comparison to other things. The medium of exchange and the standard of value are referred to as the *primary* functions of money.

Secondary Functions of Money

Economists speak of two *secondary* functions of money. It serves as a standard for deferred payments; it is the most common unit in which payments deferred until the future are stated. For example, if you borrow money to buy a new car, the loan contract will normally specify the amount of money and the dates on which repayment must take place.

The other secondary function of money is to serve as a store of value. Money is a means through which economic value can be preserved and carried forward through time. It provides generalized purchasing power, acceptable at any time and in any place. Money is not the only instrument through which economic value can be conserved. A farmer can keep wheat in storage, waiting for the right moment to get the best price; a manufacturer can keep a supply of his product in inventory, anticipating an increase in demand. But money is usually the most convenient medium to preserve economic value.

Defining money through its functions brings out a point of special significance. The material substance—coins, bills, or anything else—used at a particular time or place for money is not important. What counts is what money does or can do for those who hold it.

The Money Supply in the United States

Currency and Demand Deposits

In the American economy two kinds of money are in widespread use. The first is currency, composed of bills and metal coins, and the second is demand deposits in commercial banks. The first type, being created directly by the government, is government-issued money; the second is bank-created money.

The check is the primary means by which demand deposit money circulates through the economic system. Thus, it is sometimes called checkbook money. A check is a legal instrument through which money is transferred from one person to another. It is an order drawn against a bank by the owner of a demand deposit telling the bank to draw out of his account a sum of money and pay it to a designated person or business firm. Table 7-1

TABLE 7-1

Composition of the Money Supply *
(Billions of Dollars)

CURRENCY			
COINS	BILLS	DEMAND DEPOSITS	TOTAL
6,812	52,983	166,900	226,695

* As of February 28, 1972.
Source: *Federal Reserve Bulletin.*

shows a breakdown of the money supply in early 1972 into its three major parts, coins, bills, and demand deposits. The latter makes up the overwhelming proportion of the total money supply in active circulation in the economy. Table 7-2 shows the growth

TABLE 7-2

Growth of the Money Supply: Selected Years, 1900–1970
(Billions of Dollars)

YEAR	TOTAL	DEMAND DEPOSITS	CURRENCY	DEMAND DEPOSITS AS PERCENT OF TOTAL
1900	5.7	4.4	1.3	77.2
1905	8.7	7.1	1.6	81.6
1910	10.0	8.3	1.7	83.0
1915	11.4	9.8	1.6	85.9
1920	23.7	19.6	4.1	82.7
1925	24.9	21.4	3.5	85.9
1930	25.1	21.7	3.4	86.5
1935	25.2	20.4	4.8	80.9
1940	38.7	32.0	6.7	82.7
1945	94.2	69.1	25.1	73.4
1950	110.2	85.0	25.2	77.1
1955 *	130.6	103.3	27.3	79.1
1960	141.7	112.8	28.9	79.6
1965	168.0	131.7	36.3	78.3
1970 **	214.6	165.7	48.9	77.2

* 1900–1955 as of June 30.
** 1960–1970 as of December 31.
Source: *Historical Statistics of the United States* and *Statistical Abstract of the United States,* 1971.

of the money supply in the United States since 1900, including data on the proportion of the total money supply represented by demand deposits. This table provides statistical evidence that throughout the current century the overwhelming proportion of monetary transactions in the United States has been carried out with demand deposit money. Since 1900, demand deposit money has averaged 80.7 percent of money in circulation.

Near Moneys

Besides currency and demand deposits, the modern economy has an extraordinary variety of financial instruments with some of the attributes of money; economists call these "near moneys." The more important of these are savings deposits, shares in savings and loan associations, U.S. Government Treasury Bills, which are 90-day loans to the government, and the cash value of personally-held life insurance policies. In 1970 the combined value of these "near moneys" totaled about $719 billion, a figure several times greater than the size of the money supply.

Near moneys represent readily accessible purchasing power. But they are not money in the more formal sense; they do not serve as a medium of exchange, a standard of value, or a standard of deferred payments. Near moneys can, however, serve as a store of value. They do this even better than money itself, because normally they bring their owners a rate of return in the form of interest. Economists have also discovered that near moneys may grow in ways that are to some extent beyond control of the monetary authorities; thus, their impact on the economic system is of real significance. More on this point later.

Monetization of Debt

To arrive at a full understanding of the role of money in the economic system, we must be aware of the intimate relationship between money and debt. This relationship manifests itself in two ways. First, most of the money supply is made up of demand deposits; debt is the counterpart of this portion of the money supply. A demand deposit is an obligation (or debt) of the bank in which the demand deposit exists. Your bank owes you whatever balance remains in your checking account. Second, the great majority of demand deposits come into existence because individuals and business firms borrow from the banks, creating deposits. The process by which additional deposits are created through borrowing is at the heart of the modern system of expansion and contraction of the money supply. Economists call the creation of demand deposits through borrowing "the monetization of debt," which means that debt is the basis for a significant portion of the money supply in the modern world. The importance of this statement will be more apparent when we examine in detail the process by which demand deposits are created.

Determination of the Money Supply

How is the money supply determined? The answer is twofold, primarily because, as we have seen, the money supply itself consists of two major components—currency and demand deposits. To understand what determines the size of demand deposits we must look closely at the banking system, the primary instrument through which money is created, expanded, and contracted.

Banking in the United States has gone through a long period of development. Although in its essentials it resembles the banking structure of most other advanced countries, the American system has certain unique characteristics. One is that the United States has an extremely large number of independent banks, with branches usually limited to a single community, state, or region. In most other countries banking tends to be concentrated in far fewer banks with branches throughout the nation. But many American states have legal restrictions to inhibit or prevent the growth of branch banking.

Three types of banks need to be distinguished in order to understand the role of the banking system in the creation, expansion, or contraction of the money supply. These are commercial banks, savings banks, and the central bank.

Commercial Banks

The term *commercial bank* is used by economists and financial specialists for banks that accept demand deposits. Commercial banks are distinguished from savings banks, investment banks, and other specialized kinds of banks by virtue of this fact; only the commercial bank accepts a demand deposit. A demand deposit is not only a debt, as already pointed out, but it is a deposit payable on demand. As a practical matter, most modern commercial banks pride themselves on being "full-service" banks; they also accept savings deposits and offer a wide range of other financial services, such as estate and trust management.

Savings Banks

A *savings bank* is distinguished from a commercial bank in that it accepts only savings accounts; these are deposit accounts which cannot be transferred by check. The form of the pure savings bank most widespread in the United States is the savings and loan association or the mutual savings bank. These institutions largely get their resources from the savings of lower and middle income families and are often the source of loans for home construction. A savings bank, or the savings department of a commercial bank, plays an intermediary role; it merely channels funds from lenders (or savers) to borrowers. The commercial bank, on the other hand, has a vital role in creation of the money supply and determination of its size.

The Central Bank

A *central bank* is a bank for banks; its deposits are owned by other banks in the system. Commercial banks are required to keep a certain percentage of their funds in reserve. The central bank has the authority to determine the size of these required reserves, which consist of cash in its vaults or deposits with the central bank, that a commercial bank must have on hand to meet its customers' demands for payment in cash—i.e., currency. Required reserves are the key to the size of the money supply in the modern economy. In early 1972 the required reserve ratio was 17 percent for major banks.

The central bank in a modern nation also serves as a deposit bank for the government of the country, and provides the mechanism through which checks drawn on one bank and presented for deposit in another bank are cleared. The Federal Reserve System is the central bank of the American economy. Because the United States is such a large nation, the Federal Reserve System is divided into twelve regions, in each one of which there is a Federal Reserve Bank. Figure 7-1 shows the location of the banks within the Federal Reserve System. The basic structure of this system, which is essentially an agency of the national government, will be explained shortly.

*The Federal
Reserve System*

The Quantity of Demand Deposits

Demand deposits determine the size of the money supply, not only because they amount, on the average, to over 80 percent of the total money supply, but also because they have important, indirect influences on the currency that is actually in circulation. The volume of outstanding demand deposits at any particular time is determined within broad limits by the actions the commercial banks take on the basis of their deposit reserves. This is the first crucial principle to grasp to understand how the monetary system operates.

As previously pointed out, a demand deposit is a liability of the bank, subject to payment on demand. Thus prudent management requires that a bank keep at least some cash—or currency—on re-

155

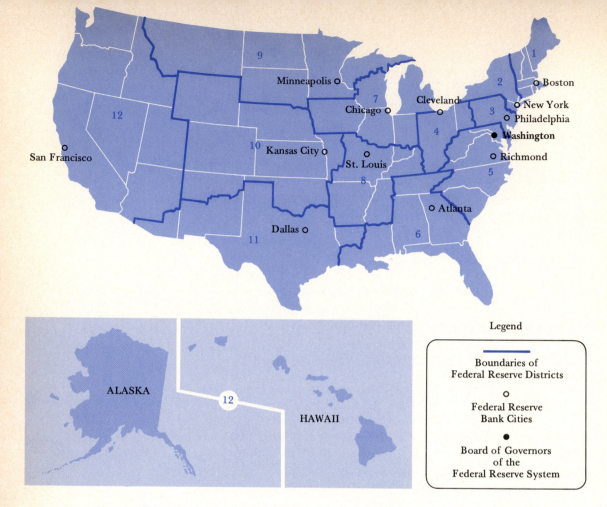

FIGURE 7-1
The Federal Reserve System.

Because of the geographic immensity of the United States, the Federal Reserve System—America's central bank—is divided into 12 Federal Reserve Districts with a Federal Reserve Bank in one of the major cities in the district and branches in other important cities. (Source: Board of Governors, The Federal Reserve System.)

Fractional reserves serve to meet the demands presented by its customers. Experience teaches, though, that on any given day the amount of cash or currency demanded by customers is unlikely to equal the bank's total deposits, even though legally a bank is liable for payment on demand of this total to its customers. Thus it is not necessary to maintain at all times a 100 percent reserve of currency. The bank knows that it can operate safely most of the time with fractional reserves, with only a percentage in cash in the vault or available quickly through deposits with the central bank as a reserve against withdrawal demands by its customers. This fact introduces the second basic principle which explains how the monetary system works: the principle of fractional reserves.

156

The Fractional Reserve Principle

In practice, this principle means that most of the time banks will find themselves with excess reserves, which become the basis for expanding deposits by making loans to new customers. This brings us to the heart of commercial banking as a business; a commercial bank supplies credit to the economy, hoping to make a profit in the process. The size of its excess reserves determines how many loans it may undertake. Other things being equal, the more loans, the more profitable the banking operation. To clarify this process, we shall now examine the mechanics of credit expansion, first by looking at the individual bank, and then, the banking system as a whole.

The Mechanics of Bank Credit Expansion

To understand how the individual bank may expand its demand deposits by making loans based upon its excess reserves, we must first understand a few essentials about the balance sheet of the commercial bank. Its balance sheet, like the balance sheet of any other private business, shows, on one side, the liabilities and net worth of the bank, and, on the other, its assets. For our purposes the most important liability is the deposit liability and the most important assets are cash on hand (or deposits in the central bank) and loans to the bank's customers. The latter are an asset because they involve a promise to pay the bank a stipulated sum at some future date.

The balance sheet of a commercial bank

Table 7-3 shows a simplified balance statement for a hypothetical bank, the Citizens Bank, just after an individual has made a deposit of $1000. The origin of this particular deposit will be dealt with later; for our simplified example let us assume that the depositor is a contractor who has just been paid for materials supplied to the federal government. He is paid by a check drawn by the United States Treasury on the federal government's account in one of the Federal Reserve Banks in the country. Note the sta-

TABLE 7-3
Balance Sheet of the Citizens Bank
Following a New Deposit

ASSETS		LIABILITIES	
1. Cash or Deposits in the Federal Reserve System	$1,000	1. Demand Deposit	$1,000
Total	$1,000	Total	$1,000

157

tus of the balance sheet. Immediately after this transaction, we abstract from the situation all the other assets and liabilities of the bank. On the liability side, the bank records an increase in deposits of $1000, the reason being that the new deposit is a debt of the bank. Under assets it records as cash (or deposits in the Federal Reserve Bank of its district) an amount of $1000. The balance sheet remains in balance because the increase in its liabilities of $1000 is matched by an equal increase in its assets.

Using Excess Reserves

Excess reserves

The principle of fractional reserves has taught the management of Citizens Bank that, on the average, it need keep only 20 percent of its deposit liabilities available to cope with cash withdrawals by its customers. Thus, the deposit reserve the bank must have available at all times for the safety of its operations is no more than $200. What shall the bank do with the remaining $800 in cash on hand? These are excess reserves for the bank, and because the bank is in business to make a profit by lending money, the management sees no reason why they should lie idle in its vaults or be unused as deposits with the central bank. Leaving aside the question of the price (or rate of interest) it will charge for a loan, we see that the bank management has a strong incentive to put its excess reserves to work by lending them to one or more new customers of the bank.

The act of lending transforms the balance sheet of Citizens Bank as shown in Table 7-4. Earlier we explained that "monetiza-

TABLE 7-4
Balance Sheet of the Citizens Bank
Following a New Loan

ASSETS		LIABILITIES	
1. Cash or Deposits in the Federal Reserve System	$1,000	1. Original Deposit	$1,000
2. Promissory Note	800	2. New Deposit Created by Loan	800
Total	$1,800	Total	$1,800

tion of debt" is involved whenever additional money is put into circulation in the economic system by the commercial banks. Suppose an individual negotiates a loan from Citizens Bank for $800, the exact amount of the bank's excess reserves. After the loan is complete, the bank creates for this customer a new deposit in the amount of $800, accepting in exchange his promise to pay for this amount. The following transformation takes place on the balance sheet of the Citizens Bank. Its liabilities increase by $800 through establishment of the new deposit, and its assets increase by an equal amount because the new customer gives the bank his I.O.U. for $800. After this entire transaction is completed, the balance sheet shows a total of $1800 in liabilities, matched by a total of $1800 in assets. Obviously there has been an increase in the money supply because the demand deposits in the economy of which the Citizens Bank is a part have now been increased by $800. If this bank were the only bank in the society and this were the only transaction, then the money supply for the entire economy would have increased by $800.

Money Creation

This process of monetary expansion is subject to much confusion, by the banking community and public alike. If you informed a commercial banker that he creates money, you would receive an indignant denial. The banker would no doubt point out that he has done no more than lend money available in the vaults of his bank. This is true enough. But it cannot be denied that the money supply has increased; in our example the total money in circulation is $1800 after this transaction, against $1000 before. Money creation takes place when the management of Citizens Bank monetizes the debt of its new customer, advancing him funds (or purchasing power) by creating a new demand deposit in exchange for his promise to pay.

Though paradoxical, there is nothing illogical or inconsistent in the contention of the bank manager, on the one hand, that he has only loaned a customer funds he already possesses and, on the other, the argument of the economist that by doing this he has, in effect, created more money. The positions can be reconciled once we understand the different vantage points from which the same transaction is being viewed.

The individual bank in this example did not expand its deposits by more than its excess reserves. It would not dare do so because of the possibility of adverse clearing balances, a real danger as long as the individual bank is part of a larger system in which there are many commercial banks. An adverse clearing balance results when a customer of the Citizens Bank draws a check on his balance, presenting it to someone who, in turn, deposits it in another bank. Sooner or later the second bank will present the check for payment to Citizens Bank, and to make payment the bank must have sufficient cash on hand (or deposits in the central bank) to honor the check when it is presented. If the management has expanded its loans beyond its excess reserves, it will be in trouble because it will not have the necessary cash or deposits in the central bank to meet the demands for payment.

Multiple Deposit Expansion

When we look at the banking system as a whole instead of the operations of a single bank within the system, an entirely different situation presents itself. An individual bank is always limited in the expansion of its demand deposits by the amount of its excess reserves, but the banking system as a whole can expand deposits by a multiple of the excess reserves existing within the system. This point is crucial; it is the source of much confusion, and accounts, furthermore, for the banker's insistence that he does not create additional money. For the individual bank, ability to expand deposits depends upon deposits being made which provide it with reserves that are not immediately needed, whereas for the banking system as a whole the opposite is the case: deposits are expanded because excess reserves are present. This statement has to be qualified to account for the actions of the central bank. By lowering its reserve requirements, the central bank can increase the excess reserves of a commercial bank, thereby enabling the bank to expand its deposits. But aside from this, and for any single bank within the system, a new deposit provides the bank with additional lending power as long as the bank operates on the principle of fractional reserves. For the individual bank, a new deposit is any deposit that comes to the bank from an outside source, as contrasted to deposits created by the bank itself through the process of lending its excess reserves to its customers. Thus a check on another bank received by a customer of Citizens Bank and deposited by this customer in the Citizens Bank will be a new deposit for the Citizens Bank.

To examine how the banking system as a whole engages in a multiple expansion of demand deposits on the basis of excess reserves, let us use another simplified numerical example. Table 7-5 traces out the process of recurring series of deposits and loan expansions which bring about a multiple expansion of the money supply, assuming that a 20 percent reserve is required throughout the banking system. Let us start with a new deposit in Citizens Bank, created by a customer depositing a $1000 check received from the United States government. Where does this money come from in the first instance? Several answers are possible, but let us assume that the customer has exported some merchandise from the United States, in payment for which gold has been received. Because individual citizens are not legally permitted to own gold, the exporter sells the gold to the Treasury of the United States, for which he receives a check in the amount of $1000. He deposits this check in Citizens Bank. The bank is now in the position described earlier in Table 7-3; it has a new deposit liability in the amount of $1000 and, as soon as the check clears through the Federal Reserve System, new cash reserves equal to $1000. With a 20 percent reserve requirement its excess reserves will be $800. The bank does not want these excess reserves to lie idle, because it earns no income from reserves in the form of cash in its vaults or held as deposits with the central bank. Citizens Bank loans $800 to Mr. Smith, who promptly uses the money as a down payment on a new car, purchased from Brown Motor Co. Smith pays with a check. The Brown firm deposits this check in its bank (the First National Bank); this is a new deposit in the amount of $800 as far as the First National Bank is concerned.

The First National Bank now finds itself with excess reserves in the amount of $640, or 80 percent of its newly acquired deposit.

TABLE 7-5
Multiple Expansion of Bank Deposits

NAME OF BANK	NEW DEPOSITS	TOTAL RESERVES	REQUIRED RESERVES	EXCESS RESERVES	NEW LOANS
Citizens Bank	$1,000	$1,000	$200	$800	$800
					↓ Loan ↓
	←Deposit ← Brown Motor Co. ← ── Purchase of Car ← ──Smith				Mr.
First National Bank	$800	$800	$160	$640	$640
					↓ Loan ↓
	←Deposit← Appliance Store ← ── Purchase ← ── Thompson				Mr.
City National Bank	$640	$640	$128	$512	$510
	Deposits	Process Continues Throughout the Banking System		Purchases	
Final Position of the Banking System	$5,000	$5,000	$1,000	$4,000	$4,000

TABLE 7-6
Successive Position of Individual Banks in Multiple Expansion of Deposits

NEW DEPOSIT	CITIZENS BANK				FIRST NATIONAL BANK	
	Assets		Liabilities		Assets	
	a. Cash	$1,000	a. New Deposit	$1,000	a. Cash	$800
	Total	$1,000	Total	$1,000	Total	$800

NEW LOAN		Assets		Liabilities		Assets	
	a. Cash	$1,000	a. Original Deposit	$1,000	a. Cash	$800
	b. Note	800	b. Loan Deposit	800	b. Note	640
	Total	$1,800	Total	$1,800	Total	$1,440

FINAL POSITION		Assets		Liabilities		Assets	
	a. Cash	$200	a. Deposits	$1,000	a. Cash	$160
	b. Note	800			b. Note	640
	Total	$1,000	Total	$1,000	Total	$800

The 20 percent reserve requirement means that it must keep available only $160 to meet adverse clearing balances. The management of the First National Bank behaves in rational economic fashion by promptly lending its excess reserves to Mr. Thompson, who spends the proceeds of his newly acquired loan of $640 for furniture and a refrigerator. The store where this sale took place deposits the check Mr. Thompson drew on the First National Bank in its bank, the City National Bank, and the process repeats itself. The City National Bank has acquired a new deposit for $640, against which it must keep a 20 percent reserve requirement of $128; thus it has excess reserves of $512 which it will wish to lend as soon as possible. Table 7-6 shows the successive balance sheet positions of these three banks as a consequence of these transactions.

The process will, in principle, repeat itself until the size of the loans made and the new deposits created from excess reserves dwindles to an insignificant amount. We find, though, that if subsequently we add up all of the transactions which have taken place, the total expansion of deposits in the system equals $4000, given the original new deposit of $1000 which the Citizens Bank received. Required reserves available in the banking system as a whole total $1000, which is 20 percent of the deposit total of $5000 now in existence, and, finally, the banking system develops during this series of transactions excess reserves equal to $4000, all of which were loaned to the customers of the individual banks. The end result of this sequence of transactions places the banking system in a position similar to the individual bank in that the sys-

Liabilities		Assets		Liabilities	
a. New Deposit	$800	a. Cash	$640	a. New Deposit	$640
Total	$800	Total	$640	Total	$640

Liabilities		Assets		Liabilities	
a. Original Deposit	$800	a. Cash	$640	a. New Deposit	$640
b. Loan Deposit	640	b. Note	512	b. Loan Deposit	512
Total	$1,440	Total	$1,152	Total	$1,152

Liabilities		Assets		Liabilities	
a. Deposits	$800	a. Cash	$128	a. Deposits	$640
		b. Note	512		
Total	$800	Total	$612	Total	$640

tem as a whole has made loans equal to the excess reserves generated in the system through the series of transactions. Deposits expanded fivefold over the initiating new deposit which made it possible for the Citizens Bank to expand its own loan to its customers.

The sequence of events traced out in Table 7-5 provides a simple but accurate numerical example of the process of credit expansion as it works for the banking system as a whole. The principle of fractional reserves governs this process, and because the banking system as a whole operates on this fundamental principle, there has been a multiple expansion of money in circulation in the form of demand deposits. In this example we assumed a reserve requirement of 20 percent, which permits an expansion five times greater than the initial deposit. A full explanation of the maximum expansion possible in a modern banking system must await our analysis of how the central bank operates within the system.

Let us summarize what we have analyzed to this point. We started with the statement that the quantity of money in the economy is determined primarily by the volume of demand deposits. The extent of demand deposits is governed by the magnitude of excess reserves within the banking system as a whole. Since individual banks operate on the principle of fractional reserves, the total volume of demand deposits can expand to some multiple of the amount of excess reserves available at a given time. Excess reserves become the strategic key to expansion of demand deposits, both with respect to the individual banks within the system and

Expansion of demand deposits summarized

163

to the system as a whole. Do not forget, however, that the individual bank is limited in its expansion capabilities to the absolute amount of its excess reserves, although the system as a whole (all banks together) can expand its deposits to some multiple of this amount. Since reserves are also the key to control of the money supply in the modern economy, it is appropriate that we now turn the discussion to analysis of the part played by the central bank in contemporary monetary systems.

The Federal Reserve System

We have stressed the importance of the central bank in the operation of the monetary system. In the United States, the central bank is the Federal Reserve System, established in 1914 primarily as a consequence of periodic failures in the nation's monetary system, which gave rise to economic collapse. Before this, the monetary supply was relatively inelastic; it was not capable of adjusting to the changing circumstances of economic life in the society.

The role of the central bank

A central bank, as pointed out, is a bank for banks. Its most distinguishing feature is its ability to create or contract reserves for the commercial banks in the system. It also serves as an agency for the clearing and collection of checks, as well as being the major source of currency in circulation. In the United States, for example, practically all of the paper currency now in circulation consists of Federal Reserve Notes, which are a non-interest-bearing debt of the Federal Reserve Banks. But these functions, important as they may be, are subsidiary to its basic task, which is to control the money supply by influencing the size of reserves held by the commercial banks.

The Federal Reserve System and Government

The Federal Reserve System in the United States is a quasi-governmental body; the Federal Reserve Banks in each of the twelve individual districts in the United States are owned by member banks in that district, which are private business firms. However, the federal government exercises control over the activities of the central bank because the President of the United States appoints the Chairman and members of the Board of Governors of the Federal Reserve System; this group makes the crucial decisions that determine the size of the reserves of the commercial banking system, which, in turn, directly influence the size of the money supply. Including the Chairman, there are seven members of the Board of Governors; each serves for fourteen years, one term expiring every two years. The idea is to make the Board indepen-

The Board of Governors

dent of political pressure. Arthur Burns, an economist formerly of Columbia University, is the current chairman.

It is important to note that this is a hybrid system. Technically the Constitution of the United States gives the Congress the power to "coin money and regulate the value thereof," suggesting that the authority and responsibility for the monetary system and its management, including the creation of money, ought to rest with the Congress. As a matter of fact, critical decisions about the expansion or contraction of the money supply are made by private firms which operate on the profit-maximizing principle within the confines of a market system. The ultimate ability of the commercial banks to influence the size of the money supply is constrained on the one hand by the central bank's control of the level of reserves, and on the other by the public's willingness or unwillingness to borrow. The system works, but it is a curious one, nevertheless; the Congress has delegated the important policy function of supplying the economy with a necessary medium of exchange to a private, profit-seeking entity. This situation was not the result of any conscious plan by the architects of a monetary system; it evolved from long historical development and experimentation with different arrangements.

Essentially the central bank has three major instruments through which it may influence the size of bank reserves: open market operations, changes in the discount rate, and changes in legal reserve requirements. Let us examine each of these in turn.

Open Market Operations

Open market operations are the most important instrument available to the Federal Reserve for controlling the reserves of the commercial banks. The Federal Reserve Banks may enter the open market to buy and sell securities, either from persons and business firms or from the commercial banks themselves. In practice, the Federal Reserve System confines itself primarily to the buying and selling of government securities, such as bonds and short-term notes called bills, although it occasionally engages in transactions in nongovernmental securities. It is prohibited by law from buying government securities directly from the Treasury, primarily because this would allow the Treasury to finance its operations by the relatively easy route of borrowing directly from a semi-governmental body.

Purchase and sale of securities

The Federal Reserve as Buyer

When the central bank decides to enter the open market to buy government bonds from the banks or the public, the effect is to pump money in the form of reserves into the commercial banking

*Money, Banking,
and the Economic
System*

*Increasing reserves
in the banking
system*

system. These reserves then become the basis for the expansion of demand deposits. How does this work? When the Federal Reserve buys a bond from a commercial bank it will pay for the bond with a check drawn on itself, and when the commercial bank deposits this check with the Federal Reserve Bank in the district in which it is located, its reserves on deposit with the Federal Reserve Bank are increased by the amount of the check. The Federal Reserve Bank which buys the bond from the commercial bank has its deposit liabilities increased by the amount of this purchase, but its assets are increased by the amount of the newly acquired security. For the banking system as a whole there is a net increase in reserves, because the check by which payment is made for the security is not drawn on any other bank in the system, but on one of the Federal Reserve Banks.

There is another important effect to be noted in conjunction with the purchase of securities through the open market operations of the Federal Reserve System. When a Federal Reserve Bank enters the open market to buy securities, its action will bid up prices. Securities, including government bonds, are bought and sold in markets like any commodity, and when demand increases the price inevitably rises. An increase in the market price of an outstanding bond is the same thing as a decline in the rate of interest for that particular bond. This is because the annual return in an absolute amount for a bond is fixed at the time it is originally issued. Hence, if it is sold at a higher price prior to its maturity, the rate of return will have declined. For example, a $1000 bond might originally have been issued at a rate of 5 percent, which would yield an annual income of $50 to the holder. If it is sold in the open market for $1100, it will still yield the new holder an annual income of $50, but his rate of return on his investment of $1100 will be only 4.54 percent. Thus, the secondary effect of open market purchases by the Federal Reserve System is to reduce interest rates. To summarize, open market buying has a twofold impact on the potential increase in the money supply. First, there is the increase in reserves within the commercial banking system, which may induce banks to expand their loans, and, second, the reduction in the rate of interest, which may make it more attractive for potential borrowers to acquire new loans.

The Federal Reserve as Seller

The Federal Reserve may also enter the open market as a seller. When the commercial banks purchase securities from the central bank they have to pay for them by drawing down their reserve deposits with the Federal Reserve Bank of their district. When they lose reserves, their lending capability declines, leading them to slow down the rate at which they increase demand deposits, or, possibly, to reduce their outstanding volume of demand deposits by not replacing loans which mature with new loans.

Selling of securities by the Federal Reserve tends to lower the market price of the securities, which may also cause interest rates to rise. This development may, in turn, affect the willingness of the public to borrow. When the Federal Reserve Banks sell securities, their liabilities in the form of deposits by the commercial banks are reduced, as well as their assets in the amount of the securities sold. The effect will be the same if securities are sold to the public rather than directly to the commercial banks. The public pays for these securities by drawing checks on their accounts in commercial banks, and when these checks are presented for payment by Federal Reserve Banks, the commercial banks will find that their reserve balances are reduced accordingly. The balance sheet of a commercial bank will show a net reduction in its liabilities, because deposit accounts are extinguished by this action, and a net reduction in its reserves, including any excess reserves. The impact on the money supply of a sale of securities by the Federal Reserve directly to the public is greater than the impact when the securities are sold directly to the commercial banks. The reason is that a sale to the public reduces demand deposits (the money supply) immediately, whereas a sale to the commercial banks only reduces their lending power, not necessarily their outstanding deposit liabilities.

The Discount Rate

The Federal Reserve also influences the reserves of the commercial banks by changes in the discount rate. Commercial banks which are members of the Federal Reserve System have the privilege of borrowing from the Federal Reserve Bank in their district when they want to increase their reserves. For this, as is normally true for any bank customer, they pay interest, usually called the discount rate. By a change in the rate charged the commercial banks, the Federal Reserve may influence the willingness of commercial banks to add to or to reduce their reserve balances. The initiative for a change in the discount rate is taken by the Federal Reserve, but a change will not in itself affect the reserves of the commercial banks, because they must decide whether to react to the change and increase or reduce their borrowing because of the change. An increase in the discount rate not only makes it more costly for the commercial banks to obtain additional reserves, but may also lead them to raise the rates they charge their customers, thereby reducing public borrowing from the commercial banks. A reduction in the discount rate tends to have the opposite effect.

167

Legal Reserve Requirements

The third important power of the Federal Reserve System is to change the legal reserve requirement appropriate to the different types of banks that are members of the system. The Congress delegated to the Federal Reserve the power to determine within broad limits legal reserve requirements for member banks. The reserve requirements may be varied within these limits by the Board of Governors. Currently, the reserve requirements for demand deposits vary between 10 and 22 percent for "city banks" and 7 and 14 percent for "country banks." City banks are those located in New York, Chicago, and 60 other designated large cities; country banks are those located elsewhere. The size of the city or town where a bank is located is one determinant of the amount of business it carries on and hence of its reserve needs. These requirements pertain to demand deposits; for savings deposits the requirements are lower. An increase in the reserve requirements reduces the amount of excess reserves at the disposal of the commercial banks, and consequently curtails their lending power. A reduction in reserve requirements has the opposite effect.

Direct Controls

The three controls we have discussed so far work indirectly to influence the money supply. The Federal Reserve has other powers which have a direct impact on the money supply. These are called selective or direct controls, because they influence the use to which banking credit may be put more than its total amount. The most important of these include control over the use of credit to purchase securities on the stock market, control over maximum interest rates that may be paid on certain classes of deposits, direct pressure on the banking community, and selective controls over consumer credit, particularly during wartime.

Sometimes securities are purchased "on the margin," which means that a customer will make a down payment on a security and then use the security as a collateral for borrowing money to cover the remainder of the purchase price. The Federal Reserve can control this use of credit by stipulating the amount of a cash down payment that the potential buyer for a security must make. During the 1920s, extreme speculation on the stock market security market was financed by extensive borrowing on the margin; once prices began to fall, the entire structure of credit erected on margin borrowing collapsed rapidly. In recent years margin requirements have averaged 70 percent and above; this means that the customer must pay at least 70 percent of the price of a security.

Direct controls on interest rates that may be paid for different types of deposits influence the composition of deposits and the movement of funds from one type of activity to another. Direct pressure, or "moral suasion," as it is sometimes called, involves closer scrutiny by the Federal Reserve of the kinds of loans that member banks are making, as well as attempts to persuade the banks to be more circumspect in their lending policies.

Selective credit controls over consumer purchasing, used during World War II and the Korean War, regulate the required down payment for purchase of a consumer durable and the length of time allowed the customer to pay off the loan. The purpose of these selective controls was to reduce the level of consumer spending for durable goods. The Federal Reserve has not had the power to impose selective controls of this type since 1952.

The Impact of Money on the Economy

Ultimately, the purpose of control over the money supply is to influence economic activity. How are these two related?

Historically, different answers have been given to this question. An influential theory, now generally called the "classical view," prevailed before the 1930s, especially before the ideas of John Maynard Keynes had an impact upon contemporary economic thought. But the "Keynesian view" has held sway since, though it has been somewhat modified in recent years and continues to undergo refinement. This view of the impact of money on the behavior of the economic system emerged from Keynes' theories about the determinants of the employment level. Third and most recent, there is the "modern monetarist view," thus described because there are points of similarity with the earlier classical view, but the framework into which the analysis of money is fitted is essentially Keynesian. The modern monetarist analysis has been largely the work of Professor Milton Friedman at the University of Chicago. His views have had a strong impact upon the economic policies of the Nixon administration, as we shall see in Chapter 9. Before undertaking a brief exposition of the essential elements in each of these viewpoints, it is important to stress that no single view is universally accepted by economists. A modern synthesis would undoubtedly involve elements of each; there are valid ideas in each particular approach.

Three viewpoints

The Classical View

The pre-Keynesian classical view rested upon the assumption that the essential function of money for the overall performance of the economic system is the medium of exchange function. This classical view also rested on a second assumption: that the "normal" status of the economic system is one of full employment for all resources. This view is particularly appropriate for a policy position of *laissez-faire,* or a minimum intervention by government in the operations of the market economy. If full employment is presumed to be the normal economic situation and if the most important function of money is to serve as a medium of exchange, two conclusions follow logically. First, any change in the money supply results in a change in spending, because money is useful only if it can be used as a medium of exchange. Second, a change in spending cannot affect production and employment because the economy is fully employed; it can affect the general price level. In formal terms, this idea is described as the quantity theory of money.

The quantity
theory of money

The classical quantity theory states that there is a direct correlation between the money in circulation and the price level. Often the quantity theory of money is presented as a truistic statement called the equation of exchange, namely $MV = PT$. This equation is a truism because it means that money supply M times the velocity of circulation of each unit of money V must equal the general price level P times total transactions T. Velocity means the number of times a unit of money turns over during a stipulated period. Thus any increase in velocity would have the same effect as more units of money in circulation and a decrease would do the opposite. It becomes an explanatory or theoretical equation if we assume that velocity is a constant and the volume of transactions is relatively stable, because of the existence of the assumption of full employment. Under the circumstances, when velocity V and transactions T are dropped from the equation it is made to read that the price level is a direct function of the money supply, namely $P = f(M)$.

The Keynesian View

After 1936, when John Maynard Keynes' monumental treatise, *The General Theory of Employment, Interest, and Money* appeared, thinking about the role of money in the economic system changed significantly. Economists still recognize that money plays an important role in determining the level of economic activity, but the process by which money influences economic activity is more subtle than that embodied in the older quantity theory. One fundamental conclusion of Keynesian economics is that the money supply primarily affects interest rates, rather than the price level. Keynes directed attention to the "store of value" function of money, as well as the medium of exchange function. He postulated the existence of a demand for money independent of the desire to have a medium of exchange. People, Keynes observed, wanted to hold money as a convenient way to store economic value over time. This demand is related to the supply of money available for this purpose through the rate of interest.

Keynes saw interest as a price which would equate the demand for money to hold as a store of value and the supply of money available to meet this need. An increase in the demand for money to hold would raise interest rates and a decrease in this demand would have the opposite effect. He called this a "liquidity preference" theory of interest; because money is the most liquid of all assets, it can readily and quickly be converted into other forms without loss.

Liquidity preference

The liquidity preference theory represented a subtle shift away from the earlier preoccupation with the medium of exchange function of money. It has an important influence on the way in which we think about the economic system, because if money affects the interest rates rather than the price level, then its impact on the economic system is altogether different. Modern economic analysis regards the primary determinants of output and employment as spending for consumption, for investment, and by governments. Anything that will affect the overall level of economic activity, including the price level, must work through its impact on the spending streams whose total equals aggregate demand. The question, therefore, is how a change in the interest rates will affect the important spending streams.

The essential points in Keynesian thinking about the way a change in the interest rates affects spending can be summarized as follows. First, there is little reliable evidence to indicate that consumer spending is especially influenced by interest; on the contrary, the chief finding of empirical research is that income is the major determinant of spending by consumer units. Second, there is much uncertainty about investment spending, although in *The General Theory* Keynes argued that investment is influenced primarily by changes in interest rates. There is support by both economic theorists and the practitioners of monetary policy in the Federal Reserve for this view of investment spending, especially for long-lived projects such as buildings and private homes. The effect of interest rates on investment in equipment is less certain. Finally, opinion is divided as to the ultimate impact of interest rates on spending by public bodies in the United States. The contemporary view generally holds that spending at the federal level is not significantly affected by the interest rates, whereas state and local spending may be influenced by changes in them. Other conditions, such as the general level of the economic activity, which bear upon the ability of state and local governments to levy and collect taxes, are probably more influential than the rate of interest in determining spending by those public bodies.

The impact of interest rates on spending

*Money, Banking,
and the Economic
System*

*The effect of
changes in the
money supply*

The Monetarist View

The modern monetarist view takes a different position with respect to the impact of money on the economic system. It is like the earlier classical view because its proponents emphasize the supply of money, rather than the rate of interest, as in the Keynesian view. But it is "modern" because unlike the earlier classical view it does not postulate a direct correlation between the money supply and the price level. Rather, modern classical monetary theorists maintain that changes in the money supply offer a better guide to probable changes in the level of employment and output than do the variables entering into aggregate demand in the Keynesian system. They do not refute Keynes' analytical framework, which postulates aggregate demand as the key determinant of output, but assert that the spending variables which enter into aggregate demand are more directly related to changes in the money supply than any other aggregates that can be measured.

What is different about the modern monetarist approach is its insistence that the key relationship is between income and the amount of money that people want to hold at any one time for *all* purposes. If this relationship is disturbed, say, by an increase in the money supply, the result will be more spending as people seek to restore what they regard as the proper balance between money on hand and their incomes. On the other hand, a reduction in the money supply would lead to less spending; with a smaller stock of money this would be the only way to restore money holdings to the appropriate level. This presumed cause and effect relationship between the money supply and spending in all forms leads the monetarists to suggest that control of the money supply is the best single tool for influencing the overall level of economic activity. We shall have more to say on this matter in Chapter 9.

Thus we find three important views contending in answer to the fundamental question of how money affects economic activity. No single view offers a definitive answer to this question, but a modern theoretical synthesis, which has not yet appeared, will have to include elements from all three. In the meantime, policy makers have to continue to exercise the best judgment possible when they approach the difficult and complex task of attempting to determine when and under what circumstances the money supply should be changed.

Questions for Review and Discussion

1. Why is it that money cannot be given a precise definition, but must be defined in terms of its most important functions?
2. What are the most important functions that money performs in any economy?
3. Explain the difference between "government-issued" money, "bank-created" money, and "near moneys."
4. What is a commercial bank? How does it differ from a savings bank? From a central bank? Give examples of each.
5. Commercial banks operate on the principle of fractional reserves. What is the nature of this principle and what is its significance for the money supply?
6. If an individual commercial bank has excess reserves in a given amount, why can it lend out only the amount of these reserves, while the banking system as a whole can lend a multiple of the system's volume of excess reserves?
7. Give examples of the kind of deposits that would be considered "new deposits" by an individual commercial bank. Why do such deposits give the individual bank a basis for credit expansion?
8. What is the most important function a central bank performs in the operation of a nation's monetary system?
9. What are the three major means through which the Federal Reserve System in the United States exercises control over the quantity of reserves available to commercial banks?
10. What will happen to commercial bank reserves, the price of outstanding government bonds, and interest rates if the Federal Reserve enters the open market and buys securities?
11. Explain how changes in reserve requirements and the discount rate can affect the money supply.
12. Contrast briefly the classical, the Keynesian, and the modern monetarist position on the impact of the money supply upon economic activity, including employment and output.

8

Principles of Economic Growth

Changing attitudes toward growth

THE ECONOMIST'S CONCERN with understanding and explaining the process of economic growth is almost as old as the discipline of economics itself, although roughly from the mid-nineteenth century until after World War II the subject of economic growth was overshadowed by preoccupation with the allocation of resources and income distribution. After World War II, in part because of an increasing awareness of the acute economic problems faced by the underdeveloped areas of the world, there was a sharp revival of interest in the subject of economic growth. By the 1950s, growth had become a matter of popular concern and discussion in the United States, for the economy apparently was performing far below its potential, and there was considerable fear that it might be overtaken by the fast-growing Soviet economy. This fear intensified when the Russians first put a man-made satellite into orbit around the earth. Since the 1950s the "growth race" between the United States and the USSR has faded into the background, although interest in matters relating to economic growth continues. But today it is the adverse effects and costs of economic growth that demand more and more of the public's attention.

In this chapter we shall concentrate on the forces that determine the growth of the national output over long periods of time, especially for the economies of advanced countries, such as the United States and the nations of Western Europe. In Chapter 18 we will resume discussion of this subject, although our attention there will be directed to the problems confronting economically underdeveloped nations.

The Meaning and Measurement of Economic Growth

There is no single definition of economic growth that is satisfactory in all respects and no single measure of economic growth. Economic growth obviously involves expansion in the output of useful goods and services during a specified period of time (normally the calendar year). But even this relatively simple definition is not wholly satisfactory; before there can be an increase in output there must be an increase in the economy's potential to produce output, or productive capacity. The point is worth stressing. In the less developed parts of the world the crucial growth problem is to increase the economy's potential for production. In the United States and other economically advanced countries the problem has sometimes been one of finding ways to utilize fully an expanding productive potential. In any event, it is important to stress that growth necessarily focuses on both *output* and the *potential for output*.

Expansion in output and in productive capacity

It is wise to recall that economic growth is a long-term phenomenon. When we discussed the principles of national income determination (Chapter 6), our interest was in a short-run situation in which the productive capacity of the economy was assumed as given. Under these circumstances, the essential problem was to identify the forces which determined the extent to which productive capacity was used. Now we must focus our analysis on change in productive capacity, as well as on changes in output that must come about if a growing productive capacity is to be continuously utilized.

Rate of Growth

Although economic growth generally means an expansion of output during a period of time, economists frequently use rate as a measure of growth, which means that the increase in output in one period is expressed as a percentage of output in a prior period. In 1971, for example, real GNP in the United States increased by a mere 2.7 percent over 1970. 1965 was a much better year, as output was 6.3 percent higher than in 1964. The rate context is a particularly useful way to make growth comparisons between countries with quite diverse economic and social structures. In order to measure the "rate" of economic growth, it is first necessary to measure output and changes in output. Normally this is done in terms of money value. But since we are concerned with real changes over the long run (this applies to potential as well as to actual output), measures of output in monetary terms must be adjusted for price level changes. Thus, any series used to calculate rates of growth for an economy over a long period of time must be reduced to real terms, which means that they must be stated in dollars of constant purchasing power. The technique for doing so was discussed in Chapter 5.

Per Capita Output

Most economists agree that *output per person* (or per capita) is the most satisfactory way to measure material or economic progress in a society. An improvement in material well-being—as distinct from less tangible satisfactions—obviously requires that, on the average, more goods and services be available for each person in the society. Hence, statistics on output are usually converted to a *per capita* basis, which is done by dividing total output (gross national product in real terms) by the population. Even this measure, though, is not entirely satisfactory. A significant portion of a country's total output may be diverted to war or other activities which do not directly increase the availability of goods and services (both private and collective) for use by the citizens of the country. This has been the case in both the United States and the Soviet Union in the post-World War II period. Much of the national output has been derived from military outlays which do not directly enhance the material well-being of citizens in either country. A more satisfactory measure of growth under these circumstances would be real consumption per capita. To get such a figure, consumption expenditures should be stated in real terms and divided by the population.

Structural Changes

Another way to examine growth is to analyze it in terms of its impact upon the structure of an economic system. Economists have long recognized that the process of economic growth involves basic changes in the economic structure of a society. In this context, the term "structure" refers to the distribution of the work force, the origin of the output, the changing nature of occupations, the distribution of population between urban and rural areas, and similar phenomena. A pioneer student of economic growth, Colin Clark, has pointed out that growth results in far-reaching changes in the structure of employment in an economy. In a less developed country, for example, the overwhelming proportion of the labor force is employed in agriculture (or primary production), mainly because the low level of productivity generally prevailing in such a society means that most of the work force has to devote its energies to providing the minimum of food necessary for physical survival. However, as economic development begins and productivity increases, particularly in the agricultural sector, labor resources are released for use elsewhere, which permits a shift of labor from primary to secondary (or manufacturing) production. As the development process continues, a society can develop more and more activities of a "tertiary" nature, such as wholesale and retail trade, professional activities, and a variety of other services. The process of growth thus involves a continuous shift of the labor force away from agriculture toward manufacturing and tertiary activity. In highly developed economies, such as the United States, a significant proportion of the labor force engages in these latter activities. Figure 8-1 shows the changing distribution of the American labor force since 1900.

As an economy expands, the origin of its national output changes too. Under the impetus of development less and less of the national product originates in the agricultural sector, whereas a growing proportion originates in the manufacturing and services sector. The structure of occupations also changes, as manual labor gives way to positions which require increasing amounts of training because they involve tasks of increasing complexity.

The Meaning and Measurement of Economic Growth

The impact of growth on employment

FIGURE 8-1
Distribution of the American Labor Force: 1900–1970.

There has been a striking decline in the proportion of the labor force engaged in agriculture and mining, coupled with an equally drastic increase in the proportion found in services (including government). The proportion in manufacturing has changed relatively little since 1900. (Source: *Statistical Abstract,* selected years.)

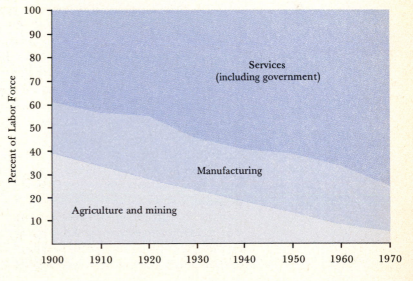

Development is also accompanied by significant geographical shifts in population, as cities grow and the rural areas become less significant. Urbanization—and ultimately "suburbanization"—is an important attribute of a growing society. These changes are not necessarily good or desirable, but they do appear characteristic of the growth experience of most societies.

The Growth of the American Economy

Recently the Department of Commerce of the United States Government published a comprehensive series of estimates on the long-term growth performance of the economies of the United States and other major countries. The United States figures and growth rates for some other leading industrial countries are shown in Table 8-1. For the period 1870–1964, which covered nearly a century, and which included the Great Depression, two world wars, as well as many lesser periods of economic fluctuations, the Department found that the growth rate of the *real* gross national product for the American economy averaged 3.6 percent a year, a figure higher than the rate for Germany, France, the United Kingdom, Italy, and Canada, all important industrial countries, but slightly lower than Japan's rate in the same period.

Long-term growth performance

If the period is broken into shorter segments, it is found that the growth rate of the United States was highest between 1870 and 1913, when it averaged 4.5 percent per year. This period coincides with the vast surge of industrialization which began in the American economy shortly after the Civil War, as well as with the era of greatest immigration into the country. The American rate of growth during this period was considerably higher than those reported for the countries already mentioned, including Japan.

Economic growth, 1870–1913

For 1913 through 1929 the rate of growth averaged only 2.8 percent per year; even though the 1920s are generally thought of as a period of sustained prosperity, the decade opened with a major recession which reduced the growth rate. There was a short, though sharp, recession in the American economy right after 1913, and again after 1920.

Economic growth, 1913–1929

From 1929 through 1965, the third segment of this long span, the growth rate rose. The average for this era was 3.1 percent per year, a significant figure because the period includes the ten depression years of the 1930s when there were catastrophic reductions in output. The main reason for the higher rate recorded in this third segment was a sharp acceleration of the rate of growth in the 1960s. Although this particular series ends in 1965, other data from the Department of Commerce show that for the 1960s

Economic growth, 1929–1965

TABLE 8-1
Growth Rates for the United States and Other
Major Nations: 1870–1964

PERIOD	UNITED STATES	JAPAN	GERMANY	UNITED KINGDOM	FRANCE	ITALY	CANADA
GROWTH RATES OF GROSS NATIONAL PRODUCT							
1870–1964	3.6	3.8	2.8	1.9	1.7	2.0	3.5
1870–1913	4.5	3.3	2.8	2.1	1.6	1.4	3.8
1913–29	2.8	3.9	0.4	0.8	1.7	1.8	2.4
1929–64	3.0	4.2	3.9	2.2	1.9	2.9	3.6
1929–65	3.1	—	—	—	—	—	—
1929–50	2.7	0.6	1.9	1.6	0.0	1.0	3.2
1950–64	3.6	9.9	7.0	3.0	4.8	5.8	4.3
1950–65	3.7	—	—	—	—	—	—
1950–60	3.2	9.4	7.8	2.7	4.6	5.8	4.0
1960–64	4.4	11.4	4.8	3.6	5.4	5.7	5.1
1960–65	4.7	—	—	—	—	—	—
GROWTH RATES OF OUTPUT PER EMPLOYEE							
1870–1964	—	—	1.7	1.1	1.7	1.6	1.7
1913–29	1.2	—	−0.1	0.4	2.0	1.5	0.7
1929–64	1.8	—	2.9	1.5	2.0	2.7	2.1
1929–65	1.8	—	—	—	—	—	—
1929–50	1.5	—	1.2	1.1	0.3	1.0	2.0
1950–64	2.3	7.8	5.4	2.2	4.6	5.2	2.2
1950–65	2.4	—	—	—	—	—	—
1950–60	2.0	6.9	5.9	2.0	4.6	4.7	2.1
1960–64	3.0	10.2	4.3	2.7	4.6	6.5	2.4
1960–65	3.1	—	—	—	—	—	—
GROWTH RATES OF PER CAPITA GROSS NATIONAL PRODUCT							
1870–1964	1.9	—	1.7	1.3	1.5	1.4	1.7
1870–1913	2.2	—	1.7	1.2	1.4	0.7	2.0
1913–29	1.3	—	0.0	0.3	1.8	1.2	0.7
1929–64	1.7	—	2.8	1.7	1.4	2.2	1.8
1929–65	1.8	—	—	—	—	—	—
1929–50	1.6	—	0.7	1.2	0.0	0.3	1.8
1950–64	1.8	8.7	5.9	2.4	3.8	5.2	1.8
1950–65	2.0	—	—	—	—	—	—
1950–60	1.4	8.1	6.9	2.3	3.7	5.2	1.3
1960–64	2.8	10.3	3.5	2.7	3.9	5.0	3.2
1960–65	3.2	—	—	—	—	—	—

Source: U.S. Department of Commerce.

179

(1960–1970) the rate of growth of real output in the American economy averaged 4 percent a year, significantly above the long-term average. As the decade ended, the growth rate dropped sharply (2.8 percent in 1969) and in 1970 it was actually negative (−0.4 percent) as real output declined by $4.7 billion. In 1971 there was a recovery, but the rate of expansion was below the rate experienced in prior post-World War II recessions. In the first quarter of 1972, though, real GNP grew at an annual rate of more than 5 percent.

Per Capita Growth

Real per capita gross national product reflects the same trends, although obviously the percentages are lower because per capita data take into account population growth. For the entire period 1870–1964, per capita real gross national product grew at an annual rate of 1.9 percent, a figure higher than the rate recorded for other major industrial countries. The period 1870–1913 also recorded the highest rate of growth for gross national product per capita, an average of 2.2 percent a year. There was a slowdown in the subsequent period, 1913–1929, when the annual average rate of growth of product per capita was only 1.3 percent. This slowdown coincided with a rapid reduction in immigration after 1921, following passage of immigration acts which effectively cut off the vast flow of Europeans into the United States. If the rate of population growth had not slowed down as a result of the reduction in immigration, the per capita rate probably would have been even lower since the 1913–1929 period also saw a reduction in the average rate of growth. For the period 1929–1965, the rate of growth of real output per capita increased, the average being 1.8 percent per year. This again reflects the sharp acceleration in the rate of growth of total output that began in the 1960s; from 1960 through 1970 real output per capita grew at an annual average rate of 2.9 percent. A declining rate of population growth helped boost the average rate for output per capita in this period. In the first half of the decade population grew at an annual average rate of 1.27 percent, but in the second half the annual rate of growth dropped to 1.08 percent.

Competition With Other Nations

The long-term data and more recent data show that, on the whole, the growth record of the American economy compares satisfactorily with other leading advanced countries. However, in the late 1950s the American economy was seriously lagging behind the growth rate of other leading nations, including the Soviet Union. Statistics for the 1950s indicate that real gross national product in the United States grew at an annual average rate of only 3.3 percent, below the rate recorded for France, West Germany, Italy, United Kingdom, Japan, and the USSR. The subnormal performance of the American economy in this particular period gave rise to fears that the American economy would soon be overtaken by the Soviet Union, a development which it was thought would put us at an immense disadvantage in the rapidly developing armaments and space race. The lagging growth rate was a factor that entered into the 1960 presidential campaign; John F. Kennedy's stress on moving America ahead undoubtedly contributed to his election.

The rapid acceleration in the growth rate in the 1960s eliminated any fear that future performance of the Soviet Union might exceed that of the United States. Further, a recent study by a Swedish economist indicates that the relatively high growth rates recorded in most European countries during the 1950s were a one-time phenomenon; they represented a catching-up because of the gap in development caused by the Great Depression and World War II. By the mid-1960s the European economies were back on the long-term trend line they would have followed if depression and war had not disrupted their economic life.

As the American economy boomed ahead during the late 1960s, partly as a consequence of the high rate of military spending resulting from the war in Vietnam, a new and different point of view on economic growth emerged. Instead of excessive concern with the inadequacies of the growth rate, as was characteristic of the 1950s, there were beginnings of what has been called an "anti-growth" school of thought. This new approach raises some fundamental issues concerning the real costs that are a consequence of rapid economic growth. It reflects aroused concern about the quality of our environment, a growing awareness that there are immense and often irreversible social costs tied to rapidly expanding industrial production. These social costs cover such diverse and adverse developments as the smog and pollution of the atmosphere resulting from the internal combusion engine and the "death" of a great body of water like Lake Erie because of the indiscriminate dumping of industrial wastes.

The anti-growth school

Growth and Public Policy

Although there is no specific legislative commitment to growth in the sense that the Employment Act established a national commitment to full employment, economic growth has become an object of American public policy. This was especially true during the 1950s, when the issue was an inadequate rate of growth. Eco-

181

nomic growth clearly belongs in the realm of public policy, but as yet there is no clear consensus on what the policy ought to be.

A number of issues are involved. First, there obviously may be a conflict between the goal of growth and other desirable goals. Rapid growth, in particular, conflicts with the desire for price level stability. This became painfully evident after 1965 when expansion induced by the Vietnam war brought inflationary pressures and increases in the general price level that did not abate even though expansion was halted in 1970. We have not yet discovered how to bring about rapid economic growth without overheating the economy and putting strong pressures on the price level. Another issue is the proper rate of growth. Is a 3 percent rate adequate? a 4.5 percent rate? If not, what is? It is probably more difficult to ascertain the "proper" rate of economic growth than it is to determine the appropriate level of unemployment. We can determine within rough limits how much unemployment is of a frictional nature, and thus know when we have reached full employment, but there is less agreement among economists, in either policy or theoretical terms, on the optimum rate of economic growth. An even more fundamental issue to which American society has not directed sufficient attention is the end to which growth is directed. This is the matter of our priorities.

Finally, there remains the problem of what the government can do to attain a given growth rate, assuming that agreement on the appropriate rate has been reached. For full employment, it is clear that the government can take the necessary steps to adjust the level of aggregate demand, which will bring the economy closer to the objective of full employment, even though the cost may be excessive inflation. When the objective is a given rate of growth, it is not entirely clear what, specifically, a government can do to achieve it.

The Sources of Economic Growth

As was pointed out earlier, economic growth presupposes an increase in the productive capacity of a society. Thus the problem of explaining the sources of economic growth reduces itself first to the question of identifying the key determinants of productive capacity. We shall attempt first to identify and discuss the immediate or strategic determinants. They are immediate because there exists a clear and direct relationship between these variables and the economy's productive capacity. Beyond them, however, is another set of determinants, more remote from the expansion of productive capacity, but nevertheless fundamental to the process of economic growth. We can lump them together under the heading of the social and economic (socioeconomic) structure of a society.

We are only beginning to understand how the socioeconomic structure affects the growth of productive capacity. This is a matter of even greater significance for the less developed nations of the world than for the advanced economies, which have over two centuries developed socioeconomic structures conducive to economic growth. Nevertheless, these second-level determinants have much to do with the success of the strategic determinants in increasing a nation's productive capacity.

Resources

The strategic determinants of productive capacity can be broadly characterized as resources and technology. Resources consist of the services of human beings and the services provided by land and capital goods. The basic economic distinction between land and capital is that capital is man-made and reproducible, whereas land (or natural resources) is not. As we saw in Chapter 2, a rise in production and the potential for output depends upon combining the services of economic resources in the most effective way possible. Thus, growth in a society's potential for production, as well as its actual production, clearly depends upon both the quantity and the quality of the resources available to that society.

A strategic determinant

It is important to think of resources as a stock of things of great variety which determine what goods and services a society can produce. Production requires that the stock of resources of all kinds be brought into play, but the upper limit of a society's ability to produce the goods and services necessary to satisfy its wants depends upon the size of that stock. This is true whether we think of resources as human beings, or as land and mineral wealth, or as capital goods or tools. Drawing all resources together as a stock phenomenon helps us understand the process by which a nation increases its productive capacity. Growth in productive capacity can occur only when there is an increase in the stock of resources that make production possible.

The stock of resources

Technology

Resources, though important to the process of economic growth, are not the whole story. The other major determinant of strategic significance is technology. In a narrow sense, technology refers primarily to the application of science and knowledge to the process of production. But the term also has broader connotations. Basically technology refers to the overall effectiveness with which resources are combined to obtain capacity and output. Resources alone do not constitute productive capacity. They must be com-

A second strategic determinant

bined, and the skill with which they are combined is a measure of the technological capabilities of the society.

As a concept it is easy enough to separate technology from resources; in actual practice it is difficult, if not often impossible. To a degree, a society's level of technological attainment is reflected in the quality of its resources, both the human resources of skill, knowledge, and education and man-made resources or capital goods. Technology is embodied in capital instruments. A striking example of this is the growth of the computer. Essentially, the computer is based upon knowledge about how data can be manipulated, but this knowledge is not meaningful in a productive sense until it is embodied in electronically operated machines which perform the necessary computations far more rapidly than even the brightest human beings.

The notion of technology is broad enough to embrace almost any change in the process of production, the introduction of a new product, new uses for old products, and the development of new methods for organizing and managing production. Technology is not easily measured, let alone defined, but there is little doubt that it is a key element in the process of economic growth. It is also one which, in spite of the difficulties involved, needs to be separated in concept and in measurement from the resources themselves. Subsequently we shall refer to some recent efforts to measure the impact of both technology and technological change on the rate of growth of the American economy.

Growth requires an enlargement of the society's productive capacity. This results from an enlargement of its resource base, an improvement in the quality of its resources, or technological change. As a matter of fact, economic growth, which is ongoing and continuous, involves combinations of all three of these. One of the tasks of the economic theorist is to disentangle the relative importance of the different sources of economic growth at varying periods of time. To put the matter differently, an economist seeks to understand why resources and technology change, and what impact these changes have on productive capacity. Before further discussion of this point, let us refer briefly to the second set of determinants of productive capacity, the socioeconomic structure of a society.

Socioeconomic Structure

Like technology, the concept of socioeconomic structure is very broad, embracing many variables which influence the economy's productive potential. Essentially, though, the term relates to fundamental institutional arrangements existing in a society that provide the setting within which the economic system operates and through which the process of growth is carried forward.

The best way to explain this term is to identify the main attributes of the economic system which ought to come under this heading. Four of these are of particular importance to the process of economic growth. First, there is the system of ownership for nonhuman resources (land and capital), including the distribution of that ownership. The basic issue is the extent to which private ownership of resources exists in a society. This is one of the fundamental distinctions between market and non-market economies. Equally important for the market economy, at least, is the distribution of ownership of economic resources. The economist is interested in the degree of equality or inequality in ownership, including the effect the distribution may have on the supply of the services of these resources.

A second important characteristic is the distribution of income, which ultimately concerns how the society's output is distributed to its citizens. The significant aspect of income distribution is its impact on the supply of effort and the services of non-human resources. Because income distribution is especially relevant to the supply of human effort, a great deal of analysis has been directed toward the relationship between incentive and income received, although no clear conclusions have emerged which are directly applicable to the problem of economic growth.

A third significant structural characteristic centers about the dominant forms of business activity in the society, especially in a market economy. This concerns the size of the basic production unit, including the kind of competition predominant in the society. Competition and the form of the producing unit have an impact on the efficiency with which resources are organized in the productive process, including the rate of technological change. These matters are treated in detail in Chapters 11 and 12. One of the issues of continuing and vital concern in this area, for example, is whether giant firms are more efficient than small or medium-sized firms. These are sticky questions for which the economist has no easy answers.

Finally, the process of growth may be influenced by the population's tastes and values. Critical factors here are the extent to which the consumer prefers new products over old and familiar products, the adaptability of the consumer to changes in the productive processes, and the willingness of business and industrial leaders to introduce new production techniques. For the United States in the 1970s, an intriguing but as yet unanswered question is the extent to which the changing life styles of some people, with less stress on materialistic goals, may influence our thinking and behavior on economic growth. But a society which strenuously adheres to traditional techniques in the realm of production is not likely to be a rapidly growing society; this is true of many less developed nations. If a society is conditioned to resist

Income distribution

Forms of business activity

The society's tastes and values

change, this will affect the rate of economic growth adversely. Without attitudes of mind responsive to change, disciplined work habits, and organized activity, economic growth is not possible.

The Labor Force

Now that we have identified both the strategic and fundamental determinants of economic growth, let us examine close-up the factors which influence the size and quality of the strategic determinants, namely resources and technology. Until the last two centuries, the labor force was the most important source of economic growth in any society; in many underdeveloped areas, it still is. The labor force can be viewed as the stock of man-hours available to the economy during a given period of time. This depends, first, upon the number of people employed and the hours they customarily work. The most important determinant of size is population. The rate of population growth depends upon birth rates, death rates and the level of immigration into the country. In the nineteenth century, when the labor force in the United States grew very rapidly, most of the growth was due to the huge influx of immigrants from Europe and other areas of the world.

*Population as
determinant of
labor force*

Because birth and death rates, as well as the immigration rate, are deeply rooted in the institutional structure of a society, they normally do not change quickly, although change is of course possible. Recently the United States has experienced a sharp decline in the birth rate, although no one knows if this is permanent. During the 1960s the birth rate steadily declined, reaching a postwar low of 18.2 children born per 1,000 population at the end of the decade. In the first quarter of 1972 the rate dropped to the lowest level ever recorded for a three-month period—15.8 births per 1,000 population. The general historical experience of Western nations has been for the birth rate to decline as the level of real output rose. But there is no clear evidence that the newly emerging nations will follow the same path, once they begin to achieve continuous economic progress. If they repeat this experience they will lessen the frightful population pressures that have left their people prey to famine and disease.

*Changing birth
rates*

The relationship between birth, death, and immigration rates also affects the age structure of a population, in itself a major determinant of the size of the labor force. A rapidly growing population will have an age structure skewed toward the younger age brackets, while the age structure of a static or slowly growing population will be skewed toward the upper age brackets. The work force is generally drawn from the portion of the population between the ages of fourteen and sixty-five. From the viewpoint of economic growth, the size of this segment is of crucial importance, simply because those who do not fall within the work force have to be supported by those who do not participate in the pro-

*Age structure and
labor force*

ductive process. Thus, a "young" or "old" population requires more effort by the labor force because there are relatively more nonparticipants.

Participation in the Labor Force

The size of the labor force is also determined by the labor force participation rate. While the population bracket that determines the maximum size of the labor force encompasses all people between the ages of fourteen and sixty-five, not everyone in this bracket is in the labor force. The length of schooling affects the labor force participation rate, as does the extent to which women, especially mothers, enter the job market.

There is no economic principle which governs precisely the size of the labor force participation rate. It depends mostly on the values and attitudes that people hold. In the early part of this century in the United States public attitudes were strongly hostile toward women—especially married women—working, except in a few special occupations, such as teaching or nursing. Now it is a commonplace for women to work, including even women with small children. Consequently, the labor force participation rate has probably risen because of changing attitudes toward the working woman.

Women in the labor force

Another factor, however, has lowered the labor force participation rate: the tendency to prolong the school years. More and more people now remain in school well into their early twenties as a growing proportion of the population pursues a college education. The long period of growth and affluence of the 1960s also spawned, especially among the young, a reaction against the work-oriented spirit of the "Protestant Ethic." The less prosperous note on which the 1970s opened, with a growing scarcity of jobs, makes it quite uncertain whether this attitude will have any significant or permanent effect on labor force participation rates.

Extended education

Finally, the supply of labor effort depends upon the number of hours worked as well as the number of people considered as a part of the labor force. To a degree, hours are regulated by law. Legislation and custom have established the forty-hour week as the norm, although the 1970s may see a further reduction in the standard work week, either through changing practices or by legislation. The four-day work week has begun to emerge in some industries, although the total hours worked remains at or close to forty.

The work week

Capital

Of the nonhuman resources important to economic growth, capital has been the most important in the modern era. Historically, land was more significant until approximately two hundred years ago. Until the beginning of the Industrial Revolution most societies, for all practical purposes, were agrarian; thus the availability of fertile land was the key to the level of production. This certainly is no longer the situation. In the modern world the supply of land is still limited, in spite of efforts being made in some parts of the world to reclaim land from the sea. But modern agricultural production relies heavily on the application of capital in the form of machines and fertilizers to increase the productivity of the land rather than solely on the original fertility of the land itself. Today capital, man-made and reproducible, is the most important nonhuman resource for the process of production.

Economists have found a significant correlation between the rate of growth of a society and the growth of its stock of capital. There are two basic ways for the capital stock to grow. One is the "widening" of capital. This occurs when a country with an expanding population and labor force enlarges its stock of capital at a rate that keeps pace with the growth in population and the labor force. Under these circumstances, the economy equips its labor force with more capital of the kind which already exists, maintaining unchanged, in effect, the ratio of capital to labor.

The second way in which the capital stock may grow is more significant; it is generally described as a "deepening" of capital. It occurs when the capital stock grows faster than the labor force, thus leading to an increase in the ratio of capital to labor. This is the kind of growth most likely to be associated with technological advance; it has the effect of giving the labor force more tools for its work. In other words, when there is a deepening of capital, more machines and tools are combined with labor than previously, a development which presumably results in a higher average output per man-hour for the society. In recent times, the deepening of capital has been more important in the process of economic growth than the widening of capital, although obviously both are essential if a society is to advance.

Finally, the enlargement of a society's capital stock involves the process of investment. In real terms investment means the diversion of resources from production for current consumption in order to enlarge the stock of capital. This means an increase in productive capacity for the economy in the future. All societies must invest, both to replenish their capital stock and to enlarge its absolute size. Without investment there can be no increase in the size of the capital stock, and without such an increase economic growth is doubtful. Investment is measured as a rate, in the sense that the amount of current output devoted to investment purposes (both replacement and new) is measured as a percentage of the gross national product. In the United States gross investment in the postwar period averaged between 15 and 17 percent of the gross national product. Table 8-2 shows the relationship between the rate of growth of the gross national product and the rate of investment in several advanced countries. This table shows that high rates of investment generally correlate with high rates of economic growth.

TABLE 8-2
Rate of Growth of GNP and Investment:
Selected Countries

COUNTRY	INVESTMENT RATE * (1960–69)	RATE OF GROWTH OF GNP ** (1960–70)
United States	16.7%	4.9%
United Kingdom	17.3	3.1
West Germany	25.2	5.9
France	23.8	7.6
Italy	20.8	7.3
Japan	32.8	18.5

* Gross investment as a percent of GNP.
** At 1963 prices and 1963 exchange rates.
Source: *Monthly Statistical Bulletin*, OECD, and *National Accounts Statistical Yearbooks*, OECD.

Education

Our capacity to grow depends upon our ability to apply technology to output. This rests upon our stock of technological knowledge. For analysis of economic growth it is appropriate to treat technology, as well as the labor supply and capital, as a stock. What causes it to grow? Technology, of course, is part of the general body of human knowledge, which means that much of our technology comes from the accumulated experience of mankind. It is also true, though, that technology as a body of specialized knowledge is capable of deliberate expansion in two ways: education, and research and development.

Through education a society increases not only its stock of general knowledge, but also its stock of technological knowledge that can be applied to the production of goods and services. Identifying education's contribution to economic growth is no simple matter. Of course not all expenditures for education should be looked upon as an investment designed to increase our stock of technological knowledge. A significant portion of expenditures for education are analogous to consumer expenditures for goods and services, for much of the demand for knowledge arises from the great satisfaction people derive from learning; it makes possible a more meaningful and happier life, apart from any contribution it may make to one's ability to earn a living. This demand should be viewed as a consumer want, which must be satisfied. There is no clear way to distinguish what percent of educational

Increasing the stock of technological knowledge

189

expenditures ought to be allocated to consumption and what percent ought to be allocated to investment. But education is reflected in improvement in the quality of the labor force, and an
improved labor force represents one way to advance the stock of
technology.

In spite of the difficulties inherent in separating education in
its role as a consumer good or service from the part which increases the stock of technology, there is a tendency among economists to treat education as an investment expenditure. Professor
Theodore Schultz of the University of Chicago found that between 1900 and 1957 the educational "investment" of the economy, when measured by its total cost, increased more than eight
and one-half times over the 1900 level, a gain significantly greater
than the estimated increase in the stock of physical capital during
the same period of about four and one-half times over the 1900
level. Between 1960 and 1970 there was a further sharp increase
in the relative importance of educational as compared to investment outlays in the American economy. In this period investment
expenditures (gross) increased by 81 percent, but educational outlays, including those for higher education, jumped by 205 percent.
Table 8-3 compares for selected years since 1960 both gross investment and educational expenditures as a percent of the gross
national product. The change in the relative importance of education is strikingly reflected in the fact that between 1960 and
1970 these expenditures jumped from 6.2 percent of the gross national product to 9.8 percent, during which time gross investment
as a percent of the gross national product actually declined.

Education as
investment
expenditure

Direct costs of
education

Table 8-3
Gross Investment and Educational Expenditures As a Percent of the Gross National Product: Selected Years, 1960–1970

	1960	1965	1968	1969	1970
Gross Investment	14.9%	15.8%	14.7%	15.0%	13.9%
Education *	6.2	7.8	8.6	9.0	9.8

* Primary, secondary, and higher.
Source: *Statistical Abstract of the United States,* 1971.

Valuable as they are, these figures do not tell the full story of
how to measure investment in education. This investment is measured not only by the direct costs reflected in the trends shown in
Table 8-3, but also by the income forgone by students in educational institutions. This is most important for students in higher
education and the last two years of their secondary education; students in lower grades normally are not in the work force, and
thus forgo no income. It has been estimated that about half of the

Income forgone

total educational costs in high school and more than half of the real educational costs in college and post-graduate education can be attributed to income forgone.

The precise relationship between investment in education and the growth in the stock of technology is obviously difficult to determine, although there is little doubt about the existence of this relationship. A clue to its magnitude is found in attempts made by economists to measure the *rate of return* on educational expenditures in the 1950s and 1960s. They found, in general, that the rates of return on investment in education were comparable to those earned in other economic activity; in some instances, the rates were higher than the return on other forms of investment expenditure, a finding which indicated some *underinvestment* in education by society. The technique employed was essentially to compare incomes earned over varying periods by persons with different levels of education (i.e., primary school, high school, and college) and reduce the higher income differentials associated with more education to a rate of return on the costs involved in acquiring more education, including both educational outlays and income forgone.

Research and Development

The second major source of increases in the stock of technology is expenditure for research and development (R and D), which is the organization of effort and the expenditure of money to develop new techniques and products. In other words, R and D is a formal attempt to advance knowledge, especially knowledge directly applicable to the process of production. It is carried out by business, government, and private institutions; although the largest part of research and development activity is performed in the private sector, most of it is financed by the public sector. For example, in 1969 over 70 percent of research and development work in the American economy was actually performed in private industry, although 47 percent of private expenditure for research and development was financed by the federal government.

Since 1955 there has been an explosive growth in R and D expenditures in the American economy; in the period 1955–1971 total outlays for research and development increased by 341 percent. In these same years research and development expenditures as a percent of the gross national product grew from 1.6 percent to 2.7 percent in 1971. Despite its growth R and D activity is not spread evenly throughout the economy. On the contrary, research and development expenditures in the American economy are highly concentrated. In 1971 the bulk of federal expenditures for research and development were directed toward space, defense, and atomic energy; these activities accounted for 79 percent of the

The rate of return on education

Growth and distribution of R and D

federal R and D dollar. In private industry and outside of expenditures connected with aerospace and national defense, most research and development expenditures are of a modest nature, primarily affecting the design and style of existing products. Furthermore, much industrial research and development is aimed at the very short run and is essentially of an applied character. The later 1970s ought to see some major shifts in emphasis, particularly if we are serious about issues of the environment and ecology. The blunt truth is that the R and D effort needed to deal with such difficult and costly issues as how to recycle wastes so as to end the destruction of the environment has hardly begun. Yet it must, if the environment is to be saved.

Declining ratio of
capital to output

The most tangible overall evidence of the effectiveness of research and development expenditures is the relationship between the stock of capital and the level of output. Statistical evidence suggests that in the last several decades there has been a decline in the ratio of capital to output, which reflects the fact that through technological change the efficiency of capital has, on the average, become greater.

Measuring the Sources of Economic Growth

Now that we have examined some of the most important strategic determinants of the economy's growth, we can ask whether there is any solid evidence of their quantitative importance. The answer is yes. In an imaginative pioneering study undertaken on behalf of the Committee for Economic Development, Edward F. Dennison sought to measure statistically the sources of economic growth in the United States for two important periods in the past, 1909–1929 and 1929–1957. His results are summarized in Table 8-4, which arranges the data to make a clear distinction be-

TABLE 8-4
Sources of Economic Growth in the United States: 1909–1957

COMPONENT	RATE OF GROWTH 1909–1929	RATE OF GROWTH 1929–1957	PERCENT OF GROWTH RATE 1909–1929	PERCENT OF GROWTH RATE 1929–1957
Real National Income	2.82%	2.93%	100%	100%
Increase in Total Inputs	2.26	2.00	80	68
Labor Inputs *	1.53	1.57	54	53
Employment	(1.11)	(0.80)	(39)	(27)
Education and Experience	(0.42)	(0.77)	(15)	(26)
Capital	.73	.43	26	15
Productivity **	.56	.93	20	32

* Adjusted for quality changes.

** Increase in output per unit of input (reflects advances in knowledge and economies of scale).

Source: Edward F. Dennison, *The Sources of Economic Growth in the United States and the Alternatives Before Us* (1962).

tween growth that results from additional inputs (or increases) in the stock of labor and capital and growth that results from improvements in education and training. Although Dennison's study was completed in the late 1950s, there were no developments in the years since that altered in any significant way his fundamental conclusions.

It is significant that whereas in the earlier period (1909–1929) the primary source of growth was an increase in resources in the form of labor and capital, in the later period (1929–1957) this was less important than growth in the quality of the labor force, growth in the stock of knowledge, or other variables. Specifically, growth in the stock of labor and capital accounted for 42 percent of the increase in output over the second period, whereas in the earlier period these two inputs accounted for 65.3 percent. Again in the 1929–1957 period an increase in the *quality* of the labor force as reflected in education and training accounted for 26.3 percent of growth, the increase in the stock of knowledge amounted to 19.8 percent, and other variables were responsible for 11.9 percent. In the earlier period the variables which reflect primarily education and growth in the stock of knowledge accounted for only 34.3 percent of the total growth recorded in the period.

Basically, Dennison's findings document the growing importance of qualitative factors such as education and improvements in the stock of knowledge as a source of economic growth in recent times. There is little doubt that this tendency will accelerate in the future, for increasingly the United States and other economies are coming to recognize that knowledge in its broadest aspects is the most critically important element in the process of economic growth. Further, knowledge is a resource in critically short supply all over the world.

We have advanced far enough in our analysis of the strategic determinants of economic growth to reach a first conclusion. Aside from the growth of the labor force, the most important single determinant of growth in any society is the amount the society is willing to invest either in physical capital or in knowledge. To grow, a nation must divert resources from production for current use and use them to provide for future capabilities and output. Investment is a grand theme of economic progress that runs like a thread through all attempts by economists (past and present) to generalize about the process of economic growth. Investment may be directed toward physical capital, it may be directed toward increasing our stock of knowledge through education, or it may involve some combination of the two. In any event, investment is the key to economic progress.

The growing importance of education and training

Investment as key to economic growth

The Theory of Economic Growth

Economists can identify the strategic variables, but modern economics does not possess a complete theory of economic growth. Much of our understanding of growth stems from the work of economists in times past. The findings of earlier economists, although not always precisely correct, still contain elements and ideas relevant today.

Adam Smith

As we noted in Chapter 2, the subject of economic growth is the full title of Adam Smith's classic work, *An Inquiry into the Causes of the Wealth of Nations*. For Smith used the term wealth roughly as the modern economist uses the term income.

Division of labor

What did Smith have to say about economic growth? His outlook was essentially optimistic, because he saw no serious obstacle to mankind's continued material progress. The fundamental source of growth in Smith's analysis is the division of labor, which stems from his belief that human beings have a natural propensity to "barter and exchange." The significance of the division of labor is twofold. First, it improves the productivity of the individual worker, because by subdividing any task into smaller and smaller parts the worker can become more and more proficient in performing any one of the sub-tasks of the larger whole. Second, Smith believed, the division of labor would open the way for increasing use of tools and machines (or capital). In his view, specialization and the use of capital were naturally linked together and in combination they would lead to continued material progress and human betterment.

Smith did not foresee any barriers to a continued improvement in material well-being by the extension of division of labor and use of more and more capital in conjunction with labor. Nor did he conceive of technology as a significant factor in the process of economic growth. Smith, of course, wrote during an early phase of the Industrial Revolution, so he could not be expected to foresee all the changes that new sources of power would bring about. The willingness and ability of the market system to use capital was tied not only to specialization of labor, but also to the existence of profit, primarily because Smith's conception of the economy rested upon a market system in which self-interest played a key role. Thus, the expectation of profit would lead the businessmen to use more capital, although the continued division of labor gave him the opportunity to do so.

David Ricardo

The optimism of *The Wealth of Nations* gave way in the early nineteenth century to pessimism about the economic system's capacity for continued growth. The switch in viewpoint resulted from the impact of the ideas of David Ricardo (1772–1823) and Thomas Malthus (1766–1834). Ricardo, a British banker and businessman as well as a leading economist in the early nineteenth century, is responsible for one of the crucial ideas in economic thought, the "law" of diminishing returns. This says, in effect, that if inputs of any resource (labor or capital) are increased while the quantity of another resource (land) is fixed, the initial result will be added output, but that sooner or later the rate of increase in output begins to slow down. Eventually, output increases may cease altogether, in spite of the fact that more units of the variable resource are being added. The significance of this principle is that a fixed supply of any resource sooner or later puts a brake on the expansion of all output.

The law of diminishing returns

Ricardo first applied the law of diminishing returns to the situation in England in the early nineteenth century, where land, obviously, was the resource in fixed supply. Thus as population grew and more labor was applied to land to produce more food, diminishing returns in food production would inevitably occur. The effect was to raise the cost of production of food and, thereby, the cost of living for workers and others. Ricardo believed that the beneficiaries of this process were the landlords, because as more and more land was brought into use to meet the growing demand for food, the price of land would have to rise. Since Ricardo assumed that the best land normally was brought into production first, this land received a surplus because of its lower production costs. The price paid for food and the derived price for land obviously had to be high enough to cover production costs on the most recent—and presumably poorest quality—land brought into production. The surplus obtained by the best lands Ricardo called economic rent. Note carefully that he used the term rent in a sense quite different from its everyday use. In Ricardo's sense and as a current economic term, economic rent is a surplus associated with the use of any resource in fixed supply.

Economic rent

The pressure on food production costs resulting from a limited supply of land also forced the subsistence wage level to rise, because workers must, at minimum, be paid a subsistence wage; that is, a wage sufficient to enable them to live and raise their families. The rise in the subsistence wage level in combination with the operation of diminishing returns resulted in a hard squeeze on profits. This is the root of Ricardo's pessimism about the ability of the economy to continue to grow. Like Adam Smith, he saw

The rent-wage squeeze

195

capital accumulation as the strategic element in economic growth, but capital accumulation depends upon the existence of profit. Thus, the reduction or elimination of profit through the rent-wage squeeze sooner or later would bring capital accumulation to a halt. When this happened economic progress itself would halt. Since the land area of the world is also limited, it was relatively easy for Ricardo to generalize and apply his scheme of thought to all economic systems. Ricardo, like Smith, could not conceive of a technology which might offset the relentless operation of diminishing returns.

Thomas Malthus

*The geometric
growth rate of
population*

Ricardo's pessimistic outlook on economic progress was strongly reinforced by the population theory developed by his fellow economist, the clergyman Thomas Malthus. In his famous *Essay on the Principle of Population,* Malthus argued that population tends to grow at a rate which would far outstrip the growth of the means of subsistence. To illustrate this principle, he suggested that the population might grow at a geometric rate, by doubling each generation, but the means of subsistence (the food supply) could, at a maximum, only grow at an arithmetic rate. Inevitably the bleak result must be famine unless the population growth is checked by moral restraint and man-made disasters like war, or natural disaster such as disease. Today the specter of overpopulation that Malthus raised is real in most of the underdeveloped parts of the world. These areas are engaged in a grim struggle to keep output growing at least as fast as the population, and in some parts of the world this struggle is being lost, with a subsequent decline in per capita real income. Even in the more advanced nations, the fear of overpopulation is emerging once again as a matter of serious concern. In the United States and the countries of Western Europe the concern centers more on the impact of excess population on the environment than on any real fear about production failing to keep pace.

*The dismal
science*

When Malthus' fears about population pressure are combined with Ricardo's views about diminishing returns because of limited land for food production, it is easy to understand why the optimism of Smith changed to gloomy pessimism only some thirty-odd years after the appearance of *The Wealth of Nations.* As a matter of fact, the views of Ricardo and Malthus resulted in economics being called during most of the nineteenth century the "dismal science."

Why—at least in the Western world and to date—have events not supported the forecasts of Ricardo and Malthus? There are at least two explanations. First, the opening up of vast food-producing areas in the central United States, Canada, and Australia in combination with cheap transportation increased the amount of land available for food production, a development clearly not foreseen by either Ricardo or Malthus in the early nineteenth century. Yet by the close of that century this development had a tremendous impact upon the availability of food for the Western world. Second, and more important, the application of technology to food production brought into being forces which more than offset the play of Ricardo's principle of diminishing return. From the mid-nineteenth century on, agriculture in the Western world was characterized by increasing rather than decreasing returns. New inventions like McCormick's reaper were in part responsible. In the United States the change was helped by the institution of the land-grant college, a social invention through which the state absorbed the real costs of research and development for agricultural production but made the results freely available to the individual farmer. Land-grant colleges—most of which are now universities—came into existence as a result of the Morrill Act, passed by the Congress in 1862. This act made grants of federal land available to the states, in return for which they were required to set up public institutions of higher education, devoted in part at least to the agricultural and mechanical arts. Some of the nation's major public universities, such as the University of California and the Ohio State University, originated as land-grant institutions.

Karl Marx

The pessimism of Ricardo and Malthus about a market system's ability to experience economic progress for a lengthy period was shared by another nineteenth-century economist, Karl Marx, the intellectual father of modern Communism. But Marx offered quite different reasons why continued economic advance was not possible. Marx was a classical economist in the sense that his basic economic ideas were derived largely from David Ricardo. The point of departure for Marx's analysis of the functioning of a market system is the labor theory of value, an explanation of exchange value first developed by Ricardo. Essentially, this theory holds that all exchange value is created by labor. Exchange value is the worth of one commodity or service in terms of another commodity or service. The Marxian labor theory is a cost of production theory of value; it only stresses factors affecting the cost (or supply) of a commodity or service. Modern economists dispute that exchange value can be determined by reference to cost factors alone; they assert that subjective factors also enter into the determination of value. These factors depend upon whether or not potential users of a good or service believe the good or service is useful. Marxian economists have not accepted this view; hence

197

Principles of Economic Growth	the labor theory of value remains the basis of Marxian economic theory.

Principles of Economic Growth

The capitalist

Central to Marx's analysis is the argument that all value created through production does not accrue to the worker as a wage. The return to any resource other than labor (such as capital or land) represents an expropriation of the surplus value created by labor. In a portion of a typical working day, the worker creates enough value to exchange for the commodities he needs to subsist. The balance of the value he creates goes to the *capitalist*, the owner of the nonhuman means of production, land and capital. In Marxian theory, since all value is created by labor, these owners have no claim upon any portion of the output. Nevertheless their position as owners of the nonhuman resources needed in production enables them to expropriate some part of the output.

According to Marx, fierce competition exists between owners of the means of production to increase the surplus value accruing to them. They compete primarily by making labor more productive, which increases the total value produced, but does not necessarily increase the proportion going to the worker. To increase the productivity of the worker requires more capital, but the ability of the individual capitalist to use capital depends upon profit. Thus, like the earlier economists, Marx links capital accumulation to the rate of profit, and sees capital accumulation as the engine of progress in his system.

The collapse of the capitalist system

The struggle among owners to increase surplus value not only drives them toward capital accumulation, but has other, more profound effects. First, capital may displace workers, creating what Marx called a "reserve army of unemployed," which puts pressure on wages, keeping them at the subsistence level. In Marxian theory the reserve army plays a role similar to the rate of population pressure in Malthus' analysis of the behavior of the economic system. Further, the attempt by the owners of capital to extract more and more surplus value from the working class leads to periodic crises for the system as a whole, primarily because the purchasing power of the working class fails to keep pace with the growth in total value. Eventually, Marx argues, the system will break down because of the increasing severity and frequency of economic crises, then to be replaced by another form of economic organization. In summary, Marx saw the market system as driven through competition to capital accumulation and economic growth, but with contradictions such that periodic breakdowns occur. Their magnitude and frequency increase until total collapse results.

Marx's prediction today

Contemporary economists, although they recognize some elements of validity in the Marxist analysis, point out that many of his predictions about the way a market society would develop proved to be incorrect. Increasingly, the market economies of Western nations have been able to prevent serious and frequent economic crises, while at the same time managing to obtain adequate rates of economic growth. Certainly the development of Keynesian economics in the 1930s provided an important theoretical base for actions to offset major fluctuations, and to stimulate economic growth.

Beyond this, however, what is the essential character of contemporary thinking about the process of economic growth? In one important sense the modern view is thoroughly different from earlier views: no modern economist has developed a grand scheme, such as the one worked out by Marx and his predecessors, which shows in sweeping strokes how the growth process unfolds in a complex and modern economic system. Modern thinking about growth is much more partial and pedestrian than earlier thinking. But there is a significant similarity, involving the theme that investment and capital accumulation hold the key to economic progress. Modern thinking about growth has not discarded this view; rather, the emphasis has shifted partly from investment in physical capital to investment in education and investment in research. Investment remains the theme of economic progress.

The Potential Growth of the American Economy

Given what we know about the past performance of the American economy, as well as a knowledge of the theoretical aspects of economic growth, what can we say about the probable growth of the economy in the future? In the spring of 1970 the Bureau of Labor Statistics of the U.S. Department of Labor undertook a massive study and made projections of the shape of the American economy in 1980. This study, like any such projection, rests upon a number of specific assumptions which will be detailed shortly. It should be understood, too, that a projection of this sort is not intended to state what will happen to the economy, but the developments that may take place if all or most of the underlying assumptions turn out to be valid.

Table 8-5 summarizes the primary findings of the Bureau of Labor Statistics on the nation's gross national product, including its major components. The data for 1968 are included in the table, as well as two projections for 1980. One is based upon an assumed annual average rate of unemployment during the 1970s of 3 percent of the civilian labor force, and the other on an assumed annual rate of unemployment of 4 percent. In view of the high unemployment rates with which the 1970s opened (4.9 percent in 1970 and 5.9 percent in 1971), these assumptions may turn out to be unduly optimistic.

TABLE 8-5
Potential Growth of the U.S. Economy to 1980
(Billions of Constant Dollars)

COMPONENT	1968	1980 3% UNEM-PLOYMENT RATE	1980 4% UNEM-PLOYMENT RATE	ANNUAL AVERAGE PERCENT CHANGE 3% UNEM-PLOYMENT RATE	ANNUAL AVERAGE PERCENT CHANGE 4% UNEM-PLOYMENT RATE
Gross National Product	$865.7	$1,427.8	$1,415.7	4.3	4.3
Personal Consumption Expenditure	536.6	903.2	895.6	4.4	4.4
Gross Private Domestic Investment	126.3	222.2	220.1	4.3	4.2
Government Purchase of Goods and Services	200.3	289.7	287.1	4.2	4.2
Net Exports	2.5	12.9	12.0	3.3	3.3

Source: U.S. Department of Labor.

Predictions for 1980

Average growth of GNP

If the economy does succeed in maintaining a 3 percent unemployment rate during the 1970s, the nation's GNP in 1980 will total $1,427.8 trillion (in 1968 prices), a percentage increase of 64.9 percent over the 1968 level. If the unemployment rate is 4 percent, then the 1980 GNP will be slightly lower, $1,415.7 trillion. This will be 63.5 percent higher than the 1968 figure. Under either the 3 or 4 percent assumptions about the unemployment rate, the annual rate of growth in the GNP will average 4.3 percent, a figure slightly below the 4.5 annual average rate established during the 1960s.

Beyond these data on the size, composition, and rate of growth of the nation's GNP as shown in Table 8-5, the BLS projections included a number of other interesting findings. The most significant of these are as follows:

Growth and change in the labor force

1. The labor force will have increased by 21.5 percent, reaching 100 million workers in contrast to 82.3 million in 1968. Moreover, it will contain an especially large supply of young workers between the ages of twenty-five and thirty-four, as the total in this age bracket is expected to be 26 million, or about a quarter of the total labor force. The educational level of the nation's labor force will also have risen substantially. The practical import of this is that an enormous number of new jobs for well-trained people will have to be created in the 1970s. The tight labor market for college graduates in 1971–1972 is an indication of this developing situation, as well as of the difficulty involved in correcting it.

Growth in labor productivity

2. Output per man-hour—or labor productivity—is expected to advance at an annual average rate of 3 percent, a figure slightly lower than the average of the 1960s. The work week is expected to decline through the 1970s at the slow pace of 0.1 percent per year,

so that by the end of the decade 38 hours will have become the standard work week. How this will be allocated by days remains to be seen, for, as mentioned earlier, there is a move underway in some industries and areas toward the four-day work week. Unless income distribution becomes less inequitable (a topic discussed in Chapter 15), a shorter work week may merely lead to more moonlighting.

3. The structure of employment is expected to continue to shift toward the service industries, including trade and government, while employment in an occupational sense will continue to shift toward the occupations which require the most education and training.

Underlying Assumptions

As indicated at the beginning of this section the BLS projections rest upon a number of assumptions. It is worth noting these and commenting upon their validity, a task which may be as speculative as the assumptions themselves.

First, it is assumed that the 1970s will see an improvement in the international climate, which is interpreted to mean that the United States will no longer be fighting a war but that the improvement will not be sufficient to permit a major reduction in armaments. What happens in the latter respect depends most upon the success of the Strategic Arms Limitations Talks (SALT). The success of President Nixon's Moscow visit in May 1972 is a hopeful sign. If there is the degree of improvement in the international climate that the BLS expects, then they expect the strength of the armed forces to drop back to the level preceding the Vietnam war. In 1964 there were 2.7 million persons in the armed forces. This would seem to imply a continuation of the draft, although this is not clear in the BLS study. One of the crucial unknowns is the amount of resources that can be directed to other purposes even with a reduction in the size of the nation's armed forces to pre-Vietnam levels, given the costly nature of modern weapons systems and the determination and power of the Pentagon to push for new weaponry.

Second, the BLS assumes that fiscal and monetary policies will achieve a satisfactory balance between low unemployment rates and relative price stability, without any reduction in the long-term economic growth rate. Fiscal and monetary policy are discussed in Chapter 9, but the experience to date of the United States and most other advanced nations raises doubts as to whether we yet possess either the knowledge or political skill to get full employment without inflation.

Finally, the projections assume that there will be no radical changes in the institutional framework of the American economy; that present social, technological, and scientific trends will continue, including values now placed upon the relationships be-

War and disarmament

High employment without inflation

Continuation of present social trends

201

tween work, education, income, and leisure; that the Congress will channel more funds to state and local governments; and, last, that the need to solve the problems posed by air and water pollution and solid waste disposal will not dampen significantly the potential long-run rate of growth. Perhaps the latter is the weakest of this particular group of assumptions, simply because so little is really known at this point about the amount of our resources that must be invested in both research and capital to solve these problems. Diversion of resources to this form of investment will obviously pay handsome psychological dividends by preserving the natural environment and making the world a better place to live, but there is no certainty that it can be done without a reduction in conventional forms of growth.

The data in the BLS study should be understood as neither a prediction nor a forecast, but simply a set of projections resting upon the assumptions discussed above and derived through some relatively simple techniques. These techniques involved an estimate of the number of people working, an estimate of the total hours worked, and an estimate of average output (productivity) per man-hour. Potential output can then be found by multiplying each of these together. The final projections, of course, can be no better than the crucial ones made concerning employment, hours of work, and trends in labor productivity.

The Costs of Economic Growth

As the economy moved into the 1970s, preoccupation with the adequacy of the growth rate had largely vanished, in large part because during most of the 1960s real gross national product grew at the exceptionally high rate of more than 4 percent per year. Concern has now shifted in an entirely different direction with regard to economic growth. Increasingly, the focus is on some of the real costs of economic growth, a development reflected not only in the public press but within the economics profession. We shall examine this question briefly, approaching it on three different levels: the immediate (or economic) costs of expansion; the environmental (or external) costs, which have received increasing attention in the last several years; and costs which, for want of a better term, we shall designate as psychological or subjective.

Economic Costs

Economic growth is not a costless proposition. We simply cannot get more output without some kind of sacrifice. The most basic economic costs are essentially a reduction in leisure, a sacrifice in current output for the sake of future production, or a combination of both. The sacrifice of current output means investment, whether directed toward capital goods, education, or research and development. To these immediate economic costs should be added a third, the possible obsolescence of skills and capital. Economic growth, especially when it results from rapid technological change, is destructive of existing products, existing methods, and existing skills. This has been called a process of "creative destruction" by the late Harvard economist, Joseph Schumpeter.

Are these economic costs worthwhile? If we want more economic growth, we have to give up either leisure or some current output (or a combination of the two) for benefits that will accrue at some future date. The farther they lie in the future the greater the uncertainty which attaches to these benefits and, consequently, the more difficult it is to make the necessary cost-benefit analysis.

Reduction in leisure and sacrifice of current output

External Costs

Economists and others have long recognized the immediate costs associated with economic growth, but concern with the qualitative aspects of our national life and the impact of growth itself on the quality of life has developed only recently. In the 1930s great strides were made in the quantitative measurements of the performance of the economy through development of the national income accounts, discussed in Chapter 5. The sequel to this development, which will absorb the energies of many economists and statisticians in the current decade, will be the development of *qualitative* measures of our economy's performance. In the meantime serious questions are being raised concerning the environmental damage or external diseconomies that increasingly appear to be part of the price we pay for a rapidly rising gross national product.

Qualitative measures of the economy's performance

Critics who concern themselves with the environmental costs of economic growth center their analysis on two major points. First, they challenge the conventional notion that growth expands the range of choice available to members of a community and so increases their welfare. As more goods and new types of goods appear on the market, older goods no longer remain available. Therefore more choices may not really be available. In the modern economy the wants of the consumer are not independent of the products created by the producer, so it is an illusion to speak of an expansion in choice when more and more products are offered by producers who at the same time create additional wants through this process. Many producers offer a range of competing products, but the differences are more apparent than real; hence more "models" of a given product does not mean more choice.

The illusion of choice

The automobile industry, with its many superficial differences in style, is a case in point.

Finally, the critics challenge the conventional assumption that there is a strong link between choice and welfare. This link in contemporary society has been weakened in part because of the fact that choosing, by itself, is necessarily time-consuming, as well as because our society increasingly emphasizes status and income in a relative sense. Keeping up with the Joneses, perhaps getting ahead of them, matters to a great many Americans. Therefore, a mere increase in goods and services does not by itself necessarily enhance welfare.

The second point raised by the critics of economic growth is that in recent years growth has brought about such a spread of *disamenities* of an environmental nature as to cast doubt upon any added welfare resulting from economic growth. The erosion of the countryside, the traffic congestion characteristic of major cities in every leading industrial country in the world, the pollution of the air and the rivers with chemical wastes, the poisoning by sewage of public beaches, the destruction of wildlife and plant life by indiscriminate use of pesticides, and all other forms of destruction of natural beauty seem to be by-products of industrialization and economic expansion. Some environmentalists fear that this upset and destruction of the ecological balance has gone so far as actually to endanger the survival of the human race.

One of the most recent warnings to this effect came from a report (*The Limits to Growth*) produced in the spring of 1972 for the Club of Rome by an interdisciplinary team from the Massachusetts Institute of Technology. (The Club of Rome is a voluntary international organization of scientists and businessmen concerned with analysis of economic, social, and environmental problems common to all nations.) In its report to the Rome group, the MIT team warned that continual population and industrial growth will both exhaust the world's mineral supplies and through pollution make the atmosphere uninhabitable. It is their argument that if present growth trends in population and output continue unchecked, the world will reach an absolute limit on growth sometime within a century. This doomsday view has not gone unchallenged by economists, as noted shortly. In any event, an increasing and critical need exists to develop techniques for measurement of the external costs of economic growth. We must do this if we are to measure the true welfare gain from a growing GNP.

Psychological Costs

The third kind of cost associated with economic growth is even more elusive and less subject to any form of quantitative measurement than those just discussed. Professor James Tobin of Yale University points to several trends associated with economic growth, which, in his judgment, have a damaging effect upon the quality of our intellectual and cultural life. First, it is well known that economic growth has brought about a decline in the average hours of work. In a sense society has chosen to enjoy some of the benefits of the rising productivity of its labor force in the form of more leisure rather than through more goods and services. It is less well known, though, that the main beneficiaries of this trend have been the manual worker and the clerical worker, with little benefit to professional and managerial workers. As a matter of fact, the increasing complexity of business and social organization has probably brought about a reduction in leisure for managerial and professional workers. Thus, there has been a redistribution of leisure as well as an overall increase in it, a redistribution which has meant less leisure for the intellectual and professional classes. To the extent that these classes are the source of most creative, intellectual activity in contemporary society, the effects may be damaging. There is a paradox here; growth itself may threaten further growth because of the adverse effect it has upon one of its key sources.

Adam Smith pointed out that economic growth requires specialization, but he did not foresee the extent to which specialization would bring about both increasing technical complexity in all fields of production and an increase in the size of the average economic unit. Both of these trends result in a growing alienation of the individual from his fellow man. Increasing technical complexity in production makes the life of the average citizen dependent upon experts whose judgment he cannot question, while the emergence of large economic units forces him to deal more and more with organizations which are impersonal and bureaucratic. These developments must be counted among the more serious psychological costs of rapid economic growth.

As pointed out earlier, the ideas of the emerging "anti-growth" school of thought have not gone unchallenged by economists. These critics point out that analyses like that done for the Club of Rome are built on the assumption that growth in output and population produces resource demands and food requirements as well as pollution, all growing at a geometric rate. Such an assumption is identical with the one that Malthus made in the early nineteenth century about population growth. But, say the critics, the anti-growth advocates claim that the technical progress needed to cope with resource demands and food requirements can grow at no more than an arithmetic rate, much as Malthus assumed two centuries ago for the food supply. Although most economists are not inclined to minimize the dangers to the physical and social environment from unrestrained population growth,

The Costs of Economic Growth

Redistribution of leisure

Alienation

Anti-growth alarmism?

205

many also are not prepared to accept uncritically the assumptions implicit in the anti-growth viewpoint. In spite of fear about forthcoming shortages, worldwide prices for many natural resources remain low, which means that serious shortages have not yet developed. Further, it is argued, there is no solid evidence that technical progress is either slowing down or unable to keep pace with the growth in demand for resources and food. In any event, the argument over the good and the bad of economic growth will continue throughout the 1970s.

Government and Economic Growth

We shall conclude this chapter with a brief comment on a theme advanced earlier: what can the government do to stimulate growth, assuming it is desirable to do so? Recent American experience leaves this unclear.

Federal policy makers understand, as do professional economists, that the key to a higher rate of growth in productive capacity is investment. What the policy maker does not have, though, is the necessary theoretical and statistical knowledge of the precise effects of particular types of investment outlays on the economy's productive potential. Should we have more investment in education, say, and less in plant equipment? Should the investment in research and development expenditure be increased? At issue here are two things. First, what can the government do to stimulate directly investment of a particular kind? In some cases, such as research and development expenditures, its role is quite direct, for the federal government supplies many of the funds needed. But in other types of investment, such as private investment in plants and equipment, the role of the federal government is much more indirect. By changing tax rates or special devices such as an investment tax credit or accelerated depreciation allowances, government may be able to stimulate or reduce investment spending, but we have no precise knowledge of the exact effect of such measures. These particular devices are a part of President Nixon's New Economic Policy. The second matter at issue is insufficient knowledge concerning the effects of more investment in plant and equipment, in more education, or in more research and development on the rate of growth of productive capacity. One hopes this knowledge will be forthcoming, but until that day the policy maker has a difficult role to play in attempting to tell us exactly what ought to be done to raise the rate of growth of productive capacity by a given amount.

Questions for Review and Discussion

1. How is economic growth defined? How is it measured? What is the basic difference between the way we measure full employment and the way we measure economic growth?

2. Give examples of the changes that take place in the economic structure of a society when the society experiences economic growth.

3. How has the long-term growth record of the American economy—both total and per capita—compared with the performance of other advanced industrial nations?

4. Give some of the reasons why it is probably more difficult for policy makers to agree on an optimum rate of economic growth than on an appropriate level of unemployment.

5. What are the immediate or strategic determinants of any increase in the productive capacity of an economy? Why are they called strategic?

6. What is the basic difference between resources and technology?

7. List some of the key factors that determine the size of the labor force available to a nation at any one time. Which of these factors are most readily influenced by public policy measures?

8. Explain what economists mean by a "widening" of capital in contrast to a "deepening" of capital. Which is the most significant for growth?

9. How does a society increase its stock of knowledge? In what way can the economic concept of investment be related to this question?

10. Why were classical economists like David Ricardo and Thomas Malthus much more pessimistic than Adam Smith about the ability of a society to continue to expand its output faster than its population?

11. In order to forecast the potential growth of the American economy over the next decade, what assumptions should be made and what factors should be taken into account?

12. What are some of the real costs of economic growth that are of increasing concern to the public and to economists? Why are they termed costs?

9

Fiscal and Monetary Policy

THE MODERN ECONOMY does not always perform fault-lessly. Action must be taken from time to time to improve its performance, and in our complex world government is the primary instrument for such action. We have reached a point in our study of macroeconomics (the whole economy) where we can apply theory to the policies a central government uses to affect the behavior of the economy. We shall begin with two fundamental questions: what do we want from the economic system, and how can we attain it?

Tasks for the Economy

People expect the economic system to do a variety of things. Gradually, though, public concern has centered around four major objectives of economic policy. These are full employment of labor and other resources, stability of prices, a satisfactory rate of economic growth, and equilibrium in our balance of international payments, which involves our trade and financial transactions with other nations. The closest we have come to embodying these objectives in national legislation is the Employment Act of 1946, which says in part, "The Congress hereby declares that it is the continuing policy and responsibility of the Federal Government to use all practical means consistent with its needs and obligations and other essential considerations of national policy . . . to promote maximum employment, production, and purchasing power." This statement, from Section 2 of the act, rather explicitly implies a commitment to at least the first two of the major policy objectives just enumerated.

Full Employment

The Employment Act of 1946 does not use the phrase "full employment," but rather specifies maximum employment, which it defines as ". . . conditions under which there will be afforded useful employment opportunities, including self-employment, for those able, willing, and seeking to work." There is no precise statistical definition of full employment, although policy makers in the United States have generally believed that an unemployment rate of between 3 and 4 percent represented, for all practical purposes, full employment. Since most European countries had lower unemployment rates during the period following World War II, a statistical definition of full employment in terms of their experience would be even lower. An unemployment rate of 4 percent or less still means a sizable number of persons without work. In 1969 the unemployment rate was down to 3.5 percent, but there were still 2.8 million persons without work. Such an average also conceals significant differences in the unemployment rate, as for teenagers and nonwhites. To illustrate, the overall unemployment rate in 1971 was 5.9 percent, but for persons between 16 and 19 years of age it was 16.9 percent, and for minorities it was 9.9 percent. Any percentage figure is a judgment, arbitrary to a degree, which must be interpreted in relation to the particular circumstances prevailing in the economy at any particular time.

Price Stability

The Employment Act does not make price level stability a specific objective of public policy, although stable prices may be implied in the phrase "maximum purchasing power." If maximum employment is achieved, then stable—or declining—prices are necessary to get the maximum purchasing power from that level of economic activity.

209

Economic Growth

Note, too, that the Declaration of Policy in the Employment Act says nothing about economic growth. Yet this objective is there by implication. If the economy is dynamic, with a growing population, labor force, stock of capital, and level of technology, it follows that there must be some rate of growth of ouput that will maximize employment, production, and purchasing power over time.

Balance of Payments

Equilibrium in the nation's balance of international economic transactions is the most recent addition to the policy goals of the American economy; not until the 1960s did it become fully apparent that the United States, like most other countries today, could have serious difficulties with its international payments position. For example, for the period 1965–1970 the excess of U.S. expenditures, grants, and loans to foreign nations exceeded our receipts from them in all forms on an average of $2.8 billion per year. In 1971, for the first time in more than a century, the United States imported more goods and services than it exported. The deficit in our trade in goods alone was $2.8 billion. In the first quarter of 1972 the deficit for all goods and services reached $3.6 billion on an annual basis. We have thus had to recognize, like other nations before us, that this is a matter of national concern which must be treated through appropriate aggregate policy measures.

The Trade-Off Problem

It is not sufficient merely to enumerate the key policy objectives appropriate to the national economy. We must also understand that these goals, however desirable, may to some extent conflict with one another. It is virtually impossible for any society to attain all its goals simultaneously. Thus we have to decide how much attainment of one goal must be sacrificed to attain another goal. The choice between goals is often a tough one for policy makers. Economists call it the *trade-off* problem.

Unemployment versus Inflation

A widely publicized example of a conflict between two goals is that between full employment and stability in the general price level. Most economists are convinced that full employment on a sustained basis can only be achieved at the cost of an unacceptable rate of increase in the general price level. In other words, the cost of ending unemployment is likely to be a dangerously high rate of inflation.

The difficulties inherent in this situation were forcefully demonstrated in 1970. The Nixon administration sought to slow down the economy in 1969 and 1970 in order to reduce the inflation rate—consumer prices rose at an annual average rate of 5.3 percent in 1969—but during 1970 prices continued to rise at an even higher rate—5.9 percent—in spite of the fact that the unemployment rate rose to over 6 percent by the end of the year. After the wage-price freeze was instituted in the summer of 1971, the upward movement of the price level abated somewhat, but there was little effect on the unemployment rate. At the end of the first quarter of 1972 the unemployment rate still stood at 5.9 percent of the labor force, little changed from the levels of the preceding twelve months.

The trade-off therefore becomes the amount of price stability we will sacrifice to get full employment or, conversely, the amount of unemployment we are willing to tolerate for the sake of price level stability. By mid-1971 it was clear that policy makers in the Nixon administration had decided that a 6 percent unemployment rate was unacceptable, hence deliberate efforts to slow down the economy were abandoned. The New Economic Policy (NEP) with its wage-price freeze and tax cuts was the administration's answer to its problem. Since the economy began to pick up steam in the first half of 1972, whether or not the freeze can succeed in holding down prices once the unemployment rate begins to come down remains to be seen.

The Phillips Curve

The reality of this particular trade-off is substantiated by simple empirical evidence. One technique often used to demonstrate the relationship between employment and changes in the price level is a device known as the Phillips Curve, named for the British economist who made the pioneering studies of the problem. A typical Phillips Curve, shown in Figure 9-1, measures the unemployment rate on the horizontal axis and the rate of change in hourly money wages on the vertical axis. The data in Figure 9-1 show a curve approximated to 1960–1970 data for the American economy. The curve relating these variables indicates that as the unemployment rate declines the rate of increase in money wages accelerates. Be careful not to attribute causal significance to this relationship. The curve in Figure 9-1 shows in graphic form what has been observed about the correlation between these variables, namely the unemployment rate and the rate of change in money wages. The same type of relationship exists between the unemployment rate and the rate of change of the price level, as shown

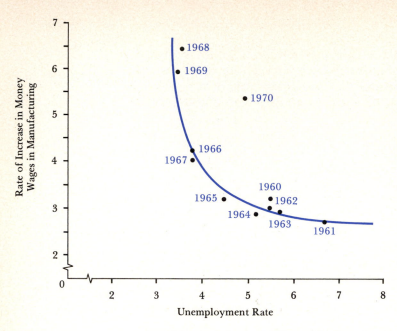

FIGURE 9-1

The Phillips Curve for the American Economy: 1960–1970.

The curve drawn approximately to fit these data shows that as the unemployment rate declined from nearly 7 percent at the start of the decade to about 3.5 percent at the end, the rate of increase in money wages (hourly rates) in manufacturing jumped from a little over 3 percent to more than 6 percent. (Source: *Economic Report of the President*, 1971.)

in Figure 9-2. A 1971 study by the Brookings Institution indicated that a 4 percent unemployment rate in the United States would entail a 5 percent inflation rate.

Most economists would agree that a main objective of government policy should be to shift the Phillips Curve to the left; this would result in a lower rate of price inflation with any particular unemployment level, or, conversely, trade off a given rate of price

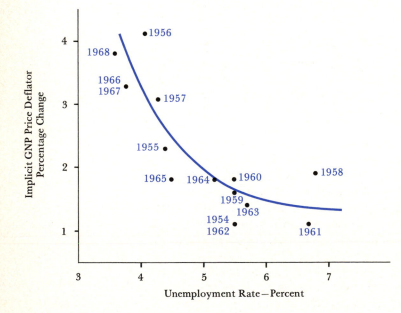

FIGURE 9-2

Price Performance and Unemployment in the American Economy: 1955–1967.

These data and the diagram are from the *Economic Report* prepared by the Council of Economic Advisers. They show that a strong correlation exists between the unemployment rate and the rate of increase in prices, as well as between unemployment and money wage rates, as shown in Figure 9-1.

inflation for a lower level of unemployment. Figure 9-3, which contains hypothetical data, illustrates how the rate of inflation associated with a 4 percent unemployment rate could be reduced from 5 to 3 percent with a shift in the curve. But our present state of theoretical knowledge does not enable us to say specifically what policy measures will shift the Phillips Curve to the left and by what amount.

FIGURE 9-3

Shift in the Phillips Curve.

An improvement in the trade-off between unemployment and inflation would involve a shift to the left in the Phillips curve, a change that might be brought about by improved worker productivity or a reduction in frictional unemployment. The result of the shift is a reduction in the inflation rate associated with 4 percent unemployment from 5 to 3 percent.

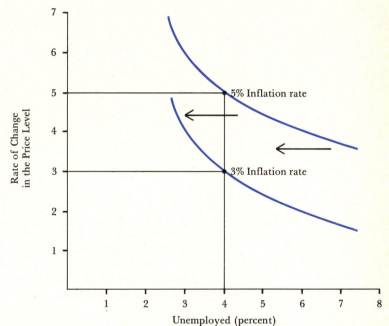

Stable Balance of Payments versus Growth

Another trade-off situation involves a basic incompatibility between equilibrium in the balance of international payments and attainment of a satisfactory rate of economic growth. Economic growth requires a high rate of investment spending, which is possible only if interest rates are low. Low interest rates, however, may cause trouble for the balance of international payments. If interest rates in the United States are low relative to those abroad, financial capital may flow out of the economy, which puts pressure on the nation's balance of international payments. In the early phase of the Kennedy administration this was an especially acute problem, since economic policy was aimed at stimulating the economy and achieving a more rapid growth rate. This had to be done at a time when the nation was faced with a deficit in its balance of payments. Thus, policy makers had to find a way to stimulate investment without forcing interest rates so low that a massive outflow of financial resources would ensue.

Interest rates and the balance of payments

213

Full Employment versus Growth

A third trade-off exists between the goals of full employment and a high rate of economic growth. Economic growth is associated with rapid technological change, either because growth brings about technological change or because technological change is a major factor leading to a high rate of economic growth. Even though growth usually tends to promote higher levels of employment, rapid technological change may result in *structural unemployment*. Structural unemployment exists when workers are displaced as a result of changes in production processes, or significant shifts in demand toward new products and services. Automated equipment frequently reduces the need not only for manual workers, but even for supervisory personnel. The automation of long-distance telephone calls—"direct dialing"—has drastically reduced the number of operators needed. Technological change may make an industry obsolete, leaving its work force with no source of employment. The high level of unemployment among skilled workers in the aerospace industries in the early 1970s was, in a sense, a form of structural unemployment; it resulted from demand changes brought about by shifts in the national priorities, as reflected in the cutback in space exploration or the elimination of the SST program. Drastic changes in the location of industry also result in structural unemployment. Unemployment after World War II in the mill towns of New England or in the mountain regions of Appalachia was of this nature. Regions, like nations, may go through stages of growth and decline, the latter resulting in serious structural unemployment.

The Analytical Framework

The goals of the modern economy and the policies necessary to attain them can be worked out within the analytical framework of aggregate demand and aggregate supply. Using tools we developed in Chapter 6, we can determine how specific policy measures will further the objectives we wish the economic system to attain. The impact of successful policy must be on aggregate demand, since demand is the most important single determinant of the overall performance of the economic system. This is true even in the long run, as in the case of economic growth.

Aggregate economic policy in the United States and other market economies embraces four distinct approaches: fiscal policy, monetary policy, incomes policy, and debt management. With these basic policy approaches a contemporary, democratic government has power to influence the aggregate performance of the economic system. Fiscal and monetary policy are analyzed in this chapter; incomes policy and debt management will be examined in Chapter 10.

Fiscal Policy in the Modern Economy

The term *fiscal policy* refers to deliberate changes in government spending for goods and services, government transfer payments, or taxes, designed to increase or decrease aggregate demand by influencing one or more of the following: output, employment, the price level, or the rate of economic growth. The stress in this definition is on the word "deliberate." Fiscal policy may also include some changes in public expenditures and taxes that are automatic in nature. These are referred to as *automatic stabilizers*. Unemployment compensation is such a stabilizer, as it works automatically to sustain some purchasing power when joblessness climbs, and is reduced in amount when the economy moves back toward full employment. We shall discuss the impact of automatic stabilizers on the economic system later in this chapter.

The ultimate impact of fiscal policy measures is on spending. To understand how fiscal policy works, we must examine the effect of deliberate changes in public spending or taxes on one or more of the major spending streams which enter into aggregate demand—spending for consumer goods and services by households; spending for new plants and equipment by business, including residential construction; and government purchases of goods and services. A fourth element in aggregate demand is the net export of goods and services, but it is relatively minor, normally averaging less than one percent of the gross national product.

Impact of fiscal policy on spending

While any change in expenditure, transfer payments, or taxation by state and local government will have an impact on the economy's aggregate demand schedule, fiscal policy is meaningful only in conjunction with the activities of the federal government. Only the federal government has the authority and the power to undertake fiscal and other policy measures aimed at the overall performance of the economic system. This does not mean that spending and taxing by state and local governments has no impact on the economy's performance. It means simply that there is no practical way to coordinate the activities of state and local governments to bring about deliberate changes in spending and taxing for the purpose of affecting the level of aggregate demand. Only the federal government can do this.

The Federal Budget

The chief instrument for fiscal policy is the budget of the federal government, a massive document showing the total of expenditures authorized and approved by the Congress and the sources of revenue—mainly taxes—that will finance these expenditures. The budget is proposed and ultimately authorized by the Congress on a *fiscal year* basis; the fiscal year runs from July 1 of one year to June 30 of the following year. It is customary to designate a specific fiscal year by the year in which the planned expenditures will terminate. Thus, in 1972 Congress approved a budget for Fiscal 1973, that ran from July 1, 1972 to June 30, 1973. For policy purposes, though, expenditures and taxes are put on an annual basis.

The impact of the budget on the spending streams can be measured on a national income accounts basis, using methods we developed in Chapter 5. A net surplus in the federal sector exists whenever government expenditures for goods and services are less than net taxes. Net taxes equal total taxes less transfer payments, which we have also designated as negative taxes. On the other hand, a net deficit exists whenever the total of federal expenditures for goods and services is greater than net taxes, the latter always being equal to taxes minus transfers. A budget surplus means that, on balance, the federal sector is pulling more out of the income stream through net taxation than it is putting back into the income stream through purchases of goods and services. A deficit means that more income is being put into the income stream through expenditures for goods and services than is being drawn out by net taxation.

Figure 9-4 illustrates this aspect of the federal budget. The horizontal axis shows values for the gross national product up to an assumed level of full employment; the vertical axis shows the surplus or deficit associated with each particular output level. The schedule in the diagram assumes a given structure of net taxes and government expenditures for goods and services. Note that the budget is in balance at an output below full employment. This indicates that the tax structure is related to a given level of government expenditures in a way that automatically generates a surplus as the economy approaches the full employment GNP. When the economy falls below a given level of output a deficit will automatically ensue. A change in policy with respect to the tax structure or the volume of government expenditures for goods and services would shift the position of the schedule shown in Figure 9-4. For example, a deliberate increase in public expenditures for goods and services shifts the schedule downward, which means that the theoretical balanced budget position is moved to a

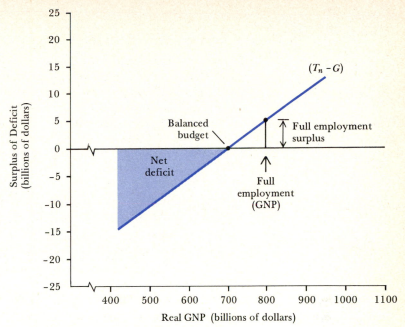

FIGURE 9-4

Federal Surplus and Deficit in Relation to the GNP.

Whenever government expenditures for goods and services are less than net taxes, there will be a surplus and the budget will have a dampening effect on the economy. But if the opposite condition prevails—net taxes are less than government expenditures for goods and services—there will be a deficit and the impact on the budget will be expansionary. (Data in billions of constant dollars.)

higher level of economic activity as measured by the gross national product, whereas a deficit would appear much sooner following a downturn in economic activity. A decrease in government expenditures (or an increase in taxes) has just the opposite effect. These changes are shown in Figure 9-5.

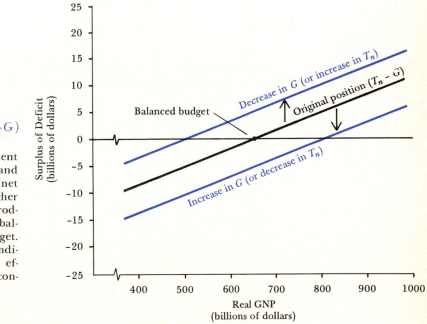

FIGURE 9-5

Shifts in the $(T_n\text{-}G)$ Schedule.

An increase in government expenditures for goods and services or a decrease in net taxes means that a higher value of gross national product is required to attain balance in the federal budget. More taxes and less expenditures have the opposite effect. (Data in billions of constant dollars.)

Full Employment Budget Surplus

A diagram of this kind is especially useful to dramatize the existence and size of a *full employment budget surplus*. This is the excess of government revenues (net) over government purchases of goods and services generated by the tax system at hypothetical full employment GNP. This analysis was developed in the early 1960s by the President's Council of Economic Advisers. Early in 1970 the Nixon administration adopted the concept of the full employment budget in the presentation of its budget message to the Congress. The economic significance of the concept is its implication that the real importance of a deficit or surplus is whether it exists when the economy is at full employment. It also demonstrates the existence of a potential fiscal dividend, the surplus automatically generated by the economy which grows in size as the full employment GNP expands under the influence of forces which make the economy grow.

The fiscal dividend   A potential fiscal dividend comes into existence and increases in magnitude as long as there are no significant changes in the basic relationship between taxes and expenditures. In a growing economy the full employment output, shown in Figure 9-6 by the vertical line at the right-hand side of the diagram, will constantly in-

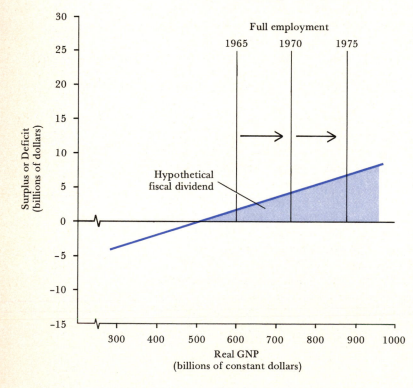

FIGURE 9-6

The Full Employment Budget Concept and the Fiscal Dividend.

With a given tax structure and pattern of federal expenditures, designed to yield a surplus under full employment conditions, the amount of the surplus will increase as the full employment level of the gross national product grows. This illustrates the notion of a "fiscal dividend." Its existence depends upon a relatively fixed structure of both expenditures and taxes. (Data in billions of constant dollars.)

crease. In the diagram this line shifts to the right. We can readily see that the full employment surplus must grow, if there are no changes in either tax rates or the structure of government expenditures. The surplus is designated a fiscal dividend because its existence may either permit future tax cuts or be the source for unrestricted grants to the states. The idea of a fiscal dividend was first broached in the mid-1960s, but spending for the Vietnam war, followed by recession and sluggish recovery in 1970 and 1971, precluded the emergence of such a surplus at that time, let alone its deployment. In 1971 the federal government's deficit on a national income accounts basis exceeded $23 billion, a figure that was being reduced as the economy began to move ahead in 1972. Proponents of federal revenue sharing to meet the pressing financial needs of the cities and states still look to a fiscal dividend provided by growth as a relatively painless means to achieve their objective. It remains unclear, though, whether the magnitude of expansion demands built into many of the Great Society programs of the late 1960s—spending for social welfare, medical care for the aged, and education, for example—are so large as to absorb much of the added revenue that a growing economy will generate for the federal sector.

Shifting the Schedule

Figure 9-4 focuses our attention on the budget as the instrument for the implementation of fiscal measures, but it does not tell us precisely what impact these measures will have on the economic system. A shift in the schedule toward a smaller full employment surplus (or greater deficits at less than full employment) can be brought about by an increase in government spending for goods and services, by a reduction in taxes, or by an increase in transfer payments. A reverse shift will require opposite changes. These shifts were mentioned earlier in reference to Figure 9-5. The magnitude of the shift (either upward or downward) initially reflects the impact of a change in expenditures or taxes on the federal budget. This shift, though, does not tell us what the ultimate impact of the change will be, even though in general any change that increases a deficit (or reduces a surplus) will be expansionary because it puts more spending into the income stream, and any move that enlarges a surplus (or reduces a deficit) will be contractive because it pulls income out of the spending stream. Policy makers, of course, require more precision than this to arrive at appropriate fiscal policy measures. To see how they attain this precision, we must determine how the shifts in the schedules shown in Figure 9-5 are brought about.

Impact on budget of change in spending or taxation

Changes in Government Expenditures

The ultimate impact of any fiscal measure depends upon both the amount by which the aggregate demand schedule is changed as a result of the fiscal action and the size of the multiplier. In Chapter 6, we stressed that the multiplier operates on any change reflected in a shift in the position of the aggregate demand schedule. Consequently, if the value of the multiplier is known, the ultimate effect of a change in the federal budget is determined by the size of the initial shift in the aggregate demand schedule. The latter is, of course, identical to the effect of a change in the federal budget.

Fiscal measures which involve a change in government expenditures have a different initial impact on aggregate demand than those which involve a change in net taxes. Any fiscal measure which involves a deliberate change in government purchase of goods and services (an increase or a decrease) will shift the aggregate demand schedule by an identical amount, assuming all other variables in the economic system remain unchanged. For example, if the federal government increased its expenditures for goods and services in a fiscal year by $10 billion (as was done more than once in the late 1960s as the war in Vietnam escalated), this would be the same as a $10 billion increase in aggregate demand during that year. Because the multiplier effect works on the initial increase, the ultimate increase in output depends upon the size of the multiplier, which was roughly estimated to have a value of 2 at the time of the 1964 tax cut. From a fiscal point of view, a change in government purchases of goods and services has the most direct and immediate effect on economic activity.

Changes in Net Taxes

Now let us assume the change in the federal budget results from a change (upwards or downwards) in net taxes, resulting either from a change in tax rates or a change in transfer payments. To illustrate, let us assume that net taxes are reduced by $10 billion. The ultimate economic effect differs from the increase in government purchases of goods and services, because a change in net taxes does not directly affect any spending stream. Its effects are indirect. The initial impact of a net reduction in taxes is to place more disposable income in the hands of individuals. When consumers find their disposable income has been increased, they will increase spending accordingly. How much more they spend depends upon the value of their marginal propensity to consume. Normally this is less than 100 percent; consequently the amount of increase in disposable income does not translate into an equal increase in consumer spending.

To summarize, the effect of a fiscal change brought about by an increase or decrease in net taxes differs in two ways from the effects of change resulting from an increase or decrease in government expenditures for goods and services. First, the effect is indirect; it has no immediate impact on aggregate demand. The effect on aggregate demand depends upon the change in disposable income and how this affects consumer spending. Second, the effect on aggregate demand is normally less than the size of the net change in taxes, because only a portion of any change in disposable income leads to more or less spending. Thus, a fiscal measure based on a change in net taxes ultimately has less effect on output than one involving a change in government purchases of goods and services.

A change in net taxes may also influence aggregate demand through its effect on investment spending, the third component of the income stream. Investment spending may be affected in two ways. If the change in net taxes is on individuals, leading, therefore, to a change in consumer spending, the business community may change its expectations concerning the profitability of investment spending. If the tax change involves corporation income taxes, then the effect on business investment is more direct, for a change in corporate taxes changes the profit outlook of business firms. Normally, a reduction in corporate taxes has a favorable effect on investment spending, whereas an increase has an unfavorable effect. But it is difficult to forecast with any precision the exact impact of a given tax change on investment expenditure. The expectations on which business bases its investment decisions are often highly subjective: one can only describe in general terms the degree of confidence the business community has in the economic policies of the government at a particular time.

Drawbacks of Changing Expenditures

We have not yet fully decided whether changes in public purchases of goods and services are more effective fiscal measures than changes in net taxes. This is the issue we must now pursue with a more detailed analysis of the effect of both kinds of change on the level of economic activity. While there is a greater direct impact from changes in government spending for goods and services, this approach to fiscal action has two drawbacks. First, it lacks flexibility. Public expenditures for goods and services allocate resources to the public sector to meet collective needs. Often these expenditures are for long-term projects—for example, development of a highway system, construction of dams and irrigation works, or other capital activities. The possibility of significant expansion or contraction in these expenditures over short periods of time is fairly remote. The flow of resources allocated to

Taxes and aggregate demand

Taxes and investment expenditure

Lack of flexibility

221

the public sector to supply social goods simply cannot be readily turned on or off to satisfy the economy's requirements for maximum output, growth, or a stable price level. Probably as government activity becomes more complex and extensive, the rigidity inherent in public expenditure programs increases rather than decreases.

*Reduction in
private investment*

A second objection sometimes raised against fiscal action based on government expenditures is that some of these expenditures may compete with private investment spending, leading to a reduction in the latter. Public housing, for example, may reduce private investment in dwellings. This criticism applies only to the increase of public expenditures for fiscal policy purposes, not to their reduction. Related to this is the fact that some would oppose increase in public expenditures because it enlarges the public sector relative to the private sector, whereas tax reduction might improve the relative position of the private sector. Reduction in federal expenditures or tax increases would, of course, have the opposite effects.

Drawbacks of Taxation

Indirect effect

Examining taxation as a fiscal measure in greater detail, we must start from the premise that a change in net taxes has less direct effect than a change in government purchases of goods and services. The smaller direct impact of a tax change as compared to a change in government demand for goods and services may be a disadvantage. But a tax change provides much greater flexibility because it has an immediate effect upon disposable income. Since the withholding system (deduction of taxes from an individual's weekly or monthly paycheck) for the income tax is an integral part of our tax system, disposable income can be changed from one month to the next by an appropriate change in tax rates. To gain this flexibility and speed, the Congress must be willing to enact the necessary legislation, since the power to impose taxes rests ultimately with the legislative branch.

Legislative Drawbacks

The delay required for Congressional action is a disadvantage common to both forms of fiscal policy. To increase or decrease government purchase of goods and services by a significant amount, or to change the rate structure of the tax system, requires that appropriate legislation be introduced in the Congress, that hearings be held before the proper committees, and that both the Senate and the House of Representatives, as well as the President, approve the changes.

Experience shows that rapid fiscal action by the Congress is, indeed, a rare occurrence, and the effects of an appropriate fiscal policy may be weakened by serious lags in implementation. A case in point is the recent experience with an income tax surtax, which was passed in 1968 in response to inflationary pressures arising from the war in Vietnam. (The surtax is an additional tax, over and above the income tax.) Although many professional economists believed as early as 1966 that a tax increase was needed to suppress the inflationary pressure caused by accelerated war spending, the Johnson administration remained unconvinced until 1967 that the inflation was severe enough to warrant an emergency tax measure. It then took the administration an entire year to persuade the Congress to impose a 10 percent surtax on personal and corporate income; there was nearly a two-year lag between economists' recognition of the need for anti-inflationary fiscal measures and the passage of the surtax legislation.

Fiscal Policy and the Budget

Aside from the relative merits of different approaches, the emphasis on and experience with fiscal policy since World War II has brought about fundamental changes in thinking with respect to the federal budget. If we look at both expenditures and taxation as stabilizing devices, we have to abandon the notion that each year the federal government must balance its outgo and its intake. Using expenditures and taxes as fiscal policy instruments is simply incompatible with the idea of an annually balanced budget. Neither a balanced budget nor a surplus or deficit *per se* is the direct object of public policy; rather, they are means to achieve particular economic ends: satisfactory employment conditions, a satisfactory price level, a satisfactory rate of growth, or a combination of these objectives. Whether the federal budget is in balance, in deficit, or in surplus is really incidental to its impact on the state of the economy as reflected in the foregoing objectives.

These remarks are not to imply that it is easy for the Congress and the executive branch to balance the federal budget, even with the best will in the world. In part, the difficulty results from the fact that public expenditure programs often have growth factors built into them; this proved to be the case with Medicare and expenditures for education, both usually deemed highly desirable. The rate of inflation affects the budget of the government, just as it does that of the typical householder. Moreover, tax collections depend on the state of the economy; even a slight dip in economic activity may cause a sharp drop in federal revenues and hence unbalance the budget. In the summer of 1971 it was estimated that for the fiscal year ending June 30, 1972 the deficit would be at least $21 billion, nearly twice the level forecast by the Nixon administration early in the year. The 1970 recession and a sluggish recovery in the first half of 1971 were the main factors responsible for turning what was expected to be a small surplus in fiscal 1971 into a deficit of over $23 billion.

Automatic Stabilizers

*Built-in flexibility
through taxes and
transfers*

Up to this point we have focused on discretionary fiscal policy; we have been concerned with changes in expenditures or taxes deliberately undertaken to influence economic activity. The modern economy also contains some built-in forces whose fiscal effect is stabilizing. To no small degree, the structure of our tax and transfer system is such that when the gross national product expands, taxes and transfers automatically interact to enlarge net taxes relative to expenditures, thus tending to create a budgetary surplus. This assumes a fixed volume of government purchases of goods and services. When national output contracts, the effect is the opposite: net taxes fall, tending to create a deficit. On the tax side, the progressive rate structure of the federal income tax is the most effective automatic stabilizer. Some transfer payments also function as automatic stabilizers, particularly unemployment compensation, which increases in volume when output and employment fall and declines when they rise.

There is an overall tendency for the federal fiscal system to generate a surplus during an expansion and develop a deficit when economic activity turns down. This tendency is said to be built in because it takes place without any deliberate change in the tax rate or government purchases of goods and services. Built-in devices usually reinforce the effects of discretionary fiscal policy. Most economists do not believe that they are strong enough to eliminate the modern economy's need for discretionary fiscal action to attain satisfactory levels of output, employment, and price. Many do feel, however, that in a minor recession or downturn, the automatic stabilizers may have enough force to prevent the economy from falling into a serious depression. During the 1970 recession, for example, disposable personal income rose each quarter, although the rate of increase slackened, reaching only 0.6 percent in the fourth quarter. Personal tax payments leveled off and actually declined in the third quarter. These developments undoubtedly helped keep consumption spending from falling.

Monetary Policy in the Modern Economy

Monetary policy has the same objectives as fiscal policy; it is the techniques for attaining these objectives that differ. While taxes and government spending are the tools of fiscal policy, the money supply is the instrument used to implement monetary policy. In this context, money supply includes demand deposits and currency in circulation.

Monetary policy works through the impact of changes in the money supply on decisions made by lenders—the financial institutions—and on those who do the spending in the economic system—households, business firms, and governments. Ultimately monetary policy must affect the aggregate level of spending, as does any policy intended to affect the behavior of the economy as a whole.

Impact of changes in money supply on spending

The Making of Monetary Policy

In the United States the body that formulates and carries out monetary policy is the Federal Reserve System. Since the Federal Reserve Banks have the power to influence the reserves of the commercial banking system, they can control the quantity of money and credit in circulation and its cost. The locus of decision-making power for monetary policy differs significantly from the locus of decision-making power for fiscal policy. For fiscal policy the power is shared by the administration in power and the Congress, whereas for monetary policy it resides wholly in the Board of Governors of the Federal Reserve Board. Since the new governors are not appointed whenever a new administration takes office in Washington, the Board has a degree of independence that does not exist for those who formulate fiscal policy. Some students of fiscal and monetary policy argue that this power to pursue an independent policy should be sharply curtailed, primarily because they believe that all tools necessary for effective policy making in the contemporary economy ought to be in the hands of the administration in power, which is responsible for maintaining satisfactory economic performance.

The Federal Reserve Board

The Rate of Interest

To understand monetary policy we must first understand how changes in the reserve position of the commercial banks lead directly to changes in the money supply and indirectly to changes in total spending within the economy. Let us examine what happens when, for example, the Federal Reserve resorts to open mar-

Changes in bank reserves and the money supply

225

ket operations to increase the reserves available to the commercial banking system. Purchases of securities in the open market by the Federal Reserve immediately put more cash reserves into the hands of the commercial banks. Since the commercial banks are basically in the business of lending money, they try to expand their loans; they now have more financial resources available for this purpose, i.e., more reserves. To induce people to borrow more, they may reduce the price they charge for getting loanable funds, which means that the rate of interest declines.

Will this lead to more spending? This is the crucial question. If some types of spending, such as the purchase of capital goods by business firms, are sensitive to the rate of interest, then a fall in interest rates should induce more investment spending. This is one example of the indirect way in which monetary policy affects economic activity. Lower mortgage rates might induce a consumer to buy a house; lower interest rates, as well as greater availability of loanable funds, might simply lead to more spending. If the Federal Reserve sold securities on the open market, this would pull reserves out of the commercial banking system, making money scarcer and, consequently, driving up its price. An increase in the rate of interest should, other things being equal, lead to less borrowing and less spending.

This is the traditional view of the way monetary policy works. Economists are now less willing to accept this view, particularly with respect to the notion that higher interest rates may be a deterrent to spending plans. During 1969 and 1970 interest rates rose to their highest levels in recent history, but without a drastic impact upon forms of spending heretofore believed to be especially sensitive to the rate of interest, particularly investment in plant and equipment and construction outlays. Both leveled off in these years, but did not decline drastically. Although economists are not willing to abandon wholly the traditional view that monetary policy works through the rate of interest and its effect upon spending, there is less certainty than there used to be concerning the strength and dependability of this relationship.

Money Balances

Besides the traditional view that monetary policy works primarily through the rate of interest, there is another and more subtle conception of how the money supply may affect economic activity. This more recent view holds that monetary policy works primarily through its impact on the *money balances* held by spending units.

The money supply and money balances

To carry on normal economic activity, households, business firms, and other spending entities must hold adequate money balances. Presumably, they will establish a normal or customary relationship between their expenditures and their stock of money balances. The size of normal balances depends, among other things, upon the frequency with which people receive money income. The more frequently a person is paid, the smaller, on the average, will be the stock of money balances he must hold to carry out his normal expenditures.

An increase in the money supply will temporarily disturb the normal relationship between money balances and the level of economic activity by increasing this ratio. This leads to more spending as households, firms, and governments seek to restore what they regard as the normal relationship between their holdings of money balances and their expenditure level. On the other hand, a decrease in the money supply resulting from Federal Reserve sale of securities in the open market would depress the ratio of money balances to the general level of economic activity below its normal value. This would lead to a reduction in spending as households, firms, and government units tried to restore what they regarded as a proper ratio. This mechanism is more subtle and, perhaps, less well understood by economists than the view of the rate of interest as the primary link between money and economic activity. Economists like Milton Friedman at the University of Chicago believe money balances may be the most powerful way in which the impact of monetary policy is felt by the economic system.

Income Velocity of the Money Supply

Actions of monetary authorities affecting the money supply may be offset by changes in the velocity of circulation of money. For example, if money is in short supply because of restrictive actions by the central bank, then the users of money will try to get more work out of each unit of money in existence. This means that each dollar will be spent more times per period. For example, the gross national product in current prices grew almost twice as fast as the money supply between 1950 and 1970; thus there had to be a corresponding increase in the turnover rate for each dollar in circulation. On the other hand, a reduction in velocity may offset an increase in the amount of money in circulation, which might nullify central bank action to ease monetary conditions and stimulate economic activity.

A widely used velocity concept is that of the *income velocity* of the money supply, which is the ratio of GNP to the money supply. Figure 9-7 shows income velocity since 1929. Statistical evidence indicates that, in general, the velocity of circulation increases during an economic expansion, while in a period of recession the velocity of money falls. In spite of cyclical fluctuations in the velocity of money, over the long run there has been a decided upward trend.

Ratio of GNP to the money supply

227

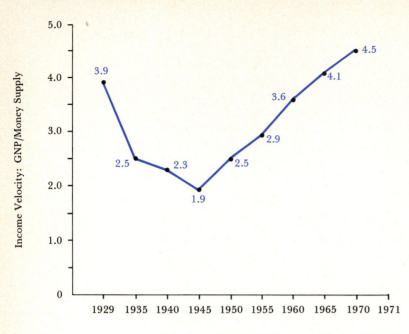

FIGURE 9-7

The Income Velocity of Money: Selected Years, 1929–1970.

Since 1945 there has been a sharp rise in the income velocity of money in the United States, which means that each unit of money is now working harder because it turns over more times in the course of a year. (Source: *Economic Report of the President,* 1972.)

Flexibility and Timing in Monetary Policy

Independence of Federal Reserve

One of the chief advantages claimed for monetary policy relative to fiscal policy is its greater flexibility. The Federal Reserve System can use such actions as open market operations, changes in the discount rate, or variations in reserve requirements to exercise a direct effect on the reserves of the commercial banking system, and through them upon the money supply. The Board of Governors of the Federal Reserve System does not have to go to the Congress for authority to act when it believes that the current economic situation requires action.

In spite of the flexibility of monetary policy, there are other serious problems attached to its use as an instrument of economic stabilization and management. The most important of these relate to timing, the magnitude of action that the Federal Reserve System should take, and various lags inherent in monetary policy.

When to act

The first issue is the question of when to act. The Board of Governors of the Federal Reserve must be able to assess the current state of the economy, including the direction in which events are moving, and decide on this basis whether action is necessary. In effect, the Board of Governors has to judge what the economic situation is likely to be six months or a year hence if no action takes place.

228

A Digression on Economic Forecasting

To understand how such decisions are made, we must consider the art and science of forecasting economic events. Broadly speaking, three approaches to forecasting have evolved in recent years, all of which are used in varying degrees by policy makers in the Federal Reserve and generally by government economists. The first and least formal is to estimate the spending intentions of the key entities whose decisions determine the size of the major spending streams making up the gross national product. This is done by questionnaires to business firms concerning investment plans, by sampling techniques, or by simple observation of recent economic activity. Housing starts (that is, new residential construction), industrial production indices, and inventory changes yield clues to future developments. Using these techniques, economists and statisticians may forecast the size of the gross national product and its key elements for short periods of time, usually no more than a year ahead.

The practice of making an annual forecast of GNP at the beginning of a year is now fairly widespread, not only among governmental bodies but also among private business firms, particularly large companies with staffs of economic analysts. Among the most important of the anticipated spending decisions that enter into this type of forecasting model are those pertaining to investment expenditures by business firms. This is because the theoretical and empirical developments of the last thirty years have demonstrated that fluctuations in investment spending are a key to understanding what is likely to happen in the economic system over the next six to twelve months. Therefore, if we can learn something of the capital spending intentions of business firms, we have a sound basis for predicting the performance of the economic system in the near future.

Another more elaborate and scientific technique is growing in significance; it involves the use of formal *econometric models* of the economic system. An econometric model embraces a set of mathematical relationships that depict the performance of the economy in terms of its crucial parts. These relationships are derived from statistical studies of the actual behavior of the economic system. The variables that enter into the model are those which, in the judgment of the model's designer, represent the key determinants of the level of economic activity. In a technical sense econometric models consist of a series of simultaneous equations, which reflect the underlying, basic relationships that econometricians and theoreticians believe exist in the economic system. As pointed out above, the only way to derive these relationships is through careful study of the behavior of the economy.

Further, and as the term "model" suggests, the series of interrelationships expressed in equations describes how the economy behaves with respect to output, employment, and other key variables such as consumption, investment, and government expenditures. By attaching data appropriate to the current situation to the equations which make up the model, it is possible to forecast the level of gross national product and its major components for intervals extending into the future. It is important to understand that econometric models are largely based upon statistical analysis of recent economic experience. This means that the relationships embodied in a model should not be projected far into the future. Key variables may change with time and changing circumstances, and econometric models must be continually updated.

Leading indicators

A third technique used to forecast the path of the economy for six months or a year hence involves a close examination of the so-called leading indicators. This approach was developed by the National Bureau of Economic Research, a private research body. The National Bureau carefully studied all the variables which fluctuate with the economic system and it developed a list of 78 cyclical indicators, some of which lead fluctuations in the general level of economic activity, some of which coincide with these fluctuations, and some of which lag behind. For immediate and selective use the Bureau specifies a "short list" of indicators: twelve leading indicators, eight that are coincident, and five lagging indicators. Some of the more important leading indicators on this list include new orders for durable goods, new building permits, the length of the work week for production workers in manufacturing, the prices of common stocks, and corporation profits after taxes. Coincident indicators include personal income, industrial production, retail trade, and the unemployment rate. The most important lagging indicators are business expenditures for new plant and equipment, the unemployment rate for persons unemployed fifteen weeks or more, commercial and industrial loans outstanding, and interest rates on short-term business loans. Through a painstaking study of particular statistical time series that have proved over the years to be either leaders, laggers, or coincident, the National Bureau has found certain series that are especially helpful for indicating that a turn in economic activity is likely to take place. Thus, policy makers find the series of leading, lagging, and coincident indicators, now published at regular intervals by the U.S. Department of Commerce, an invaluable tool for forecasting.

Economic forecasting is a science insofar as it relies upon reasonably accurate relationships derived from past experience to predict what is likely to happen in the near future. But it is an art in that much personal judgment and skill enter into it. No wholly scientific basis for forecasting has been established; at this time we have neither a theory to explain how all the variables which determine economic activity are related to one another, nor adequate statistical information on which forecasts may be based.

Further Problems of Monetary Policy

Even though the Federal Reserve authorities may have decided when action is necessary, other problems are involved in the application of monetary policy. Decisions must be made on *how much* and *what kind* of action are needed. The latter usually comes first; the Board of Governors must choose among several alternatives. Should it raise or lower the discount rate? Should it change reserve requirements? Or should it enter the open market and buy (or sell) securities?

If the Board decides to change the discount rate, this indicates that it believes the problem is best resolved by measures affecting the rate of interest; this also means its action is aimed directly at spending. But it must have some notion of the extent to which spending decisions will be affected by a given change in the rate of interest.

Changing the discount rate

Since open market operations, or changes in reserve requirements, directly affect the reserves of the commercial banking system, action in this direction suggests an attempt to influence the behavior of lenders in the first instance. Before acting, the Board ought to have an idea of how large a change in the reserves of the commericial banks is necessary to make an impression on the general level of economic activity. Even given past experience, these are matters of judgment; no precise knowledge exists to tell the Board of Governors the exact change in reserves or rate of interest needed to achieve a particular effect on the performance of the economic system.

Open market operations and changes in reserve requirements

The Time Lag

In addition to questions involving the magnitude of the action, the Federal Reserve authorities must also have some notion of how much time will elapse before spending decisions are affected. Spending decisions, after all, are the ultimate determinants of what happens in the economy. No precise statistical information exists on the exact length of the lag between the application of monetary policy and its full effect upon the economic system, although there seems to be a growing consensus among economists that the impact of Federal Reserve policy is spread over a period of six to twelve months.

Financial Intermediaries

Besides lacking precise information on the magnitude of action required and the length of time before the full effects of any action are felt, those charged with applying monetary policy have other troubles. Since World War II, the economy has seen rapid growth of a variety of new types of financial institutions which lend money. These financial intermediaries include savings and loan associations, insurance companies, personal finance companies, credit unions, and other entities.

Nonbanking institutions

These intermediaries are all engaged in lending activities, but essentially they are nonbanking institutions. Their importance lies in the fact that their activities are to a degree beyond the control of the Federal Reserve, even though they have become an important source of funds for potential borrowers. To the extent that these intermediaries can supply borrowers with funds, even at a time when the Federal Reserve is attempting to reduce spending, monetary policy has lost some of its potency as an instrument for the control of economic activity. As a consequence, we can expect increased pressure from a variety of sources, including the Congress, for legislation involving more control over the activities of financial intermediaries.

Uneven Impact

Still another problem affecting monetary policy is that its ultimate impact upon spenders may be both uneven and unfair. A large corporation often has adequate financial reserves, and thus is not forced to go into the money market to get funds for expansion. On the other hand, the small firm has fewer internal financing resources, and must depend upon bank credit for some of its operations. Consequently, in a period of tight money, the pressure of monetary policy may be felt most acutely by small business, leaving large corporations relatively unaffected by central bank policies. Since the spending decisions of large corporations generally have more impact on the economy than those of small businesses, some of the effectiveness of monetary policy has been lost. Industrial concentration—the tendency for industries to be dominated by a handful of large firms—may also be furthered under these circumstances.

Economists have long recognized that different investment expenditures differ significantly in their sensitivity to a change in the rate of interest. For example, expenditures for buildings, including residential housing, are believed to be much more sensitive to a change in the rate of interest than are business expenditures for inventories, or even new equipment. Thus, a stringent monetary policy which leads to a sharp rise in the rate of interest affects investment spending unevenly. Whether such uneven effects are desirable from the standpoint of a social policy is a matter of key importance.

Recent Criticisms of Monetary Policy

The problem of the timing and magnitude of monetary policy is so difficult that some critics now believe that often the action of the Federal Reserve will be destabilizing rather than stabilizing. Essentially, economists critical of discretionary action by the central bank argue that because we lack sufficient knowledge of both the timing and the impact of action, it would be better if there were no discretionary policy actions. Rather, the basic policy of the Federal Reserve should be to make certain that the money supply grows at a reasonably consistent rate, that is, the amount of annual increase necessary to maintain a growing economy. The economic reasoning behind this proposal is that the money supply is more influential in the determination of output than any other single variable. Given the inadequacy of the Federal Reserve forecasts, the best thing the central bank can do to promote stability in output, employment, the price level, and the rate of economic growth is to allow the money supply to grow at a constant rate.

Discretionary vs. automatic increases in the money supply

The foregoing views stem largely from the research of Professor Milton Friedman, a leading critic of discretionary monetary action by the Federal Reserve. In monumental empirical and historical research into the relationship between money and the level of economic activity Friedman has documented statistically his view that the most effective thing the Federal Reserve can do is fix an automatic rate of increase in the money supply at roughly 4 percent per year. Professor Friedman sees in his studies a strong correlation between the growth of the money supply and the national output, and feels that discretionary action has more often been destabilizing than stabilizing. Therefore, the best way to get stability in the economy is to get stability in the growth of the money supply, something that the Federal Reserve could do if willing.

The Friedman view: pro and con

Critics of the Friedman position stress two major points. First, the argument for a constant rate of increase in the money supply is, in their judgment, a form of wishful thinking resting on the false hope that we can thus avoid the hard necessity of dealing realistically and forcefully with the behavior of the economic system. Since there is nothing automatic in the functioning of the modern economy, effective performance in output, employment,

233

the price level, and the rate of economic growth requires active management. Furthermore, meaningful management demands an active fiscal and monetary policy; responsibility cannot be avoided by resorting to an arbitrary rule such as Professor Friedman proposes. Second, critics of this position declare that the evidence of a close relationship between the money supply and the level of economic activity is vitiated to some degree because research has neglected the impact of changes in velocity. Changes in velocity could be a powerful factor operating to offset any automatic increase in the money supply at a constant rate. There may be more stability of velocity in the long run than in the short run, as suggested by the findings of Professor Friedman, but the evidence for the short run suggests that the velocity of circulation is highly unstable. Keep in mind that the long run is a consequence of decisions and events which are made and take place within a short-term context. Thus it would be unwise to ignore short-term changes in velocity and rely only on a presumed long-term relationship between the money supply and the general level of economic activity.

Now that we have examined the principles of modern fiscal and monetary policy, let us turn to a discussion of their workings in the last ten to twelve years. The period since 1960 offers a kind of grand laboratory experiment in the application of modern fiscal and monetary techniques, as not only has there been a variety of problems—ranging from stagnation and unemployment through war and inflation—but three administrations have had an opportunity to try out their ideas on the proper role of these two policy instruments in the modern economy.

Fiscal Policy in the 1960s

Although economists have understood since the 1930s how government expenditures and taxes affect aggregate demand, not until the 1960s was an administration in Washington persuaded to take an aggressive stand in favor of fiscal action to influence the economy's performance. Before the 1960s, it is true, there were occasional actions with respect to both expenditures and taxes which had desirable effects upon the economic system. But favorable results were more often than not an accidental outcome of changes made for other reasons.

President John F. Kennedy's administration was the first to accept fully the fundamental idea of modern fiscal policy: that the federal budget ought to be managed in a manner calculated to have a direct influence on economic activity. The individual most responsible for persuading the Kennedy administration to embrace this modern theoretical view was Professor Walter Heller of the University of Minnesota, who served as Chairman of the Council of Economic Advisers from 1960 to 1965. When the Kennedy administration came into office in 1961 the unemployment rate was excessively high (more than 6 percent) and the economy was not growing rapidly enough to utilize its full potential. One of the first actions of the Council of Economic Advisers was to develop impressive statistical evidence showing the gap between the growth of the economy's potential for output and its actual output. This gap had existed since the mid-1950s and had grown progressively larger. Figure 9-8 shows the close relationship between unemployment rates and the gap between actual and potential output for the period 1955–1961.

The problem confronting the Kennedy Council of Economic Advisers was to explain the sluggish behavior of the economy since the mid-1950s. In a brilliant piece of economic analysis, the Council concluded that the structure of the federal tax system was

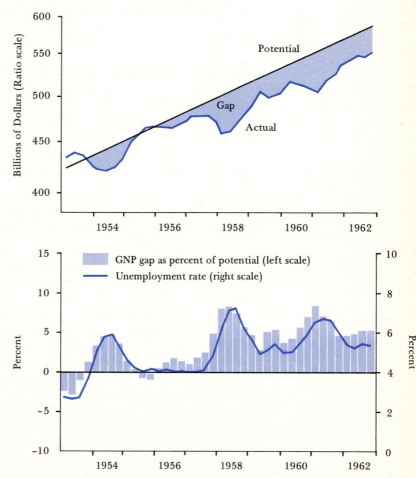

FIGURE 9-8
Gross National Product, Actual and Potential, and Unemployment Rate.

This figure gives a striking graphic presentation of the "gap" hypothesis, which asserts that from 1955 onward there was a growing gap between the economy's actual output and its potential output. This analysis was the basis for the most important economic policy developments in the first years of the Kennedy administration. (Source: *Economic Report of the President,* 1963.)

the main source of trouble, primarily because as the economy approached full employment, the tax system automatically tended to generate a large budgetary surplus, thus creating a "fiscal drag" which slowed the pace of economic activity. From their analysis the Council developed the notion of a full employment budget surplus, an important concept discussed earlier in this chapter. (Review Figure 9-6 and discussion on p. 218.) According to the Council's reasoning, the emerging full employment surplus acted as a brake on expansion because offsetting increases in private investment were insufficient to push the economy to full employment. To resolve this dilemma the Council proposed major reductions in the rates for personal and corporate income taxes. The proposal was a bold one for that time because the federal government in 1961 already had a budgetary deficit and to call for a tax reduction on top of an existing deficit when the economy was not in a severe recession was contrary to the conventional wisdom of the era.

The Tax Cut of 1964

The Council, through the Administration, pressed all during 1962 and 1963 for a massive tax cut to eliminate the gap between actual and potential output. Not until 1964, following the assassination of President Kennedy, did Congress finally enact a tax cut, which in total amounted to $11 billion. Of this figure about $8.5 billion went for a cut in personal income taxes, the balance going to corporate income tax. In explaining the rationale of the tax cut, the Council showed how the resulting increase in disposable income would stimulate output and employment through its impact on the spending stream, especially on consumer spending. The Council stated that each dollar added to disposable income by the tax reduction would lead to further spending of about 92 cents. Research by the Council discovered that the multiplier effect applicable to the initial increase in spending resulting from the tax cut was approximately two. Consequently, the ultimate effect of a tax reduction of about $8.5 billion on personal incomes would be to increase consumer spending by about $16 billion. Besides these immediate effects, the additional output generated by the tax cut normally would induce more investment spending. This plus the expected increase in consumption spending would, it was hoped, eliminate most of the gap between actual and potential output. In its *Annual Report* issued in January 1966, the Council reviewed the effects of the 1964 tax cut and concluded that by December 1965 the overall impact of the tax cut amounted to $30 billion, a figure close to the estimated amount needed to close the gap between potential and actual output. By the end of 1965 the unemployment rate was approaching 4 percent, the target of the Council's policies during the early 1960s.

The New Economics

For advocates of fiscal policy, the 1964 tax cut was a watershed event. It demonstrated conclusively the effectiveness of fiscal action as a means of achieving full employment and a satisfactory rate of economic growth. The 1964 experience was regarded as proof of the public acceptance at last of Keynesian ideas born out of the Great Depression of the 1930s. The period from 1960 to 1965 in which Heller and economists of similar views had key roles in the formulation of economic policy is often described as an era of triumph for the "new economics," meaning that the leaders in the administration and Congress approved two basically Keynesian ideas: that the level of aggregate demand is the key to influencing the level of economic activity, and that fiscal measures are the most potent instrument for influencing the level of aggregate demand. But the extent to which there had been political acceptance of fiscal policy as an effective economic instrument was overstated. In 1966–1967 the administration and Congress were extremely reluctant to raise taxes to combat inflation, even though such a course was strongly recommended by professional economists. (See p. 223.)

The application of Keynesian economics

Proponents of monetary policy, especially those influenced by the ideas and careful research of Professor Friedman, have challenged the contention of the "new economists" that fiscal policy was *primarily* responsible for the expansion that began approximately in 1961 and carried the economy to full employment by the end of 1965. These critics not only challenge the claim that the 1964 tax cut was a spectacular success, but also the basic idea behind it, namely that fiscal measures are the most significant way to influence the level of total spending. We shall shortly examine further the current conflict between "fiscalists" and "monetarists" with respect to economic stabilization and public policy.

The Surtax of 1968

A second major experiment with fiscal policy took place in 1968. In response to inflationary pressures and the overheated state of the economy engendered by the rapid growth of government expenditures after escalation of the Vietnam war in 1966, the Johnson administration advocated and the Congress finally acquiesced in the passage of a 10 percent surtax. The law specified that the rate would drop to 5 percent on January 1, 1970 and the entire tax would expire in mid-1970. Congress also imposed mandatory reductions on government expenditures for the 1969 fiscal year.

The surtax, which applied to individuals and corporations, plus the expenditure cuts, were expected to convert a budget deficit of $11.9 billion in fiscal 1968 to a surplus by the close of fiscal

237

1969, thereby substantially reducing the expansionary pressures at work in the economic system. Fiscal 1969 did end with a surplus of $4.6 billion. The response of the economic system to the fiscal measures taken in June 1968 was not nearly so rapid nor so obvious as the response to the 1964 tax cut. Throughout the second half of 1968 and all of 1969 real output expanded without any significant reduction in the rate of increase in the general price level.

The slow response of inflationary pressures to anti-inflationary fiscal brakes suggests that the problem of managing a high employment economy without inflation is more complex than previously thought. A study concluded in 1971 by Arthur M. Okun, last Chairman of the Council of Economic Advisers under President Johnson, concluded that the surtax did reduce inflationary pressures in 1968–1970, but the impact on consumer spending was not strong enough to end the inflation. Other economists have suggested that consumers were fully aware of the temporary nature of the tax; hence they reduced their savings rather than consumption expenditures when confronted with a decline in disposable income. Saving as a percent of disposable income did decline in both 1968 and 1969, as compared to 1967, and rose again in 1970, thus lending some credence to this view.

The Recent Record of Monetary Policy

As we have observed, no national administration before the Kennedy administration had accepted the basic theoretical tenets of modern fiscal policy. This was not the situation with monetary policy. The Board of Governors of the Federal Reserve has for many years both understood the theoretical basis for monetary policy and been willing to apply this theory to the management of the economic system.

Results of restrictive policy, 1951–1962

There are some clearly discernible trends in the application of monetary policy over the past two decades. First, policy in the eleven-year period from 1951 through 1962 was clearly restrictive, as the dominant concern during the era was inflation; the Board of Governors of the Federal Reserve appeared determined to keep inflationary pressures under control by permitting relatively slow growth in the money supply. For this period the money supply grew at an annual average rate of approximately 1.7 percent. In 1953 there was a very sharp reduction in the rate of growth of the money supply over the preceding year and in 1957 and 1960 the money supply in absolute amount actually decreased. The sharp reduction in 1953 was followed by a recession in 1954, as the reduction in 1957 was by a recession in 1958. The 1960 reduction apparently did not trigger a recession the next year, although the real rate of growth in 1961 slowed perceptibly from what it had been the prior year. Critics of Federal Reserve policy in the 1950s assert that it was a major factor in bringing about the sluggishness of the economy that became evident after 1955. Money supply statistics for this period offer some support for the argument that there does appear to be a close correlation between the slow rate of growth in the money supply and the slow rate of growth of the economy.

Economic Policy in the Nixon Administration

The second significant fact is the distinct shift in monetary policy after 1962; beginning in 1963 the rate of growth of the money supply accelerated sharply. For the six-year period from 1963 to 1968 the average annual rate of growth in the money supply was 4.6 percent, a figure almost three times greater than the average during the earlier eleven-year period. Each year during this time the rate of growth in the money supply accelerated, except for 1966, when there was a sharp contraction in the money supply during the first half of the year. It is also important to note that beginning in 1967, precisely when the Johnson administration became increasingly concerned with the necessity for cooling off the economic system because of the inflationary impact of the Vietnam war, the rate of growth of the money supply (currency plus demand deposits) reached a level higher than at any time since the 1950s, namely a rate of expansion of 6.6 percent in 1967 and 7.8 percent in 1968.

Results of expansionary policy, 1963–1968

Not until late in 1968 did the Federal Reserve begin to apply the monetary brakes and slow down the rate of monetary expansion. In 1969 money grew by 3.1 percent, but the rate jumped again to 5.4 percent in 1970. Money expansion in 1967 and 1968 in combination with the widely recognized lag in the impact of monetary policy on spending decision may help account for the slow response of the economy during 1968 and early 1969 to both the fiscal and monetary measures taken to control the inflationary pressures. During the first half of 1971 there was again a sharp expansion in the money supply, the annual rate of increase in the first six months of the year being over 10 percent. But in the last half of 1971 the money supply remained virtually unchanged, followed by another sharp expansion in the first quarter of 1972.

Applying and easing the monetary brakes, 1968–1972

Economic Policy in the Nixon Administration

When the Nixon administration assumed office early in 1969 the first priority for the domestic economy was to bring inflation under control. Ever since the escalation of the Vietnam war in 1966, the price indices had been rising at an ever-increasing rate.

Employment was not the problem, for in 1968 the unemployment rate was down to 3.6 percent of the civilian labor force, the lowest level since 1953. But consumer prices rose in 1968 by 4.2 percent, with every indication that the rate of increase would be even higher in 1969. This turned out to be the case, for in 1969 the consumer price index rose by 5.4 percent.

President Nixon named a University of Michigan economist, Paul W. McCracken, to be Chairman of the Council of Economic Advisers. McCracken, who had been a Council member in the Eisenhower administration, was charged with the delicate task of bringing down the inflation rate without causing an unacceptable increase in the unemployment rate. As our earlier discussion of the Phillips Curve (p. 211) inidcates, this kind of trade-off is not easy to bring about.

The Nixon "Game Plan"

Gradualist approach

Early in 1969 the Council of Economic Advisers put together what the press later began to call the Nixon "game plan" for inflation control. McCracken committed the administration to a gradualist approach which would attempt to cool off the economy enough to break or dampen the inflationary psychology which three years of sharply rising prices had engendered, but not cool it abruptly enough to cause unemployment and a recession. Basically, the Council expected to achieve this by slowing down the rate of growth in both federal expenditures for goods and services and the money supply. In both cases they were successful; federal government expenditures for goods and services dropped from an annual rate of increase of 9.7 percent in 1968 to only 1.8 percent in 1969, and the rate of growth in the money supply (currency plus demand deposits) slowed from an annual rate of 7.8 percent in 1968 to 3.1 percent in 1969. The latter was below the approximate 4 percent annual rate of money growth that monetarists regard as desirable.

In addition to what it regarded as the gradualist approach inherent in these measures, for nearly its first two years the administration firmly rejected any incomes policy. We shall explore fully in Chapter 10 the meaning of an incomes policy, but, essentially, such a policy is concerned with controlling rates of increase in money incomes to ease strong pressures on the price level. At his first press conference President Nixon expressly rejected an incomes policy for his administration, especially the tactic of "jawboning," the somewhat derisive term given to presidential exhortations to labor and management to hold down both wages and prices because of inflation. Specifically, the President said:

I do not go along with the suggestion that inflation can be effectively controlled by exhorting labor and management to follow certain guidelines. I think that is a very laudable objective for labor and management to follow. But I think I am aware of the fact that leaders of labor and the leaders of management, much as they personally want to do what is in the best interests of the nation, have to be guided by the interests of the organization they represent.

So the primary responsibility for controlling inflation rests with the national administration and its handling of fiscal and monetary affairs.

In 1969 the administration took a lukewarm attitude toward retention of the surtax, due to be reduced from 10 to 5 percent on January 1, 1970 and to expire altogether in mid-1970. By the end of 1969 the administration had decided not to ask Congress for an extension of the surtax. Critics of the administration's approach to inflation control believe that the rejection of any form of an incomes policy in 1969 and the failure to press for retention of the surtax were serious mistakes.

Given the normal lags between the initiation of economic policy and anticipated results, 1970 became the decisive test year for the success of the Nixon administration game plan. By the end of the year it was clear that the game plan had failed. Setbacks for the administration in the 1970 elections confirmed the economic impact of this failure on voter behavior. Unemployment rose from the 3.5 percent rate of 1969 to a rate of 6.2 percent at the end of 1970. When 1970 began there were 3.1 million persons without jobs; by December, the jobless total had jumped to 5.1 million people. During 1970 the consumer price index rose by another 5.9 percent, a higher rate than in either 1969 or 1968. The unhappy outcome of the game plan has been dubbed "stagflation," an unlovely term for a combination of stagnation and unemployment with continued inflation.

Failure of the game plan

From Gradualism to Activism

As 1971 began it was clear to most observers that the administration game plan was being junked, although obviously there was no public pronouncement to this effect. What was not so obvious was the shape economic policy would take during the final two years of President Nixon's first term. Early in 1971 it appeared that the administration had decided to concentrate on expanding output and reducing unemployment, even given the risk that this would usher in a new cycle of inflationary pressures. Several developments pointed in this direction. In its 1971 *Annual Report,* the Council of Economic Advisers forecast that the GNP would reach a level of $1,065 billion (in current prices) during the year,

241

a rate of advance that, if continued, would bring the unemployment rate down to about 4.5 percent by mid-1972. The Council also forecast that by then the inflation rate would be in the 3 percent range. Actual GNP reached $1,046.8 billion in 1971 and all prices rose by 4.6 percent as measured by the GNP deflater.

Two important comments by the President lent support to the view that the administration was now committed to an activist policy of economic stimulation. The first was his statement to a newsman following a television interview that "I am a Keynesian," which implied his willingness to use fiscal measures vigorously to stimulate the economy. The second was his strong endorsement in his budget and economic messages to the Congress of the concept of the full employment budget, a topic we explored earlier (pp. 218–219).

Non-intervention

By mid-1971, though, it was becoming clear that the shift from gradualism toward activism, designed to reduce the unemployment rate even at the cost of rekindling inflationary fires, was more apparent than real. At the end of June, just as it became evident that the federal deficit for the 1971 fiscal year would be in excess of $23 billion, the President announced that Secretary of the Treasury John Connally would henceforth be the "chief economic spokesman" for his administration. This announcement, with its implied downgrading of the influence of McCracken within the administration, was followed by a statement by Secretary Connally that the Nixon administration would not institute a wage-price review board, impose mandatory wage-price controls, ask the Congress for any tax cuts to stimulate the economy, or increase federal spending as a stimulant. This statement represented an astonishing 180-degree turn from the activist policy position that the Nixon administration had been groping toward since early 1971. Even more astonishing was the Secretary's statement that the notion of a 4 percent unemployment rate as a desirable norm—a workable and pragmatic measure of full employment— was ". . . a myth; it has never happened . . . save in wartime, not in the last quarter of a century." Through this statement, the Nixon administration became the first national administration in the post-World War II era to cast doubt upon the policy objective of full employment inherent in the Employment Act of 1946. Secretary Connally's statement was followed a few days later by a frank admission from Chairman McCracken that the goal set in January for a GNP in 1971 of $1,065 billion was beyond reach without fiscal stimulus of a magnitude that would unleash anew the inflationary pressures which had lessened slightly during the first half of 1971. McCracken's statement indicated, too, that the goal of a 4.5 percent unemployment rate and a 3 percent inflation rate by mid-1972 were now beyond reach, as they were tied into the forecast of a $1,065 billion GNP for 1971.

This non-interventionist position was extremely short-lived, for in a dramatic announcement on August 15 the President established a new economic policy. Not only did he move to a complete wage-price freeze (for more details, see Chapter 10), but stated that he would ask the Congress for tax cuts to stimulate the economy. These would take the form of a revival of the investment tax credit, the elimination of excise taxes on automobiles, and an acceleration in the already scheduled increases in personal exemptions under the income tax. The President also devalued the dollar and imposed a 10 percent surtax on imports, a move that aroused fears of a return to protectionism (see Chapter 17).

This sudden shift from the non-interventionist position taken in late June was largely accounted for by the continuing lethargy of the recovery and the drastic worsening of the nation's export-import balance. Unemployment hovered around 6 percent through June and July, while only moderate progress was made in the struggle to bring the price level under control. Most non-administration observers felt that the really pressing problem was the continued inflation, hence the drastic expedient of a wage-price freeze. The fear of potential inflation later in the year was sharply enhanced when it became known that the Federal deficits for the two fiscal years ending June 30, 1972 might range as high as $45 billion, deficits far larger than recorded in any two-year period since the end of World War II. The most recent figures place the overall federal deficit for this period at $61.8 billion. Moreover, Milton Friedman had sounded warnings that the expansion of the money supply during the first six months of 1971 at an annual rate in excess of 10 percent would generate strong inflationary pressures six to nine months later. The overall impact of these developments made the administration realize that some domestic action was called for if the deteriorating trends in both the domestic economy and our international economic relations were to be improved. Hence, the New Economic Policy.

To implement the New Economic Policy the administration established a Pay Board and a Price Commission, and asked the Congress to approve an investment tax credit, eliminate the excise tax on automobiles, and provide relief for the individual taxpayer by speeding up the increases in the personal exemption and standard deduction which were scheduled to go into effect in 1973. Authority for establishing the Pay Board and the Price Commission came from the Economic Stabilization Act, which was extended in the fall of 1971 for an additional two years. The Pay Board consisted of five members each from labor, business, and the public, but the Price Commission was composed of seven members, all of whom were to represent the public. Labor's representatives left the Pay Board in March 1972, following a break with the administration over appropriate rates of increase for

The New Economic Policy

Pay Board and Price Commission

243

wages under the New Economic Policy. The general guidelines followed by the Pay Board and the Price Commission were 5.5 percent per year for wage increases and 2.5 percent per year for price increases. The new policy was introduced with a 90-day wage-price freeze, followed by Phase II, in which the original stringency of wage and price control was somewhat relaxed.

How successful has the new economic policy been? The results are mixed. During the last four months of 1971 there was a definite slowdown in the inflation rate, both as reflected in the consumer price index and the price deflator for the gross national product. The first four months of 1972 saw some resurgence of price level pressure, especially for the gross national product deflator, which increased at an annual rate of more than 5 percent. This was countered, though, by a sharp increase in real gross national product in the first quarter of 1972, up by more than 5 percent at annual rates over the last quarter of 1971. The unemployment rate remained stubbornly resistant to the policy changes, for it averaged 5.9 percent during the first four months of 1972, the same as in 1971. It was apparent by mid-1972 that the economy was again on the move, but the new economic policy had not succeeded in ending the inflationary threat nor in bringing the unemployment rate down to a satisfactory level.

Fiscal versus Monetary Policy

Our review of recent American experience with fiscal and monetary policy suggests two things. First, it indicates a growing acceptance by the government of the idea that fiscal and monetary measures ought to be used vigorously to promote a satisfactory level of employment, stability of prices, and an adequate rate of economic growth. Second, it shows that neither professional economists nor those responsible for the execution of public policy agree completely on the relative desirability and effectiveness of different types of policy measures.

In spite of current controversy and some disagreement among economic theorists over the relative merits of different policy measures, there is agreement on one fundamental point: *total* spending is the short-run key to the size of output, the level of employment, the stability of the price level, and even the rate of economic growth. From this it logically follows that the way to influence the performance of the economy is through measures which touch upon spending decisions and thereby affect the total spending in the economic system. Public policy, to be effective, must have an impact upon aggregate demand.

Then what is the status of specific policy measures? Basically, economists understand how the elements which enter into the fiscal or monetary policy categories may influence spending in the economic system, but they are unsure of the exact quantitative dimension to be given to these policy measures. For example, with respect to fiscal policy it is quite clear that taxes affect consumer spending because they influence disposable income. The same is true for the transfer expenditures made by governments. Economists agree on the direction of this impact, but they cannot predict the precise quantitative effects of a given change in taxes or transfers. Government purchases of goods and services pose a similar problem. Government spending is obviously an important part of aggregate demand. When such expenditures change, aggregate demand also changes, but uncertainties arise once we pass beyond the initial effect of a specific change. We cannot anticipate the exact value of the multiplier under a particular set of circumstances.

There is general agreement among economists that a change in the money supply will have some impact upon the decisions lenders make, which, in turn, will influence spending. But as with fiscal measures, policy makers lack the quantitative knowledge to predict exactly what will take place with any given change in the money supply.

Still unresolved are some fundamental theoretical questions concerning the relative effectiveness of fiscal versus monetary measures. On this point there exists a basic division in point of view, which probably will not be reconciled without much more empirical research and more experience in the application of both fiscal and monetary policy. The prevailing view since 1960, essentially Keynesian, holds that the most effective way to manage the modern economic system is by mixing fiscal and monetary policy with the greater emphasis upon fiscal policy. The proponents of this view tend to favor changes in tax rates as the best and most flexible instruments of economic policy.

Spokesmen for the alternative monetarist viewpoint argue that there is little empirical evidence to support the claim that fiscal measures in particular are the most effective way to manage a modern economic system. On the contrary, modern monetary theorists are strong advocates of the straightforward proposition that the money supply is the most important single determinant of the level of the economic activity. Thus, total spending and with it the performance of the economic system, are best influenced by controlling the supply of money. Further, modern monetary theorists are critical of monetary policy as currently practiced by managers of the central banking system in the United States. They do not believe that forecasts can be sufficiently accurate to provide a basis for current short-term policy decisions involving change in the money supply. Rather, they prefer to have

The Keynesian view

The monetarist view

the money supply expand at some reasonably stable annual rate. This, they believe, would result in sufficient spending to keep the rate of expansion of real output in a satisfactory relationship to the advance in productive capacity. In sum, monetary theorists are critical of the notion that active management of the economy is necessary, and they are dubious of the effectiveness of traditional fiscal policy, not to mention the techniques of monetary management characteristic in the past of the Board of Governors of the Federal Reserve System.

Essentially, the monetarists operate on the premise that the economy is inherently stable; hence its effective management does not require continuous and close attention. The Keynesian school continues to dispute this, adhering to the belief that a market economy is inherently unstable, and, consequently, should be controlled by active and vigorous management. Which view will ultimately prove to be correct cannot be determined now, but must await the results of further research, empirical testing, and experimentation.

Questions for Review and Discussion

1. What are the four most important objectives of public policy pertaining to the overall performance of the economic system? Which of these objectives are set forth either explicitly or implicitly in the Employment Act of 1946?

2. Why may there be a conflict between goals, giving rise to a "trade-off" problem? Explain how the Phillips curve illustrates this point.

3. What is meant by the term "fiscal policy"? What are the instruments of fiscal policy in the modern economy?

4. How does a full employment budget work? What is the relationship between a full employment budget surplus and a fiscal dividend?

5. Give some reasons why a cut in taxes might be preferable to an increase in government expenditures for goods and services as a stimulus to the economy. Give reasons for the opposite approach, namely an increase in government expenditures rather than a tax cut.

6. What are the major limitations policy makers are likely to encounter in the application of fiscal measures, both to stimulate and to restrain the economy?

7. Why do most economists believe that the idea of an annually balanced budget for the federal government is obsolete?

8. What is meant by "built-in flexibility"?

9. Explain the term "monetary policy." What are the instruments of monetary policy in the modern economy?

10. Contrast the role played by the Congress in the implementation of a fiscal policy with its activities in respect to monetary policy.

11. Explain the role of money balances in determining the effect that changes in the money supply may have on the level of economic activity.

12. Review the most important fiscal and monetary developments during the 1960s and the Nixon administration's first term. What decisions were of special significance?

10

The Impact of Incomes Policy and the Public Debt

WE HAVE JUST CONCLUDED detailed examination of fiscal and monetary policy, the two most important policy instruments available for management of the modern, mixed economic system. But this is not the whole story. Increasingly the federal government has discovered that attainment of the production and employment goals implied in the Employment Act of 1946 brings in its wake new problems, for which appropriate policy measures must be devised. Two of these are incomes policy and debt management, and we shall now consider these policy areas and their relation to management of the national economy.

Incomes Policy

One of the most acute problems of all advanced economies since World War II has been the tendency for prices to rise sharply as the economy approaches full employment. This conflict between price stability and full employment is, as we saw earlier, nicely dramatized in the device of the Phillips Curve, which shows the trade-off that may exist between inflation and employment. To cope with this problem, modern nations have had to develop new policy approaches, generally known as "incomes policy" or "income and wage policy." The theoretical basis for these new policy approaches to money income in an economy nearing full employment is not nearly as well developed as the theoretical basis for contemporary monetary and fiscal policy.

In a broad sense, an incomes policy deals with the question of how rapidly money income in all forms (wages and salaries, rents, interest, and profits) may advance in an economy with full or nearly full employment. The need for an incomes policy arose out of the realization that a genuine conflict exists between full employment and price level stability. Incomes policy is concerned with the crucial problem of maintaining full employment without inflationary pressure. Its goal is to establish conditions under which money incomes can advance without creating intolerable inflationary pressures in the form of rising production costs.

Changes in all forms of money income

The theoretical basis for an incomes policy is that, in the aggregate, incomes received by persons who supply resources to the economic process are costs of production for the firms which produce the national output. Consequently, the rate at which money incomes increase in a growing economy will affect production costs and, ultimately, the general level of prices. Thus an incomes policy must be rooted in microeconomics, or analysis of individual firm, industry, and consumer behavior. It must rest upon an understanding of the relationship between production costs, payments made to the suppliers of economic resources, and the effect of these factors on the price at which various amounts of output will be produced. Incomes policy requires knowledge of the significant links between the economics of the individual firm, the market structure of which the firm is a part, and the aggregate performance of the economic system.

Theoretical basis of incomes policy

Wage-Price Guideposts

The United States made its first serious attempts to develop a national incomes policy in 1962, when the Council of Economic Advisers in its *Annual Report* set forth a series of guideposts for noninflationary wage and price behavior. The guideposts were intended to stipulate the conditions under which wage and other money incomes could rise without causing increases in unit labor costs that would put inflationary pressure on the economic system. In this landmark 1962 *Annual Report* the Council first analyzed the problem of the growing gap between the economy's potential for output and its actual output. The Council foresaw the possibility that if measures taken to eliminate the gap were successful, strong pressures would be put on the price level as the economy approached full employment. The national interest required development of a policy setting the rate at which wages and other money incomes might advance without being inflationary. In developing this policy, the Council argued that in peacetime mandatory controls over wage and price decisions were neither desirable nor practical in the market-oriented economic system of the United States. Nevertheless, the Council asserted that employees and employers who have discretionary power with respect to price, wage, and other income decisions should realize that the national interest is involved in their decisions. This being the case, the government should set up guideposts to help hold price, wage, and other income adjustments to non-inflationary levels.

The Nature of the Guideposts

In essence, the Council asserted that if wage and other increases in money incomes are to be non-inflationary, they should, on the average, be no greater than the average gain in productivity for the economy as a whole. If all increases in money incomes are held within this limit, factor costs per unit of output for the economy as a whole should be stabilized, eliminating any inherent market forces tending toward a general increase in the price level. The economic rationale for this policy rested partly upon the assumption that, under competitive market conditions, prices tend to equal unit production costs. In its discussion the Council of Economic Advisers heavily stressed increases in money wage rates. Since wage and salary payments account for 65 to 70 percent of the national income, adherence to the guideposts for wage adjustments would do the most good in keeping total unit costs on a noninflationary basis. It can readily be generalized that this policy implies that all forms of money income ought not to advance any faster than the average gain in productivity for the entire economy. The policy as set forth by the Council applied to the economy as a whole, not necessarily to each individual industry.

As we shall see, the Council suggested appropriate adjustments for individual industries, if their condition varied from the conditions prevailing in the economy as a whole. In a practical sense the guidepost policy meant that prices might be stabilized, while money incomes advanced at the same rate at which productivity (output per man-hour) was increasing. This was thought to be between 3½ and 4 percent per year. In a broader sense, the wage-price guidepost policy amounted to a recommendation that the society ought to participate in the benefits of improved productivity through higher money incomes rather than through stabilized money incomes and falling prices. Perhaps the Council merely recognized a fact of modern economic life: that prices and costs generally tend to be flexible upwards, but are most inflexible toward any downward movement. Consequently, the practical way to translate advances in productivity into improved economic well-being is by permitting all forms of money income to rise at the same rate at which output per man-hour is rising. This approach is fraught with difficulties, but the underlying economic reasoning is valid.

The Rate of Productivity

When it explained this policy in the 1962 *Report,* the Council proposed using the overall trend of productivity increases as a guide for action. However, economists and statisticians recognize *Adjusting for* that the rate at which productivity may advance varies widely *uneven changes* from industry to industry. It also changes erratically from year to year. Thus the Council had to meet the possibility that in some industries productivity would increase more rapidly than in the economy as a whole and in other industries it would move less rapidly.

As a general guide, the Council stated that if the rate of productivity change for an industry exceeded the average for the economy as a whole, unit labor costs in that industry would decline, and hence the appropriate action in that industry would be a decline in prices. On the other hand, if productivity in an industry rose less rapidly than the average for the economy as a whole, unit labor costs would increase, and therefore prices should rise. If there were no major shifts in demand, the price increase in an industry with a slower rate of productivity increase should lead to a reduction in quantity demanded, whereas the industry whose prices declined because of its higher rate of growth in productivity should see some increase in quantity of its output demanded. Thus, the relative change in prices in industries with differential rates of change in productivity would bring about a corresponding shift in quantity demanded and resources used. This would reflect the fact that the one industry is relatively more efficient than the other. Other things being equal, we should expect the price mechanism to operate like this. Beyond this, the Council stipulated certain special conditions that might provide for some exceptions to the guideposts; these were related primarily to a special need to attract labor or capital to a particular industry.

Validity of the Guideposts

Guideposts and
the distribution
of national income

We cannot say categorically whether the wage-price guideposts policy as originally stated in 1962 was sound. It is difficult to fault the arithmetic of the guideposts as a mechanism for keeping increases in money income within non-inflationary bounds. Given the existing distribution of the national income between wage and non-wage income, if all money incomes rise at an annual rate no greater than the average annual increase in productivity, the results would be non-inflationary. This is so because any increase in the costs to the producer of obtaining economic resources would be offset by stepped-up production. Further, the guideposts would not alter the existing distribution of the national income between wage payments and nonwage income such as rents, interest, and profits. The policy presumes that the economy starts with an acceptable distribution of the national income, for nothing in the guideposts policy will lead to a different—and possibly fairer—division of the national income between wage and nonwage or property income.

The correlation between productivity trends in an industry and the price adjustments that take place within the industry has been substantiated by some important statistical evidence. Figure 10-1, taken from a *Report* of the Council of Economic Advisers,

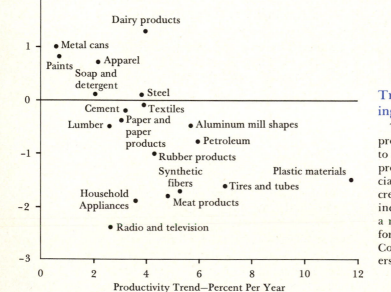

Figure 10-1

Price and Productivity Trends in 19 Manufacturing Industries.

The correlation between productivity and prices ought to show that a high rate of productivity gain is associated with either price decreases or a low rate of price increase. These data provide a rough statistical verification for the hypothesis. (Source: Council of Economic Advisers, 1965.)

shows a close correlation between price increases or decreases and productivity trends characteristic of some 19 different manufacturing industries for the period 1959–1964. In general, the figure shows that the industries with the highest rate of productivity increase in the period were also the industries which experienced a downward trend in the prices for their commodities. On the other hand, the industries with a low rate of increase in productivity had price increases. These data lend statistical support to the Council's recommendation on how industries should act with respect to price changes if their rate of change in productivity departs significantly from the average for the economy.

Effect of the Guideposts on Personal Income

We have observed that the guideposts policy provides only for price stability, not for an overall decrease in the general price level. This presents no problem for persons and groups in the economy who can increase their money incomes at the same rate at which productivity is rising. But it is a hardship for those whose incomes are fixed, particularly retired persons and others who derive their incomes primarily from transfer payments. Theoretically, of course, the society can make compensating adjustments in the money incomes of these people, and unless some such compensation is made, a successful guideposts policy, over a long period of time, would bring about a systematic shift in the distribution of income away from those whose incomes are relatively fixed toward those whose incomes are variable. If the fixed income population is largely composed of the aged, the disabled, and others outside the work force, many of whom are poor, this means that the society would achieve price level stability at the expense of those least able to participate effectively in the economic process. Successful implementation of a guideposts policy must therefore provide for reasonable periodic adjustments in the money incomes of this segment of the population so that its economic position will not worsen relative to other groups.

Hardship on fixed incomes

Incomes Policy in the 1960s

Analysis of the economy's performance between 1961 and 1965 indicates that wage advances were generally kept within the boundaries established by the guideposts policy. In this period the unemployment rate was significantly reduced from the high levels of the end of the 1950s. In its 1969 *Report,* the Council of Economic Advisers pointed out that between 1961 and 1965 average hourly compensation in the private, non-farm sector of the economy rose at an annual average rate of 4 percent, which for all practical purposes was about the same as the rate at which productivity increased. Thus unit labor costs remained virtually unchanged, resulting in no significant change in the price level.

But as the unemployment rate began to move below 4 percent toward the latter part of 1965 and as the expenditure buildup for the war in Vietnam accelerated, pressures for wage and salary adjustments rose so rapidly that the guideposts policy broke down in 1966. The breakdown began with the settlement of key strikes in the airline industry and the New York City subway system through wage adjustments far in excess of the guideposts. It then spread rapidly to other industries. For 1966, the median wage adjustment negotiated through collective bargaining arrangements was 4.8 percent, a figure well above the average increase in output per man-hour during the year. Between 1966 and 1969, a growing demand for labor generated by the surging output of the economy made possible wage settlements consistently in excess of productivity gains, as suggested by the incomes policy. Thus, for all practical purposes, the American economy's first experiment with a policy for money income adjustment in an era of rapidly expanding demand collapsed.

The guideposts policy broke down under pressure primarily because the government lacked the necessary means to make it effective. The federal government had no real power to force income and wage settlements to adhere to productivity guidelines. At best, the policy was one of exhortation and persuasion ("jawboning"), which worked effectively only as long as powerful groups and firms representing both organized labor and management were willing to adhere voluntarily to the guidelines for wage, price, and income adjustments. Aside from occasional pressure that might be exerted on some sectors by the threat of antitrust action, or the possibility of releasing some materials from governmental stockpiles, the federal government discovered in this period that there was little it could do when confronted with a wage or income settlement which broke through the suggested guidelines.

The collapse of the guideposts

Jawboning

Income Policy and the Nixon Administration

As pointed out in the last chapter, the Nixon administration came into office firmly opposed to any incomes policy, especially wage-price guideposts of the kind attempted by the Kennedy and Johnson administrations. President Nixon's chief economic adviser, Paul McCracken, told a Congressional committee in 1969 that a ". . . guidepost policy is unlikely to have a significant effect when inflationary pressures are strong."

By mid-1970, though, when inflation was proving more stubborn than originally anticipated, the administration began to edge toward intervention into wage and price setting processes. At that time the President created three new mechanisms aimed at influencing wage and price decisions. These included a National Commission on Productivity, to suggest means to improve the productivity of the nation's labor force and thereby diminish the impact of increased wage costs on prices; an "inflation alert" system that required the Council of Economic Advisers to give wide publicity to wage and price settlements deemed especially inflationary; and a federal purchasing review board intended to see that the buying practices of the federal government did not contribute to inflation.

By the end of 1970, even though it was clear that the 1969–1970 "game plan" to end inflation had failed, the administration still maintained the public stance that no incomes policy was necessary. This was true in spite of the fact that Arthur F. Burns, a close adviser of the President and Chairman of the Board of Governors of the Federal Reserve System, argued strongly for an incomes policy throughout most of 1970. Specifically, Burns urged creation of a Federal Wage-Price Review Board, a proposal that was endorsed in mid-1971 by a group of 13 Republican senators.

During the spring of 1971 the Nixon administration began to hedge somewhat on its public stand against an incomes policy. The Davis-Bacon Act, which requires government construction contractors to pay prevailing union scale wages, was suspended, an action intended to restrain wage increases in the construction industry. At the same time the President established wage stabilization machinery for the construction industry, a move that might be interpreted as a "mini" incomes policy, since it was limited to a single industry. Some discreet jawboning also took place as the President urged labor and management to exercise restraint in bargaining under way during the spring in such major industries as automobiles, telephone and telegraph, railroads, and steel. This had little effect; settlements averaged 30 percent over a three-year period.

In an abrupt shift in June 1971 the administration backed wholly away from any incomes policy. At the time, Secretary of the Treasury John Connally, the President's chief economic spokesman, stated that the administration would not establish a wage-price review board; institute wage-price controls, even though the Congress voted standby authority for such controls; ask the Congress for any tax reductions; or increase federal expenditures to stimulate the economy. The federal budget deficit of more than $22 billion for the fiscal year ending June 30, 1971 and

Income Policy and the Nixon Administration

Early measures

Tentative moves toward an incomes policy

255

the rapid expansion of the money supply in the first six months
of the year were believed by many observers to be the major reasons why the administration in midyear not only backed away
from an incomes policy, but took a strong anti-interventionist position.

This stance did not last long, though. On August 15, the President again abruptly reversed the administration's course, an-
nouncing a series of measures designed to stimulate the lagging
economy, which at midsummer saw the unemployment rate hov-
ering near 6 percent and prices still rising at rates Federal Reserve Chairman Burns called "unacceptable and dangerous." The
most stringent measure was a 90-day "freeze" on wages, prices,
and rents, an action which the President hoped would slow down
inflation for an interim period during which the administration
could develop more suitable policies to deal with the price level
problem. The freeze was accompanied by creation of a Cost of
Living Council, headed by the Secretary of the Treasury, whose
task would be to develop a permanent incomes policy. Other measures included a request to Congress for tax cuts, cutbacks in federal spending and employment (Chapter 9), and devaluation of
the dollar in the foreign exchange markets (see Chapter 17).

Early in October President Nixon announced Phase II of his
new economic policy, the most important part of which, from the
viewpoint of an incomes policy, was the establishment of the Pay
Board and the Price Commission. The 90-day freeze on all wages
and prices gave way to a less stringent arrangement which, for stabilization purposes, divided the economy into three sectors. Very
large businesses (firms with annual sales of $100 million or more)
and unions were still subject to strict controls, requiring approval
from either the Pay Board or the Price Commission before wage
and price increases could go into effect. Intermediate size firms
(annual sales between $50 and $100 million) and unions were
only required to report wage and price actions, while all other
units would be controlled through spot checks and case investiga-
tions. Basically, the October modifications in the new economic
policy meant that the administration's incomes policy sought to
control wages and prices by concentrating primarily on the large
and strategically placed business firms and labor unions. It was
expected that if wage and price decisions could be controlled in
these pacesetting units the effects would spill over into the rest of
the economy. The success of Phase II, as pointed out in Chapter
9, has been spotty; the inflation rate was definitely slowed, but
not so much as the administration originally hoped.

*Commitment to an
incomes policy*

Phase II

Toward an Effective Incomes Policy

The experience of the American economy to date indicates a clear conflict between the twin goals of full employment and price level stability; the closer we get to full employment, the greater the pressure on the price level. Further, experience suggests that it is difficult to use the traditional instruments of monetary and fiscal policy for the fine adjustments needed as the economy nears full employment. Successful control of the price level through traditional techniques of monetary and fiscal policy is likely to lead to an unacceptable unemployment rate. If this is so, what is to be done? The real roots of the problem can be found in the market power that exists in key sectors of the economy. Large corporations and labor unions possess significant control over the prices received for their products and services. Under full employment conditions, such power is readily exercised. We must put more effort into finding new techniques to restore competitive conditions if we are to resolve the conflict between full employment and price level stability.

Market power and price stability

Alternatives

Are there other approaches to an incomes policy than those which involve some form of income and price controls, either temporary or permanent? Professor Sidney Weintraub of the University of Pennsylvania suggests imposition of a surtax upon the corporate income tax to go into effect whenever wage and salary settlements exceeded acceptable guidelines. The guidelines would, like the guideposts policy, be based upon productivity gains. Weintraub suggests that the surtax should be some multiple of the percentage figure by which a wage or salary settlement exceeds the desired level. The basic purpose of his proposal is to stiffen corporate resistance in collective bargaining by imposing a heavy financial penalty on corporations which exceed the guidelines. The underlying assumption is that in key sectors prices are "administered" (see Chapter 12), which means they are set on the basis of production costs rather than competitive market conditions.

Penalties for violations of guidelines

Another approach is the development of a system of deferred compensation, which would automatically come into play whenever the economy reached full employment (4 percent or less of the labor force unemployed). Under this arrangement, the federal personal income tax would be used to skim off any wage or salary settlement in excess of the desired guideline. The excess would

Deferred compensation

257

not be taxed away, like the 1968–1970 surtax, but held in trust for release at a later date; hence the term "deferred compensation." The surplus held in this fashion might be added to an individual's social security benefits, plugged into the unemployment compensation system, or merely held to be released whenever the economy needed a fiscal stimulus.

The Public Debt and Its Management

A final set of public policy measures deals with the public debt. The broad term *debt management* refers to all policies involving the size of the public debt, interest paid on it, and the effect that these factors have on the level of economic activity. We shall consider first, in a general way, how the public debt affects economic activity, including analysis of some of the conventional and generally incorrect views held by the public on the significance of debt for operation of the economic system. Then we shall analyze management of the debt in a technical sense, stressing especially the things the Treasury may do about the debt which bear upon the economy's performance. Before proceeding with the analysis, we must examine certain aspects of the role of debt, private as well as public, in the economic system.

Public and Private Debt

Private vs. public debt

As of December 31, 1970 total outstanding debt, public and private, in the American economy amounted to a figure equal to 1.6 times the 1970 gross national product. Private debt constituted the overwhelming proportion of this amount, representing 73.7 percent of the total, or $1,356.9 billion. Table 10-1 shows the major components of the public and private debt for selected years since 1929.

Aside from corporate borrowing, the other major sources of private debt are borrowing to finance homes (mortgages), borrowing by consumers for installment purchases, and borrowing by small businessmen and farmers. As Table 10-1 indicates, corporate borrowing accounted for about 57 percent of all private debt outstanding in 1970. The magnitude of private debt is rarely mentioned in discussions of the debt, although at the end of the 1960s it was nearly three times the combined public debt for the federal government and all state and local governments.

The portion of the debt that receives most attention in the press and general conversation is, of course, the debt of the federal government. One major reason is that this debt is closely associated with fiscal measures of the kind discussed in Chapter 9.

TABLE 10-1

Public and Private Debt, Selected Years: 1929–1971

(Billions of Dollars)

YEAR	FEDERAL DEBT	STATE AND LOCAL DEBT	TOTAL PUBLIC DEBT	CORPORATE DEBT	INDIVIDUAL AND NON-CORPORATE DEBT	TOTAL DEBT
1929	$16.5	13.6	30.1	88.9	72.9	191.9
1935	35.5	16.1	50.5	74.8	49.7	175.0
1940	44.8	16.4	61.2	75.6	53.0	189.8
1945	252.5	13.4	265.9	85.3	54.7	405.9
1950	218.1	21.7	239.8	142.1	104.3	486.2
1955	232.5	41.1	273.6	212.1	180.1	665.8
1960	242.3	64.9	307.2	302.8	263.3	873.3
1965	275.3	98.3	373.6	454.3	416.1	1,244.0
1970	339.9	143.3	483.2	774.1	582.8	1,840.1

Source: *Economic Report of the President,* 1972.

As a matter of fact, some of the hostility directed toward fiscal policy as an instrument of economic stabilization probably stems from the fact it often leads to "deficit spending" and an increase in the public debt. The federal government cannot incur a deficit without a corresponding increase in the federal debt, while a surplus may permit a reduction in the size of the federal debt. Given many people's unfounded fears of any growth in the federal debt, it is understandable that some of this fear is transferred to the use of fiscal policy as a measure for economic stabilization. In contrast, the public does not link monetary policy with changes in the debt position of the federal government.

The Federal Debt Today

At the end of 1971 the outstanding debt of the federal government was $424.1 billion, 40.5 percent of the gross national product. The federal government's outstanding debt was, in other words, equal to more than one-third the value of the nation's total production. Holders (or owners) of the public debt include commercial banks, mutual banks and insurance companies, private corporations, state and local governments, individuals and families, as well as other financial organizations, including nonprofit institutions, corporate pension funds, etc. At the end of 1971, 41.5 percent of the federal debt was held either by U. S. government agencies or the Federal Reserve System; 16 percent was held by commercial and other banks; 1.6 percent by insurance companies; 6.7 percent by other business firms and nonprofit organizations; 4.8 percent by state and local governments; 18.3 percent by individuals; and 11.1 percent by foreign residents, governments, and international organizations.

*Holders of the
public debt*

259

In any discussion of the public debt and its ownership it is important to understand that, although the debt is an obligation of the government, to the person owning a portion of the debt it is an asset. The owner of a government bond has an asset which promises him a sum of money at a future date.

Misconceptions about the Public Debt

Bankruptcy

*The myth of
national
bankruptcy*

Although many people are interested, and often dismayed, by the absolute size of the public debt, this figure is not of any particular economic significance. To understand why this is true, we need to examine some of the commonly held views about the role of debt in the economic system. Perhaps the oldest and most feared notion, as well as the one with the least analytical foundation, is the idea that in some sense the nation is going to be driven into bankruptcy by a large debt. This view derives from a false analogy between what the nation can do and what the individual (including private corporations) can do. We know that if an individual persistently spends more than his income, sooner or later he will find himself without assets and unable to meet the claims that creditors have upon him. When this happens the individual is bankrupt. The economically unsophisticated fear that the same thing may happen to the nation; that someday a host of creditors will descend upon the nation's capital and demand payment for the national debt. As a matter of fact, creditors are demanding payment every day, so to speak, because large portions of the national debt mature at periodic intervals. The Treasury of the United States generally refunds the federal government's "IOU's" being presented for payment, which means simply that it issues new debt certificates to take the place of those which have matured. The new certificates of indebtedness (that is, bonds) are not necessarily issued to the same people, but overall the portion of the debt which has come due may be replaced by newly issued securities. This is a routine Treasury operation.

*Treasury bonds
as debt
certificates*

*The power to tax
and to coin money*

Those who fear that a heavy burden of indebtedness will bankrupt the nation generally do not realize that the federal government has the power to tax, and hence can always raise the money to pay off a maturing obligation if it so chooses. More important is the fact that the federal government has the power—granted by the Constitution—to coin money. Not that this would be a desirable policy, but if by some strange circumstance all of the debt was presented for payment, the Congress could, in theory and fact, simply coin (or print) enough currency to pay it off. This would be a desperate remedy, for it would flood the economy with more money, leading to serious inflation and other problems. However, the debt could be paid off.

The only significant resemblance between the debt of the nation and the debt of the individual occurs when a large part of the national debt is owned by foreigners. To repay foreign-held debt the nation must acquire foreign currency (or foreign exchange); the most logical way to do this is to export more goods and services than it imports. Thus, repayment of foreign-held debt requires a diversion of part of the nation's output from domestic to foreign use, and in this sense a real burden is imposed upon the economy. In 1971, it will be recalled, foreigners held only 11.1 percent of the national debt.

This is not the case for repayment of internally held (or domestic) debt. The domestic debt is owned by some of us and ultimately must be paid off by taxing all of us sufficiently to provide funds for those who happen to hold government securities. Thus the repayment of the domestic debt, as well as its annual servicing through interest charges, involves a transfer of income from the society at large to the persons and entities which hold some portion of the debt. Given this fact, and given, too, the undisputed fact that the modern state can both create money and obtain money through its taxing power, it should be clear that there is no economic foundation for the idea that the nation will become bankrupt because of the existence of a debt.

Shifting the Debt Ahead

A second time-honored, though unfounded, belief concerning public debt is that through debt we are in some vague and undefined fashion transferring an awesome burden to our children, our grandchildren, or even our great-grandchildren. This popular misconception has been accepted uncritically even by some recent presidents of the United States. A good way to understand the fallacy inherent in this view is to examine the financing of expenditures during World War II. As pointed out earlier, a large proportion of these expenditures was financed by borrowing, but this did not result in any transfer of the real costs of the war to the future. The real costs of World War II resulted from the diversion of resources at that time (labor and nonhuman resources) away from the production of consumer goods and services toward the production of war goods. With limited exceptions, there was no significant way for the generation that lived through and fought the war to shift the burden of the war to the future, in spite of the fact that it resorted to deficit financing to underwrite an important share of the expenditures undertaken in connection with the war.

261

What was shifted to the future? Obviously, a large part of the absolute size of the federal debt today was incurred during World War II. But there has been no shift of the burden. What has taken place has been a transfer of income in the form of interest payments from society at large to those who happen to hold a portion of the debt. This has not involved shifting a burden from one generation to the next, but merely a rearrangement of income by virtue of the existence of the debt among persons living and working in the society today. This rearrangement of income results because interest on the debt is a transfer payment. Thus, the larger the debt, the larger the amount of annual interest charges, and the larger the transfer of income from all taxpayers to individuals and other entities who own the debt. In the final analysis, debt is simply a technique for financing a public activity at a particular period of time; in its economic effects it is no different from financing by taxation.

Significant Debt Ratios

Ratio of Debt to GNP

What is important in appraising the impact of the debt on the economy's performance is the *ratio* of the debt to the gross national product. There are two reasons for this. As mentioned earlier (p. 260), those who own government securities have an asset they can readily turn into purchasing power. The larger the size of the debt relative to the gross national product, the greater the pool of potential spending power at any time. Such a pool constitutes a potential inflationary danger spot under full employment conditions. A second reason for concern is that any increase in the ratio of the debt to the gross national product also signifies an increase in debt service charges—interest on the debt— relative to the economy's output. These are transfer payments that must be financed out of taxation. Inasmuch as ownership of the debt is more concentrated in the upper than lower income groups, transfers of this type tend to have a regressive economic impact.

It is interesting to see what has happened to this ratio over the last four decades. Figure 10-2 shows this. In 1929, for example, the last year of the great surge of prosperity of the 1920s, the federal debt was equal to 16 percent of the gross national product. By 1940, primarily as a consequence of deficit spending during the 1930s, the ratio had climbed to 44.9. The sharpest increase occurred during the World War II era, from 1940 to 1945, when it reached 119.2 percent of the gross national product in 1945. Since the end of World War II the ratio has declined steadily until

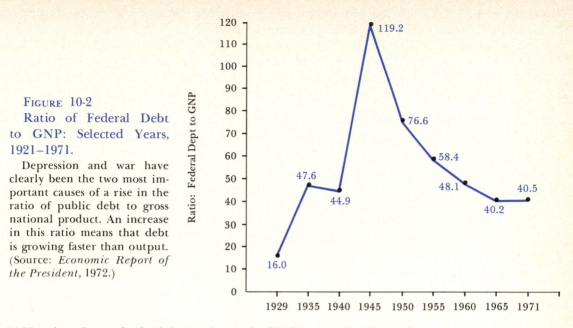

FIGURE 10-2

Ratio of Federal Debt to GNP: Selected Years, 1921–1971.

Depression and war have clearly been the two most important causes of a rise in the ratio of public debt to gross national product. An increase in this ratio means that debt is growing faster than output. (Source: *Economic Report of the President,* 1972.)

1965, when it reached 40.2. By the end of 1971, though, the ratio had increased slightly to 40.5. Except for the sharp increase during World War II and a small bulge in the last few years (the Vietnam war), the federal debt has generally grown more slowly than the gross national product.

From 1940 to 1945 the debt rose by 463.6 percent, an astronomical increase which reflects the extent to which deficit financing was used in World War II. Between 1945 and 1971 the absolute size of the debt increased by a mere 67.9 percent; in this period, too, the ratio of debt to the gross national product experienced a decided decline. Between 1960 and 1970, the absolute size of the federal debt increased by only 40.3 percent, whereas private debt rose by 130.2 percent and state and local government debt increased by 120.8 percent. These figures should put into a better perspective the role and position of debt in the economy. Figure 10-3 shows the ratio of public to private debt since 1929.

Interest on the Debt

The ratio of interest on the debt to gross national product is perhaps equally significant in analyzing the role of public debt—particularly the federal debt—in the economic system. Interest charges are transfer payments, as we discovered through examination of gross national product statistics in Chapter 5; therefore their size in relation to the gross national product is some indication of the extent to which the public debt imposes a transfer burden on the economic system. For the last decade there has

Ratio of interest on debt to GNP

263

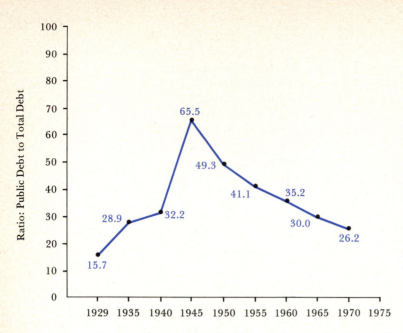

100
90
80
70
60
50
40
30
20
10
0

Ratio: Public Debt to Total Debt

65.5

49.3

41.1

35.2

28.9

32.2

30.0

15.7

26.2

1929 1935 1940 1945 1950 1955 1960 1965 1970 1975

FIGURE 10-3
Public Debt as a Percent of Total Debt: Selected Years, 1929–1970.

A healthier perspective on the overall significance of public debt is obtained by measuring it as a percent of total (public and private) debt in the economy. War and depression are the major reasons for a rise in the ratio. (Source: *Economic Report of the President,* 1972.)

been practically no change in the ratio of interest charges to the gross national product. In 1959 this ratio was 1.2, but by 1970 it had risen by only .2 percentage points to 1.4.

The Public Debt and the Economy

The debt as an inflation threat

The two most widely held conceptions of how debt affects the economy are unfounded but there are ways in which the debt and its size are of genuine economic significance. First, ownership of a portion of the debt means that the owner has in his possession not merely an asset, but a highly liquid asset that can readily be converted into purchasing power with little risk of loss in the value of the asset and little inconvenience. This is especially true if a significant portion of the debt is of a short-term rather than a long-term character. At the end of 1971, slightly more than 45 percent of federal marketable securities had a maturity date of less than one year.

As stated previously, the larger the size of the debt the greater the stock of liquidity available to the individuals and business firms who hold it. In this sense a large debt is an inflationary threat to the economy: it makes available spending power which can be brought into play quite quickly, and which, for the most part, is beyond control of the monetary authorities.

Deflationary impact of the debt

There is yet another way in which the public debt affects the overall performance of the economy. The annual interest charges on the debt, as has already been pointed out, constitute a transfer of income from society at large (the taxpayers) to those who own the debt. Contrary to the liquidity inherent in the debt, the transfer aspects of a large debt may depress aggregate spending. The reason for this lies in the fact that the individuals, corporations, and other financial institutions that own the debt are often in the upper income brackets, and thus less inclined to spend any additional interest income received through ownership of the debt, whereas the taxpayers, being spread across all of the income brackets, may, on the average, have a lower propensity to save than those who own the debt. Thus if the transfer of interest income on the public debt is financed by taxation it may have a deflationary impact on the economic system.

Debt Management

Management of the debt in a technical sense concerns the decisions made by Treasury officials that pertain not so much to the size, but to the timing and type of securities that will be sold to finance budget deficits and the retirement of securities when the existence of a surplus in the governmental accounts makes it possible to reduce the debt. Management of the debt, in other words, involves making decisions related to its structure: what portion is to be held in very short-term securities and what portion in long-term obligations. Such decisions must be made both when the debt is being increased and when it is being reduced. Decisions on the structure of the debt are also made in conjunction with refunding activities, because refunding, which takes place frequently, gives the managers of the debt an opportunity to adjust its structure in terms of the maturity dates of the various kinds of obligations that make up the overall debt structure.

The timing and type of government securities

As of the end of 1971, 45.5 percent of the marketable public debt was in the form of short-term issues, with the balance in long-term Treasury bonds. Short-term issues, mostly Treasury bills and notes, have a maturity date of less than one year. This structure may be contrasted with the situation at the end of 1946, when only 32.7 percent of the marketable debt in the hands of the public was in the form of short-term issues. In an economic sense this means that at the end of 1971 the pool of "liquidity" available to the public in the form of debt instruments quickly convertible into purchasing power was much larger than it was at the end of World War II. A short-term issue is a more liquid instrument than a long-term Treasury bond.

The current structure of the debt

Specialists believe that long-term debt management ought to be counter-cyclical, that is, the structure of the debt ought to be arranged to dampen down the effects of fluctuations on the eco-

**The Impact of
Incomes Policy and
the Public Debt**

*Adjusting the debt
to economic
fluctuations*

nomic system. This would entail measures to lengthen the debt structure during a boom, which would reduce the amount of liquidity available to the general public for any given size of the national debt, and to shorten the debt structure in a recession or depression, which would raise potential liquidity. A debt structure is lengthened by managing the overall debt so that the proportion of the total made up of long-term securities is increased; shortening it involves increasing the proportion of debt held in short-term Treasury obligations.

This viewpoint is not unchallenged; some economists who oppose counter-cyclical debt management argue that such a policy would significantly affect interest charges on the debt and do so at the wrong time. If debt management attempts to lengthen the structure in periods of prosperity, the result will be higher interest charges on the overall debt, because interest rates are highest during periods of prosperity. Moreover, the interest rate on long-term obligations is normally higher than the interest rate on short-term obligations. On the other hand, if the Treasury attempts to shorten the debt structure during a recession, then it is precluded from borrowing at long-term when interest rates are most favorable from the borrower's standpoint. At best, technical management of the debt requires a balance between a structure which minimizes the impact of the public debt on fluctuations in the economic system, and one which minimizes the interest charges to the Treasury, given the existing size of the public debt. This balance is not easily attained

The Economist as Adviser

The last four decades have seen an enormous expansion in the application of theoretical economic knowledge to key issues of public policy, a development which has thrust economists increasingly into important policy-making roles in government and business. During this era the policy implications of the "Keynesian Revolution" of the 1930s have been so fully accepted that the idea is now almost commonplace that the federal government should use its fiscal and monetary powers to minimize economic fluctuations and bring the economy to full employment. The Employment Act of 1946, including establishment of the President's Council of Economic Advisers, formally marked this achievement, even though it was not until the 1960s that a national administration was finally persuaded to act on the basis of these principles.

But the struggle to employ theoretical knowledge in the wise management of the national economy is far from ended. The key to full employment without an unacceptable rate of inflation still largely eludes us, although this will probably be our major problem throughout the 1970s. Certainly economists in government, in the academic community, and in business will continue striving to perfect their theoretical knowledge, but it is still more likely that even greater efforts will be made to translate theoretical knowledge into policies to resolve the array of problems that face us. History may not label this era "The Age of the Economist," but it will certainly recognize that the essentially economic nature of most of our problems demanded more economic expertise.

Questions for Review and Discussion

1. What is meant by the term "incomes policy"?

2. Why did the guideposts policy of the eartly 1960s seek to relate wage increases to productivity?

3. Why would a policy that succeeded in limiting increases in money in all forms to a rate equal to the rate of increase in productivity leave the factoral distribution of the national income unaltered? Would this be good or bad?

4. Give examples of groups in the economy that might be hurt by a successful incomes policy.

5. Describe and contrast the Nixon administration's approach to an incomes policy with that of its predecessors.

6. What proportion of total debt outstanding in the economy is represented by the federal debt? By state and local debt? By private debt?

7. Name some of the main groups (including persons) who own the federal debt. Do owners of the debt regard it as an asset or a liability?

8. Is the idea that a large public debt may drive a nation into bankruptcy valid? Why or why not?

9. Explain why both the repayment of the domestic debt and its annual servicing through interest charges involve a transfer of income.

10. Why is it essentially incorrect to say that the use of debt to finance part of the money outlays for World War II resulted in a shift of the burdens of that war to the children and grandchildren of the World War II generaion?

11. Give some examples of possible adverse effects of a large public debt upon the economic system.

12. What is debt management? Who are the managers of the public debt?

11

Prices and the Allocation of Resources

Microeconomic analysis

THE PROBLEMS OF INFLATION in a fully employed economy cannot be solved wholly with the tools of macroeconomic analysis. The roots of inflation are at the microeconomic level, a significant fact for the type of analysis we are concerned with in this and the next two chapters. Specifically, we shall focus on price determination, the allocation of economic resources among alternative uses, and how these functions are performed in a market economy. Our procedure in these chapters is to develop specific analytical techniques and then use them to construct theoretical models through which we can analyze the behavior of the market economy. Keep in mind the abstract nature of these analytical tools. To use them successfully requires liberal doses of imagination. But when used with care and imagination they are invaluable in helping us make sense out of the complex network of the modern company.

Prices and the Market System

Prices play a crucial role in the operation of the market economy. At every level of activity, from the government to the household, prices exercise a powerful influence on what people and organizations do, what happens to our standard of living, and what we produce and consume. Technically, price is the exchange value of a good or service expressed in terms of money; it measures the command that a commodity or service has over other commodities or services. For example, a newly constructed house selling for $36,000 is worth 15 times a newly produced car which lists for $2400. Thus, price in relation to resource allocation is closely related to the process of exchange.

Exchange value in money terms

Relative Prices

In microeconomic analysis the economist focuses on relative price, the price of one thing relative to or compared to some other thing. Changes in relative prices are of strategic importance in the market economy because they are the means of expression for consumer preferences. The basic idea of consumer sovereignty is that the desires of the consumer determine what is to be produced. This in turn provides a guide to the effective and profitable use of economic resources. This theoretical model does not always exist in the real world, where producers, through advertising, for example, often influence the consumer as much as the consumer influences them. It is practically impossible to watch television these days without being told that Brand X toothpaste will practically guarantee a smile with devastating sex appeal or that Brand Y coffee may save a marriage from collapse because heretofore the wife had not discovered a coffee good enough to please her husband's demanding tastes. Consumer advocates like Ralph Nader have drawn attention to this fact.

Administered Prices

Price determination by market forces is not the only way prices are set. They may be set by some authority, as is the case with government-established prices. Government control over prices is common in the regulated industries—telephone, telegraph, power, and transportation, for example—where some kind of public commission usually exists to set prices and exercise control over output and, often, the entry and exit of firms into the industry. A recent example of government intervention was the wage-

Determining prices by fiat

price freeze that President Nixon ordered in mid-August 1971. The freeze was lifted at the end of ninety days, but through the Price Commission the government has retained control of price decisions in key industries. In some cases a private firm may be able to establish the price of a commodity or a service independent of market forces. This is possible when a merchant or firm is the only supplier of a good or service in a given geographical area. When prices are determined by fiat, in government or in private, economists say that they are administered. As we shall see, price in the modern economy is often determined by a mixture of administered decisions and the interplay of market forces. Finally, some prices are set by custom; people come to regard a particular price as proper and just, irrespective of the play of market forces. The ten- or fifteen-cent cup of coffee at the lunch counter is a case in point.

Demand and Supply Schedules

Our interest is not only in the process of establishing prices, but also in situations characterized by different degrees of competitiveness. To explain price determination in the market, economics has developed two fundamental analytical tools, a demand schedule and a supply schedule, which were introduced in Chapter 3. In this chapter we shall use them to examine the process of price determination in a generalized market situation and then, in a sense, go behind these schedules to explain why they assume a particular shape and slope. Demand and supply schedules depict human behavior in the market setting; thus, when we explain their nature, we are explaining an aspect of human behavior.

The Process of Price Determination

We start our analysis with a condensed review of points made in Chapter 3. Recall from our discussion there that demand in an economic sense is more than mere desire. It embraces both the willingness and the monetary means to acquire a good or service. To the economist, demand is a schedule showing at a given time (and on the assumption that other things are constant) the quantities of a good or service that an individual (or group) is willing to purchase at alternative prices.

*Demand and
supply contrasted*

Supply in an economic sense is also a schedule. But whereas demand measures the purchaser's response, supply depicts the response of producers to price. The supply schedule shows the quantities of a good or service that the supplier is willing to place on the market at a particular time at alternative sets of prices.

The demand schedule involves a relationship between price and quantity demanded. The quantity demanded is the dependent variable; its value depends upon and changes in response to changes in price, the independent variable. This is an inverse functional relationship: quantity demanded varies in response to changes in price. It is important to note that price does not vary in response to changes in the quantity demanded.

The supply schedule also embodies a basic relationship between quantity supplied and price, but, in contrast to the demand schedule, this relationship is a direct one. The amount supplied, other things being equal, varies directly with the price. Economists say that the demand schedule has a negative slope (it slopes downward to the right), and the supply schedule has a positive slope (it slopes upward to the right).

Price Determination in the Market

Given demand and supply schedules for a commodity, we can review the principles of price determination in a particular market. This is done most easily with a numerical example. Table 11-1 contains schedules representing the demand for and supply of crude oil. The price which will ultimately prevail in this market depends upon the interaction between these two schedules. Suppose for the moment that the current market price of crude oil is $2.75. The schedules show that at this price the quantity of crude oil demanded is greater than the quantity supplied. Obviously the price of crude oil will be bid up because the excess of demand is competing for the limited amount actually being offered for

A numerical example

TABLE 11-1
Demand and Supply for Crude Oil

QUANTITY DEMANDED (MILLIONS OF BARRELS)	PRICE (PER BARREL)	QUANTITY SUPPLIED (MILLIONS OF BARRELS)
559	$2.60	547
558	2.65	548
557	2.70	549
556	2.75	550
555	2.80	551
554	2.85	552
553	⟶ 2.90 ⟵	553
552	2.95	554
551	3.00	555
550	3.05	556
549	3.10	557
548	3.15	558
547	3.20	559

271

sale in this market. The price increase will set off a series of events. First, a rising price brings more crude oil into the market, but at the same time reduces to some extent the demand for crude oil. Assuming no outside interference in the market, this process will continue until the quantity demanded and the quantity supplied are equal. When this happens market price will be in equilibrium. Given the schedules in Table 11-1, this price will be $2.90. After this price is reached, no further change in price will take place as long as the schedules remain fixed.

To complete our discussion, let us examine what would take place if, initially, the price of crude oil were $3.05. In this case the reverse of the situation just described occurs; the quantity of crude oil being supplied to the market exceeds the quantity demanded. Some suppliers find that they cannot sell all the oil they offer on the market at the prevailing price and, rather than allow it to remain unsold, they take a lower price. It is expensive to store oil and wait for a better price. As a result the price of crude oil starts to fall. The price change draws more buyers into the market and pushes some suppliers out of the market, thereby reducing the quantity of oil being supplied. This process of downward adjustment must continue until the market again achieves a balance between quantity supplied and quantity demanded. Price will again be in equilibrium.

Equilibrium in the Market

This process is shown graphically in Figure 11-1, where we have plotted the demand and supply schedules given in Table 11-1. Note carefully that price is plotted on the vertical axis, whereas quantity demanded and quantity supplied are plotted on the horizontal axis. This is the conventional procedure. By connecting the points representing quantity demanded at every possible price we graph the demand schedule, and by doing the same thing for the quantity supplied we graph the supply schedule. Equilibrium exists for both price and quantity at the point of intersection of the two schedules. At any price above this level there is disequilibrium because the quantity supplied exceeds the quantity demanded. Price will fall. At any price below this level there is a different type of disequilibrium because the quantity demanded exceeds the quantity supplied. Consequently the price will rise. In this hypothetical market the price of crude oil continues to change, other things being equal, until it reaches the level determined by the intersection of the demand and supply schedules. Once this happens, there is no further tendency for market price to change; the market price and equilibrium price for crude oil are identical. The equilibrium price clears the market of the amounts offered by suppliers and the amounts purchased by demanders.

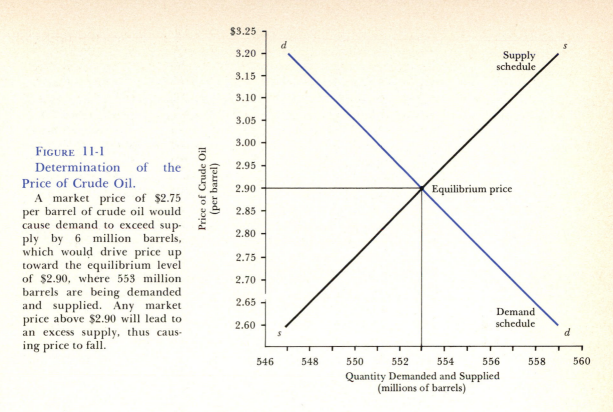

FIGURE 11-1

Determination of the Price of Crude Oil.

A market price of $2.75 per barrel of crude oil would cause demand to exceed supply by 6 million barrels, which would drive price up toward the equilibrium level of $2.90, where 553 million barrels are being demanded and supplied. Any market price above $2.90 will lead to an excess supply, thus causing price to fall.

Price of Crude Oil (per barrel)

Quantity Demanded and Supplied (millions of barrels)

Supply schedule

Equilibrium price

Demand schedule

Characteristics of Equilibrium Price

The Role of Human Behavior

There are several points to observe about an equilibrium price and its determination. First, equilibrium price depends upon the interaction between demand and supply forces in the market. These forces, which are expressed as schedules, represent human behavior. We should not think of them as immutable laws, but rather as tendencies. As Alfred Marshall once said, "a law of social science . . . is a statement of social tendencies; that is, a statement that a certain course of action may be expected under certain conditions from the members of a social group." [1]

The Role of Time

A second important matter involves the relationship between equilibrium price and time. Explicitly or implicitly, there is a time dimension inherent in every demand or supply schedule, even though the economist in his analytical work rarely designates any specific period of time appropriate to the schedules. De-

---

[1] Alfred Marshall, *Principles of Economics*, 8th ed. (London: Macmillan and Company, 1925), p. 33.

273

*Market, short-term,
and long-term
equilibrium*

mand and supply must necessarily refer to the quantities purchased or offered at prices that prevail during a set period of
time. The type of diagram shown in Figure 11-1 is said to be
static because it cannot show the passing of time.

For analytical purposes it is useful to set up some hypothetical
time periods appropriate to equilibrium price. These periods are:
market equilibrium, short-term equilibrium, and long-term equilibrium. The circumstances which define these periods originate
with supply rather than demand. In market equilibrium, supply
is limited to the quantity currently placed on the market. There
is no time, in other words, for supply to be adjusted through
production adjustments by business firms. In short-term equilibrium there is enough time for supply to vary within the limits of
the existing productive capacity of all firms currently operating in
a particular industry. Long-term equilibrium is a period of sufficient duration for supply to be adjusted by variations in the size
of the industry, through the entry or exit of firms or a change in
the size of existing plants in the industry. In the automobile industry, for example, a recent long-term upward adjustment in
supply took place when the Chevrolet Division of General Motors
built a new plant to produce the Vega. Less recently, a downward adjustment of a long-term nature took place when the Stu-
debaker Motor Company ceased production of automobiles.

Change in the Equilibrium Price

A third observation about equilibrium price concerns the process
by which it may change. Change of this kind is not the same as
change in market price as the latter moves toward equilibrium.
Change in an equilibrium price will occur only if there has been
a shift in either the demand or the supply schedule. Changes in
demand and supply must be distinguished from changes in quantity demanded or in quantity supplied; the latter involve a movement along a given schedule. A change in a demand (or supply)
schedule is a shift in the position of the schedule, such that at the
same array of prices either more or less will be demanded (or supplied) than before.

Figure 11-2 illustrates a change in equilibrium price brought
about by an increase in demand for crude oil. A growing scarcity
of natural gas, an alternative fuel, might account for such an increase. The demand schedule shifts upward and to the right from
dd to $d'd'$. At all prices shown, more crude oil will be purchased
than previously. Since the supply schedule has not changed, the
increase in demand has led to an increase in the price of crude
oil. A decline in demand would have had the opposite effect. Similarly, changes in an equilibrium price may be brought about by
an increase or a decrease in supply.

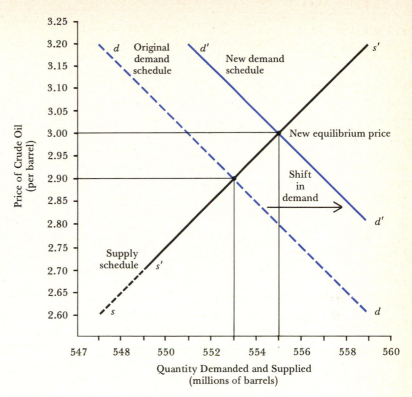

FIGURE 11-2

Increase in the Demand for Crude Oil.

When the demand for crude oil increases—shown by a shift in the demand curve to the right—the price will rise to $3.00 per barrel and output will jump to 555 million barrels. The higher price brings forth the larger supply, given the upward slope of the supply curve.

Laws of Price Behavior

This discussion of equilibrium price and changes in equilibrium price can be summarized in three general "laws" of price behavior.

> 1. In a competitive market, price tends to settle at a level at which the quantity demanded and the quantity supplied are equal.
> 2. An increase (decrease) in demand with supply unchanged will cause price to rise (fall).
> 3. An increase (decrease) in supply with demand unchanged will cause price to fall (rise).

In our analysis of market price determination and equilibrium price, we have been dealing with an impersonal process in that no participant by his own action has been able to determine the outcome of the pricing process. Under such circumstances price is the result of the freely expressed preferences of all market participants, consumers and suppliers alike. This is the essence of the economist's concept of a competitive market. Prices determined in this manner are not arbitrary. They are not the result of the exercise of economic power over price by anybody or any entity. The absence of any power over price is a key to understanding the competitive market. The competitive market idea does not

The concept of a competitive market

275

purport to describe all markets in the real economy. Rather it is a benchmark, if you will, a means to analyze critically actual market behavior in the real economy.

A final point. Price serves as a rationing device. It excludes from the market and thus from consumption persons without the means to pay. Ponder some of the implications of this fact. Societies, we all know, usually decide that price should not exclude certain groups from the consumption of essential goods or services—rent subsidies and low-cost medical care for the aged, for example. In such cases either the individuals or groups must be given more income, or the goods and services must be made available at prices other than those which would prevail in response to market conditions alone.

Price Changes and Resource Allocation

The processes of equilibrium price determination examined so far pertain primarily to developments within one industry. How do changes in relative prices affect resource allocation in the entire economic system?

*Movement of
resources in response
to increased demand*

Let us analyze what happens when demand increases. According to our second "law" of price behavior, an increase in demand, other things being equal, will lead to an increase in price. Well and good. But what happens after this? If other things are equal, all other prices in the economic system must be unchanged. If this is true then firms in the industry experiencing the increase in demand will enjoy larger profits than the rest of the economy. More resources will be drawn into that industry as firms expand their output in pursuit of better opportunities for production and sale of their products. This is how a change in relative prices affects resource allocation in the economic system. Resources are drawn toward the industry in which product price has risen relative to prices in other industries.

*Movement of
resources in response
to decreased demand*

When demand decreases, the "law" of price behavior indicates that prices will fall. If an industry experiences a decline in the price of its output relative to prices elsewhere, profits and the scale of production for firms in the industry are adversely affected. Resources will leave the industry, seeking employment in other industries where prices are higher. Thus a relative decline in price tends to force resources out of an industry and elsewhere in the economic system.

*Movement of
resources in response
to supply changes*

Changes which originate on the supply side also affect resource allocation in the economic system. For example, any increase in supply with demand unchanged depresses the market price for a good or service. A fall in price, as we have just seen, pushes resources away from an industry. On the other hand, a reduction in supply increases price, assuming demand is unchanged. This pulls resources toward the industry.

Changes in supply may result from technological developments which lower production costs, or from changes in the price that all firms in an industry have to pay for resources. Any change which disturbs a preexisting equilibrium price in a particular market will affect resource allocation. It does not matter whether the initiating change comes from demand or supply in a given market. The growth in recent years of the petrochemical industry is largely a consequence of the development of plastics, which substitute for metal, wood, and other materials. To the extent that such substitution takes place, labor and capital are drawn into the petrochemical industry. Another historic example of technological change is the substitution of nylon for silk, with drastic consequences for resources used in silk production in Japan. The decline in the demand for pure silk forced the silkworm farmers to find alternative employments, an adjustment process that was often difficult and painful for the individuals.

A Closer Look at Demand

We have saved until now a fundamental question about the nature of demand. Why does the economist view demand as a schedule linking price and quantity? There are two facets to this question. We need to know why the relationship between price and quantity is central to the phenomenon of demand and also why quantity demanded varies inversely to price.

The Predominance of Price

Obviously a number of factors influence an individual's decision to purchase a particular good or service at a particular time. Besides price, the most important would include income, tastes of the buyer, prices of other goods and services, expectations about future prices, not to mention basic physical needs. It would be hard to find instances where one or more of these factors did *not* have an important influence on our decision to buy a particular commodity or service. Yet, though there are many considerations in the buying decision, both historical evidence and economic analysis suggest that price is the factor of greatest strategic significance. Therefore, the basic demand relationship is between price and quantity demanded. The technique of analysis is to assume that all other variables remain constant, which permits us to examine how the variable "quantity demanded" changes in response to the variable "price."

Influences on the decision to buy

277

Income and Substitution Effects

Two explanations may be advanced to answer the question why quantity demanded varies in inverse relation to price. Let us take the easier one first. Whenever the price of a particular commodity or service declines, other things being equal, there are income and substitution effects which enable the buyer to buy more of the good or service at the lower price. If the price of a commodity goes down, to the consumer this is the equivalent of having more income. His real income has increased. The buyer may, if he desires, purchase more units of the good than he was purchasing before its price changed. Of course, the reverse is true if the price goes up. This phenomenon is the *income effect* of a price change, assuming the prices of other goods and services are unchanged. For example, a reduction in the price of gasoline might lead to more driving and bigger gasoline sales, whereas a price increase could lead to a decision to use the car less, and thus to a decline in sales.

There is also a *substitution effect*. If the price of a given commodity falls, the purchaser may substitute consumption of this commodity for some other good. When the price of poultry falls, we eat more fried chicken and less hamburger. Again we note that a price decrease causes the buyer to consume more of the commodity than he has been doing. On the other hand, if the price goes up he will, if possible, substitute some other good or service for the commodity in question. Higher poultry prices will stimulate the consumption of more hamburger, unless beef prices have undergone a comparable rise in price.

The income and substitution effects offer commonsense explanations of why the quantity of the good purchased varies inversely with its price. But we need a broader-based explanation to analyze rational consumer behavior. How does the consumer obtain maximum satisfaction from expenditure of a limited income? This is an important economic question which bears not only on consumer behavior, but also on the behavior of the business firm.

The Principle of Utility

A basic philosophical explanation for the negative slope of the demand curve depends on the concept of utility. This approach originated with the "pleasure-pain" hypothesis of Jeremy Bentham, an eighteenth-century British social philosopher best known for his exposition of the doctrine of utilitarianism, sometimes called the "greatest happiness principle." Bentham argued that man is a rational creature motivated by a desire to maximize pleasure and minimize pain. In economics, pleasure is the satisfaction or utility derived from the consumption of goods and services. Disutility (or pain) is the effort needed to acquire the goods and services that offer satisfaction. While our wants are, perhaps, capable of indefinite expansion, at a given time a specific want will eventually be satisfied if we continue to consume successive units of a good or service.

Thus the utility or satisfaction derived from consumption must necessarily decline as more units of the good or service are consumed during a given span of time. A commonplace example is the morning cup of coffee. Many people can't really get going until they have had the first cup of coffee. Even a second helps, but a third and fourth become less and less attractive. The utility of each added cup drops rather fast. Even the most intensive wants must eventually become satiated.

An example of declining utility

Marginal Utility

This is the nub of the matter. The marginal—or added—utility derived from consumption of successive units of a good or service has to decline. If this is true, and if it is also true that the price a person is willing to pay for a good or service roughly reflects the satisfaction or utility he gets from its consumption, then it follows that consumers will be unwilling to purchase successive units of a good or service except at a lower price, other things being equal. We now have the underlying explanation for the downward slope of the demand curve: *the principle of diminishing marginal utility.*

The principle of diminishing marginal utility

This principle, besides helping to explain the basis for the demand schedule, also tells us that the utility of a commodity or service depends upon its scarcity, other things being equal. The more units of a commodity available to the consumer, the smaller the usefulness of any single unit to the consumer; hence the more we have of any one item, the lower the price we will pay to acquire more of that item. On the other hand, the fewer the units of the good or service available, the greater the usefulness or value of any single unit to the buyer; therefore the higher the price he will pay to acquire an additional unit. The confirmed morning "coffee addict" would probably pay considerably more than the customary dime, if only a single cup of coffee were available to satisfy a large thirst. But since a person's need for morning coffee is rather quickly satisfied, the utility of each cup drops rapidly. Lunch counters often offer a second cup for five cents, but beyond that there is little point in cutting the price, for few people derive much satisfaction from a third cup at a particular sitting. Value, according to the utility principle, does not depend upon total utility; it is marginal utility, or the satisfaction derived from the last unit consumed, that determines the price. And price, as we have seen, depends upon scarcity.

*The paradox of
value*

Since utility involves the satisfaction a person derives from consumption, it is clearly a subjective concept, and cannot be precisely measured. At times this is troublesome. But the principle of diminishing marginal utility aids greatly in explaining other phenomena in economics which, from time to time, have posed difficulties. One such as the "paradox of value," which we encountered in Chapter 3; the utility concept explains that water and air are cheap because they are plentiful, whereas gold and precious stones are scarce and thus valuable.

Consumer behavior

The concept of utility is also useful in explaining rational behavior on the part of the consumer. A rational consumer with a limited income will try to maximize the satisfaction he gets from consuming the things he can afford given his income, tastes, and other considerations.

*Maximizing
satisfaction*

The principle of diminishing marginal utility explains how the consumer acts. To maximize satisfaction from the expenditure of a fixed income the consumer should try to allocate his spending for different items so that the last dollar spent for a particular good or service will bring him satisfaction equal to the final dollar spent on all other goods and services. If he did not behave in this fashion—either by cool calculation or rough approximation—he could increase his total satisfaction by shifting his spending to some other good or service. To illustrate, our early morning coffee drinker may well prefer to purchase a doughnut rather than a third cup of coffee because he gets more satisfaction from the doughnut that he would from the third cup of coffee.

Put simply, the principle of rational consumer behavior says that the consumer ought to allocate his money income so that the last dollar spent for each product or service will yield him the same amount of extra utility. This means the marginal utility *per dollar spent* is equalized for all items. This proposition can be expressed in mathematical form. For example, the consumer is in equilibrium when

$$\frac{MU_a}{P_a} = \frac{MU_b}{P_b} = \frac{MU_c}{P_c}, \text{ etc.}$$

In other words, the consumer maximizes utility when the marginal utility (MU) of each commodity or service consumed divided by its price (P) equals the marginal utility of every other product or service consumed divided by its price. (The subscripts a, b, c in the equation refer to different commodities.) The ratio of marginal utility to price for all products and services consumed is equal. This appears relatively abstract, but there is an everyday explanation for it. Rational behavior requires us to adjust our expenditures to get the most out of them.

The Concept of Elasticity

The foregoing discussion stressed the key idea that the quantity demanded varies inversely in relation to price. This is the essence of the "law of demand." Another dimension of demand, however, is of great importance to the economist. It is not enough merely to know that the quantity demanded varies inversely with price; we must also know how responsive quantity demanded is to a change in price. Economists want to know the extent to which quantity demanded changes when price changes. This kind of knowledge is needed for supply as well as for demand. *Elasticity* is the technical name given to the responsiveness of either quantity demanded or quantity supplied to a change in price.

The responsiveness of demand and supply to price

Economists distinguish three types of demand or supply schedules by reference to their elasticities. (We will discuss only the demand schedule, although obviously the same ideas apply to the supply schedule.) An *elastic* demand schedule is one for which quantity demanded is highly responsive to a change in price, whereas an *inelastic* demand schedule is one in which quantity demanded does not respond significantly to a change in price. A demand schedule of *unitary elasticity* is one in which the quantity demanded changes in the same proportion as price.

Three degrees of elasticity

Expenditure and Price

Although these distinctions are quite general, we can determine quantitatively the elasticity of a demand schedule. The easiest and most direct method is to examine what happens to the total expenditures for a commodity (price times quantity) when price changes. If total revenue increases (decreases) when the price is reduced (increased), the demand is elastic. On the other hand, if total revenue decreases (increases) when the price is reduced (increased), the demand is inelastic. If there is no change in total revenue with either an increase or a decrease in price, demand is of unitary elasticity. Figure 11-3 illustrates the three types of elasticity.

Coefficient of Elasticity

The second and more complex technical measure of elasticity involves the use of a *coefficient of elasticity*, which for any given demand schedule measures the responsiveness of quantity demanded

281

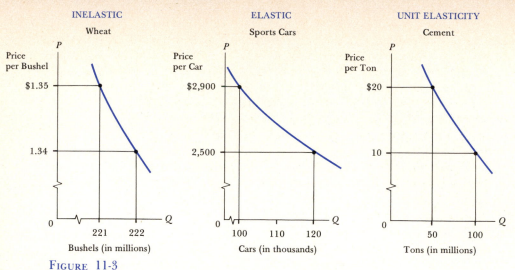

| INELASTIC | ELASTIC | UNIT ELASTICITY |
| Wheat | Sports Cars | Cement |

FIGURE 11-3

Types of Elasticity.

An *inelastic* demand is shown in the left-hand diagram. In this case a drop in the price of wheat by 2 cents a bushel also leads to $9,000 less revenue. In the center diagram an *elastic* demand is shown: cutting the price of sports cars by $400 increases total sales by $10 million. Finally, the right-hand diagram shows *unitary elasticity,* in which a reduction in price has no effect on total revenue. In all three cases more was sold at the lower price.

to a change in price by comparing them in percentage form. If this coefficient is greater than one, demand is elastic; if the coefficient is less than one, demand is inelastic; and if the coefficient is equal to one, demand is of unitary elasticity.

For example, let us assume a retailer is selling 50,000 packs per month of a well-known brand of cigarettes at 35¢ per pack. A new tax of 5¢ per pack is imposed on cigarettes; the retailer passes it on to the consumer by raising the price to 40¢ per pack. After this change, the retailer's total sales decline to 49,000 packs per month. However, his total revenue has gone from $17,500 per month to $19,600 per month, which must indicate that the demand is inelastic. The coefficient of elasticity is determined by dividing the percentage change in quantity sold (2.0%) by the percentage change in price (14.3%). The resulting coefficient is .14, which is significantly less than one and thus indicates a highly inelastic demand.

The Determinants of Elasticity

Elasticity is significant because it gives a numerical indication of the degree of control a seller may exercise over the price of the commodity or service. In general, if the demand schedule for a commodity or service is inelastic it suggests that the seller has some significant amount of control over the price he can charge for his wares. In our example, the inelastic nature of the demand

The seller's control over price

for cigarettes enables the retailer to pass the full amount of the tax on to the consumer. A relatively elastic demand schedule gives the seller little or no control over price. A wheat farmer, for example, has no power to raise the price he gets for his crop; he must accept the price determined by the totality of market forces. In Chapter 12 we shall see more fully how the elasticity concept is useful for understanding the various types of market situations in the modern economy.

Several factors determine the elasticity of demand for any particular commodity or service. The most important of these include the extent to which substitutes are available for the commodity or service, the size of expenditure on the good or service in relation to income, whether the product is regarded as a necessity or a luxury, and the durability of the commodity. Generally, demand is elastic for products for which there are acceptable substitutes; for which expenditure is large in relation to income; which are thought of as luxuries; and which are durable. Demand is inelastic for goods or services for which there are few acceptable substitutes; for which the expenditure is small in relation to the income of the buyer; which are viewed as necessities; and which are not durable. To confirmed cigarette smokers, as in our example, a five-cent increase in price per pack may be a nuisance, but it will not deter them from purchasing cigarettes.

The concept of elasticity is very significant in advertising. One of the purposes of advertising is to reduce the elasticity of the demand schedule for a particular product or service. Advertising that stresses the importance of one brand compared to another brand is trying to do this. If it succeeds, the seller will have more control over price and a stronger market position.

Individual Demand and Total Demand

So far, we have discussed the principle of demand primarily by reference to the individual and his response to price, given his preferences, his income, and other variables which may influence the amount of a commodity or service he wishes to buy. We have seen that the demand relationship is founded on the individual; the concept of utility—or, more appropriately, marginal utility—supplies the rationale for consumer behavior. But economic analysis is also concerned with total demand for a particular commodity or service. Although both individual demand and total demand are difficult to measure statistically, the concept of total —or, as it is sometimes called, "market demand"—has significance and validity. In effect, it is the summation of all the individual demand curves for a particular commodity or service. We pointed out above that one purpose of advertising is to reduce the elasticity of demand for a particular product, thereby giving the seller more control over the price. But the advertiser is concerned about more than his own product; he also wants to increase market demand. The automobile manufacturer, for example, hopes his advertising will not only make the demand for his car less elastic, but also increase the total demand for automobiles.

The Principle of Supply

Let us now turn to the other side of the coin and consider the forces which shape the supply curve. In economic analysis, supply is a schedule showing the quantity of a commodity or service that the supplier places on the market at various possible prices. As for the demand schedule, there is a time dimension to the supply schedule. But demand and supply differ in the relationship between quantity and price. For the supply schedule this relationship is direct: the quantity supplied varies directly with the price. The basic principle of supply is that the higher the price, the greater the amount offered in the market; the lower the price, the less the amount offered in the market.

The Nature of the Firm

Economic analysis is largely concerned with demand originating with the individual consumer. On the supply side, the counterpart to the individual consumer in a market economy is generally the business firm. The firm may be a small single proprietorship or a gigantic corporation; in either case, it decides on the quantity of output it will offer on the market at various prices. Thus the business firm occupies a central and strategic position in a market system. The firm in some form exists in practically all societies. In the American economy it makes the key decisions on output and supply.

We are not now concerned with the legal structure of the business firm—whether it is organized as an individual proprietorship, a partnership, or a corporation. We are concerned with the firm as an economic unit whose major function is to combine economic resources in a production process and transform them into economically useful goods and services.

Balancing Profits and Costs

In a market setting, the business firm in the short and the long run is motivated by the pursuit of profit. For the private firm the pursuit of profit is the way in which it realizes its self-interest. The economist generalizes this to maintain that firms attempt in a broad sense to maximize their profits. Profit maximization, as we have seen, is the peg upon which the economist hangs the analysis of business firm behavior.

The firm's pursuit of profit does not by itself account for the nature, shape, and slope of the supply schedule. Normally the firm makes a profit by producing an output and selling it in the market, but in order to decide how much output to produce, given an array of possible prices, it must take into account the costs of production. These costs are the payments a firm must make to the owners of economic resources (i.e., those who own labor and nonhuman resources needed for production) to induce them to supply the services of their resources.

Once the firm has obtained the necessary resources, it combines them to produce an output. For the typical firm, the decision about production and supply involves a comparison between revenue expected from the sale of output, which in turn depends upon both the price and the quantity of output, and the costs incurred at varying levels of output. Thus, the supply schedule depends directly on the nature of the costs and their behavior as output changes. Armed with this understanding, we can see how firms operate on the supply side of the equation and determine what is going to take place in the market.

The Nature of Production Costs

All costs are payments that firms must make to owners of economic resources to induce them to supply the services of these resources. But production costs may be *explicit,* which means that they involve actual money outlays, or *implicit,* which means that resources are being used but no money outlays are involved. Implicit costs arise when the firm uses resources which it owns or which the owners of the firm own; hence no money outlays are necessary. In small firms, for example, the labor of the owner-manager is a common type of implicit cost, often such individuals do not pay themselves an actual money salary equal to the salary they might receive if employed by another firm. Farmers and other small businessmen often do not charge themselves a rent for land owned and used in their operation, although there are costs involved in its use.

Opportunity Costs

Whenever resources are used to produce a commodity or a service, some cost is involved. If a resource has several alternative

285

Prices and the
Allocation of
Resources

*The return to a
resource in its best
alternative use*

uses, there is always a cost involved in its use in a particular activity. The owner of the resource forgoes the income he could have obtained by allowing it to be used in another way. The term *opportunity cost* designates the return a resource can command in its next best alternative use. This concept underscores the fact that a firm's use of resources it may own does not mean it has no production costs. The cost is measured by the return the firm could get by putting the resources into their best alternative use. The salary an owner-manager could command elsewhere as a hired manager is an opportunity cost arising out of operating his own business. The opportunity cost of a college education is the income the student could have earned by going to work instead of to college.

Fixed and Variable Costs

Another way to classify costs is by distinguishing between fixed costs, sometimes called "overhead costs," and variable costs. Fixed costs are constant regardless of the level of production. The rent a firm pays for the building that houses its production facilities is a fixed cost. The rent must be paid each month, whether or not the firm actually produces an output that month. Property taxes and the salaries of management are often fixed or overhead costs.

Variable costs, as the term suggests, change as the level of production changes. Wage costs are a good example: as a firm expands its output it must hire more labor, and hence the element of labor cost expands with the increase in output. In the automobile industry, for example, production line workers are hired and fired with the ebb and flow of demand for automobiles. They are the variable factor and their total wage bill represents a major form of variable costs for the industry. Steel, glass, and other materials, of course, are also variable costs in automobile production. On the other hand, and apart from a major economic downturn, it is rare for the engineering, accounting, sales, and managerial staffs to change in size with short-term fluctuations in the demand for automobiles.

Note that variable costs are meaningful primarily in relation to the short-term production period, which we defined earlier as a period of time during which supply can be varied within the limits of existing plant size. In the long run, when the size of the industry may change because plant size is changing within the industry, all costs become variable.

Marginal Cost

Finally, let us note that it is important to distinguish between cost per unit of output and total cost. Much subsequent analysis concerning cost behavior will be formulated on the basis of unit rather than total cost. This is especially true for the concept of marginal cost, a fundamental notion for economic analysis. Marginal cost is the addition to total cost which results from a firm's production of an additional unit of output. To illustrate, assume it costs an extra $25 in labor and materials to produce one additional automobile per day in an automobile plant. The $25 is the marginal cost of the added output.

The concept of marginal cost is similar to marginal utility in that it involves change in one variable (cost) as a result of change in another variable (output). This type of change is described as "behavior at the margin" and is a key to much economic analysis. It simply means that we seek to analyze and understand change by looking at it in very small doses. Actual change does not always happen like this, but it is a useful way to proceed.

Economic Profit

An exact understanding of costs is important, too, in defining more precisely the meaning of profit in an economic sense. This is not the same thing as the bookkeeping profit of a business enterprise. Bookkeeping profit is generally the difference between total revenue and explicit costs. If accounting techniques were sufficiently advanced—which they are not—to recognize that costs spring fundamentally from the economic concept of opportunity costs, or income forgone, then there would be no essential difference between the economic and the accounting concept of costs. To the economist, profit is a surplus over and above all necessary costs—explicit and implicit—which the firm may incur in the process of producing goods and services. Economic profit is what the firm pursues and attempts to maximize in the short or the long run. Table 11-2 provides a simple numerical example of the difference between bookkeeping and economic costs. The data represent receipts and costs for a small individually owned manufacturing firm. In determining the accounting—or bookkeeping—profit the owner does not take into account his opportunity costs, which represent what he might be able to earn working as a hired manager for an enterprise of similar size and nature. This procedure yields a profit of $19,600. But when the owner's implicit (opportunity) cost is included in the calculation, the profit figure drops to $9,600. This is the true economic profit for the firm.

TABLE 11-2

Bookkeeping and Economic Profits

COMPUTATION OF BOOKKEEPING PROFIT

1. Gross Sales		$55,000
2. Explicit Costs		
a. Rent	$3,000	
b. Wages and Labor	8,000	
c. Interest on Loan	2,400	
d. Materials Used	22,000	
3. Total	$35,400	_____
Bookkeeping Profit (1–3)		$19,600

COMPUTATION OF ECONOMIC PROFIT

1. Gross Sales		$55,000
2. Explicit Costs		
a. Rent	$3,000	
b. Wages for Labor	8,000	
c. Interest on Loan	2,400	
d. Materials Used	22,000	
3. Total Explicit Costs	$35,400	
4. Implicit Wage of Owner	10,000	
5. Total of Implicit and Explicit Costs (3+4)	$45,400	_____
6. Economic Profit (1–5)		$9,600

The Behavior of Costs

Costs, both total and unit, change in response to changes in output. Since production costs are the major factor behind supply, an explanation of the behavior of costs will also explain the shape of the supply schedule.

Table 11-3 contains a set of cost data for a hypothetical firm producing bicycles. The same data are given in graphic form in Figure 11-4. The cost data are expressed on a unit basis. Unit costs are derived by dividing total cost by output; they are based on the behavior of total costs as the firm varies its level of output. The table shows unit fixed costs, unit variable costs, total unit costs, and marginal cost. The most significant aspect of the cost data in the table and the figure is that unit variable costs, unit total costs, and marginal cost initially decline as production is expanded, but eventually, after reaching a low point, begin to rise.

*Initial fall and
subsequent rise of
production costs*

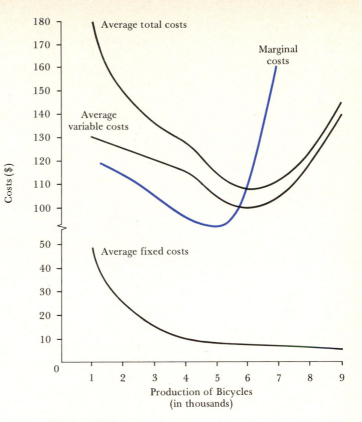

FIGURE 11-4
Weekly Cost Data for
the Production of Ten-
speed Bicycles.

Unit (average) variable
and unit (average) total costs
must decline as long as marginal costs are smaller, but
when marginal costs become
larger these costs will also
start to rise. Unit (average)
fixed costs always decline
while output is expanding.

TABLE 11-3
Weekly Cost Data for
the Production of 10-speed Bicycles

OUTPUT	TOTAL FIXED COST	TOTAL VARIABLE COSTS	TOTAL COSTS	AVERAGE FIXED COSTS	AVERAGE VARIABLE COSTS	AVERAGE TOTAL COSTS	MARGINAL COSTS
1,000	$50,000	$131,000	$181,000	$50.00	$131.00	$181.00	
							$119.00
2,000	50,000	250,000	300,000	25.00	125.00	150.00	
							110.00
3,000	50,000	360,000	410,000	16.67	120.00	136.67	
							100.00
4,000	50,000	460,000	510,000	12.50	115.00	127.50	
							65.00
5,000	50,000	525,000	575,000	10.00	105.00	115.00	
							75.00
6,000	50,000	600,000	650,000	8.33	100.00	108.33	
							135.00
7,000	50,000	735,000	785,000	7.14	105.00	112.14	
							225.00
8,000	50,000	960,000	1,010,000	6.25	120.00	126.25	
							300.00
9,000	50,000	1,260,000	1,310,000	5.56	140.00	145.55	

Unit fixed costs, of course, do not follow this pattern. They will continue to contract as long as output increases, because they do not increase or diminish as the level of output rises or falls. Therefore, the larger the level of output the smaller the fixed costs for a unit of output.

The numerical example and diagram illustrate an important point: economists regard cost curves as being typically U-shaped, although in reality the bottom of the U may extend over a very large range of output. Nevertheless, unit cost behavior is assumed to be of this nature. Costs decline as output expands, eventually reaching a minimum level, following which they rise if production continues to expand and press against the limits of firm capacity.

The Law of Diminishing Returns

The crucial economic problem is to account for the initial fall and subsequent rise in unit production costs. Economic analysis explains this behavior by the "principle of diminishing marginal productivity," also called the "law of diminishing returns" and the "law of variable proportions." This "law" is one of the most fundamental in all economic analysis; it involves a basic relationship between the input of a particular resource and the resulting output, on the assumption that all other resources are held constant. The essence of the principle is:

> *If increasing quantities of one economic resource are used in conjunction with a fixed quantity of other resources, then, after a certain point, each successive unit of the variable resource will make a smaller and smaller addition to the total output.*

How does this principle apply to a typical firm? In the short run, the fixed resource is the size of the physical plant, including land available for the firm's operations. The variable resource is its labor supply. Thus, if the firm varies its production within the confines of a fixed quantity of plant and land by changing the amount of labor it uses, its unit costs of production will initially decline as it expands operation toward the most efficient point of production. Eventually, though, its cost of production will begin to rise as it tries to spread more and more labor over a fixed quantity of other resources.

Table 11-4 contains hypothetical data on the behavior of output in response to variation in the quantity of one resource (labor), given a fixed quantity of other resources (land and capital). Figure 11-5 plots these data in a graph showing the relation between inputs of labor and total product. A close examination of these data and the diagram will not only clarify the meaning of the principle of diminishing marginal productivity, but also show

TABLE 11-4
Output of Bicycles and Labor Input

LABOR INPUT	OUTPUT	OUTPUT PER WORKER *	MARGINAL OUTPUT PER WORKER **
10	100	10.0	
			15.0
20	250	12.5	
			17.5
30	425	14.2	
			17.0
40	595	14.8	
			15.0
50	745	14.9	
			13.5
60	880	14.7	
			13.0
70	1010	14.4	
			10.0
80	1110	13.9	
			9.0
90	1200	13.3	
			0.0
100	1200	12.0	

* Total output divided by labor input. This equals average product per worker.

** Amount of output added on the average per additional worker. Note: Workers are added in groups of 10.

why this principle underlies cost behavior, given prices for the economic resources which enter into the production process. Figure 11-5 shows that initially, as the labor input increases output expands more than in proportion to the increase in the input of the variable factor. This phase of production involves increasing returns, which, in turn, means that production costs decline. Eventually a point is reached at which output response is less than in proportion to the input of the variable resource. In Figure 11-5 this is the phase of diminishing returns. Unit production costs begin to rise at this point. If the firm continued to push ahead with use of the variable resource, given no change in its other resources, it would eventually reach a point at which no further increase in output was obtainable. In Figure 11-5 this is the point of absolute diminishing returns. Any use of the variable resource beyond this point results in an absolute decline in output: further rise in unit costs without any additional output. Normally no firm operates in this range; the U-shaped portion of the typical cost curve for the business firm corresponds to the range of output lying within the phase of increasing returns and the phase of decreasing returns.

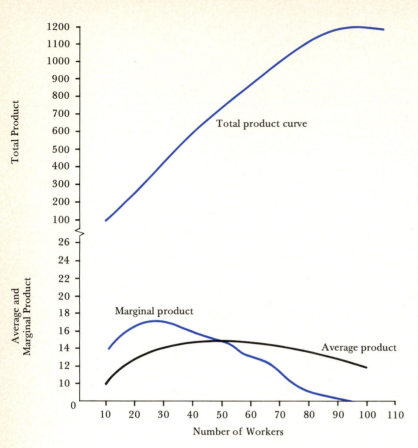

Total product curve

FIGURE 11-5

Output and Labor In-
put: Principle of Dimin-
ishing Marginal Productivity.

Output increases in greater
proportion than labor input
up to a level of labor use of
50 workers. This is the phase
of increasing returns and corresponds on a cost curve diagram to declining unit variable costs. Beyond this level
of labor use output increases
less than in proportion to
labor input, the range of decreasing returns. On a cost
curve diagram this corre-
sponds to rising unit variable
costs.

Marginal product

Average product

Number of Workers

The Marginal Product

Figure 11-5 also contains a curve labeled "marginal product."
This is the addition to total product resulting from the employment of one more unit of the variable factor. Note carefully that
marginal product first increases as output is expanded through
the use of the variable factor and then begins to decline, reaching
zero at the point where diminishing returns in an absolute sense
are encountered. The marginal product curve is the physical expression of the principle of diminishing marginal productivity
and forms the physical basis for the behavior of the marginal cost
in Figure 11-4 and in Table 11-3.

*The principle of
diminishing
marginal
productivity*

The Supply Curve and Time

The crucial lesson of this discussion is that cost behavior is determined primarily by the operation of the principle of diminishing

returns. More than any other single factor, this principle accounts for the positive slope of the supply curve. But this is not the end of the story; the supply curve, like the demand curve, has a time dimension attached to it.

In discussing the supply curve economists distinguish between the *long run* and the *short run*. In the short run the size of the productive plant is fixed, which means that output can be varied only within the limits of a given plant capacity. In the short run, therefore, capital and land are the fixed resources and labor is the chief variable resource. The short-run behavior of the unit variable costs and marginal costs curve reflects the use of additional quantities of labor with a fixed amount of capital and land. The long run is a period of time sufficient to permit variation in the size of the plant. Therefore, in the long run all resources become variable.

Economists generally agree that even in the long run the typical cost curve will eventually turn upward, which means that there is some practical limitation to the optimum size of a production plant. The reason for the increase in the level of costs, even in the long run, is still to be found in the principle of diminishing productivity. The limiting resource in the long run appears to be managerial ability, for even with the increased use of sophisticated tools such as the computer, there is an upper limit to the size of an enterprise that can be effectively controlled. If this were not true then there would be no absolute upper limit to the size of a physical plant; theoretically, the output of an entire industry, such as automobile production, could be produced most economically from one single plant.

Single plant industries may exist in a small geographic area, but not for the entire nation. However, the size of a plant must be distinguished from the size of a firm. A single firm may operate one or more plants, and there may not be the same limitation to the growth of the size of the firm as the principle of diminishing productivity imposes on the growth of the size of the plant.

Economies of Scale

Economists have found that in the long run the behavior of costs is affected by *economies of scale,* some of which are internal and some external. Economies of scale are cost-reducing forces which come into play as the size of the plant or the size of an industry increases. Internal economies of scale take place within the plant as it grows in size. They may include a greater specialization in management and labor; more effective use of capital because some machinery may be available only for a minimum size of operation; greater access to sources of finance; or economies in marketing. All of these may result from the simple increase in the size of the plant. Internal economies of scale do not nullify operation of the principle of diminishing returns; they merely shift all cost curves to a lower level as the scale of operations becomes larger.

External economies of scale are those which benefit the firm as a result of the growth of the industry of which it is a part. These may include lower costs for the materials purchased by the firm because a larger industry makes it possible for suppliers to specialize. A larger industry may justify the establishment of training schools which provide better skilled and more productive labor. A large industry may also be better able to support specialized services, such as research, which may benefit the firm. In other words, the firm's costs may be reduced not by its own action but because the industry of which it is a part has grown enough to permit internal economies of scale to develop elsewhere, particularly among the firms which supply the industry.

The Business Firm and Resource Allocation

We are now in a better position to examine how the actions of a firm affect resource allocation in the economic system. As pointed out earlier, the firm occupies a strategic position in a market economy; it makes the basic decisions that determine how resources ultimately are allocated among alternative uses. Demand expresses the preferences of consumers and other ultimate users of the goods and services produced, but the response of suppliers operating within firms influences the pattern of resource allocation within the economic system.

Demand for Labor

The firm has to make two vital decisions that bear upon resource allocation. First, it must decide upon the scale of operation within the limits of its existing plant. Primarily, variation of output within a firm's existing plant means variation in labor used. Output expansion requires more labor. There are a limited number of sources of additional labor available to the firm. It may, first of all, draw on people who have been unemployed. This is likely to occur when output expansion is part of an overall expansion which brings the economy out of a recession or depression. If the economy is fully employed, however, the situation is different, because with full employment additional labor can come only from other firms in the same industry, from other industries, or by bringing new workers into the labor force. In any event it is likely that the firm will have to bid up the price it pays for labor;

*Demand for labor
in a fully employed
economy*

as this happens, some reallocation of labor resources from other economic sectors will take place. When total demand is such that output is pushed toward full capacity, bidding by the individual firm for more labor resources will also add significant pressure to the price level.

Demand for Land and Capital

The firm must also make a long-run decision whether to expand or contract the size of its plant. This decision will affect not only the allocation of labor resources among alternative uses, but also the use of capital and land. Thus, in the long run, the allocation among alternative uses of all economic resources is determined for the market sector of the economy by decisions made at the level of the firm.

Profit Maximization

The economist assumes there is rational behavior underlying the decision-making process of the firm in a market context. As has been stressed repeatedly, rational behavior in an economic sense is maximizing behavior. For the consumer, rational behavior means maximizing the satisfaction he gets from consumption, given the constraints of a limited income, personal tastes, prices, and other variables. The pursuit of self-interest by producers leads the firm to try to maximize its profit for the good and simple reason that profitability is the most important single criterion by which the success of an enterprise is judged in a market system. Profit in this context means economic profit, the surplus of revenue over all costs of production, explicit and implicit.

Since profit maximization is the underlying theme which runs through all market analysis concerned with the behavior of the firm, it is essential to understand what this means and does not mean! When the economist talks of profit maximization for the firm in the context of the market he does not mean that profit is the only explanation for business behavior. Obviously, many other factors influence the behavior of a business firm, just as many things besides price influence the behavior of the consumer. These include such important but elusive variables as power, prestige, survival, service, and continuity, to name but a few. But over time and in many different kinds of market situations, profit is the single most important—or most strategic—factor to which we can point in explaining the behavior of the business firm in a market setting. Profit maximization is the foundation stone of an elaborate structure of analysis which examines how firms behave in a variety of market situations. We shall consider this behavior and its impact on resource allocation in the next chapter.

Profit vs. other motivating factors

295

Questions for Review and Discussion

1. What is the technical meaning of price? What is the meaning of relative price? What is its significance?

2. Cite some examples of prices set outside the market process.

3. Explain the basic ideas involved in the concepts of demand and supply schedules. What is unique about these concepts?

4. What is an equilibrium price? How does it differ from any observed price?

5. What are the three general laws of price behavior?

6. Trace the manner in which a decline in demand for a particular product will affect relative prices and the allocation of resources within the economy.

7. Explain the principle of diminishing marginal utility and why it provides an explanation for the shape of the demand schedule.

8. How can a rational consumer maximize the satisfaction obtained from spending his income? What does this have to do with price?

9. Give some reasons why the idea of demand elasticity is important for understanding the way a market economy works. What are the determinants of demand elasticity?

10. How does the concept of opportunity costs aid in understanding the nature of the costs incurred by the typical business firm?

11. Explain the law of diminishing returns and its relationship to the behavior of production costs.

12. What are economies of scale? What is the difference between internal and external economies of scale?

12

Competition and the Allocation of Resources

COMPETITION IS A FACT OF LIFE in the business world. Nearly every firm in the American economy must make its production decisions with an eye to what rival firms are doing. But the degree of competition varies greatly from industry to industry; while automobile production in the United States is concentrated among four corporations, several thousand companies manufacture the machine tools used in heavy industry. In this chapter, we shall consider how the firm's behavior is affected by the competitive environment in which it operates. Our major concern will be to determine the market conditions that yield maximum efficiency in the use of economic resources.

The Structure of Competition

The different competitive situations which influence the behavior of the firm are called the structure of competition. The most important factors that determine this structure in any given industry are:

1. The number of firms in the industry.
2. The ease with which firms enter or exit from the industry.
3. The nature of the product or service produced.
4. The extent of the firm's control over the price of the commodity or service produced.
5. The techniques the firm employs to market its output.

Though not exhaustive, this list provides a useful basis for the study of four models of market situations that economists use to examine the behavior of the firm under varying conditions. These models are pure (or perfect) competition, monopolistic competition, oligopoly, and monopoly. They are representative of market situations that prevail in important sectors of the economy, although it must be stressed that no market in the actual economy corresponds in every respect to a particular model. Moreover, in the real economy the dividing lines between different market situations are not as clear and sharp as those separating the models. But the models establish performance criteria the economist can use to evaluate the effectiveness of the market structures that do exist.

These models not only enable us to understand some important characteristics of different market situations, but also permit us to define more precisely the meaning of competition as it relates to resource allocation and the behavior of the firm. Two forms of competition are important to economic analysis: price competition, that is movements in price which affect resource use and the competitive position of the individual firm; and nonprice competition, which embraces all efforts to improve the competitive position of the firm by means other than price changes. In price competition the price changes in response to demand and supply forces, whether or not the individual firm wishes or initiates such price changes.

The major forms of nonprice competition include changes in the quality and design of a product, advertising, and special services to the consumer. Quality and design changes embrace a variety of practices, including annual model changes in automobiles, new packaging techniques, different styles of a commodity for different groups (such as wide and narrow ties for men), not to mention technical improvements that lead to better quality and lower prices. Many forms of nonprice competition lead to a real improvement in consumer welfare by increasing the choice open to the consumer. But it is also true, especially for advertising and some alleged design changes, that nonprice competition can be spurious, adding only to costs and little to real improvement in consumer welfare. Much of the contemporary consumer movement is directed at the elimination of questionable and misleading forms of nonprice competition.

The Model of Pure Competition

Pure competition describes a market structure characterized by a very large number of firms producing a standardized product. The number of firms must be so great that no single firm can by its own action control the price of the commodity produced. The closest we come to pure competition in the actual economy is in agriculture, where we find markets in which the number of farms producing a given commodity (such as wheat) is so large that no individual farmer can influence the price of wheat by adding to or withdrawing from the supply on the market.

Many firms with no single seller controlling price

Pure competition is also characterized by relative ease of exit from or entry into the market. There are no precise standards to measure this, but clearly it is much easier to enter into or exit from agricultural production than, say, steel production. When there are many firms in an industry, the typical firm is small; thus it is easier to acquire the resources necessary to enter the industry. This is less true today than it used to be, for now capital equipment worth $50,000 to $100,000 may be needed just to get started in farming. Nevertheless, the labor, land, and equipment (i.e., the capital) needed to enter agricultural production are more readily obtainable by an individual than are the quantities required for entry into most kinds of manufacturing.

Relative ease of entry and exit

Since there are many sellers of the commodity and the product in pure competition is standardized, buyers are indifferent to the identity of the seller. Thus it does the seller no good to advertise. One does not see Farmer Smith advertising in a local newspaper that his brand of wheat is superior to the brand produced by other farmers. The buyer does not care where the wheat comes from as long as it is up to the standard he requires.

The Model of Monopolistic Competition

Monopolistic competition shares a number of characteristics with pure competition. First, the market characterized by monopolistic competition has a large number of sellers, but not so many that the individual seller has absolutely no control over the price. Monopolistically competitive industries abound in many sectors of the economy, particularly retailing and distribution. Grocery stores, drugstores, and department stores are common examples.

Many firms with the seller exercising some control over price

Usually location is the factor that gives one retail store some slight edge over its competitors. In monopolistic competition, many small firms produce similar products and services, but typically there are not so many that the individual seller is completely without control over the price at which he sells his wares.

Monopolistically competitive industries are often characterized by *product differentiation,* which, as the term suggests, refers to real or imagined differences between the products of different sellers. There may be real differences in product quality, variations of the shape or packaging, differences in the services offered in conjunction with the sale of the product, or merely extensive advertising which tries, often successfully, to give the potential buyer the idea that product A is somehow superior to product B. The bewildering variety of breakfast cereals is a familiar form of product differentiation. Most of us realize there are no differences of substance in the many varieties of cereals derived from the same basic product—wheat or rice—even though we may have favorites. Any activity by the seller which causes the potential buyer to differentiate his product from another seller's product can be called product differentiation. In the modern, complex economy there seems to be no limit to the ingenious techniques sellers employ to establish some idea of difference with the buyer.

Entry into and exit from an industry characterized by monopolistic competition is relatively easy. The retail sale of gasoline and other petroleum products illustrates this. In almost any well-traveled area new filling stations appear and disappear at frequent intervals; the new firms enter this activity and leave it without great difficulty.

Industries marked by monopolistic competition must indulge in a significant amount of "nonprice" competition to secure additional sales and customers. Obviously a firm may compete by changing price if it has some control over the price. In monopolistic competition, then, a firm may use variations in price as well as variations in other ways, such as services performed in conjunction with the sale of a commodity, advertising, or qualitative changes in the product.

The Model of Oligopoly

*Relatively small
numbers of firms
with the seller
exercising
significant control
over price*

Oligopoly is a type of market structure especially common in the contemporary American economy, in which the number of producers or sellers is relatively small. The phrase "relatively small" is not precise, but it means, in effect, a number of producers so small that no single seller can act without taking into account the fact that his rivals will react in some fashion to whatever he does.

This is not necessarily the situation in monopolistic competition, where the number of sellers may be so large that no one seller has to worry particularly about the reaction of a rival to any action he may take. In oligopoly one must always be concerned with the reaction of rivals. Thus one of its most significant characteristics is the mutual interdependence of the sellers.

Oligopoly is found largely among the major manufacturing sectors of the American economy. Steel manufacturing, automobile manufacturing, chemical production, rubber tire production are a few examples. Because of the large size of the producing unit and the small number of firms, entry of new firms into oligopolistic industries is both difficult and rare. Nor is exit a common occurrence in these industries. The financial troubles that plagued the Penn Central Railroad Company in the last several years offer dramatic testimony on this point. After a failure to raise a desperately needed $200 million through a federally guaranteed loan, the company was forced into bankruptcy in June 1970. Yet it continues to operate as a railroad, hauling passengers and freight, and what its ultimate destiny will be no one really knows.

Difficult entry and rare exit

Oligopolistic industries may produce either a standardized or a differentiated product. The firms in an oligopolistic industry usually have significant control over the price of their products, although nonprice competition is also significant.

The Model of Monopoly

Monopoly is a market situation in which there is a single seller for a commodity or service with few, if any, acceptable substitutes. For a monopoly of any sort to exist in the economic system there must be formidable barriers to the entry of new firms into that particular industry. In monopoly the firm has a high degree of control over price; as a matter of fact, it really controls price because it does not have to contend with competing firms. Under monopoly there is identity between the firm and the industry. A common example is a telephone company with a government franchise that gives it the exclusive right to operate in a given area. The only restraints on the rates that the phone company charges are those imposed by the Federal Communications Commission and state regulatory agencies.

Single seller with price restrained only by regulation

Market Models and Resource Allocation

The four models for market structures can be regrouped into two basic categories: industries characterized by many sellers (or producers), and industries with a few producers or sellers. Pure competition and monopolistic competition are in the first category. These market arrangements are most likely to be found in either agriculture or the services and trade sector of the economy. In the second category are oligopoly and monopoly. Oligopoly is most likely to exist in manufacturing, especially the large mass production industries, monopoly in public utilities.

To complete the analysis of resource allocation in a market economy begun in Chapter 11, we turn now to two basic questions. How does the firm behave in these different market situations, or under varying degrees of competition? And how does this behavior affect resource allocation? Our analysis is based on the assumption that the firm is a profit-maximizing entity. Our purpose is to gauge the degree to which alternative types of market structures contribute to the efficient use of society's real resources.

Competition with Many Producers

Let us begin this analysis by examining how firms behave in industries with many producers, the situation in pure competition. This is not necessarily the most realistic market model, but it demonstrates the principles necessary to understand firm behavior in any type of market conditions. The purely competitive market model is the source of important criteria for appraising the conditions under which society can reach an *optimum* with respect to resource allocation. (An optimum is a condition that cannot be improved by any change in the pattern of resource use.)

Marginal cost and marginal revenue

To understand how the firm acts in any kind of market setting, we utilize the concepts of marginal revenue and marginal costs. Marginal cost, as pointed out in Chapter 11, is the addition to the firm's total cost resulting from production of one more unit of output. Marginal revenue is a similar concept; it is the addition to the firm's total revenue (price times quantity sold) when the firm produces and sells one added unit of output. Marginal cost and marginal revenue are essential to an explanation of the firm's search for maximum profits. Throughout the discussion we shall continue to use the term "firm" as economists do, for any individual producer, from a single wheat farmer to a corporate giant on the order of General Motors.

Demand under Pure Competition

Recall the two most important features of the purely competitive market: the firm has no control over price, and the individual firm is only one of an extremely large number of firms in the industry. In practical terms, this means that any one firm can produce as much as it is physically capable of producing in a period of time and within the limits of its capacity and that it can dispose of its output in the market without affecting price in the market. Thus, to the individual firm demand appears unlimited at the level of the existing price.

Demand unlimited from viewpoint of individual firm

Note this most carefully. Demand is unlimited from the viewpoint of any single firm, because the firm can sell all of its production without depressing price. This does not mean, though, that demand is unlimited for the output of the entire market of which the firm is a part. For example, the individual wheat farmer has no fear that if he produces more bushels per acre he will depress the price of wheat. He knows that at the prevailing price the market will absorb all he can produce, because he is such a small part of the total supply. Translated into graphic terms, this means that the individual firm in the purely competitive market views demand as a horizontal line at the level of existing market price. Such a demand schedule is shown in Figure 12-1. Technically, we

FIGURE 12-1

Individual Demand in a Purely Competitive Market.

To the producer in this type of market, demand is perfectly elastic, which means he can sell all he can produce at the prevailing market price. A horizontal schedule depicts this situation. Here market price and marginal revenue are also identical.

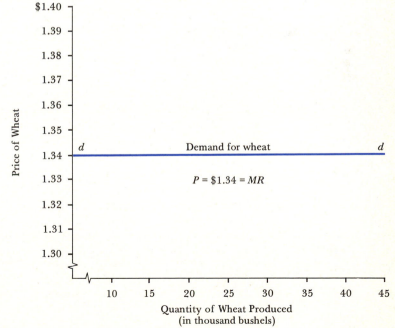

$P = \$1.34 = MR$

Quantity of Wheat Produced
(in thousand bushels)

**Competition and
the Allocation of
Resources**

*Marginal revenue
the same as price
in pure competition*

say that in a purely competitive market, demand for the output of
any single producer is perfectly elastic.

Two things require clarification at this point. First, what determines price? As in any market, it depends on the interaction between total demand and total supply. Figure 12-2 shows the establishment of the market price for wheat, which is the price paid
the individual wheat farmer. Second, what does marginal revenue
mean in pure competition? Since marginal revenue is the addition to total revenue derived from the production and sale of one
additional unit of output, and since, too, all added units of output can be sold at the same price, it follows that marginal revenue
and price are the same in the purely competitive market. The single firm does not have to reduce the price to sell more of its output. If it had to, marginal revenue would be less than price, but
this is not the case in pure competition.

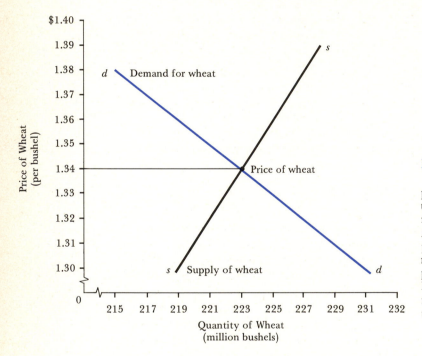

FIGURE 12-2
Determination of the
Market Price for Wheat.
   The market price of $1.34
per bushel is determined by
the interaction of total demand *dd* and total supply *ss*.
At a higher price—say $1.36
per bushel—demand would
run ahead of supply, causing
price to rise. Only one equilibrium price is possible in a
market at any particular
time.

We can now examine how the firm determines how much it
will produce under pure competition. We assume the firm is motivated by a desire to maximize its profit within the limits of its
existing productive capacity and that it has full knowledge of
market price and of production costs and their behavior as output
changes.

The Principle of Profit Maximization

Under such conditions, the basic economic principle governing the behavior of the firm is this: output will be adjusted to the point at which marginal cost and marginal revenue are equal. The firm must do this to maximize its profit. Whenever marginal revenue is greater than marginal cost, total profit can be increased by expanding production, but whenever marginal cost is in excess of marginal revenue, total profit is increased by reducing production.

*Maximum profit
achieved when
marginal cost
equals marginal
revenue*

This principle is readily demonstrated with the simply hypothetical data given in Table 12-1 and plotted in Figure 12-3. In the table we find a set of cost data and an assumed price for the product. The cost data include average total cost, average variable cost, and marginal cost. Marginal revenue is the same thing as price. Table 12-1 also contains a column showing total cost and total revenue; total cost is equal to output times average cost, whereas total revenue is equal to output times price. The difference between total revenue and total cost is, quite obviously, the total profit the firm will obtain at various levels of output. A careful examination of the data in the table shows that total profit is maximized when the firm's level of output is at the point where marginal cost and marginal revenue are equal. This exact level is 29,000 bushels of wheat. Further examination of these data indicates that at any level of output less than 29,000 bushels, marginal revenue exceeds marginal cost and the firm has not yet reached the scale of operations at which its total profit is maximized. Accordingly, it should adjust its production volume upward. On the

TABLE 12-1

Cost and Revenue Data for a Wheat Producer

OUTPUT *	MARGINAL REVENUE (PRICE)	AVERAGE TOTAL COST	MARGINAL COST	TOTAL COST	TOTAL REVENUE	PROFIT OF LOSS	
10,000	$1.34	$1.360	$1.36	$13,600	$13,400	− $200	
15,000	1.34	1.330	1.27	19,950	20,100	150	
20,000	1.34	1.320	1.29	26,400	26,800	400	
25,000	1.34	1.320	1.32	33,000	33,500	500	{ Profit
29,000	1.34	1.322	1.34	38,338	38,860	⟶ 522 ←	{ Maximization
30,000	1.34	1.330	1.38	39,900	40,200	300	
35,000	1.34	1.360	1.54	47,600	46,900	− 700	
40,000	1.34	1.400	1.68	56,000	53,600	− 2,400	
45,000	1.34	1.460	1.94	65,700	60,300	− 5,400	

* Bushels of Wheat.

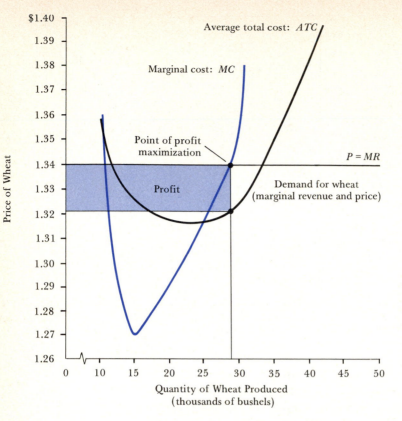

FIGURE 12-3
Cost, Price, and Profit Data for a Wheat Producer.

Profit is maximized when output is adjusted to the level at which marginal cost and marginal revenue are equal; in the figure this takes place at a level of 29,000 bushels of wheat. The shaded area shows total profit.

other hand, at a level of output in excess of 29,000 bushels, marginal cost is greater than marginal revenue and again the firm has departed from the profit-maximizing position. Now it should adjust its volume of production downward.

In Figure 12-3 profit maximization is at the intersection of the marginal cost curve and the marginal revenue schedule, the latter being at the level of existing price in this market. But Figure 12-3, because it is based on unit cost data, does not reveal directly the firm's total profit. To achieve this we need to plot total revenue and total cost, which is done in Figure 12-4. Here profit maximization is at an output level at which the vertical distance between the total revenue curve and the total cost curve is greatest; this is also the output at which marginal cost and marginal revenue are equal.

Balancing Gain and Cost

All this may seem unnecessarily abstract and unrealistic. But actually the principle of equality between marginal cost and marginal revenue is merely a formal way to describe behavior in which expected gain is balanced against expected cost. All firms must do this to decide on their scale of output. When a major au-

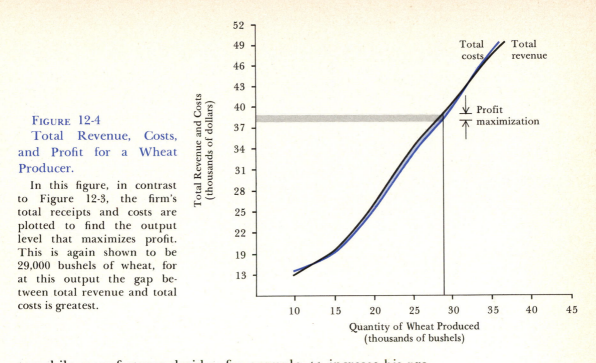

FIGURE 12-4
Total Revenue, Costs, and Profit for a Wheat Producer.

In this figure, in contrast to Figure 12-3, the firm's total receipts and costs are plotted to find the output level that maximizes profit. This is again shown to be 29,000 bushels of wheat, for at this output the gap between total revenue and total costs is greatest.

tomobile manufacturer decides, for example, to increase his production for the next quarter, he must balance the cost of hiring more labor and buying more materials against a judgment about the added revenue the firm will receive if the additional cars produced are sold. No rational producer can escape making such a calculation. Procedures for doing this may be highly formal, specifically attempting to estimate the revenue expected at different levels of output and weighing it against anticipated costs. Or the procedures may be very informal, involving little more than hunches or the manager's judgment of what will happen when the firm varies production under alternative conditions.

Minimizing Losses

The principle of equality between marginal cost and marginal revenue is also useful in explaining how a firm may minimize its losses, if market price is not high enough to cover the firm's average costs of production. Just as a firm will maximize its profit by adjusting output to the level at which marginal costs and marginal revenue are equal, it will minimize its losses by doing the same thing, *if* price is high enough to cover average variable costs of the firm, but not high enough to cover the firm's total average costs.

Table 12-2 contains data for a situation in which the price confronting the firm is not above the firm's average total costs at all levels of output, but is above its average variable costs. Under

307

TABLE 12-2

Price, Average Total Costs,
and Average Variable Cost Relationships
for a Business Firm

OUTPUT *	AVERAGE TOTAL COST	PRICE **	AVERAGE VARIABLE COST	MARGINAL COST	TOTAL COST	TOTAL VARIABLE COST	TOTAL REVENUE	PROFIT OR LOSS
10,000	$1.36	$1.28	$0.36	$1.36	$13,600	$3,600	$12,800	$ −800
15,000	1.33	1.28	0.66	1.27	19,950	9,900	19,200	−750
20,000	1.32	1.28	0.82	1.29	26,400	16,400	25,600	−800
25,000	1.32	1.28	0.92	1.32	33,000	23,000	32,000	−1000
30,000	1.33	1.28	0.99	1.38	39,900	29,700	38,400	−1500
35,000	1.36	1.28	1.07	1.54	47,600	37,450	44,800	−2800
40,000	1.40	1.28	1.15	1.68	56,000	46,000	51,200	−4800
45,000	1.46	1.28	1.24	1.94	65,700	55,800	57,600	−8100

* Bushels.
** Price = Marginal revenue

these circumstances it pays the firm to produce some output, even though it suffers losses at all levels of output. The firm minimizes its losses by producing at the point of equality between marginal cost and marginal revenue because production that more than covers the variable costs will reduce the losses experienced if the firm shuts down completely. This point would lie between 15,000 and 20,000 bushels of wheat. Should the firm shut down, its loss would equal its total fixed costs. As long as production yields revenue somewhat greater than its variable—or "out of pocket"—costs, it will not lose as much money as it would if it shut down completely.

Halting Production

The relation between price and variable cost also tells us when the firm should shut down operations altogether. A complete halt in production is rational economic behavior when price is not high enough to cover the variable costs of the firm. Losses will be minimized by stopping production, because then they will be limited to the total fixed costs of the firm. Production under these conditions would only add to the loss total. Figure 12-5 shows these two situations. In the left-hand diagram, price is higher than average variable cost for some output levels but below average total cost for all output levels. Losses are minimized when marginal revenues are equal. In the right-hand part of the figure price is below both average total cost and average variable cost. Now there is no level of output that would reduce the losses of the firm below the amount it would experience with a complete shutdown of operations.

FIGURE 12-5
Minimizing Loss and
Plant Shutdown.

In diagram A the firm is better off by producing an output *OQ* because price exceeds its average variable costs in the output range *NM*. By producing at the point at which *MR* equals *MC*, the firm will have a smaller loss than if it shut down completely. But in diagram B the firm is better off not to produce at all, as there is no output level at which price is higher than its average variable costs.

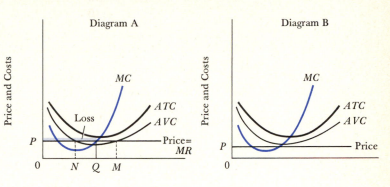

Thus the marginal cost curve plays a key role in determining how much the firm will offer on the market, given a price situation over which it has no control. To put the matter differently, the marginal cost curve is the short-term supply curve for the firm operating in a purely competitive industry. This is logical simply because this cost schedule shows the quantities that will be put on the market at different possible prices, given the principle that profit miximization requires output to be adjusted to the point at which price and marginal cost are equal. If we assume that all the firms in a particular industry have approximately identical cost curves, then it follows that the supply curve for the whole industry is nothing more than the summation of the marginal cost curves for all firms in the industry. Market price is then determined by the interaction between total demand for the output of that industry and the reaction of all firms in the industry, the latter being determined by the shape of the marginal cost curve for the individual firm. Figure 12-6 on the next page shows the industry supply curve constructed by multiplying the marginal cost data in Table 12-1 by the number of firms in the industry. The outcome in the market thus depends upon supply conditions that prevail at the level of the individual firm.

Supply curves for the firm and the industry

Equilibrium of the Firm and Resource Allocation

Our discussion so far has assumed that the individual firm is operating with a fixed productive capacity, the short-term equilibrium position of the firm. Since the productive capacity of the individual firms—and consequently the productive capacity of the whole industry—is fixed, the resources most directly affected by the action of the firm are those that enter into variable costs. For

The responses of resources to changes in output

309

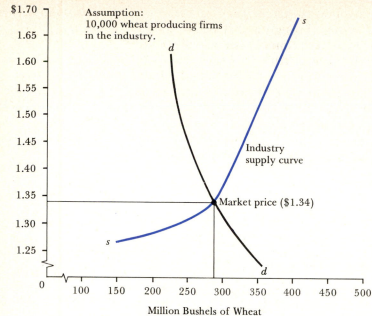

FIGURE 12-6
Industry Supply Curve
for Wheat Production.

Since the amount each firm will supply in a competitive industry is governed by its marginal costs, the supply curve for the entire industry (*ss*) is obtained by adding together the marginal cost curves for all firms in the industry. On the assumption that the firms have identical cost curves, this result is obtained by multiplying the output for each firm at a given level of marginal costs by the number of firms in the industry.

the economy as a whole, as well as for individual industries, variable costs depend primarily upon the amount of labor used. As long as there is inequality between marginal cost and marginal revenue there will be a movement of resources into the firm and hence into the industry, or out of the firm and hence possibly out of the industry. If the firm discovers that its marginal revenue exceeds its marginal cost, the profit maximization principle compels it to expand output, and to do this it will need to employ more labor and other resources which enter into variable costs. Thus, resources will be allocated toward the firm and the industry to which it belongs as long as production is expanding. On the other hand, if marginal cost exceeds marginal revenue, the firm will contract production, which involves using less labor and other resources. If these resources cannot be employed in other firms within the industry, they will either revert to the ranks of the unemployed or seek employment in other activities and other sectors of the economy. Under these circumstances, therefore, resources will be allocated away from the firm and the industry to which it belongs.

Equilibrium in the Long Run

Let us now examine firm and industry behavior in the long run. We continue to assume that purely competitive conditions exist in the industry under examination. Recall that the long run is a period of time which permits the individual firm to vary the size of its operations and permits the entry or exit of firms into the industry. Thus, the long run involves sufficient time to make adjustments on the supply side, either through a change in the size of the individual plant or through variations in the size of the industry itself. Generally, since the typical firm in a purely competitive industry is small, most changes in the long run take the form of expansion or contraction in the number of firms in the industry. We shall thus frame our analysis in terms of this type of change, although the principles involved also apply to changes in the size of the typical plant operating in the industry. Reality is, of course, much more complex than this.

Entry of New Firms

Let us begin by assuming that at the moment the typical firm has an economic profit, after having adjusted its output to profit-maximizing level. We also assume that the industry's existing profit level exceeds that obtainable elsewhere in the economic system; otherwise no new firms and resources would be drawn into the industry. In other words, the individual firm is in equilibrium, although the industry as a whole is not.

The effect on total industry supply

The role of economic profit—which is a surplus over and above all necessary explicit and implicit costs of production—is to draw new firms (hence resources) into this industry. But as new firms come into the industry, total industry supply is increased, which in turn causes the market price to fall. This process is shown in Figure 12-7. Here the supply curve shifts to the right, although there is no change in the level of total demand in the in-

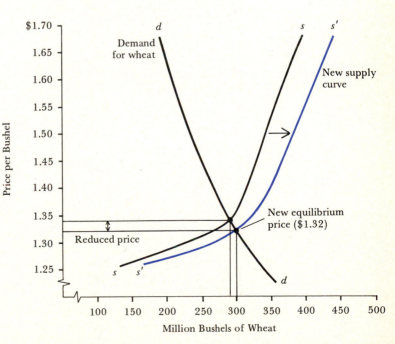

FIGURE 12-7
Shift in Industry Supply Curve and Change in the Price of Wheat.

The entry of 2,000 new firms into the industry shifts the total supply schedule to the right, from *ss* to *s's'*. This results in an increase in equilibrium output for the industry to 300 million bushels of wheat and a fall in price from $1.34 to $1.32 per bushel.

dustry. We see in operation here another law of price determination: an increase in supply reduces price, other things unchanged.

The individual firm sees these events as a downward shift in the level of the demand curve for its output, which, under purely competitive conditions, appears to the firm as a horizontal line at the level of existing price. But any downward shift in the demand curve confronting the individual firm requires it to readjust its level of output; when demand shifts down, marginal cost will exceed marginal revenue and the firm will no longer be producing the output that maximizes its profit. With an enlarged supply coming from the entry of new firms into the industry, the individual firm can reach a new profit-maximizing position only by adjusting output downward and finding a new equilibrium position.

Duration of Resource Flow

*The industry in
long-run
equilibrium*

If we are correct in assuming that as long as any economic profit exists in the industry there is a reason for more firms to enter the industry, then resources will flow into the industry until all firms in the industry are in a position in which price just covers all their average total costs. Then there will no longer be an incentive for new firms to come into the industry, and each individual firm in the industry will find itself in a long-run equilibrium position. Such a situation for the typical firm is shown in Figure 12-8.

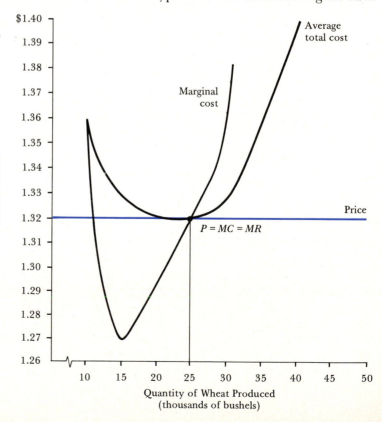

FIGURE 12-8

Long-run Equilibrium for the Competitive Firm.

Falling prices brought about by the entry of new firms into the industry force the typical firm into a long-term equilibrium in which price and marginal cost are equal at the output at which average total costs are lowest.

Note carefully the meaning of this position. The firm, as close examination of Figure 12-8 reveals, is operating at an ouput level at which its average total costs are lowest, but all economic profit has disappeared. This does not mean that the firm is not earning a return—or a bookkeeping profit—from the resources it owns, including the labor of the owner. It does mean that the rate of remuneration on all of its resources, including internally owned labor and other factors, is no greater than can be obtained elsewhere in the economic system.

Note, too, that in this long-run competitive equilibrium position, marginal cost and marginal revenue are equal, which means the firm is at an optimum with respect to profit maximization, even though all economic profit has disappeared. Each individual firm in the industry will produce less than before because as more firms enter the market, the share of any single firm will be smaller. For the industry as a whole, price will be lower but total consumption of the product will be greater (see Figure 12-7). Thus competition in the long run provides more output at lower cost to the consumer, even though each individual firm finds itself in a less comfortable position: its economic profit—or surplus— has disappeared and it is producing less, even though all of its resources are earning returns equal to what they could command in alternative uses.

The Social Significance of Pure Competition

In the social (as distinct from the individual) sense effective performance means the ability of the system to satisfy a maximum of consumer wants at the lowest possible real cost in terms of resources used. Does a purely competitive market structure lead to such a result?

There are three important points to be made. First, in the long-run competitive equilibrium position for the typical firm there is equality between price and the firm's lowest level of average total unit costs. This means that each firm in the industry and the industry as a whole are producing the maximum output of goods or services desired by the consumer at the lowest possible price, given the technological considerations inherent in the cost curve of the firms in the industry. Economic profit, a pure surplus, has disappeared; price covers only the necessary cost of the resources needed to produce the output. Price presumably reflects consumer preferences because it measures the marginal utility to the consumer of the final unit of the commodity produced. Therefore, there is no difference between the cost of producing the final unit consumed and the utility the consumers derive from

Maximum output at lowest price

313

its consumption. This is an optimum position for the consumer.

In the long-term equilibrium position, price also equals marginal cost for each firm in the industry. An optimum allocation of resources within the industry has been reached. If all industries in the economy were purely competitive, then an optimum in resource use would exist in the entire economy. Marginal cost, let us not forget, measures the worth of resources in alternative lines of production. Consequently, an equality of marginal cost and price in all industries would mean that there were no better uses for the resources. No improvement in well-being, no gain in satisfaction, could be obtained by shifting resources.

Finally, it should be understood that the output at which production costs are lowest is the point of maximum efficiency in production. Efficiency in an economic sense is the greatest possible output at the lowest possible cost in terms of resource input. This is not the largest output obtainable, but the maximum output at the lowest real cost. Given the technology embodied in the supply curve, and given, too, the prevailing prices for economic resources, this position is to be found only at the low point of the average cost curve of the typical firm. The analysis presumes, moreover, that cost curves are the same for all firms in the industry.

Output Determination under Monopolistic Competition

With this discussion of the purely competitive model as a backdrop, let us examine how the behavior of the firm is affected by a different type of market structure, monopolistic competition. Under monopolistic competition the number of producers is large, but the individual firm has some control over the price at which its product is sold. In other words, a degree of monopoly power exists in the market situation.

The individual producer in a monopolistically competitive industry sees the demand curve for his output as a schedule with a slight negative slope, in contrast to the horizontal schedule viewed by the producer in a purely competitive market. Moreover, the existence of a downslope to the demand curves, even though small, indicates that there is some leeway in such markets for product differentiation. For example, if the producer increases his price he will lose some but not all of his buyers, as he would in pure competition. Product differentiation makes this possible. It means, too, that the buyer is not necessarily wholly indifferent

to his source of supply. Generally, entry into or exit from a monopolistically competitive industry is relatively easy.

Marginal Revenue and Price

One important result of the negative slope that characterizes the
demand curve under monopolistic competition is that marginal
revenue and price are no longer identical. Figure 12-9 shows this
difference. Marginal revenue at any particular level of output is
normally less than price; to sell additional units of output the
price must be reduced, not only on the last unit sold but on all
units. Mathematically, of course, this means that each unit sold
adds less to total revenue than the price at which it is sold. The
significance of this will become more apparent when we examine
the long-run competitive position of the firm in this type of market structure.

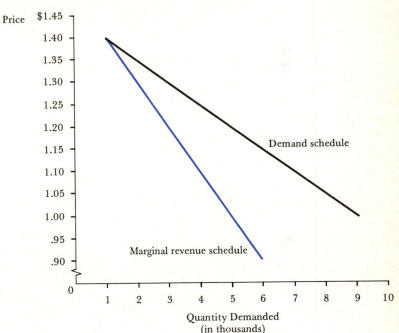

FIGURE 12-9

Demand Schedule and
Marginal Revenue Sched-
ule for Ten-speed Bicycles.

Because the demand sched-
ule as seen by the firm under
monopolistic competition is
downsloping, marginal revenue no longer coincides
with price. As the figure
shows, the marginal revenue
schedule will drop off even
more sharply than the de-
mand curve.

Under monopolistic competition we find once again that to
maximize profit the firm must adjust its output to the level of
equality between marginal revenue and marginal cost. As a practical matter, in the short run the results will be similar to the situation in pure competition, even though price and marginal cost
will not be equal. Figure 12-10 depicts the short-term equilibrium position of a firm operating in an industry with monopolistic competition.

Table 12-3 contains hypothetical cost and revenue data for a

*Monopolistic
competition in the
short run*

315

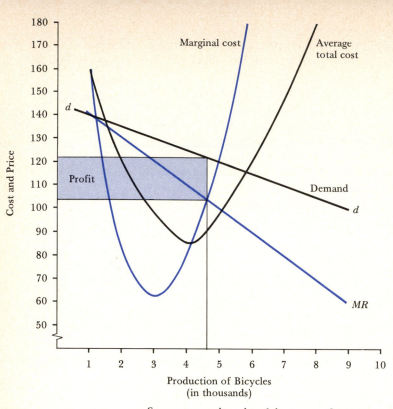

Marginal cost

Average
total cost

Profit

Demand

d

MR

Cost and Price

Production of Bicycles
(in thousands)

FIGURE 12-10
Short-term Equilibrium
for a Firm Producing
Ten-speed Bicycles under
Monopolistic Competition.
The firm in this market situation will seek to adjust its
output to the point of equality between marginal revenue
and marginal cost, which in
the figure lies between an
output level of 4,000 and
5,000 units. Note that price
remains above marginal cost,
unlike the situation in the
purely competitive industry.

firm operating in this type of market situation. The major difference between Tables 12-3 and 12-1 is in the marginal revenue
curve and the demand schedule. The demand schedule in Table
12-3 is constructed so that more output can be sold only as the
price declines; consequently the marginal revenue schedule departs from the demand curve. Given these data, the firm in
monopolistic competition will act like a firm in a purely competitive industry: it will try to maximize its profit by adjusting out-

TABLE 12-3
Cost and Revenue Data for a Firm Producing 10-speed Bicycles
Under Monopolistic Competition

| | COST DATA | | | DEMAND DATA | |
OUTPUT	AVERAGE TOTAL COST	MARGINAL COST	PRICE	QUANTITY DEMANDED	MARGINAL REVENUE
1,000	$160.00	$160.00	$140.00	1,000	$140.00
2,000	120.00	80.00	135.00	2,000	130.00
3,000	100.00	60.00	130.00	3,000	120.00
4,000	95.00	80.00	125.00	4,000	110.00 ⎰ Profit
5,000	100.00	120.00	120.00	5,000	100.00 ⎱ Maximization
6,000	120.00	220.00	115.00	6,000	90.00
7,000	150.00	330.00	110.00	7,000	80.00
8,000	180.00	390.00	105.00	8,000	70.00

put to a level at which marginal revenue and marginal cost are equal. In this case the necessary equality will be obtained at roughly 4600 units of production.

The long-run situation in an industry structure characterized by monopolistic competition shows significantly different results from those brought about under pure competition. The existence of profit—or loss—serves the same purpose in monopolistic competition as in pure competition: it draws new firms into the industry or forces some firms to leave the industry. However, the long-run equilibrium position which will result from the entry or exit of firms differs in an extremely important way from that of pure competition.

Entry of New Firms

Let us assume the representative firm in the industry is making an economic profit. As in pure competition, the entry of new firms, assuming no change in industry demand, increases total supply, which in turn causes the demand curve confronting each single firm to shift downwards and to the left. Eventually, the continued entry of new firms into the industry will push each firm's demand curve down to the level at which market price just covers average total costs, as happens in pure competition. Equality between price and average total cost will be at an output which, for the typical firm, is less than the output representing its most efficient point of operation. Figure 12-11 shows the long-term equilibrium position of the firm under monopolistic competition. Price equals average total cost, but the point at which the demand curve is tangent to the average cost curve lies to the left of the average cost curve's low point. Output has been adjusted so

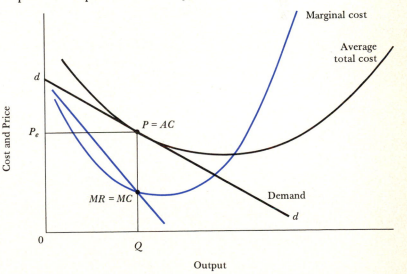

FIGURE 12-11
Long-run Equilibrium for a Firm under Monopolistic Competition.
In the long run under monopolistic competition, price adjusts to equality with the firm's average total costs (economic profit is eliminated), but output is less than the level which minimizes average total cost. Other things being equal, firms under monopolistic competition produce a smaller output at a higher price than do firms in a purely competitive industry.

that marginal cost and marginal revenue are equal, but price remains greater than marginal cost. Thus two conditions differ significantly from those found in the long-run equilibrium position of the firm under pure competition. Price, though equal to average total cost, exceeds the low point of the latter. And price is greater than marginal cost.

Misallocation of Resources

These differences are significant from the point of view of efficient resource allocation among alternative uses. First, the price-cost relationship indicates that there is overcrowding in the industry, which forces the typical firm to produce below its most efficient point of operation. If it expands production to the most efficient point, represented by the low point of its average total cost curve, it immediately experiences losses. This indicates that the monopolistically competitive industry cannot use all its available resources effectively without losses.

Second, the fact that price is in excess of marginal cost means that from the consumer's point of view the industry has less than an optimum allocation of resources. The utility of the goods or services produced with the last unit of resources employed in the industry is greater than the value of these resources in any alternative use, as represented by marginal cost. Hence, for optimum resource allocation, more resources ought to come into the industry. But there are already too many firms. These results are paradoxical; they stem, nevertheless, from the structural characteristics of a monopolistically competitive market.

If the demand curve for the output of the typical firm in monopolistic competition is relatively elastic—that is, it approaches the horizontal—the firm's long-term equilibrium position does not vary a great deal from the position it would achieve under pure competition. Nevertheless, monopolistic competition will result in resource misallocation and, thus, less consumer satisfaction, unless technology or economies of scale are such that costs, on the average, are lower than those which might exist under purely competitive conditions. Then these advantages may offset the disadvantages which confront the firm because of the negative slope of ts demand curve.

Some Long-Term Advantages

Other things being equal, the long-term results under monopolistic competition appear less desirable than the long-term results under pure competition if society's goal is an optimum allocation of resources among alternative uses. In reality, of course, other things are seldom equal. Thus we should examine some circumstances which may offset this less than optimum resource allocation.

First, since the monopolistically competitive industry does not necessarily involve a standardized product, a greater variety of goods or services may be available to the consumer under such conditions than under pure competition. This may be a positive social advantage; the consumer has more choice, which most economists argue is desirable.

Second, we have assumed identical cost conditions for firms in monopolistically competitive industries and purely competitive industries. This may or may not be the case; we do not know enough about the extent to which cost conditions do differ. On the average, firms are larger in monopolistically competitive industries, in part because of difficulties of entry and in part because technological conditions favor larger production units. The modern supermarket illustrates both points. Self-service, a major feature of the supermarket, requires not only large departments well stocked with a variety of goods attractively displayed, but also adequate parking facilities. More space is needed in addition to the advanced technology, and it is therefore more difficult now to enter the retail grocery business. If this is true, then typically cost curves in monopolistically competitive fields will be lower than those of the smaller firms characteristic of pure competition.

Third, some excess capacity is not necessarily a bad thing. In many industries there are seasonal fluctuations in demand, which can be met without severe fluctuations in price if some excess capacity exists in individual firms and the industry as a whole. Moreover, there is something to be said for building capacity in anticipation of demand, for growth in an industry will push prices upward if the overall productive capacity of the industry fails to expand.

Finally, a monopolistically competitive market often promotes nonprice competition, which may take a variety of forms, some of which are in the consumer's interest. As we have seen, if firms compete to improve the quality of the product, the consumer is bound to benefit. Even when quality changes are more imaginary than real, they may play a role similar to price competition, by putting the producer under pressure to provide maximum value for a given price.

Increased consumer choice

Lower cost curves

Advantages of excess capacity

Quality improvements

Competition with Few Producers

Under pure and monopolistic competition industries are composed of many producers. But how do firms behave in industries with few producers? And what effect does the concentration of production within a few firms have on resource allocation?

Industries with few producers play a far larger role in the contemporary American economy than those characterized by a large number of producers. We pointed out earlier that the major heavy manufacturing industries are largely oligopolistic in structure and the public utilities, which provide such vital services as transportation, communications, and electrical power, tend to be monopolies. The model of the purely competitive market helps us understand behavior in such industries and its social consequences.

Output under Monopoly

We shall approach the subject of price, output behavior, and resource allocation in industries with few producers by first examining the situation found in monopoly, which lends itself more readily to analysis with our present tools than does oligopoly. Further, the issues of social well-being posed by monopoly are more clearly delineated than those associated with oligopoly.

*National vs. local
monopolies*

We have defined monopoly as a market situation in which all of the output is produced by a single firm; barriers to the entry of new firms must be strict enough to maintain this condition. Technically, monopoly exists only so long as there are no acceptable substitutes for the commodity or service. Monopoly is not very extensive on the national scene, primarily because there are few commodities or services for which there are absolutely no acceptable substitutes. But local or regional monopolies of various kinds are relatively common. Consolidated Edison, the power company in the New York City metropolitan area, is a typical example. Monopoly has its roots in a great variety of factors, of which economies of scale, limited markets, ownership of strategic resources, patent control, and the possession of an exclusive franchise are the most important.

From an economic point of view the monopolistic firm behaves like any other, assuming the objective of profit maximization. This means application of the profit-maximizing rule of adjusting output to the point at which marginal cost and marginal revenue are equal. Note, though, that the existence of monopoly in an industry does not guarantee profit; further, a monopolist might be constrained from maximizing his profits by the fear that such behavior will either lead to government regulation or tempt other firms to overcome the barriers to entry into his market.

The major long-run difference between monopoly and other competitive structures is that in the absence of pressure resulting from the entry of new firms into the industry, economic profit is not eliminated. Practically, this means that price remains above average total costs, and price is greater than marginal cost. Figure 12-12 shows the long-run profit-maximizing position of a monopoly, the shaded area being the profit that results from monopoly. Lack of new firms in the industry keeps price above average cost. The monopolist enjoys a pure surplus and too few resources are allocated to the monopolized industry. Whenever price is greater than marginal cost in an industry, the utility derived from the last resources employed is greater than their utility elsewhere. From the social point of view, therefore, monopoly normally results in an underutilization of resources.

FIGURE 12-12

Long-run Equilibrium for a Monopoly.

The major difference between a monopolistic firm and firms in non-monopolistic industries is that there is no threat of entry of new firms into the industry. Thus, there is no downward pressure on demand and the monopolist continues to receive economic profits, as indicated in the shaded area.

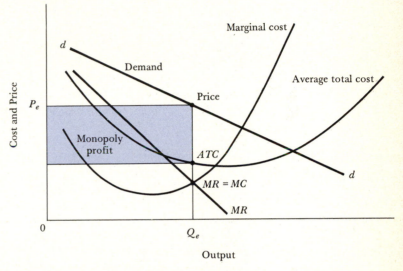

This analysis of the monopolistic firm rests on the assumption of profit maximization. This motive may not exist in all monopolies for a number of reasons. First, a strict interpretation of the profit-maximizing rule may lead to demands for regulation. The monopolist does not enjoy the "protection" afforded by a large number of firms in other market situations, and therefore any attempt to maximize profit draws attention to him. Second, profit maximizing, as already suggested, may attract new firms to the industry, in spite of the barriers to entry. Conceivably, if high profits continue for long periods, other firms may succeed in breaking down the entry barriers. Finally, monopolists frequently do not know the demand curve for their output well enough to maximize short- and long-term profit.

In some industries, economies of scale are such that a single firm can produce the output required by the market at a lower average cost than can many small firms. If the product or service produced by such an industry is deemed vital to the public, as in

321

the case of electrical power, then a "public utility" exists and its price and output will be subject to regulation by some government agency. In the next chapter we shall consider the economic and social issues raised by the need to regulate price and output for industries serving the public.

The Social Consequences of Monopoly

Our analysis shows that the unregulated monopolist will, if he attempts to maximize profit, adjust his output to the point at which marginal revenue and marginal cost are equal. This applies to both short- and long-term behavior, but in the long run economic profit will not be eliminated because new firms cannot enter the industry. What are the consequences of this situation for society?

Price exceeds marginal cost

First, unregulated monopoly leads to a misallocation of resources because price remains greater than marginal cost. This point has already been touched upon. Too few resources will be allocated to the monopolistic industry and as a consequence too many resources will be allocated elsewhere. Misallocation of resources may occur under monopolistic competition, but it is likely to be far more severe under monopoly.

Economic profit

Second, under monopoly an economic profit continues to exist in the long run. Thus profit loses its social purpose, which is to draw additional resources into the industries where the relationship between price and cost indicates that the consumer desires more output. But under monopoly economic profit becomes a private tax levied on the consumer, the benefits of which accrue to the owners of the monopoly. Monopoly also causes a less favorable distribution of income than would exist under competitive conditions. The monopolist's income is higher than it would be under more competitive conditions, and this gain is at the expense of a loss in real income to consumers, who pay higher prices than they would under more competitive conditions.

Loss of incentive to innovate

Finally, monopoly power may run counter to economic efficiency and progress. Price remains above average total cost and the monopolist is not forced to produce at the low point of his cost curve; hence the firm is not operating at its most efficient level. The continued existence of monopoly profit may reduce the firm's incentive to innovate—to introduce new techniques of production and new products. Research by the late Jacob Schmookler of the University of Minnesota indicates that, on the average, very large firms have to spend more than small ones to produce an invention worth patenting, a finding that casts doubt on the view that giant firms are the technological leaders in our society. Innovation is a major source of progress in the market economy. Although some economists suggest that the assurance of monopoly profit may be beneficial to innovation, this is distinctly a minority viewpoint. The adverse social consequences of monopoly far outweigh any good that might spring from this type of market arrangement.

The undesirable rating we have given monopoly as compared to other market structures rests upon the assumption that the shape and level of the cost curves are identical in all alternative market situations. However, the economies of scale in some industries may result in lower costs if a single firm produces the output than if it is produced by a large number of smaller firms. As we noted earlier, however, this kind of a situation, particularly if the industry is a public utility, often leads to some regulation of the monopolist's price and output.

Oligopoly in the Economy

Pure monopoly, with the exception of the public utilities, is a relatively rare phenomenon in the economic system. More characteristic of many important industries in the economy is oligopoly, which, it will be recalled, is a market situation characterized by a very few producers. "Few" is not a precise term, but here we mean a number of producers so small that a state of mutual interdependence exists in the market. Each seller is uncertain how his rivals will react to any action on his part, such as a change in price or output, and in planning his own action the producer must take into account his rivals' possible reaction. While this is also the case for the firm in monopolistic competition, its importance is much greater in oligopoly where there are few firms, each keeping careful check on the others. Oligopolistic market structures are characterized by a high degree of uncertainty. This, perhaps, is the dominant feature of oligopoly.

High degree of uncertainty

Exclusion of New Firms

Most oligopolies in the American economy effectively bar the entry of new firms into the industry. To a large degree this is a result of the economies of scale which often exist in heavy manufacturing and make it impractical for more than a few firms to attempt to supply the output demanded by the general public. Oligopolies may produce a differentiated or an undifferentiated product, but in either case there is usually a significant amount of nonprice competition.

**Competition and
the Allocation of
Resources**

*Growing
concentration in
manufacturing*

Size of Firms

Oligopoly probably originated because technological considerations for certain types of production make large firms necessary in relation to the size of the market. But the bigness required in the producing units is in itself a major barrier to the entry of new firms, for gigantic financial resources are necessary to start a new firm in the industry. Table 12-4 shows the extent of oligopoly in the contemporary American economy, giving data for industries in which a relatively small number of firms is responsible for the major portion of output. For the industries shown in the table, most of whose leading firms are well known, no more than four firms account for 40 percent or more of the industry's output. In most cases the percentage is much higher.

TABLE 12-4
Oligopoly in the American Economy

INDUSTRY	VALUE OF SHIPMENTS MADE BY		NUMBER OF FIRMS IN INDUSTRY[a]
	FOUR FIRMS	EIGHT FIRMS	
Primary aluminum	95[b]	100	7
Electric light bulbs	93	97	36
Linoleum	89	98	15
Breakfast cereals	87	96	35
Cigarettes	81	100	7
Typewriters	79	99	17
Household laundry equipment	79	95	31
Motor vehicles and parts[c]	79	83	1,655
Household refrigerators	72	93	99
Soap and detergents	72	80	641
Tires and tubes	71	90	105
Tin cans	71	83	99
Phonograph records	71	79	157
Computers and related machines	67[a]	80[a]	213
Distilled liquors	55	72	70
Steel mills and blast furnaces	49	66	162
Farm machinery and equipment[d]	45	59	1,481

[a] In 1963; data for 1966 not available.

[b] Estimated; not disclosed by census.

[c] Industry includes many small-parts manufacturers. In 1963, four firms made 99 percent of passenger cars, 81 percent of trucks, and 83 percent of buses.

[d] Industry includes small equipment manufacturers. In 1963, four companies shipped 72 percent of tractors and 69 percent of harvesters.

Source: Department of Commerce, Bureau of the Census, *Value-of-Shipment Concentration Ratios by Industry, 1966* (Washington, D.C., 1968).

Not only is oligopoly all-pervasive in the American economy, but the concentration in economic power it reflects is also growing. Figure 12-13 shows the percentage of manufacturing assets owned by the 200 and 100 largest corporations for the period 1925–1969. As the chart indicates, there has been a decided increase in the degree of concentration in manufacturing since the early 1950s. As of 1969 there were more than 194,000 manufacturing corporations in the American economy, but the 200 largest—or barely 0.1 percent of the total—controlled over 60 percent of manufacturing assets!

Oligopoly in the Economy

FIGURE 12-13

Change in Concentration of Corporate Manufacturing Assets Compared to Most Active Merger Periods: 1925–1969.

The merger movement in the American economy is far from dead! Since 1952 the 200 largest manufacturing corporations in the American economy have increased their control of assets in this sector from less than 50 to just over 60 percent. (Source: Reports prepared by Willard F. Mueller, Federal Trade Commission.)

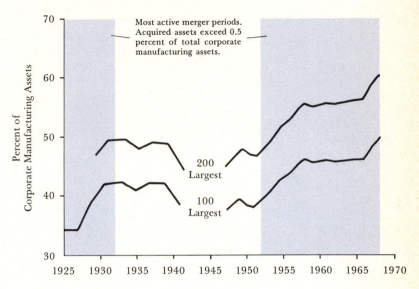

The Cost Situation

It is difficult for the economist to generalize about the nature of the firm's behavior in an oligopolistic industry. On the cost side, the situation confronting the oligopolist does not differ in its essentials from that of any firm in any industry. The oligopolist, like the firm in pure competition, in monopolistic competition, or in monopoly, must be concerned with the behavior of his average costs and his marginal costs as output expands. Because of the importance of the economies of scale under conditions of oligopoly, the declining phase of the average cost curve will probably prevail over much of the range of output within which the oligopolist operates.

In most other market situations, including monopoly, price is determined by the way firms react to their cost situation, in the light of the individual firm's demand curve. The sum of these reactions gives us the supply response, which, in combination with total market demand, sets the price. In oligopoly, however, the situation is not so simple, primarily because the individual firm cannot act without considering the reaction of its rivals.

325

Thus demand as seen by the individual firm is not independent of the reaction of rival firms, as it is in other market situations.

The Kinked Demand Curve

Economists have developed a theory which suggests that the demand curve as seen by the firm in an oligopolistic industry has a radically different shape than is typical of the demand curve in other market structures. This theory is represented by the "kinked" demand curve: demand under oligopoly appears to have a sharp kink—or bend—at the level of the existing market price. This principle does not tell us how price gets to that level, but it does deal with the probable behavior of an oligopolist when he is confronted with the possibility of changing the current price. In oligopoly, moreover, prices are administered: they are set by management on the basis of cost and profit calculations, rather than competitive market forces.

A kinked demand curve is shown in Figure 12-14. The oligopolist sees his demand at any level above the prevailing price as a relatively flat curve; in technical terms this means that in the range of price above the current price, demand is highly elastic. On the other hand, the demand curve below the prevailing price

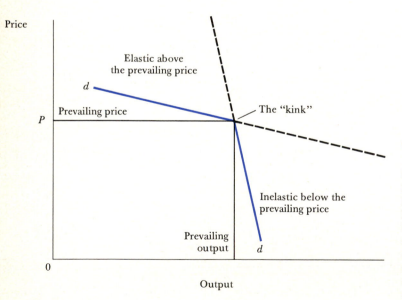

FIGURE 12-14

The Kinked Demand Curve in Oligopoly.

When there are few firms in an industry a producer has little incentive to raise or lower price because he has little to gain in either case. If he raises price he may lose sales because his rivals do not follow his lead, but if he cuts price he will not gain sales either because they may follow his lead. Either way he loses.

is a relatively steep curve, thus quite inelastic. This happens because the number of firms is small. If each firm reacts to what other firms do, then, should one firm raise its price, it will lose sales to other firms unless they follow suit. On the other hand, if the individual oligopolist reduces his price, his rivals will do the same thing; hence, cutting price will not gain sales of any significance.

Price Rigidity

Practically, this reasoning means that price competition is frequently ruled out because of the nature of oligopoly. The oligopolist sees no point in trying to gain customers by reducing price, and he knows that if he attempts to raise the price and exploit an imagined monopoly position he will lose sales. Firms in oligopoly are highly reluctant to engage in price competition because they know it is unlikely to yield any significant gain in either sales or revenue for the firm. This gives us the basic theoretical explanation of why price rigidity and nonprice competition are such a strong characteristic of oligopoly.

Reluctance to engage in price competition

If it is also correct that economies of scale result in oligopolistic firms which operate on the part of the cost curve where average costs are still declining, then it follows that each firm in the industry will reap significant gains from advertising that is directed at increasing total demand for the product. The individual firm's profit will be increased, too, because a shift to the right of the demand curve increases the differential between price and average cost. This possibility is shown in Figure 12-15, where the kinked demand curve for a typical oligopolist shifts to the right, presum-

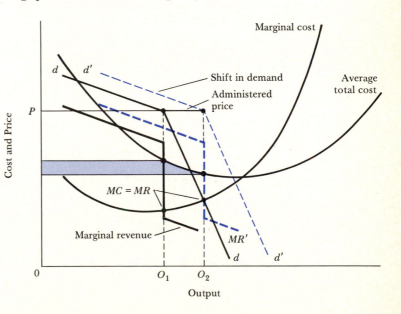

FIGURE 12-15
Shift in Demand under Oligopoly.

The combination of a kinked demand curve and economies of scale may improve an oligopolistic firm's profit position with an increase in demand. Note the shaded area that shows the increased differential between price and average total cost. The benefits of the situation are not passed on to consumers, though, for price need not change.

ably because a successful advertising campaign benefited the entire industry. Note carefully that this does not necessarily mean that the individual firm has gained sales at the expense of the other firms in the industry, although this is always a possibility in advertising.

Price Leadership

*Incentive for
collusion*

The precarious position of the oligopolistic firm with respect to the dangers of price competition gives these firms a strong incentive to engage in some form of collusion, although this is clearly illegal in the United States under the antitrust laws (see Chapter 13). Whether one considers it collusion or not, *price leadership* is commonplace under oligopoly. It involves a tacit agreement on the part of the firms that a particular firm will be the leader in establishing the "proper" price and the remainder of the firms will follow suit. Price leadership has been common in steel, agricultural machinery, newsprint paper, and other industries. The existence of price leadership does not, of course, preclude other forms of competition. Particularly, it does not reduce the incentive to use advertising to increase total sales for all firms in the industry, which, as just pointed out, may increase profits if the firms are operating on the downsloping side of their average cost.

Oligopoly and Society

*Advantages and
disadvantages of
oligopoly*

From society's viewpoint, oligopoly has several unhappy consequences. As already pointed out, administered prices lead to some degree of price rigidity. This is not always undesirable, although there is the danger that when demand conditions change the firm will change its output rather than its price. For the oligopolistic firm, in other words, a decline in demand may be met by a reduction in employment and price increases rather than a decline in price. This type of behavior is fairly common, as the data in Figure 12-16 show. The graph compares price behavior in recent years in oligopolistic industries with competitive industries. The analysis suggests, too, that even though the behavior of an oligopolistic industry is to a degree indeterminate, price tends to remain above average total costs for most firms. This is primarily caused by barriers to entry; as a result, economic profits are obtained by firms in these industries. Table 12-5 shows rates of profit prevailing in various oligopolistic industries whose barriers are effective to differing degrees. It is also most likely that oligopoly price is above marginal cost, which clearly indicates resource misallocation.

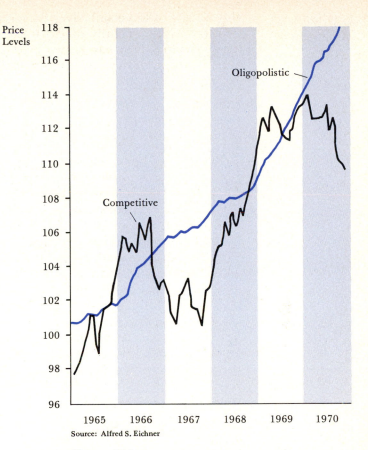

FIGURE 12-16
Comparison of Competitive and Oligopolistic Prices at Wholesale: 1965–1970.

A simple and dramatic story is told by this figure: prices in oligopolistic industries are flexible in one direction only—upward—while prices in competitive industries move both ways. There was a "mini" recession in 1967 and a more pronounced and longer recession in 1970. (Source: Alfred S. Eichner.)

Source: Alfred S. Eichner

TABLE 12-5
Average Profit Rates for 30 Industries, 1950–1960,
Classified by Barriers to Entry

VERY HIGH BARRIERS	AVERAGE PROFIT RATE, 1950–60	SUBSTANTIAL BARRIERS	AVERAGE PROFIT RATE, 1950–60	MODERATE TO LOW BARRIERS	AVERAGE PROFIT RATE, 1950–60
Automobiles	15.5	Primary aluminum	10.2	Glass containers	13.3
Chewing gum	17.5	Biscuits	11.4	Tires and tubes	13.2
Cigarettes	11.6	Oil refining	12.2	Shoes (diversified)	9.6
Ethical drugs	17.9	Steel	10.8	Rayon	8.5
Flat glass	18.8	Soap	13.3	Gypsum products	14.4
Liquor	9.0	Farm machinery	8.8	Canned fruits and vegetables	7.7
Nickel	18.9	Copper	11.5	Meat packing	5.3
Sulphur	21.6	Cement	15.7	Flour	8.6
		Shoe machinery	7.4	Metal containers	9.9
				Beer	10.9
				Baking	11.0
				Bituminous coal	8.8
				Textiles	6.9
Class average	16.4	*Class average*	11.3	*Class average*	9.9

Source: William N. Leonard, *Business Size, Market Power, and Public Policy* (New York: Thomas Y. Crowell, 1969).

In defense of oligopoly, it is only fair to point out that technological considerations and economies of scale may make for decreasing average unit costs in these industries. Society must weigh
the advantages of decreasing costs and their impact upon prices
against the resource misallocation that results from a price in excess of marginal cost. Though economic profit continues to exist
over the long run under oligopoly, as with monopoly, the existence of nonprice competition, a characteristic of the oligopolistic
firm, may be a redeeming element which is not present with monopoly. But economics still needs more effective data on the actual
performance of the oligopoly in the market economy.

Competition and the Market System

In order to evaluate the market system as an instrument for satisfying individual wants under differing degrees of competition, we
need to pose three basic questions. Does it produce the goods and
services wanted by the consumer? Does it produce the maximum
of goods and services preferred by consumers at the lowest possible prices? Does it produce these goods and services using the
most advanced techniques of production? These are the key criteria for evaluating the system. We shall proceed on the assumption that identical cost curves prevail under all circumstances—a
large assumption, which obviously is not always correct—and also
that demand conditions are known, which implies both that consumers know their own preferences and are aware of alternatives,
and also that firms know their demands. Our examination of the
models for different types of market structures revealed that the
model of pure competition led to results which were most nearly
optimum with respect to all three criteria, provided that the level
of costs was the same in all circumstances.

Pure competition comes closest to realizing the ideal of consumer sovereignty because producers cannot exercise any economic
power (i.e., control over price) and can only respond to the
wishes of the consumer. We have seen that pure competition
forces firms in the market to produce the maximum amount but
at the lowest possible price and with the latest production techniques. This means that we are getting the best possible results
with respect to economic efficiency. From a social point of view,
resource allocation is at an optimum in the long run under pure
competition because price equals marginal cost in all industries.
But seldom, if ever, in the real world economy do we find economic conditions which exactly resemble those that exist in the
purely competitive model. Cost conditions are not identical, and

consumers as well as suppliers do not have full knowledge of their wants and of alternatives available to them. What then is the usefulness of such an abstract model? Its real value does not lie in answering the tough question of how we ought to organize society and its economic activity, but in giving us useful criteria to evaluate the performance and the efficiency of the market system.

We must analyze the effectiveness of the market system not only as an instrument for the satisfaction of individual preferences, but also from a broader social perspective which takes into account the fact that the desires and preferences of the individual are only a part of the picture. From this wider perspective, we find its effectiveness seriously limited.

First, the market can only respond to preferences expressed through money expenditures. The market honors individual preferences based upon the existing distribution of money incomes, but that distribution will not necessarily satisfy the full range of human wants. There are powerful needs (both individual and social) which society cannot afford to neglect. Second, consumers frequently lack the kind of knowledge posited by the pure theory of a market system, and thus may not be able to express their preferences either fully or accurately. Under such circumstances resource allocation may not be optimum. Third, the market is not a proper instrument for the allocation of resources to satisfy social (or public) wants. Public goods and services are vital in our society, but they do not carry the same kind of price tag as goods and services produced and designed to satisfy individual wants. Fourth, the market may not measure adequately both social costs and social revenues, although both must be taken into account if society is to reach an optimum allocation of resources. Finally, it appears that forces inherent in the market system often lead to a breakdown in competition, particularly under the impact of modern technology and the economies of scale. These comments mean, in effect, that the operation of the market system in a social sense is something less than perfect. This, then, is the ultimate rationale for public policies directed toward modifying the workings of the market system in the social interest. These matters are discussed in Chapter 13.

Questions for Review and Discussion

1. List the most important factors that determine the type of competitive structure that may exist in any industry.
2. What are some of the major forms of nonprice competition common in the economy? List some examples of each.

3. Describe briefly the essential features of each of the four major models economists use to characterize structural differences between market situations.

4. Explain why the point of profit maximization for a firm in any market situation is one at which marginal cost equals marginal revenue. Why does this represent a form of rational behavior by the business firm?

5. How does a firm in a purely competitive industry behave in the long run? What is the broad social significance of this kind of competitive structure?

6. Contrast the major long-run differences in terms of price, output, and profit for firms operating in a monopolistically competitive industry with those in a purely competitive industry.

7. What is the major difference in the long run between monopoly and other types of market structures, including oligopoly, monopolistic competition, and pure competition?

8. Give some reasons why monopoly is bad from the social point of view.

9. What role do economies of scale play in the emergence of oligopoly in an industry?

10. Explain why price stability is likely to be characteristic of oligopoly and the "kink" in the typical demand curve that confronts the firm in this situation.

11. List some of the shortcomings as well as some of the advantages of oligopoly for the economy and the society.

12. What are the key criteria by which the market system should be evaluated as an instrument for the satisfaction of individual preferences?

13

Public Policy and the Allocation of Resources

AT THE END of Chapter 12 we pointed out that there are many reasons why the market mechanism does not always function in the social interest and why government is called on to intervene in the market economy. Public policy is normally directed toward modifying the price and output pattern that would result from the market mechanism operating unchecked. The rationale for such policy is the belief that unrestrained market behavior will lead to socially undesirable results. The value judgment involved here is made through the political process in a democratic society.

There are four distinct forms of public policy of vital importance with respect to resource allocation: government regulation of price and output, promotion and maintenance of competitive conditions in an industry, restriction of competition, and public ownership. The first two have been most significant in the United States, although restrictions on competition often occur in the agricultural sector of the economy. Public ownership is not uncommon in the power industry at the municipal level, but it has not been of major national significance.

Four types of policy

333

Public Policy and the Regulated Industries

No economic principle can tell us under precisely what conditions government regulation of price and output is necessary or desirable. Historically, though, two major categories of industry have been subject to regulation in the United States: those often described as "natural monopolies," or public utilities, and public transportation.

Natural Monopolies

Public utilities

The phrase "natural monopoly" applies to an industry where monopoly rather than competition seems the most feasible way to produce and distribute a commodity or service. A natural monopoly arises whenever economies of scale tend to make competition impractical and contrary to efficient allocation of resources. A natural monopoly becomes a public utility if the good or service it produces is indispensable to large groups of people. Enterprises which supply water, electricity and natural gas, and telephone and telegraph service are the best known public utilities. Since economies of scale make it possible for a single firm to supply electrical power, heat, or communications facilities for a city, state, or region at a lower real cost than two or more competing firms, competition is wasteful. Competing electrical power companies, for example, would result in unnecessary expense and duplication of services. Hence public utilities are typically monopolistic.

Transportation

*Single carrier with
sole operating rights*

Transportation frequently assumes all the characteristics of a natural monopoly, although there may be competition between different forms of transportation: for example, rail transport competes with road transport, and air transport may compete with both. Nevertheless, within a particular transport industry a single carrier, most often a railroad or small feeder airline, may be given sole operating rights over a route. Generally, this involves routes that serve small cities or towns. It would be wasteful to duplicate rail lines or even some air routes. In the airline industry, the Civil Aeronautics Board often awards routes on major trunk lines to at least two carriers to preserve a semblance of competition. But while there are elements of both monopoly and competition in transportation, historically transportation has been subject to regulation in the American economy.

Private Ownership of Regulated Industries

One other characteristic of the regulated industries in the United States must be underscored: for the most part ownership of these industries has remained private. In other nations, particularly in Europe, the situation is different. Public (or government) ownership of railroads, airlines, telephone and telegraph services, electrical power and natural gas production, is common today and has been for decades. In the United States, private ownership has made it necessary to regulate transportation and the public utilities to avoid the exploitation inherent in unrestrained monopoly. Over the years a system of regulation for these industries has been developed through laws passed in Congress and further defined in Supreme Court rulings and the operation of regulating agencies. It is uncertain whether this system functions more effectively in the public interest than does the system of public ownership. There is a growing body of opinion critical of the regulatory process, but no consensus on how it should be changed.

Before we examine the techniques the United States has evolved to regulate natural monopolies and transportation, let us see how important the regulated industries are to the economy as a whole. Table 13-1 contains data on this matter. For example, in

TABLE 13-1
Percentage of National Income Originating and
Employment in the Regulated Industries: 1970

INDUSTRY	PERCENT OF NATIONAL INCOME ORIGINATING	PERCENT OF EMPLOYMENT
TRANSPORTATION	3.7	3.5
Railroad Transportation	0.9	0.8
Bus Transportation	0.3	0.4
Motor Freight	1.4	1.4
Water Transportation	0.3	0.3
Air Transportation	0.5	0.5
Pipeline Transportation	0.1	0.1
Transportation Services	0.2	0.2
UTILITIES		
Electric, Gas, Sanitary Services	1.8	0.9
COMMUNICATIONS		
Telegraph, Telephone, Broadcasting	2.1	1.5
TOTAL: Regulated Industries	7.6	5.9

Source: *Survey of Current Business*.

1970, 7.6 percent of the national income originated in the regulated industries. In the same year these industries were responsible for 5.9 percent of total employment in the economy, and 7.4

percent of the private wages and salaries paid by all industries (including government) in the economy. It is apparent that these industries play an important role in the structure of the American economy.

The Regulatory Commissions

In the United States, the historic pattern for the control of privately owned natural monopolies and transportation firms involves creation by legislative authority of a regulatory agency or commission with broad powers to establish and control the prices charged by the industry. These agencies are usually referred to as *independent regulatory commissions*. The first such bodies were established in the New England states before the Civil War, although their powers were largely advisory. Following the Civil War, commissions with mandatory powers to regulate rates charged by grain elevators, warehouses, and railroads were established in several midwestern states.

National and state regulatory commissions

Regulatory commissions now exist on both the national and the state level. The national regulatory commissions are responsible for regulating public utilities and transportation in interstate commerce, and the state bodies regulate intrastate activity. The regulatory commissions are called "independent" because they are presumed to operate as a fourth branch of government, subordinate neither to the executive, the legislative, nor the judicial branches. The commissions carry out legislative and judicial functions under a broad grant of power from a state legislature or the Congress of the United States. The federal regulatory commissions are made somewhat independent by having their members appointed for terms which extend beyond the term of the President, who normally makes appointments to these bodies subject to approval by the Congress. At the state level the members are usually appointed by the governor or elected by popular vote.

Sources of regulatory power

The regulatory commissions must function under broad guidelines laid down by the legislature. Congress (or the state legislature) may delegate legislative power, but it must also define the limits of its delegation. In practice, the regulatory commissions often operate with a wide discretion, although their decisions are subject to judicial review through the court system. These commissions can, of course, only exercise powers specifically conferred upon them by the legislature or the Congress. In 1894 the United States Supreme Court (Regan *v.* Farmers' Loan and Trust Co.) clearly established the legislature's right to create a commission to carry out the intent of the legislature as expressed in legislation. In the United States five federal commissions have jurisdiction over the interstate activities of the natural monopolies and the transportation industry. These commissions, which were established at different times by the Congress, regulate the activities of specific industries. Table 13-2 summarizes the key information concerning the five major Federal regulatory agencies.

TABLE 13-2
Major Federal Regulatory Agencies

AGENCY	DATE ESTABLISHED	NUMBER OF MEMBERS	TERM YEARS	NUMBER OF STAFF MEMBERS	JURISDICTION
Interstate Commerce Commission	1887	11	7	1,929	Railroads: motor carriers: shipping by coastwise, intercoastal, and inland waters; oil pipelines: express companies: freight forwarders: sleeping car companies
Federal Power Commission	1920, 1935	5	5	1,131	Electric power, natural gas and natural gas pipelines, water-power sites
Securities and Exchange Commission	1934	5	5	1,360	Securities and financial markets, electric and gas utility holding companies
Federal Communications Commission	1934	7	7	1,458	Radio, television, telephone, telegraph, cables
Civil Aeronautics Board	1938	5	6	770	Airlines

Source: Charles F. Phillips, Jr., *The Economics of Regulation* (Richard D. Irwin, 1969).

At the national level, the oldest regulatory body is the Interstate Commerce Commission, established in 1887. In the post-Civil War era railroads developed rapidly, often under monopolistic conditions, which they frequently exploited by discrimination in the rates they charged. Originally, the ICC was created to regulate the railroads, but its authority has since been expanded to include oil pipelines, motor carriers, and water carriers.

Interstate Commerce Commission

As the oldest federal regulatory agency, the ICC has served as a model for other regulatory bodies. In 1920 the Congress established the Federal Power Commission, initially to regulate power projects on navigable rivers. In 1935 its authority was broadened to include regulation of the interstate transmission of electricity, and in 1938 the FPC was given jurisdiction over the interstate transportation and sale of natural gas.

Federal Power Commission

*Public Policy and
the Allocation of
Resources*

*Securities and
Exchange
Commission*

The Securities and Exchange Commission was organized in 1934 to administer the Securities Act of 1933 and the Securities Exchange Act of 1934. The necessity for the SEC became apparent after the stock market crash of 1929 revealed widespread abuses in the securities markets during the boom of the 1920s. This commission regulates the conditions of the sale of new securities and some of the practices of stock exchanges. It also has the authority to regulate the finances and corporate structures of electric and gas utility holding companies.

The Federal Communications Commission was established in 1933. It regulates radio and television broadcasting and interstate telephone and telegraph services.

The most recently established federal regulatory commission is the Civil Aeronautics Board, created in 1938, which has regulatory control of commercial air transportation.

The Legal Foundations of Regulation

For the federal government the legal basis of regulation of industries is found in Article I, Section 8, of the U. S. Constitution. This is the interstate commerce clause, which gives the Congress power "to regulate commerce among the several states." Almost from our beginnings as a nation, the Supreme Court has interpreted the commerce clause in a broad and liberal fashion, enabling the federal government to engage in a variety of regulatory activities. Chief Justice John Marshall, in a classic decision (Gibbons *v.* Ogden) in 1824, extended the concept of interstate commerce to embrace all the processes through which trade is carried on; this interpretation established a basis for far-reaching federal regulation of economic activity.

In the individual states, regulation is derived from the police power of the state—the authority of a sovereign state to legislate for the protection of the health, safety, morals, and general welfare of its citizens. The courts have given the states extremely wide latitude under these powers to regulate all kinds of business activities. In a 1934 case (Nebbia *v.* New York), the United States Supreme Court said, "a state is free to adopt whatever economic policy may reasonably be deemed to promote the public welfare and to enforce that policy by legislation adapted to its purpose." Thus, the right of federal and state government to regulate economic activity—particularly to set prices or rates—is clearly established, although the Court recognizes that such regulation cannot violate individual rights safeguarded by the Constitution and that the activities of all regulatory bodies must be subject to judicial review.

The Key Issues in Regulation

In the regulation of a natural monopoly producing a commodity or service to be sold through the market there are two main issues to consider. The first is the establishment of a fair market price for the commodity or service; the second is determining an equitable rate of return on the investment by the regulated firm. The two issues are closely linked.

Fair market price

Obviously a regulatory commission cannot decide on a fair rate of return on the production facilities owned by a natural monopoly unless it has some conception of their economic worth. The second aspect of regulation, therefore, centers on determining the proper value of the properties or production facilities of the regulated monopoly. In the language of public utility regulation this is called determination of the *rate base*.

Fair rate of return

Establishing both the rate base and the rate of return requires the commission to limit the amount of profit the monopoly will be allowed to obtain. Most controversy concerning regulation of natural monopolies in the United States has revolved around the meaning of a fair rate of return and determination of proper value for the properties of the public utility. There are no obvious or simple answers to these issues, for they involve both legal and economic questions of great complexity.

The Legal Aspects of Regulation

In a famous decision in 1898 (Smyth *v.* Ames), the Supreme Court declared that the rate—or price—charged for the product or service of a public utility ought to be calculated to yield "a fair return on the fair value" of the utility's holdings. But in this case, as in subsequent decisions, the Supreme Court did not state specifically what constitutes a fair rate of return. In a series of decisions subsequent to Smyth *v.* Ames, the Court went on to assert that no single rate is fair at all times and that regulation does not necessarily guarantee a fair rate of return to the firm. Thus it is still not very clear what constitutes a fair rate of return.

*"Fair return on
fair value"*

In general, courts in the United States have argued that two broad standards ought to guide regulatory agencies in determining the rate of return applicable in particular situations. The first of these is the "cost of capital" standard: the rate of return ought to be sufficient to enable a regulated industry to attract into the industry the financial capital needed for the firm to continue to

*Two standards:
cost of capital and
comparability of
earnings*

339

operate. The second is the "comparability of earnings" standard: the rate of return ought to be comparable to that prevailing in other industries with corresponding risks. Since judicial doctrine holds that no single rate of return applies in all circumstances, the idea of a fair rate of return necessarily represents a zone of reasonableness within which rates may fluctuate.

Determining fair value

The other key question raised by the "fair return on fair value" doctrine of the Smyth *v.* Ames decision concerns the meaning of fair value for the properties of the regulated industry. As with the rate issue, the Supreme Court did not try to define this quantity precisely. It suggested, though, two theories of value that the regulatory body could consider in establishing rates: determination of value on the basis of original cost, and determination of value on the basis of reproduction cost. Industries subject to regulation would obviously favor the latter in a period of rising prices and the former when prices are falling.

The "fair return on fair value" doctrine stood until 1944, when, in Federal Power Commission *v.* Hope Natural Gas Pipeline Co., the Supreme Court changed its thinking and said that regulatory bodies are not bound to any special theory of valuation for the purpose of determining the value of the properties of the utility to be employed in setting rates. Specifically the Court said:

> Rates which enable the company to operate successfully, to maintain its financial integrity, to attract capital, and to compensate its investors for the risks assumed certainly cannot be condemned as invalid, even though they might produce only a meager return on the so-called 'fair value' rate base.

The courts have not been willing to designate a particular rate as "fair," although in a 1923 case (Bluefield Waterworks) some guidelines were suggested. These included rates in comparable industries, a rate that would attract the necessary financial capital, current economic conditions, the risks of the enterprise, the cost of financial capital, and the financial history and policies of the enterprise. These guidelines involve questions that usually cannot be answered with precision.

The regulatory body must not only determine a fair rate of return and incorporate this into the cost curves of the firm, but also set the price for the service at the lowest level at which the utility can operate profitably and still supply the needed services. In 1912 Justice Oliver Wendell Holmes of the United States Supreme Court once summarized the problems involved in the regulation of the public utility (Cedar Rapids Gas Light Co. *v.* Cedar Rapids):

> On the one side, if the franchise is taken to mean that the most profitable return that could be got, free from competition, is protected by the Fourteenth Amendment, then the power to regulate is null.

On the other hand, if the power to regulate withdraws the protection of the amendment altogether, then the property is naught. This is not a matter of economic theory but of fair interpretation of a bargain. Neither extreme can have been met. A midway between them must be hit.

Economic Aspects of Regulation

The economic issues involved in regulating a natural monopoly are illustrated in Figure 13-1, which shows the cost curves and revenue curves for a monopoly subject to regulation. First let us examine what would happen in the absence of regulation, assuming the monopolist is free to act so as to maximize his profit. Given the demand and cost curves shown in the diagram, the monopolist, in the absence of regulation, produces an output of OQ_1, which sells at the price of OP_1. This is the profit-making maximizing output based on equality between marginal cost and marginal revenue. From a social point of view this outcome is undesirable because price significantly exceeds average cost and output is less than possible at some other configuration.

The problem of the regulatory body is to set price at the level which will represent the best price from the social point of view and yet not impair the economic health of the regulated utility. Our discussion presumes that the cost curves shown in Figure 13-1 include the rate of return (profit) to the monopoly which the regulatory commission deems fair and equitable. Ideally, the com-

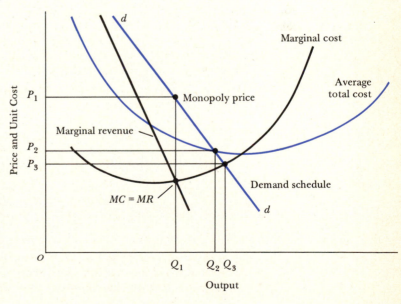

FIGURE 13-1
Regulation of a Natural Monopoly.

In the absence of regulation the monopoly will produce an output that maximizes its profit, output OQ_1, at which marginal revenue and marginal cost are equal. The regulated price will be determined by the output OQ_2, insuring a price that will cover all costs, provide a reasonable rate of return, and entail a larger output than under unrestrained monopoly pricing.

mission ought to set the price for the product or service of this
public utility at a level which will result in an optimum use of resources, where *price is equal to marginal cost.* But the commission cannot employ this principle because setting the price (i.e.,
rate) equal to marginal cost results in losses to the monopolist
since this price lies below average total cost. In Figure 13-1, the
marginal-cost price is OP_3, which would lead to an output of
OQ_3. This is the dilemma facing the regulatory body: the socially
optimum situation necessarily entails a price beneath cost, but for
the economic survival of the public utility this condition cannot
endure indefinitely.

*Setting price equal
to average cost*

The solution the regulatory body may follow is to set price
equal to average cost. In Figure 13-1 the price OP_2 leads to an
output of OQ_2. For society this has the advantage of eliminating
the monopoly profit and bringing price closer to marginal cost
than it would be in the absence of regulation. In Chapter 12 we
saw that monopoly distorts the distribution of income in favor of
the monopolist, and there is no socially valid justification for this.
A price set at OP_2 covers all the socially necessary production
costs for the public utility, including a "fair rate of return" on the
value of its properties. This is all that is necessary to insure equitable treatment of the industry.

If a regulatory commission wished to go beyond this and follow
the marginal cost principle of output pricing in order to get the
most effective allocation of resources, then the only real alternative is for society to subsidize the monopoly. In this event, society
must balance the gain represented by lower price and more efficient allocation of resources to this industry against the cost to society as a whole of the subsidy given to the industry. This
requires a value judgment; economic analysis cannot supply an
easy or direct answer.

Public Policy and Maintaining Competition

Public utilities and transportation, though important, do not account for the bulk of activity in the American economy. The
overwhelming proportion of economic activity takes place in industries and sectors of the economy where some degree of
competition is present, and where it is not necessary directly to
regulate prices and output through a commission.

We stressed in Chapter 12 that the social rationale for competition is the fact that it forces producers to act in accord with the
interest of society at large, securing the maximum output of desired goods and services at the lowest possible real cost and with
the latest techniques of production. But we also pointed out that

the prevalence of oligopoly in the economy leads to less competition, if not outright collusion. This has led to the development of public policies designed to enforce and maintain competitive conditions in key sectors of the economic system.

Policies promoting competitive conditions have been directed primarily toward heavy manufacturing, the segment of the economy in which tendencies toward concentration are greatest. In agriculture, where conditions most nearly resemble those of the purely competitive model, public policy has aimed at reducing the impact of competition on the individual producer. These policies are examined later in this chapter. In retail and wholesale trade and services, conditions are greatly diversified, depending largely on the size of a particular city or region. Some authorities estimate that approximately two-thirds of trade and service activity is carried on under reasonably competitive conditions, but in the other one-third severe restrictions on competition may exist.

Heavy manufacturing the main target

Tendencies Toward Oligopoly

Economists by no means agree upon the current strength of forces making for concentration in oligopolistic industries. In the United States the years from 1870 through 1905 were characterized by mergers in manufacturing. This was the heyday of the "trusts," a word which in this context described any business practice involving a combination of firms in restraint of trade. More precisely, a "trust" was an arrangement whereby the owners of stock in two or more competing firms transferred their securities to a body of trustees, receiving in exchange certificates which entitle them to their share in the pooled earnings of the jointly managed companies. This type of organization was first devised by promoters of the Standard Oil Combination in 1879. By getting rebates from the railroads on its shipments and by cutting prices in one region at a time to drive local rivals out of business, Standard Oil acquired control of all important pipelines and 90 percent of the nation's petroleum refining capacity. In 1911 the Supreme Court (Standard Oil Company of New Jersey *v.* the United States) ordered the combination dissolved.

The trusts

The merger movement since 1880

Between 1880 and 1910 there were an estimated 3500 mergers through trusts of major manufacturing corporations in the United States. From 1905 until 1935 the concentration trend shifted to public utilities, with the creation of many gigantic holding companies. The Public Utility Holding Company Act of 1935 brought this trend under control. After World War II the merger movement in American industry and commerce came to life again in the form of the "conglomerates," a new type of merger of firms in different industries. The size and impact of the conglomerate merger movement is discussed later in this chapter.

Today there are diverse forces at work in the manufacturing sector which make for more concentration and less competitive conditions. During most of this century, output in manufacturing has risen more rapidly than the number of manufacturing plants, which indicates that average plant size is increasing. Economies of scale are the principal cause of this increase. Companies, too, have tended to grow in size as managerial innovations make it possible for a single company to bring more and more plants under its control. The computer, for example, is a tremendously effective instrument for extending the range of managerial control.

Expansion in plant size

Mergers of companies in the same or closely related industries may be inspired by the expectation of tax advantages and other financial gains. Xerox Corporation is a good example of the diverse forces tending toward industrial expansion. The company's original growth was based upon ownership of a key patent (xerography), but later growth resulted from acquisitions of firms in other industries and development of new and related products. On the basis of its worldwide acquisition of xerography patents, the corporation produced a wide array of photocopying and photographic equipment, but through the acquisition of other firms it has expanded into such diverse fields as educational publishing, information handling systems, research for military and aerospace technology, and medical diagnostic equipment. The parent corporation has at least twenty subsidiaries scattered across the globe.

Financial gains in merger

On the other hand, any tendency toward concentration is lessened by growth in the size of particular markets, a development which enables more firms to exist in an industry. Innovations which reduce transportation costs allow competition to spread over a larger area than would otherwise be the case. Interindustry competition is probably more real than in the past, partly because more and more of the largest firms in major sectors of the economy have sought to diversify their outputs.

Lessened concentration through growth of market

General Motors is a case in point. Although its main business is the production of passenger automobiles and trucks, it has expanded into a variety of other fields, including diesel locomotives, earthmoving equipment, electronic navigation and control systems, and household equipment such as refrigerators, freezers, washers, driers, ranges, and air conditioning units. Through its subsidiary, the General Motors Acceptance Corporation, the company has been financing automobile purchase loans on a major scale.

The Anti-Monopoly Tradition
of the United States

There exists in the United States a deeply rooted anti-monopoly tradition, which holds both that monopoly is bad and that competitive conditions ought to be the rule rather than the exception in most parts of the economy. The economic argument behind this tradition states that competition is a socially desirable force. There is also a legal argument which puts the weight of law in favor of competition and against monopoly.

Effect of the Common Law

The legal basis for public policy which seeks to enforce competitive conditions in industry springs from the English common law, a body of non-legislative principles developed by court decisions over a long period of time. It originated in England during the latter part of the Middle Ages, and is based primarily upon decisions that courts handed down in cases involving private parties. It is a part of America's legal heritage and tradition as well as England's. Broadly speaking, the common law embodies in non-legislative form concepts and ideas of what is right and just.

In Britain and the United States the common law took the position that restraints upon trade or commerce were not in the public interest. This meant not only that contracts and agreements that restrained trade were unlawful but also that any attempt to create restraints on trade was unlawful. In the nineteenth century the courts interpreted the common law to hold invalid all contracts that involved practices such as the curtailment of output, division of territories between companies, fixing of prices, and pooling of profits.

Restraint upon trade not in the public interest

The basic difficulty with the common law is that it does not have any preventive features. As it evolved in Anglo-Saxon countries, persons and firms hampered by restraint of trade or attempts to monopolize could bring suit for damages, but this was the only recourse open to them. There was no way for a government to act directly against such practices. In the United States, especially, the common law proved inadequate to cope with the trust and merger movement that gained momentum after the Civil War. It became increasingly evident during the late nineteenth century that legislative restraint was necessary if monopoly was to be prevented and reasonably competitive conditions were to be maintained in the major industries of the American economy.

Inadequacies of the common law

345

Antitrust Legislation in the United States

The competition sought by antitrust legislation in the American economy is not, be it understood, the pure competition of economic theory. The rationale for these policy measures rests partly on the economic concept of the social desirability of competition, and partly on the hostility of the common law to monopoly. American antitrust legislation aims at the creation of effective or workable competition. It is generally recognized that the economist's idealistic model, with its large number of competing firms, cannot be attained in most industries, given the impact of modern technology and the economies of scale that result from mass production. What is sought is a situation in which competition in the form of an active rivalry among producers is effectively present with results at least roughly similar to those in the model of pure competition. In other words, "workable" competition within any given industry implies that the producer is limited in what he can do to control price, and consequently, that the market forces him to produce in line with the preferences of the consumer, to use the most effective techniques of production, and to keep prices somewhere near the socially necessary costs of production.

The Laws

The extent of the post-Civil War trust movement, in combination with growing public clamor for regulation, was behind the passage of the Sherman Act by the Congress in 1890. This act, more commonly known as the Sherman Antitrust Act, remains the most important single legislative act designed to promote and maintain competitive conditions in industry. It has two important sections. The first states, in effect, that every contract or combination, in the form of a trust or otherwise, or conspiracy in restraint of trade, is illegal. Persons who make such a contract or engage in any combination or conspiracy can be deemed guilty of a misdemeanor and, if convicted, punished by a fine not in excess of $50,000 or imprisonment not in excess of one year. The second provision of the act holds that any person who monopolizes or attempts to monopolize or who combines or conspires with other persons to monopolize any part of trade or commerce can be deemed guilty of a misdemeanor and punished by a fine not in excess of $50,000 or by imprisonment not in excess of one year.

The Sherman Act was based on the interstate commerce clause of the Constitution. But the Sherman Act did not give precise definition to such critical phrases as "combination and conspiracy," "restraint of trade," or "attempts to monopolize." Some authorities argued that this was unnecessary because the phrases were presumed to have precise meanings under the common law; in fact, interpretation of the Sherman Act was left to the courts and subsequent legislation.

The Sherman Act was followed by other major federal laws, all of which aimed at maintaining competitive conditions in industry. Four additional acts, with the Sherman Act, make up the principal body of American antitrust legislation. These are the Clayton Act (1914), the Federal Trade Commission Act (1914), the Robinson-Patman Act (1936), and the Celler Act (1950).

The Clayton Act was in effect an amendment to the 1890 law, designed to strengthen the Sherman Act by closing some loopholes discovered later. Specifially, the Clayton Act prohibited certain practices when the effect of these practices was to "substantially lessen competition or tend to create a monopoly." The most important practices struck down by the Clayton Act were: price discrimination not justified by differences in grade, quality, or quantity of commodity sold; tying contracts, in which a buyer agreed to refrain from purchasing a competitor's goods as a part of a contract made with the seller; combinations in restraint of trade brought about through the acquisition of the shares of competing firms; and the use of the interlocking directorate, which involves the same person or persons serving as directors in competing companies, a device to establish monopoly control.

The Clayton Act of 1914

The Federal Trade Commission Act set up the regulatory commission of the same name and made it responsible for discouraging "unfair methods of competition" through the issuance of cease and desist orders. The Federal Trade Commission is largely a watchdog agency which polices against seller misrepresentation.

The Federal Trade Commission Act of 1914

After passage of the Federal Trade Commission Act, no further antitrust legislation was passed until the Robinson-Patman Act of 1936. This act was designed to spell out the price discrimination provisions of the Clayton Act. Specifically, it sought to prevent chain stores and other large retailers from obtaining from wholesalers quantity discounts that might adversely affect the economic position of small rival firms. As antitrust legislation this act was not aimed at protecting the consumer, but rather at protecting the small producer from the competition of a large firm.

The Robinson-Patman Act of 1936

The Celler-Kefauver Anti-Merger Act of 1950 was designed to close another major loophole of the Clayton Act by preventing mergers carried out by acquisition of the assets of competitors. Mergers of this nature are illegal only if their effect is to lessen competition substantially or tend to create a monopoly. This act has not proved sufficient to halt mergers of the conglomerate type, which usually involve firms in different industries, for, like

The Celler-Kefauver Anti-Merger Act of 1950

most antitrust legislation, the Celler-Kefauver Act assumes that mergers will involve competing firms in the same industry.

Interpretations by the Courts

Enforcement of antitrust legislation rests with the Antitrust Division of the Department of Justice, although the ultimate meaning of the laws depends on the interpretation of the courts. The attitude of the federal courts and the U.S. Supreme Court has undergone several changes since the first antitrust legislation came into existence. In 1911, in a famous case involving dissolution of the Standard Oil Company, the Supreme Court adopted what is known as the "rule of reason" doctrine. According to this doctrine, the Court said that when Congress passed the Sherman Act in 1890 it intended to make unlawful only "unreasonable" combinations in restraint of trade. Basically, this doctrine made for a looser and more flexible interpretation of the Sherman Act, because it gave both the Antitrust Division and the courts considerable discretion as to the kind of business practice that would be in violation of the law.

Later, during the 1920s, the Supreme Court, acting under the rule of reason doctrine, held that the existence of monopoly power which was not abused was not in violation of the Sherman Act. In 1945, though, in a case involving the Aluminum Company of America (Alcoa), then the sole producer of ingot aluminum in the United States, the Court reversed its attitude and held that monopoly power, even though not abused, was in violation of the Sherman Act unless the monopoly was "thrust upon" the company; that is, the company must be the passive beneficiary of monopoly. This was not the case with Alcoa. It became a monopoly originally through its exclusive control of patent rights, and then by control over bauxite deposits and generation sites for hydroelectric power needed in aluminum manufacture.

Since 1945 the inclination of the Court has been toward a stricter interpretation of the Sherman Act with greater limitation on monopoly power which might be abused in oligopolistic industry, strengthening the Alcoa ruling. In a 1946 decision, in a case involving the American Tobacco Company, the Court held in effect that oligopoly, too, could be unlawful under the provisions of the Sherman Act, even though a monopoly did not exist. But the American Tobacco Company case did not resolve the issue of whether oligopoly sometimes operates in the social interest. The government charged that American Tobacco deliberately conspired to influence the price of cigarettes and monopolize the industry so as to discourage the expansion of smaller firms. Obviously these conditions are not present in all oligopolies. Oligopoly usually means a lack of competition in the conventional sense of many firms engaged in active rivalry with one another. But as our economic analysis has shown, it does not necessarily follow that oligopoly is inefficient, or that the public interest would be served by replacing a few firms in an industry with many smaller firms.

There is, however, a strong tendency for oligopolists to engage in collusion, and this must be prevented. In 1960 29 manufacturers of heavy electrical equipment, along with 45 company officials, were charged with conspiring to fix the prices for their equipment and divide the market among themselves. The conspiracy, which involved some of the major firms in the industry, was discovered when examination of bids submitted by the firms on government contracts revealed a pattern indicating collusion. The firms and officials involved either pleaded guilty or offered no defense in the criminal suits brought against them.

Collusion among electrical equipment manufacturers

Probably the most effective method is to enforce the antitrust laws rigorously. The government has major roles to play, both as the instrument through which the antitrust laws are enforced, and as a watchdog against excessive mergers in any single industry.

The Conglomerate Merger Movement

In the 1950s and 1960s a new wave of mergers swept over American manufacturing, reaching a peak of intensity between 1966 and 1968. The recession that began in 1969 and continued through 1970 slowed this merger activity, but it is unlikely that this latest movement toward concentration in American industry has run its full course.

During this period the share of assets in manufacturing held by the top 200 manufacturing corporations increased from less than 50 percent to more than 60 percent. As of 1968 the top 100 corporations held a larger share of manufacturing assets than had been held by the top 200 just eight years earlier. There are approximately 200,000 manufacturing corporations in the United States with assets totaling about $600 billion. Thus the top 200, which control nearly two-thirds of these assets, represent only one-tenth of one percent of the total manufacturing corporations. Figure 12-13 on p. 325 showed the trend toward concentration over a 34-year period.

Trend toward industrial concentration

Unlike the merger movements of the nineteenth century and the 1920s, the most recent wave of mergers has been predominantly of the conglomerate type, in contrast to the "horizontal" and "vertical" types. A horizontal merger involves firms which produce closely related products and sell them in the same mar-

Horizontal, vertical, and conglomerate mergers

349

ket; for example, the acquisition of one automobile manufacturing firm by another. A vertical merger is one in which the firms have a buyer-seller relationship. Thus, a manufacturing firm might acquire a firm that supplies it with a key raw material or components of the product it produces. Conglomerate mergers may involve acquisiton of firms producing the same product, but in different geographic markets, the acquisition of firms producing products that are not directly competitive, or some combination of the two. Textron, which ranks among the 100 largest industrial corporations in the United States, is typical of the modern conglomerate. Originally a textile manufacturing firm, it is now a diversified manufacturing enterprise with operations in four major product categories: consumer products, aerospace, industrial products, and metal products. Its operating divisions produce an enormous variety of products, including rocket engines, commercial helicopters, chain saws, bathroom fixtures, cooking ware, watchbands, ball bearings, automobile parts, and specialized steel products, to name but a few. It has more than a dozen subsidiaries, including such well known firms as Bell Aircraft, Sheaffer Pen, Speidel, Talon, and Spencer Kellogg.

Conglomerates and the Law

Since conglomerate mergers often do not directly lessen competition in a particular industry or geographic area, they have proved difficult to deal with under existing antitrust legislation. Even though companies merged in a conglomerate may not be directly competing, many economists believe that conglomerates do lessen competition in the economy; in particular, they point to the practice of reciprocal selling and the growth of conglomerate interdependence and forbearance. Simply put, reciprocal selling is the practice of taking your business to firms which bring their business to you, a practice that is enhanced as a conglomerate spreads its control over more and more firms in diverse industries. Conglomerate interdependence and forbearance simply refers to the development of mutual tolerance and cooperation among large corporations brought into close contact with one another as part of conglomerates. The effect is to lessen competition.

The answer to the conglomerates and their possible adverse effect upon competition is not clear. Antitrust policy to date has not been successful in coping with this most recent form of concentration. Some authorities in this area suggest that the antitrust laws should be amended to require that before a merger involving very large firms could occur, the Federal Trade Commission must find that the merger does not substantially lessen competition, and that the merger is in the public interest. Such an approach would shift the burden of proof on the firms involved to show that there would not be an adverse impact on competition, rather than forcing the government to determine that there had been a lessening of competition before acting under the antitrust laws.

The Future of Competition

The future effectiveness of antitrust action in the economy rests to a large degree on factors now unknown. In the first place it depends upon whether competition under contemporary conditions is seriously on the decline. Solid evidence on this point is scarce, although in many areas the economy is more competitive in the sense that more choice is available to the consumer than twenty or thirty years ago. Technological change, which has brought about an increasing variety of products, is largely responsible. The results are mixed, though, for product diversification by a single firm is also a vehicle for enlarging the firm's market power.

Mixed effect of technological change on competition

It is also uncertain whether competition will decline in the future. This depends upon future technological change, particularly whether or not it is a force tending to reduce the number of firms because of its impact upon the scale of plant. Concentration in financial resources also threatens competitive conditions. Giant firms not only have access to more internal sources of income in the form of retained earnings, but their size and influence often give them a favored position for getting credit from outside sources.

The impact of concentrated financial resources

The American economy is unique among the major industrial nations of the world in its effort to foster and maintain competitive conditions through legislation. The number of actual prosecutions under American antitrust laws has not been great, but this is not the vital point. The very existence of such laws has been a strong force to maintain reasonable competitive conditions in important sectors of the economy. Most of the older industrial states of Europe have permitted the legal existence of cartels—a price-fixing and market-sharing arrangement—which are designed primarily to protect the interests of the producer rather than the consumer. In Western Europe it has only been since the creation of the Common Market—or the European Economic Community—that there has emerged a serious antitrust policy designed to eliminate combinations and maintain reasonably competitive conditions.

The Restriction of Competition:
The Case of Agriculture

When we turn our analysis to agriculture we find that public policy has moved in an entirely different direction. The fundamental difference is that in agriculture the objective of public policy has been to offset, if not to nullify, the working of the competitive market. Some critics describe our agricultural policies as "legalized cartelization," which may be contrasted to efforts to enforce competitive conditions in other sectors of the economy and to regulate natural monopoly and transportation. Although agricultural production is carried out under conditions that most nearly resemble those of our purely competitive model, since at least the late 1920s strenuous efforts have been made to prevent these competitive conditions from fully working themselves out in agricultural prices, outputs, and resource allocation.

For nearly the entire twentieth century agriculture has fared worse than the other sectors of the economy. The farmer does not see unrestrained competition in agriculture as any kind of blessing. He thinks it has left him less well off in terms of income than persons in the other parts of the economy. Essentially, the "farm problem" of the twentieth century is an income problem. Per capita incomes in agriculture have persistently lagged behind per capita incomes in the rest of the economy. Farmers have fought consistently and with considerable success since the 1930s for legislation which in one way or another offsets the workings of the competitive market. The end purpose of their efforts has been to improve the income position of agriculture as an industry, relative to the rest of the economy. In spite of these efforts, though, per capita farm income is only about 70 percent of per capita income in other sectors.

Parity

The origin of the modern farm problem can be traced back to at least 1914, a watershed year for the farmer and his position in the economy. Before 1914 the farmer's income position was approximately equal to the rest of the economy, but since 1914, with the exception of the two World War periods, this income position has declined. World War I stimulated agricultural output, but demand did not keep pace after the war. Out of the experience of a worsening relative income position during the 1920s, came the idea of *parity* prices as a means of demonstrating the farmer's unfavorable position relative to other sectors of the economy. Parity is the ratio of today's prices received and paid out by the farmer to those of some period when the farmer's income position was more equitable, as compared to the non-agricultural sector.

The relative movement of prices received and prices paid determines the farmer's economic position as compared to the rest of the economy. Prices paid are his costs of production and prices received determine his gross income. The *parity ratio* is calculated by dividing an index of prices received by an index of prices paid, including interest, taxes, and wage payments as well as family living items and other production costs. A decline in this ratio indicates that the farm sector is faring less well than the rest of the economy, while an increase in the ratio indicates improvement in the farmer's living conditions. Farmers have sought a parity ratio calculated on a base of the average prices paid and received during the period 1910–1914, when the relationship between prices received and prices paid was favorable to the agricultural sector of the economy. Table 13-3 contains data on prices

TABLE 13-3

Prices Received and Paid by Farmers: 1961–1971

YEAR	PRICES RECEIVED *	PRICES PAID *	PARITY RATIO **
1961	94	88	83
1962	96	90	83
1963	96	91	81
1964	93	92	80
1965	98	94	82
1966	105	98	86
1967	100	100	79
1968	103	104	79
1969	108	109	79
1970	110	114	77
1971	112	120	74

* 1967 = 100
** Percentage Ratio of index of prices received by farmers to index of prices paid on 1910–14 base and adjusted to reflect government payments to farmers.
Source: *Economic Report of the President,* 1972.

received, prices paid, and the parity ratio for recent years. These same data are plotted in Figure 13-2. As can be seen in the figure, the parity ratio has moved downward in recent years.

If we accept the argument that since 1914 the farmer's economic position has been less favorable than that of other groups, how can he obtain income parity? There are three alternatives. First, as we have seen, parity can be sought through the market by measures that attempt to raise the average prices received by farmers relative to the average prices paid. This is an industry-wide approach; the measures taken affect all farmers, large and small, rich and poor, but their effect is indirect since they act upon prices in the market.

Raising prices received relative to prices paid

A second alternative is direct payments to farmers whose incomes do not measure up to some level deemed acceptable and just by the population at large. The first approach is characteristic of agricultural policy in the American economy; the second has not been tried and there is little evidence to suggest that farmers want direct income subsidies.

Direct payments to farmers

353

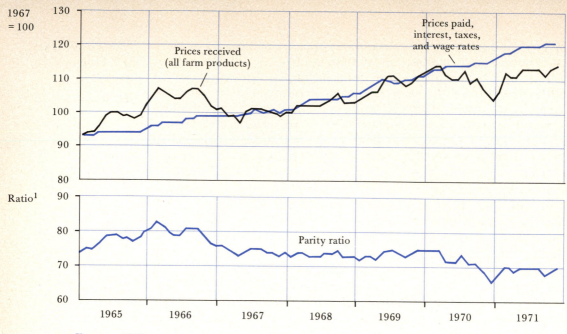

1967 = 100

Prices received
(all farm products)

Prices paid,
interest, taxes,
and wage rates

Ratio[1]

Parity ratio

1965   1966   1967   1968   1969   1970   1971

FIGURE 13-2
Prices Received and Paid by Farmers: 1965–1971.

In the last few years farm prices (the black line in the top part of the figure) have not quite kept pace with the prices farmers pay for their inputs (the upper blue line). Thus the parity ratio has fallen slightly, as shown in the bottom part of the figure.

The collective bargaining approach

Third, there is the collective bargaining approach, favored by the National Farmers Organization (NFO). This involves organizing farmers to bargain over price with processors, using the threat of withholding output from the market to raise prices. The other major farm organizations—the Farmers Union, the Farm Bureau Federation, and the National Grange—have not taken this approach. In any analysis of parity it must be kept in mind that income parity is ultimately at stake, even though the controversy surrounding the problem of agriculture in the American economy for many years now has been expressed in terms of prices.

Demand and Supply in Agriculture

Relatively inelastic demand

The agricultural problem and the farmer's income position are rooted in several demand and supply characteristics peculiar to agricultural production. First, the demand for agricultural products is believed to be relatively inelastic with respect to income and to price. Income inelasticity means that the aggregate demand for food and fiber does not grow as rapidly as demand for other goods and services when the real income of the society increases. Note that demand will not increase in an absolute sense; obviously as the population grows and as people have more

354

money, more is spent for food and other agricultural products. But the rate of growth of demand is less than for other products.

Price inelasticity of demand for agricultural products has the effect of reducing the farmers' total revenue whenever prices of agricultural commodities fall. With an inelastic demand, total expenditures for a commodity at a lower price are less than at a higher price. Since this tends to be the nature of demand for many agricultural products, the farmer's income position worsens whenever prices fall. The individual farmer operates in a highly competitive market without control over the price he receives for his output, and his natural reaction to a fall in price is to protect his income position by increasing production. In a purely competitive market, in which the demand curve appears horizontal to the individual producer, obviously any single producer can increase his own revenue by selling more. However, if all farmers do this the result will be a glut on the market which will further reduce price and, further damage the income position of the individual farmer. Rational action for the individual farmer is self-defeating for farmers as a group.

Another important characteristic of agricultural production involves supply conditions. For several decades now the supply of agricultural commodities has been increasing relatively more rapidly than demand, a development due largely to the extremely rapid growth in agricultural productivity that began in the late 1930s and continues apace. New seeds, the increased use of fertilizers, more effective herbicides, and larger and more sophisticated machines are the chief factors responsible for this situation. Persons outside agriculture are sometimes unaware of this, but since the dreary decade of the Great Depression there has been a real revolution in agricultural production. Output per farm worker has tripled since then; in recent years productivity in agriculture has increased at an annual rate of about 6 percent, a figure nearly double that of other industries in the economy. The impact of this revolution is dramatically revealed by data which show that in 1930, 10 people were supplied food by the work of one farmer, whereas by 1950 one farmer fed 15 people, and by 1964 the figure had more than doubled to 32. The rapid improvement in agricultural productivity in combination with the income and price inelasticity of the demand for agricultural output is the real root of the agricultural problem. In the market the result has been that agricultural prices and incomes do not grow as rapidly as prices and incomes elsewhere. An estimated 23.2 million persons left agriculture between 1930 and 1969, but this migration out of agriculture has not been sufficiently great to overcome the relative lag in prices. Hence per capita incomes of persons remaining in agriculture are lower than those prevailing in other sectors of the economic system.

The Restriction of Competition: The Case of Agriculture

Supply of agricultural products outstripping demand

*Public Policy and
the Allocation of
Resources*

*Programs to remove
agricultural land
from production*

Controls on Production

The fundamental policy response to this problem has been development of programs designed to support parity prices for agricultural commodities. These policies had their beginnings in the 1930s and have continued since then, although much modified in detail over the years. Given the strong incentives for the individual farmer to expand his production, the policy of supporting agricultural prices tends to result in an accumulation of commodity surpluses, a problem which has varied in seriousness and has led to experimentation with various forms of production control. The federal government has experimented with direct controls on production, plans for acreage limitations, soil bank programs, "set aside" arrangements, and other techniques designed to take agricultural land out of production by paying farmers not to produce on it. The common aim of these programs has been supply management, reducing the pressure on agricultural prices by reducing production. The difficulty with this approach has been that the payments received for holding land idle have not been enough to compensate for the income lost through non-production. Hence there has been a strong incentive to increase output on the remaining land by more intensive production methods.

Critics of agricultural policy in the United States argue that because the problem is essentially one of resource allocation, price supports impede the necessary downward adjustment in the size of the agricultural sector that market forces appear to require. Subsidies to the entire industry through support programs are deplored on the ground that they do not help those most in need, the lower-income farmers. Price support programs tend to aid all farmers, rich and poor, in the same fashion, which is not equitable. They would prefer a program of direct subsidy to low-income farmers and the elimination of support prices. Rich farmers, moreover, are often the owners and managers of very large business enterprises, so they know how to take advantage of government policies far better than do small farmers. This, the critics maintain, is another reason why present programs should be replaced with direct income support arrangements.

Public Ownership and Resource Allocation

In the beginning of this chapter public ownership was cited as a fourth major policy approach to the government's role in resource allocation. But because of a deeply rooted hostility to any form of government intervention and an attitude that regards almost any restriction on private market power as a form of creeping socialism, public ownership has not received much serious consideration in the United States. [Nationally, the Tennessee Valley Corporation (TVA) is the outstanding example of a public corporation devoted to power production and distribution.] The regulatory commission with rate- or price-fixing power remains the dominant technique used to control industries heavily vested with a public interest.

Although the foregoing is true at the national level, it is also true that at the local level public ownership is relatively widespread, particularly in transportation and the production and distribution of electrical power.

One state, Nebraska, has a complete public power system for both production and distribution of electrical power. The Nebraska system was created as a means of providing power for irrigation, but as it spread over the entire state, private ownership of power production and distribution facilities was eliminated. Some municipal transportation systems are also publicly owned. In 1968 production enterprises owned and operated by federal, state, or local governments accounted for only 1.4 percent of all enterprises in the nation. Public enterprises were responsible for only 1.8 percent of all employment. The employment figures cited should not be confused with total public—or government—employment. They refer only to persons employed in enterprises producing a good or service for sale in the market, but owned and operated by a unit of government. These figures would indicate that socialism in the United States has a long, long way to creep before it becomes a dominant force in the organization and ownership of production activity in the nation.

Advantages

The case for or against public ownership of utilities is by no means clear-cut. Rational arguments can be readily marshaled on both sides. Those favoring public ownership hold that it would lead to more effective management by eliminating the division of responsibility and authority that now exists under the American system of regulated private ownership. In the present system the managers in charge of the enterprise are responsible to private owners, and their objective is to maximize short- and long-run profits, even though they must answer to a public body which has to reconcile the private interests of the utility with society's interest. It is also argued that under public ownership it would be easier to engage in marginal cost pricing, because public ownership could do this without a subsidy to private interests. Society could, thereby, get a more effective allocation of its economic resources.

357

Drawbacks

Opponents of public ownership maintain that government-directed enterprises are not necessarily efficient, partly because they are subject to public pressure, which makes for uneconomic decisions and, further, that the control of such enterprises may be in the hands of political appointees who are unqualified to manage giant utilities. It is also argued that under public ownership the flexibility of operations may be impeded or adversely affected by bureaucratic rules and regulations. The empirical evidence is not definitive. One can readily find in the American economy examples of inefficient operation under private ownership, and just as readily discover in the European countries outstanding examples of efficient operation under public ownership. Whether private or public ownership results in efficiency in production and maximization of the social interest probably depends on the particular circumstances that surround ownership conditions—whether public or private—in any industry.

The Effectiveness of Public Policy
and Resource Allocation

In this chapter we have examined some of the ways in which the government intervenes in the operation of the market sector of the economic system. In the American economy there is a basic commitment to the idea of private ownership of nonhuman means of production and to the free exercise of individual initiative and action with respect to the use of economic resources. But there is also a fundamental social interest in the efficacy of the market system. As stressed earlier, the social interest is in the results of the system in operation; society wants the system to work so that we get the maximum output of the goods and services people want at the lowest possible prices and with the most efficient production techniques. Government intervention has come about through the political process primarily in those areas where the public and its representatives have found the performance of the market sector wanting. In general, it is agreed that intervention is necessary when competitive conditions are not feasible, as is sometimes true for transportation and nearly always true for such natural monopolies as utilities. Intervention is also necessary when competitive conditions will not be maintained without it. How effective have these policies been in terms of the social interest?

In the sphere of natural monopoly and to a lesser degree in

public transportation it is reasonable to conclude that regulation of prices and output through the independent regulatory commission has been in the social interest. Prices generally have been lower and outputs greater than they would have been without regulation, for there is strong economic and empirical evidence that in the absence of regulation monopoly pricing practices would prevail. The most serious criticism to be directed toward the regulatory pattern in the United States is that too often the commissions have tended to become spokesmen and protectors of the economic interests of the industry they are supposed to regulate, rather than active and vigorous guardians of the public interest. This is perhaps the basic weakness of the regulatory commission arrangement. Our long experience with the regulatory commissions indicates that their effectiveness depends on the quality of the people appointed to these agencies, and on the attitudes of the courts toward the problems of regulation.

The policy of maintaining competitive conditions in industry, as manifested in the Sherman Act and other antitrust legislation, has not enjoyed perfect success, but the existence of such legislation has been a meaningful deterrent to emergence of the more flagrant forms of collusion and cartelization characteristic of industry in Europe. The antitrust laws are not designed, obviously, to create industry structures resembling those of the economic model of pure competition. Today's significant economies of scale and technological forces favoring large-scale producing units make such a solution clearly impractical. However, in the absence of monopoly and collusion, effective and workable competition can attain desirable social results with respect to prices, outputs, and resource allocation. This is more likely to be the result under conditions resembling monopolistic competition—i.e., many firms—than under oligopoly, where fewness tempts collusion.

With respect to the impact of industrial concentration on resource allocation and efficiency, antitrust legislation gives no definitive answers to some of the problems posed by oligopoly, and, more recently, the conglomerate type of merger. In the last analysis, judgment must be suspended until we have more evidence on the broad social effects of oligopoly in many industries. It is true that the oligopolistic industries can take advantage of the economies of scale and introduce technological change fairly rapidly, and to the extent that they do this and pass the benefits on to the consumer through lower prices and better products, the social interest is being served. On the other hand, oligopoly offers strong incentives for collusion, which leads to the elimination of price competition, and an overall behavior pattern may emerge which is similar to the behavior characteristic of monopoly.

The problems posed by the conglomerates are somewhat different. Too often their objective appears to be the sheer acquisition

The Effectiveness of Public Policy and Resource Allocation

Regulatory commissions as protectors of regulated industries

of financial power, with little regard to economic efficiency, product improvement, or any other of the usual economic considerations. Firms are acquired and discarded at will, much as feudal barons juggled their land holdings to enhance their power. Conglomerate corporate structures often become so complex that parent companies have little awareness of the workings and needs of their subsidiaries, and insufficient knowledge of how to improve their products. Effective policies for many of the problems posed by the conglomerates have yet to be devised.

We may need someday to put absolute limits on firm size, but public opinion has not yet reached this point. More time and more experience will, perhaps, show us better ways to attain social effectiveness in resource allocation, pricing policy, and output decisions in the sectors of the economy with large oligopolistic and conglomerate concentrations.

Questions for Review and Discussion

1. What are the four major types of public policies used to cope with the market system's failure to achieve socially satisfactory results with respect to price behavior and the allocation of economic resources among alternative uses?

2. Explain the meaning of natural monopoly and why industries so characterized must be regulated.

3. What is an independent regulatory commission? Give examples of such commissions in your state and at the federal level.

4. How do the federal regulatory commissions get their authority to control private business?

5. What is the meaning of the doctrine of fair return on fair value? How did this doctrine come into existence?

6. Use cost and demand curves to explain the economic problems confronting a regulatory body that attempts to set price and output for a natural monopoly.

7. Why did British and American common law prove inadequate as a basis for preventing the growth of monopoly and maintaining competitive conditions in industry in this country?

8. What important legislative acts in the United States have attempted to maintain competitive conditions in the economy? How successful has this policy approach been?

9. Discuss the "rule of reason" doctrine and other key interpretations for the enforcement of antitrust legislation resulting from decisions of the U.S. Supreme Court.

10. How does the conglomerate merger movement of the post-World War II era differ from earlier merger movements in American history?

11. Explain how the concept of parity prices originated and came to be used by American farmers to demonstrate the adverse income position of agriculture relative to the rest of the economy.
12. What peculiar features of agricultural demand and supply help explain the persistent nature of the modern farm problem?

14

The
Distribution
of Income

In this and the following chapter we shall consider the distribution of income in the American economy. Here we will deal with broad principles, and in Chapter 15 with the spectrum of public policies designed to modify the market-determined distribution of income. Income distribution and resource allocation are closely related, for, as we saw in the case of agriculture, the level of resource use in a sector or industry is a prime factor in determining the income earned by persons in that sector or industry.

Measurement of Income Distribution

Functional income distribution

In any discussion of the distribution of income it is necessary to distinguish between functional income distribution and personal income distribution. Functional distribution (or, as it is sometimes called, factoral distribution) is the allocation of the national income to the owners of the economic resources that contributed to its production—land, labor, and capital. Functional income distribution is directly related to the play of market forces, since it depends both upon the price paid to the owners of economic resources for their services, and on the extent to which the resources are actually used. For any given year, functional income distribution can be determined by dividing the national income into wage and salary payments, interest payments, rents, and profits.

Personal income distribution, on the other hand, is the division of money income among individuals and families, a topic we shall consider closely in Chapter 15. It should be noted that income distribution among persons and families depends largely on the functional distribution of income, so that we must clearly understand how market forces distribute income before we can gauge the effectiveness of the economy in promoting the welfare of all citizens.

As groundwork for our discussion of resource pricing, the key in understanding the role of market forces in income distribution, we need to know something about the measurement of income distribution—what the economist's statistical measures tell about the inequality or equality in our society.

The Meaning of Income Distribution

The Lorenz Curve

A widely used device for measuring income distribution—and inequality—is the *Lorenz curve*. As we saw in Chapter 4, this technique arrays the cumulative percentage of spending units on the horizontal axis of a graph and the cumulative percentage of money income received by the spending units on the vertical axis. The curve connecting these points is shown in Figure 14-1. The 45-degree line represents complete equality in the distribution of income: 20 percent of the spending units receive 20 percent of the income, 40 percent of the spending units receive 40 percent of the total income, and so on. Inequality in income distribution is measured by the extent to which the curve representing the actual distribution of income departs from the 45-degree line. Income distribution in the United States in 1968 is shown by the lower curve in the diagram. Table 14-1 contains the data plotted in Figure 14-1 on the distribution of money income among spending units (families plus unrelated individuals) in the United States in 1968.

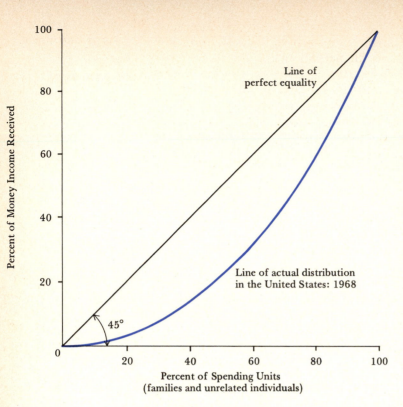

FIGURE 14-1
The Lorenz Curve.
Shown in this diagram is the actual distribution of income among all spending units (families and unrelated individuals) in the United States for 1968. Compare this distribution with Figure 4-2 (Chapter 4), which is for families only, as the latter is a bit less unequal than a distribution including unrelated (or single) individuals. Why is this? (Source: Bureau of the Census.)

Patterns of Distribution

Sources of income inequality

As the data of Table 14-1 and the diagram in Figure 14-1 suggest, income distribution in the United States is quite unequal. One-fifth of families and individuals at the upper end of the income scale receive 42.5 percent of the total money income, whereas at the lower end 20 percent of the families receive only 3.7 percent of the total. The top 5 percent of income recipients got 16.8 per-

TABLE 14-1
Distribution of Money Income in
the United States: 1968 *

RANKING OF SPENDING UNITS	MONEY INCOME RANGE	PERCENT OF INCOME RECEIVED
Lowest fifth	Under $3,150	3.7%
Second fifth	$3,150–$6,100	11.1
Middle fifth	$6,100–$8,800	16.5
Fourth fifth	$8,800–$12,500	26.2
Highest fifth	Over $12,500	42.5
Top 5 percent	Over $19,700	16.8
Top 1 percent	Over $32,000	4.9

* Families and unrelated individuals.
Source: Bureau of the Census.

cent of all money income. These figures differ slightly from those of Chapter 4 (Figure 4-2), which pertain to families only, while those in Figure 14-1 embrace families and individuals. In contemporary society there are at least four major sources of income inequality. These include differences in basic earning ability, inequality in the ownership of economic resources, inequality of opportunity—particularly for minority groups, and regional differences in supply and demand conditions for economic resources.

Judging Inequality

The question of how much equality or inequality of income distribution ought to exist is a complex and emotion-laden matter. The Lorenz curve in Figure 14-1 shows a substantial spread in income distribution, but it cannot tell us whether this distribution was either too unequal or too close to perfect equality. Unlike an optimum allocation of resources, the optimum range of income distribution is not guided by any established principles of economic analysis. Too much inequality simply outrages our sense of justice and fair play. It means some segments of the population are not receiving the equal opportunity of the American ideal. Excessive inequality indicates, too, that a significant amount of poverty exists in the society, which is ethically and morally undesirable. It also happens to be inefficient in an economic sense. On the other hand, some people fear that too much equality will damage the economy's performance by lowering incentives to produce. If the economist could answer the question of what constitutes too much of either equality or inequality, most of the difficulties that now becloud the issue of income distribution would vanish.

Behind the role of market forces in income distribution was an idea of considerable power and significance. It is that owners of economic resources ought to receive a return (or income) in proportion to the contribution their resources make to output. This distributional principle is embodied in the chief economic theory bearing on income distribution, the theory of diminishing marginal productivity.

Human experience has demonstrated, however, that we must make the differences in income received by families and individuals less than the differences in the contribution of the resources that they own to output. The contribution a resource makes to output is never completely a function of the abilities of the person who happens to own the resource at a particular time. Ownership of nonhuman resources is not determined by ability alone; inheritance gives some people material advantages over others from the day they are born. Personal abilities, too, are not distributed equally. Heredity does not endow individuals with uniform

Sources of income inequality

365

intelligence or strength, and educational opportunities and training are not equally available to all.

The Pricing of Economic Resources

The first step in examining the role of market forces in the determination of income distribution in society today is to analyze the
process of resource pricing. As already pointed out, functional income distribution depends upon the price paid for the services of
an economic resource, and the extent to which resources are employed. Resource pricing deals primarily with the process of establishing prices for services of labor, land, or capital in a market
system. Resource pricing also says something about profit determination, although profit in a pure economic sense is a surplus
rather than a price. Nevertheless, it is proper to examine profit
and its role as we discuss the general process of resource pricing.
We will first examine some general principles which apply to the
demand for the services of any resource, and then consider special
characteristics of the market for labor, land, and capital.

The Demand for an Economic Resource

A derived demand

The demand for the services of an economic resource is a *derived*
demand. It is based upon the demand for the final goods and services produced through the use of the resource. In using an economic resource, the firm will employ the profit maximization principle. It will use more units of any resource up to the point at
which the anticipated gain from the last unit employed will be
just equal to the cost to the firm of that last unit. When the firm
decides how many units of a particular type of economic resource
it will use, it must consider two things. It has to know the
amount added to its total cost of production by use of a single ad-

*Marginal resource
cost*

ditional unit of the resource. This is the marginal resource cost.
It must also know the increase in the firm's total revenue that will
result from the use of an additional unit of the resource. This is
the marginal revenue product.

The pursuit of maximum profits requires the firm to adjust its
use of any resource to the point at which the marginal revenue
product of the last unit used is just equal to the marginal resource cost. This is simply a formal enunciation of a commonsense principle. When a firm makes a decision about resource use
it compares the gain to be achieved from using more resources to
increase its output with the cost of adding the resources.

Demand in Pure Competition

How do we move from the generalized principle relating to the
amount of resources used by the firm to the shape of the demand
curve for any resource? The answer lies in the behavior of marginal revenue product, which depends upon the physical productivity of the resource and the price for which the final product
sells. Table 14-2 contains data on the productivity of a variable

TABLE 14-2

The Demand for a Resource (Labor) in a
Purely Competitive Market

LABOR INPUT	TOTAL PRODUCT	MARGINAL PHYSICAL PRODUCT	PRODUCT PRICE	TOTAL REVENUE	MARGINAL REVENUE PRODUCT
1	5		$2.00	$10	
		20			$40
2	25		2.00	50	
		18			36
3	43		2.00	86	
		17			34
4	60		2.00	120	
		15			30
5	75		2.00	150	
		13			26
6	88		2.00	176	
		12			24
7	100		2.00	200	
		11			22
8	111		2.00	222	
		9			18
9	120		2.00	240	
		0			0
10	120		2.00	240	

resource, which is labor, and the price at which the product produced with this resource sells in the market. In this table we assume that the firm operates in a purely competitive market;
therefore there is no change in product price as the firm increases
its production. Be sure to note how marginal revenue product
(MRP) is derived. Its value depends not only on the marginal
physical product—or the marginal productivity of labor (the variable resource)—but also on the product price. Since the marginal
physical product declines with the use of each additional unit of
labor, it follows, too, that marginal revenue product will decline.
The table shows that the total revenue derived from employment
of more units of labor by this hypothetical firm increases, but the
addition to total revenue does not increase as successive units of

labor are used. This, of course, is what marginal revenue product means: the increase in total revenue resulting from the use of an additional unit of a given resource.

If we know the cost to the firm of using additional units of a resource (in this instance the wage of labor), we see that the marginal revenue product schedule is, in effect, a demand schedule for the resource. In our example, the profit maximization rule tells us that the firm will use labor units up to the point at which the marginal revenue product for added labor is equal to its cost. A demand schedule for labor or any resource indicates the quantity of the resource that a firm would use, given various prices for the resource. This is exactly what the schedule marginal revenue product does; it is a demand schedule for the resource.

Demand in Other Market Situations

We have assumed up to now that the firm is in a purely competitive market, which means that the price it receives for its product is constant. What happens to marginal revenue product, and with it the demand schedule for a resource, if the firm is in a market that is not purely competitive? Recall that except under pure competition the typical firm cannot sell all its output at a constant price. Price must normally be reduced for the firm to dis-

TABLE 14-3

The Demand for a Resource (Labor) in
an Imperfectly Competitive Market

LABOR INPUT	TOTAL PRODUCT	MARGINAL PHYSICAL PRODUCT	PRODUCT PRICE	TOTAL REVENUE	MARGINAL REVENUE PRODUCT
1	5		$2.00	$10.00	
		20			$37.50
2	25		1.90	47.50	
		18			29.90
3	43		1.80	77.40	
		17			24.60
4	60		1.70	102.00	
		15			18.00
5	75		1.60	120.00	
		13			12.00
6	88		1.50	132.00	
		12			8.00
7	100		1.40	140.00	
		11			4.30
8	111		1.30	144.30	
		9			−0.30
9	120		1.20	144.00	
		0			−12.00
10	120		1.10	132.00	

pose of additional units of output, all other conditions being constant. Table 14-3 contains data for a firm operating in a market where the price of its product must fall if it wishes to sell the added output produced with more units of labor. The major difference between the results in this table and those in Table 14-2 is that the schedule representing marginal revenue product declines more steeply. For each added unit produced with additional units of labor, the price must drop. Consequently, marginal revenue product declines more rapidly than it does when price remains constant. The practical consequence is that the demand curve for labor in this type of market situation is less elastic than it is under pure competition.

Figure 14-2 plots the marginal revenue product curve derived from the data in Tables 14-2 and 14-3 as two separate demand schedules for labor, showing the difference between the two results. Even a quick glance at Figure 14-2 indicates clearly that the demand schedule for labor under other than purely competitive conditions is steeper than that which prevails under pure competition.

Let us summarize. The most important influences on the shape of the demand curve for labor are the physical productivity of labor, the price at which the product produced with the labor is sold, and the type of market structure facing the firm. These principles also apply to the demand for the other economic resources,

FIGURE 14-2

Demand for Labor Schedules (Pure Competition and Imperfect Competition)

In any industry other than a purely competitive one, the demand curve for labor—or any resource—will be less elastic, which means that at any given price for the resource less will be used.

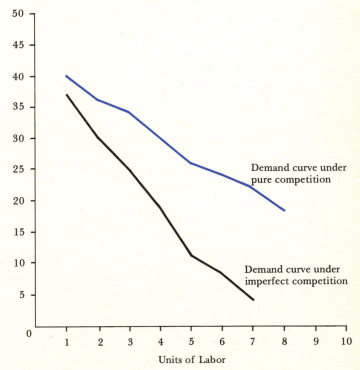

capital and land. The principle of diminishing marginal productivity explains why the physical productivity of a resource declines as additional units are used, while the theory of demand tells us that, other things being equal, more units of a commodity or service can be sold only as the price declines. We thus are led to the general proposition that the demand curve for an economic resource has a negative slope.

Market Behavior and Resource Supply

Although the principle of diminishing marginal productivity underlies the demand for an economic resource, no single principle offers a basis for a similar generalization about the supply of an economic resource. The market price for any resource depends upon both demand and supply considerations, but the only general statement we can make about resource supply is that, other things being equal, the higher the price for the services of a particular resource, the larger will be the amounts offered in any particular market. Because supply conditions vary widely with the kind of resource under consideration, the most appropriate procedure is to analyze supply conditions as they apply in the pricing of specific economic resources.

Wage Determination in the Market Economy

We shall begin with an analysis of how the market determines the prices paid for labor. About three-quarters of the national income consists of compensation to employees; Table 14-4 shows wage and salary payments in the American economy as a percent of the national income for selected years since 1929. This share has been

TABLE 14-4
Wage and Salary Payments as a Percent
of the National Income: Selected Years, 1929–1971

YEAR	WAGE AND SALARIES
1929	58.9%
1935	65.2
1940	64.2
1945	67.8
1950	64.1
1955	67.8
1960	71.0
1965	69.8
1971	75.4

Source: *Economic Report of the President* (1972).

relatively stable over the years, which underscores the importance of understanding how wages are determined.

Defining Terms

To the economist a "wage" is not only the price paid for the supply of human effort, but also the rate of pay per unit of time.
Therefore the wage is the price paid for units of labor service
supplied in the market per unit of time. In our analysis the term
"wage" will refer to income earned from the supply of human effort of all kinds, including mental effort.

In analyzing wages and wage rates we must understand the distinction between the money wage and the real wage. The latter is
the purchasing power of the money wage—what the money wage
will actually command in exchange for the goods and services. Our
main interest here is in the process by which the money wage is
established in a market setting.

Demand and Supply of Labor

To understand wage determination, we need to call on demand
and supply schedules once again. As we saw in the preceding section, the demand for labor is a schedule showing the quantity of
labor a firm is willing to use at different possible wage rates. On
the other side of the market equation is the supply of labor, a
schedule showing the amounts of labor offered in the market at
various wage rates. Economists have long maintained that the supply curve for labor has a positive slope, which means that, other
things being equal, more units of a particular type of labor in a
particular market situation will be forthcoming only if the price
of those units (in other words, the wage) is increased. The
steepness—or elasticity—of the labor supply curve depends primarily on employment opportunities elsewhere, because, as a general proposition, a firm or industry can obtain additional labor
only by bidding it away from alternative employment opportunities. The better the alternative employment opportunities for a
particular type and grade of labor, the higher the price a firm or
industry has to pay to secure additional units of this labor.

*Positive slope of
supply curve for
labor*

On a philosphical level, the positive slope of the supply schedule may be explained by the disutility of work. If work involves
disutility it must be compensated for at an increasing rate if more
work is to be forthcoming. This applies to the supply of labor in
a general sense; special considerations enter into the determinants
of supply of a particular type of labor at any special time and
place. For example, the supply of such highly skilled workers as
tool and die machinists may be quite scarce in an industry; hence
the supply curve for such workers will rise sharply. Under some

circumstances, it might be almost vertical, showing scarcity to be so extreme that no more labor effort could be obtained at any price.

Wages under Pure Competition

*Equilibrium level
in use of labor*

If we assume that a firm is in a purely competitive market with respect both to resources used and output produced, we can construct a simple model showing how market forces and only market forces determine wages. A purely competitive market in resources means that the individual firm cannot by its own action affect the wage rate it must pay to get labor. It also means that the suppliers of labor cannot by their action influence the wage they will receive for their services. For the firm in a competitive market the marginal resource cost for added units of labor is the going wage it must pay. The typical firm attains equilibrium in the use of labor when it has adjusted the units of labor used to a level at which the marginal revenue product and the marginal resource cost are equal. In other words, the firm uses labor until the marginal cost of the last unit of labor hired is equal to the wage. This position is depicted in Figure 14-3, which shows the equilibrium position of the typical firm in a purely competitive industry.

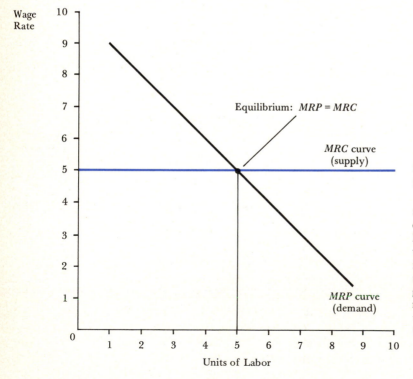

FIGURE 14-3
Equilibrium of the Firm in Labor Use in a Purely Competitive Market.
In this kind of market situation the firm's supply curve for labor appears as a horizontal line at the existing wage rate. Since it cannot by its action affect this wage, this is also the firm's marginal resource cost. Equilibrium in labor use exists when the MRC ($5) equals the firm's MRP ($5).

Wage determination in the entire industry depends, though, upon the interaction between the demand of all firms in the industry for labor and the total supply of labor in that particular industry. It is thus the interaction of demand and supply for the industry as a whole which determines the level of wages confronting the individual firm. For a particular industry the demand for labor is the summation of the demand of all firms, whereas the supply schedule depends on the amount of labor with the necessary skills that is available to that industry. The supply schedule for the industry has a positive slope typical of resource supply curves, showing that more labor is forthcoming only as the money wage is increased. Wages in a purely competitive industry result solely from interaction between demand and supply for labor in the entire industry. Figure 14-4 illustrates this process; it shows how the equilibrium wage rate in an industry is determined, using supply and demand schedules.

Wages under Pure Competition

A simplified model of wage determination

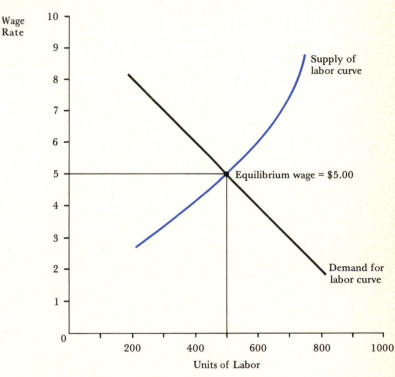

FIGURE 14-4
Industry Wage Determination.

If wage rates in an industry were determined solely by market forces, the equilibrium wage and employment level in the industry would be at the point of intersection of the demand and supply curves for labor. This is the kind of market depicted in the figure.

Although the model shown in Figure 14-4 depicts a situation in which market forces alone determine the wage level, in reality this condition seldom exists. Pure competition in the market for economic resources, including labor, is the exception rather than the rule, just as it is in markets for goods or services. One reason for this is the existence of unions and the impact they may have on wage rates. Another is that in many markets the number of

373

firms is small; hence the action of individual firms may affect the wage rate.

Nevertheless, some useful insights can be drawn from this simplified model of wage determination. First, the equilibrium position for the firm as well as the industry is one of equality between the wage rate and marginal revenue product. Since the latter depends on the marginal productivity of labor, wage rates under purely competitive conditions will reflect the contribution of labor to output. Second, the wage rate is also equal to marginal resource cost as seen by the firm, which means that the firm is in an optimum position with respect to the use of labor in the industry. Finally, the model shows that the level of wages is affected by shifts in either the demand or supply schedule for labor. A change in the demand schedule for labor results normally either from a change in the demand for a final product, or from new production processes and other developments that raise the productivity of labor. Shifts in the supply schedule, on the other hand, reflect factors which affect the conditions under which varying amounts of labor will be forthcoming in the market. Among such factors must be included the power and influence of unions, legislation affecting hours of work and the length of the work week, expectations concerning future wages, and changing attitudes toward work vs. leisure. Other things being equal, we can expect, therefore, that an increase (decrease) in the demand for labor will raise (lower) wages, and an increase (decrease) in the supply of labor will lower (raise) wages.

Wages under Non-Competitive Conditions

The real world of markets and wages is excessively complex, but economists have identified two situation that are fairly representative. These are *monopsony* and *bilateral monopoly*. Let us examine each to see what light it throws upon the determination of wage rates under conditions more closely approximating those we will find in the market economy.

Monopsony

Monopsony is a situation in which a firm (the buyer of labor) is so large relative to the market that, for all practical purposes, it is the *sole* source of demand for labor. It is especially common in small communities where a single company is often the dominant element in the labor market. In Pontiac, Michigan, for example, the General Motors plant dominates the labor market. This situation obviously requires labor with particular skills.

The economic significance of monopsony is that the firm, when it increases or decreases the quantity of labor it uses, may affect the wage rate. The firm is a monopoly buyer for labor, and thus may cause wages to rise when it demands more labor, or wages to fall when it demands less labor. Under these circumstances the marginal resource cost to the firm is no longer the same as the money wage.

In our prior discussion we assumed that the money wage would not change when the firm used more or less of a given type of labor, so that the marginal resource cost to the firm for more units of labor was identical to the money wage it had to pay to get these units. This was the situation in pure competition. In monopsony this is no longer the case. Instead, if the wage rate rises when the firm adds to its labor force, then its marginal resource cost will rise even more rapidly. To get additional units of labor it must not only pay a higher wage for the additional unit, but for all workers.

These circumstances will not deter the firm from seeking to maximize profit; the firm still tries to adjust its use of labor to the level at which the marginal resource cost and the marginal revenue product for the last units of labor are equal. But there will be other effects which make the outcome different from what we find in pure competition, and which, further, bear on the situation that will exist if the workers under monopsony succeed in establishing a trade union.

The results of wage determination under monopsony are depicted in Figure 14-5. Contrast this outcome with wage determination in a competitive industry, as shown in Figure 14-3 (p. 372). Figure 14-5 indicates that under monopsony the marginal resource cost curve lies above the supply curve for labor.

FIGURE 14-5
Wage Determination under Monopsony.

In contrast to the purely competitive industry, the equilibrium wage rate may be lower and the level of employment less. The equilibrium level of labor use for the firm remains at the point of equality between marginal resource cost and marginal revenue product.

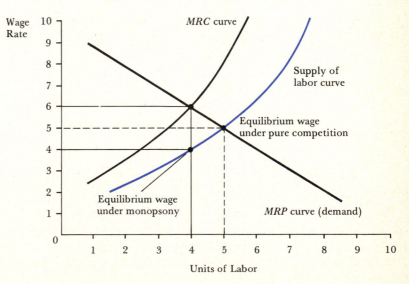

The firm adjusts its use of labor to the point of intersection of the marginal revenue product curve and the marginal resource cost curve, but this results in a wage rate below the wage which would exist under competitive conditions. It also results in a smaller amount of labor employed in the monopsonistic industry. Equality between the wage rate and marginal revenue product no longer exists. Note that the monopsonistic situation is similar to monopoly in the product market: the economy gets a smaller output for which it must pay a higher price. In this instance there is less employment and the wage rate is lower.

Bilateral Monopoly

A single firm facing a single supplier of labor

In bilateral monopoly, the firm as the buyer of labor has a monopsony position, but it is also confronted by a single seller of labor. Such a condition exists when there is a strong union that can bargain on behalf of all of the workers in a particular industry; from a practical standpoint the firm confronts a single supplier for labor resources. This is the case in the steel industry, where the firms confront a powerful union, the United Steelworkers, which bargains for all production workers.

Effect of bilateral monopoly on the wage rate

The probable results of bilateral monopoly in a market situation are readily illustrated with a diagram such as Figure 14-6. The upper limit to the wage is at the intersection of the marginal resource cost curve and the marginal revenue product curve of the firm, point *a* in the figure. This is the upper limit because the firm cannot and will not pay a wage that exceeds the value to it of the last unit of labor employed. On the other hand, the lower limit to the wage bargain is shown by the intersection of a perpendicular line dropped from point *a* with the supply curve

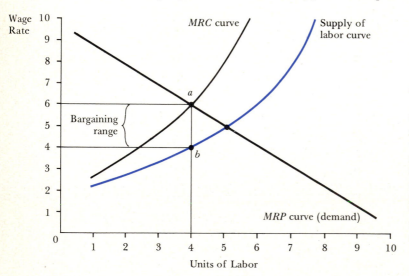

FIGURE 14-6
Wage Determination under Bilateral Monopoly.

In this type of situation the actual wage level is indeterminate, but will lie somewhere within a bargaining range whose upper limit is set by the firm's requirement that the wage cannot exceed its marginal resource cost and whose lower limit is determined by the supply curve for labor.

of labor. This is point *b* in the figure. The trade union will not accept a wage below the wage rates embodied in the basic labor supply curve of the industry. Thus there is a margin for bargaining, and the actual wage rate will be somewhere between these limits.

Unfortunately, the model cannot predict what the actual wage will be; it can only indicate the limits within which bargaining must take place, this being the process by which the wage rate comes to be established. Note that the diagram tells us that the competitive wage lies between the upper and the lower limits, and, consequently, the wage determined through the bargaining process may be either above or below the competitive wage, depending upon the relative strength of the parties involved in the bargaining process.

Trade Unions and Wage Rates

A Definition of Unions

By far the most important single characteristic of the market model of pure competition is that buyers and sellers have no control over the price at which they buy or sell. As applied to wages this means that neither the buyer of labor (the firm) nor the seller of labor (the worker) can affect the wage rate. Reality, though, is quite different. As we have seen, firms can frequently influence the wage rate they must pay for the labor they need, and, on the other hand, workers have not allowed this situation to go unchallenged. They have created organizations whose purpose is to strengthen the bargaining position of the worker *vis-à-vis* the employer. These organizations are commonly called labor or trade unions.

Organizations to strengthen the bargaining position of the worker

Essentially, a trade union is an organization of employees designed to exert pressure and influence on the employer to secure higher wages and better working conditions. Some unions, called craft unions, are organized on the basis of a trade or craft. Others, organized on the basis of the industry in which the workers are employed, are called industrial unions. The carpenters' union is an example of the craft type, while automobile workers belong to an industrial union. In the United States and other modern nations, trade unions engage in collective bargaining on behalf of their members, which is to say they attempt to get sufficient strength to bargain with the employer as a representative of all or a majority of employees over wages and working conditions. We shall take a close look in Chapter 15 at the legal foundations of collective bargaining and the development of the trade union movement in the United States.

Craft vs. industrial unions

Restricting the Labor Supply

Organized labor uses a variety of techniques to influence wages and improve working conditions. One of the most common is to restrict the supply of labor; other things being equal, a reduction in labor supply will raise the price paid for labor. This is an application of the most elementary economic principle of demand. Trade unions, however, must take into account the fact that restricting the labor supply may also reduce employment, given the normal downward slope of the demand curve for labor.

The willingness of a trade union to restrict labor supply in the expectation of higher wages will therefore depend on its intuitive or actual knowledge of the elasticity of the demand for the labor it represents. If the demand for labor in a particular industry is highly inelastic, then the trade union has much room for maneuvering because significant changes in the wage rate can take place without adversely affecting employment. For example, in the automobile industry the demand for tool and die workers is highly inelastic, because the number needed is small in relation to the total work force and their skills are vital to the manufacture of automobiles. But if the demand for labor is elastic, caution is in order because a vigorous attempt to restrict labor supply would significantly reduce employment. This might adversely affect the trade union itself. It would not benefit a trade union in the long run to raise wages if the cost of doing so was an increase in unemployment large enough to turn members or potential members against the union. Unskilled assembly line workers in the automobile industry represent a job category for which the demand may be relatively elastic. However, a strong union can overcome this situation even for the unskilled.

Historically, different means have been used by organized labor to restrict the supply of workers. These range from support of laws restricting immigration to policies that limit the number of persons who can enter a particular trade or occupation. The craft union may enhance its control of the supply of labor through high initiation fees and long apprenticeships. Trade unions can also gain effective control of the labor supply through pacts with management. A closed-shop arrangement requires union membership prior to employment, a practice which is now illegal in all states. More prevalent is the union-shop agreement, which provides that newly employed workers must join the trade union after a specified period.

Unions in Bilateral Monopoly

The industrial unions hold sway over the total labor supply in the major manufacturing sectors of the economy, particularly in those industries characterized by oligopoly. The United Steel Workers and the United Automobile Workers are well-known examples. The bargaining process in industries where there are a number of oligopolist firms and a large industrial union is, perhaps, more accurately characterized as bilateral oligopoly rather than bilateral monopoly. But the results of the bargaining process are about the same as under bilateral monopoly. That is, the actual wage is not determined, but will eventually be found within the upper and lower limits set by the forces stressed in our earlier discussion involving Figure 14-6. One basic aim of an industrial union is to bargain for a minimum wage level to apply to all workers in the industry. In doing this the union must take into account the effect of its actions on employment. If it attempts to get a wage too far above the competitive level, the impact on employment will be adverse, thereby weakening the union. But if the bargaining wage is only slightly above the competitive level, employees will see no great advantage in union membership. The union's judgment of the elasticity of the demand schedule will affect its actions.

Unions in Monopsony

In one type of market situation it is apparent that a trade union may not only be able to raise wages above the competitive level, but also to increase employment. This is a situation of monopsony in the labor market. Monopsony, as we saw, results in a wage below both the competitive level and the marginal revenue product of the firm, as well as less employment. Figure 14-5 on p. 375 shows this situation. Here the union has ample space to maneuver, because it is possible to increase the wage rate and to increase employment, bringing both closer to the level that would prevail in a competitive situation. Hard bargaining in this situation can raise wages but not at the cost of employment. Aside from this special situation, in which labor is exploited because of the monopoly position of the employer, the trade union must pay attention to the elasticity of the demand schedule for labor, which will significantly affect what it can do as a bargaining entity in terms of raising wages and without seriously affecting the level of employment.

Increasing wages and employment

Other Forms of Factor Income

Wage and salary payments constitute the largest single source of income to the owners of economic resources (see Table 14-4), but they are not the only form of factor income. Other types of income are associated with the use of resources in production and, therefore, are a source of money income to persons and families. These are rents, interest payments, and profits, although strictly speaking profit is a residual, not a factor payment. Table 14-5 contains data for selected years since 1929 on the breakdown of national income into the major components. In the table note there is a component called "proprietors' income." It is income which goes to the owners of non-corporate business firms. It is really a combination of profits, wages for labor supplied by the individual owner or partners of the proprietorship, and other types of returns.

TABLE 14-5
Major Components of the National Income
(Percentages for Selected Years: 1929–1971)

YEAR	WAGES AND SALARIES	PROPRIETORS INCOME	RENTAL INCOME	INTEREST INCOME	CORPORATE PROFITS
1929	58.9	17.5	6.2	5.4	12.0
1935	65.2	18.9	2.8	7.2	5.9
1940	64.2	16.1	3.5	4.1	12.1
1945	67.8	17.3	3.1	1.2	10.6
1950	64.1	15.6	3.9	0.8	15.6
1955	67.8	12.6	4.2	1.2	14.2
1960	71.0	11.2	3.8	2.0	12.0
1965	69.8	10.1	3.4	3.2	13.5
1971	75.4	8.0	2.9	4.2	9.5

Source: *Economic Report of the President* (1972).

Conventional procedures in national income accounting do not give us statistical results which correspond neatly with the economist's conceptual framework for resource pricing, namely returns associated with the services of labor, land, and capital. It is least difficult to discuss wages as an income source, because wage and salary income clearly result from the use of labor as an economic resource in the production process. But this does not necessarily follow for rent and interest. In the complex modern economy these components of the national income are not directly linked to the services of land and capital in production. Rent and interest are income derived from ownership, although what is owned may not be a resource which enters directly into production, but a financial "claim" such as a bond, which yields income. Yet rent and interest, not to mention profit, are important sources of income originating in the market sector. Utilizing the principle of resource pricing developed earlier in this chapter, we will now examine the forces that determine their magnitudes.

Rent as an Income Source

The garden-variety definition of rent is the price we must pay for the use of any kind of a durable good, whether land, machinery, or a building. This is the concept of rent employed in the national income accounts, as shown in Table 14-5. Rent in this sense is seen as a payment made for the services which durable goods provide in production. If this is the case, the process of rent determination can be analyzed in the same way we analyze the process of wage determination. We start by assuming that a demand schedule exists for the services of the various nonhuman resources used in production, and that this demand schedule can be derived ultimately from the productivity of these resources. We say, in effect, that behind the demand schedule for any durable good used in production, there is a curve showing the marginal physical productivity of the good; when this is translated into value terms, we have the demand schedule for the particular good. The schedule has a negative slope because of the principle of diminishing marginal productivity. If we assume the existence of a supply schedule for a durable good whose services are useful in production, then the price paid for its services will depend upon interaction between demand and supply forces. Other things being equal, the larger (or smaller) the demand relative to supply, the higher (or lower) will be the rent paid for a unit of land, a machine, or a building in any given market situation.

The price for the use of a durable good

Ricardo's Theory of Rent

This is the simplest way to analyze rent as a form of factor payment today, but in the past rent has had a different meaning to economists that is worth examining briefly. Rent was considered to be the price paid for the services of a natural resource that is fixed in supply. Land, obviously, best fits this description, and, therefore, rent has been regarded as a form of money return peculiarly associated with the use of land in production. This concept originated with David Ricardo, a British economist in the early nineteenth century. Ricardo understood that land was not man-made, and thus not reproducible, but also that the amount of arable land in existence was relatively fixed. Technically, the supply schedule for land of a given type is perfectly inelastic, because such land cannot be produced by the normal processes of production.

Ricardo's theory, which explains how the price paid for the use of land in production is determined, contains two significant

Fixed and nonreproducible resources

381

The Distribution of Income

Land rent as a pure economic surplus

points. The first is that land rent is a pure economic surplus which emerges whenever the price received for a commodity produced on land exceeds the cost of producing that commodity. For example, if the value of wheat produced on a specific unit of land exceeds the costs (labor and materials) involved in producing it, then there is a surplus over and above the production costs which must be attributed to the innate or natural qualities of the land itself. This is what Ricardo meant when he described rent as a pure economic surplus. The second point in Ricardo's theory is that economic rent emerges only as land units of different quality are brought into production.

Suppose a quantity of wheat is produced on a unit of land and the price for wheat is just high enough to cover the production costs on the land. If demand for wheat increases, the farmer will have to bring into production land less suitable for wheat, to satisfy the increased demand. Now the farmer finds that the wheat produced on the first unit of land yields a surplus above his production costs. This is economic rent. Figure 14-7 illustrates this principle. Each successive unit of land shown has a higher production cost. The last unit—*E*—is one on which price just covers labor and other costs. But the other units, *A* through *D,* yield a surplus, shown by the shaded area. If the demand for wheat declined—i.e., *dd* shifted to the left—it would no longer be possible to use unit *E* in production.

According to Ricardo, the excess of revenue over cost is a pure surplus because it is not a necessary payment to bring into exis-

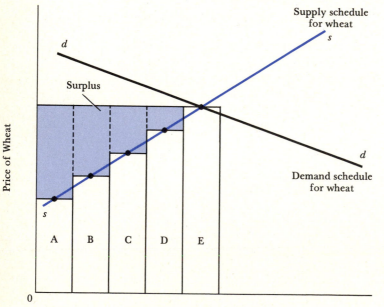

FIGURE 14-7

The Concept of Economic Rent.

The rectangles labeled *A* through *E* represent units of land of differing productivity or fertility. The non-shaded areas in each rectangle represent production costs, and the shaded area the surplus (economic rent) that emerges whenever the price in the market rises higher than the necessary production costs on any single unit.

tence a supply of the resource. The land was already there. It is fixed in amount and not man-made. Ricardo also pointed out that rent is a return which is price-determined, rather than price-determining; the level of demand relative to the available supply determines the price paid for its use, which is the key to whether or not a surplus emerges on land of different grades. Rent in the Ricardian sense is not a production cost.

This view of rent contains important insights into the nature of money returns that accrue to any resource fixed in supply, but as a theoretical proposition it is not adequate to deal with all situations in which the return to the owner of a resource is described as a rent. It is more satisfying, as well as simpler, to use the word rent to mean a payment made for the use of any resource of a durable nature which has value in the productive process, whether or not the supply is totally fixed (perfectly inelastic), or the resource is man-made.

The Single Tax

An interesting byproduct of Ricardo's rent theory was the emergence in the mid-nineteenth century in the United States of the "single-tax" proposal of Henry George, a self-educated economist and social philosopher. George proposed that all economic rent should be fully taxed as unearned income. In urban areas it is value created by society which should be recaptured by society, and in agricultural areas it is value that results from the original and natural properties of the soil. Henry George was not thinking of rent in the ordinary sense but as a pure surplus in the Ricardian sense. He thought that if the state taxed fully all economic rent, no other taxes would be necessary, hence the phrase "single-tax." No major political entity has yet tried to apply George's interesting ideas on taxation wholly, although some urban areas in Canada and Australia do use "site value" taxation. The term refers to the economic rent on land in an urban area; such rent is a function of the location of the land. Thus, a tax levied on the economic rent of urban land is said to be a tax on the site value of the land.

Taxation only on economic rent

Interest as an Income Source

Interest is the other form of property income that concerns the economist. Unlike rent and wages, interest is not calculated as an absolute amount but as a rate. This means we measure interest as the price paid for the use of a sum of money for a unit of time, but express it as a percent. The calendar year is the normal unit

Measuring interest as a rate

of time used for the calculation of interest. Thus, a rate of interest of 5 percent means a payment of $5.00 for the use of $100.00 for a period of one year. The practice of measuring interest as a rate has some practical advantages. It permits a direct comparison between the cost of acquisition of loanable funds and the rate of return earned on a physical asset, such as a building, an item of equipment, or some other form of capital good. Profitability of capital is normally computed, too, as a rate of return by expressing the net income the asset earns per year as a percent of initial cost. Second, interest, unlike wages and rent, is not a return paid directly for the services of a productive resource. Money is not a productive resource, but a means of exchange. The acquisition of money (or loanable funds) provides an individual with purchasing power through which he can get command over economic resources. If these yield a return, they will justify payment for the use of the money. Obviously, this rationale does not apply to borrowing for consumer loans.

As the data in Table 14-5 indicate, the significance of interest as a source of income has grown appreciably since World War II, especially in the last decade. Like rent, interest is no longer readily associated with the services of a specific economic resource, although historically it has been linked with capital goods and the rate of return they earn. Under competitive market conditions the rate of interest and the rate of return on capital will tend to be equal. But this does not mean, as economists once believed, that the rate of interest is determined by the rate of return on real capital.

Interest rates and rate of return on capital

The Price of Loanable Funds

Probably the most useful approach is simply to regard interest as a price paid for the use of loanable funds. Since interest is a price, it can be explained with the analytical tools economists employ whenever they deal with price phenomena: demand and supply schedules. The demand schedule for loanable funds will have the negative slope typical of any demand schedule, because, other things being equal, the amount of money people are willing to borrow increases as the price of borrowing (i.e., interest) falls. The demand for loanable funds originates with households (which borrow funds to purchase consumer goods and services), business firms (which borrow funds to purchase capital goods), and governments (which borrow funds to purchase schools, highways, buildings, and a variety of other public goods and services). Economists believe that the supply schedule for loanable funds is positive, the flow of funds into the market increases as the price paid for their use rises.

The demand and supply of loanable funds

Analyzing Interest as a Price

Money available for borrowing at interest is like any other commodity or service that has a market price in that those who control the supply can reasonably be expected to offer more in the market as the price of loanable funds increases. Loanable funds come from three major sources: current saving by business firms and consumers, the drawing down by business firms and households of cash balances accumulated in a prior income period, and credit creation by the banking system. A supply schedule for loanable funds represents the time rate of flow into the market of funds in relation to the price that they command, whereas the demand schedule represents the time rate of flow out of the market by those who want to use the funds for the purposes already enumerated. The market rate of interest is thus determined by an interaction between the demand for and the supply of loanable funds. This process is depicted in Figure 14-8. But interest rate determination is much more complex in the real world.

Short-Run and Long-Run Rates

Although we have spoken about the rate of interest, there actually exists in the economy a complicated structure of interest *rates,* which vary widely in level and the type of financial obligation represented. Generally, interest rates are lowest for loan transactions of a very short-run nature or with a minimum risk, such as Treasury notes for periods of three to six months. Interest for

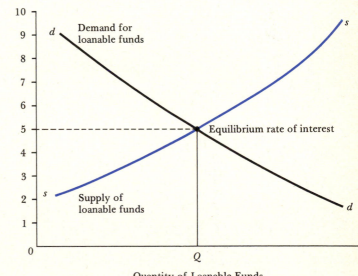

FIGURE 14-8
Determination of the Rate of Interest.
The familiar concepts of demand and supply enable us to explain how interaction between the demand for and the supply of loanable funds establishes the equilibrium rate of interest in a particular market. Interest is a price that balances the flow of funds into the market with the demand for their use.

these notes comes closest to being a "pure" rate. Rates are high when a loan is for twenty to thirty years or when there is a greater risk element, as is usually present in loans to consumers.

In the past few years the interest rate structure has ranged from approximately 4 to 6 percent on three-month Treasury bills, the short-term obligations of the United States Government, to more than 9 percent for mortgages on new homes. Small loans to individual consumers may have rates as high as 40 percent or more, although many people do not know this when they borrow. For example, it has been standard practice in automobile finance companies simply to calculate for the purchaser of a new car the amount he must pay per month and the number of months he must make payments. The rate of interest, if mentioned at all, was often buried in the small print of the loan contract. The government now requires that all loan contracts stipulate the real rate of interest. This is a consequence of the 1970 "Truth in Lending" legislation. Figure 14-9, which traces the recent behavior of key interest rates in the American economy, reveals the differences between various types of interest rates. But it also shows that all interest rates tend to move together.

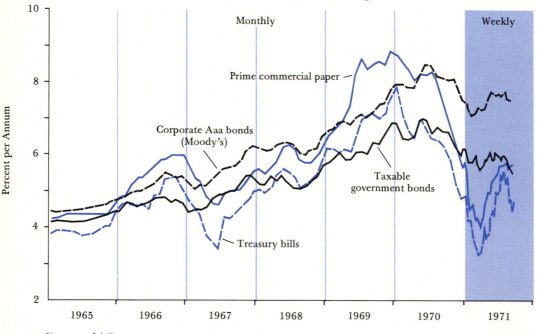

FIGURE 14-9

Bond Yields and Interest Rates.

The figure shows the close movement of four of the most important types of interest rates in the economy. Corporate Aaa Bonds refers to the long-term rate for loans to the safest private corporations; the prime commercial rate is the short-term (4 to 6 months) rate extended by major banks to their "best" business customers. (Source: *Current Economic Indicators,* 1972.)

The Federal Government and Interest Rates

Although market forces play a significant role in determining the level of the various rates that are a part of the general structure of interest, they operate within a framework in which the federal government is more than just another borrower. Basically, the federal government exerts its powerful influence on interest rates in two ways. First, it is far and away the largest single borrower of funds in the American system. In effect, it is in an oligopolistic position and thus can influence the price it pays for loanable funds. Second and even more important, the government can and does manage the supply of loanable funds through the Federal Reserve. The Federal Reserve, as we saw in Chapter 7, can pump reserves into the commercial banking system or pull reserves out. Its action affects the ability of commercial banks to make loans and, consequently, the price paid in the market for loanable funds.

*The largest
borrower of funds
in the economy*

Given the role of the federal government in the market for loanable funds, it is clear that interest rates are not wholly market-determined. For a period during and after World War II interest rates were kept by the government at low levels. In view of the enormous increase in expenditures caused by the war, the government was forced into heavy borrowing, thus expanding the public debt. To hold the annual interest charges on the debt as low as possible, the Treasury supported the price of government bonds in the market at a stipulated level. This prevented a rise in interest rates. For whenever the price of long-term government bonds drops the rate of interest climbs. This arrangement was ended in 1950 with an accord between the Treasury and the Federal Reserve. The Federal Reserve wanted to end this arrangement because Treasury support of the price of government bonds kept the Reserve from carrying out monetary policy through its normal open market operations. To pull money out of the banking system it would normally sell bonds, thus forcing their price down. But it could not do this if the Treasury was committed to a floor for bond prices. Given the large size of its outstanding obligations, the federal government could still resume support operations and exercise a very significant influence on the level of the interest rate.

Rent, Interest, and Resource Allocation

Since rent and interest can be looked at as prices, both figure significantly in the allocation of resources.

The Distribution of Income

Rent and the stock of durable goods

Recall that rent is a price paid for the use of a durable good, such as land, a building, or machinery. The price a user will pay for the services of a particular good must reflect the value of those services to the user. In this way rent allocates the existing supply of durable goods among alternative uses given the expected productivity of the services of the goods in these various uses. Rent also serves another economic role by indicating whether additional units of durable goods ought to be produced. Obviously, this does not apply to land, which is not a reproducible asset, but it does apply to buildings, which may be enlarged for more efficient production, and to machinery. If current rents are high relative to the cost of producing additional units of a particular type of durable good, then it may be profitable for a supplier to produce and sell more units. Thus, rents not only allocate the existing supply of durables (including land) among alternative uses, but also are a key element in the process by which society determines whether its stock of durable goods should be increased.

What holds for rent for the most part also pertains to the rate of interest. Aside from consumers who use loanable funds for consumption expenditure, most borrowers need money to secure resources they use in production. This is clearly true for the private firm, which borrows to finance capital equipment, and it is often true for a governmental unit, although it is difficult to calculate an expected rate of return on public capital expenditures such as highways, parks, schools, hospitals, conservation of resources, and other activities at the federal, state, and local level. In any event, interest rates have an allocative role in that they direct loanable funds to projects where expected rates of return are highest.

Interest rates and the allocation of output between present and future consumption

Interest enters into resource allocation in a second way. As long as a portion of the supply of loanable funds comes from current savings and people's willingness to save is sensitive to the rate of interest, then interest may affect the allocation of output between present and future consumption. For example, if a rise in interest rates induces people to save more, this could lead the economy to allocate more current output to production of capital goods, with favorable effects on future consumption. The importance of the rate of interest in this case depends upon the response of saving and investment decisions to changes in the rate of interest, a matter on which there is considerable disagreement among economists today. Some studies show that long-term capital investment in housing and other structures is sensitive to changes in interest rates, but no clear and strong evidence exists on the sensitivity of other types of investment to such changes. Saving is generally believed to be more influenced by income changes than by changes in the rate of interest.

Profit in the Economic System

The final income source we wish to consider in this chapter is profit. Throughout our discussion we have referred to the concept of profit, both in connection with national income and its measurement in Chapter 5 and as a factor in price determination and resource allocation in Chapters 11 and 12. We know profit is a form of income, just as wages, rents, and interest are forms of income. But it is a special form with a unique role to play in the operation of a market system. It is to this aspect of profit we now turn.

Essentially profit, or the expectation of profit, is the sparkplug for innovation and change. Profit is a pure surplus; it is the excess of income over all necessary (or economic) costs involved in production. Unlike wages and salaries, rents, and interest, which are payments that must be made to secure the resources needed for production, profit is the residual, the surplus, left after all costs, both explicit and implicit, have been met.

The sparkplug
for innovation
and changes

In Chapter 11 we saw how the price mechanism works with respect to the behavior of the firm and the allocation of resources. The desire for and expectation of profit leads the business firm to adjust its output and thus the amount of resources it uses. In a market economy, the business firm expands or contracts output (and its use of resources) until profit is maximized. In the long run profit in the economic sense may vanish, except under monopolistic or oligopolistic market conditions. Then the income of the firm may be sufficient to cover its costs, but any economic surplus in the form of profit will disappear.

The Entrepreneur

But surely there is more to profit than this. Why is it justified? To understand the role that profit plays in a market system we must also understand the role assigned to the entrepreneur. Traditionally, economic analysis associates profit as a form of income with the activities of the entrepreneur. In classic economic theory, he is far more than just the manager or the owner of an enterprise. The entrepreneur's basic function in a market system is not only to bring together the resources—land, labor, and capital—necessary to carry on production, but also to innovate and assume the risks inherent in combining resources to produce a commodity or service with the expectation that demand will exist and the good or service produced can be sold. The view of the entrepreneur as the principal source of innovation was set

The entrepreneur
as risk taker

forth most notably in the 1930s and 1940s by Joseph Schumpeter, a Harvard economist.

Profit can thus be seen as reward for innovation and risk. If it did not exist, much of our economic activity would not take place. There is no guarantee of profit in a market system. There is always the risk that an enterprise will be unable to sell what it produces and have a loss rather than a profit.

A further word about innovation. Although innovations are expected to reduce production cost or expand the range of choice open to the consumer, there is no guarantee that new productive techniques will turn out to be more economical than existing techniques, or that new products or services will be accepted by the consumer. Nevertheless, a dynamic economy must have continuous innovation in both the processes of production and the range of goods and services available to the consumer.

Of course, it is the expectation of profit—not assured profit—which motivates the entrepreneur. Profit in a market system is the catalyst for change; it is the lure necessary to get individuals and business firms to assume the risks of innovation.

Questions for Review and Discussion

1. What is the difference between factoral and personal distribution of income?
2. Does a Lorenz curve tell us when the distribution of income is either too unequal or too equal? If not, what does a Lorenz curve explain?
3. What is meant by calling the demand for the services of any economic resource a "derived demand"?
4. What is marginal resource cost? Marginal revenue product? How can these concepts be used to explain the quantity of any economic resource—land, labor, or capital—that a firm will use?
5. How does the principle of diminishing marginal productivity enter into an explanation of the nature of the demand curve for an economic resource?
6. If wages are determined in a purely competitive market, what effect does this have on workers' ability to bargain for higher wages?
7. Explain monopsony. What effect does monopsony have on the wage level and the amount of employment?
8. Why is the wage level said to be indeterminant when the market structure is one of bilateral monopoly?
9. What is the difference between a craft union and an industrial union? Which type of union structure is likely to predominate in oligopolistic industries?
10. Explain why David Ricardo regarded land rent as a pure economic surplus. Does this concept of rent have any validity today?

11. If interest is the price paid for loanable funds, what are the major sources of demand for loanable funds? Of supply?

12. Explain why profit is simultaneously a surplus (thus not an economic cost) and one of the key forms of income in a market system.

15

Public Policy and the Distribution of Income

INCOME IN THE MODERN ECONOMY is derived either from the market, which depends upon factor prices and employment, or from transfer payments, which provide income to persons who do not or cannot participate in the productive process. Up to now we have concentrated primarily upon the role of market forces in income distribution. In this chapter we shall scrutinize the way in which public policy affects the distribution of income. Our prime concern is with the distribution of income to persons, although obviously some attention has to be given to factoral distribution as well.

The activities through which modern governments affect income distribution may be sorted into two broad categories. First, there are public actions designed to help people improve their ability to derive income from market sources. Second, there are public policy measures which bypass the market process and provide income directly to individuals through transfer payments. Policy measures in this category are usually directed at income losses through unemployment, old age, illness, or the accidental and premature death of a wage-earner, among other things. Such income losses are sometimes caused by failures or inefficiencies in the working of the market economy (for example, mass unemployment), and sometimes by personal misfortune which may or may not be the individual's fault. Recent policy in this area has been concerned with the kinds of poverty that are largely untouched by programs dealing with these traditional sources of economic insecurity. However, these two basic categories provide the framework through which we shall examine the most significant public policy measures designed to modify the pattern of income distribution resulting from the play of market forces.

We shall begin by analyzing the role of trade unions in the economic system, because their history, development, and relationship to government are an excellent example of policy measures that influence the individual's ability to get income through the market system. Then we shall review public action that provides income to persons threatened by economic insecurity, concluding the chapter with an examination of poverty in the American economy and what is being done about it.

Trade Unions in the American Economy

The modern trade union movement began in England when the Industrial Revolution established the factory system, although in the United States trade unions did not begin to flourish until the latter third of the nineteenth century. Prior to the Civil War a few unions were organized, mostly on a craft basis and generally of a local character. No important attempt to establish a national labor union took place until after the Civil War.

The first trade unions

The first national labor organization of any consequence in the United States, the Knights of Labor, was formed in 1869. Although the Knights of Labor was organized to improve working conditions and wages for manual workers, its membership was somewhat unusual: it included not only workers but also small farmers, small businessmen, and even professional people such as doctors and lawyers. The Knights of Labor was also very active in social reform, particularly in movements for improvement of public education, abolition of child labor, establishment of an income tax, and the public ownership of transportation facilities, especially railroads. The Knights grew rapidly, even spectacularly, reaching a peak membership of about 700,000 in 1886. Thereaf-

The Knights of Labor

393

ter, though, the membership declined just as rapidly, primarily because there was not enough unity of purpose among the diverse groups included in its membership to hold it together as a cohesive force.

Samuel Gompers and the AFL

The contemporary American labor movement really began in 1881 with the establishment of the Federation of Organized Trade and Labor Unions, which changed its name to the American Federation of Labor in 1886, the year in which the Knights of Labor reached its largest membership. The American Federation of Labor was the creation of Samuel Gompers, its first president and president until his death in 1924. More than any other person, Samuel Gompers shaped the character of the labor movement prior to the Great Depression of the 1930s.

The son of a Jewish cigarmaker of Dutch extraction, Samuel Gompers was born in London but came to the United States at the age of thirteen. His formal schooling ended at the age of ten, following which he became a cigar worker like his father. In the sweatshops of New York City's East Side, it was often the custom for workers to chip in to pay the wages of one worker while he read aloud to the others. Because Gompers had a strong voice, he often had this chore and used it to educate himself and develop his ideas and philosophy.

Two basic principles dominated his drive to establish and lead the trade union movement in the United States. First, the craft was the basis upon which the labor movement had to be founded. Second, the movement had to stick to the basic issues of improved wages and improved working conditions for the working class. It must not, at all costs, become involved in crusades to reform society; this, Gompers believed, had led to the downfall of the Knights of Labor. His approach was simple and pragmatic, sometimes described as "business unionism." His political philosophy was straightforward. He accepted private property and was content to operate within the market system, but constantly tried to get a larger share of the output for members of his union. He insisted that the Federation not identify itself with any political party, but adhere to the practical principle of rewarding the friends of labor and punishing its enemies at the polls. These basic elements in the economic, social, and political philosophy of Samuel Gompers set the tone for the American Federation of Labor during its first half-century.

"Business unionism"

*The growth of the
trade union
movement*

The trade union movement grew slowly from 1881 to 1900, but at the turn of the century a period of rapid growth began. By 1904 union membership in the country was over two million, approximately 8 percent of nonagricultural employment. This spurt in membership was followed by another period of slow growth which continued until World War I, when membership more than doubled, reaching slightly more than five million by 1920. The 1920s were years of retrogression for the labor movement, and by 1933 membership had fallen to less than three million. Immediately thereafter the dual impact of the Great Depression and the beginning of the New Deal in Washington brought about a fantastic rise in union membership. The era from 1933 until the end of World War II witnessed the most rapid growth in union membership in the history of the country. At the end of World War II membership in all trade unions in the United States reached nearly 15 million persons, nearly 36 percent of nonagricultural employment.

The Rise of the Industrial Union: The CIO

In this long span of time, labor unions not only grew but changed in character and membership. During the 1920s the American economy underwent a significant transformation, marked by the spectacular growth of enormous mass-production industries for automobiles, steel, rubber tires, chemicals, and other goods. In these industries the assembly line dominated the production process, and since most of the workers were unskilled or semi-skilled, they were not particularly suited to the craft form of labor organization. The American Federation of Labor clung stubbornly to its view that the craft was the only viable basis for a union organization, a view which undoubtedly accounted for the decline in union membership during this period.

The need for unskilled and semi-skilled labor

This attitude was not seriously challenged until the 1930s, when the combination of the depression, mass unemployment, and the forceful, colorful leadership of the glowering John L. Lewis, president of the United Mine Workers, created within the AFL a Committee for Industrial Organization. The CIO held that the mass production industries ought to be organized on an industrial rather than a craft basis. The pressing events of the 1930s forced the AFL leadership to accept at least a temporary departure from their time-honored philosophy of craft unionism, although the leadership hoped that later they would be able to incorporate the industrial unions into the old-line craft structure of the Federation.

The founding of the CIO

A series of strikes in combination with a drastic change in the climate of legal and governmental attitudes toward unions brought astounding success to the organizing efforts of the CIO under the leadership of John L. Lewis. Unfortunately for the unity of the labor movement, the differences between the craft and the industrial approach to union organization proved too great to allow both to exist in one organization; consequently, in

395

1935 John L. Lewis took his newly formed industrial unions out of the American Federation of Labor to establish a rival organization, the Congress of Industrial Organization. This basic split in the American trade union movement existed until 1955 when, after long and difficult negotiations between the leadership of the AFL and the CIO, the two organizations once again merged into a single labor organization, now known as the AFL-CIO.

After the rapid membership growth between 1933 and 1945, another plateau was reached; since 1945 growth in membership has been relatively slow, although there was a sharp upward spurt between 1950 and 1955 and since 1965 the trend is again upward. In 1970 trade union membership in the United States was 20.7 million, 27.5 percent of nonagricultural employment. Table 15-1 shows the growth of trade union membership in absolute figures and as a percent of nonagricultural employment for selected years since 1880. Figure 15-1 shows absolute membership and membership as a percent of the labor force for the period since 1930.

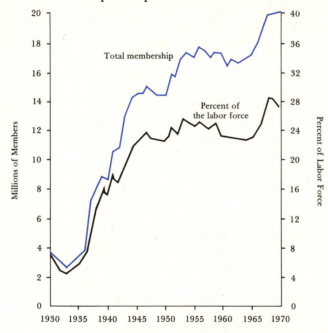

**Figure 15-1
Trade Union Membership since 1930.**

Since 1930 membership in American trade unions has jumped nearly sixfold, although the growth has not been so rapid in the period since World War II. Since about 1950 the labor force has grown slightly more rapidly than trade union membership. (Source: *Statistical Abstract of the United States,* 1971.)

The Legal and Political Environment
of the Union Movement

Trade unions organize workers in a craft, trade, or industry to enable them to influence market forces to better their wages and improve their working conditions. But how far a union can go toward these objectives is heavily influenced by the legal and political environment within which it must act.

TABLE 15-1
Trade Union Membership
Selected Years: 1880–1968

YEAR	MEMBERSHIP (IN THOUSANDS)	PERCENT OF NONAGRICULTURAL EMPLOYMENT
1880	200.0	2.3%
1890	372.0	2.7
1900	865.5	4.8
1910	2,140.5	8.4
1920	5,047.8	16.3
1930	3,392.8	8.8
1933	2,857.0	11.5
1934	8,980.0	28.9
1945	14,796.0	35.8
1956	17,490.0	33.4
1960	17,049.0	31.4
1968	19,297.0	28.4
1970	20,700.0	27.5

Source: *Statistical Abstract of the United States.*

Early Hostility

In a legal sense, the federal government gave little or no support
to trade unions before the New Deal of the 1930s. The government's hostility toward the trade union movement during the
nineteenth century and again in the 1920s arose partly from the
fact that the courts, under the common law, tended to regard
unions and their activities as criminal conspiracies in restraint of
trade. Thus trade union activities were frequently curbed by the
use of the injunction, a court order that could prevent a strike or
other action. In 1842, the Supreme Court held in Commonwealth
v. Hunt that unions as such were not criminal conspiracies in restraint of trade. But their legal right to exist was still not firmly
established and the conspiracy doctrine was still used in labor
cases, especially if a jurist held that the ends sought by the union
were illegal. Furthermore, the judiciary frequently held that the
methods unions used to obtain their objectives, such as strikes,
walkouts, and boycotts, were illegal devices in restraint of trade
and could therefore be prevented by injunctions. Up until the
1930s the law remained vague, making it possible for the personal
philosophy of the individual jurists to play a predominant role in
determining how the power and action of unions might be constrained.

Not only were the courts before the 1930s generally hostile to
the normal activities of the trade union, but they also often ruled
unconstitutional legislation designed to improve working conditions, especially legislation that would regulate the working con-

*Unions viewed as
conspiracies*

397

ditions of women and children. The Sherman Antitrust Act of 1890, while aimed primarily at monopolistic practices by business firms, was used by the courts to curtail or restrain trade unions, since the act declared illegal all combinations in restraint of trade.

The Acceptance of Unionism

A fundamental reversal in the legal and political climate of opinion occurred in the United States at the onset of the Great Depression of the 1930s. The pace of change accelerated greatly during the first New Deal Administration (1933–1936) of Franklin D. Roosevelt.

One of the first significant legislative acts of this period was the Norris-LaGuardia Act, passed in 1932, prior to the advent of the New Deal. This law made unenforceable in the federal courts agreements which trade unionists called "yellow-dog" contracts. A "yellow-dog" contract is one in which an employee agrees as a condition of employment not to join a union at any time during his employment, the penalty being dismissal. This highly effective deterrent to unionization had been widely used by employers and blessed by the judicial system prior to 1932. The second provision of the Norris-La Guardia Act placed severe limits on the use of the injunction, hitherto liberally used by courts friendly to employers.

The Norris-LaGuardia Act

The next important advance in labor legislation came in 1935, with the passage of the National Labor Relations Act, popularly known as the Wagner Act after its chief author, the late Senator Robert Wagner of New York. This act, which has been called the Magna Carta of labor, explicitly recognized for the first time in the United States the right of workers to organize and bargain collectively with their employer. In addition, the act established the National Labor Relations Board to carry out its provisions. The NLRB does this, first, by holding plant elections to determine what labor organization, if any, should be accepted as the bargaining representative for the workers, and, second, by making certain that employers do not engage in any of the unfair labor practices included in the act. The NLRB has the power to issue "cease and desist" orders to carry out its role in the administration of the act, although these orders may be appealed to the courts to determine their ultimate validity. A cease and desist order makes an employer stop using a practice the NLRB finds in violation of the act.

The National Labor Relations Act

Collective bargaining

The key provision of the National Labor Relations Act requires that employers bargain collectively and in good faith with their employees, a proviso which put the full power of the federal government behind the drive toward unionization and collective bargaining. This act and the Norris-LaGuardia Act gave an especially strong impetus to organization of workers in the mass production industries. It is doubtful that the Committee on Industrial Organization, which took the lead in organizing these industries, could have succeeded in this monumental undertaking without the legal and political support embodied in this historic legislation.

The Postwar Situation

Immediately after World War II the American economy experienced a sharp increase in the number of strikes, as well as a substantial rise in the general price level, a development for which organized labor, rightly or wrongly, received much blame because of its postwar wage demands. By this time many people felt power had swung too far to the side of organized labor. One result was further labor legislation, which somewhat readjusted the balance of power between labor and management back toward management. The Labor Management Relations Act of 1947 (also known as the Taft-Hartley Act) did this by establishing a number of "unfair labor practices" applicable to employees, not just employers as under the Labor Relations Act of 1935, and by making certain labor practices illegal. Among these are the secondary boycott and the jurisdictional strike. A secondary boycott involves a strike or other action against one employer to compel him to bring pressure on another employer with whom a union has a dispute. A jurisdictional strike is a strike called to force an employer to recognize one union rather than another.

The Taft-Hartley Act

The Taft-Hartley Act also strengthened the position of the individual worker *vis-à-vis* the union by making a closed-shop agreement in labor-management contracts illegal, and by permitting the states to pass legislation to make even the union shop illegal. (In a closed shop an individual must be a member of a trade union before he can be employed; in a union shop an individual must join the union within a specified period after he is hired by a firm.) As a result of the Taft-Hartley Act a number of states passed so-called "right-to-work" laws, which held in effect that no person can be excluded from employment because of membership or non-membership in a labor organization. The practical impact of "right-to-work" legislation is to make the union shop illegal. Such legislation now exists in nineteen states, none of them major industrial states. Further, the Taft-Hartley Act provided for an 80-day "cooling-off" period for strikes in industries which might imperil the national health or safety. This waiting period is enforced by injunction, compulsory mediation, and compulsory fact-finding. Nevertheless, the national emergency provisions of the Taft-Hartley Act have not proved especially effective as a

The end of the closed-shop agreement

means for dealing with major labor disputes. In two instances (1948 and 1950) involving John L. Lewis and the United Mine Workers the injunction was ignored, even though in the 1948 coal strike heavy fines were levied upon Lewis and the union. In 1959 a steel strike lasted 116 days before an injunction was instituted and a 1964 dock strike lasted about the same number of days after an injunction was ended.

*The Landrum-
Griffin Act*

Organized labor was—and remains—strongly opposed to this act, although it probably has not seriously weakened the labor position in the economy. The shift in public attitude away from the pro-trade union feeling of the 1930s was manifested in the most recent major legislation affecting organized labor, the Landrum-Griffin Act of 1959. This act, whose legal title is the Labor Management Reporting and Disclosure Act, is designed to reduce or eliminate corrupt practices within trade unions and make trade unions more democratic. It provides for stricter control over union elections and greater regulation of their internal affairs. Specifically it provides for the secret election of union officers, a guarantee of free speech and the right of assembly of rank and file union members, and the filing of detailed financial reports by trade unions.

Trade Union Activity and Current Issues

The basic objective of a trade union in any industry is to secure sufficient control over the labor force to become the sole bargaining agent for the employees in that industry. A union seeks through the bargaining process to negotiate a collective agreement, an understanding between the firm and the union on a number of major points. First, and often the most important among these, is the status of the union. Much of the labor strife in this country in the 1930s revolved around this issue; workers went on strike or engaged in pitched battles with forces of the employers simply to gain recognition for the union. At the least the union sought recognition as the bargaining agent for its members; often its goal was to become the exclusive bargaining agent for all employees.

*The union as
bargaining agent*

*Rates of pay,
working conditions,
hiring and laying
off workers*

Second, an agreement must deal with the level of wages, including different rates of pay for different jobs, the effect of minimum wage rates on employment, and other economic factors including hours of work. Third, a union contract will embrace all facets of working conditions concerning the employee. Finally, a collective agreement normally specifies the principles that govern seniority and how they will be applied in hiring and laying off workers. Attention is given to procedures for the redress of grievances by union members. All these points are usually covered in a conventional collective agreement. Since World War II, unions have become increasingly alert to the fact that wage increases are threatened by inflationary advances in the general price level, so it has also become a common practice for contracts to include a clause providing automatically for cost-of-living adjustments in the basic wage rate. Such adjustments are often tied to changes in the index of consumer prices.

Unions Today

The trade union movement in America has come a long way since the floundering Knights of Labor in the 1880s. Currently nearly 25 percent of the civilian labor force is organized in trade unions, many of which have more than 100,000 members. The key mining, transportation, and manufacturing sectors of the economy are tightly organized, and these sectors set basic patterns for prices and wages that influence the economy as a whole. The Harvard economist John Kenneth Galbraith is one of the strongest proponents of the view that in approximately one-half of the economy prices are set by the action of great corporations and the trade unions in the industries these corporations dominate. President Nixon's Phase II program for controlling inflation also embodied this view of how the economy works, for it rested upon the assumption that the Pay Board and Price Commission would succeed if they could control the wage and price decisions within the three to five hundred largest corporations in the nation.

The power of unions

Students of the American labor movement are now wondering whether the movement has reached a plateau of achievement; there have been no spectacular advances in trade union membership since the great surge forward in the 1930s. One reason, perhaps, for the lack of significant recent growth in trade union membership is that employment in the goods-producing industries (agriculture, manufacturing, mining, and construction) appears stabilized; the greatest growth has been in the service industries (trade, services, the professions, and government). These now employ about 50 percent more people than the goods-producing sector. Furthermore, the trade unions have not had notable success in enlarging their membership in retail and wholesale trade and other services, although growth in union membership among public employees has been quite rapid in the last five to six years. The American Federation of State, County, and Municipal Employees (AFSCME) has more than 400,000 members and is one of the fastest-growing unions in the country.

Slow growth of unions

The Future Role of Labor

A close look at the current status of the labor movement suggests two firm conclusions. First, there is no question that the trade union is firmly established in a legal sense and is a key part of the economic system in the United States. Second, collective bargaining has become a basic part of the process of wage determination in key sectors of the economy. The crucial wage decisions are the outcome of market forces and the relative strength of the parties involved in the bargaining process, organized labor and management.

Conservative tendencies in unions

A look ahead reveals a number of important issues which remain unresolved, but are bound to have an impact upon the character of the labor movement. Two seem particularly important. First, the trade union movement in the United States appears to have lost some of the dynamic excitement of the 1930s, when it not only organized massive numbers of workers, but was also an instrument for progress and reform. Historically, organized labor has fought for and supported such broad measures as free public education, banking and monetary reform, regulation of the stock market, adequate retirement income through a system of social security, aid to agriculture, the progressive income tax, control of private monopoly power in the business sector, a system of universal medical care, and expansion of the public sector. Politically, organized labor was one of the main elements in the New Deal coalition that President Franklin Roosevelt put together in the 1930s, and that formed the political and economic basis for the post-World War II Democratic administrations of Harry Truman, John Kennedy, and Lyndon Johnson. A difficult problem of organized labor today is recapturing some of the idealism of the movement in the 1930s. Rightly or wrongly, the leadership of the trade union movement today appears to many to have become excessively conservative, concerned only with power and the material prosperity of its members and not with contemporary issues like war, racism, and the destruction of the environment. Probably the main reason that this viewpoint is relatively widespread—among young people at least—is that most of the leadership in the AFL-CIO strongly supported the Vietnam policies pursued by the Johnson administration. The union movement is not hostile to efforts to save the environment, but it fears that some of the highly zealous supporters of the environmental and ecological causes are not enough interested in the adverse effect on jobs of some actions taken in the name of the environment. The recent debate over the merits of the supersonic transport plane (the SST) is a case in point. Environmental groups were practically unanimous in their opposition to continued development of the SST, but the unions, fearing the loss of jobs, just as strongly favored continued federal funding for the project. This, perhaps, is the fate of any institution that has successfully made the transition from a protest movement to a "going concern."

Second, no real solution is yet in sight for resolving major strikes between labor and management, especially when management may be a public body, such as a municipality, and labor may perform a vital public function, such as police or fire protection. It seems obvious to many impartial observers that the strike has become too costly a means to attain a settlement of differences between labor and management when the public interest is vitally involved, as happens when a strike completely shuts down the operation of a great city. We need techniques more sophisticated than the strike to settle a growing proportion of our labor disputes. They will not be easy to find, for the strike is labor's most effective weapon. Given labor's long, bitter, and often bloody struggle to achieve its present status, it is difficult to see any alternatives to the strike likely to meet with organized labor's approval. There is little in the post-World War II experience, including the recent experiences under Phase II of the Nixon administration, to give labor much confidence in the impartiality of government. President George Meany of the AFL-CIO and three other labor members of the Nixon administration Pay Board resigned from that body in March 1972 because they believed the decisions on pay increases under the President's program were not fair to organized labor. The specific issue was a decision of the Pay Board to scale down a pay increase a union won after a long strike.

Increasing costliness of strikes

Economic Insecurity in the American Economy

No aspect of income distribution is more pressing—or more controversial—than public policies that are aimed at alleviating economic insecurity or poverty. Economic insecurity means a threat to the livelihood of the breadwinner in a family; it may arise from malfunctions of the economic system, in a depression or recession, from loss of income because of retirement, or from serious injury, illness, and other unexpected personal misfortunes. In this context, economic insecurity is not the same thing as poverty. Poverty exists when an individual or family has inadequate income relative to a standard defined as the minimum for the society. According to the Social Security Administration, an income of less than $3,972 would place a family of four below the poverty line. The criterion for defining poverty in terms of income will obviously change as the level of material well-being for the entire society changes and also will vary with family size. A poverty level income in the 1970s is far different from a poverty level income in the 1930s.

Obviously economic insecurity and poverty are related, al-

The meaning of economic insecurity

Economic insecurity vs. poverty

403

though for analytical purposes it is desirable to treat them separately. Economic insecurity may plunge a family or individual into poverty, particularly if the loss of income is prolonged. It is important to note, for this is especially relevant now, that measures taken to deal with the problem of economic insecurity do not necessarily eliminate poverty. This is one of the paradoxes of our time, for in the last half-century extensive programs have been undertaken to eliminate economic insecurity in the American economy; in spite of them, the economy still has an unreasonably large portion of its population living below the poverty line and economic insecurity still exists. We shall soon examine this paradox.

Unemployment

Basically, there are three key causes of economic insecurity under contemporary conditions. First, there is loss of income through *Mass unemployment* unemployment. There have been periods of severe, and sometimes prolonged, unemployment in the American economy. During the Great Depression of the 1930s, mass unemployment occurred all over the country and persisted for longer than a decade. There is also loss of income for a shorter period caused by unemployment in certain occupations, particularly those of a seasonal character. From 1948 through 1970, unemployment in the American economy averaged more than 3.2 million workers, and the rate of unemployment was above 5 percent in ten of those years. There were only four years in which unemployment was 3.5 percent or less, a figure that can reasonably be defined as "full employment." The average unemployment rate was 4.7 percent of the civilian labor force during this period.

All unemployment is not necessarily due to cyclical fluctuations in the level of economic activity. Some of it is structural in character; it arises out of technological change, innovation, and other *Structural unemployment* dynamic developments that stimulate demand for new skills and make some existing skills obsolete. Even though our knowledge of fiscal and monetary policy makes it probable that mass unemployment as was experienced in the 1930s is a thing of the past, unemployment remains a major source of economic insecurity.

Retirement

A second major cause of economic insecurity in an industrial society is the loss of earning power through retirement. As the economy's character has changed during the last century from an essentially rural and agricultural society to a highly industrialized and specialized economic system, a mandatory retirement age has become the practice in many areas of the economy. For too many individuals retirement may be an economic catastrophe, because they have not been able through their working lives to accumulate sufficient savings and assets to provide an adequate income once they leave the labor force. Furthermore, retired persons are quite likely to confront heavy medical expenses because of the aging process. The unhappy consequence of the loss of income through retirement too frequently has been to force older citizens into a standard of living below the poverty line. Recent estimates indicate that over 20 percent of retired couples in the United States live in poverty, and another 20 percent live precariously close to the poverty line.

Injury and Illness

A third major source of economic insecurity is the loss of income because of accidental injury or illness for the wage earner in a family, or because of the premature death of the wage earner. The 1964 *Economic Report of the President* pointed out that at least a tenth of American families were without a male head, and a large proportion of these were economically imperiled because of the premature death of the male wage earner. Emerging patterns of living in the nation are thrusting women in ever greater numbers into the dominant position as the major breadwinner in some families. In 1971 women accounted for 37.7 percent of all employed persons, in contrast to 33.0 percent a decade earlier. Two decades ago women made up only 30.3 percent of the employed labor force. Rapidly changing attitudes that take a more liberal view of the family, marriage, and the traditional role of woman as a housewife and mother no doubt account in part for the accelerating pace with which women are entering the labor force. Another factor is the necessity for many families to have two breadwinners in order to keep up with the image of American living standards continuously and subtly promoted by television and other media advertising.

The emerging role of women in the economy

Injuries and illness, though no longer the major source of economic insecurity, are not to be dismissed lightly. For many families a major illness or a serious accident results in complete financial catastrophe, because they must operate on an economic margin too narrow to permit them to cope with any serious or unexpected financial drain on their resources. The "working poor" are clearly in this position.

Public Policy and Economic Insecurity

Workmen's Compensation

Public policy measures designed to lessen economic insecurity date back to the early part of this century, when programs were first undertaken to compensate workers for loss of income resulting from industrial accidents or occupational disease. These programs are generally described as "workmen's compensation." Prior to development of workmen's compensation legislation in the United States, a worker injured on the job had no recourse except to bring a suit against his employer. To collect damages he had to prove that the employer had been negligent, which was extremely difficult for a worker to do. Most wage earners simply did not have resources to hire adequate legal help, and consequently most such negligence suits were lost. Early in the twentieth century, though, public dissatisfaction with this procedure became so intense that the states finally began to enact workmen's compensation legislation.

Workmen's compensation

Basically, workmen's compensation laws require employers to make specified payments to workers who have been disabled or injured as a result of employment. The legislation does not attempt to assign blame for an accident. Instead, industrial accidents are regarded as a social cost to be met through legislation. Originally these laws were limited to industrial accidents, but most of them have now been broadened to include occupational diseases within their coverage. Legislation of this kind has been a state rather than a federal responsibility. The methods used to finance compensation for an industrial accident or occupational disease vary from state to state, although in about half the states the law requires employers to take out insurance against the risks of disability their workers may incur. In other states insurance may be voluntary, but often the law in these states will not permit the employer to resort to the common law defense if he does not have insurance. As a matter of practice, most employers carry insurance to compensate them for the risks of industrial accidents and occupational disease.

Safety regulations

Workmen's compensation laws have not only helped provide income for the disabled worker, but they have also given business firms an incentive to improve their practices, especially those pertaining to safety on the job. Insurance rates can be set to give a favorable rate to firms where the accident rate is low. In addition, over the last century most states have adopted safety regulations of greater scope and complexity; this has also been an important factor in the long-term reduction of industrial accidents in the

United States. The average cost to the employer of insurance to cover compensation for injured employees is about one percent of the payroll, which is not excessive in view of the potential benefits.

Unemployment Insurance

A second type of public policy concerned with the elimination of economic insecurity is state unemployment insurance, which, in the United States, dates back to the 1930s. Unemployment insurance came into effect when the Social Security Act of 1935 established methods for dealing with the loss of income because of old age and retirement. Unlike the Social Security system, however, unemployment compensation in effect was left in the hands of the states. To make certain that the states would enact unemployment insurance laws, Congress imposed a federal tax on all employers' payrolls, but provided that nine-tenths of the tax imposed would be returned to those states which imposed an equivalent tax of their own to finance an unemployment insurance program. This meant that no state would be placed at a competitive disadvantage by the program, unless it failed to enact appropriate legislation. As a result of this action, by July 1937 all states had established unemployment insurance programs.

The economy now has an effective nationwide system of unemployment insurance administered by the states. Unemployment insurance laws cover the majority of workers in the economy, although wage earners in agriculture, domestic servants, and casual laborers generally are excluded. State laws are such that about 80 percent of all wage and salary earners are covered under the unemployment insurance acts.

Scope of unemployment insurance

As a general principle, state laws require that a worker must have been employed a certain number of weeks or have earned a certain amount of wages (or both) to be eligible for unemployment benefits. Usually he must be able to work and be available for work in order to continue to receive his benefits. The basic purpose of unemployment compensation is to provide income maintenance for the worker when the loss of employment is involuntary. In general, unemployment benefits are either a fixed amount or related to the earnings of the worker while employed. The latter is the practice of a majority of the states, but there generally is a ceiling on the size of the benefit a worker may receive. The goal appears to be benefits at about 50 percent of the wage, although some states make an additional allowance for dependents. There is wide variation of maximum benefit among the individual states, ranging from about $30 a week in some Southern states to as high as $66 a week in Hawaii. In most instances, the range is between $40 and $50 a week, a level below the poverty

Unemployment benefits

line. Unemployment benefits are paid after a waiting period, normally a week, and in most of the states there is a maximum number of weeks during which the unemployed worker is eligible for benefits. This is most often 26 weeks. Special action by Congress extended the length of the benefit payment period in the 1958, 1961, and 1971 recessions.

Social Security

The most comprehensive existing American legislation aimed at economic insecurity is the Social Security Act of 1935. This act, which was essentially a product of the Great Depression, set up a system of retirement benefits. It is now known as Old Age Survivorship and Disability Health Insurance (OASDHI). Unlike workmen's compensation or unemployment insurance, this is wholly a federal program. Its coverage is more comprehensive than that of either workmen's compensation or unemployment insurance, and its benefits are also more nearly adequate.

*The Social
Security Act of
1935 and
amendments*

When the Social Security Act was first passed in 1935, its major purpose was to establish a system of benefits for retired workers or the survivors of retired workers. In 1950 the act was amended to provide benefits for workers who were permanently and totally disabled, and in 1965 the act was further amended to provide medical care for the aged. As it now exists, the Social Security program embraces a system of benefit payments for retired workers, a system of benefits payable for the survivors of retired workers, a system of disability income payments, and medical care for the aged. Initially, the act did not extend coverage to certain employees, particularly agricultural workers, domestic workers, and the self-employed, but subsequent amendments have generally brought all the groups that were originally excluded into the Social Security system. As now constituted, the law even applies to the professions, including lawyers and physicians; employees of nonprofit organizations and state and local governments now have the option to participate in the Social Security Act.

*Direct transfers
vs. payroll taxes*

When Congress in the 1930s was considering social security legislation it faced two options. It could, on the one hand, provide for direct transfer payments to retired and disabled persons, financing the system by the income tax or any of the taxes that are part of the federal revenue structure. Alternatively, it could provide for a system of benefits related to the individual's prior earnings and financed by a tax on payrolls. Congress chose the latter option, although most other countries have elected the first solution to the problem of retirement income for the aged.

The American system of Social Security is financed by two taxes, one of which is imposed on the wages paid by the worker and the other on the employer's payroll. The rates are identical and they apply (as of 1973) to the first $10,800 of the worker's earnings. This has the effect of making the tax regressive, since everyone with an income of $10,800 or less will pay the same effective rate, but the effective rate will be smaller for persons whose income is greater than $10,800. For example, in 1973 a person with an income of $10,800 paid at a combined effective rate (employee and employer) of 11.0 percent of his income under the Social Security tax. This amounts to $1188. But a person with an $18,000 annual income would pay the same identical amount—$1188—because only the first $10,800 of income is subject to Social Security taxation. This, though, is an effective tax rate of only 6.6 percent. This is significant, for Social Security taxes, which now account for nearly 25 percent of the total tax receipts of the federal government, are the fastest-growing source of federal revenue, second only to the individual income tax in revenue produced. By 1986 the combined employee-employer rate for Social Security will be 11.2 percent on maximum covered earnings of $12,000, given present provisions of the law. It has been estimated that Social Security taxes take more money than does the income tax from the three-fifths of the population who pay both taxes, and there is increasing concern over the essentially regressive character of the Social Security tax. Critics of the present arrangement urge reforms to lessen the burden this tax imposes upon those in the lower income brackets. Among the reforms proposed are shifting a part of the costs of financing Social Security benefits to general revenues, allowing Social Security taxes paid by the individual to be credited against his or her income tax liability, and lifting the wage base ceiling, thereby making all wages and income from self-employment subject to the payroll tax.

The benefits paid to a retired worker under the Social Security Act depend upon two things. A minimum benefit of $84.50 a month (as of 1973) is paid to any worker eligible for benefits under the act, irrespective of the amount of past income earned or the amount earned at the time of his retirement. Above this minimum benefit, the sums a retired worker receives depend upon his prior earnings and whether he has a dependent. The benefits payable are in graduated amounts based upon earnings up to $10,800 a year. The additional benefits allowable for dependents are calculated as a percent of the primary insurance benefit. The formula used to determine benefits based upon the employee's average monthly wage is complex, but under the schedule in effect in 1973 the minimum benefit for a person was $84.50 per month and the maximum $404.50 per month, although it will be many years before anyone qualifies for a pension of the latter size.

The present Social Security tax

The present Social Security benefits

Medicare

The most important single extension of the Social Security Act is Medicare, which was added in 1965 and provides a system of compulsory hospital insurance for all persons over 65 covered by either the OASDHI or the Railroad Retirement System. Persons over 65 who were not covered by these acts were also included in Medicare. The Medicare system of insurance offers hospital care (including all services rendered in a hospital) for up to 90 days, services rendered for up to 100 days in a skilled nursing home, and up to 100 home visits by a nurse following the patient's release from a hospital or nursing home. In addition, four-fifths of the costs of outpatient diagnostic tests are covered by Medicare. Increased benefits for Medicare under Social Security are financed by an increase in payroll taxes, which began at a rate of 0.35 percent in 1966 and is scheduled to rise to 1.10 percent by 1986.

Voluntary medical insurance

The Medicare addition to the Social Security Act also provided for a program of voluntary medical insurance which pays up to 80 percent of the charges after the first $50 for the services of physicians and surgeons, 100 home health service visits, and part of the costs of mental illness up to $250.00 per year. These benefits are financed by a payment of $5.80 per month by the insured person, matched by an equal contribution from the general revenue of the federal government. It is estimated that the benefits under the Medicare program meet approximately one-half of the medical expenses of the aged person.

Workmen's compensation, unemployment insurance, and the Social Security Act, including Medicare, make up the main public policy measures the United States has developed in this century to cope with economic insecurity. No matter how these programs are financed, they transfer income to the victims of economic insecurity who have suffered a loss of income.

There are two basic economic issues involved in solving the problem of economic insecurity. First, there is the perennial matter of the proper level of benefits for those who suffer a loss of income as a result of the various risks inherent in an industrial society. Second, there is the issue of how to finance these benefits. To the extent that economic insecurity is treated as a social problem, benefits will be financed by taxation. An exception is workmen's compensation, which is financed through private insurance even though the impetus for the program came from the government. A key issue in financing is the kind of tax to use. It is necessary to avoid regressive taxes, which defeat the purpose of the programs by imposing an undue burden on those most in need of benefits. Society does not yet fully understand that these programs basically involve income transfers, and there is no agreement on the extent to which both benefits and the taxes which finance the benefits ought to favor individuals and families that live on the brink of economic insecurity.

Poverty in America

We have concentrated so far on the public policy measures directed toward replacing income lost because of economic insecurity. Although economic insecurity has long been recognized as a major source of poverty in modern society, not until early in the 1960s did policy makers begin to realize that existing measures designed to alleviate economic insecurity, even though moderately successful, could not eliminate poverty in the American economy. The recognition that poverty was endemic and widespread in American society came in part from the impact of *The Other America,* a remarkable work published in the early 1960s by Michael Harrington. Harrington, whose phrase "the invisible poor" has become almost a household word, made it starkly clear that there existed within the United States a vast and desolate world and culture of poverty, largely untouched by the affluence of the majority of the population. Harrington's analysis received strong backing from studies made in the early 1960s by the President's Council of Economic Advisers to determine what persons in the population would not be helped by the pending tax cut which was designed to push the economy to a full employment level of production. These developments are the origin of current interest and concern for the continuous state of poverty in the United States.

The "invisible poor"

The Poverty Level

Poverty is relative. Its meaning in a given situation depends upon the level of income used as the criterion for determining who is poor. Obviously, this measure will differ from one society to another, as well as change through time. Poverty should not be confused with inequality, because unless we should achieve perfect equality in the distribution of income, the people at the lower end of the income scale will be relatively less well off than those at the upper end. But they need not be poor. Poverty has to be defined in relation to an absolute level of income meaningful for a society's time and circumstances.

Poverty vs. inequality

In 1964 the Council of Economic Advisers defined the poverty level as an annual income of $3,000 for a family of four, or $1500 for a single individual. These criteria placed approximately seven million families below the poverty line and another five million

Current definition of poverty line

411

single individuals in the same category. In total, the Council reported that about 30 million Americans were poor on this basis. More recent criteria worked out by the Social Security Administration put the minimum level of subsistence for a nonfarm family of four at $3,972. By this figure, it is estimated that in 1971 about 25.5 million persons lived in households below the poverty line. This may be compared to the estimated figure of 40 million in 1960. Since 1959 the number of poor people in the nation has declined at an annual average rate of 4.9 percent except for 1970, when the number of persons living below the poverty line increased by 5.1 percent. This was the consequence of the recession that the economy suffered in 1970.

Note, though, that the mere movement of families above the poverty line may give a misleading impression of progress; it may only mean that a family has moved from a "poor" to a "near-poor" status. The Social Security Administration describes persons and families as "near-poor" if their incomes are only about one-third higher than the basic poverty level. The Council of Economic Advisers reported that in 1967, 16.2 percent of all households could be classified as "poor" and 5.9 percent as "near-poor." Together these totaled 13.9 million households.

Who are the poor? We need to locate the individuals and families most likely to be poor under present circumstances. What are the causes of poverty? Can we identify the primary elements that cause poverty and are responsible for its continued existence in an affluent society? What has been done about poverty in this society? Is it possible to eliminate poverty and, if so, what must be done? We shall tackle these questions in turn.

Identifying the Poor

The poverty gap

Though there may be disagreement concerning the income level that marks the poverty line, it is possible, nevertheless, to identify the individuals and families which fall below it. According to the Council of Economic Advisers,* in 1967 there were approximately 10.2 million poor households, representing slightly less than 12 percent of the population. The latter figure, though still substantial, is sharply down from the estimated 30 percent of the population below the poverty line at the close of World War II. Figure 15-2 shows trends since 1948 in the absolute number and the incidence of poverty in the United States. Note that the 1970 recession caused both measures to increase. The CEA pointed out in its 1969 *Report* that the "poverty gap" dropped from $13.7 bil-

* The 1969 Report of the CEA contains one of the most comprehensive analyses of poverty in the United States, readily available. The situation has not changed significantly since these data were published, except perhaps to worsen slightly after the 1970–71 recession.

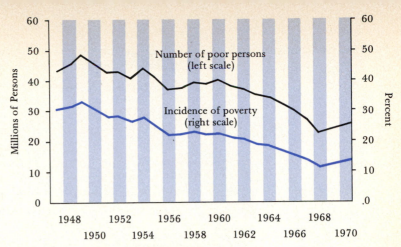

FIGURE 15-2

Number of Poor Persons and Incidence of Poverty.

The upturn in the number of poor persons as the 1970s began reflects the 1970–1971 recession. The number in poverty also rose in earlier recessions, notably in 1948–1950, 1953–54, and 1957–58. (Source: Council of Economic Advisers, 1972.)

lion in 1959 to $9.7 billion in 1967. The gap rose, though, to $11.4 billion in 1970, again because of the recession. The "poverty gap" is the difference between the actual incomes of the poor (in the aggregate) and the incomes that would be necessary to place them above the poverty line. It gives us a rough estimate of the dollar cost of the statistical elimination of poverty.

Contrary, perhaps, to popular opinion, the incidence of poverty in the United States is greater in rural than in urban areas, although urban poverty appears to receive most of the publicity in the nation's press. In 1967, 23 percent of the population in the rural areas outside of metropolitan counties was classified as poor, with the heaviest concentration in the South and the Appalachian Mountain belt stretching from Tennessee and Kentucky through Pennsylvania into New York State. The Council of Economic Advisers also found quite a high incidence of poverty (19 percent) in the smaller cities and towns outside the major metropolitan areas. In the central cities the incidence of poverty was 16 percent, but in the suburbs of the central cities only 9 percent. *Rural and urban poverty*

The majority of the poor are white, although the treatment of poverty in the popular press has, perhaps, led many people to believe that the majority are nonwhite. As of 1967, 71 percent of all poor families were white and 83 percent of all poor unrelated individuals were white. However, the incidence of poverty is far higher among nonwhites than among whites; the Council found that on the average about one household in three was poor among nonwhites, while the comparable figure for whites was only one household in seven. *The white poor*

Figure 15-3 contains a profile of poverty in the United States as of 1970, both for families and for unattached individuals. It shows that the poor in America are likely to be found among four major groups. First there are the nonwhites. Data for 1970 show that 30.9 percent of nonwhite households are poor—this embraces more than seven million persons—and 46.4 percent of nonwhite unattached individuals are living below the poverty line. For *Nonwhites*

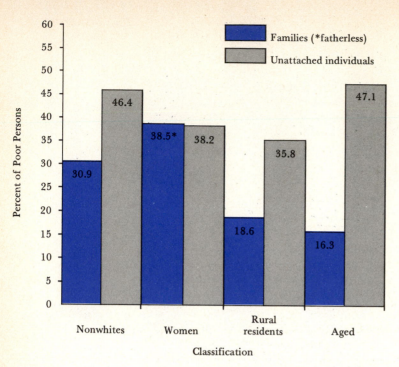

Percent of Poor Persons

30.9   46.4   38.5*   38.2   18.6   35.8   16.3   47.1

Nonwhites   Women   Rural residents   Aged

Classification

FIGURE 15-3
Profile of Poverty in the United States in 1970.
The largest proportion of families below the poverty line is among fatherless families, followed by families that are nonwhite, rural, or with a head 65 years old or older. These are the four main groups in which poverty for the family and for unattached individuals is most likely in the United States today. (Source: *Current Population Reports,* 1971.)

1971 the U. S. Department of Commerce reported that 33.6 percent of the nation's black population is poor. Thus the odds are significantly higher that a nonwhite will be poor.

A second important group with a high incidence of poverty is the aged, especially the single aged. This is true even though they are the chief beneficiaries of income transfers under the Social Security program. In its comprehensive 1969 report on poverty in the United States, the Council of Economic Advisers stated that more than 22 million persons received retirement income under the provisions of the Social Security Act. In spite of this, 16.3 percent of households in which the head is 65 or older remained below the poverty line; the situation was much worse for the unattached elderly person, for 47.1 percent of these individuals were living in poverty in 1970. The leading factor in the reduction of poverty among the aged has been increased Social Security benefits, although the level of benefits remains too low to eliminate poverty in this group.

Households headed by women constitute the third group in which there is a high incidence of poverty. In 1970, 38.5 percent of families headed by a woman were below the poverty line. For nonwhite families the percentage was much higher, 59 percent. For white families the figure was 28.6 percent. These families are the prime beneficiaries of the welfare system, which has increasingly come under attack during the last decade, and which we shall discuss in the last part of this chapter.

The old

Families with a female head

The fourth major group in which poverty is most likely to be found are farm families, although the proportion of these families below the poverty line has drastically declined in the last decade, at least for whites. As of 1970, 18.6 percent of all rural families were below the poverty line; the percentage for whites was 16.2 and for nonwhites 58.1. A significant part of the improvement has come from the migration of people from rural areas, rather than from any general overall improvement in agriculture resulting from the farm programs. Government aid to agriculture has not been a significant factor in helping the poor farmers, chiefly because most of the aid goes to the large producers who are geared to producing for the agricultural market.

In addition to nonwhites, the aged, families without a male breadwinner, and rural families, there are poor people who do not fit neatly into any of these categories. They make up only about 3 percent of the total number of poor. There are a variety of reasons why they are poor, some of which are attributable to the individual himself and some of which are caused by forces over which he has no control. Illness is often a factor in such situations, as is inadequate education and training. But for one reason or another these people cannot participate effectively in the market economy and earn enough income to lift themselves out of poverty.

The Causes of Poverty

There is no one way to classify the causes of poverty. Either the poor do not possess sufficient resources to obtain an adequate income through the market, or the transfer mechanisms of society do not provide them with sufficient income. We can, though, place the specific causes of poverty in three general categories, which identify key elements in the problem.

Overall Causes

First, there are causes of a general nature, applicable to the whole economy and resulting primarily from malfunction in the economic system. Unemployment clearly belongs in this category. This type of poverty can be treated by providing income to people in the event they are unemployed (i.e. unemployment compensation), or better still by public policy measures to maintain full employment conditions. A significant portion of the reduction in poverty in the American economy since World War II simply results from the fact that in these years the economy has had reasonably full employment; hence jobs have been available

415

and there has been a significant reduction in the incidence of poverty.

There is also a hard core of "unemployables" in the labor force, estimated to be equal to between one and two percent of the civilian labor force. These are the chronically ill, the physically handicapped, many unskilled, and others who for psychological and physical reasons cannot hold a permanent job.

Regional Causes

A second cause of poverty is regional or geographic. Events occur that lead to a significant decline in the economic base of a particular region. The poverty in Appalachia and some of the southern parts of the United States is of this nature, since it is caused by a decline in demand for the area's resources. Poverty with a regional or geographic basis affects nearly all of the residents of the area; generally it is not significantly affected by the levels of prosperity in the rest of the economy. Unless poor people in these regions can migrate to other areas, they will remain poor as long as nothing is done to overcome the adverse conditions which brought poverty to the region in the first place.

Individual Causes

*Discrimination,
arbitrary retirement
programs, etc.*

Finally, there is a heterogeneous group of causes that impinge primarily on the individual or his family, rather than the whole society or a region. This grouping embraces discrimination, arbitrary retirement programs, absence of educational opportunity, the lack of an economically useful skill, insufficient ambition, or simple personal misfortune, such as an illness or accident not adequately compensated for by either private insurance or public transfers.

Poverty in the Black Ghetto

*The black ghetto
as a colony*

One of the acute pockets of poverty in the United States is found in the black ghettos of our great cities. Since World War II there has been a vast migration of blacks into the central cities of the United States and a countermigration of whites into the suburbs. The result has been the creation of a black core—the urban ghettos—in the central part of most large American cities. At this time there is little or no sign of a reversal of these trends; current projections indicate that by 1985 black majorities will dominate such cities as Chicago, Philadelphia, St. Louis, Detroit, Baltimore, New Orleans, and Cleveland. As of 1970 it is estimated that there were 13.6 million blacks living in the central cities, a figure that is expected to rise to 20.3 million by 1985. Nonwhites have lower incomes than whites generally and are more likely to be below the poverty line (see Figure 15-4), but the problem of poverty is especially severe in the central areas of our major cities because of overcrowding, poor housing, poor schools, inadequate government services, and a critical shortage of opportunities for employment. Mountains of research have demonstrated conclusively that blacks in America are systematically discriminated against in education, jobs, and housing; although there undoubtedly has been some improvement, it is not inaccurate to view the black

Poverty in the Black Ghetto

FIGURE 15-4

Percent of Whites and Nonwhites (Families and Unrelated Individuals) Below the Poverty Line: 1959–1970.

Although the proportion of both whites and nonwhites below the poverty line has shown a significant decline since 1959, nonwhites still represent a much higher proportion of such families than do whites. The odds are more than three to one that a person from a nonwhite family will be poor rather than one from a white family. (Source: *Current Population Reports,* 1971.)

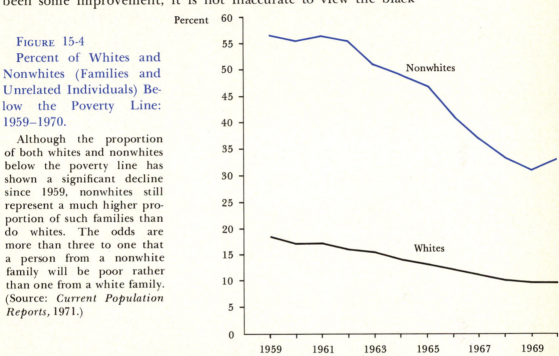

ghettos of American cities today as internal colonies exploited by the white majority. The ghetto world has a relatively low per capita income and a high birth rate; its work force is unskilled and lacks capital; local markets are underdeveloped; its only basic export is its unskilled labor power. Under such circumstances, the ultimate solution to its problems may have to take the form of a massive infusion of capital from external sources, much as in the underdeveloped—or "third world"—countries.

Not only is there extensive geographical segregation and isolation of the black and nonwhite population from the rest of society, but the economic position of blacks has been and remains distinctly inferior to that of the dominant white majority. In 1970, for example, the average income of black families was only 63.6 percent of that of white families. Further, 56 percent of black families had incomes of less than $6,000 in contrast to 31.7 percent of white families. At the upper end of the income scale, 17.8

417

percent of white families had incomes in excess of $15,000, but the corresponding percentage for blacks was 6.1. Table 15-2 shows the distribution of family income for white and black families in 1970.

TABLE 15-2

Distribution of Family Income for White
and Black Families: 1970

INCOME RANGE	PERCENT OF WHITE FAMILIES	PERCENT OF BLACK FAMILIES
0–$1,999	9.0	18.8
$2,000–3,999	11.6	19.7
$4,000–5,999	11.1	17.5
$6,000–9,999	26.2	25.2
$10,000–14,999	24.3	12.7
$15,000–24,999	14.3	5.5
Over $25,000	3.5	0.6

Source: U.S. Department of Commerce, *Current Population Reports*.

The incidence of poverty is much greater among blacks and nonwhites generally than it is among whites. Figure 15-4 shows the percent of whites and nonwhites whose incomes fall below the poverty line for the years 1959 through 1970. For both groups there has been significant improvement in the last decade, but the proportion of nonwhites with incomes below the poverty line is still more than three times greater than the proportion for whites.

One interesting fact emerges from the data in Figure 15-4: a vigorous economic expansion does much to improve the economic status of the nonwhite minority. The proportion of nonwhites below the poverty line began to decline relatively rapidly after 1965, when the Vietnam war buildup pushed the economy to full employment. The lesson is not that war is needed, but that full employment is the essential complement to all other measures in the way of investment in education, job training, and improved housing if a real impact is to be made in reducing the glaring disparities between the economic status of whites and nonwhites in this country.

Anti-Poverty Programs in the

American Economy

We have asked what this society has done about poverty. Aside from attempts to eliminate the poverty that develops out of economic insecurity, there have been two other basic approaches to this problem. The first belongs under the general heading of public assistance, or, as it is more commonly known, "welfare." This approach provides aid in various forms to persons and families who do not qualify for some or sufficient aid under economic insecurity programs. The second approach, glamorously called "the war on poverty" under the administration of President Kennedy, was brought to its most developed legislative form during the administration of President Lyndon B. Johnson. The Nixon administration expanded and modified some of the Kennedy-Johnson programs and inaugurated anti-poverty measures of its own, while discarding the phrase "war on poverty."

Welfare

Public assistance, which is financed in part by grants-in-aid to the states from the federal government, helps four kinds of persons or families: the aged, the blind, the permanently and totally disabled, and families with dependent children (known as AFDC, for Assistance to Families with Dependent Children). In 1971 over 13 million persons received aid under one or more of the programs. Table 15-3 shows by category the number and percent of persons who received public assistance in 1971. In spite of the magnitude of this expenditure and the number of families receiving some form of public assistance, it is estimated that these programs reach only about a fourth of the families whose incomes fall below the poverty line.

Aid to the aged, the blind, the disabled, and families with dependent children

TABLE 15-3
Persons Receiving Public Assistance: 1971

CATEGORY OF RECIPIENT	NUMBER	PERCENT OF TOTAL
Children	7,421,000	55.5
Mothers	2,483,000	18.6
Fathers	126,000	0.9
Aged	2,082,000	15.6
Blind or disabled	1,254,800	9.4
Total	13,366,800	100.0

Source: U.S. Department of Health, Education, and Welfare.

The largest sums under public assistance go to families with dependent children. This is the side of "welfare" that has caused most controversy and dissatisfaction among the recipients, those who administer the program, and the general public. Significant changes in the AFDC have recently been proposed, as we shall

The welfare family

419

see, and more can be expected, particularly in view of widespread public unrest with the existing program. Part of the problem of the welfare program, especially the AFDC portion, is that the income received is rarely enough to boost a family above the poverty line. In 1971 the average payment to a welfare family of four varied from a low of $60 per month in Mississippi to a high of $375 per month in Alaska. In all but four states welfare payments have been below the established poverty level of $3,972 per year (1971). Under existing law, each state establishes its own "need standard"—the amount required for the necessities of family living. But more than half the states paid less than their own established standard of need. The federal courts have liberalized the rules governing conditions under which a family with dependent children can secure aid, particularly by overturning the controversial "man in the house" rule, which had denied AFDC benefits to children when a man not legally responsible for their care lived with the family. The courts also declared invalid some state residency requirements for public assistance. A 1967 amendment to the Social Security Act gave AFDC mothers a slight incentive to work, by providing that their welfare benefits would not be reduced by the full amount of any additional earnings. Before this, there had been for all practical purposes a 100 percent tax on the additional earnings of AFDC mothers able to work. The law was changed in 1971 to require adult welfare recipients to sign up for work or training, or lose part of their benefits.

The War on Poverty

The approach to poverty now known as the "war on poverty" had its beginnings during the 1960 Presidential campaign, partly as a response to conditions President Kennedy saw in West Virginia when he was campaigning for the Democratic nomination. It embraces a number of legislative acts, beginning in 1961 with the Area of Development Act, followed by the Manpower and Development Training Act in 1962. After the assassination of President Kennedy, President Johnson continued with the program, pushing the Economic Opportunity Act through the Congress in 1964. In general, the policy reflected in these acts differed from policies embodied either in traditional programs aimed at economic insecurity or in the more controversial welfare programs. Essentially, the approach of the Economic Opportunity Act was to attempt to eliminate the *causes* of poverty, especially by trying to help the unemployed become employable through education, work experience, and vocational training. The most important programs attempted under the Economic Opportunity Act were the Community Action Programs, the Job Corps, and Vista, domestic equivalent of the Peace Corps. The latter two were combined into a single agency by the Nixon administration in 1971. Late in 1971 legislation extending the Office of Economic Opportunity for two additional years was vetoed because the bill extending the program contained a comprehensive child development program for all income levels. Congress failed to override the presidential veto. Late in 1972, Congress completed action on a new bill extending the major programs under OEO.

In spite of the grandiose title of "war on poverty," the program undertaken under the Economic Opportunity Act was really small in scale. It is difficult to appraise the results that were achieved, primarily because the resources that might have gone into poverty programs were diverted to the war in Vietnam. Estimates are that no more than about 6 percent of the poor were reached under these programs. Perhaps their most important results were in changing the direction of governmental efforts in the poverty area. In contrast to previous programs, the "war on poverty" did not seek to solve the problem of poverty simply by increasing existing benefits for those below the poverty line, but by attacking some of poverty's fundamental causes, particularly those affecting young people. This approach will almost certainly be attempted again in the future; in the long run the only meaningful way to resolve the problem of poverty is to attack its basic causes and so create conditions in which people can be productively employed.

New Approaches to the Poverty Problem

In the 1970s there is widespread dissatisfaction with poverty programs, both among those who ought to benefit from the programs and among the general public. There is a growing awareness that current policies either offer inadequate assistance to bring people above the poverty line, or are not able to break the vicious circle of poverty in which families and young people found themselves trapped. New approaches have to be found if the nation is to eliminate poverty. There is a paradox here: the Council of Economic Advisers in its 1969 *Report* stressed that the poverty gap in the United States was only slightly more than *one percent* of the nation's gross national product, a relatively small magnitude. The paradox is even more startling if we compare this to the amount of the gross national product absorbed when the war in Vietnam was at its peak, approximately 3.5 percent. Thus, as many observers have pointed out, what is really lacking in the drive to eliminate poverty in the United States is not the resources, but the will. And the will alone is not enough; there must also be more effective mechanisms, because recent experiences clearly demonstrate that existing policies are woefully inadequate.

Guaranteed Income

One new idea being discussed more and more widely is some form of guaranteed family income, a plan variously described as a system of family allowances, a negative income tax program, or, simply, a guaranteed income. In the last several years a variety of suggestions have been offered by academic economists as well as other responsible groups and interested parties, and surprisingly, the idea of an income guarantee appears to be gaining support from conservatives as well as liberals. Conservative economist Milton Friedman is a strong supporter of the idea of a negative income tax, as is James Tobin of Yale University, a former member of President Kennedy's Council of Economic Advisers.

*Assurance of a
minimum income*

Whatever the label applied to it, this approach involves a guarantee by the government of a minimum income for every family, the minimum being related to family size. It abandons the notion of a means test, or proof that the applicant is in dire economic straits. Instead, eligibility is to be a matter of right, and payment is to be based on the extent to which the family's income falls short of a stipulated level. It is because payment to a family is at least equal to the difference between the income earned by the family and the minimum guarantee that this kind of plan is called a "negative income tax." As the earnings of a family rise toward the guaranteed level, the amount of aid received necessarily diminishes.

*A break-even level
of income*

The guaranteed-income approach differs from past methods because it is possible to build into the plan incentives for the family to work and improve its economic position. This is done by establishing a break-even level of income—level at which no further benefits are received from the government—at a higher level than the minimum guarantee. This makes certain that a family's assistance is not reduced by an amount equal to increase in its earnings. One of the chief criticisms of the way welfare programs have operated in the past centers on this point: whenever a welfare recipient got income from any other source welfare payments were reduced by a like amount; thus, there were no incentives to work and get off public assistance.

Table 15-4 shows how such a program might work, assuming a minimum guarantee of $4,000 for a family of four with no income and a break-even (or cutoff point) of $6,000 in earned income for the receipt of income supplements—or negative income taxes. As this example is constructed, the income supplement is reduced by $670 for every additional $1,000 that the family earns. This is the marginal tax rate on additional income and its magnitude determines the level of the break-even income. A lower marginal rate raises the break-even point.

TABLE 15-4
A Negative Income Tax Plan

EARNED INCOME	INCOME SUPPLEMENT	TOTAL INCOME
None	$4,000	$4,000
$1,000	3,330	4,330
2,000	2,660	4,660
3,000	1,990	4,990
4,000	1,320	5,320
5,000	650	5,650
6,000	None	6,000

The proponents of guaranteed income do not claim that adoption of this program would eliminate all other existing forms of public assistance. It would eliminate some of the inequalities and cumbersome procedures of the present welfare system, particularly those associated with AFDC. Furthermore, it would be a direct frontal assault on poverty, placing income in the pockets of people who do not benefit from existing programs. Realistically, a guaranteed family income should be viewed as a supplement to existing programs; it would be false to suggest that such a program would significantly reduce total outlays for welfare in all of its various forms. But the additional burden on the economy would be relatively slight.

The Nixon Administration
Family Assistance Program

The concept of a guaranteed family income (negative income tax) was partially translated into policy in August 1969 when the Nixon administration proposed a major reform in the welfare program, which the President called a Family Assistance Plan. As originally proposed, a family of four would receive a guaranteed federal payment of $1,600 per year if it had no income. As its income increased the family would be eligible for federal payments on a decreasing scale until its earnings reached $3,920 per year. The House of Representatives passed a bill in April 1970 that embodied the essential features of the Family Assistance Program, but the legislation never got out of the Senate Finance Committee, where liberal members of the committee opposed it because the benefit payments were too low and conservatives said that it was too costly. Consequently, 1970 ended without Congressional action on welfare reform.

In 1971 the House Ways and Means Committee introduced a

new welfare reform measure, which embodied the President's Family Assistance Plan but also contained some additional features. The bill also increased Social Security benefits and extended Medicare coverage. In the realm of welfare reform the two most important provisions were the Opportunities for Families Program and the Family Assistance Plan. The Opportunities for Families Program provided for child care, public service employment for 200,000 persons, and manpower training and placement program. Families with an employable adult, including families with a full-time working father at low wages, are eligible for this aspect of the program. The act also requires that all employable adults eligible for benefits under the program register for work or training. The Family Assistance Plan modified the original Nixon proposal by raising the minimum benefit available for a family of

TABLE 15-5
Proposed Payments Under the
Family Assistance Plan

EARNINGS	FAMILY ASSISTANCE PAYMENT	TOTAL INCOME
a. Family of 2:		
None	$1,600	$1,600
Earnings of		
$720	1,600	2,320
$1,200	1,280	2,480
$1,800	880	2,680
$2,400	480	2,880
$2,940	120	3,060
b. Family of 4:		
None	2,400	2,400
Earnings of		
$720	2,400	3,120
$1,800	1,680	3,480
$2,400	1,280	3,680
$3,000	880	3,880
$3,600	480	4,080
$4,140	120	4,260
c. Family of 8:		
None	3,600	3,600
Earnings of		
$720	3,600	4,320
$1,800	2,880	4,680
$3,000	2 080	5,080
$4,200	1,280	5,480
$5,400	480	5,880
$5,940	120	6,060

Source: House Ways and Means Committee.

four with no income to $2,400 and the minimum benefit that a family of eight would receive to $3,600. The cutoff point for federal assistance for a family of four was raised to $4,260 and for a family of eight $6,060. Table 15-5 shows the proposed schedule of payments under the new plan. Compare these data with the hypothetical plan in Table 15-4.

This proposal would shift more of the costs of welfare program to the federal government. Under existing programs 56 percent of the cost is borne by the federal government, but the new proposal would shift 75 percent of the cost to the federal government. For states where welfare payments are higher than the proposed federal minimums, the legislation contained provisions to guarantee that their welfare costs would not increase over 1971 levels because of the new federal legislation. In 1972 this welfare reform measure passed the House of Representatives, but no action was taken in the Senate, thus effectively ending hopes for reform.

The McGovern Proposals

Early in 1972 Democratic Presidential candidate George McGovern proposed a much more sweeping version of the negative income tax than the welfare reform scheme embodied in President Nixon's Family Assistance Plan. Although in mid-1972 many details were either missing or obscure, the basic idea behind the McGovern plan was to replace entirely the existing welfare system by a program that would provide a basic guarantee of $1,000 per year for every person in the nation. The effect of this would be to establish a minimum income guarantee of $4,000 for a family of four with no income. Only the very poor would actually get $1,000 per person, for the basic grant would replace the present personal exemption of $750 per person under the federal income tax. Thus, families with taxable income would see a portion of the grant go for taxes, since it, like all other income, would be subject to taxation as income under the federal income tax laws. Another major point of difference between the McGovern and Nixon proposals was that the break-even point under McGovern's plan for a family of four would be $12,000, as contrasted to the approximate figure of $4,300 for earned income under the President's proposal. There was such a storm of controversy concerning the ultimate cost to the taxpayer of the McGovern plan that Senator McGovern in the late summer revised his program to place emphasis upon a minimum guaranteed income for a family of four of $4,000 and more job opportunities. The McGovern and Nixon plans share acceptance of the principle of the negative income tax and as intent to equalize welfare payments across the country.

A broad version of negative income tax

The Government as "Employer of Last Resort"

Another new approach to the elimination of poverty is to have the government become the "employer of last resort." This has been recommended by two national advisory committees in recent years, the first being a National Commission on Technology, Automation and Economic Progress, which made its report in 1966, and the other being the National Advisory Committee on Rural Poverty, which reported to the President in 1967. Basically, such a program provides that the government be ready to provide employment to every person able and willing to work, if that person is unable to find a job through normal market channels. Public support for this approach seems to be much stronger than for a guaranteed annual income, according to public opinion polls, and it has been attempted recently on a small scale. In 1971 Congress voted $2.2 billion to finance 150,000 public service jobs in state and local government in the field of recreation, education, health, public safety, and environmental improvement.

The term "employer of last resort" is, perhaps, a misnomer, for the proponents of this approach to the elimination of poverty really do not want a gigantic "make-work" along the lines of the emergency measures taken during the Great Depression of the 1930s. The creation of dead-end jobs that provide neither meaningful satisfaction to the employee nor any output of real value to the society should be avoided. What is needed is a system of public service jobs that offer hope for a productive career and are not stigmatized as charity or work relief. Such a program will require more imagination and ingenuity than has been shown so far in any programs of public employment.

A Concluding Comment

Poverty still exists in the American economy. In spite of our affluence, some poverty in America is as bad as it is anywhere in the world, including the least-developed nations. The effort required to eliminate poverty is not great in relation to the size of our gross national product, although we still face a formidable task in finding the appropriate means to tackle this vast and important task on our domestic agenda. No one at this juncture in our history knows the proper approach, but it is valid to say that we have the resources and the means to eliminate poverty, if we can only discover the will and the right mechanisms. It is an outrageous scandal that poverty of such dimensions and degradation continues to exist in the most affluent of contemporary societies. It is clear that jobs and income are the most important ways to lift people out of their poverty status, but this will not be done by waiting for normal growth to eliminate poverty through a process of attrition. A deliberate effort is needed. We must also recognize that there are many persons now poor who cannot by any conceivable means become economically productive in a meaningful sense. But these persons must be provided for by transfer payments of sufficient size to bring them out of the poverty range. Beyond this, the national effort must be directed toward the children of the poor so that they can break out of the vicious circle that now characterizes the subculture of poverty in the United States, and thereby become productive citizens.

Questions for Review and Discussion

1. Why did the AFL succeed as a labor organization while the Knights of Labor failed? Does the AFL-CIO still adhere today to the basic philosophy of Samuel Gompers?

2. What were the major reasons for the rapid growth of the union movement in the 1930s?

3. What effect did the Commonwealth *v.* Hunt decision have on the trade union movement in America?

4. Explain why the Norris-LaGuardia Act and the National Labor Relations Act were so important to organized labor.

5. What is the basic difference between economic insecurity and poverty? Does the elimination of economic insecurity necessarily lead to the elimination of poverty?

6. List the major sources of economic insecurity in our modern industrialized society.

7. Explain the nature and success of the major public policy measures adopted in the United States since the 1930s to deal with problems of economic insecurity.

8. Why is it correct to describe our Social Security system as an income transfer system rather than an insurance program?

9. Should poverty in the United States be viewed as a relative or absolute matter? What difference does such a definition make to measured progress in the elimination of poverty?

10. Identify the major groups in American society that are likely to have a high incidence of poverty. Can the concentration of poverty in such groups be readily explained?

11. List the major causes of poverty in contemporary America.

12. Explain the principles involved in the negative income tax approach to the elimination of poverty.

16

Principles of the International Economy

IN THE FINAL THREE CHAPTERS our concern is with the international economy, the network of trade and financial relationships between all the nations of the world. From the viewpoint of the United States, we shall examine its important characteristics, analyze specific economic principles that apply to the world as a whole, and discuss the major developments that have shaped the international economy in this century.

The Balance of International Payments and the Rate of Exchange

We shall lay the foundation for our analysis by discussing two major economic concepts essential to understanding the workings of the international economy and its relation to the domestic economy. They are the balance of international payments and the rate of exchange.

To grasp the nature and importance of a nation's balance of international payments, we must analyze the process of international payments as it relates to trade between nations. Figure 16-1 is a simplified illustration of the essential character of transactions between countries, showing how payments must be made when goods and services are exchanged. This diagram is a useful point of departure for our detailed discussion of the balance of international payments statement and the rate of exchange.

The Balance of International Payments and the Rate of Exchange

A simple model of international payments

FIGURE 16-1

Basic Elements in International Transactions.

A key point about international trade transactions is that the foreign exchange market enables importers of goods to pay in their national currency and exporters to get paid in their national currency. Thus the American importer of British bicycles buys British currency with American currency in the foreign exchange market to pay for the bicycles.

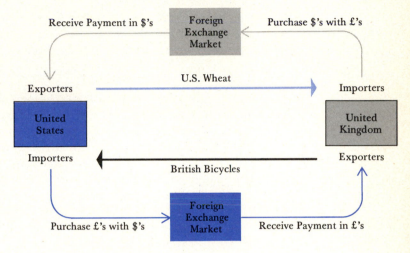

Exchange and Payment

Figure 16-1 shows a "model" of payment for goods exchanged between two countries, the United States and the United Kingdom. Both countries export and import goods and services, but let us begin with exports from the United States and trace several typical transactions. For example, if the United States exports automobiles, chemicals, and wheat, there will be a flow of American goods to Great Britain. On the other hand, if the United States imports British automobiles or bicycles, the flow of goods is to the United States. All trade is like this. What is extraordinary about international trade is that goods and services flow across national boundaries, which calls for payments in different kinds of money. In the United States the monetary unit is the dollar; in Great Britain the monetary unit is the pound sterling. This creates a problem because both American and British exporters want to be paid in their own money. Importers, as well, want to pay in their own money. Consequently machinery has to be established to transform payments made in one type of monetary unit into another type of monetary unit.

When goods are exported to the United Kingdom, British importers must go first into the foreign exchange market, where they exchange pounds for dollars. The dollars they purchase with their pounds in this market are eventually used to pay exporters in the United States. Thus the American exporter receives payment in his own currency, even though the goods will be sold in Britain for British currency. The process is reversed when the United States is the importer. Pounds are purchased in the foreign exchange market and then used to pay the exporters in Great Britain.

Foreign exchange markets are not located in any one place, but exist wherever there are banks and other financial institutions which undertake transactions in all currencies in use in different countries. This market plays a key role in the international exchange of goods and services; subsequently, we shall analyze how the rates at which different national currencies exchange for one another are established.

The situation is complicated somewhat by the introduction of gold into the discussion. For centuries gold has been used as a form of international money, and it remains in use today, although it is no longer lawful in the United States for private citizens to own and use gold in this way. Nevertheless, gold can be used to obtain foreign currencies when payments need to be made to foreign nationals. In the example illustrated in Figure 16-1 gold might have been shipped from the United Kingdom to the United States as a means of getting dollars so that British importers could settle their obligations to U.S. exporters. The role gold has played in international trade and finance will be discussed fully in the next chapter.

The example just cited relates primarily to the exchange of and payment for goods. But this is only one of many types of international transaction. Services, for example, are also traded internationally, among them shipping, insurance payments, banking facilities, and tourist expenditures. International transactions also embrace loans made by the citizens of one country to foreign citizens, the repayment of loans, and the flow of interest and dividend payments between residents of different countries. All these transactions require the use of the foreign exchange market. Whenever business involving different currencies is carried out there must be a means to convert value measured in one currency into value measured in another currency. This is the essential purpose of the foreign exchange market. The price at which different national currencies exchange for one or another is called the *exchange rate*.

The Balance of International Payments

Our simple model of international transactions leads us to the balance of international payments statement, the major accounting device for trade between nations. The balance of international payments statement summarizes for a period of time— normally the calendar year—*all* the international economic transactions that have taken place between residents of one country and residents of another country or of the entire world. Normally, the statement is constructed in terms of relationships between the residents of one country and the residents of the rest of the world. "Residents" means not only individuals, but business firms, governmental units, and international organizations located in a particular country.

The most useful way to analyze a balance of international payments statement is to examine the specific types of transactions it contains. By definition, international economic transactions always require residents of a country to make payments to residents of foreign nations or to receive payments from them. The transactions can be measured in the currency of the country whose balance of international payments is under discussion or in foreign currency. The former is the usual practice and the one we shall follow as we analyze the balance of payments from the vantage point of the United States.

Figure 16-2 summarizes the payments effect of transactions contained in the balance of international payments statement. The chart is constructed to show the two basic types of transactions involved. First, examine closely the transactions in which American residents make payments to foreigners. Transactions of this type supply dollars to foreign residents. It is equally correct to say that these transactions create a demand for foreign currency (i.e., for-

The Balance of International Payments and the Rate of Exchange

The major accounting statement for international trade

Payments to and from foreigners

FIGURE 16-2
The Payments Effect of U.S. International Transactions.

A key fact to remember: all international transactions involve either payments to foreign residents or payments by foreign residents to U.S. residents. Consequently they can be viewed as creating either a demand for foreign exchange (supply of dollars) or a demand for dollars (supply of foreign exchange).

Payment to Foreign Residents

↓

Creates Demand for Foreign Exchange or Supply of Dollars

↓

MAJOR SOURCES

1 U.S. Imports of goods and services
2 U.S. Loans to foreign nations and residents
3 Transfers (government and priviate) to foreign nations and residents

Payments from Foreign Residents

↓

Creates Demand for Dollars or Supply of Foriegn Exchange

↓

MAJOR SOURCES

1 U.S. Exports of goods and services
2 Repayment of U.S. loans or loans by foreigners to U.S. residents
3 Transfers from foreigners to U.S. residents

eign exchange) by American residents. Now look at transactions that involve payments from foreigners. In the foreign exchange market, these transactions create a demand for dollars by foreign residents. But it is equally correct to say that such transactions create a supply of foreign exchange for American residents. Thus, all international transactions have two sides—demand and supply —when looked at in terms of their impact upon the demand for and the supply of domestic money and foreign money. This is a point to remember in a few pages, when we see how the exchange rate is determined.

Let us examine Figure 16-2 in greater detail. Under transactions that give rise to payments to foreigners, we find three major subcategories. First, there are imports of goods and services by American residents. Included in this category are not just imports of commodities, but the purchases of shipping and other services (including insurance), tourist expenditures, expenditures by U.S. military personnel stationed abroad, and interest and dividend payments to the foreign owners of American securities (i.e., bonds and stocks).

Categories of
imports

The second major subcategory includes lending and related financial transactions between American residents and the rest of the world. If Americans loan money to other countries and their residents, dollars will be made available to foreigners, but an American demand for foreign exchange may also be created. Americans may lend to British residents by purchasing the bonds of a British corporation. They use dollars to acquire through the foreign exchange market the sterling necessary to buy the bonds in Britain's financial market, a transaction that has the dual effect of making dollars available to British residents and creating a demand by American residents for British currency.

Lending

Economists describe the outcome of financial and lending transactions as either an export or import of capital. Note that capital in this context has a financial connotation, which differs from its use elsewhere in our economic analysis. Thus, when Americans lend abroad the result is an outflow of capital. Repayment of loans or borrowing from abroad would lead to an inflow of capital. In the post-World War II period capital outflows from the United States were a significant source of dollar supply for nations all over the globe.

Outflow and inflow
of capital

The third major subcategory of transactions involving payment to the rest of the world is transfers. There are two kinds. First, there are U.S. government transfers to foreign governments for economic or military assistance. These are often called economic or military *grants,* for unlike an intergovernmental loan, they are not expected to be repaid. Second, there are transfers by individuals, usually described in balance of payments terminology as unilateral transfers and gifts. Throughout the postwar period

Transfers

Economic and
military grants

grants by the United States government for military and economic purposes were a major source of dollar exchange for the rest of the world. The United States also has an old tradition of private, unilateral transfers, such as CARE funds, relief to impoverished nations, or the funds sent to Israel through the United Jewish Appeal. All transfer payments supply the rest of the world with dollars. On occasion, they may represent a form of demand for foreign exchange, but they are more likely simply to add to the world supply of dollar exchange.

Now let us examine the major subcategories of transactions requiring foreign residents to make payments to American residents. Since World War II the most important type of transaction in this category has been the export of goods and services by the United States to the rest of the world. These transactions not only included the export of merchandise but the purchase of transportation and shipping services by foreign residents from Americans, the purchase of insurance by foreigners from residents of the United States, and interest and dividend payments to American owners of foreign securities.

Exports of goods and services by the United States to the rest of the world create a demand for dollars because exporters in the United States ultimately expect to be paid in dollars. But the exchange of foreign currencies for dollars in the foreign exchange market also supplies residents of the United States with foreign monies. A second subcategory of transactions involving payments by foreigners to U.S. residents is financial in nature. These transactions may involve the repayment of loans by foreigners to Americans or lending by foreigners to American residents. Lending and repayment normally operate in both directions. The effect of a foreign loan to an American resident is the opposite, economically speaking, of a loan by an American resident to a foreigner. A foreign loan supplies the American resident with foreign exchange, although at the same time it may create a demand for dollars if lending takes the form of, for example, the purchase of an American bond by a foreigner.

Transactions that, on balance, involve foreign lending to the United States are called "capital inflows." During most of the time in recent years the United States has exported more capital than it has imported, which means that it has been a net lender rather than a borrower. On the other hand, in the period before World War I, as well as throughout most of the nineteenth century the United States was, on balance, a net importer of foreign capital. The capital balance between the two world wars was mixed in character, primarily because of the chaotic state of foreign exchange markets and the international economy, both as an aftermath of World War I and as a consequence of the Great Depression of the 1930s.

Unilateral transfers and gifts

Categories of exports

The recent U.S. capital balance

433

Finally, there are transfer payments originating with foreigners. Transfers may involve payments to American residents, just as they involve payments by U.S. residents to foreigners. In recent decades, transfers from abroad have not been of major significance to the American balance of international payments position. As already pointed out, most international transfers in recent years have been an outflow from the United States, because of the large-scale military and economic grant programs of the American government.

The Balance of Payments in Recent Years

Current Account

To see how the elements of the balance of payments interlock, let us consider data for the American economy for 1960–1971. These data are found in Table 16-1, organized to show both receipts and payments by residents of the United States in four categories of transactions, including errors and omissions. In the table the first group of transactions is under the heading "Current Account." These transactions cover the export and import of goods and services, including the several subcategories discussed earlier. In 1971 total payments to residents in the United States from abroad (the demand for U.S. dollars) amounted to $65.9 billion, whereas total payments by American residents to the rest of the world (the supply of dollars) equaled $65.2 billion. The United States in

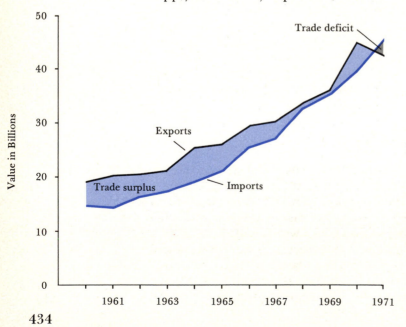

FIGURE 16-3

U.S. Merchandise Exports and Imports: 1960–1971 (billions of dollars).

During the last decade the American trade surplus has gradually diminished, finally being replaced by a trade deficit in 1971. This was the first time since 1893 that the United States imported more goods than it exported. (Source: *Economic Report of the President,* 1972.)

TABLE 16-1
U.S. Balance of Payments, 1960–1971
(Billions of Dollars)

CATEGORY	1960–64 AVERAGE	1965–69 AVERAGE	1970	1971
Current Account				
Exports of goods and services	31.3	47.0	62.9	65.9
Merchandise	21.7	31.3	42.0	42.8
Military sales	0.6	1.1	1.5	1.9
Investments income	5.1	8.6	11.4	12.7
Other services	4.0	6.0	8.0	8.5
Imports of goods and services	−25.4	−42.6	−59.3	−65.2
Merchandise	−16.2	−20.5	−39.9	−45.6
Military expenditure	−3.0	−4.1	−4.9	−4.8
Investment income	−1.2	−2.8	−5.2	−4.8
Other services	−5.0	−7.2	−9.4	−10.0
Balance on goods and services	5.9	4.4	3.6	0.7
Capital Account *				
Net long-term capital	−2.9	−1.8	−1.5	−4.1
Net short-term capital	−1.1	−0.2	−0.5	−2.5
Balance on capital transactions	−4.0	−2.0	−2.0	−6.6
Transfers				
Government transfers **	−2.9	−3.7	−3.8	−4.4
Private transfers	−0.7	−1.1	−1.4	−1.5
Balance on transfers	−3.6	−4.8	−5.2	−5.9
Errors and Omissions	−1.0	−1.0	−1.1	−10.9
Surplus (+) or deficit (−)	−2.7	−3.4	−4.7	−22.7
Financed By:				
1. Reduction in U.S. reserves ***	1.0	—	3.3	3.1
2. Increase in U.S. liabilities to foreigners	1.2	—	1.4	19.6
3. Decrease in foreign liabilities to U.S.	0.5	3.4	—	—
	2.7	3.4	4.7	22.7

* Private capital
** Including government loans
*** Gold and foreign exchange
Source: *Federal Reserve Bulletin.*

1971 had a small net surplus on its current account of $700 million, but recorded the first merchandise trade deficit since 1893.

As Figure 16-3 shows, imports have grown much more rapidly than exports in recent years, partly because since the mid-1960s the dollar has been in excess supply in world financial centers, though its rate of exchange did not reflect this until the Nixon administration devalued the dollar in the latter part of 1971. Prior to this the dollar was "overvalued" in terms of foreign currencies, which impeded sales of U.S. exports abroad, stimulated

435

imports, and encouraged American firms to invest abroad. The current account is not in balance, for the demand for dollars to buy American goods and services was slightly larger than the supply of dollars generated by American purchases from abroad. This particular condition is called an active current account balance. If total payments had been larger than total receipts the balance would be labeled passive.

Capital Account

U.S. as net exporter of capital

The next section is the Capital Account. The transactions included here yield a net negative balance of $6.6 billion. In 1971 the transactions that involved either lending or loan repayment by American residents to the rest of the world exceeded lending or loan repayments by residents of the rest of the world to American residents by this amount. In other words, the United States in 1971 was a net exporter of capital, which also means that it supplied the rest of the world with 6.6 billion dollars. Note that up until 1971 the current account surplus was greater than the dollar outflow resulting from capital transactions. The long-term capital balance largely represents U.S. acquisitions of plant and equipment abroad.

Transfers

Next we turn to the "Transfer" section of the American balance of payment statement. In 1971 U.S. government transfers totaled $4.4 billion, private transfers $1.5 billion, resulting in a grand total *outflow* of dollars through transfers in the amount of $5.9 billion. The item "Errors and Omissions," shown as the last section is both a balancing item and one that reflects inaccuracies in the data-gathering process. The "Errors and Omissions" item was extraordinarily large in 1971, reflecting an exceedingly large volume of unrecorded private capital outflows from the United States. For the most part these took the form of purchase of foreign exchange by American citizens and business firms, partly to acquire short-term foreign securities because of interest rate differences between the United States and other nations, and partly in the expectation that the foreign exchange value of the dollar would be allowed to drop. Thus those who had acquired foreign currencies could buy back dollars at a cheaper price, making a profit on the transaction.

To sum up, the United States in 1971 paid out more dollars than it received, which meant that overall it had a net deficit in its international economic transactions of $22.7 billion. This deficit was financed partly by an outflow of gold from the United States, partly by the willingness of foreigners to increase their dollar balances, and partly by a reduction in foreign currencies or claims against foreigners held by U.S. residents. The methods used to finance the deficit are summarized in the bottom part of Table 16-1.

Determination of the Rate of Exchange

Financing the deficit

Later in this chapter we shall discuss fully the concepts of equilibrium and disequilibrium as applied to the balance of international payments, but at this point certain peculiar features of the recent payments deficit of the United States are worth noting. The United States clearly has had a *deficit* in its international economic transactions for more than a decade, but before 1971 it differed from the deficits experienced by most nations in their relations with other countries. Normally a deficit occurs when a nation's current account expenditures exceed its receipts. For a deficit on current account there must be offsetting capital flows or gold flows. In the United States, at least prior to 1971, the problem was not a deficit arising out of current account transactions. As Table 16-1 showed, the receipts the United States derived from current transactions prior to 1971 clearly exceeded the payments it had to make. The deficit came about because the outflow of funds from the United States resulting from capital transactions and transfers (government and private) far exceeded the surplus generated by current account transactions. In a sense the deficit was not due to any inability of the American economy to earn foreign exchange by exporting goods and services, but rather to the fact that its capital and transfer activities provided the rest of the world with more dollars than the rest of the world needed to cover its current account deficit with the United States.

The origins of the payments deficit

Determination of the Rate of Exchange

We now turn to the process by which market forces determine the rate of exchange, a prelude to our discussion of the international monetary system and balance of payments equilibrium and disequilibrium. The balance of payments shows transactions with other countries, but these transactions require the buying and selling of foreign currencies, and we must understand these processes. The *rate of exchange* is the price at which one currency is converted into another currency, for example, the rate at which dollars are converted into British sterling, or British sterling into American dollars. The introduction of the rate of exchange into international transactions causes a complication not present in the domestic economy. In international economic transactions

The rate of exchange

one must not only compare the price of the goods and services being traded in the currency of one or more countries, but also the prices of the currencies of the countries that engage in trade.

When a consumer in California buys a good produced in Ohio, he does not have to convert his dollars into another type of money at a particular price, as he must when he purchases a good made abroad (though the actual conversion is usually handled by a bank). For example, if the Californian purchases a British automobile he must consider not only the price of the automobile in Britain plus transportation costs, but also the price that must be paid to get the British currency needed to buy the automobile. This price—which is the rate of exchange of dollars for sterling —also determines what the price of the car will be in the United States.

Of course, the dollar price the dealer establishes will ultimately determine whether an American buys the automobile, but this price may fluctuate *not* because of a change in the price of the automobile in Great Britain measured in British currency, but because of a change in the rate at which British currency exchanges for American currency. For example, when the Nixon administration devalued the dollar in 1971, this raised the price in dollars of foreign goods and services. On the other hand, it made U.S. goods and services cheaper for foreigners. Thus, it is important to understand how the exchange rate influences international economic transactions, and equally important to understand the process by which the rate of exchange is determined, given the play of market forces.

The Foreign Exchange Market

The term "foreign exchange market" refers to any place where currencies of all nationalities are bought and sold. Generally this can be done through any bank in a major city, but most transactions take place in banks in or near the major ports of export and import or in the leading international financial centers, such as New York, London, Paris, or Zurich. There are also specialized dealers in national currencies located in these areas. If you have traveled abroad you are familiar with the process of exchanging currency.

Foreign Exchange: Demand and Supply

Since the rate of exchange is a price, we can use the fundamental tools of economic analysis developed for price phenomena, demand and supply schedules. Figure 16-4 contains demand and supply schedules to show how the market price of British sterling is determined in terms of the United States dollar. The price being established is the dollar exchange rate for British sterling. On the horizontal axis we measure the quantity of British pounds being exchanged, and on the vertical axis we measure the price of British sterling in dollars. A demand schedule for sterling has the normal negative slope of any demand schedule, showing that as the price in dollars of British pounds decreases more pounds will be demanded by American residents. This presumes no change in the price of the goods and services available in Great Britain for purchase with British money. Given this assumption, a decrease in the exchange rate for sterling in dollars makes British goods and services cheaper for persons holding dollars. Hence the quantity of sterling demanded, other things being equal, will increase as its price measured in dollars declines.

The supply schedule in Figure 16-4 has a positive slope like any other normal supply curve, showing that more units of British money are offered through the market as its price increases. Those who hold sterling and desire to exchange it for dollars get a better buy each time the price of sterling in dollars goes up. If the price of goods and services in the United States in dollars remains constant, then an increase in the exchange rate of sterling for dollars gives them greater purchasing power each time they exchange a unit of British currency for a unit of American currency. The supply schedule for sterling is also the reverse of a demand schedule for dollars, whereas the reverse of the demand schedule for sterling is a supply schedule for dollars. The reason is that people who want British currency offer dollars in exchange

FIGURE 16-4

Determination of the Market Rate of Exchange (Price of British Sterling in U.S. Dollars).

The rate of exchange is a price which, like any other price, goes up when the demand increases and drops when demand declines. Thus the dollar cost of British currency will go up when there is an increased demand for British goods and fall when the opposite happens.

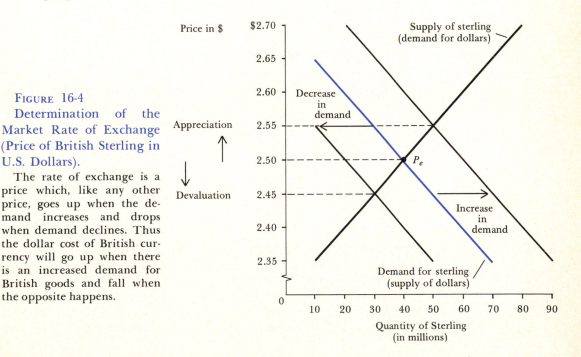

and those who want American dollars offer British sterling in exchange. This is a difficult and subtle point which demands careful thought.

The Market Rate of Exchange

Given the existence of demand and supply schedules for the pound sterling, the market rate of exchange will be determined at the point of intersection of these two schedules. In the diagram this is shown at the point P_e, a dollar price for sterling of $2.50. If the exchange rate were determined solely by market forces, the dollar would exchange for British money at this rate. Under these circumstances an increase in the demand for sterling, shown by a shift to the right in the demand schedule, leads to an increase in the price of sterling in dollars. After the increase in demand the dollar price of sterling climbs to $2.55 This is an appreciation in the foreign exchange value of British currency, which makes British goods more expensive for American residents and American goods cheaper for British residents. This is what happened to foreign currencies generally when the Nixon administration devalued the dollar in 1971. For example, a commodity that costs £1 in Great Britain prior to the shift in demand would have an American price of $2.50 (disregarding transportation costs). After the increase in demand and the appreciation in the foreign exchange value of sterling the American price becomes $2.55, even though the good continues to sell for £1 in Great Britain.

On the other hand, a decrease in the demand for sterling, indicated by a shift in the demand curve to the left, leads to a fall in the foreign exchange value of sterling. The new price is $2.45. This change is a depreciation in the dollar exchange value of British currency, which makes goods and services in Great Britain cheaper for persons with dollars. This depreciation of the pound also makes American goods and services more expensive for British residents.

Stabilization of Exchange Rates

Whenever exchange rates are determined by market forces alone they are likely to fluctuate, sometimes over a very wide range. Since wide fluctuations in exchange rates are undesirable in the eyes of governments and other participants in the international economy, most governments take measures from time to time to keep exchange rates reasonably stable. In extreme situations, a government can simply declare a particular rate of exchange for its currency in terms of other currencies to be the official rate, forbidding transactions in foreign currencies at any rates other than the official one. This requires a full-fledged system of exchange control, including the administrative machinery and techniques to enforce the official rate.

Governments rarely resort to the extreme of complete exchange control, unless they face severe problems in their international economic relationships. In an earlier era, the "gold standard" helped maintain stable exchange rates (as you will see in the next chapter), but it has not existed in meaningful form since the early 1930s. A more appropriate and widely used technique attempts to hold fluctuations in the rate of exchange within relatively narrow limits, but permits market forces to determine the fluctuations in the rate of exchange within these limits. In most instances the basic exchange rate is established by governmental action. To maintain exchange rates within the set limits and without resort to exchange controls, a government must have foreign exchange to draw upon and use in the foreign exchange market. It must also be prepared to use domestic currency for this purpose.

The International Monetary System

The balance of payments statement and exchange rates are the visible evidence of the existence of an international monetary system, which consists of the institutions, practices, and other arrangements through which international trade and transactions are carried forward. Let us begin this discussion by recalling some of the aspects of the domestic monetary system discussed in Chapter 8. A brief restatement of the features essential to any monetary system is a useful prelude to analysis of the international monetary system.

The first function of a monetary system is to provide the society with an acceptable medium of exchange. As we know, money has other functions, but from the standpoint of the international monetary system, the medium of exchange is the critical one. Second, as strongly stressed in the earlier analysis, the monetary system must provide for control over the money supply. In practice, this means there must be a mechanism to expand and contract the money supply in accordance with the needs and demands of the economy as a whole. It will be recalled that the central bank—in the United States the Federal Reserve System—has emerged as the principal instrument for control over the quantity of money in circulation.

*Functions of the
domestic monetary
system*

Finally, the domestic monetary system must be so constructed and maintained as to create confidence in the basic monetary unit. A nation must be convinced that its monetary unit is sound and will continue to hold its basic value. A decisive loss of confidence in the monetary unit will endanger the structure of the monetary system itself. Historically, an excessive supply of money has been the most significant reason for the destruction of confidence. This point is particularly applicable to the international economy.

The domestic monetary systems in nearly all major nations of the world have generally shifted away from the use of metal (gold or silver) toward various forms of credit including bank notes, as the primary medium of exchange. The chief determinants of the money supply today are found in managed systems in which administrative decisions are made within the central bank. But the international monetary system has not evolved nearly as far in this direction.

To explain how the international monetary system differs from domestic monetary systems, the best procedure is to analyze what it must do.

Exchange: Gold, Currency, Credit

*Establishing
machinery for
currency
conversion*

First, the international monetary system has to serve as a clearinghouse for payments between residents of different countries. This involves the establishment of machinery for conversion of the currency of one country into the currency of another country, a task we have already discussed. Beyond this, the international monetary system must establish an international medium of exchange, some form of international money, recognized and accepted by all countries, individuals, and other entities that participate in the system. As in most domestic monetary systems, a variety of things have served as an international medium of exchange, but the oldest form of international money, still important today, is gold.

*Gold as an
international
medium of
exchange*

Gold has almost always been accepted internationally in payment for goods and services. From early in the nineteenth century until the onset of the Great Depression it was so dominant a form of international money that the international monetary system was called the gold standard. Since World War II the United States dollar and, to a lesser extent, the British pound sterling have assumed the role of international money. This was not the result of deliberate action or design. After World War II, the dollar was in demand virtually everywhere because the United States, untouched physically by the war, was the major source of supply for many of the goods and services needed for postwar rebuilding. Hence it became normal for nations to accept the dollar as a form of international money, just as they would accept gold, especially since gold was in extremely short supply for international exchange after World War II. (In the 1930s most of the world's gold supply had moved to the United States, partly because of the rise of Nazism in Germany and the fear of war and partly because of political unrest in Europe during the Great Depression.)

Different types of credit may also serve as forms of international money, particularly "drawing rights" that nations may have on holdings in the International Monetary Fund. This agency was established in 1944 as a new international institution designed to supply funds—or credit—to nations with balance of payments problems. We shall have more to say about international borrowing in the next chapter. The essential point here is that in addition to the foreign exchange function, the international monetary system must in some way provide an acceptable medium of exchange to *all* the nations of the world.

International Reserves

There is another task for an international monetary system. It must supply nations engaged in trade, commerce, and other international transactions with access to *international reserves*. The international reserves of a nation consist of its stock of an internationally recognized medium of exchange, such as gold, national currencies widely accepted internationally, or claims on the International Monetary Fund which can be used to make international payments. We can draw an analogy between international reserves and the process by which the money supply is expanded or contracted in the domestic economy.

An adequate supply of international reserves is an essential for a smooth flow of commerce, trade, and other international transactions. Any nation needs international reserves because its international transactions are not always in balance; in any particular period the foreign exchange a nation obtains through its international transactions will not necessarily equal the amount that it needs in the same period. For example, in a particular year a nation may spend more abroad than it earns, thus incurring a deficit in its international payments position. If it wants to avoid restrictive measures on trade and commerce, or perhaps severe fluctuations in the exchange rate for its currency, then it must have international reserves upon which it can draw to meet the deficit in its international transactions.

The need for international reserves

International Equilibrium and Disequilibrium

The crucial role of international reserves in the international monetary system brings us to the problem of equilibrium and disequilibrium in the world economy. Recall from our earlier discussion of the balance of international payments statement

443

*Equilibrium in a
nation's balance of
payments*

that as an accounting statement this device is always in numerical balance. But this does not mean that a nation has an equilibrium in terms of its trade and payments position with the rest of the world. A nation may have a disequilibrium in its economic transactions with the rest of the world. Let us define these terms more precisely.

Equilibrium in a nation's balance of international payments means that the nation is obtaining the amounts of foreign exchange and international reserves it needs for its usual international transactions through "normal" sources of supply for foreign exchange. In this context, a normal source of supply is one that is dependable over time. Goods and services a nation produces for sale fall into this category, because in the long run the major source of foreign exchange for any nation lies in its export capacity. But there are also some lending (or capital) transactions regarded by economists as normal, although these may change with time and circumstances.

Historically, borrowing at long term was a normal source of supply of foreign exchange for many nations. In most of the nineteenth century, for example, the United States was a net debtor: American citizens borrowed at long term from the more developed areas of the world, which gave the American economy access to needed foreign exchange. At that time most borrowing and lending was by private citizens and private business, although in World War I large-scale intergovernment lending emerged as a major factor in international transactions.

Since World War II, a new variable has entered the picture, one which many initially thought would be temporary, but which has continued as a significant source of foreign exchange, especially for developing countries. This is the grant—not loan—from the more developed to the less developed areas in the world. This means of making foreign exchange available to less developed nations has continued for more than a quarter of a century, in spite of many difficulties and growing resistance to continued grants by the taxpayers of the more developed countries, so that grants, along with exports and long-term loans, should be considered a normal source of supply for foreign exchange.

When a nation is neither drawing down nor building up its stock of international reserves, we may say that it has achieved an equilibrium in its balance of international payments. Such equilibria are normally transitory. The dynamic and often unstable nature of international economic relationships makes it extremely unlikely that any nation will be able exactly to match its demand for foreign exchange with available sources of supply for any very long period of time.

We can draw together this discussion by pointing out that since all nations, in their international economic transactions, are confronted from time to time with disequilibria, only a viable international monetary system can prevent the chaos that would result if each country tried to settle its international accounts unilaterally. Except for special circumstances, such as the period of economic reconstruction after World War II when the dollar was in short supply over most of the world, disequilibria tend to be randomly distributed between nations. This means that a nation confronted with the necessity of drawing down its international reserves because of, say, an unfavorable trade balance, should sooner or later find its international economic position reversed and thus be able to rebuild its inventory of reserves.

The Basis for International Trade

An international monetary system really exists to ease the flow of goods and services between nations. This brings us to another key question in international economics: why do nations trade with one another? And why do nations specialize in some goods and services and not others?

In the broadest sense, the basis for specialization and trade lies in a nation's endowment with economic resources, including the physical environment. We can make this statement more specific by examining five major aspects of resource endowment that reflect differences between nations and regions. Some of these are conditions beyond the control of human beings; others can be changed by human action, making trade and specialization a dynamic phenomenon.

Five major aspects of resource endowment

Climate and Natural Resources

First, there are great differences in climate and natural resources among nations. We all know that some countries are well endowed with the kinds of land, mineral deposits, and climatic conditions that favor the production of particular goods. For example, a warm climate is essential to production of citrus fruit. Climatic and environmental conditions differ widely over the surface of the globe, being little subject to change by human effort. If there were *no* other differences between nations, this fact alone would account for much specialization and trade.

Human Resources

The second aspect of resource endowment is human resources and the supply of labor in different nations and different regions. The state of human resource endowment is the result of the entire history and development of a nation, not of any natural or innate differences in ability between people in different parts of the world. The quantity and quality of human resource supply depend on many factors, including educational levels, the development of skills, and the rate of population growth.

Capital Goods

Contrast between developed and underdeveloped nations

Third, the supply of physical capital varies widely between countries. Some countries, such as the United States and those in Western Europe, are richly endowed with capital goods in the form of tools, machinery, and buildings, key instruments in the productive process. Many other nations, though, have few capital goods relative to their other resources. India, like most other underdeveloped nations, is a "capital-poor" country. It is important to note that since capital goods are man-made, the quantity of capital goods in a nation is something that human beings can, within limits, control. Differences in capital-goods endowment between nations are not natural, but like the skills, education, and technical abilities of a nation's labor force they are the product of a long evolution. Thus nations can enlarge and improve their holdings of the physical capital necessary for production. As they do this, they also change the basis for specialization and trade.

Proportion of Resources

A fourth aspect of the general proposition that the ultimate basis for trade resides in differences in resource endowment centers on the fact that the proportions in which a nation possesses different types of economic resources vary widely. For example, some nations, especially underdeveloped countries, have plenty of human labor relative to land and capital. Others, like Australia, have an abundance of land relative to other resources. The point is that the productive process always entails differences in the proportion in which resources are combined; consequently, nations especially endowed with one kind of a resource relative to other kinds will be in a favorable position to produce those goods and services that use a relatively large input of the plentiful resource. To illustrate, wool production requires little capital, little manpower, but much land. Thus Australia is in a favorable position to produce wool cheaply because it has much land relative to both capital and people.

Politics and Society

Finally, there is a catchall aspect that pertains to a nation's general political and social conditions. Some countries have stable and long-established governments, others are beset by chronic instability in government. The stability of a government, as well as the skill and efficiency of governmental employees, play a major role in the development of specialized skills and, thus, the basis for trade. Governmental stability and integrity are essential, too, for the development of a nation's private and social capital stock.

Our discussion to this point may be summarized as follows. Trade is primarily a consequence of specialization. People, regions, and nations trade with one another because they specialize. In an economic sense, specialization results from the supply of economic resources, the quality of these economic resources, and the proportion in which different types of resources exist in a region or nation. Trade also serves as a substitute for the movement of resources between nations, some of which is physically impossible.

A nation's resource endowment translates ultimately into real differences in the cost of production for various commodities and services. These real differences are the input of resources necessary for a particular output. A real cost difference means that it takes fewer resources to produce a given product in a given region or country than in another region or country. In a world economy, where national currencies are exchanged for one another through the foreign exchange market, real differences in production costs between nations are reflected in differences in money costs and prices.

Cost Advantage

Economics has developed two principles—or "laws"—to explain the direction that specialization and trade by a nation will take. These are the principle of *absolute* cost advantage and the principle of *comparative* cost advantage.

Absolute Cost Advantage

A nation has an absolute cost advantage in the production of any commodity or service in comparison to other nations when it can produce the commodity or service with an absolutely smaller input of real resources than is possible elsewhere. To illustrate, a nation in a tropical region can produce tropical fruit with less input of resources than a nation in the temperate zone. Conceivably the latter might produce tropical fruit under hothouse conditions, but its real cost in terms of resources used would be much greater. An important part of the world's trade is based on the principle of absolute cost advantage.

Ability to produce a commodity with smaller input than elsewhere

447

*Degree of difference
in absolute cost
advantage*

Comparative Cost Advantage

What happens when a nation is so favorably endowed with resources of all types that it is probably more efficient in the production of nearly everything than other nations? The problem of trade under these conditions attracted the attention of David Ricardo, an early nineteenth-century economist. He first formulated the principle of *comparative cost advantage,* which remains valid as an explanation for a high proportion of specialization and trade in the world economy. A nation has a comparative cost advantage with respect to another nation whenever its absolute cost advantage in one particular commodity is relatively greater than its absolute cost advantage in another or a series of other commodities, or when its absolute cost *dis*advantage in a particular commodity is relatively smaller than its absolute cost disadvantage in another or a series of other commodities. There may be absolute cost differences between countries for a whole range of commodities, but the degree of difference—or comparative difference—often varies widely for particular commodities.

Ricardo's Example

When Ricardo first developed the principle of comparative cost advantage early in the nineteenth century, he employed a simple example involving two commodities and two countries. The countries were England and Portugal and the commodities were wine and cloth, which presumably could be produced in both countries. Let us use an example like Ricardo first employed. It is oversimplified, but nevertheless illustrates the basic economic forces at work in a complex market situation. For a measure of resource input we shall use one man-day of work, ignoring for the sake of simplicity the contribution of other resources to the output of a particular commodity. This procedure enables us to see clearly both the absolute cost differences and the comparative cost differences that may exist in a trade situation.

We begin with the assumption that in England a single man-day of work will produce either 150 bottles of wine or 300 yards of cloth. Wine or cloth are the alternative uses for England's resources. One man-day of work is the absolute real cost of production of either 150 bottles of wine or 300 yards of cloth. In Portugal we find an entirely different situation. Here one man-day will produce either 100 bottles of wine or 100 yards of cloth. The reasons for such differences in the effectiveness of one man-day of work in England or Portugal can be attributed to the differences in natural resource endowment, climatic conditions, the skill of labor, capital supply, and other conditions. These are the factors, it will be recalled, that account for real differences in production costs.

So far, a man-day of work in England produces *more* of both commodities than does a man-day of work in Portugal, no matter what the underlying reasons. From an economic standpoint, England is more efficient than Portugal in the production of both commodities. England, in other words, has an *absolute* cost advantage for the production of both wine and cloth. It might seem logical, then, to suggest that England should produce both commodities. But this is not the case, for England's comparative cost advantage differs for the two commodities. Let us see what this means.

England's advantage over Portugal in the production of wine is in a ratio of 1.5 to 1, which means that a man-day of work in England produces 150 bottles of wine as compared to only 100 bottles of wine in Portugal. On the other hand, England's advantage over Portugal in the production of cloth is on the order of 3 to 1, because one man-day of work in England produces 300 yards of cloth as compared to 100 yards in Portugal. Thus England has a *comparative* cost advantage with respect to the production of cloth. It is not only more efficient in producing both of these commodities than Portugal, but its degree of efficiency in cloth production is much greater than in wine production. This is the important principle that Ricardo discovered and to which he gave formal expression.

Cost Advantage and Trade

Let us see how the principle of comparative advantage works to enable a nation to gain from trade by specialization on the basis of a comparative cost advantage. Table 16-2 contains our hypothetical data on wine and cloth production in England and Por-

TABLE 16-2
The Principle of Comparative Cost Advantage

PRODUCTION	RESOURCE INPUT (ONE MAN-DAY OF WORK)	
	England	Portugal
Cloth (yards)	300	100
Comparative cost ratio, England to Portugal = 3:1		
Wine (bottles)	150	100
Comparative cost ratio, England to Portugal = 1.5:1		
Domestic Terms of Trade		
England: 2 yards cloth = 1 bottle wine	Portugal: 1 yard cloth = 1 bottle wine	

tugal. Note that in England one man-day will produce either 150 bottles of wine or 300 yards of cloth, whereas in Portugal a man-day of labor produces only 100 bottles of wine or 100 yards of cloth. The table also shows that the comparative cost advantage for England in the production of wine is 1.5 to 1 and in the production of cloth is 3 to 1.

Equally important, though, is the internal ratio at which these commodities exchange for one another in both England and Portugal. This is called the domestic terms of trade. Within England, given the possibility that a man-day will produce either 150 bottles of wine or 300 yards of cloth and assuming competitive conditions, the ratio of exchange within England will be one unit of wine for two units of cloth. Put another way, the price of a bottle of wine in terms of cloth is two yards of the latter. On the other hand, in Portugal one bottle of wine exchanges for one yard of cloth. This means that the price ratios—or relative prices —for wine and cloth differ between the two countries, which reflects the underlying comparative differences in real production costs. This fact establishes *a basis for gains from trade* by both countries, even though England is more efficient economically in the production of the two commodities. England gains as long as it can get a bottle of wine for anything less than two yards of cloth. On the other hand, Portugal gains if for a bottle of wine it can get anything more than one yard of cloth. If a price ratio for these commodities is established which differs from the ratios that prevail in the absence of trade, then both countries can gain from trade.

Let us assume that trade gets started on the basis of an international price ratio of 1 bottle of wine for 1.5 yards of cloth. This international price ratio must fall within limits established by the internal cost (price) ratios in the countries concerned, otherwise there would be no reason for trade. Let us suppose that such a ratio does exist.

If England specializes in cloth production, it will be able to exchange the surplus cloth for wine at a price of 1.5 yards of cloth for 1 bottle of wine, which clearly is for England a saving of half a yard of cloth per bottle of wine obtained. If England chose to produce its own wine, then for every bottle of wine produced it would have to give up 2 yards of cloth. The cloth price of wine is 2. To put it another way, the international price quoted above permits England to get through trade 1 bottle of wine for every 1.5 yards of cloth produced, a clear gain over what could be obtained if all production was carried on internally. Portugal also surely gains through trade because it receives for each extra bottle of wine produced 1.5 yards of cloth rather than only the one if the country did not engage in trade. For Portugal the international cloth price of wine is higher than its domestic price. Both countries, therefore, find an advantage in trade because both countries will be able to consume more cloth and wine than they would be able to do if they did not engage in trade, but produced themselves all the cloth and wine they consumed.

Table 16-3 illustrates the gains derived from trade. Without trade England will produce and consume 200 yards of cloth and 50 bottle of wine; just how it allocates its labor input of one manday between cloth and wine production depends upon the relative intensity of the English demand for these two commodities. Remember, though, that the comparative cost data in Table 16-3 show that the ratio at which cloth can be transformed into wine by shifting resources is 2 yards of cloth for 1 bottle of wine. So if only 200 yards of cloth are produced, the balance of its labor input can be used to produce 50 bottles of wine. In Portugal 70 yards of cloth and 30 bottles of wine are produced with an equal amount of each commodity being consumed.

An example of the gains from trade

Table 16-3
The Gains from Trade: England and Portugal

WITHOUT TRADE

	England		Portugal	
	Production	Consumption	Production	Consumption
Cloth (yards)	200	200	70	70
Wine (bottles)	50	50	30	30

The combined production of England and Portugal is 270 yards of cloth and 80 bottles of wine.

WITH TRADE

	England				Portugal			
	Prod.	Exports	Imports	Cons.	Prod.	Exports	Imports	Cons.
Cloth (yards)	300	100	—	200	—	—	100	100
Wine (bottles)	—	—	67	67	100	67	—	33

International price: 1.5 yards of cloth = 1 bottle of wine

Net gain for England:
  17 bottles of wine

Net gain for Portugal:
  3 bottles of wine
  30 yards of cloth

After trade total production is greater by 30 yards of cloth and 20 bottles of wine.

Now what happens when trade is opened up between the two countries and each one specializes in the commodity in which its comparative cost advantage is most favorable? England will produce 300 yards of cloth and Portugal 100 bottles of wine. If an international price of 1.5 yards of cloth for 1 bottle of wine exists and England exports her surplus cloth production of 100 yards, she will receive in exchange 67 bottles of wine. This means she is able to consume 17 more bottles of wine than previously, which is England's gain from specialization and trade. Portugal, on the other hand, is able to get 100 yards of cloth in exchange for her export of 67 bottles of wine. After trade we find that she is consuming 30 more yards of cloth than before trade and 3 more bottles of wine. For both nations together total production has gone up by 30 yards of cloth and 20 bottles of wine.

How the gains from trade are shared between the two countries depends upon how close the international price lies to the internal price—domestic terms of trade—in one or the other country. The closer the international price gets to the domestic price ratio in one of the countries, the less that country will gain from trade. To illustrate, if the international price moved to 1.75 yards of cloth for 1 bottle of wine—which is closer to the price in England—the English would get only 57 bottles of wine in exchange for the export of their surplus cloth production of 100 yards. The gain would be 7 bottles rather than 17. Once trade is opened between the two countries, the international price will depend upon the relative intensity of the demand of the countries for the products in which each of them specializes.

*Production of
commodities and
services for greatest
absolute cost
advantage and
least absolute cost
disadvantage*

From both a policy and practical standpoint, the most important lesson of the principle of comparative advantage follows: Given conditions of free trade between countries, a market system tends to establish price ratios that direct production into commodities and services in which a nation's absolute cost advantage is greatest or in which its absolute cost disadvantage is least. In either case, it will specialize in the production of the commodity or commodities in which it has a *comparative* advantage. In our example these were cloth in England and wine in Portugal. Moreover, this principle not only says that countries will be better off if they specialize and trade on the basis of comparative advantage, but that total production of traded commodities or services will be increased. The basic argument in favor of free trade between nations rests upon the principle of comparative cost advantage. It should be recognized that the argument implies a static situation in which gain is maximized on the basis of an *existing* distribution of economic resources between nations. It ignores the drive of nations toward economic self-sufficiency, their desire to change their resource base and broaden the foundations for both specialization and trade. For this reason, they may reject the idea of free trade.

Barriers to Trade

In spite of the powerful theoretical arguments in favor of free trade that flow from the Ricardian doctrine of comparative advantage, most industrial and developing nations over the last 200 years have erected barriers to the free movement of goods and services across international borders. The major exception to this policy was England, which early in the nineteenth century embarked upon a free trade course which lasted until the collapse of the gold standard in the Great Depression. In England the victory of free trade reflected the triumph of the emerging industrial capitalists over the landowning classes in the post-Napoleonic era. The industrial class wanted free trade so that imports of cheap grain from the newly developed grain-producing areas in North America would expand, the object being to keep food prices and thereby wages low.

Much more common in the history of Western nations in the nineteenth and twentieth centuries and underdeveloped nations in the post-World War II era is the imposition of restrictions on trade. Two types of trade barriers are widely used: the tariff and the quota.

Tariffs

A tariff is a tax imposed on a good imported into a country. Most tariffs today are protective, which means they are designed to reduce or eliminate the amount of goods that can enter into a nation from abroad. Sometimes, though, tariffs are designed to produce revenue, as was the case in the United States in the nineteenth century. A revenue tariff cannot be so high as to keep foreign goods out, or it defeats its purpose of raising money for the government. Tariffs are generally imposed in two ways: *ad valorem,* which means as a percentage of the value of an imported good; or *specific,* which is a flat amount per physical unit imported. The essential purpose of a protective tariff is to raise the selling price of a foreign good, thus making it possible for domestic producers to get a larger share of the market. If the home commodity subject to the tariff is produced and sold in a highly competitive market, the result of the tariff will be to bring more firms into the industry, but if the industry is not competitive, the effect of the tariff will be to increase the profits for existing firms in the industry.

Quotas

A quota differs from a tariff in that it is a direct physical limitation upon the amount of a commodity that can be brought into a country. It works differently from a tariff because the latter operates through the price system by raising the price for the imported good. Whether a tariff will significantly alter the quantity of a good being imported depends upon the elasticity of demand for the commodity subject to the tariff. But a quota imposes an exact limitation on the amount that can be imported. A quota, like a tariff, will raise the price for domestic producers of the good subject to the import restriction, but it also confers a monopoly gain on the importer or importers fortunate enough to secure a quota license. Quotas often create a strong inducement to bribe public officials simply because the necessary license to import may have enormous economic value. In the United States quotas have been extensively used to protect domestic sugar producers.

Sometimes public health rules may be used to keep out imports that compete with domestic production as well as to protect against the influx of contagious disease. Governments, too, may act in a restrictive fashion if they deliberately follow a policy of purchasing goods in the domestic market, even though foreign-made goods might be cheaper.

Questions for Review and Discussion

1. Trace the basic steps involved in the export of American products to England, showing how exporters receive payment in their currency (dollars) and importers make payment in their currency (pounds).
2. Why do American imports create a demand for foreign exchange (foreign currency) or a supply of dollars? Why is the one the converse of the other?
3. If American residents purchase the bonds of a British corporation, what effect does this have on the supply of dollars and the demand for pounds in the foreign exchange market?
4. What is a rate of exchange?
5. Explain why a depreciation in the dollar exchange rate for the British pound would make it more difficult for American firms to sell in Britain.
6. What major functions must any international monetary system perform?
7. What are international reserves? Why are they essential for the effective functioning of the international monetary system?
8. Explain the conditions that must be present if a nation is to experience equilibrium in its balance of international payments.
9. How can trade between nations be explained on the basis of their differences in endowment with economic resources?
10. Explain absolute and comparative cost advantage.
11. Why does the principle of comparative cost advantage lead to the conclusion that free trade between nations is desirable?
12. What is the significance for the free trade argument of the fact that free trade rests upon the existing distribution of the world's resources?

17

Change and Upheaval in the International Economy

THIS CHAPTER WILL ANALYZE the changes that have beset the international economy in the twentieth century. This has been an era of great turbulence, punctuated by wars and a massive depression, resulting in profound changes in the structure and character of the world economic system. In spite of such upheavals the world has steadily grown more economically interdependent, a trend that will undoubtedly continue for the rest of the century. We shall analyze these changes by discussing the impact of major events on the two key elements of the international economic system: the international monetary system and the structure of world trade.

The Experience of the Nineteenth Century

We cannot understand the cataclysmic upheavals of this century
without some appreciation of how the international monetary system and the structure of world trade were shaped by events in the
nineteenth century. From the end of the Napoleonic wars in 1815
to the outbreak of World War I in 1914 the nations of the world
enjoyed nearly universal peace. The nineteenth century was also
dominated by the philosophy and policy of *laissez faire* in the role
of government in domestic and international economic affairs.
Thus the system that evolved in the nineteenth century extended
the market principle throughout the world through organization
of trade and payments among the major industrial nations and
their colonial possessions. During this era an intricate worldwide
structure of trade and payments slowly evolved. The structure
was European-centered, or, more accurately, British-centered, for
throughout the nineteenth century Great Britain and Western
Europe were the pivot on which the industrial world turned.

This period saw the extension of the market system as a technique for the organization of economic activity over most of the
civilized world. Colonial areas in Africa, Asia, and the Middle
East, which emerged from the explorations and outward thrust of
the European powers beginning in the sixteenth century, were
brought during the nineteenth century into a closely knit trade
and payments network. Figure 17-1 illustrates this network of
trade and payments: goods and services flowed outward from
major industrial centers to the less developed regions in exchange
for a return of agricultural products and industrial raw materials.
This system was multilateral; a nation or region did not have to
offset exactly its deficit (or surplus) with another region. In a
multilateral system nations can utilize surpluses acquired in trade
with some nations or regions to offset deficits incurred elsewhere.

A multilateral system cannot work without an effective international monetary system constructed around some universally accepted medium of exchange for all international transactions.
This role was played by the international gold standard, the financial counterpart of the worldwide trade network illustrated in
Figure 17-1. As a monetary system, it provided a medium of exchange, gold; international reserves, also gold; a system of
exchange rates; and, finally, a mechanism for adjustment whenever nations had disequilibria in their balance of international
payments.

FIGURE 17-1

The Nineteenth-Century System of Multilateral Trade.

When read clockwise, the diagram shows the mainstreams in the system of multilateral trade that emerged in the nineteenth century. The arrows show the direction of flow and represent a balance of exports over imports for the regions involved. The flows shown represent the trade patterns as they existed in the late 1920s, just prior to the collapse of the gold standard and the nineteenth-century structure of trade. (Source: The League of Nations, *The Network of World Trade,* Geneva, 1942.)

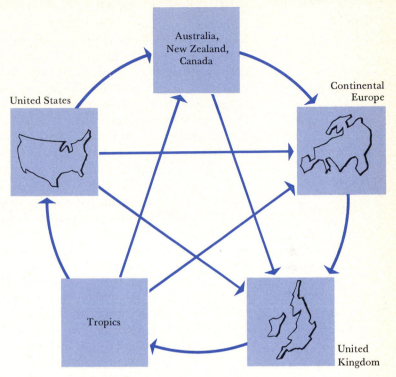

The International Gold Standard

The Rules of the Game

The world's monetary system was on the gold standard approximately from 1814 to 1914, although technically the gold standard lasted until its final collapse in 1933. Like any monetary system, the gold standard provided the world economy with an international medium of exchange to transfer purchasing power between countries; arrangements giving nations access to international reserves they could draw upon when needed; and a mechanism to attain adjustment when a nation confronted a disequilibrium in its balance of international payments.

For a nation to be "on" the international gold standard, it had to define its currency unit in terms of gold, that is, establish by law a basic gold content for the currency unit. This gold content was known as the "par value" for its currency. Such action was tantamount to establishing a fixed and official price for gold in

Currency defined in terms of gold

457

the country concerned, a price normally set on the basis of prevailing market prices for gold being traded for other purposes.

Definition of a nation's currency unit in terms of gold was the first requisite for membership in the "gold standard club." The second was convertibility of currency and all other forms of money into gold upon demand by private citizens, which means that gold circulates freely as a form of money. Under the gold standard gold coins actually existed, but were not in wide circulation; instead gold certificates, redeemable in gold upon demand, were issued by the government. This condition has not existed in the United States since the early 1930s, when the United States left the gold standard. Finally, to maintain stability in the rate of exchange under the gold standard system, it was essential that private citizens be free to export and import gold and hold title to it.

These conditions constituted the rules of the game for the gold standard system. In the climate of world opinion in the nineteenth century it was the ultimate sign of international respectability for a nation to be a member of the gold standard club, and membership depended on adherence to these rules.

The Exchange Rate

How did the gold standard system work? Let us first consider what happened to the exchange rate. Under the gold standard, the basic exchange rate was determined by the gold content of the domestic currency. For example, before 1914 British currency —the pound sterling—had a legal gold content 4.85 times greater than the American dollar, which meant that the basic rate of exchange between American and British currency was 4.85 dollars for each British pound. This rate was known as the mint par value of exchange. The actual market rate of exchange—that is, the price ·of sterling in dollars in different exchange markets throughout the world—could not vary from this figure by more than a few cents. Anyone who wanted to acquire sterling in exchange for dollars would not be willing to pay more for a unit of sterling than the mint par value price—$4.85—plus a slight additional charge to cover the cost of shipping the appropriate quantity of gold from the United States to Great Britain. If faced with a higher rate, the customer could exchange dollars for gold at the official price, then ship the gold to the United Kingdom to be sold for British currency at the British mint par value.

Reserves

The international monetary reserves available to a nation under the gold standard system consisted of the gold stock held by the treasury of the country. The size of the gold stock varied with the ebb and flow of trade and other transactions with other nations. An export surplus generated by current transactions led to an inflow of gold as foreigners sought to obtain domestic exchange by shipping gold and trading it for domestic currency. On the other hand, an import surplus had the opposite effect, an outflow of gold.

In the era in which the gold standard flourished, the domestic monetary system in most countries rested upon the size of the nation's stock of gold. Expansion and contraction of the domestic money supply depended upon its metallic base, which, in turn was affected by the tempo of international trade. For a gold standard country, the change in the gold stock which led to a change in the domestic money supply provided the mechanism for corrective action when the nation confronted a disequilibrium in its international payments position.

Expansion and Contraction

How did this corrective mechanism for a disequilibrium work under international gold standard conditions? Assume that the United States experienced a persistent import surplus in its current transactions with the rest of the world. To meet its payments obligations in excess of the amount of foreign exchange earned by current exports, the nation would either have drawn upon its existing stocks of foreign exchange or upon its international reserves (i.e., gold) to get the necessary foreign exchange. If the deficit persisted after existing inventories of foreign exchange had been exhausted, gold would inevitably leave the country. Under gold standard conditions this was the only means remaining by which the nation's citizens could obtain the foreign exchange to meet their outstanding obligations.

In analyzing the effects of a prolonged outflow of gold, we must keep in mind that gold played a strategic role in a country's domestic monetary system, providing the ultimate base for the expansion (and contraction) of currency and various forms of credit money. Consequently, a loss of a portion of the gold base for a nation's monetary system forced a contraction in the money supply.

Most economists and other financial experts in the nineteenth century believed that a contraction in the money supply ultimately brought about a fall in the general price level. They started from the assumption that normally resources are fully employed. In this case, following a contraction of the money supply neither output nor employment, but the price level would change. Thus, the following sequence of events would occur: an outflow of gold, a reduction in the domestic money supply, and ultimately a fall in the general price level. Abroad, the inflow of gold would reverse this sequence of events.

The practical impact of these changes was that, in relative

The nation's stock of gold

Gold in the domestic monetary system

Outflow of gold followed by contraction in the money supply

Contraction in the money supply followed by fall in the price level

459

terms, prices declined in the country losing gold and increased in the gold-receiving countries, although there would be no change in the exchange rate between the countries concerned. The fall in prices in the United States increased American exports because domestically produced goods were now cheaper relative to foreign produced goods. Imports would be reduced for the same reason.

The drop in prices in the United States served as the corrective mechanism to end the nation's imbalance in international transactions. This was a critically important attribute of the gold standard system. It meant that the burden of adjustment for an international disequilibrium was thrust upon the domestic economy. In the nineteenth century, this was not considered a serious problem; economists and others believed that the substance of adjustment was a change in the price level, not a contraction of output or an increase in unemployment.

*Change in the
price level as
corrective
mechanism*

Because the gold standard rules of the game established fixed exchange rates, there was no possibility for attaining an adjustment to disequilibrium by a change in the exchange rate. As a matter of fact, manipulation of the exchange rate would have been regarded by the London bankers who managed the system as the ultimate in irresponsibility. The adjustment mechanism under the international gold standard was called the "price-specie-flow" system, because the process involved the flow of specie (i.e., gold) between nations, followed by price adjustments which ultimately brought about changes in trade that corrected the disequilibrium. It is necessary to understand, too, that the system operated through market forces, without any requirement for government action other than the legal establishment of a *par value* in terms of gold for the currency of a nation. Beyond this a government had only to continue to follow the rules of the gold standard game.

*Price-specie-flow
system*

Collapse of the Gold Standard

The collapse of the international gold standard did not come dramatically; it was a gradual process, which extended from the onset of World War I to September, 1931, when Great Britain left the gold standard once and for all. The system, which had lasted more than a century, was fatally weakened by disruptions to international trade, loss of confidence in national currencies, and internal disturbances in the economies of the major trading nations, all of which stemmed from World War I. During the war, nations had temporarily abandoned the gold standard by suspending convertibility of their currencies and other forms of money into gold. In the 1920s, attempts were made to reestablish the gold system through restoration of convertibility for the major currencies of

A gradual ending

the world. But trade and payments patterns had been so badly disrupted by the war that the system never again achieved the effectiveness it had enjoyed before 1914.

The death blow to gold was delivered during the Great Depression, a catastrophe coming on the heels of a worldwide financial crisis in 1929. The depression ushered in an era of near-anarchy in trade and international payments, as nation after nation scrambled and fought to protect its own economic position, irrespective of the cost to other countries. At this time the cost of staying on the gold standard became too high. In the 1930s, depression-wrought internal collapse made it impossible for most countries to further deflate prices, employment, and output to cope with their international payments problems. They were forced instead to sacrifice exchange rate stability, which meant abandonment of the international gold standard.

To go off the gold standard, a country had to suspend convertibility of all forms of money into gold upon demand, eliminate the *private* citizen's freedom to import and export gold, and end the circulation of gold as a form of money at home. Economists date the formal end to the gold standard from Great Britain's suspension of convertibility for sterling in September 1931, for Britain had always been the center and spark of the system. The United States suspended convertibility in 1933.

For the rest of the 1930s exchange rates were set mostly by government action. Governments did attempt to maintain rates at fixed levels with a variety of devices including equalization or stabilization funds through which governments bought and sold foreign exchange in order to offset market fluctuations. As a last resort, governments used exchange control to fix—or set—the price of foreign currency, making it illegal to buy or sell at any other rate. Under exchange control, a government, not market forces, determines the rate of exchange. Chaos in the international monetary system during the 1930s was worsened by a frequent resort to quotas, excessively high protective tariffs, and other measures aimed at restriction of trade and payments between countries. The intricate structure of trade and payments built up so laboriously in the nineteenth century was shattered in this ten-year period of economic anarchy. Nation after nation sought to save, to protect, and to insulate its economy from the effects of the worldwide depression, usually at the expense of international trade and payments and of its neighbors.

The Bretton Woods System

From 1939 to 1945, while World War II raged, trade and international payments were further disrupted and distorted. During the conflict, though, it became increasingly evident to the Allied leaders that there had to be a far-reaching reconstruction of the international monetary system and the world trade network when peace came. It was also apparent from the experience of both the 1930s and World War II that the world economy could not return to the nineteenth-century system, which rested wholly on the free play of market forces and accorded a strategic role to gold. Yet planners and economists concerned with postwar reconstruction wanted to retain some of the advantages of that system, particularly its multilateral character and the exchange rate stability so characteristic of the pre-1914 era. To rebuild a system and to achieve these results, a conference was held in 1944 at Bretton Woods, New Hampshire to work out the basic outlines of the post-World War II international monetary system, one which remained largely intact until the crisis of mid-1971 when the dollar was devalued. At present the international financial and economic community is still struggling to reconstruct and renovate the world's monetary system. The task will take most of the rest of this decade.

The International Monetary Fund

Forty-four nations, led by the United States and Great Britain, took part in the conference that set up the basic framework for the 1945–1971 international monetary system. The Soviet bloc countries did not participate. This conference created the International Monetary Fund, the key institution of the Bretton Woods system. As its name implies, the IMF is a fund (or pool) of gold and national currencies. These currencies are on deposit with the Fund and made available to member states under stipulated conditions. In other words, nations may draw on funds in the IMF to meet temporary deficits in their balance of international payments. To establish the IMF, the participants in the Bretton Woods conference agreed to pool a stipulated amount of their gold and their national currency. The size of a nation's quota was determined by its relative economic standing. Original contributions to the fund by the charter states totaled $8 billion. Since then the fund has grown in size to $28.9 billion and the current membership includes 106 nations.

   In addition to providing a pool of gold and national currencies, the International Monetary Fund offers a mechanism for attaining exchange rate stability, and for the orderly adjustment of exchange rates when economic conditions make this necessary. Exchange rate stability was achieved by an agreement between the member states to set rates in the immediate postwar period, using the American dollar as a benchmark reference. That is to say, each member country was required to declare a par value for its currency in relation to the dollar, which in turn had a fixed value in terms of gold. The rates were set at levels which it was hoped would be compatible with international equilibrium. Machinery was provided to adjust the exchange rate whenever necessary. A ten percent change in a country's rate of exchange was permitted without approval of the Fund, but for an adjustment beyond this figure approval of the Fund was required. In this way the IMF was designed to prevent disruptive and competitive exchange rate changes of the kind that had caused repeated monetary crises in the 1930s.

A basic purpose of the IMF was to create a stock of international reserves in the form of "drawing rights" on the Fund that nations might utilize when necessary. These international reserves are in the form of the total payments made to the fund in gold and national currencies by the members. They are made available to member states as temporary loans in accordance with formulas based upon the size of the individual contribution. An underlying assumption was that balance of payments disequilibria would be distributed randomly among the countries of the world; hence no single national currency would be in constant demand. It was also assumed that most of the time a balance of payments disequilibrium confronting a particular country would be temporary. Under these circumstances, a nation could augment its own reserves when needed by drawing upon the resources of the fund. Since any disequilibrium was expected to be short-lived, the nation would soon be able to repay the loan.

Drawing rights

Evolution of the Bretton Woods System

As a matter of fact, developments in the postwar period have been quite different from what was envisaged by the architects of the IMF. The main reason was the massive worldwide dollar shortage which existed for approximately a decade after the end of World War II, roughly from 1945 to 1955. The dollar shortage occurred because the dislocation and destruction of the war left the United States as the only major source of supply for the goods and services that much of the world needed for reconstruction. Thus massive trade imbalances developed between the United States and many parts of the world, especially Western Europe.

The dollar shortage

The Role of the Dollar

To a large degree this shortage was covered by the grants for economic recovery made by the United States to nations in Western Europe and to other countries between 1945 and 1955. The European Recovery Program—commonly called the Marshall Plan, after U.S. Secretary of State George Marshall—was the

The dollar as international reserve currency

463

chief means by which the United States made dollars available to Europe in this period. The U.S. dollar also emerged as a key form of international money, alongside gold and drawing rights in the International Monetary Fund. It must be stressed that this was not the result of any group or nation's design, but of the peculiar circumstances existing in the decade immediately following World War II. The widespread demand for the dollar made it readily acceptable throughout the world. Furthermore, Bretton Woods made the dollar the basic standard of reference by which the exchange rate for other currencies was determined. These factors led to the use of the dollar as a reserve currency. Many nations, in other words, were willing to hold U.S. dollars as international reserves, along with gold and drawing rights in the International Monetary Fund.

Between 1945 and 1971 the legal gold content of the dollar, as determined by the Congress, remained unchanged. Though private individuals (American or foreign) could not do so, U.S. laws permitted foreign official holders of dollars to obtain gold for these dollars if they desired. The term "official holders" means governments and international organizations such as the International Monetary Fund or the World Bank, formally known as the International Bank for Reconstruction and Development. Founded at the Bretton Woods conference, the World Bank was established to provide loans for the reconstruction of war damage and for developing nations. Like the IMF, it got its basic resources from subscriptions by member states, which now total more than 100. The bank also sells its own bonds to raise funds for lending.

The Gold Exchange Standard

Out of these practices evolved the gold exchange standard, an international monetary system in which the dollar played a key role as an international money, as an international reserve, and as the standard by which exchange rates of other currencies are defined. It was called a "gold exchange standard" (as opposed to a gold standard) because official holders of dollars could exchange them for gold. In the eyes of other nations this meant that the dollar was as valid as gold in holdings of international reserves. The survival and effectiveness of this system depended upon confidence that the dollar would remain a viable unit of international exchange, convertible into gold upon demand for official holders. In the absence of such confidence, other nations would have been less willing to hold international reserves in the form of dollars, which could threaten the entire structure of the international monetary systems as it painfully evolved over the last twenty-seven years. In the late 1960s the system faced the beginnings of the current crisis, a development to which we now turn.

Recent Crises in the International Economy

To comprehend the nature of the crisis for the Bretton Woods system which began in the late 1960s, we must understand the special and peculiar relationships between the dollar as a key currency, the necessity for international reserves, and the balance of payments deficit of the American economy. At the root of this crisis was the Bretton Woods system's excessive dependence upon the U.S. dollar as a reserve currency. By the mid-1950s, the "dollar shortage" was, for all practical purposes, over, even though the dollar continued to play a key role as a reserve currency. The growing volume of world trade and commerce, which accelerated rapidly after the mid-1950s, required a corresponding growth in international reserves.

*Excessive
dependence on
the dollar*

The Gold Drain

If nations do not feel that their stocks of international reserves are adequate, they may resort to undesirable restrictions on trade, or to the use of exchange control, even if only temporarily. In the world today there simply is not enough gold to meet the reserve requirements for a growing volume of trade; consequently, the U.S. dollar continued in its strategic role as a reserve currency. This was the nub of the difficulty, for international reserves in the form of dollars entered into the system only as the result of a balance of payments deficit on the part of the United States.

Recall that prior to the 1970s the balance of payments deficit of the United States took the peculiar form of an outflow of dollars as a result of foreign investment and government grants in excess of the inflow from a favorable balance on current account transactions. Thus, the United States' large deficits pumped reserves into the international economy, but, paradoxically, continued American deficits undermined foreign confidence in the dollar as a reserve currency. If as a consequence of prolonged payments deficits by the American economy foreigners built up their holdings of dollars beyond a level they considered prudent, they could convert a part of their dollar holdings into the more stable and enduring form of international currency, gold. This happened on a significant scale in the late 1960s, resulting in a sharp drain on U.S. gold reserves. Figure 17-2 shows U.S. holdings of monetary gold reserves for selected years from 1946 to 1971. For a short while during this crisis, the outflow of gold from the United States grew so heavy that it was feared that the entire international monetary structure faced actual collapse. The solution to

*Conversion of
dollar holdings
into gold*

465

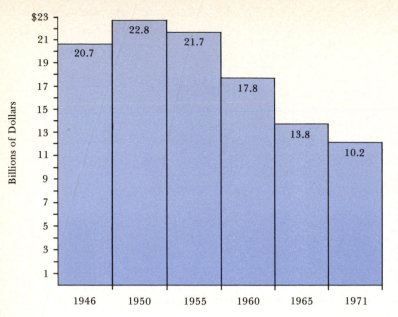

the problem lay in somehow lessening the dependence of the international monetary system upon a single national currency, no matter how strong it appeared at any particular time. To resolve the problem a conference was held at Rio de Janeiro in 1967, the outcome of which was a major innovation in the structure of the Bretton Woods system.

The Rio Conference

The purpose of the Rio conference, which was attended by the 106 members of the International Monetary Fund, was to develop a mechanism to add to the world's stock of international reserve and, at the same time, lessen the dependence of the international economy upon a single national currency as a reserve. The U.S. dollar of course occupied the latter role. The Rio conference created a new type of reserve in the form of special drawing rights, or "SDRs," on the IMF. These new reserves are also called "paper gold," since member states will accept them in international economic transactions, either to pay deficits or to meet their reserve needs. Hence, the SDRs play the role of international money. These special drawing rights are created by the directors of the International Monetary Fund, but only with the approval of 85 percent of the fund participants. This means that the directors of the fund do not have unlimited power to create reserves, and further, SDRs are to be created only when there is acute need for additional reserves over and above the normal source of reserve used in the international economy. This "paper

Special drawing rights

gold" is available to International Monetary Fund members in proportion to their quotas in the fund.

The 1971 Crisis

The Rio conference bought some time but failed to correct the fundamental weaknesses in the world's monetary system that had been revealed by the events of the 1960s. A more serious crisis burst upon the world monetary scene in mid-August 1971, when the Nixon administration took the drastic action of suspending for foreign holders the convertibility of the dollar into gold. This action marked a critical turning point for the Bretton Woods system.

The continued deterioration of the U. S. balance of payments during 1969, 1970, and 1971 led to this crisis. Between 1965 and 1970 the overall deficit averaged $3.4 billion, but jumped to $4.7 billion in 1970. (See Table 16-1.) In 1971, when for the first time since 1893, the United States had a deficit in its foreign trade, the overall deficit in the balance of payments reached the staggering total of more than $22 billion.

Early in August a Congressional subcommittee issued a report stating, among other things, that the U.S. dollar was overvalued, a point of view that was long held by critics of the crisis confronting both the United States and the international monetary system. Such overvaluation of the dollar—which meant that its price was too high in terms of foreign currencies—made American goods and services more expensive and foreign goods and services relatively cheaper, thus contributing to the trade and payments imbalance of the United States. The situation was worsened by domestic inflation in the United States and by large-scale speculative outflows of funds from the United States in 1971 as expectations developed that the dollar might be revalued in terms of foreign currencies. Speculators stood to gain by exchanging dollars for foreign currencies and buying back dollars at a later date at a cheaper price in terms of the foreign currencies they had acquired.

Overvaluation of the dollar

Devaluation

The upshot of all this was that by August 1971 the deterioration of the United States' balance of payments had reached such a magnitude and the pressure on the nation's dwindling gold stock was so great that some drastic action had to be taken. In August the United States had gold and other reserves equal to about $13 billion, against which there were potential obligations of around $60 billion. On August 15, President Nixon suspended the convertibility of the U.S. dollar into gold and imposed a 10 percent surtax on imports. The basic effect of the suspension of con-

Suspending the convertibility of the dollar

467

vertibility was a *de facto* devaluation of the dollar in terms of foreign currencies. For a time after the August action the dollar was allowed to "float," which meant that its basic foreign exchange value was being determined by the play of market forces. The counterpart to the dollar devaluation was an appreciation in the foreign exchange value of most other currencies, which was expected to lead to improvement in the U.S. balance of payments.

During the autumn of 1971 extensive talks and negotiations took place between the United States and the major industrial nations, the object being to bring some order out of the confusion set in motion by the August 15 action. In mid-December President Nixon and Pesident Pompidou of France announced they had reached agreement that the U.S. dollar should be revalued through a change in the price of gold and there should be a prompt realignment of exchange rates between major currencies. Shortly thereafter an agreement was concluded in Washington in which the dollar was devalued 8.57 percent by an increase in the price of gold from $35 to $38 per ounce, and the currencies of West Germany and Japan were revalued upward by 13 and 17 percent respectively. These two countries were the ones with which the United States had the greatest deficits. The United States also agreed to the immediate lifting of the import surcharge.

The action taken in December 1971 eased the crisis confronting the international monetary system, but did not resolve the more fundamental and long-term problem of reexamination and reform of the basic structure of the Bretton Woods system. Still unsettled, too, is the future role of the dollar as a reserve currency, the role of gold, and whether the International Monetary Fund will undergo more transformations in the near future. We now turn to some of the issues raised by these questions.

Alternatives to the Present System

No one who has studied the turbulent history of the international economy in this century would argue that the evolution of the international monetary system is nearly complete. Undoubtedly there will be further changes in its structure and the way it functions, in both the near and distant future. Development of the international monetary system has been somewhat analogous to the development of domestic monetary systems in advanced countries; it has evolved from a situation in which the basic form for international reserves was metal—gold—toward a system in which, increasingly, international reserves are nothing more than entries on the books of the International Monetary Fund. We have already seen the domestic evolution of the primary form of money from metal, such as gold or silver, to an entry in the books of the central and the commercial banks. Domestic monetary systems are closer to being fully managed systems than the international monetary system, because the major countries have strong and effective central banks. This stage of development has not yet been achieved in the international monetary system.

A Central Bank for the International Economy

One of the key proposals made in recent years for a further transformation in the Bretton Woods system comes largely from the writing and thinking of Professor Robert Triffin, a Yale University economist and authority on the international monetary system. He suggests, in effect, that the International Monetary Fund be transformed into a true central bank, with authority to create international reserves on the basis of need, rather than only with the approval of an overwhelming majority of members of the fund, as is now the case. Triffin's plan would require member states to deposit in the IMF a portion of their reserves, which the IMF could then use as a base for creating additional international reserves to lend whenever appropriate to deficit countries. The IMF would be transformed from an organization providing a pool of gold, national currencies, and special drawing rights, to an organization able to create reserves as economic conditions dictated—a true central bank for the international economy. Such a change would reduce—if not eliminate—the dependence of the international monetary system upon deficits in the American balance of payments to supply it with international reserves, as well as dependence upon the uncertainties of gold mining and the supply of gold for the world economy.

The Triffin plan

The difficulty in the Triffin plan is that it would require member states to surrender some national sovereignty to an international organization, the International Monetary Fund. The power to create reserves that would be accepted internationally as a medium of exchange would also enable the IMF to create purchasing power, which might be used to transfer a part of the output of one member state to the uses and benefit of another member state. Whether nations are willing to transfer this kind of power from the market system to an international organization such as the IMF remains to be seen.

Flexible Exchange Rates

Among other proposals being advanced currently for the further reform of the Bretton Woods system is the elimination of its commitment to fixed exchange rates. It is argued that exchange rates should be free to fluctuate in response to the demand and supply conditions pertaining to the different currencies. This of course would lessen a nation's dependence on international reserves. When the nation had a deficit in its balance of payments, the foreign exchange value of its currency would tend to depreciate relative to other currencies and this would begin to correct its balance of payments problem. The corrective process would involve automatic changes in exchange rates sufficient to change trade and payments balances in the amount needed to restore equilibrium. Under such an arrangement there would be little need for international reserves.

Proponents of a flexible exchange rate system argue that with the degree of stability and growth in the international economy at this time, it is unlikely that fluctuations in the rate of exchange would be excessive if the tie to a fixed exchange rate system were broken. Opponents argue that stability and the elimination of uncertainty in international economic transactions will be furthered by exchange rates that are subject to change only when special circumstances warrant it. There is little doubt that debates over the desirability of pushing the IMF further toward becoming an international central bank and the merit of fluctuating versus fixed exchange rates will continue and ultimately have an impact upon the future shape of the international monetary system.

Postwar Problems of World Trade

As we have seen, during the nineteenth century nearly all parts of the world were linked together in an intricate network of trade and commerce, which rested fundamentally upon the market system and the international gold standard. Like the international gold standard, this nineteenth-century network was shattered by the triple impact of World War I, the Great Depression, and World War II. Not only did the cataclysmic events of the twentieth century disrupt this mechanism, but in the aftermath of World War II three major developments changed irrevocably the relationships between various parts of the world that had been an integral part of the nineteenth-century trade structure.

Emerging Nations

The first was the political independence achieved during and immediately after World War II by practically all of the colonial areas that, in the nineteenth century, had been tied both economically and politically to the nations of Western Europe. In an economic sense the role of the colonial areas before World War I was to provide primary products (foodstuffs and industrial raw materials) to the more developed nations and serve as outlets for some of their exports of manufactured goods. This trade pattern reflected the comparative advantage which existed at that time, given the pre-World War I distribution of economic resources between the European countries and colonial areas. After the colonial areas became independent states, they were determined not only to maintain their independence, but to minimize and break the economic ties that had held them in a subordinate and subjugated status as parts of a colonial empire. Economically this meant that these countries were no longer satisfied with their existing resource endowment and, consequently, no longer willing to accept a pattern of specialization and trade based upon their supplying the developed nations with natural resources.

Now that the emerging nations aspire to diversify their economies, resources which had been used in the past to promote the export of one or two primary commodities are being used internally to expand the economic base of the country. India, for example, has undertaken a series of five-year plans to speed development. As a consequence some former colonial countries have serious balance of payments problems, which force them to seek extraordinary sources of finance to sustain their international economic position. Economic aid from the developed countries partly fills the gap. These new nations are breaking out of the old pattern of specialization and trade carried over from the nineteenth century, but have not yet fully found how they fit into the emerging structure of world trade.

Attempts to diversify economies

Temporary Eclipse of Industrial Nations

A second impact of World War II was the temporary eclipse of both Western Europe and Japan as centers of the international economy, particularly manufacturing and trading centers. Before the war Japan and Western Europe were leading surplus areas in the production and export of manufactured commodities. World War II left their economies almost wholly devastated; both regions were heavily dependent on outside help. This led to serious imbalances in the world trade structure, even though of a temporary nature. Once recovery and rebuilding was completed, both Japan and Western Europe entered into international trade with a new vigor and competitiveness which has further transformed the post-World War II network of international trade.

The Soviet Bloc

Finally there was the emergence of the Soviet bloc after World War II, a development which, in spite of some reduction in tensions and loosening of trade restrictions, shattered prewar trade patterns between Eastern and Western Europe. Before World War II the Soviet bloc countries of Eastern Europe were primarily agricultural, but under the impact of the postwar developments and the Cold War they sought to industrialize and diversify, permanently changing economic relationships between Eastern and Western Europe. In spite of this, though, and as tensions lessen, there is a growing volume of trade between Eastern and Western Europe.

American Policy and the Reconstruction of World Trade

The task of rebuilding the structure of world trade after World War II concerned all of the major trading countries of the world, especially those of Western Europe and Japan, but our discussion will focus primarily upon the American role and American policy objectives. This does not mean that what was done was determined wholly by the United States, although in the early period of reconstruction—the later 1940s and early 1950s—the American role was a dominant one. Consequently, the structure that emerged strongly reflected American views of the nature of the world economy and its trade network.

It is never easy to analyze the very complex motives for a major economic power like the United States, but the events following World War II suggest that three major objectives dominated American policy from the mid-1940s through the 1960s:

1. Rebuilding the war-ravaged economy of Western Europe. This rated the highest priority of the American postwar policy agenda.
2. Active promotion of the economic—and, it was hoped, with it the political—integration of Western Europe.
3. Freeing trade and commerce from the many restrictive practices which developed in the 1930s and during the war.

Immediate Aid

Rebuilding the damage to the economy of Western Europe wrought by World War II was achieved in several stages. In the three years following the end of hostilities in Europe, 1945 through 1947, the United States poured money into the area, the bulk of it directed toward the immediate relief of people in the war-torn nations. Some aid was channeled through the United Nations Relief and Rehabilitation Administration (UNRRA), but other sums were made available through grants to individual nations, particularly those made in 1947 to Austria, France, Italy,

Greece, and Turkey, all of which were facing serious internal political disorders and the threat of a Communist takeover. In addition, the United States made emergency, large-scale loans to Great Britain, whose difficulties were especially severe after the abrupt termination of lend-lease at the end of the war. Before the United States entered World War II the Roosevelt administration undertook to "lend or lease" war equipment to Great Britain, primarily as a way of helping the British in their struggle against Germany and of getting around an American law that prohibited the United States from lending money to belligerent nations. This technique was used all during World War II to assist our allies, including the Soviet Union. In this early phase, more than $16 billion in outright grants and long-term loans was extended to these nations.

The Marshall Plan

By 1947, though, it was apparent that the reconstruction of the economies of Western Europe required more than emergency relief. In June 1947, Secretary of State George Marshall proposed that the United States supply large-scale aid to Western European countries if they would coordinate their efforts and work together in a recovery program, designed not merely to tide them over the hardships resulting from the war but to improve their productive capacity to deal with the fundamentally changed economic situation brought about by the war. At this time the nations of Europe had a massive deficit in their balance of international payments, a deficit which could be overcome only by rebuilding and enlarging their productive capacity enough to develop an export surplus to offset the loss of prewar sources of income from abroad. Marshall's proposal led to the European Recovery Program, which went into effect in 1948 and became popularly known as the Marshall Plan. It proved phenomenally successful, even though it was terminated ahead of the anticipated ending date in 1952 because of the outbreak of the Korean War in 1950 and Western Europe's preoccupation with rearmament beginning in 1949 with the formation of NATO (the North Atlantic Treaty Organization). During the approximately two and a half years in which the Marshall Plan was fully effective, the United States made available more than $10 billion in grants to the economies of Western Europe. By the early 1950s recovery in Western Europe was substantially complete, a conclusion sustained by the fact that prewar levels of production were restored in practically all countries and the balance of payments problem on the continent was reduced to manageable proportions.

Large-scale aid to Western Europe

473

Military Assistance

The third phase of American policy toward Western Europe began in the early 1950s, when, under the pressures of rearmament, American aid shifted from essentially economic to military in character, a consequence of the establishment of NATO and attempts to create a European defense system. Military assistance in varying degrees, including the maintenance of large American forces in Western Europe, has continued to the present.

Free Trade in the Postwar World

The European Economic Community

Economic integration in Western Europe has been primarily a European accomplishment, although throughout the postwar period there was strong American support for efforts to move in this direction. The earliest important attempt at some kind of economic integration came in 1952 when the Coal and Steel Authority was created. This arrangement involved the establishment of a free market in the products of the coal and steel industries for six countries in Western Europe which were to become the nucleus for the European Economic Community: France, Western Germany, Italy, Belgium, Holland, and Luxembourg. The movement toward economic and political integration was largely the offspring of Jean Monnet, father of the French Recovery Program during the Marshall Plan era, and Maurice Schumann, Foreign Minister of France in the late 1940s and early 1950s. The success of the Coal and Steel Community was directly responsible for establishment of the European Economic Community through treaty in the later 1950s. The European Economic Community, generally called the Common Market, was set up to establish a free trade area for all goods and services and to provide for the free movement of labor among the six member states.

Although the European Economic Community is an arrangement designed to create a free trade area over much of Western Europe, it also has a common tariff policy against the rest of the world. The basic goals for abolition of all tariffs and import quotas in commodities traded within the area, establishment of a common system of external tariffs, and the free movement of both money capital and labor between Common Market countries were to be established over a twelve- to fifteen-year period, beginning on January 1, 1958. As of 1970 these objectives were largely achieved.

The first major expansion in membership in the Common Market came in January 1972 when Great Britain, Denmark, and

Ireland were formally accepted into membership. For Britain this was a momentous step, as Britain had boycotted the Community in the 1950s and had its membership application vetoed by France in 1963. With the entry of these three countries, the Common Market embraces a population of 246 million, which accounts for nearly 40 percent of total world trade. Political union through the creation of supranational institutions of government, which would transform the Community into a genuine United States of Europe, is far from being achieved.

The Trade Expansion Act

American policy strongly supported the move toward European integration. In the early 1960s the United States hoped that the European Economic Community would be the nucleus of a larger free trade area embracing not only most of Western Europe, but the United States and Canada as well. The Kennedy administration's 1962 Trade Expansion Act, which gave the President broad authority to negotiate tariff reductions over a five-year period, rested on the assumption that Great Britain would soon enter the Common Market, which was expected to create the opportunity for negotiations to eliminate tariffs on many of the products traded between Common Market countries and the United States.

Tariff reduction and elimination

The 1962 act was partially stimulated by the realization that success of the Common Market created a potential competitive threat for the American products in foreign trade, a situation best dealt with by creating an even larger free trade area. Therefore the Trade Expansion Act gave the President additional authority to negotiate arrangements and eliminate tariffs wholly on products in which both the Common Market and the United States together accounted for 80 percent or more of world trade. Since this would have included a very long list of products if Great Britain had entered the Common Market as originally contemplated, the final result of successful negotiations would have been an enormous free trade area embracing most of the Atlantic community. France's 1963 veto of Britain's application to enter the Common Market made this aspect of the Trade Expansion Act practically a dead letter, for without Great Britain as a member, there were few commodities in which the Common Market and the United States together accounted for more than 80 percent of the world's trade.

Free Trade as American Policy

The roots of these postwar American policies aimed at freeing trade and commerce from restrictive practices are found in the

*The "most favored
nation" principle*

1930s, when, under the impetus of President Roosevelt's Secretary of State, Cordell Hull, the Reciprocal Trade Agreements programs were instituted. In 1929, on the eve of the Great Depression, the United States enacted the highest tariffs in its history (the Smoot-Hawley Act). Some economists view this action as a major factor in bringing on the depression. In any event, in the 1930s under Hull's leadership the United States reversed the policy of high tariffs and began to move toward freer trade with all countries. The Reciprocal Trade Agreements program was designed to negotiate mutually advantageous tariff reductions between the United States and other countries. It rested upon the assumption that movement toward free trade was a desirable public policy objective, and that the trade reduction should be nondiscriminatory. This objective is carried out through the "most-favored nation clause," which states that the benefits of any trade reduction achieved through negotiation should be extended equally to all other countries with which the signatories of a trading pact have trade relationships. The principle of the most-favored nation has governed American policy throughout the postwar period.

GATT

The architects for the postwar reconstruction of the international monetary system and the network of international trade had hoped to create an International Trade Organization as a counterpart of the International Monetary Fund, but the charter for the ITO was rejected by the United States Senate. However, its place was taken in part by the General Agreement on Tariffs and Trade (GATT), negotiated in 1946 and 1947 and signed in 1947 by some 23 nations, including the United States. This general agreement embodies three major principles: equal and nondiscriminatory treatment for all countries, negotiations for the mutual elimination and reduction of tariffs, and agreement to work toward the complete elimination of all quotas as a technique for restricting trade between nations.

*The Kennedy
Round*

Since GATT was established in 1947 several rounds of trade negotiations have taken place, all of which have had some influence on expanding world trade, as well as bringing about a general reduction in tariffs by the member countries. The most recent round of negotiations was called the "Kennedy Round," because it was based upon the authority given the President in the Trade Expansion Act of 1962. An assessment of the success of the Kennedy Round, completed in 1967, indicates that about 70 percent of the dutiable imports in the participating countries were affected by these negotiations and that two-thirds of the tariff reductions stemming from the negotiations amounted to 35 percent or more. Moreover, the nations that participated in the Kennedy Round accounted for some three-fourths of the world's trade.

Protectionism Today

For the past third of a century the United States has committed itself to the free trade philosophy. Recently, though, a rising tide of protectionist sentiment has developed in the United States, particularly in the industries most vulnerable to the competitive impact of the rebuilt and modernized industries of Japan and Western Europe. Some of the industries that feel most threatened by foreign competition include bottled liquors (28), textile goods (47), rubber footwear (23), leather goods (30), table china and kitchen articles (32), nonferrous metals (45), sewing machines and parts (35), and motorcycles and bicycles (17). The figure in parentheses represents imports as a percent of total supply, which the U.S. Department of Commerce defines as domestic production plus imports. Imports are thus a higher percentage of domestic production than is indicated by these figures.

It is too early to say whether the growing pressure for protection through higher tariffs and quotas will succeed in reversing the trends of the past third of a century and lead into a new era of excessive nationalism in the world economy, a development which would seriously threaten the multilateral structure of trade and payments that has evolved since 1945.

Essentially, the argument for freer trade rests upon the venerable doctrine of comparative advantage, a principle which shows that in a market system, freedom to export and import will force nations to specialize in the production and export of the commodities in which they have a comparative advantage and import those in which their comparative position is least desirable. The rationale for both economic and welfare reasons for free trade is that the output of the entire trading area will be maximized. This means that all the participants in trade will have more to consume than they would in the absence of trade. The case for free trade rests upon the assumption that resources—labor and capital, especially—are immobile between nations, an assumption of dubious validity in the face of the explosive recent growth of multinational corporations. We shall examine this phenomenon in the next section.

Against the case for free trade are various traditional arguments that stress the desirability of protecting domestic industry from foreign competition, the bulk of which have little economic merit, but often do have an enormous emotional appeal, especially when couched in terms of protecting domestic wage levels from presumably lower paid, less efficient, and less meritorious foreign competition.

Economists seriously doubt the merit of most of these arguments, except possibly for the view that tariffs should be used

**Change and
Upheaval in the
International
Economy**

*The infant-
industry argument*

from time to time to protect industries that are trying to get started in the face of intense foreign competition. This is the "infant industry" argument, which has validity because the doctrine of comparative advantage takes as given the existing distribution of resources, a condition that many nations do not want to accept. In other words, free trade will maximize output and consumption in the trading area as long as the existing distribution of resources is maintained. But if a nation wants to expand its resource base and perhaps diversify its capabilities, then free trade will not necessarily maximize output. Thus about the only major argument economists will accept in opposition to freeing trade from restrictions, particularly quantitative restrictions such as quotas and other devices, is the argument for protecting industries while they get a start.

The Multinational Corporations

A new development that may require some changes in the traditional economic analysis of the basis and benefits of free trade is the multinational corporation—giant business corporations whose operations span the globe. This is a relatively new phenomenon in the international economy, but one, nevertheless, which has aroused intense interest and concern.

The contemporary international corporation is primarily a product of the vast outflow of investment funds from the United States over the last two decades. This does not mean that this development is exclusively American, as giant corporations from many different nations are found in the ranks of the "multinationals." Some of the best known names include Olivetti (Italy), Shell (Holland), Bayer (Germany), Unilever (Great Britain), Alcan Aluminium (Canada), and General Motors (the United States).

But between 1950 and the end of the 1960s the value of U.S. investments abroad increased nearly five times, from $31.5 billion to $143.4 billion. Of the latter, about two-thirds was private investment and the largest share of this was direct investment by U.S. multinational corporations in productive facilities abroad. Within the last decade U.S. direct investments in manufacturing facilities alone have increased threefold.

The economic significance of the development of multinational operations is to outdate traditional economic thinking about the immobility of some economic resources and thus the basis for trade between nations. Specifically, the multinational corporation has become a vehicle for the ready transfer of financial capital, management skill, and technology from one country to another.

The revolutionary developments in communications and transportation technology of the last few decades have made possible the international mobility of these resources.

In the 1950s, when the international economy was still living in the shadow of the earlier dollar shortage, American policy makers argued that the outflow of capital from the United States was highly desirable, especially because it would be an instrument to make American technology available to less developed or wartorn economies. This has happened to a far greater degree than was then foreseen, one unexpected result being the development of multinational corporations so large and powerful that they raise serious questions for domestic economies.

In the United States organized labor, in particular, has reacted strongly to the multinational corporations, arguing that, in effect, employment has been exported through their operations. The production-line worker does not enjoy the same mobility as management, financial capital, and technology in large multinational operations. Labor spokesmen claim that it has become more profitable for many large companies to export their capital, technology, and managerial skills to foreign-owned subsidiaries, rather than export the goods themselves. The result is unemployment in the American economy.

Opposition of labor to the multinational corporation

It is too soon to assess the full impact of this development on the future pattern of international trade, but clearly this development has injected a new factor into the process of trade between nations, one that has not yet been explained adequately by economic theory.

The Future of U.S. Trade

The emergence of giant U.S. multinational corporations as a new factor in the international economy is only one of several recent developments that raise important questions about the future competitive position of the United States in the world economy. As pointed out earlier, one of the more serious aspects of the United States' balance of payments problem has been the steady deterioration in the nation's balance of merchandise trade. In the early 1960s the excess of exports over imports for merchandise averaged around $5 billion, but in the last few years it slipped to an average of between $1 and $2 billion, and in 1971 the United States had its first actual trade deficit in 78 years.

As the Nixon administration began to prepare a comprehensive trade bill early in 1972, it was confronted with substantial evidence that the international competitive position of the American economy has worsened in the last couple of decades. For example,

Declining U.S. share of world trade

between 1950 and 1970 the U.S. share of world trade steadily declined, while the share of the Common Market countries and Japan expanded spectacularly. Specifically, the U.S. share of the trade among major industrial nations has dropped from one-third to one-fifth during this period.

A number of factors are involved in the changed position of the United States in the world economy. Some reflect the success of American policies of the early postwar era, which, as we have seen, helped restore to economic health the war-torn economies of West Germany and Japan, two of America's most intense competitors. The upsurge in trade of the Common Market is in part, too, testimony to the success of earlier policies, for the United States had strongly supported the concept of economic union and integration in Western Europe. Other factors, though, are unrelated to these developments and also play a role in the changed competitive position of the American economy. The most important of these have been the inflation fueled by the Vietnam war, the lag in the growth of productivity that also began to manifest itself in the late 1960s, and the structural shifts in the American economy toward services instead of goods or manufacturing production.

*High technology
vs. low technology
products*

Analysis of the structure of American exports and imports shows that over the last 10 to 15 years there has been a steady increase in the export surplus obtained from products which embody advanced technology in their production. These "high technology" products include chemicals, machinery, electronics, automobiles, aircraft, and instruments, to name but a few. On the other hand, growing deficits have been recorded in "low technology" and labor intensive products, such as textiles, steel, fabricated metals, newsprint, housewares, and shoes. Farm products have maintained a fairly constant surplus, but there has been a growing deficit in raw materials and fuels, including iron ore, copper, lumber, pulp, cotton, oil, and coal. It is estimated that by the end of the decade the nation will have to import up to 50 percent of its raw material requirements, in contrast to about 30 percent at present.

There is plentiful evidence that the nation faces a much more competitive situation internationally than at any time in this century. The high technology goods are one area in which the nation continues to maintain a strong trade position, but even in this area its advantage has begun to narrow. This, too, is the area in which the most intense competition is being felt from other advanced nations. Since technological advance remains one of the keys to competitiveness, the recent decline in the rate of productivity growth must be halted and reversed. This task has been accorded high priority by the Nixon administration.

The early years of the 1970s have been watershed years in the international economy. They have seen the end of the post-World War II era, a period of difficult and prolonged struggle for the restoration of a multilateral system of world trade and the building of a viable monetary order. Absolute free multilateral trade remains an unrealized and idealized dream, but a practical and reasonably free system does exist, even though there remain many barriers to trade in the form of quotas, tariffs, restrictive taxes, and other devices. Similarly, the international monetary system is far from a completed structure, but there do exist workable arrangements to finance trade, manage balance of payments deficits, and accumulate reserves. The world economy can look forward not only to a more competitive world economic order, but, let us hope, to a strengthening of the forces making for freedom in the international movement of goods, money, and people.

Questions for Review and Discussion

1. What three essential conditions are the "rules of the game" for the international gold standard?

2. Explain the mechanism by which exchange rate stability was maintained under the international gold standard.

3. If the United States experienced a persistent import surplus on current account under gold standard conditions, what corrective mechanisms would come into play?

4. Give the major reasons for the final collapse of the international gold standard during the 1930s. How did the United States leave the gold standard?

5. List the major ways in which the international monetary system established as a result of the 1944 conference at Bretton Woods differed from the old international gold standard.

6. How did it happen that after World War II the U.S. dollar became a major form of international money? What are the drawbacks of an international monetary system tied so closely to a particular national currency?

7. What were the major developments that led up to the 1970 crisis in the international monetary system, a crisis that resulted in the United States' formal suspension of any conversion of the dollar into gold?

8. Why are Special Drawing Rights in the International Monetary Fund called "paper gold"?

9. List some of the major alternatives proposed for further transformation of the Bretton Woods system.

10. List the major objectives of American economic policy toward Western Europe in the post-World War II era.

11. What major principles are embodied in GATT (the General Agreement on Tariffs and Trade?

12. What possible consequences will the growth of multinational corporations have on international trade?

18

Economic Development: The International Setting

OUR ATTENTION in the last two chapters was riveted mainly on the economically powerful nations that control the flow of goods around the world. But the economically weak nations, which account for about 60 percent of the world's population, produce barely 18 percent of the world's goods and services. This is why poverty is an increasingly difficult economic problem for the world community, ranking only slightly below the need to end the threat of nuclear war.

The Magnitude of World Poverty

To grasp the magnitude of poverty on a world scale, we must first decide how to measure it. Once agreement on measurement is achieved, we must determine the extent of poverty on a world scale. How many nations are poor and where are they?

The Standard of Living

Poverty in an economic sense relates to the level of material well-being, what is popularly called the standard of living. As we noted in Chapter 15, the most widely used measure of the standard of living is real income per person. It is a simple and direct way to indicate the average amount of goods and services a nation can offer its citizens. But it is not the only way to determine whether a nation is economically developed or underdeveloped. There are many others, including life expectancy at birth, infant mortality rates, per capita food consumption (measured in calories), the literacy of the population, the proportion of the economically active population which is unemployed, the proportionate distribution of the employed population among major forms of economic activity, and personal consumption as a proportion of the national income.

Real income per person

Table 18-1 contains recent data from the United Nations on per capita real income for major areas of the world, including key nations in each area. A survey of the table clearly indicates that the economically advanced nations are located in Western Europe, North America, and a few other places, while most of the underdeveloped countries are in Africa, Asia, the Middle East, and Latin America.

In many of the less developed areas and nations there is a much greater lag in the collection and publication of reliable statistics than in more advanced areas. Still economists can speak of the international "poverty line" as a per capita figure of slightly less than $500; it is based on average per capita income worldwide.

The international poverty line

Poverty and Population

Since poverty and population problems often go hand in hand, Table 18-2 contains data on the distribution of world population according to this same classification. This arrangement of data helps put the magnitude of poverty into the proper perspective. For example, the four areas (Africa, Asia, the Middle East, and Latin America) with the overwhelming majority of the underde-

Table 18-1
Per Capita National Income by Area and Selected Countries: 1958, 1965, 1968
(in United States dollars)

AREA	1958	1965	1968
Africa	$100	$130	n.a.
Ghana	140	233	198
Kenya	69	89	218
Libya	110	665	1,239
Nigeria	49	68	n.a.
South Africa	314	460	550
United Arab Republic	111	161	n.a.
Asia	$80	$100	n.a.
Afghanistan	67	69	n.a.
Burma	53	61	67
Ceylon	118	133	131
India	64	89	71
Indonesia	82	78	86
Japan	290	721	1,122
Pakistan	62	95	121
Philippines	193	218	250
Middle East	$180	$290	n.a.
Cyprus	450	600	622
Israel	630	1,097	1,158
Jordan	141	231	n.a.
Syria	155	160	214
Turkey	180	245	321
Latin America [1]	$250	$340	$370 [2]
Argentina	489	728	609
Brazil	139	193	271 [2]
Chile	328	419	449
Mexico	272	412	511
Peru	163	218	246
Uruguay	541	574	552
Soviet Union	$940	n.a.	$1,351
Western Europe	$730	$1,250	$1,440
EEC Countries [3]	724	1,312	1,592
Austria	588	967	1,145
Greece	326	567	679
Norway	871	1,453	1,808
Spain	305	589	663
Switzerland	1,195	1,929	2,294
United Kingdom	1,013	1,478	1,451
Oceania	$940	$1,350	$1,570
North America	$2,061	$2,821	$3,454

[1] Including the Caribbean and Central America.
[2] 1967 data.
[3] Belgium, Netherlands, France, West Germany, Italy and Luxemburg.

Source: United Nations, *Monthly Bulletin of Statistics,* 1971.

veloped nations also have most of the world's population. In 1970, the estimated world population was 3.6 billion; nearly three-quarters of it was located in these parts of the globe. Of more ominous portent for the future is the fact that recent rates of population growth are significantly higher in the "third world," as residents of the underdeveloped countries are sometimes described.

TABLE 18-2

Population by Area and
Estimated Rates of Growth: 1970, 1963–1969

AREA	1970 POPULATION (IN MILLIONS)	ESTIMATED RATE OF GROWTH, 1963–1969 [1]
Africa	341.9	2.4
Asia	1,907.7	2.6
Middle East	96.5	2.6
Latin America [2]	283.1	2.9
Soviet Union	242.8	1.1
Europe [3]	462.0	0.8
Oceania [4]	19.3	2.0
North America [5]	226.8	1.2
Total	3,580.1	

[1] Based on rates in major countries only.
[2] Includes the Caribbean and Central America.
[3] Includes East and West Europe.
[4] Australia only.
[5] The United States only.
Source: United Nations, *Demographic Yearbook*, 1971.

Tables 18-1 and 18-2 are useful because they dramatize the magnitude of the problem of world poverty, but they do not tell us about another critical aspect of this situation. This is the growing gap in income between the rich nations and the poor nations in the world. In spite of more than two decades of effort to solve the economic problems of underdeveloped countries, the gap between the rich and the poor has widened rather than narrowed.

Widening gap between rich and poor nations

Table 18-3 shows the distribution of world income in relation to population for 1950 and for 1964, the most recent date for which worldwide data of this type are available. These data indicate that the share of world income for countries included in the three lower quintiles declined between 1950 and 1964, whether or not data for the United States are included in the table. The three lowest fifths in the table embrace the underdeveloped countries which make up the poorest 69 percent of the world's population. These data reveal that the poorest three-fifths of the world's people received 13.2 percent of world income in 1950, but only 11.1 percent in 1964, a clear indication of the growing gap between rich and poor. On the other hand, the richest 40 percent

TABLE 18-3
International Distribution of Income
(1950, 1964)

WORLD POPULATION	PERCENT OF INCOME (U.S. INCLUDED)		PERCENT OF INCOME (U.S. EXCLUDED)	
	1950	1964	1950	1964
Lowest fifth	3.5 ⎫	2.9 ⎫	5.5 ⎫	4.1 ⎫
2nd fifth	4.2 ⎬ 13.2	3.5 ⎬ 11.1	6.4 ⎬ 19.3	4.9 ⎬ 14.6
3rd fifth	5.5 ⎭	4.7 ⎭	7.4 ⎭	5.6 ⎭
4th fifth	16.3	22.5	21.4	24.4
Highest fifth	70.5	66.4	59.3	61.0

Source: James H. Weaver and Leroy P. Jones, "International Distribution of Income: 1950–1964," *Journal of Economic Issues,* December, 1968.

increased their income share from 86.8 percent in 1950 to 88.9 percent in 1964. In 1970 the situation was even worse, for the 73.5 percent of the world's population living in Africa, the Middle East, and Latin America received but 13.8 percent of the world's estimated income.

Figure 18-1 illustrates these wide disparities between relative shares in population and income. Obviously, we must still find means to overcome the human misery that accompanies under-

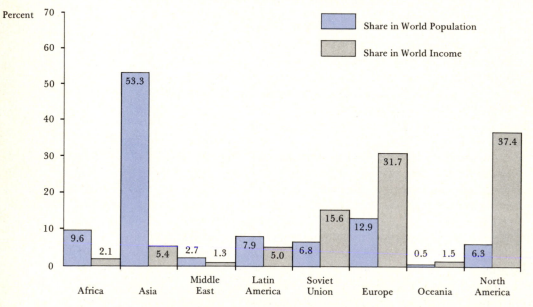

FIGURE 18-1
Distribution of World Population and Income by Geographic Area: 1970.
The diagram reflects one of the most serious aspects of the international problem of economic development: the wide disparity between the share of the world population found in Africa, Asia, the Middle East and Latin America and the share of these areas in world income. (Source: United Nations data.)

development. The achievement during the 1960s was especially disappointing, for these years were to be the "Decade of Development." It is sad but true that the world spends many times as much for armaments as it does for economic development.

Characteristics of the Underdeveloped Countries

Economically underdeveloped nations share many characteristics, though all nations have their own individual differences. Understanding what they face in common is essential if we are to find solutions to world poverty. The most useful frame of reference is the broad division of economic activity into agricultural and industrial sectors; for, over the wide span of history, development has involved a shift of people and resources from the agricultural into the industrial sector, including the production of services.

Agricultural and industrial sectors

Low Productivity

The most common characteristic of underdeveloped nations is low productivity for labor and other resources. Nations, like people, are poor primarily because they lack skill and effectiveness in using resources. This is especially true in agriculture; a large proportion of the labor force is tied up in food production in countries where people must battle to produce enough crops to survive. This situation was common to Western nations more than two centuries ago; their rapid economic development became possible only after drastic improvement in agricultural labor productivity. It was the agricultural "revolution" of the seventeenth century that paved the way for the nineteenth century Industrial Revolution.

Thus, an underdeveloped nation must first discover how to improve productivity in agriculture. During the last two decades this has become increasingly apparent to leaders in the underdeveloped nations, who have grown more willing to direct investment and resources into agriculture. This is a partial reversal of an earlier attitude among underdeveloped countries that the short cut to economic development was primarily through industrialization.

Agricultural productivity and development

The proportion of the labor force working in the agricultural sector is one of the best indicators of a country's degree of development. As economic development unfolds less and less labor is necessary to produce the basic food and fiber; this process has been underway for a long time in the more advanced nations. In the United States, for example, less than 5 percent of the labor force is now employed in agricultural production. The few exceptions to this generalization include Denmark and New Zealand, developed nations with a high proportion of their labor force in agriculture. In these countries agriculture is a major export industry and as such a major factor in the high level of development they have achieved. The technology for rapid agricultural advance exists, but poor nations lack the means and often the inclination to utilize it, preferring time-honored—though inefficient—methods in many cases. The problem is as much cultural as it is economic in many countries; deeply-rooted patterns of behavior block the introduction of new techniques.

*Disguised
unemployment*

In the underdeveloped nations the problem of low average productivity in agriculture is compounded by the "disguised unemployment" that often exists in rural regions. In disguised unemployment ostensibly people are working, but they really contribute little to actual output. The productivity of many agricultural workers in underdeveloped nations is so low that they could be shifted to other sectors of the economy without reducing agricultural output. Surplus agricultural labor could be used productively in other sectors, but all too often no sectors of sufficient size exist in underdeveloped economies. This is a baffling paradox; these countries have *too* many people in agriculture of whom many are unproductive, yet there are no places where they can be productively employed.

Lack of Markets and Capital

Economic progress in any nation depends to a considerable extent on specialization in production, which must rest upon a large and growing network of markets for exchange of commodities. To complement the markets there must be an effective monetary system. The size of the market also has a direct impact on the productivity of labor because specialization makes people more proficient at their tasks. In underdeveloped nations markets are also limited by a lack of transportation and communication facilities, such as roads, rail systems, or even a postal system, and by the absence of financial institutions to supply credit and other services needed for exchange on a market basis. The consequence is not only that specialization is limited, but that regions and villages must be self-sufficient. Production therefore takes place in extremely small units, which seriously inhibits the growth of factors that improve productivity.

*Limited markets
and financial
institutions*

*Labor wasted for
lack of capital*

A third significant characteristic of underdeveloped countries is an overall scarcity of capital, the major means by which a society improves the productivity of human labor and other resources. In the long view, the key distinction between a developed and less developed economy is the extent to which capital is available to the productive process. Modern advanced countries, such as the United States, are rich in capital, both absolutely and relative to other resources. Poor nations are confronted with extreme shortages of capital, especially relative to other resources. Many underdeveloped countries, such as India, have abundant labor available because of their large populations, but their labor cannot produce effectively for lack of capital resources to complement its efforts. The scarcity of capital is reflected in the low level of per capita energy consumption in underdeveloped countries, which is about only one tenth as great as in the advanced nations.

An especially acute shortage is found in social overhead capital, also called the infrastructure of a society. Social overhead capital, taken for granted in a developed society, includes facilities for energy production, communications, transport, and education. It is a key element in the development process, extremely expensive to acquire and slow to have an impact on the productivity of a society. Educational systems are a case in point. No nation can be modern and productive without a large investment of resources in the education of its citizens, but the process by which acquired knowledge leads to improved productivity is slow and arduous. Severely limited in their social overhead capital, underdeveloped countries must devote a disproportionate share of their meager saving and investment to overcoming this handicap.

Primitive Technology

A fourth characteristic of underdeveloped nations is the primitive technology in production in many sectors of the economy, a situation closely related to the general scarcity of capital. In nations like Pakistan or the Congo, plows made of wood or even rude sticks often represent the level of agricultural technique available. Capital instruments spread technology; they represent the physical embodiment of the techniques available in economically advanced countries. One need only observe agricultural production in the Great Plains area of the United States to grasp the relationship between capital and technology. In this region a few people produce large quantities of agricultural commodities, primarily because they work with abundant equipment which in design and construction reflects the best in technology. Technology in underdeveloped countries is often further retarded by inadequate educational systems.

Problems with Saving, Exports, and Investment

The problems caused by scarcity of capital and primitive technology are both perpetuated and compounded by the fifth characteristic of the underdeveloped nations: a low capacity to save and invest. Obviously, this is a consequence of the low level of income and productivity. Low income means a very narrow margin for saving; thus the proportion of output that can be invested in new productive facilities lags seriously behind the more advanced countries. Also, most underdeveloped countries are basically agricultural; even if they do save there is no easy way to transform resources released from agriculture into the kinds of capital they need to industralize. In addition, many underdeveloped nations have a highly unequal distribution of income and a wealthy class with no strong disposition to save and invest. In the underdeveloped nations far too many wealthy citizens use their high incomes for extremely ostentatious forms of consumption, or tuck their savings away in safe places like Swiss banks. If they do invest their savings, they are more likely to put them into real estate or commercial ventures than industry or agriculture.

Exports limited to primary products

A sixth troublesome characteristic of many underdeveloped countries is that export capability is often concentrated in one or two crops or minerals. Underdeveloped countries export primary products (food, fiber, and minerals), which often are subject to sharp price fluctuations in world markets, and for which demand is relatively inelastic with respect to both income and price. Prices fluctuate because supply cannot be adjusted to market conditions as readily as can supply of manufactured commodities. This makes it difficult for underdeveloped countries to get capital through development of an export surplus, which would be an alternative to direct transformation of savings into industrial capital. Furthermore the terms of trade, the ratio at which the output of one country exchanges for the output of another, are often adverse to the underdeveloped countries, given the inelastic demand and the uncertain price outlook for primary products.

The risks of foreign investment

An alternative to obtaining capital through an export surplus or increased domestic savings is importing capital from abroad. Unfortunately, many obstacles confront the underdeveloped country that tries to attract capital from foreign sources. Private investors may feel an underdeveloped nation is a poor risk. Its government is often unstable, the labor force is poorly trained or unskilled, and the absence of social overhead capital compounds the difficulties and risks confronting private capital flows. Intergovernmental aid substitutes to some extent for an insufficient inflow of private capital, but in the post-World War II period foreign economic assistance has not been on a scale large enough to give underdeveloped countries all the capital they need.

Government and Society

We have considered six economic characteristics of underdeveloped countries. But the problems of development are not all economic. One of the most significant is that governments in many underdeveloped countries tend to be weak and ineffective, especially plagued by scarcities of trained personnel. Citizens in developed countries take for granted the existence of stable gov-

Ineffective governments

ernments staffed by qualified people. But no modern society developed effective governmental structures overnight, and many economically underdeveloped nations are former colonies whose rulers did little to train the population in administration and government. Thus they have been confronted since their independence with the awesome problem of literally learning from scratch how to administer and govern effectively.

The shortage of trained personnel extends to the business sector in the many underdeveloped countries that lack an entrepreneurial or "middle" class able and willing to undertake the task of economic innovation. Innovation involves not only risks, but the foresight and imagination to introduce new techniques of production, new ways of doing things. Many underdeveloped countries have not yet been able to gather together enough effective entrepreneurs, in or out of government.

Absence of entrepreneurs

Underdeveloped nations are often hampered by a structure of values and beliefs which gives people no incentive to adopt new methods. They are traditional societies, where existing ways of doing things often have the prestige of the centuries to support them. To some extent a social structure which inhibits change is a consequence of underdeveloped educational systems, for education is the most effective way to show people the advantages of new ways. Again we see that educational development and the elimination of poverty are closely interrelated. Without good government a society cannot advance economically; social stability is essential for saving to grow, as it must if investment is to take place. And investment gives a society the physical and educational capital that enables it to adopt the most effective production techniques.

Resistance to change

Thus underdeveloped nations frequently remain trapped in a vicious circle of poverty. Their productivity is low, which means that their income is low; this is the real meaning of their poverty. But this happens because of their low ability to save, a consequence of low income. They cannot divert resources into the formation of industrial, social, and educational capital on the scale needed to break out of the vicious circle. Until a way is found to create a progressive improvement in their rate of saving and investment, the underdeveloped nations will, like some citizens of more advanced countries, remain poor because they are poor.

The vicious circle of poverty

The Population Explosion

In the early nineteenth century, as we saw in Chapter 8, Thomas Malthus voiced the fear that population would outrun the world's capacity to feed itself. Malthus referred to the situation in England and the West at that time. Fortunately, the Industrial Revolution, with its dramatic impact on the productiveness of labor, pushed the Malthusian problem into the background. Throughout the nineteenth and twentieth centuries the rate of growth of output in the Western world far outstripped the rate of growth of population, so that real per capita incomes rose dramatically.

Overpopulation and world poverty

This has not happened in the rest of the world where the grim specter Malthus first raised is now an ominous fact. The United Nations Conference on the Human Environment, held in Stockholm in June, 1972, showed that even the developed world is aware of the dangers of expanding population, although Western nations do not really face the population crisis which confronts the two-thirds of the world's people who now live in serious poverty. The solution to world poverty is enormously complicated by the relentless pressure of population on the limited resources of the underdeveloped parts of the world. Overpopulation is the most explosive of all the problems confronting poor nations.

The History of World Population

The character of the problem is perhaps best seen in the long-term perspective of human habitation on the earth. Figure 18-2 shows that from roughly 250 A.D. until approximately the onset of the Industrial Revolution in the mid-eighteenth century, the world's population grew at a snail's pace. But shortly after this point its rate of growth began to accelerate, giving rise to the con-

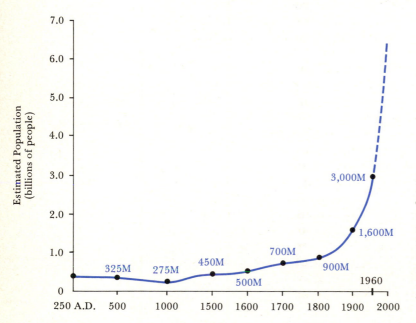

FIGURE 18-2

World Population Since 250 A.D.

The sharply rising world population curve not only illustrates how rapidly and dangerously world population is growing, but how much the time span required for a doubling of population is being compressed. [Source: Dean Fraser, *The People Problem* (Bloomington: Indiana University Press, 1971).]

sequences we call the "population explosion." Not only has total population expanded, but the rate of population growth has accelerated. This is the source of the population problem.

A brief examination of these data shows that the current population explosion is unlike anything the world has ever faced. Although its immediate and major impact is still upon the underdeveloped areas, increasingly its effects are spreading to the rest of the world, reflected in the growing concern that our high consumption patterns are leading to the destruction and exhaustion of our supply of natural resources.

Second, the acceleration in the rate of population growth has drastically reduced the number of years required for the population to double. And estimates of the trend of world population to the year 2000 predict that growth will be concentrated heavily in the underdeveloped regions. Few statistics dramatize more starkly the ominous problem of poor nations.

Causes of the Population Problem

The basic causes of the population explosion are fairly obvious. One is the dramatic improvement in public health, especially since World War II. The spread of modern medical techniques has drastically lowered the death rate in underdeveloped countries. For example, in some countries modest expenditures for DDT spraying to eliminate malaria have cut the death rate by as much as 40 percent in a single year and by over 75 percent in a single decade. In Turkey malaria control reduced the death rates from 28 per 1,000 persons to 10 per 1,000 persons in only six years. Western Europe experienced comparable reductions in death rates only over many decades.

Improvements in public health

Another factor has been the introduction of new seed grains—the so-called "Green Revolution"—which has enabled food production to expand rapidly enough to sustain growing populations. Contrary to popular opinion, rising fertility rates have not been the major reason for the population problem, at least not in the underdeveloped areas of the world. In the Western world, particularly in the 1940s and 1950s, there was an upward surge in the birth rate, but this seems to have passed its peak. The higher level of education combined with the growing concern with ecology and the environment will probably cause the birth rate in the advanced nations to keep falling. Paradoxically, humanitarian considerations require mankind to do everything possible to reduce the death rate, particularly the rate of infant mortality, but in doing so we compound the already grave problem of improving conditions for the two-thirds of the world's population living in poverty.

The Green Revolution

We must stress one basic difference between the current situa-

493

tion in underdeveloped countries and the experience of Western nations, a difference that helps us understand the difficulty of solving the population explosion. In the West, especially Europe and North America, economic development preceded a fall in the death rates; the impact of medical science on the human life span came *after* economic development had taken place. Basically the situation in the underdeveloped countries has been the reverse. The death rate declined before any significant development took place.

Consequences of Rapid Population Growth

Many specific economic consequences, which are particularly critical in underdeveloped areas, are associated with rapid population growth. First, rapid population growth changes the age structure of a nation's population drastically. High birth rates and falling death rates not only increase family size but lead to a much higher ratio of children to adults. In advanced countries about 25 to 30 percent of the population is below fifteen, the age at which people are usually considered to enter actively into the labor force. Many underdeveloped countries have as much as 40 to 45 percent of their population below this age, a proportion that may swell even more as long as population is growing rapidly. The consequences from the standpoint of economic development are serious.

*Change in age
structure of
populations*

A growing population with large families and a high proportion of the family members under the age of fifteen will have an adverse effect upon the society's ability to save. Large families put pressure on consumption, which increases the difficulty of saving at the national as well as the family level. In addition, a rapidly growing population with an age structure skewed toward the young changes the kinds of investment needed. Rapid population growth requires more social investment, particularly in housing and education. Not only does social capital absorb large quantities of resources, but much of it contributes only indirectly to increased productivity, and even then only after a long period of time. This makes it more difficult to increase the rate of output enough for the society to keep ahead of population pressure.

*Increased need for
social investment*

The Requirements for Development

The fundamental requirement for development in any society is to apply capital and technology to the process of production with enough scope and vigor to expand output faster than population. Human effort and time are the ultimate resources of any society;

everything else complements them. In order to raise the productivity of labor and other resources, and thus improve the standard of living, a society must reduce the time and effort needed to produce. Experience of the advanced nations indicates that this has largely been brought about by applying capital and technology—including education as a resource—to the process of production.

The Role of Saving and Investment

To improve production this way, the society must first be able to generate sufficient saving. Second, the saving must be invested with enough skill so that the resulting output expansion outpaces population growth. If this fails, growth will be inadequate, living standards will not improve, and the problems of poverty will worsen.

Obviously circumstances differ from country to country, but economists have developed a rough rule of thumb for estimating the amount of saving and investment required to put an underdeveloped economy on the path to economic progress. Experience suggests that to get a unit of income a society must invest about three times as much of its resources into capital equipment. Technically, what economists define as the *capital-output ratio*—the ratio of capital to output on the average—is equal to at least three. If the rate of population growth averages three percent a year, a realistic figure for most economically underdeveloped countries, a satisfactory rate of economic growth would require an annual rate of investment equal to nine percent of the national income simply to keep pace with the growth of population. If the underdeveloped country wants its output to grow at a rate one percent faster than population growth, so that some improvement in per capita real income takes place, it would have to invest annually 12 percent *net* of its national income. This simple example does not allow for replacement of capital; gross investment would have to be significantly higher to include it. These figures underscore the enormous difficulties economically underdeveloped countries face, for many of them have not been able to devote much more than five or six percent of their national income to capital formation. It is not unrealistic to stress that a doubling of effort is needed simply to achieve a most modest rate of advance in per capita income.

Minimum capital-output ratio

Table 18-4 shows saving and investment rates typical of many underdeveloped countries during the past decade. The data in the table also underscore the critical need to reduce the rate of population growth in all underdeveloped countries, if only because of the severe scarcity of resources for capital formation.

We have seen that economic development is not just a simple

TABLE 18-4

Saving and Investment as a Percent of GNP: Average for 1960–1967

	SAVING RATE	GROSS INVESTMENT RATE
Underdeveloped countries	15.0	17.8
Africa	13.1	16.7
South Asia	11.3	13.9
East Asia	11.0	15.6
Latin America	16.3	17.7
Middle East	14.8	19.8
Industrialized countries	21.7	21.2

Source: *Partners in Development, Report of the Commission on International Development* (New York, Praeger, 1969).

matter of increasing the rate of saving and finding techniques to invest the savings in productive equipment. It is a much more complex problem, which involves creating the human skills, knowledge, and management techniques that must accompany the growth of capital. The world's poor nations are trying to accelerate the process and do in a few decades what took centuries elsewhere.

The tough question is: How is this to be done? First, we will approach these questions by analyzing the specific economic and political changes needed to create an atmosphere in which growth will flourish. Second, we shall examine how such changes may be brought about. It is not especially hard to say what should be done, but it is clearly difficult to specify the *means*. To keep the matter in perspective, we must realize that development is essentially a problem in political economy. There cannot be a separation of the political and economic elements in the process of development.

The Role of Government

The need for continuity

We have noted that one of the most critical needs for an underdeveloped nation is stable, effective, and honest government. Development is a long-term process and demands an environment of stability and continuity. Without it, the odds against satisfactory development are enormous, because the gains from investment are realized only over time. For example, it would be very hard to persuade a society that developing a school system is worthwhile unless it is certain that this will lead to greater skill and productivity for labor, if not in the present generation then at least in the next. No such assurance is possible without the stability that only government can provide.

The government has a number of specific duties to further economic development in an underdeveloped nation. It must often be the instrument to mobilize savings for investment purposes, because private capital markets are either nonexistent or woefully weak. Taxation is the fundamental means it can use, and if the government is neither competent nor responsive the tax system will be unfair and enough savings will not be mobilized. A closely related task of government is the extensive investment in *social* capital needed for development.

All experience to date indicates that economic planning is an absolute necessity for development. In the West the lack of population pressure gave market forces time to develop as the chief carriers of the development process. In poor countries today time is an unavailable luxury; their problems are too urgent. Government planning must be the major carrier of development.

Finally, government provides a link to obtaining foreign financial aid, both in grants from more advanced countries and in private investment originating abroad. Private foreign investment is especially dependent upon good government; if instability reigns the investor's risks increase at an alarming pace, and foreigners will be reluctant to invest.

Social and Cultural Changes

In addition to development of stable and effective government, there must be a broad cultural transformation in a developing country. As the economy changes from a subsistence and village economy to a market system built around effective government, profound changes are likely to occur in the family, the systems of ownership, political institutions, religious practices, and the degree of urbanization. Economic development rarely leaves any aspect of society untouched to some degree. Frequently the consequences of this change and upheaval in established folkways, institutions, and behavior patterns are painful and troublesome.

We have already noted that economic development demands an entrepreneurial class. This class may come from the government, or it may come out of the private sector, but it is absolutely essential for development. Members of an entrepreneurial class, whether imaginative businessmen or innovative public servants, expect and should receive extraordinary rewards, both financial and nonfinancial. The return for entrepreneurial effort may be social prestige, political position, or economic success, but there must be some extra return if the entrepreneurial role is to be performed effectively.

Among the basic attitudes required for development, none are more important than those pertaining to work. A developing society must be disciplined with respect to work. Advanced nations with high standards of living may be less concerned about the need for work and discipline, but this luxury is not permitted to a poor society that wants to stop being poor. A poor society must put a premium on efficiency; it must want to get things done effectively with the least cost in real terms, i.e., in terms of the resources that go into production.

Land and Agriculture

Beyond the need for attitude changes and a transformation in techniques of production, particularly in the rural areas, many underdeveloped countries badly need land reform. First, small farmers and peasants must become landowners; otherwise they lack incentive to produce effectively and introduce new techniques, as is underscored by the frequent failure of attempts to transform and modernize agriculture through programs that collectivize the land, making farmers and peasants into government employees. Second, reform should not lead to an ownership structure in which holdings are excessively fragmented and too small for effective production techniques. If this happens, neither changes in attitude nor improvements in agricultural production will take place.

Prospects for the needed transformation of agriculture appear more favorable today than many experts thought possible only a decade ago. In the optimistic years immediately after the end of World War II, underdeveloped countries overemphasized investment in industry, to the comparative neglect of agriculture. Industrialization looked like the clear road to development because the more developed nations are industrialized nations. Since then, however, underdeveloped countries have shifted their emphasis toward agriculture. More than ever before they recognize the real need to improve agricultural productivity, if only to feed rapidly growing populations. Furthermore, they now generally recognize that the surplus they need for investment must come out of the agricultural sector. Developments in the area of fertilizers and high-yielding varieties of seed for rice and wheat—the "Green Revolution"—promise relief for the problem of hunger and may lead to rapid and low-cost increases in agricultural production that would release resources for other productive sectors.

Capital

Even if cultural transformations are achieved, they will not in themselves insure the success of any development effort.

A society has three major sources for capital in both a financial and a real sense. There is the possibility of a voluntary increase in savings, although the low average income in underdeveloped nations makes this unlikely. Thus there is a low margin for saving. Another effective way for an underdeveloped nation to increase the saving rate is through taxation. Without honest and effective government, however, this will not work. Finally, saving in a *real* sense can be increased by mobilizing underemployed labor in the agricultural sector. The difficulty is that all too frequently there is no easy way to employ this labor on capital construction projects. It cannot be readily transferred to the urban areas. Even if it could, needed social investment in the form of housing, schools, and transport facilities does not exist. The best way to use the labor available from disguised unemployment is in direct and simple capital formation projects in the rural areas, such as construction of houses, schools, roads, irrigation systems, wells, and other capital which does not demand complicated equipment.

The second crucial problem associated with saving and capital formation in the underdeveloped country is how to transform savings into actual output of more capital goods. Through taxation or an increase in private saving, a government in an underdeveloped country may increase the money resources available for capital formation, but since the capital goods industry itself is underdeveloped or even nonexistent, an increase in output of capital goods does not automatically follow. To some extent the growth of capital goods can be achieved indirectly through exporting an agricultural surplus. This earns foreign exchange, which can be used either to import specific capital goods or the goods needed to create a capital goods industry. An underdeveloped nation must also use foreign aid to get the kinds of capital needed to transform its saving into the actual output of capital goods. Finally, and as previously pointed out, surplus labor in the agricultural sector can be directly used for the production of simple capital goods.

International Assistance

Several times in this chapter we have mentioned the need for foreign economic assistance to help underdeveloped nations over the saving and investment hump. Historically, there have been two major ways for a nation to augment its resources from external sources. First, through development of an export surplus any nation can get goods and services not available domestically. Second, an inflow of private foreign investment provides a nation with resources, either directly by the construction of facilities and plants within the country by foreigners, or indirectly by making foreign exchange available through long-term loans. This foreign exchange may be used to finance needed imports, which augment domestic output.

499

Foreign Aid

What is different about the post-World War II era is that international assistance has shifted from a private to public character. Since 1945, the international economy has witnessed the emergence of large-scale efforts to transfer wealth from richer to poorer nations through programs of foreign aid. Public international assistance takes two forms. First, there are key international organizations, namely the International Bank for Reconstruction and Development (better known as the World Bank) and various specialized agencies of the United Nations which administer international economic and technical assistance.

Second, there are loans and gift programs which originate with governments in the more advanced countries and are directed to governments in less developed countries. These are called intergovernmental transfers or aids. In recent years international assistance from all sources has totaled $12 to $13 billion per year, although its magnitude measured as a percent of the output of the advanced countries appears to have diminished. Table 18-5 shows the amount and source of intergovernmental aid flowing to less advanced countries in the world economy. However, a significant portion of aid in all forms transferred to underdeveloped nations has involved military rather than economic assistance, which does not contribute in any meaningful way to economic development.

TABLE 18-5
Intergovernmental Aid to Underdeveloped
Countries: Selected Years *
(billions of U.S. dollars)

TYPE OF AID	1956	1961	1963	1967	1968
Grants	$5.2	$9.7	$10.3	$11.0	$10.5
Loans	0.5	0.6	1.5	2.3	2.4
Other	—	0.9	0.2	0.3	0.5
Total	$5.7	$11.2	$12.0	$13.6	$13.4

* Noncommunist Countries.
Source: *Partners in Development, Report of the Commission on International Development* (New York, Praeger, 1969).

According to data in the 1972 *Annual Report* of the President's Council of Economic Advisers, economic assistance by the United States to all parts of the globe averaged $4.6 billion per year for the period 1962–1970; more than half of this—$2.4 billion—was in loans rather than grants, which averaged $2.2 billion per year in this same period. In contrast, direct American expenditures overseas for military purposes, including grants, averaged $3.8 billion per year during the 1962–1970 period. These data on military outlays do not include the more than $100 billion expended to date in the Vietnam war.

The pressure on underdeveloped countries to devote resources to military purposes can only have adverse effects on their ability to expand production and cope with their overwhelming population problems. It is one of the great tragedies of the postwar era that global expenditures for armaments far outstrip expenditures for development. Recent estimates indicate that the world is spending annually nearly $200 billion dollars on armaments, a staggering figure compared to the relatively small amounts of wealth transferred from the more advanced to the less advanced countries.

In spite of the unhappy aspects of foreign aid, including evidence that its relative importance is declining, public international assistance is certain to continue. The world community of nations has recognized somewhat haltingly that the market system, operating through traditional channels of trade and private foreign investment, is not enough to transfer wealth on a scale necessary to spur development in the underdeveloped nations.

*Limited capacity
to absorb aid*

Whether or not the aid effort made by advanced countries is adequate, there is a second question here of equal importance: the ability of underdeveloped nations to absorb aid. If all resources now tied up in military expenditures were transferred into expenditures for development, the funds would far exceed the capacity of the underdeveloped nations to absorb assistance from abroad. The 1968 United Nations Conference on Trade and Economic Development recommended aid in the 1970s of around $20 billion per year, a figure significantly higher than the amount of foreign aid now available, but far less than the amount the world is spending on armaments. We have already seen the reasons for this limit. Many nations may lack a skilled work force and a managerial class, a stable government, or the kind of value structure needed to absorb productively a large influx of financial resources. If too much is poured into a nation lacking a suitable environment, the result may be waste and the allocation of money income to the wrong persons, rather than a productive use of resources to speed up the process of economic development.

Success and Failure:
The Cases of Mexico and Indonesia

Although the underdeveloped nations have an array of common characteristics and problems, during the last couple of decades

501

they have by no means been uniformly successful in breaking out of the vicious circle of poverty in which most of them are trapped. Mexico and Indonesia offer a dramatic contrast between success and failure in the development sweepstakes.

Mexico nearly doubled its per capita national income in the period 1958–1968, while Indonesia in the same time span saw its per capita income figure first decline by about 5 percent and then climb laboriously to a figure not quite 5 percent higher than it was at the start of this period. Why the difference in performance between two countries that were both poor and stagnant not too long ago?

Mexico's development success story involves a number of factors, not the least of which was the overthrow of the dictatorial Díaz regime in 1910; this unleashed a torrent of energy that had been repressed for nearly forty years. To this must be added the expropriation of foreign-owned oil and railroad investments in 1937–38. These expropriations led to a foreign boycott, but this only stimulated the nation's internal development further. To these political and social developments must be added a highly favorable climate of cooperation between the business community and the government bureaucracy—at least with respect to economic development.

Out of this has come a many-pronged approach to the elimination of national poverty, an approach that offers an almost textbook-like model of what needs to be done to spur development. Out of the 1910 revolution came land reform, which made possible improved farming methods, including irrigation, better use of machinery, and an American-style extension program, all of which helped raise agricultural productivity. With the expropriation of foreign-owned oil and the railroads, came the impetus for more public investment in social overhead capital. To those factors must be added the development of an educational system emphasizing technical training and the establishment of a system of domestic banks and credit institutions geared to meet the needs of the economy for investment funds.

Indonesia presents an unhappy contrast to this dynamic picture. Its essential situation for many decades—both under Dutch colonial rule and as an independent state since 1949—has been near-stagnation in per capita income and little change in the structure of production and employment. Although there has been some slight improvement in the last few years, the basic outlook remains gloomy. Indonesia still depends heavily on the export of a single crop—rubber—as its major source of foreign exchange, although it does have other natural resources to exploit, namely vegetable oil, tin, coal, and petroleum. As compared to other poor nations, Indonesia is relatively well supplied with natural wealth.

But little has come of this, at least as far as economic development is concerned.

The major reason for Indonesia's stagnation appears to be a lack of the right combination of leadership and political framework—a combination that would promote the imaginative entrepreneurship needed to get the process of economic development started. This did not happen under the Dutch colonial regime and it did not happen after independence. The parliamentary democracy that came after independence failed to face the problems of economic development confronting the nation; it left a legacy of stagnation and inflation. A dictator named Sukarno, who succeeded the parliamentary government, set up a "guided economy" that managed mainly to destroy Dutch, Chinese, other foreign, and even much Indonesian private business leadership without replacing it by an effective public entrepreneurship and without developing any large-scale investment program. The history of Indonesia during most of the post-World War II era is the story of a potentially rich and productive nation floundering without any effective economic leadership. The results are what economic analysis would lead us to expect; stagnation and economic failure.

Perspectives on Economic Development

Economists and others have struggled for more than two decades to find practical and theoretical solutions to the problem of world poverty. Realism dictates that although some progress has been made in alleviating massive worldwide poverty, the maximum accomplished has been to prevent an overwhelming disaster. There has been sufficient output growth in many underdeveloped countries to bring about slight improvement in per capita real income, but not much more than that. But while two-thirds of the world lives thus in poverty, the more advanced countries have accelerated their rate of growth, widening the gap between the less developed and the developed. The world has learned much about economic development in this decade, but no spectacular shortcut to economic progress for an underdeveloped nation has yet been discovered. And, in truth, there is no undiscovered "secret" to economic development. Two-thirds of the world's population is striving to achieve in decades something that in the more fortunate and advanced parts of the world took at least two centuries to accomplish. Progress has been made, knowledge does exist, and, one hopes, the solution of the problem is not beyond human capabilities.

The outlook

503

Questions for Review and Discussion

1. What is the most widely used indicator of the degree of economic development experienced by a nation? What are some of the limitations of this indicator?

2. List the most important characteristics common to the majority of underdeveloped nations.

3. What is disguised unemployment? How can this segment of the labor force be used to further the development process?

4. What factors account for the rapid acceleration of population growth after the mid-eighteenth century?

5. What are the major economic consequences of rapid population growth, especially for economically underdeveloped nations?

6. How does the rate of population growth play a critical role in determining an appropriate rate of investment for an underdeveloped nation?

7. List some of the major economic and political changes necessary to create an atmosphere in which economic growth will take place.

8. Why do most authorities regard the emergence of an entrepreneurial class as crucial to the success of programs for economic development?

9. What role does land reform play in the process of economic development? What kind of land reform is needed in many underdeveloped nations?

10. What is the Green Revolution? How did it come about and what does it portend for the underdeveloped nations?

11. Explain the means by which an underdeveloped country may increase its saving rate. What problems confront such a country in transforming saving into productive capacity?

12. Are the needs of the underdeveloped two-thirds of the world for economic growth and development likely to clash seriously with the emerging worldwide concern with pollution, environmental decay, and the exhaustion of the world's nonrenewable resources?

Suggestions for Further Reading

Paperbound editions have been cited wherever available.

Chapter 1: The Nature of Economics

Boulding, Kenneth E., *Economics as a Science*, New York, McGraw-Hill Book Company, 1970, Chapter 1.

Brown, Robert, *Explanation in Social Science*, Chicago, Aldine Publishing Company, 1963.

Heilbroner, Robert L., *The Worldly Philosophers* (revised edition), New York, Simon & Schuster, 1967.

Heller, Walter W., *New Dimensions of Political Economy*, New York, W. W. Norton & Company, 1967, especially Chapter 1.

Keynes, John Neville, *The Scope and Method of Political Economy* (4th edition), Clifton, N.J., Augustus M. Kelley, Publisher, 1917.

Lekachman, Robert, *The Age of Keynes*, New York, Random House, 1966.

Marshall, Alfred, *Principles of Economics* (9th edition, 2 vols.), New York, The Macmillan Company, 1961, especially Chapters 1–4.

Mundell, Robert A., *Man and Economics*, New York, McGraw-Hill Book Company, 1968.

Nourse, Edwin G., *Economics in the Public Service*, New York, Harcourt Brace Jovanovich, 1953.

Okun, Arthur M., *The Political Economy of Prosperity*, New York, W. W. Norton & Company, 1969, Chapter 1.

Chapter 2: An Overview of the Economy

Galbraith, John Kenneth, *American Capitalism* (revised edition), Boston, Houghton Mifflin Company, 1956.

Ginzberg, Eli, Hiestand, Dale L., and Reubens, Beatrice G., *The Pluralistic Economy*, New York, McGraw-Hill Book Company, 1965.

Heilbroner, Robert L., *The Making of Economic Society* (3rd edition), Englewood Cliffs, N.J., Prentice-Hall, 1970, Chapter 1.

Stigler, George J., *The Theory of Price* (3rd edition), New York, The Macmillan Company, 1966, Chapter 2.

Chapter 3: Principles of the Market Economy

Grossman, Gregory, *Economic Systems*, Englewood Cliffs, N.J., Prentice-Hall, 1966.

Heilbroner, Robert L., *The Making of Economic Society* (3rd edition), Englewood Cliffs, N.J., Prentice-Hall, 1970, Chapters 2 and 3.

Henderson, Hubert, *Supply and Demand*, New York, Cambridge University Press, 1958, Chapter 2.

Smith, Adam, *An Enquiry Into the Nature and Causes of the Wealth of Nations* (6th edition), New York, Barnes & Noble, 1950, Book I.

Chapter 4: Principles of the Public Economy

Galbraith, John Kenneth, *The Affluent Society*, Boston, Houghton Mifflin Company, 1971.

Heilbroner, Robert L., and Bernstein, Peter L., *A Primer on Government Spending* (2nd edition), New York, Random House, 1970.

Phelps, Edmund S. (ed.), *Private Wants and Public Needs* (revised edition), New York, W. W. Norton & Company, 1965.

Schultze, Charles L., *The Politics and Economics of Public Spending*, Washington, D.C., The Brookings Institution, 1968.

Smith, Adam, *An Enquiry Into the Nature and Causes of the Wealth of Nations* (6th edition), New York, Barnes & Noble, 1950, Book V.

Chapter 5: National Product and Its Measurement

Abraham, William I., *National Income and Economic Accounting*, Englewood Cliffs, N.J., Prentice-Hall, 1969.

Peterson, Wallace C., *Income, Employment, and Economic Growth* (revised edition), New York, W. W. Norton & Company, 1968, Chapter 2.

Schultze, Charles L., *National Income Analysis* (3rd edition), Englewood Cliffs, N.J., Prentice-Hall, 1971.

Silk, Leonard S., and Curley, M. Louise, *A Primer on Business Forecasting with a Guide to Sources of Business Data*, New York, Random House, 1970, Chapter 5.

United States Department of Commerce, *The National Income and Product Accounts of the United States, 1929–1965*, Washington, D.C., 1966.

United States Department of Commerce, *Survey of Current Business.* (Data on gross national product and other income measures found in July issues each year.)

Suggestions for Further Readings

Chapter 6: Principles of Output Determination

Economic Report of the President. Also contains the *Annual Report* of the Council of Economic Advisers. Published in January of each year, Washington, D.C., U.S. Government Printing Office.

Gilboy, Elizabeth W., *A Primer on the Economics of Consumption,* New York, Random House, 1968.

Lekachman, Robert, *The Age of Keynes,* New York, Random House, 1966.

Peterson, Wallace C., *Income, Employment, and Economic Growth* (revised edition), New York, W. W. Norton & Company, 1968.

Chapter 7: Money, Banking, and the Economic System

Bernstein, Peter L., *A Primer on Money, Banking, and Gold,* New York, Random House, 1968.

Board of Governors of the Federal Reserve System, *The Federal Reserve System: Purposes and Functions* (5th edition), Washington, D. C., 1963.

Chandler, Lester V., *The Economics of Money and Banking* (5th edition), New York, Harper & Row, 1969.

Duesenberry, James S., *Money and Credit: Impact and Control* (2nd edition), Englewood Cliffs, N.J., Prentice-Hall, 1967.

Shapiro, Eli, et al., *Money and Banking* (5th edition), New York, Holt, Rinehart and Winston, 1968.

Chapter 8: Principles of Economic Growth

Committee for Economic Development, *Economic Growth in the United States,* New York, CED, 1969.

Fabricant, Solomon, *A Primer on Productivity,* New York, Random House, 1969.

Heller, Walter (ed.), *Perspectives on Economic Growth,* New York, Random House, 1968.

North, Douglass C., *Growth and Welfare in the American Past: A New Economic History,* Englewood Cliffs, N.J., Prentice-Hall, 1966.

Phelps, Edmund S. (ed.), *The Goal of Economic Growth* (revised edition), New York, W. W. Norton & Company, 1969.

Chapter 9: Fiscal and Monetary Policy

Committee for Economic Development, *Further Weapons Against Inflation: Measures to Supplement General Fiscal and Monetary Policies,* New York, CED, 1970.

Friedman, Milton, and Heller, Walter W., *Monetary vs Fiscal Policy,* New York, W. W. Norton & Company, 1969.

Heller, Walter W., *New Dimensions of Political Economy,* New York, W. W. Norton & Company, 1966.

507

Suggestions for Further Readings

Okun, Arthur M. (ed.), *The Battle Against Unemployment* (revised edition), New York, W. W. Norton & Company, 1972, Parts 1–3.

Okun, Arthur M., *The Political Economy of Prosperity*, New York, W. W. Norton & Company, 1969.

Pechman, Joseph, *Federal Tax Policy* (revised edition), New York, W. W. Norton & Company, 1969.

Silk, Leonard S., and Curley, M. Louise, *A Primer on Business Forecasting with a Guide to Sources of Business Data*, New York, Random House, 1970, Chapters 1–4.

Chapter 10: The Impact of Incomes Policy and the Public Debt

Hamovitch, William (ed.), *The Federal Deficit: Fiscal Imprudence or Policy Weapon*, Boston, D. C. Heath and Company, 1965.

Okun, Arthur M. (ed.), *The Battle Against Unemployment* (revised edition), New York, W. W. Norton & Company, 1972, Part V.

Ott, David J., and Ott, Attait F., *Federal Budget Policy* (revised edition), Washington, D.C., The Brookings Institution, 1969.

Perlman, Richard (ed.), *Inflation: Demand-Pull or Cost-Push*, Boston, D. C. Heath and Company, 1965.

Shultz, George P., and Aliber, Robert Z. (eds.), *Guidelines, Informal Controls, and the Market Place*, Chicago, University of Chicago Press, 1966.

Chapter 11: Prices and the Allocation of Resources

Leftwich, Richard H., *The Price System and Resource Allocation* (4th edition), New York, Holt, Rinehart and Winston, 1970, Chapters 3, 4, 8.

Mansfield, Edwin, *Microeconomics: Theory and Applications*, New York, W. W. Norton & Company, 1970, Chapters 2–6.

Chapter 12: Competition and the Allocation of Resources

Averitt, Robert T., *The Dual Economy*, New York, W. W. Norton & Company, 1968.

Caves, Richard, *American Industry: Structure, Conduct, Performance* (second edition), Englewood Cliffs, N.J., Prentice-Hall, 1967.

Galbraith, John Kenneth, *The New Industrial State*, Boston, Houghton Mifflin Company, 1969.

Leftwich, Richard H., *The Price System and Resource Allocation* (4th edition), New York, Holt, Rinehart and Winston, 1970, Chapters 9–12.

Mansfield, Edwin, *Microeconomics: Theory and Applications*, New York, W. W. Norton & Company, 1970, Chapters 8–11.

Mueller, Willard F., *A Primer on Monopoly and Competition*, New York, Random House, 1970.

Shepherd, William G., *Market Power and Economic Welfare: An Introduction*, New York, Random House, 1970.

Weiss, Leonard W., *Case Studies in American Industry*, New York, John Wiley & Sons, Inc., 1967.

Chapter 13: Public Policy and the Allocation of Resources

Heady, Earl O., *A Primer on Food, Agriculture, and Public Policy*, New York, Random House, 1967.

Heilbroner, Robert L., *The Making of Economic Society* (3rd edition), Englewood Cliffs, N.J., Prentice-Hall, 1970, Chapter 6.

Leonard, William N., *Business Size, Market Power, and Public Policy*, New York, Thomas Y. Crowell Company, 1970.

MacAvoy, Paul W. (ed.), *The Crisis of the Regulatory Commissions*, New York, W. W. Norton & Company, 1970.

Mansfield, Edwin (ed.), *Monopoly Power and Economic Performance* (revised edition), New York, W. W. Norton & Company, 1968.

Mueller, Willard F., *A Primer on Monopoly and Competition*, New York, Random House, 1970, especially Chapters 8, 9, 11.

North, Douglass C., and Miller, Roger L., *The Economics of Public Issues*, New York, Harper & Row, 1971.

Owen, Wyn F. (ed.), *American Agriculture: The Changing Structure*, Boston, D. C. Heath and Company, 1969.

Ruttan, Vernon W., Waldo, Arley D., and Houck, James P., *Agricultural Policy in an Affluent Society*, New York, W. W. Norton & Company, 1969.

Schultze, Charles L., *The Distribution of Farm Subsidies: Who Gets the Benefits*, Washington, D.C., The Brookings Institution, 1971.

Chapter 14: The Distribution of Income

Leftwich, Richard H., *The Price System and Resource Allocation* (4th edition), New York, Holt, Rinehart and Winston, 1970, Chapters 13–15.

Mansfield, Edwin, *Microeconomics: Theory and Applications*, New York, W. W. Norton & Company, 1970, Chapters 12–13.

Chapter 15: Public Policy and the Distribution of Income

Batchelder, Alan B., *The Economics of Poverty* (2nd edition), New York, John Wiley & Sons, 1971.

Bok, Derek, and Dunlop, John T., *Labor and the American Community*, New York, Simon & Schuster, 1970.

Bowen, William G., and Ashenfelter, Orley, *Labor and the National Economy* (revised edition), New York, W. W. Norton & Company, 1973.

Budd, Edward C. (ed.), *Inequality and Poverty*, New York, W. W. Norton & Company, 1968.

Chamberlain, Neil W. (ed.), *Contemporary Economic Issues*, Homewood, Ill., Richard D. Irwin, 1969, Chapters 2–3.

Cohen, Sanford, *Labor in the United States* (3rd edition), Columbus, Ohio, Charles E. Merrill Publishing Company, 1970.

Suggestions for Further Readings

Hamilton, David, *A Primer on the Economics of Poverty*, New York, Random House, 1968.

Harrington, Michael, *The Other America: Poverty in the United States*, New York, The Macmillan Company, 1970.

Lampman, Robert J., *Ends and Means of Reducing Income Poverty*, Chicago, Markham Publishing Company, 1971.

Tabb, William K., *The Political Economy of the Black Ghetto*, New York, W. W. Norton & Company, 1970.

Will, Robert E., and Vatter, Harold G. (eds.), *Poverty in Affluence: The Social, Political and Economic Dimensions of Poverty in the United States* (2nd edition), New York, Harcourt Brace Jovanovich, 1970.

Chapter 16: Principles of the International Economy

Ellsworth, Paul T., *The International Economy* (4th edition), New York, The Macmillan Company, 1969.

Kenen, Peter B., *International Economics* (2nd edition), Englewood Cliffs, N.J., Prentice-Hall, 1967.

Pen, Jan, *A Primer on International Trade*, New York, Random House, 1967.

Snider, Delbert A., *Introduction to International Economics* (5th edition), Homewood, Ill., Richard D. Irwin, 1971.

Chapter 17: Change and Upheaval in the International Economy

Balassa, Bela (ed.), *Changing Patterns in Foreign Trade and Payments* (revised edition), New York, W. W. Norton & Company, 1970.

Dowd, Douglas F., *America's Role in the World Economy: The Challenge to Orthodoxy*, Boston, D. C. Heath and Company, 1966.

Economic Report of the President, Washington, D.C., U.S. Government Printing Office, 1969 *Report*, Chapter 4; 1971 *Report*, Chapter 5.

Johnson, Harry G., *The World Economy at the Crossroads: A Survey of Current Problems of Money, Trade and Economic Development*, New York, Oxford University Press, 1965, especially Chapters 2, 3, and 4.

Chapter 18: Economic Development: The International Setting

Alpert, Paul, *Economic Development*, New York, Free Press, 1963.

Baldwin, Robert E., *Economic Development and Growth*, New York, John Wiley & Sons, 1966.

Committee for Economic Development, *Assisting Development in Low-Income Countries*, New York, CED, 1969.

Heilbroner, Robert L., *The Great Ascent*, New York, Harper & Row, 1963.

Hirschman, Albert O., *The Strategy of Economic Development*, New Haven, Yale University Press, 1958.

Lewis, W. Arthur, *Some Aspects of Economic Development*, New York, Panther House, 1970.

Maddison, Angus, *Economic Progress and Policy in Developing Countries,* New York, W. W. Norton & Company, 1970.

Randall, Laura (ed.), *Economic Development: Evolution or Revolution,* Boston, D. C. Heath and Company, 1964.

Ranis, Gustav (ed.), *The United States and the Developing Economies* (revised edition), New York, W. W. Norton & Company, 1973.

Ward, Barbara, *The Lopsided World,* New York, W. W. Norton & Company, 1968.

Suggestions for Further Readings

511

Glossary of Economic Terms

All italicized terms in the definitions are themselves defined elsewhere in the glossary.

Ability-to-pay principle   The principle that taxes should be based on a person's income or wealth because it is thought that the marginal dollar has less value for a richer person than a poorer one.

Abscissa   In a rectangular coordinate system, the horizontal axis, known mathematically as the x axis. Compare *Ordinate*.

Absolute cost advantage   A situation where a nation can produce a commodity or service with an absolutely smaller input of real resources than is possible in any other nation.

Administered prices   Prices set independent of market forces by firms possessing some degree of economic power.

Adverse clearing balances   Shifting of deposits from one bank to other banks.

Aggregate demand   Total flow of money expenditures in the economic system during a given time period.

Aggregate demand schedule   Total expenditures forthcoming from the spending entities of the economic system at each and every possible level of the *GNP*.

Aggregate supply   The amount of goods and services produced by all firms in the economy in a period in response to demand expectations.

Aggregate supply schedule The total supply of goods and services forthcoming from all firms in the economy at each and every possible level of the *GNP*.

Antitrust laws Legislation prohibiting restraint of trade. These laws are intended to preserve free competition in the economy.

Assets Resources owned by persons, firms, or the government. They can be either monetary claims or physical things, i.e., land, buildings, etc.

Automatic ("built-in") stabilizers Government *fiscal policies* that automatically tend to generate a budget surplus during expansionary periods and develop a deficit when the economy contracts.

Average cost Total cost per unit of output.

Balance of international payments The formal accounting statement of all payments made between a nation and other nations of the world.

Benefit principle The idea that taxes should be paid in proportion to the benefits received by individuals from government activity.

Bilateral monopoly A market situation in which the firm as the buyer of a resource has a *monopsony* position, but is confronted by a single seller of the resource.

Capital Man-made things used to produce goods and services in conjunction with *labor*. In economics capital is not *money* or *assets*.

Capital consumption allowance A monetary measure of the quantity of *capital* used up during a production period.

Capital deepening A change in capital stock leading to an increase in the ratio of *capital* to *labor*.

Capital inflows International transactions that, on balance, involve foreign lending to the United States.

Capital-output ratio The ratio of a nation's *capital* to its total production.

Capital widening An enlargement of *capital* stock to keep pace with the expanding *labor force* and thus maintain the existing ratio of *capital* to *labor*.

Capitalism An economic system in which the means of *production* are privately owned and the allocation of resources is performed by a free market system. Individual motivations and choices are considered important.

Cartel A combination of business firms acting to reduce competition and promote their own interests to the detriment of the public (illegal in the United States).

Central bank A bank whose deposits are owned by other banks in the system. The Federal Reserve Bank is the central bank in the United States.

Ceteris paribus "Other things being equal." Much economic analysis makes use of this principle, which assumes that outside influences on an economic model remain constant. The economist uses this assumption because it is difficult to isolate economic variables from a variety of influences.

Check A legal instrument by means of which money is transferred from one person to another.

Closed shop A requirement that employees be members of a union prior to their employment.

Coefficient of elasticity The ratio of the percentage change in quantity demanded to a percentage change in the price.

Collective bargaining The practice of unions, representing all or a majority of employees, bargaining with employers over *wages* and working conditions.

Collective ownership Government ownership of all major instruments of *production*. There are various degrees of collective and private ownership arrangements in most societies.

Commercial banks Banks that accept *demand deposits* in addition to their other services.

Common Market The European Economic Community, set up to establish a free trade area for all goods and services and mobility of *labor* among its member states.

Comparative cost advantage A situation where a nation's *of a*
cost advantage with respect to another nation in one particular commodity is relatively greater than its absolute cost advantage in any other commodities.

Competition A technical term economists use to describe the effort of two or more parties, acting independently, to secure the business of a third party by offering the most favorable terms. See also *Perfect competition.*

Competitive market A market situation in which prices are set as a result of freely expressed preferences of all traders. No trader has enough power to set the price himself.

Conglomerate merger Merger of business firms operating in separate and distinct markets.

Constant prices Prices from which the price-level changes have been eliminated by dividing the data valued in current prices by an appropriate *price index*. This procedure makes it possible to compare real changes over time.

Consumer sovereignty The principle that the desires of the consumer determine what is to be produced in a *market economy*.

Consumption In economics, the using up of goods and services in the satisfaction of human wants. Output not consumed during the *income* period in which it is produced is considered an addition to the existing stock of *wealth* of the economy.

Consumption function A schedule showing total consumer expenditures forthcoming at various levels of *disposable income*.

Craft union A union organized to include all members of a particular craft, such as a carpenters' union.

Current prices *Prices* that prevail in a particular period of time.

Debt management Decisions relating to the structure of governmental debt, such as the proportion to be held in long- or short-term obligations. These decisions could be used as measures to counter business fluctuations.

Debt ratio The ratio of the national debt to the *gross national product*.

Demand The desire plus the ability to purchase a good or service.

Demand curve The graphic representation of a *demand schedule*.

Demand deposit A liability or debt of a commercial bank, payable on demand.

Demand schedule Computation of the quantities of a commodity that buyers would be willing to purchase at each and every price of the commodity.

Depression A phase of the business cycle marked by industrial and commercial stagnation, scarcity of money and goods, low prices, poor expectations, and mass unemployment.

Derived demand The demand for the service of a resource that is based on the demand for the final good or service produced with the use of the resource.

Devaluation of currency A reduction in the definition of a currency in terms of gold or foreign currencies.

Diminishing marginal utility The principle that satisfaction (*utility*) declines with the consumption of successive units of a good or service.

Discount rate Interest paid by Federal Reserve member banks when borrowing from the *Federal Reserve System*.

Disguised unemployment A situation common to underdeveloped regions, where people are at work but really contribute little to output. It is a case of low *marginal productivity*.

Disinvestment Reduction in the economy's stock of goods on hand.

Disposable income *Personal income* less personal income taxes.

Distribution of income The distribution to resource owners of output (*real income*) of a society, based on the contribution of resources used in *production*. The phrase also is used to mean the distribution of money income to spending units, i.e., families and single individuals.

Division of labor A characteristic feature of the present-day economy, in which jobs are divided to permit specialization in one particular function. Modern mass production depends upon division of labor, which lends itself to mechanization and avoids wasteful duplication of tools.

Durable goods Consumer goods that provide a continuing flow of useful services to their owners. Examples are automobiles, refrigerators, and housing.

Econometric model A set of mathematical relationships depicting the performance of the economy in terms of its crucial parts, based on statistical analysis of economic experience.

Economic analysis The scientific study of economic relationships.

515

Economic efficiency The greatest possible output at given cost in terms of resource input.

Economic forecasting A logical extension of the technique of historical analysis, used to predict the future direction of economic activity.

Economic growth The long-term expansion of output of useful goods and services caused by an expansion of the economy's productive capacity.

Economic indicators Variables that fluctuate with the economic system. There are leading, lagging, and coincident economic indicators. Leading indicators are sometimes used in forecasting.

Economic model An abstract framework of relationships representing the economic system and its parts, which seeks to explain the behavior of persons and institutions in the economy.

Economic policy The means that individuals, groups, or a whole society may utilize to achieve objectives that are primarily of an economic nature.

Economic principle A broad statement that embodies a useful and meaningful relationship between observed economic events; a generalization that explains economic behavior.

Economic profit The surplus of revenue over all costs of production, *explicit* and *implicit*.

Economic rent A surplus associated with the use of any resource in fixed supply.

Economic resources All things used and necessary in the production of economically valuable goods and services.

Economics The systematic study of the production, distribution, and use of scarce resources of a society so as to satisfy the maximum number of wants. It is the study of choices among alternatives in a situation of *scarcity*.

Economies of scale Economies in production that can be achieved by increasing the scale of output.

Elastic demand A situation in which the quantity demanded is highly responsive to a change in the price of the commodity, as is the case with luxury items.

Elasticity The extent to which quantity demanded changes when *price* changes. (It can actually be the responsiveness of either quantity demanded or quantity supplied to a change in price.)

"Employer of last resort" An anti-poverty plan in which the government must be ready to provide employment for all who cannot otherwise find work.

Employment Act of 1946 One of the most important pieces of economic legislation in United States history, which committed the federal government to "promote maximum employment, production, and purchasing power." The act also established the Council of Economic Advisers to report to the President on the economy.

Entrepreneur One who takes the initiative in combining the resources of *land, capital,* and *labor* to produce goods and services. He bears the risk for his business policy decisions in his attempts to earn profits.

Equilibrium A situation in which there is no tendency for economic variables (such as price, income, or employment) to change.

Equilibrium income level The particular level of *income* in the economy where *aggregate demand* and *aggregate supply* are in balance.

Equilibrium level of output An output of the economy at which *aggregate demand* and *aggregate supply* in the schedule sense are equal.

Equilibrium price A *price* that equates the quantity demanded with the quantity supplied. It balances the behavior of buyers and sellers, thus clearing the market.

Ex ante Intended or planned. (Ex ante savings are *planned* savings.)

Ex post Actual or existing. (Ex post savings are *actual* savings.)

Excess reserves The amount of reserves over the fractional reserves needed for cash demands on a bank's deposits.

Exclusion principle The idea that if a person cannot pay the price for a good or resource he is excluded from its use or consumption.

Explicit costs Actual *money* outlays required in the *production* of output.

External diseconomies A harmful effect on one or more persons or firms that results from the action of another person or firm.

External economies A favorable effect on one or more persons or firms that results from the action of another person or firm.

Externalities Benefits or costs accruing to some individual, firm, or group not involved in a specific market transaction. They may exist in production or consumption.

Factoral income distribution Another term for *functional income distribution.*

Factors of production *Land, labor, capital,* and the role of the *entrepreneur.* These are *economic resources* used in the production of useful goods and services.

Fair rate of return An equitable return on investment that regulatory commissions allow to *natural monopolies.*

Fallacy of composition The mistake of assuming that what is true of one part will necessarily be true of the whole. This is a common problem pertaining to aggregation in economics: what is good for a single family or firm may not be good when all families or firms are involved.

Federal Reserve notes Non-interest-bearing debt of Federal Reserve banks, used as common currency.

Federal Reserve System The twelve Federal Reserve banks that are the central banks for the U.S. economy. It is a quasi-governmental agency.

Federal Trade Commission An agency of the federal government

517

with the power to investigate unfair methods of competition and practices in restraint of trade, and to prosecute violators of certain antitrust laws.

Firm An economic unit whose major function is the transformation of *economic resources* into outputs of useful goods and services.

Fiscal dividend The added tax revenue that the economy tends automatically to generate and that will grow in size as the full employment *GNP* expands, given a fixed tax structure.

Fiscal drag A large budgetary surplus that might be created by the tax system as the economy approaches *full employment*. It may act as a brake on economic expansion.

Fiscal policy Deliberate changes in government spending, *transfer payments,* or taxes, designed to increase or decrease *aggregate demand*.

Fiscalists Economists who believe *fiscal policy* is the most effective instrument of government economic policy.

Fixed (overhead) costs Costs that are constant regardless of the firm's level of production.

Foreign exchange market Any place in which currencies of all nations are bought and sold.

Foreign exchange rates See *Rate of exchange*.

Full employment The absence of involuntary unemployment in an economy.

Functional relationship A relationship of two or more variables such that the value of one depends upon the value of the other. Economic relationships can in this way be expressed in mathematical or symbolic form.

Functional income distribution (also called *Factoral income distribution*) The allocation of the *national income* to the owners of the *economic resources* that contributed to its *production,* namely *land, labor,* and *capital.*

Functions of money A medium of exchange and a standard of value are primary functions. The secondary functions are a standard for deferred payments and a store of value.

Gold exchange standard The *international monetary system* in which the dollar defined exchange rates and official dollar holders could exchange them for gold.

Gold standard A monetary system where the value of currency is based on gold and convertible to it on demand.

Grants-in-aid Federal government revenues shared with states. They are earmarked for specific purposes.

Green revolution The development of high-yielding varieties of seed grains, which has had a dramatic impact on the agricultural output of developing nations.

Gross investment Investment in the real *capital* of the economy, including replacement of worn-out capital.

Gross national product (GNP) The value in current prices of all final goods and services produced by the economic system during the calendar year.

Guaranteed family income An anti-poverty plan that guarantees a minimum *income* for every family. Often called the *negative income tax*.

Horizontal merger A merger involving firms that produce closely related products and sell them in the same market.

Identity equation An equation stating an equality that is true by definition. For example, total output of the economy is equal to the sum total of investment, consumption, and government expenditures in a closed economic system. $GNP = (C+I+G)$.

Implicit costs Resources obtained by a firm without money outlays.

Income The flow of output of an economy over a time period. Also used to mean the flow of receipts to households during a time period.

Income effect The effect of a price change on a consumer's *real income*.

Incomes policy Policy concerned with an acceptable rate for advancement of money income in all forms without creating intolerable inflationary pressures (in the form of rising production costs) as the economy nears *full employment*.

Increasing returns A phase of production where, when the variable input increases, output expands more than in proportion to the increase in the input.

Indirect business taxes As used in *national income* accounting. All taxes levied on business firms except the corporate income tax.

Indivisibility of public goods A characteristic of public goods such that the benefits received by one person are received by all persons. National defense and fire protection are examples.

Industrial union A union organized to include all members in a particular industry, for example the United Automobile Workers.

Inelastic demand Situation in which the quantity demanded does not respond significantly to change in price. This is usually the case with necessities in the consumer's budget.

Inflation Any increase in the general price level that is sustained and non-seasonal in character.

Interest The price paid for the use of loanable funds. The *rate of interest* is the price paid per time period.

Interlocking directorates The practice of the same person or persons serving on the boards of directors of competing companies.

International Monetary Fund An international organization whose members agree to certain rules for determining exchange rates. Loans are made to member countries from the assets of the Fund.

International monetary system A system of institutions, practices, and policies to facilitate international exchange.

Investment An increase in the real *capital* stock of the economy. (See *Net investment* and *Gross investment*.) To the economist, investment means the purchase of investment goods (buildings, machinery, etc.) produced during the year. Financial transfers (the purchase of stocks and bonds) or purchase of a five-year-old factory, for example, would not be called investment.

"Invisible hand" A famous phrase from *The Wealth of Nations* by Adam Smith. The desire for personal profit within the framework of a competitive economic system works like an "invisible hand" to guide the system toward the greatest welfare for all.

Jawboning The use of exhortation and persuasion by the government to affect wage and price decisions.

Kinked demand curve A bend in the *demand curve* of an *oligopoly* that occurs at the existing market price, suggesting possible behavior of the oligopolist when confronted with the possibility of changing price.

Knights of Labor The first nationwide labor association in the United States, organized in the last third of the nineteenth century.

Labor Human energy used in the production of goods or services. It may be mental or physical.

Labor force The stock of man-hours available to an economy during a given period of time.

Labor theory of value The theory that all exchange value is created by labor. It is the basis of Marxian economic theory.

Laissez faire The principle of minimum intervention by government in the operation of a market economy.

Land All natural things used in the production of useful goods or services. Also called *natural resources,* it includes land, minerals, water, or any other material things used in production that are not man-made.

Law of Demand The principle that the quantity of a commodity demanded is inversely proportional to the price of the commodity. In other words, consumers will buy more of a product when its price is low and less when its price is high.

Law of diminishing returns The principle that, when inputs of any resource are increased while the quantity of another resource is fixed, eventually the rate of increase in output slows down. The fixed supply of the one resource acts as a brake on the output.

Law of supply The principle that the quantity of a commodity producers are willing to supply varies directly with the price of the commodity. At higher prices the quantity supplied is greater than at lower prices.

Law of variable proportions Another term for the *law of diminishing returns*. It is also called the *principle of diminishing marginal productivity*.

Liabilities Monetary obligations or debts owed by persons or firms.

Liquidity preference The theory that people prefer to hold assets in the form of money because it is more readily converted into other forms than other assets. Hence, money is "liquid."

520

Long-term equilibrium A period of time long enough to permit market supply to be adjusted by variations in the size of the industry.

Lorenz curve   A graphic means to compare the equal distribution of income against the actual distribution. It is also used for comparisons of the distribution of assets or wealth.

Margin requirements   The required cash down payment on the purchase of securities; the amount is controlled by the Federal Reserve System.

Marginal cost   The addition to the firm's total cost when it produces one additional unit of output.

Marginal product   The addition to total product resulting from the employment of one more unit of the variable factor.

Marginal productivity   The increase in output caused by the addition of one unit of resource input.

Marginal productivity of labor   The increase in output caused by the addition of one unit of labor input.

Marginal propensity to consume   The proportion of any given increment of income spent for consumption purposes.

Marginal propensity to save   The proportion of any given increment of income saved. (1 − marginal propensity to consume.)

Marginal resource cost   The addition to total cost created by the use of a single additional unit of a given resource input.

Marginal revenue   The addition to total revenue that results from the sale of one more unit of output (the rate of change of total revenue).

Marginal revenue product   The increase in total revenue resulting from the use of each additional variable input.

Marginal utility   The utility derived from the use or consumption of successive units of a good or service.

Market economy   An economy whose basic coordinating mechanism for decisions of buyers and sellers of products and resources is through a system of markets and prices.

Market equilibrium   A time period in which supply is limited to the quantity already produced and placed on the market.

Monetarists   Economists who view the *money supply* as the single most important determinant of the price level and the general level of economic activity, including employment.

Monetary policy   A change in the money supply undertaken with the intent to influence output, employment, the price level, the rate of *economic growth,* or the *balance of international payments.*

Monetization of debt   The creation of *demand deposits* by bank lending.

Money   Anything serving as a medium of exchange facilitating the economic processes of production, distribution, and consumption.

Money supply   Currency and *demand deposits* in use as money in an economy.

Money wage   The amount of a wage in money terms.

521

Monopolistic competition A type of market structure with a large number of sellers who possess some degree of control over their selling price. Product differentiation is usually a characteristic of this type of competition.

Monopoly A market situation where there is a single producer or seller for a commodity or service with few, if any, substitutes. By definition the firm comprises the industry.

Monopsony A market situation in which a firm is so large relative to the market that it is the sole buyer of resources. (Usually refers to a firm that is the sole purchaser of labor services.)

Multiplier effect The principle that total and ultimate changes in output will be greater than the amount by which the *aggregate demand schedule* has shifted. It is determined by the *marginal propensity to consume.* $(k = \dfrac{1}{1-mpc})$

National income Aggregate earnings of persons and property arising from the production of goods and services in an economy during a specified time period (usually a calendar year).

Natural monopoly A market situation in which monopoly rather than competition appears to be the most feasible and efficient arrangement for the production and distribution of a commodity or service. *Public utilities* are examples.

Near-monies Financial instruments with some of the attributes of money. They are savings deposits, shares in savings and loan associations, U. S. Treasury bills, and cash value of personally held life insurance policies.

Negative income tax Proposed government payments to a family to equal the difference between income earned and a minimum guaranteed income level.

Net exports The difference between a nation's exports and imports.

Net investment The amount by which the economy's total stock of wealth has increased in the current *income* period. It is the total output of investment goods less the amount of replacement investment.

Net national product (NNP) The net output of final goods and services produced by the economy during the calendar year. It is the *gross national product* less *capital* used up in *production* (depreciation).

New economics The use of Keynesian theories to influence the level of *aggregate demand.*

Non-price competition All behavior designed to improve the competitive position of the firm by any means other than price changes. Examples are advertising, improved product design, or special services offered to customers.

Normal distribution A theoretical frequency distribution in statistics often used in economics to predict the behavior of a group on the basis of the behavior pattern of a smaller sample of the group.

Normative economics Branch of economics concerned with what ought to be, as opposed to descriptive or *positive economics.*

Not-for-profit sector A large variety of economic activities producing goods and services for the public on a nonprofit basis.

Oligopoly A type of market structure common in the United States, in which there are relatively few producers or sellers and they have control over prices and entry into the market. As rivals they are mutually interdependent and collusion often results.

Open market operations The buying and selling of securities by the Federal Reserve as a means of affecting the reserves of commercial banks. This procedure in turn affects the *money supply* of the economy.

Opportunity cost The return that a resource can command in its next best alternative use.

Ordinate In a rectangular coordinate system, the vertical axis, known mathematically as the *y* axis. Compare *abscissa.*

Paradox of value The phenomenon that because a good has *utility* it does not necessarily have economic value, and because a good has economic value it is not necessarily useful. The crucial factor in determining value is scarcity of a good relative to the desire for it; this is the basis of economic value.

Parity The ratio between prices received by the farmer and prices paid in some "ideal" prior period.

Perfect competition A model of a market structure in which firms produce a standardized product but no firm has control over the market price.

Personal income The current money income actually received from all sources by persons and households during an income period. It includes government transfers and interest income.

Personal income distribution The division of money income among families and individuals.

Phillips curve A graphic technique (curve) demonstrating the relationship between employment and changes in the price level. It shows the trade-off between *full employment* and *inflation* or price-level stability.

Positive economics The branch of economics concerned with what is. It attempts to describe and explain the economic system and its workings.

Post hoc ergo propter hoc Literally, "after this, therefore because of this." A common fallacy in economics, it assumes that because one event precedes another the first event is the cause of the second.

Poverty line A criterion proposed by the Social Security Administration as the minimum level of subsistence income for a family.

Price The exchange value of a good or service expressed in terms of money.

Price deflators An index of the price level that will convert data in current prices to data in constant prices.

Price discrimination The practice of charging different prices to different customers for the same product or service.

Price index A statistical device for comparing the amount by which prices have changed during a given period of time. A specific year is chosen as the base year and prices in all other years are measured as a percentage of the price in this base year.

Price leadership A tacit agreement on the part of firms in an industry that one firm will be the leader in establishing the price and the others will follow suit.

Price system A device that coordinates the desires of buyers and the response of sellers, thereby serving as a mechanism for the organization of *economic resources* and the production of goods and services.

Principle of diminishing marginal productivity See *Law of diminishing returns.*

Private property One of the legal institutions of *capitalism*. Individuals are allowed to own personal property and also the non-human means of production.

Product differentiation A characteristic of the *modern economy* where firms attempt by brand names and advertising to convince the public that a certain kind of a particular commodity should be purchased.

Production The creation of *utility* or economic value to satisfy human wants.

Productive capacity The economy's potential to produce useful goods and services. It is limited by the stock of *capital* goods, the available *labor force,* and the level of *technology*.

Productivity Output produced per unit of resource employed.

Productivity of capital Output produced per unit of *capital* employed.

Productivity of labor Output produced per unit of *labor* employed. It can be measured per man or per man-hour.

Profit The excess of income over all economic costs involved in the process of production—a surplus or residual.

Profit maximization A principle stating that the output of a firm will be adjusted to the point at which *marginal cost* and *marginal revenue* are equal.

Progressive tax rate A tax rate that increases as the tax base increases. The present federal income tax is a progressive tax.

Propensity to consume The proportion of any given income level spent for consumption purposes.

Proportional tax rate A tax rate that does not change as the tax base changes. The percentage rate of tax paid is constant.

Public utility An industry in which there is public regulation of a vital good or service that is produced more efficiently by a single firm than by many firms. Natural gas and electric power are examples.

Public sector That part of the economy in which decisions of a collective or public nature predominate; the realm of government.

Quantity theory of money The theory that there is a direct correlation between the money in circulation and the price level, expressed in the classical equation $MV = PT$, which reduces to $P = f(M)$.

Rate of exchange The price at which different national currencies exchange for one another.

Real income The purchasing power of income.

Real wage The purchasing power of a money wage.

Recession A downturn in economic activity, one phase of the business cycle. Decreased investment, falling incomes, falling consumption, and increased unemployment are characteristic of this phase.

Reciprocal buying or selling The practice of taking a firm's business to firms that bring business to it.

Regressive tax rate A tax rate that declines as the tax base increases. (Often taxes, such as the sales tax, are regressive in practice but not in design.)

Relative price The price of one commodity compared to the price of another commodity.

Rent A price paid for the use of any kind of a durable good, whether land, machinery, or buildings.

Required reserves (also called *legal reserve requirement*) Commercial banks are required by law to hold cash reserves equal to a certain percentage of their deposits. This puts an upper limit on the amount of credit banks can extend.

Reserves Cash in a bank's vault or on deposit with the central bank to meet cash demands of customers.

Revenue-sharing The federal government's sharing of its revenues with states on an unrestricted basis.

Right-to-work laws Laws to the effect that no person can be excluded from employment on the basis of his membership or non-membership in a union.

"Rule of Reason" doctrine In antitrust cases the theory that the Sherman Act only outlaws unreasonable combinations in restraint of trade.

Savings bank A bank that accepts only savings accounts, for example, savings and loan associations and mutual savings banks. Savings banks cannot create *demand deposits*.

Scarcity The supply of *economic resources* is limited relative to the demand.

SDRs Special Drawing Rights, issued by the International Monetary Fund, often called "paper gold" and serving as international currency.

Selective credit controls Controls on consumer credit imposed by the Federal Reserve during World War II and the Korean War to regulate the required down payment for the purchase of a consumer durable and the length of time allowed the customer to pay off a loan.

Semi-social goods Goods possessing some of the attributes of both social and private goods. They are only partially indivisible, which means they can be priced to a degree on an individual basis. Education and medical care are examples.

Sherman Act The first antitrust legislation in the United States (1890), which outlawed restraint of trade and the monopolization of commerce.

Short-term equilibrium A time period long enough to permit market supply to vary within the limits of existing productive capacity.

Social balance The relative distribution of resources between the public and private sectors.

Social benefits A gain that accrues both to society as a whole and to individuals, but for which an individual does not have to pay directly.

Social costs A disadvantage to society resulting from private production but not necessarily reflected in the money costs to the individual producer of acquiring the resources needed for production. Pollution is a social cost of production that the market system does not measure.

Social goods Goods and services that are wholly indivisible and may entail substantial *external economies*. They are usually distributed to society without any charges based upon benefits received.

Social overhead capital The *capital* of a society, consisting of facilities for energy production, communications, transportation, and education. It is also called the *infrastructure* of a society.

Social Security A social welfare program in the United States where employees receive old-age retirement benefits depending upon their previous earnings. Both employer and employee contribute by means of a payroll tax.

Social wants Wants by individuals in a society for government services, largely determined through the political process.

Socialism An economic system in which the society or social system owns the major means of production. Some form of planning is required to perform the allocation process.

Specialization of labor The division of tasks in an economy, allowing it to perform more efficiently and obtain the benefits of mass production. Another term for the *division of labor*.

Spillover effects Another term for *externalities*. Some benefits or costs associated with the production or consumption of a good spill over to third parties (parties other than the buyer or seller).

Stagflation A combination of stagnation and unemployment with continued inflation.

Structural unemployment The displacement of workers as a result of technological change in production processes or a shift in demand toward new products and services.

Substitution effect   The effect of a price change on the substitution of commodities for each other by the consumer.

Supply   The amount available of a good, service, or resource.

Supply curve   The graphic representation of a *supply schedule*.

Supply schedule   The quantities of a commodity that producers will supply at each and every price of the commodity.

Surtax   A tax levied on another tax payment as the base.

Tax base   The object upon which a tax is levied, such as income, sales, property, etc.

Tax impact   The person legally responsible or charged with making the tax payment.

Tax incidence   The ultimate bearer of the burden of a tax payment.

Technological change   Growth of the stock of knowledge used in the production of goods and services.

Technology   Man's entire stock of knowledge and skills.

Terms of trade   The ratio at which the output of one country exchanges for the output of another country.

Third World   A term for the poor countries of the world who are facing problems of backwardness, underdevelopment, and poverty.

Tight money   Monetary policy with a restrictive impact on economic activity. Usually associated with high interest rates.

Total cost   Output times average cost for a firm.

Total profit   The difference between a firm's total revenue and its total cost.

Total revenue   Total output of a firm times the selling price of the output.

Trade union   An organization of employees whose purpose is to strengthen their bargaining position for higher wages or better working conditions.

Transfer payments   Disbursements by the government for which it receives no products or services in return at the time. Items such as *Social Security* payments to the aged, *unemployment compensation,* and certain business subsidies are included because they channel tax revenues back to businesses and households without directly absorbing resources.

Trust   Any business combination involving restraint of trade.

Unemployment   The situation of workers involuntarily out of work.

Unemployment compensation   One of the government stabilization policies providing payments to the unemployed.

Unemployment rate   The percent of the civilian labor force that is out of work as measured by the U.S. Bureau of Labor Statistics.

Unintended investment   Unforeseen inventory accumulation in the economic system. This is the means by which actual saving and actual investment are brought into equality in the economy.

Union   See *Trade union*.

Union shop   Requirement that newly-employed workers become members of the union after a specified time period.

Unitary demand elasticity Quantity demanded changes in the same proportion as the price changes.

Utility The ability of a good or service to satisfy a want.

Variable costs Costs that change as a firm's level of production changes.

Vertical merger A merger involving firms in a buyer-seller relationship, for example a manufacturing firm and its supplier of raw materials.

Wage The price paid for units of labor service supplied in the market per unit of time.

Wage-price controls Government controls over the level of wages and prices in the economy.

Wage-price guideposts Conditions or standards set by the government for non-inflationary wage and price behavior.

Wealth The stock of material things possessing economic value in an economy, measured at a single instant of time.

Welfare state The government's assumption of responsibility for systems of old-age pensions, *unemployment compensation,* medical care, and provision of income for families unable to participate in the productive process.

Workable competition A practical approach to the preservation of competition within the economy. It stresses the realistic, rather than the idealistic, concept of competition.

Workmen's compensation Legislation requiring employers to make specified payments to workers who have been disabled or injured on the job.

"Yellow dog" contract A contract where an employee agrees as a condition of employment not to join a union. Yellow-dog contracts are illegal in the United States.

Index

532